W9-BBS-885

Copyright, Congress and Technology: The Public Record

Copyright, Congress and Technology: The Public Record

Volume I:
The Formative Years, 1958-1966

Volume II:
The Political Years, 1967-1973

Volume III:
The Future of Copyright, 1973-1977

Volume IV : CONTU:
The Future of Information Technology

Edited with an introduction by
Nicholas Henry.

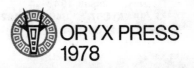 ORYX PRESS
1978

Operation Oryx, started more than 15 years ago at the Phoenix Zoo to save the rare white antelope—believed to have inspired the unicorn of mythology—has apparently succeeded. The operation was launched in 1962 when it became evident that the animals were facing extinction in their native habitat of the Arabian peninsula.

An original herd of nine, put together through *Operation Oryx* by five world organizations now number 47 in Phoenix with another 38 at the San Diego Wild Game Farm, and four others which have recently been sent to live in their natural habitat in Jordan.

Also, in what has come to be known as "The Second Law of Return," rare biblical animals are being collected from many countries to roam freely at the Hai Bar Biblical Wildlife Nature Reserve in the Negev, in Israel, the most recent addition being a breeding herd of eight Arabian Oryx. With the addition of these Oryx, their collection of rare biblical animals is complete.

Copyright © 1979 by Nicholas Henry

Published by The Oryx Press
3930 E. Camelback Road
Phoenix, AZ 85018

Published simultaneously in Canada

Printed and Bound in the United States of America

Library of Congress Cataloging in Publication Data (Revised)

Main entry under title:

Copyright, Congress, and technology.

CONTENTS: v. 1. The formative years, 1958-1966—
v. 2. The political years, 1967-1973.
      1. Copyright—United States—Collected works.
I. Henry, Nicholas, 1943-
KF2994.A1C57   346'.73'0482   78-23747
ISBN 0-912700-13-0 (v. 1)

TO MILES

Contents

Acknowledgements

I am indebted to a great many people in compiling these books, especially to Ms. Valari Elardo, my graduate assistant, who spent untold hours over a smoldering photocopying machine copying the necessary documents. Ms. Gwen Weaver has been both efficient and cheerful in putting out the necessary typing, and officials at the National Commission on New Technological Uses of Copyrighted Works have been cooperative and forthcoming in permitting me to reprint some of their important research in Volume IV.

Ms. Phyllis Steckler, President of The Oryx Press, deserves recognition for her perceptiveness in seeing the need for this set, as well as her personal encouragement.

Of course, and as always, I am indebted to my understanding wife, Muriel, and my children, Miles and Adrienne, for their support in the completion of this project. This set is dedicated to them.

NH
Tempe, Arizona

Introduction to the Set

Copyright, Congress, and Technology: The Public Record is a compendium of selected public documents that were published during the remarkable effort to revise American copyright law which occurred during the twenty-one years between 1955 and 1976. Simply as an example of the policy-making process, the campaign waged to change U.S. copyright law is fascinating in and of itself; few pieces of legislation have taken as long to be enacted as a revised copyright law. This four-volume set, however, is designed not only to trace the development of the Copyright Act of 1976, but also is meant to set the record straight in the areas of how the new copyright law affects the use of new information technologies, notably photocopiers and computers, for the benefit of librarians, educators, authors, publishers, and public officials. The impact of copyright on these technologies is both profound and complex, and perhaps the most simple way of conveying the thinking of policy-makers and interest groups in their effort to resolve copyright and technology is to provide a format that allows them to speak for themselves.

These volumes also describe the actual policy-making process as it related to the attempt to revise the United States Copyright Act of 1909 in a manner that would accommodate the new information technologies, notably photocopying and computer-based information storage and retrieval systems. These are the primary "neo-publishing" technologies (in the sense that they permit the massive republishing of copyrighted works by the populace), and the "politics of neo-publishing" was the effort to reconcile these technologies with copyright law.

While there are other neo-publishing technologies, those that have engendered the greatest concern among copyright owners and copyright users are photocopiers and computers. Of these two, the photocopier is preeminent. There are approximately 600,000 photocopiers in this country alone, churning out an estimated 30 billion copies every year. Most of these copies are made in public and research libraries, and empirical studies of photocopying use patterns in libraries indicate that as much as 60 percent of all the photocopies made each year may be of copyrighted publications. Increasingly, publishers are convinced that their sales of periodical subscriptions and books are being undermined by popular and massive photocopying practices, and that this is particularly the case for publications in science and technolgy.

The other major neo-publishing technology is the computer. There are more than 100,000 computer-based information storage and retrieval systems in the United States. While we know that these systems are reformatting and disseminating vast quantities of the information on demand and at an incredibly rapid rate, we do not know what proportion of that information may be protected by copyright. Some material, certainly, that is processed by computers is protected by copyright, and it is highly unlikely that information system operators and programmers are soliciting the permission of the copyright owners to use their material to any significant degree, if at all.

Both copyright owners and copyright users perceive copyright law to be virtually the only public policy that is concerned with the relationships among the new neo-publishing technologies, intellectual creativity, intellectual property, and, to quote the Constitution (Article I, Section 8), the paramount social value of promoting "the Progress of Science and useful Arts . . .". Revising copyright law to accommodate the new information technologies thus is a public policy of some consequence.

Two conclusions may be drawn from the public record about copyright law revision. One is that the process represented, and no doubt will continue to do so, a politics of technological elites. Copyright is one of the least recognized but most important public policies of our time, affecting an industry of vast magnitude. In fact, the "knowledge industry" comprises the largest single segment of the American economy, and it has been estimated by economists that the knowledge industry accounts for a third of the Gross National Product. More than 40 percent of the nation's economic growth is attributable to advances in education, and the "copyright industries" alone are the equivalent size of mining, banking, and utilities. Copyright is not merely big business, it is the biggest.

In light of the implications of the new information technologies and copyright law, it is both discomfiting and surprising to learn how small the group is that has been debating how to reconcile technology and copyright during the past three decades. The elitism of this debate is brought out in these volumes. The same names appear and reappear with frequency, but the overwhelming reality remains that public policy for new information technologies has affected and will affect far more people than those who have been talking about it. We have here a case of very small elites "representing" very limited elements of society that nonetheless are forming public policy for the new information technologies.

Why is this elitism the case? A major reason appears to be that the sheer complexity of the subject inhibits participation. Yet, complexity is a growing fact of political life in techno-bureaucratic societies, such as ours. Political decision-making in twentieth century America deals with technology, and technology is complicated. Those who understand the complex technological issues of modern political life (or who say they do) become the policymakers. Nowhere is this better illustrated than in the instance of what some have called "the politics of neo-publishing." As the reader will quickly discern, very small elites have made a public policy that affects us all.

The second conclusion that one may draw from reading these public documents, is that the politics of neo-publishing is frankly Marxist. Revising copyright law was a political brawl involving the redistribution of political and economic power between haves and have-nots. While it was not a class war in the traditional sense, the politics of neo-publishing clearly is, to use Marxian language, a fight between the owners of a means of production and the users of their products. Indeed, the formal terminology of copyright law reflects the language of Marxism: copyright "owners" and copyright "users." The neo-publishing technologies have provided an opportunity to the "exploited masses" of copyright users. By dint of these technologies, proletarian copyright users may become bourgeois copyright owners. Publishers, the historic owners of the means of intellectual production, are witnessing the undermining of their ownership through the popular use of new information technologies. As Marshall McLuhan has noted "in an age of Xerox, every man is a publisher."

Copyright is the single public policy concerned with the economics of commercial publishing. It is predicated on the idea that a would-be publisher must put up a considerable amount of capital in order to begin publishing—that is, in order to control a means of production. It follows, therefore that publishers ought to be granted certain monopolistic rights or "exclusive license" to their products. This is what copyright does, or at least did, until the neo-publishing instruments made their debuts. These technologies are redistributing a means of production and, in so doing, are undermining copyright as a standing public policy. For these reasons, the documents included in this set can be understood most satisfactorily as a Marxian class conflict—owners against users.

While such conclusions may be interesting, and perhaps even important, the major reason why this set will be useful to most readers is that an enormous amount of confusion surrounds the impact of the new copyright law on librarians, authors, educators, and publishers. Thus, these volumes are organized in such a way that they will be of optimal use to these professionals in tracing how the thinking of their colleagues has evolved just as information technologies have developed.

Volume I of *Copyright, Congress, and Technology: The Public Record* focuses on those early public documents that emerged between 1958 and 1966. The discerning reader will note that the tone of the copyright proceedings in these years is substantially different from the tone found in public documents emerging in 1967 and beyond. I have referred to this phenomenon elsewhere as "noetic politics," or the peculiar style of politics that derives from knowledge, logic, and the scientific method.[1] We see in these documents a conscious effort by the participants in copyright politics to devise legislation that will work for the benefit of all society. The normal, grubbing interest-group politics that we associate with the legislative process is relatively absent, although there are many moments of passion and greed.

It was during this period that the Register of Copyrights commissioned thirty-four scholarly studies on copyright, and issued a major report in 1961 that was hailed as a seminal work in the area. Experts, lawyers, and policy-makers of various stripes were consulted on a continuing basis during these years, and the Commission on New Technological Uses of Copyrighted Works (CONTU) was first proposed. All these instances and others represent an effort to form policy on the basis of knowledge rather than on the basis of the political power of particular interest groups.

As noted, however, this tone changes—and I think rather precipitously—in the years following. In the 1967 Congressional hearings, for example, we see spokespersons for various groups calling each other names during their testimony. The balance of power in the dispute appears to shift away from copyright owners (largely publishers and authors) and toward copyright users (largely librarians and educators), but not necessarily for reasons of wise public policy (although it may well turn out that way). Rather, the gains made by copyright users over the interests of copyright owners are made because the users have the votes and the owners do not. Thus, Volume II covers the years

1967 through 1973, and the tone throughout is overtly political, although there is some hard and creative analysis available in these years, which is included.

The third volume in the retrospect reprints documents emerging between 1973 and 1977, including pertinent selections from the several Congressional hearings on copyright law revision. An effort has been made to include those public documents that point the way toward the future of copyright. The entire Copyright Act of 1976 also is reproduced.

Volume IV, *CONTU: The Future of Information Technology*, concludes the set. It reproduces the ground-breaking studies sponsored by the National Commission on New Technological Uses of Copyrighted Works, which dealt with computer software, photocopying and copyrights, public photocopying practices, library photocopying and the economics of periodical publications. The Commissions final report, the result of years of testimony by experts from across the nation, concludes the volume.

Taken together, the four volumes are a collection that should be both convenient and authoritative in guiding copyright users and owners through the maze of copyright, technology, and public policy.

NH
Tempe, Arizona

---

1. See: Nicholas Henry, *Copyright/Information Technology/Public Policy. Part I: Copyright/Public Policies* and *Part II: Public Policies/Information Technology.* New York: Marcel Dekker, Inc., 1975 and 1976.

Introduction to Volume II

In 1967, the year that begins this volume of *Copyright, Congress, and Technology: The Public Record,* a remarkable event occurred. A Copyright Law Revision Bill passed the House on April 11th, only to die later in the Senate. The 1967 *Report* of the Register of Copyrights notes the drama that accompanied that passage, and his *Report* begins Volume II.

The Register's 1967 and 1968 *Reports* are followed by House *Report No. 83,* which is possibly a classic statement on copyright issued by Congress. While the legislative reports accompanying the hundreds of bills on copyright law revision are often repetitive as they pertain to the conflict between copyright and technology, House *Report No. 83* perhaps stands as the single most cogent statement on copyright law revision and the implications of the new information technologies.

Senate *Report No. 640* follows, which accompanied the Bill to Establish a National Commission on New Technological Uses of Copyrighted Works. Both House *Report No. 83* and Senate *Report No. 640* later proved to be significant bones of contention between copyright owners and users.

Perhaps some political background is in order. In June, 1966, a series of six meetings between educators, authors, publishers and copyright officials was held in the Register's office in order to arrive at a compromise over fair use, photocopying, computers and educational broadcasting. The series, instigated by education interests, with attendance on a limited invitation basis, lasted a total of approximately 100 hours of closed sessions and included twenty-three to twenty-six participants. From all accounts, librarians evidently were not present at any of these meetings, which later became known as the "summit conferences."

The summit conferences were conducted in an atmosphere of relative good will. In terms of fair use, a viable compromise was reached: fair use would include the four criteria specified in the 1964 bill. In addition, educators won assurances in House *Report No. 83* and in Section 504(c)(2) of the forthcoming revision bill that would "insulate a teacher who honestly and reasonably believes what he was doing constituted a fair use from excessive liability for minimum statutory damages." Educators, however, had relented in their turn. Harry N. Rosenfield, counsel for education's Ad Hoc Committee, wrote that on Copyright Law Revision, "the compromises thus affectuated carried with it the agreement by the Ad Hoc Committee to forego its insistence" upon its proposed Section 111, which called for exemption from liability of limited educational copying. The Copyright Office appeared to effectively seal this bargain in the following month, with its issuance of a report on July 22, 1966, which indicated "educational groups are mistaken in their argument that a 'for-profit' limitation is applicable to educational copying under the present law." House *Report No. 83* adopted both the compromises of the summit conferences and the Copyright Office's report as valid and acceptable.

Also abandoned by the negotiators at the summit conferences were the plethora of copyright clearinghouse proposals. Compulsory licensing systems, whether managed by public or private bureaucracies, were discarded as unworkable. A statutory system that provided access to copyrighted material unless the owner responded to the user's request within a specific time span received somewhat more attention. But educators were concerned about to whom requests should be made and the possibility of excessive charges, while owners were concerned about losing rights as a result of legitimate delays in responding to requests. Eventually, nothing was decided. The discarding of a possible copyright clearinghouse was a nominal retreat for owners that probably few people regretted, including the owners themselves; no one really knew precisely what the ramifications of a copyright clearinghouse would be.

When the summit conferences were concluded, librarians were unsure as to where they now stood in the debate. The chief library spokesman archly observed that although the agreements emerging from the 1966 negotiations seemed to permit librarians to continue serving their readers with photocopies more or less as they had been doing, it also appeared that they had been foreclosed from taking full advantages of the newer technologies. Librarians also believed that they had "suffered a substantial defeat" by the elimination of the "not-for-profit" principle, and were curious as to why the new exemption for teachers in infringement suits did not include the same benefit for librarians in nonprofit libraries.

The 1967 Copyright Law Revision bill, as it emerged from committee, had adhered to the agreements of the 1966 summit conferences. For the most part, so did House *Report No. 83*. An integral aspect of the compromise called for a legislative history, issued under the imprimatur of an appropriate congressional committee, which sanctioned approved educational practices under the copyright law. In many respects, House *Report No. 83* was this legislative history and sanctioned these practices. It stated that, "The committee sympathizes with the argument that a teacher should not be prevented by uncertainty from doing things that he is legally entitled to do and that improve the quality of his teaching. It is therefore important that some ground rules be provided for the application of fair use in particular situations." Thus, the *Report* sought to "provide educators with the basis for establishing workable practices and policies."

In more specific terms, *Report No. 83* assured educators that fair use was "broad enough to permit reasonable educational use, and education has something to gain in the enactment of a bill that clarifies what may now be a problematical situation." Furthermore, "the new language of Section 107 makes it clear that . . . fair use can extend to the reproduction of copyrighted material for purposes of classroom teaching." The "non-profit character of the school" was also a factor in determining fair use.

The House Judiciary Committee admitted in the *Report* that "a question that has never been resolved involves the difference between an 'entire work' and an 'excerpt.' " If an "entire work" referred to a "self-contained" portion (e.g., a poem or an article) in a collection of works, the "privilege of making a single copy" requested by educators "appears appropriately to be within the scope of fair use." An "entire collective work" (e.g., an encyclopedia volume or a magazine) and a "sizable integrated work published as an entity" (e.g., a novel) did not seem to be covered by the doctrine. Excerpts from such works were covered by the doctrine, however, and the *Report's* authors concluded that even multiple copies could be made from excerpts, if they were not "self-contained" or "substantial in length."

Finally, recognizing the widening character of the neo-publishing dispute, the Judiciary Committee stated that "the doctrine of fair use could apply to all stages in the operations of information storage and retrieval systems, including input, and output in the form of visual images or hard copies." Beyond this, however, "the committee does not favor any statutory provision that would exempt computer uses specially from copyright control or that would specify that certain computer uses constitute fair use." Similarly, library photocopying was "a subject better left to flexible adjustment," despite the fact that the American Council of Learned Societies and the U.S. Department of Health, Education and Welfare had "argued that the problem is too important to be left uncertain, and proposed adoption of a statutory provision allowing libraries to supply single photocopies of material under limited conditions."

While these statements represented some concessions to copyright users and some genuine clarifications of the proposed law, other portions of House *Report No. 83* and developments related to it were regarded with deep suspicion by educators. A major reason for this distrust was found in the new bill (S. 2216) that dealt with the establishment of a National Commission on New Technological Uses of Copyrighted Works. S. 2216 was introduced by Senator John McClellan, and passed by the Senate on October 11, 1967. The Ad Hoc Committee believed that the wording of Section 1(b)(2) of S. 2216, as amplified in Senate *Report No. 640*, obviated Section 107 of the 1967 Copyright Revision bill (S. 597), which defined fair use in terms of the accords reached at the summit conferences. Section 1 (b)(2) of S. 2216 read: "the purpose of the commission is to study and compile data on the reproduction and use of copyrighted works of authorship . . . by various forms of machine reproduction."

Senate *Report No. 640*, which accompanied S. 2216, explained that although it "is not the intent of the committee that the Commission should undertake to reopen the examination of those copyright issues which have received detailed consideration during the current revision effort, and concerning which satisfactory solutions appear to have been achieved," the Commission nevertheless would be expected to consider the copyright ramifications of photocopying. "Photocopying in all its forms presents significant questions of public policy, extending well beyond that of copyright law. No satisfactory solutions appear to have emerged in the limited consideration devoted to this problem during the current revision effort."

Because of Section 1(b)(2) of S. 2216 and the amplifications in Senate *Report No. 640*, the Ad Hoc Committee noted "with dismay the failure to exclude from the Commission's scope of duty the matter of 'fair use' by photoduplication and recording." Harold Wigren, on behalf of the Ad Hoc Committee, wrote the Register to state that Section 1 (b)(2) of S. 2216 "reopens the entire issue of photocopying and fair use of copyrighted materials for schools, an issue which we all assumed was settled by the agreements that the House Committee adopted in its report."

In short, Section 1(b)(2) and *Report No. 640* were, by themselves, adequate reasons for the Ad Hoc Committee to regard "the compromise agreement as having been abrogated, and therefore will be free to return to its original position or take some other position. . . ." There were additional reasons, however. Perhaps the sentence in House *Report No. 83* that engendered the greatest objections by copyright users was: "Where the unauthorized copying displaces what realistically might have been a sale, no matter how minor the amount of money involved, the interests of the copyright owner need protection."

In the view of the Ad Hoc Committee, the phrase "no matter how minor the amount of money involved," flew in the face of the combined consideration of all four fair use criteria and wiped out the other three criteria. At the very least, it vitiated the meaningfulness of the section on fair use in the 1967 bill in terms of authorizing limited educational copying. As organized education stated during the Congressional hearings, "The Ad Hoc Committee *never* accepted—and does *not* accept—any compromise agreement whereby it forgoes its original proposal for a limited statutory exemption. . . . The Ad Hoc Committee no longer is bound by any such compromise. . . ."

Fostering such reactions on the part of education were some statements uttered during the 1967 congressional hearings. These statements had no official sanction, but nonetheless seemed to be successful in unnerving educators relative to technology and copyright.

Chief among the witnesses who worried educators were the representatives of the Committee to Investigate Copyright Problems (CICP). No doubt, the CICP's role as a disinterested party increased users' apprehensions, as its testimony was supportive of owners' calls for a copyright clearinghouse. Howard A. Meyerhoff, president of the CICP, stated that fair use was "at best inconclusive" and only "a temporary guideline" because it could never "solve the real problems" of the increasing need of copyright users for multiple copies of materials, and the fact that copyright compensation constituted the total income for owners. "Therefore, we feel that the present provision for fair use, while making possible some types of research of copyrighted material in computer and microfilm storage devices, cannot solve the 'computer problem,' let alone the direct copying problem. At best, it serves as a temporary safety valve, until some clearinghouse system is established." With the advent of a copyright clearinghouse, Meyerhoff concluded, "the concept of fair use should lose it importance and die off as some form of vestigial tail."

Meyerhoff's reasoning recalled lawyer Norton Goodwin's remarks before the Subcommittee that also related fair use to the necessity of recognizing neo-publishing technologies. By applying copyright to all "recorded literary works," publishers would be "in a position to close the 'fair use' loophole by providing the right to make licensed copies of the work via automation," and thus render the doctrine moot.

Educators professed themselves aghast at such logic, despite the fact that it rested entirely on the copyright clearinghouse concept, a notion discarded at the summit conferences in 1966.

It is, perhaps, ironic that education interests were voicing such concern over new information technologies, when only two years earlier they had used the potentiality of the same technologies to worry authors with the possibility of getting "up-to-date and going on a payroll." Nevertheless, educators seemed determined not to abide by the agreements of the summit conferences.

The reasons given by educators to justify their abrogation of the summit conferences are not entirely satisfactory. The congressional witnesses who disparaged the lasting value of fair use appeared independently of any interest group, and were careful to tie in their remarks with the unlikely establishment of a copyright clearinghouse. Yet, the Ad Hoc Committee spokesmen claimed that this alone was reason enough for education to withdraw from the 1966 agreements.

The description of the proposed duties of the National Commission on New Technological Uses of Copyrighted Works in Senate *Report No. 640* would appear to accept the agreements of 1966, as embodied in the 1967 bill. The proposed Commission would have had to deal with technological uses of copyrighted material on the basis of those agreements, if S. 597 had passed into law. It seems unreasonable to suppose (as one infers educators did suppose) that the Commission's recommendations could overturn a duly enacted copyright law, particularly the law's provisions on machine reproduction, which educators admitted adhered to the compromise of 1966. Yet, the Ad Hoc Committee believed that statements in *Report No. 640* and Section 1(b)(2) of S. 2216 by themselves were adequate reasons for education to break the 1966 accords.

A more understandable objection of the Ad Hoc Committee was to the sentence in House *Report No. 83* that referred to excessively small possible losses of publication sales as a ground for instituting infringement proceedings. But, even after the Ad Hoc Committee was guaranteed in late 1969 that the objectionable line in *Report No. 83* would not appear in the forthcoming Senate report and would be deleted in any future House report, the committee nevertheless decided, according to the minutes of the Ad Hoc Committee meeting of July 27, 1970, "that because of changes in facts, circumstances, needs and times it would be perfectly proper to breach the agreement."

These concerns by copyright users, and the reactions of copyright owners, are reflected in the Senate hearings of 1967 that follow Senate *Report No. 640.* The Senate hearings were nearly as massive as the House hearings on copyright law revision of two years earlier, although the proceedings were conducted with considerably less concern. In fact, the only time that the full Subcommittee appeared during the Senate hearings was on April 11th, which happened to be the day that vocalist Julie London testified.

Selection from *Report No. 91-1219* of the Senate Judiciary Committee's Subcommittee on Patents, Trademarks and Copyrights sums up the status of copyright law revision at the end of the process's second decade. As it notes, little had changed during the last several years of the revision process.

The Register of Copyrights' annual *Reports* of 1969 through 1973, which follow selections from *Report No. 91-1219,* reflect the politics of the times. As the Register notes in his 1969 *Report,* "the program for general revision entered the 91st Congress with a noise that, if not exactly a whimper, was certainly far from a bang." And, the succeeding *Reports* of the Register indicate that the legislative effort to revise copyright law maintained that peculiar status for the next few years.

But, if "low-key" describes the legislative side of the revision campaign during these years, that is far from an appropriate assessment of the judicial side.

In June, 1968, Williams & Wilkins Company initiated a copyright infringement suit against the Library of the National Institutes of Health (NIH) and the National Library of Medicine (NLM). The Williams & Wilkins case was the first judicial test specifically concerned with copyright infringement resulting from photocopying practices.

Williams & Wilkins is a small publishing firm heavily involved in the biomedical field. It publishes thirty-seven journals, twenty-six of which are produced in conjunction with various professional societies. Spokespersons for the company stressed that, while it had brought suit for infringement, the harm being done by photocopying was not only to itself, but also to the societies for whom it published. Thus, spokespersons for the company insisted that the "target of the suit is not the 'casual user' who makes a single copy of an article for his own use, but organizations that offer copying services involving formal records and numerous employees."[1]

The NLM and NIH photocopying operations are very large in scale, and in that sense represented an arguable case for economic damage induced by neo-publishing practices. When Williams & Wilkins filed its suit in 1968, NLM in that year had supplied about 120,000 photocopies of copyrighted journal articles comprising approximately 1.2 million pages. In 1970, NIH furnished photocopies for about 86,000 requests, which totaled roughly 930,000 pages. William M. Passano, then president of Williams & Wilkins, contended that by projecting the records kept by NLM and NIH, one concludes that "1,000,000 pages of our journals were photocopied by the 200 leading libraries in the United States in 1968." He also stated that the subscription list of *Soil Science*, a journal published by his firm, "has remained static for the past several years, and individuals and institutions which logically should subscribe to it are photocopying it to death."

Passano was something of a maverick in the publishing field, and initiated his suit against the wishes of his colleagues, who felt that it would incur more resentment from librarians and educators than the industry could afford. Passano himself noted that publishers "are loath to risk offending such good customers as libraries and educators and, as a matter of fact, are unwilling to take this risk if one of their number is willing to pull their chestnuts out of the fire for them. Several years ago we reluctantly concluded that if the issue of uncontrolled photocopying was to be settled, we would have to go it alone." Passano, in fact, was approached by vice president Robert Frase of the American Association of Publishers, who had been commissioned by the industry to dissuade Passano from initiating his rumored suit. Passano, who met with Frase in the afternoon, told him that the suit had been filed that morning.

There can be little question that Passano believed in what he was doing. In one speech, he boarded the ecology bandwagon and contended that, "like the exhaust from automobiles or the spraying of DDT, uncontrolled photocopying is inexorably destroying its environment, which in this case is certain kinds of copyrighted material, most particularly scientific periodicals." In 1967, Williams & Wilkins published the only book in the implications of neo-publishing that is directed toward a popular audience: George A. Gipe's *Nearer to the Dust: Copyright and the Machine;* one would hesitate to evaluate it as an unbiased account. Finally, the firm is probably the only publishing house in the world that has established a system whereby it collects photocopying royalties from libraries that purchase the microfilm editions of its journals.

In a sixty-three page opinion delivered in February, 1972, U.S. Court of Claims Commissioner James F. Davis recommended in favor of the Williams & Wilkins Company. In so doing, he struck down every claim of federal offi-

---

1. An extended discussion of the case, including the sources for the quotations of William Passano and others that follow, can be found in: Nicholas Henry, *Copyright/ Information Technology/Public Policy. Part II: Public Policies/Information Technology.* New York: Marcel Dekker, Inc., 1976, pp. 75-79 and 90-98.

cials and copyright users, who contended that ownership of copyright was not determined, Williams & Wilkins was not the real party in interest, Williams & Wilkins was not infringed, fair use justified the government's practices, and license had been granted under the "Gentlemen's Agreement" of 1935. Davis recommended that the Williams & Wilkins proposal for a licensing system similar to the arrangement used in music publishing be considered seriously by the government.

Davis's recommendation to the U.S. Court of Claims was taken as a very grave turn of events by everyone involved. In the wake of the Williams & Wilkins recommendation, the Information Industry Association held a special seminar for copyright users and owners in order to discuss its implications for knowledge management, and the American Library Association urged its members to mobilize and resist the recommendation's implications for library service, particularly that of interlibrary loans. Williams & Wilkins, realizing the poor public relations effects that its suit might engender, took out advertisements in library journals explaining the principal points of the Davis ruling.

To the surprise of virtually all observers, on November 27, 1973, the seven-judge U.S. Court of Claims reversed the recommendation of its commissioner by a 4:3 decision. In rendering its decision, the court largely relied on, to use its own words, the "court-created" doctrine of fair use as its chief means of resolving the "troublesome problems" of new information technologies as they related to copyright. On May, 28, 1974, the U. S. Supreme Court agreed to hear the case on appeal.

Nine months later, on February 25, 1975, the Supreme Court of the United States announced its decision: Deadlock. The justices voted 4:4, with Justice Harry A. Blackmun disqualifying himself for undisclosed reasons. (It was thought in some circles that Blackmun, once a resident counsel with the Mayo Clinic, disqualified himself on the basis of close associations with persons in the medical profession.) Moreover, the Court added to the frustration inherent in any deadlock by refusing to write an opinion on the matter. The effect of the tie was to uphold the anticopyright verdict of the Court of Claims. Warren Weaver, Jr., writing in the *New York Times,* observed that the court's stalemate "seemed certain to promote efforts on two other fronts to clarify the situation. More court challenges will almost certainly be brought, probably dealing with broader aspects of the issue, and renewed pressure will be exerted on Congress to legislate a solution."

The ambivalence of the American courts on the impact of technology on copyright did not diminish the importance of the *Williams & Wilkins* case to the participants in the politics of neo-publishing. Its significance to them is indicated by the number of *amicus curiae* briefs filed by interested parties. At the Court of Claims level alone, *amicus curiae* briefs were filed by twenty-one organizations: the National Education Association, the American Library Association, the Association of Research Libraries, the Medical Library Association, the American Association of Law Libraries, the American Medical Association, the American Dental Association, the Mayo Foundation, the University of Michigan Medical School, the University of Rochester School of Medicine and Dentistry, the American Sociological Association, the Modern Language Association, the History of Science Society, the American Society for Testing and Materials, the National Council of Teachers of Mathematics, the Authors League, the Association of American Publishers, the Association of American University Presses, the American Institute of Physics, the American Chemical Society, and the dean of the Faculty of Medicine of Harvard University.

Another fourteen *amicus curiae* briefs were filed at the Supreme Court level by the end of April, 1974. Some of these briefs were from the same organizations that had submitted them earlier, notably the American Society for Testing and Materials, the National Council of Teachers of Mathematics, the Authors League, the American Chemical Society, the Association of American Publishers, and the Association of American University Presses. Most, however, were from other groups such as the American Guild of Authors and Composers, Behavioral Publications, Inc., Edwin H. Morris and Company, Harcourt Brace Jovanovich, Inc., Macmillan, Inc., the Society for Industrial and Applied Mathematics, the Magazine Publishers Association, and the Information Industry Association. The more important briefs are reproduced here.[2]

Beyond these shows of increasing and genuine support by copyright owners for Williams & Wilkins (filing *amicus* briefs is not cheap), certain publishers and professional societies formed a Committee on Copyright Protection. The committee solicited financial support for covering Williams & Wilkins' legal fees in its appeal to the Supreme Court. Its chairman, Curtis G. Benjamin of McGraw-Hill, said early on that "I confidently predict that 50 to 100 publishers will contribute to this cause," and noted that nine publishers and six professional societies had contributed from $100 to $5,000 prior to any formal solicitation by the committee.

While the *Williams & Wilkins* case was little more than an exercise in frustration, it could well be that the federal bureaucracy will evolve into the major determinant of public policy for the new information technologies, displacing the role of the courts and even of Congress. In point of fact, the bureaucracy has considerable leeway in defining the procedures and applicability of the public domain policy. For example, in 1973 the director of the National Institutes of Health inserted in the *Federal Register* a ruling which stated, in effect, that NIH could reproduce any research funded in whole or part by NIH, and could authorize others to do so by any means they chose, regardless of any copyright on the research that may be held by an author or journal. Because of liberal public funding of health-related research, such a policy affects an enormous portion of this kind of information. A number of journal editors responded to this ruling with the question, "Who owns our journals?" Nevertheless, NIH officials have held firm.

Relatedly, a variant of the public domain policy, that of "express license," also may undermine any pro-owner consequences that may emerge from the denouement of the *Williams & Wilkins* case. Express license refers to a privilege that the Federal government has had since 1965, which permits the government to stipulate that research publications funded with federal money may not be copyrighted under any provisions that preclude the government's copying or translating the publications without paying royalties. The government currently uses its express license privilege on a sporadic basis, but if it

---

2. The complete documentation of *Williams & Wilkins* is in: Marilyn McCormick, compiler, *The Williams & Wilkins Case: The Williams & Wilkins Company v. the United States*. Volume One. New York and London: Science Associates/International, Inc. and Mansell Information/Publishing Limited, 1974.

were to expand it and extend express license to nongovernmental users of federally sponsored research publications, the federal photocopying and copyright issue might well be rendered academic.

The bulk of the documents pertaining to *Williams & Wilkins* are reproduced here, although not all the *amicus curiae* are included for reasons of space. Nevertheless, documents pertaining to *Williams & Wilkins* comprise most of the public record reproduced in Volume II, and this is appropriate: The case represents the sole instance of judicial involvement in the complexities of technology and copyright, and these documents conclude Volume II.

NH
Tempe, Arizona

Copyright, Congress and Technology: The Public Record

Volume II:
The Political Years, 1967-1973

Annual Report of the Librarian of Congress
June 30, 1967

Efforts to obtain a general revision of the U.S. copyright law, which go back more than 40 years, passed another milestone in fiscal 1967, but as the year ended it was clear that a lot of hard traveling lay ahead. Passage of the bill by the House of Representatives was an undeniable achievement, but the satisfaction one could take in a hard-won and not unqualified victory was tempered by the knowledge that some major problems remained unsolved.

As the year began, the House Judiciary Subcommittee on Patents, Trademarks, and Copyrights under the chairmanship of Representative Robert W. Kastenmeier of Wisconsin, was in the middle of a series of 51 executive sessions devoted to detailed examination and redrafting of the bill. These sessions continued into September 1966, and the bill as revised by the subcommittee was reported unanimously to the full House Judiciary Committee on September 21, 1966.

Meanwhile, on August 2, 1966, the Senate Judiciary Subcommittee temporarily resumed hearings on the bill. Under the acting chairmanship of Senator Quentin N. Burdick of North Dakota the sole issue considered at this series of hearings was the liability of community antenna television systems (CATV) for copyright liability. This immensely difficult, economically important, and politically explosive question was also the subject of pending litigation and was closely related to a controversial program of CATV regulation adopted by the Federal Communications Commission. The issue of CATV liability had occupied a great deal of the House subcommittee's time and had produced a compromise proposal, which came to be known as the "Kastenmeier proposal," generally making the extent of liability of a CATV system depend on its impact on the copyright proprietor's market. This proposal was discussed at length during the Senate hearings and, while some progress was made, it was obvious that much more work remained to be done.

On October 12, 1966, the full House Committee on the Judiciary reported the revised bill without further amendment. House Report No. 2237 (89th Cong., 2d sess.), which comprises 279 pages including 141 pages of explanatory text, is an unusually valuable addition to the legislative history of the general revision bill. It examines virtually every provision of the bill in detail, recording the committee's reasoning behind its decisions on substantive issues and the intention behind its choice of statutory language. In a statement printed in the *Congressional Record* on October 19, 1966, Representative Richard H. Poff of Virginia, the ranking minority member on the subcommittee, stated:

> The Judiciary Committee is proud of its work on H.R. 4347 and the time, deliberation, and careful consideration given every issue and argument regarding every component part of the proposed new copyright law. But those of us who are involved in the legislative phase of this program are particularly appreciative of the work of the Copyright Office: the 6 years of studying the past revision efforts and present and future needs of a new law; the forum and climate provided by the Copyright Office for the 3 years of debating and discussing the innumerable proposals for revision and continuing efforts of the Copyright Office to find consensus on issues of controversy. We are appreciative of the Copyright Office's contribution to our subcommittee's executive deliberations in presenting objective analysis of every position on every issue to the subcommittee and providing the subcommittee with the expertise of almost 100 years of administering the copyright laws.

The 89th Congress adjourned less than two weeks after the bill was reported, but in its revised form it was introduced in the 90th Congress by Senator John L. McClellan (S. 597) and by Representative Emanuel Celler (H.R. 2512). It was considered by the newly constituted membership of the House Judiciary Subcommittee, again chaired by Representative Kastenmeier, in executive sessions on February 20, 24, and 27, 1967, and some further revisions were agreed upon. The bill was reported unanimously to the full committee on February 27, and was again reported to the House on March 2, 1967. Report No. 83 runs 254 pages, including 144 pages of detailed analysis; it also includes minority views by Representatives Byron G. Rogers of Colorado and Basil L. Whitener of North Carolina devoted to the jukebox issue and an additional dissent by Mr. Whitener on the bill's treatment of CATV.

It was becoming increasingly apparent, as the bill moved toward the House floor, that unreconciled conflicts on the issues of jukebox performances and CATV transmissions remained, and that there was danger that one or both of these issues could defeat the bill. The bill was considered by the House Rules Committee on March 8, 1967, and although full debate on the House floor was authorized, the tenor of the arguments forecast trouble on the floor.

Consideration by the House of Representatives of H.R. 2512 started at 10 a.m. on Thursday, April 6, 1967. Throughout the long day the House considered the complex and technical bill. The lengthy debate, acrimonious at times, and the endless quorum calls, focused on the two unresolved issues: jukeboxes and community antenna systems. It was clear that these important, unresolved, economic issues were blocking consideration of the entire bill on its merits, and at 7 p.m. the managers of the bill made the decision to take the bill off the floor, and the House recessed. The revision program had come close to disaster.

It was obvious that there was no point in resuming debate unless the issues of April 6 could be reconciled. In the next four days several crucial compromises were reached in direct negotiations, and on Tuesday, April 11, an amended bill was passed by the House after mild debate with the remarkable vote of 379 yeas to 29 nays. Fairly radical changes were made in three areas: jukebox, CATV, and instructional broadcasting. There were drastic revisions in the compulsory licensing provisions establishing copyright liability for jukebox performances; the provisions dealing with community antenna transmission were dropped entirely, theoretically leaving CATV systems fully liable for copyright infringement; and the exemptions for instructional television were considerably broadened. On the other hand, the structure and content of the bill had remained substantially intact, and there was reason to hope that at least some of the compromise solutions would stick.

Meanwhile, the Senate Judiciary Subcommittee had resumed full-scale consideration of the bill, under the joint chairmanship of Senators McClellan and Burdick, on March 15, 1967. The record of the 1967 Senate hearings, which lasted 10 days and ended on April 28, 1967, nearly equals that of the House hearings in size and content. The Senate subcommittee did not consider CATV in its 1967 hearings since it had already heard testimony on the issue several months earlier.

Of the several other areas that emerged as full-blown issues at the Senate hearings, by far the most important was the problem of the use of copyrighted works in automatic information storage and retrieval systems. The "computer problem" could well turn out to be the most important issue in the history of the copyright law, but the Senate hearings and other extensive discussions of the question during fiscal 1967 made clear that a legislative solution is not at hand.

As the 20th-century technological revolution continues relentlessly to reshape and expand the availability and efficiency of methods of communication, new groups arise to challenge the exclusive rights that authors have traditionally been given under the copyright law. Two years ago the most significant problems in copyright law revision came from jukebox performances and educational copying, today they come from community antenna television systems and computers, and two years from now there may well be new interests whose future will be directly affected by the copyright law. This acceleration makes the enactment of a revised copyright statute increasingly difficult at the very time that the act passed in 1909 is proving increasingly inadequate.

The present law is essentially a 19th-century copyright statute, based on assumptions concerning the creation and dissemination of authors' works that have been completely overturned in the past 50 years. A 20th-century copyright statute is long overdue in the United States, and the present need for a revised law that will anticipate the 21st century is undeniable. Yet again and again it has seemed that abstract agreement on this need for complete revision gives way to concrete disagreement on particular provisions to appear in the new statute. As time goes on the problems become increasingly complex, the economic and political power of the special interests becomes greater, and the conflicts on particular issues become more intense. It was obvious as the fiscal year ended that a great deal more patience, acumen, and hard work would be demanded before the goal of the general revision program can be attained.

Annual Report of the Librarian of Congress
June 30, 1968

Fiscal 1968 was a year of present disappointment but continued hope for enactment of the bill for general revision of the copyright law. The revision bill, which had been passed by the House of Representatives on April 11, 1967, had also been the subject of 10 days of full-scale hearings in 1967 before the Senate Judiciary Subcommittee on Patents, Trademarks, and Copyrights. As the fiscal year began, the program for general revision appeared to have gained substantial legislative momentum.

Much of this momentum was lost in fiscal 1968. A combination of circumstances, arising primarily from the continuing controversy between copyright owners and cable television (CATV) operators, caused the Senate subcommittee to defer action on the revision bill during the 90th Congress. At the end of the fiscal year the proponents of the bill found themselves facing a difficult period of reappraisal, new decisions, and redrafting.

Although CATV turned out to be the most serious issue the revision bill has ever encountered, the first part of the fiscal year was occupied with another important problem: the use of copyrighted works in automatic information storage and retrieval systems. This issue, which had emerged during the course of the Senate hearings, pointed to the need for a meaningful and objective study of the interrelationships between the copyright law and the new information-transfer technology before definitive legislative solutions could be found. Accordingly, the Copyright Office prepared draft language for a bill to establish a national commission within the legislative branch to study the long-range implications of this problem and to recommend legislative solutions.

This draft bill was circulated, and on July 25, 1967, a large group of interested parties met under Senate subcommittee auspices to discuss its content and language. The response to the proposal was generally affirmative, and after undergoing some revision the bill was introduced as S. 2216 by Senator John L. McClellan on August 2, 1967. The commission bill was favorably reported by the Senate Judiciary Committee on October 11, 1967 (S. Rept. 640, 90th Cong., 1st sess.), and was passed by the Senate on October 16, 1967. The bill was then referred to the House Judiciary Committee, which deferred action because the general revision bill had been sidetracked.

S. 2216, a Bill to Establish in the Library of Congress a National Commission on New Technological Uses of Copyrighted Works, provides for a 23-man commission composed of the Librarian of Congress as chairman, two Senators, two Representatives, seven members selected from authors and other copyright owners, seven members selected from users of copyrighted materials, and four nongovernmental members selected from the general public. The Register of Copyrights would serve as an ex officio member. The purpose of the commission would be to study the reproduction and use of copyrighted works in "automatic systems capable of storing, processing, retrieving, and transferring information," and also "by various forms of machine reproduction." Within three years after its creation the commission would recommend to the President and the Congress "such changes in copyright law or procedures that may be necessary to assure for such purposes access to copyrighted works, and to provide recognition of the rights of copyright owners."

Anticipating the early enactment of a general revision bill that would substantially lengthen the duration of copyrights already in effect, Congress had adopted in 1962, and again in 1965, two measures extending the length of copyrights otherwise due to expire. These extension acts were effective only through the end of 1967, and as the year wore on it became increasingly obvious that no general revision legislation could be passed before the deadline. Proposals to introduce a third extension bill, however, were met with strong efforts to add an amendment or rider providing a moratorium on copyright infringement actions against CATV operators. This produced an impasse that threatened not only the temporary extensions of copyright but also the revision program itself. In an effort to break the deadlock the Copyright Office in August 1967 held a series of meetings culminating, on August 24, with a meeting attended by nearly 50 persons representing all of the interested groups. As a result of this meeting a temporary accommodation was reached and on October 3, 1967, Senator McClellan introduced Senate Joint Resolution 114, extending expiring renewal copyrights through December 31, 1968. Senator McClellan's statement in the *Congressional Record* explained that the measure was being introduced without the provision for a CATV moratorium in view of assurances by the major copyright proprietors that they would not institute copyright infringement suits against CATV operators without ample advance notice, as long as discussions in good faith between the interested parties were continuing toward the goal of "contractual arrangements" and "appropriate legislative formulas." The interim extension bill was passed by the Senate on October 19, 1967, and, after a short hearing in the House of Representatives on October 26, 1967, at which the Register of Copyrights was the only witness, it was passed by the House, becoming Public Law 90–141 on November 16, 1967.

The temporary agreement between the copyright owners and the CATV interests also resulted in a long series of meetings and discussions of their mutual problems and proposals for solutions. These meetings continued throughout the fiscal year and might conceivably have produced a compromise settlement had not the Supreme Court agreed, in December 1967, to review the decisions of the lower courts in *United Artists Television, Inc.* v. *Fortnightly Corp.* These decisions had held that certain activities of CATV systems constitute infringement under the present copyright law of 1909, and the prospect of a Supreme Court decision in the case effectively stalled the progress of the revision bill for the rest of the fiscal year.

As movement toward revision came to a standstill, the Register of Copyrights and others undertook efforts to preserve at least some of the accomplishments and momentum that had been achieved during the 90th Congress. These efforts took the form of proposals for a "skeleton" bill that would contain a number of the largely uncontroversial parts of the general revision bill while leaving such hotly disputed issues as cable television liability for separate consideration in the 91st Congress. The proposal for a skeleton bill came to an end on April 18, 1968, when, during a meeting sponsored by the Senate subcommittee, a letter from Senator McClellan to the Register of

Copyrights dated April 17 was made public. In his letter Senator McClellan made clear that, because "this approach presents serious and unavoidable complications," he was unable to support or recommend it. On the other hand, he expressed himself as favoring "action at the earliest feasible date on the entire revision program" and indicated his willingness to "recommend to the Subcommittee that the Senate should act first on this legislation in the next Congress" and to introduce another interim extension of expiring copyrights. In a statement delivered at the same meeting the Register of Copyrights accepted the failure of the skeleton bill approach but warned of the dangers confronting the revision program and the need for cooperative effort to avoid them.

The principal purpose of the April 18 meeting was to discuss, under Senate subcommittee auspices, the liability for certain uses of copyrighted material in computers and other new devices while the question is being studied by the proposed National Commission on New Technological Uses of Copyrighted Works. Although there were some differences of opinion, the maintenance of the status quo during this period seemed generally acceptable to representatives of both owners and users.

On May 22, 1968, as he had promised, Senator McClellan introduced Senate Joint Resolution 172 to extend the duration of expiring renewal copyrights through December 31, 1969. The measure was passed by the Senate on June 12, 1968, and by the House on July 15 and became law on July 23 (Public Law 90–416). The effect of this and the earlier extension enactments is to continue in force until the end of 1969 subsisting renewal copyrights that would have expired between September 19, 1962, and December 31, 1969. These extensions apply only to copyrights previously renewed in which the second term would otherwise expire; they do not apply to copyrights in their first term, and they have no effect on the time limits for renewal registration.

The fiscal year in general revision came to its climax on June 17, 1968, when the Supreme Court handed down its historic CATV decision in the *Fortnightly* case. The Court's decision, which is discussed below, held that the CATV operations involved in the suit were not "performances" of copyrighted material and were therefore free of copyright liability. This ruling substantially altered the balance of bargaining power on the cable television question. It did not have the effect of killing the revision program, but it emphasized both the urgency and the difficulty of finding a formula for the settlement of this important issue before any further progress toward general revision will be possible.

COPYRIGHT LAW REVISION

MARCH 8, 1967.—Committed to the Committee of the Whole House on the State
of the Union and ordered to be printed

Mr. KASTENMEIER, from the Committee on the Judiciary, submitted
the following

REPORT

[To accompany H.R. 2512]

The Committee on the Judiciary, to whom was referred the bill
(H.R. 2512) for the general revision of the copyright laws, title 17 of
the United States Code, and for other purposes, having considered the
same, report favorably thereon without amendment and recommend
that the bill do pass.

PURPOSE

The purpose of H.R. 2512 is to enact a general revision of the U.S.
copyright law, constituting title 17 of the United States Code, in light
of the profound technological and commercial changes that have taken
place since the 1909 revision. The present bill is an outgrowth of
H.R. 4347 which was introduced on February 4, 1965, in the 89th
Congress. After extensive hearings and thorough deliberations on
H.R. 4347 by Subcommittee No. 3, the committee reported favorably
an amended version of H.R. 4347 (H. Rept. No. 2237, 89th Cong.,
second sess., Oct. 12, 1966). The present bill is substantially identical
with H.R. 4347 as so amended and reported by the committee. The
changes proposed by the committee from H.R. 4347 as introduced, reflected consideration of a number of the issues as they became clarified by the hearings and subsequent discussions. The purpose of these
proposed changes is indicated below in the sections of this report captioned "Summary of Principal Provisions" and "Sectional Analysis
and Discussion." A comparative print showing (1) the reported bill,
(2) existing law, and (3) the provisions of H.R. 4347, 89th Congress
as introduced will be found in the section captioned "Changes in Existing Law."

SECTION 106. EXCLUSIVE RIGHTS IN COPYRIGHTED WORKS

General scope of copyright

The five fundamental rights that the bill gives to copyright owners —the exclusive rights of reproduction, adaptation, publication, performance, and display—are stated generally in section 106. These exclusive rights, which comprise the so-called "bundle of rights" that is a copyright, are cumulative and may overlap in some cases. Each of the five enumerated rights may be subdivided indefinitely and, as discussed below in connection with section 201, each subdivision of an exclusive right may be owned and enforced separately.

The approach of the bill is to set forth the copyright owner's exclusive rights in broad terms in section 106, and then to provide various limitations, qualifications, or exemptions in the 10 sections that follow. Thus, everything in section 106 is made "subject to sections 107 through 116," and must be read in conjunction with those provisions.

The exclusive rights accorded to a copyright owner under section 106 are "to do and to authorize" any of the activities specified in the five numbered clauses. Use of the phrase "to authorize" is intended to avoid any questions as to the liability of contributory infringers. For example, a person who lawfully acquires an authorized copy of a motion picture would be an infringer if he engages in the business of renting it to others for purposes of unauthorized public performance.

Rights of reproduction, adaptation, and publication

The first three clauses of section 106, which cover all rights under a copyright except those of performance and display, extend to every kind of copyrighted work. The exclusive rights encompassed by these clauses, though closely related, are independent; they can generally be characterized as rights of copying, recording, adaptation, and publishing. A single act of infringement may violate all of these rights at once, as where a publisher reproduces, adapts, and sells copies of a person's copyrighted work as part of a publishing venture. Infringement takes place when any one of the rights is violated: where, for example, a printer reproduces copies without selling them or a retailer sells copies without having anything to do with their reproduction. The references to "copies or phonorecords," although in the plural, are intended here and throughout the bill to include the singular (1 U.S.C. § 1).

Reproduction.—Read together with the relevant definitions in section 101, the right "to reproduce the copyrighted work in copies or phonorecords" means the right to produce a material object in which the work is duplicated, transcribed, imitated, or simulated in a fixed form from which it can be "perceived, reproduced, or otherwise communicated, either directly or with the aid of a machine or device." As under the present law, a copyrighted work would be infringed by reproducing it in whole or in any substantial part, and by duplicating it exactly or by imitation or simulation. Wide departures or variations from the copyrighted work would still be an infringement as long as the author's "expression" rather than merely his "ideas" are taken.

"Reproduction" under clause (1) of section 106 is to be distinguished from "display" under clause (5). For a work to be "reproduced," its fixation in tangible form must be "sufficiently permanent or stable to permit it to be perceived, reproduced, or otherwise communicated for a period of more than transitory duration." Thus, the showing of images on a screen or tube would not be a violation of clause (1), although it might come within the scope of clause (5).

Preparation of derivative works.—The exclusive right to prepare derivative works, specified separately in clause (2) of section 106, overlaps the exclusive right of reproduction to some extent. It is broader than that right, however, in the sense that reproduction requires fixation in copies or phonorecords, whereas the preparation of a derivative work, such as a ballet, pantomime, or improvised performance, may be an infringement even though nothing is ever fixed in tangible form.

To be an infringement the "derivative work" must be "based upon the copyrighted work," and the definition in section 101 refers to "a translation, musical arrangement, dramatization, fictionalization, motion picture version, sound recording, art reproduction, abridgment, condensation, or any other form in which a work may be recast, transformed, or adapted." Thus, to constitute a violation of section 106(2), the infringing work must incorporate a portion of the copyrighted work in some form; for example, a detailed commentary on a work or a programmatic musical composition inspired by a novel would not normally constitute infringements under this clause.

Use in information storage and retrieval systems.—Although it was touched on rather lightly at the hearings, the problem of computer uses of copyrighted material has attracted increasing attention and controversy in recent months. Recognizing the profound impact that information storage and retrieval devices seem destined to have on authorship, communications, and human life itself, the committee is also aware of the dangers of legislating prematurely in this area of exploding technology.

In the context of section 106, the committee believes that, instead of trying to deal explicitly with computer uses, the statute should be general in terms and broad enough to allow for adjustment to future changes in patterns of reproduction and other uses of authors' works. Thus, unless the doctrine of fair use were applicable, the following computer uses could be infringements of copyright under section 106: reproduction of a work (or a substantial part of it) in any tangible form (paper, punch cards, magnetic tape, etc.) for input into an information storage and retrieval system; reproduction of a work or substantial parts of it, in copies as the "print-out" or output of the computer; preparation for input of an index or abstract of the work so complete and detailed that it would be considered a "derivative work"; computer transmission or display of a visual image of a work to one or more members of the public. On the other hand, since the mere scanning or manipulation of the contents of a work within the system would not involve a reproduction, the preparation of a derivative work, or a public distribution, performance, or display, it would be outside the scope of the legislation.

It has been argued on behalf of those interested in fostering computer uses that the copyright owner is not damaged by input alone,

and that the development of computer technology calls for unrestricted availability of unlimited quantities of copyrighted material
for introduction into information systems. While acknowledging
that copyright payments should be made for output and possibly some
other computer uses, these interests recommended at least a partial exemption in cases of reproduction for input. On the other side, the
copyright owners stressed that computers have the potential, and in
some cases the present, capacity to destroy the entire market of authors
and publishers. They consider it indispensable that input, beyond
fair use, require the consent of the copyright owner, on the ground
that this is the only point in computer operations at which copyright
control can be exercised; they argue that the mere presence of an
electronic reproduction in a machine could deprive a publisher of
a substantial market for printed copies, and that if input were exempted there would likewise be no market for machine-readable
copies.

In various discussions since the hearings, there have been proposals
for establishing voluntary licensing systems for computer uses, and
it was suggested that a commission be established to study the problem and recommend definitive copyright legislation several years from
now. The committee expresses the hope that the interests involved
will work together toward an ultimate solution of this problem in the
light of experience. Toward this end the Register of Copyrights
may find it appropriate to hold further meetings on this subject after
passage of the new law. In the meantime, however, section 106 preserves the exclusive rights of the copyright owner with respect to
reproductions of his work for input or storage in an information
system.

Public distribution.—Clause (3) of section 106 establishes the exclusive right of publication: The right "to distribute copies or phonorecords of the copyrighted work to the public by sale or other transfer
of ownership, or by rental, lease, or lending." Under this provision
the copyright owner would have the right to control the first public
distribution of an authorized copy or phonorecord of his work, whether
by sale, gift, loan, or some rental or lease arrangement. Likewise,
any unauthorized public distribution of copies or phonorecords that
were unlawfully made would be an infringement. As section 109
makes clear, however, the copyright owner's rights under section
106(3) cease with respect to a particular copy or phonorecord once he
has parted with ownership of it.

Rights of public performance and display

Performing rights and the "for profit" limitation.—The right of
public performance under section 106(4) extends to "literary, musical, dramatic, and choreographic works, pantomimes, and motion pictures and other audiovisual works" and, unlike the equivalent
provisions now in effect, is not limited by any "for profit" requirement.
The approach of the bill, as in many foreign laws, is first to state the
public performance right in broad terms, and then to provide specific
exemptions for educational and other nonprofit uses.

The committee has adopted this approach as more reasonable than
the outright exemption of the 1909 statute. It found persuasive the

arguments that the line between commercial and "nonprofit" organizations is increasingly difficult to draw, that many "nonprofit" organizations are highly subsidized and capable of paying royalties, and that the widespread public exploitation of copyrighted works by educational broadcasters and other noncommercial organizations is likely to grow. In addition to these trends, it is worth noting that performances and displays are continuing to supplant markets for printed copies and that in the future a broad "not for profit" exemption could not only hurt authors but could dry up their incentive to write.

As will be discussed below in connection with section 114, the bill does not recognize a right of public performance in sound recordings. However, the committee adopted the recommendation, put forward by producers of audiovisual works and book publishers, that the exclusive right of public performance should be expanded to include not only motion pictures but also audiovisual works such as filmstrips and sets of slides. The amendment of section 106(4), which is consistent with the assimilation of motion pictures to audiovisual works throughout the bill, is also related to amendments of the definitions of "display" and "perform" discussed below.

Right of public display.—Clause (5) of section 106 represents the first explicit statutory recognition in American copyright law of an exclusive right to show a copyrighted work, or an image of it, to the public. The existence or extent of this right under the present statute is uncertain and subject to challenge. The bill would give the owners of copyright in "literary, musical, dramatic, and choreographic works, pantomimes, and pictorial, graphic, or sculptural works" the exclusive right "to display the copyrighted work publicly."

With the growing use of projection equipment, closed and open circuit television, and computers for displaying images of textual and graphic material to "audiences" or "readers," this right is certain to assume great importance to copyright owners. A recognition of this potentiality is reflected in the proposal of book publishers and producers of audiovisual works which, in effect, would equate "display" with "reproduction" where the showing is "for use in lieu of a copy." The committee is aware that in the future electronic images may take the place of printed copies in some situations, and has dealt with the problem by amendments in sections 109 and 110, and without mixing the separate concepts of "reproduction" and "display." No provision of the bill would make a purely private display of a work a copyright infringement.

In H.R. 4347 as introduced, the operative word in clause (5) was "exhibit." This term proved confusing and objectionable because of its common usage in referring to the performance of motion pictures. As recommended by the Register of Copyrights, therefore, the committee has substituted the word "display" here and throughout the bill.

Definitions

Section 106 of the 1965 bill included a subsection defining the terms "perform," "exhibit" (i.e., "display"), and "publicly" but, since these terms also occur in other sections, their definitions have been moved to section 101. Each of these definitions has also undergone some amendment.

Under the definitions of "perform," "display," "publicly," and "transmit" now in section 101, the concepts of public performance and public display cover not only the initial rendition or showing, but also any further act by which that rendition or showing is transmitted or communicated to the public. Thus, for example: a singer is performing when he sings a song; a broadcasting network is performing when it transmits his performance (whether simultaneously or from records); a local broadcaster is performing when it transmits the network broadcast; a community antenna service is performing when it retransmits the broadcast to its subscribers; and any individual is performing whenever he plays a phonorecord embodying the performance or communicates the performance by turning on a receiving set. Although any act by which the initial performance or display is transmitted, repeated, or made to recur would itself be a "performance" or "display" under the bill, it would not be actionable as an infringement unless it were done "publicly," as defined in section 101. Certain other performances and displays, in addition to those that are "private," are exempted or given qualified copyright control under sections 107 through 116.

To "perform" a work, under the definition in section 101, includes reading a literary work aloud, singing or playing music, dancing a ballet or other choreographic work, and acting out a dramatic work or pantomime. A performance may be accomplished "either directly or by means of any device or process," including all kinds of equipment for reproducing or amplifying sounds or visual images, any sort of transmitting apparatus, any type of electronic retrieval system, and any other techniques and systems not yet in use or even invented. As amended by the committee, the definition of "perform" in relation to "a motion picture or other audiovisual work" is "to show its images in sequence or to make the sounds accompanying it audible." The showing of portions of a motion picture, filmstrip, or slide set must therefore be sequential to constitute a "performance" rather than a "display." The purely aural performance of a motion picture sound track, or of the sound portions of an audiovisual work, would constitute a performance of the "motion picture or other audiovisual work"; but, where some of the sounds have been reproduced separately on phonorecords, a performance from the phonorecord would not constitute performance of the motion picture or audiovisual work.

The corresponding definition of "display," as amended, covers any showing of a "copy" of the work, "either directly or by means of a film, slide, television image, or any other device or process." The phrase "motion picture" before the word "film" has been omitted to avoid confusion. Since "copies" are defined as including the material object "in which the work is first fixed," the right of public display applies to original works of art as well as to reproductions of them. With respect to motion pictures and other audiovisual works, it is a "display" (rather than a "performance") to show their "individual images nonsequentially." In addition to the direct showings of a copy of a work, "display" would include the projection of an image on a screen or other surface by any method, the transmission of an image by electronic or other means, and the showing of an image on a cathode ray tube or similar viewing apparatus connected with any sort of information storage and retrieval system.

The definition of "publicly" in connection with performance and display has also undergone some amendment. As explained at pages 23–24 of the Register's Supplementary Report, one of the principal purposes of the definition was to make clear that, contrary to the decision in *Metro-Goldwyn-Mayer Distributing Corp.* v. *Wyatt*, 21 C.O. Bull. 203 (D. Md. 1932), performances in "semipublic" places such as clubs, lodges, factories, summer camps, and schools are "public performances" subject to copyright control. To accomplish this result, the committee has restored the wording of the 1964 bill: under clause (1) of the definition, a performance or display is "public" if it takes place "at a place open to the public or at a place where a substantial number of persons outside of a normal circle of a family and its social acquaintances is gathered."

The term "a family" in this context would include an individual living alone, so that a gathering confined to the individual's social acquaintances would normally be regarded as private. The Department of Defense proposed that the definition be further amended to exclude "an official meeting or gathering of officers or employees of the United States Government"; the committee did not accept this recommendation, but notes that most routine meetings of business and governmental personnel would be excluded because they do not represent the gathering of a "substantial number of persons."

Clause (2) of the definition of "publicly" in section 101 makes clear that the concepts of public performance and public display include not only performances and displays that occur initially in a public place, but also acts that "transmit or otherwise communicate a performance or display of the work to the public by means of any device or process." The definition of "transmit"—to communicate a performance or display "by any device or process whereby images or sounds are received beyond the place from which they are sent"—is broad enough to include all conceivable forms and combinations of wired or wireless communications media, including but by no means limited to radio and television broadcasting as we know them. Each and every method by which the images or sounds comprising a performance or display are picked up and conveyed is a "transmission," and if the transmission reaches the public in any form, the case comes within the scope of clauses (4) or (5) of section 106.

Under the bill, as under the present law, a performance made available by transmission to the public at large is "public" even though the recipients are not gathered in a single place, and even if there is no direct proof that any of the potential recipients was operating his receiving apparatus at the time of the transmission. The same principles apply whenever the potential recipients of the transmission represent a limited segment of the public, such as the occupants of hotel rooms or the subscribers of a community antenna television service; they are also applicable where the transmission is capable of reaching different recipients at different times, as in the case of sounds or images stored in an information system and capable of being performed or displayed at the initiative of individual members of the public. To make these principles doubly clear, the committee has amended clause (2) of the definition of "publicly" so that it is applicable "whether the members of the public capable of receiving the performance or display receive it in the same place or in separate places and at the same time or at different times."

SECTION 107. FAIR USE

General background of the problem

The judicial doctrine of fair use, one of the most important and well-established limitations on the exclusive rights of copyright owners, would be given express statutory recognition for the first time in section 107. The claim that a defendant's acts constituted a fair use rather than an infringement has been raised as a defense in innumerable copyright actions over the years, and there is ample case law recognizing the existence of the doctrine and applying it. The examples enumerated at page 24 of the Register's 1961 Report, while by no means exhaustive, give some idea of the sort of activities the courts might regard as fair use under the circumstances: "quotation of excerpts in a review or criticism for purposes of illustration or comment; quotation of short passages in a scholarly or technical work, for illustration or clarification of the author's observations; use in a parody of some of the content of the work parodied; summary of an address or article, with brief quotations, in a news report; reproduction by a library of a portion of a work to replace part of a damaged copy; reproduction by a teacher or student of a small part of a work to illustrate a lesson; reproduction of a work in legislative or judicial proceedings or reports; incidental and fortuitous reproduction, in a newsreel or broadcast, of a work located at the scene of an event being reported."

Although the courts have considered and ruled upon the fair use doctrine over and over again, no real definition of the concept has ever emerged. Indeed, since the doctrine is an equitable rule of reason, no generally applicable definition is possible, and each case raising the question must be decided on its own facts. On the other hand, the courts have evolved a set of criteria which, though in no sense definitive or determinative, provide some gage for balancing the equities. These criteria have been stated in various ways, but essentially they can all be reduced to the four standards which were stated in the 1964 bill and have been adopted again in the committee's amendment of section 107: "(1) the purpose and character of the use; (2) the nature of the copyrighted work; (3) the amount and substantiality of the portion used in relation to the copyrighted work as a whole; and (4) the effect of the use upon the potential market for or value of the copyrighted work."

The controversy over the related problems of fair use and the reproduction of copyrighted material for educational and scholarly purposes began well before the hearings. This problem in copyright law revision received much attention from witnesses at the hearings, and from the committee thereafter.

The fair use provision in H.R. 4347, as introduced, had been reduced to a bare statement that "the fair use of a copyrighted work is not an infringement of copyright." This approach was supported by a wide range of interests on the ground that the doctrine should remain as flexible as possible, and that any attempt at definition could freeze the concept and open the door to massive, unreasonable abuses. On the other side a number of witnesses representing various educational and scholarly organizations criticized the provision as vague and nebulous, and stressed the need of teachers and scholars to be certain whether what they were doing constituted fair use or infringement. They recommended restoration of a part of the provision in the 1964 bill referring to "fair use * * * to the extent reasonably necessary or incidental to a legitimate purpose such as criticism, comment, news reporting, teaching, scholarship, or research."

The group representing educational and scholarly organizations argued further that the doctrine of fair use alone is insufficient to provide the certainty that teachers and other nonprofit educational users of copyrighted material need for their own protection. They emphasized that teachers are not interested in mass copying that actually damages authors and publishers, but that they need to be free to make creative use of all of the resources available to them in the classroom, and that this necessarily involves some reproduction and distribution of copyrighted works such as contemporaneous material in the press, isolated poems and stories for illustrative purposes, and the like. Representatives of the educational group contended that a statute subjecting the use of modern teaching tools to requirements for advance clearance and payment of fees would inhibit use of teachers' imagination and ingenuity, and they proposed adoption of a specific, limited exemption for educational copying that would apply the "not-for-profit" limitation of the present law. They also proposed an amendment of section 504(c) that would allow a court to withhold any award of statutory damages against innocent teachers.

The proposal for a specific educational copying exemption was vigorously opposed by authors and publishers, among a number of others. They characterized the educators' arguments as saying, in effect, that since it is increasingly easy to infringe, violations should be made legal. They maintained that the present "for profit" limitation has nothing to do with copying, and that the argument for exempting educational uses on the ground that they are noncommercial overlooks the serious losses and destruction of incentive that uncompensated educational uses would cause to authors and publishers, particularly in the textbook, reference book, and scientific publishing areas. They stressed that education is the textbook publisher's only market, and that many authors receive their main income from licensing reprints in anthologies and textbooks; if an unlimited number of teachers could prepare and reproduce their own anthologies, the cumulative effect would be disastrous. Because photocopying and other reproducing devices are constantly proliferating and becoming easier and cheaper to use, it was claimed that the future of some kinds of publishing is at stake, and that solutions should be sought through reasonable voluntary licensing or clearance arrangements rather than an outright exemption that would hurt authorship, publishing, and ultimately education itself.

The implications of these opposing positions extend far beneath the surface of the specific arguments and involve fundamental questions of social policy. The fullest possible use of the multitude of technical devices now available to education should be encouraged. But, bearing in mind that the basic constitutional purpose of granting copyright protection is the advancement of learning, the committee also recognizes that the potential destruction of incentives to authorship presents a serious danger.

The sharp exchanges between the representatives of authors and publishers and those of educators and scholars at the hearings did not conceal their recognition of common aims and of the need for reasonable accommodation. Several productive meetings were held in June 1966; while no final agreements were reached, the meetings were generally successful in clarifying the issues and in pointing the way toward constructive solutions.

After full consideration, the committee believes that a specific exemption freeing certain reproductions of copyrighted works for educational and scholarly purposes from copyright control is not justified. As shown by a Copyright Office study dated July 22, 1966, the educational groups are mistaken in their argument that a "for profit" limitation is applicable to educational copying under the present law. Any educational uses that are fair use today would be fair use under the bill.

On the other hand, recognizing the need for greater certainty and protection for teachers, the committee has amended section 504(c), as explained below, to insulate a teacher who honestly and reasonably believes what he was doing constituted a fair use from excessive liability for minimum statutory damages. It has also amended section 107 to restore a statement of the four criteria, quoted above, to indicate that a fair use may include "such use by reproduction in copies or phonorecords or by any other means specified by [section 106]," and to characterize a fair use as generally being "for purposes such as criticism, comment, news reporting, teaching, scholarship, or research."

The intention of the committee with respect to the application of the fair use doctrine in various situations is discussed below. It should be emphasized again that, in those situations or any others, the committee has no purpose of either freezing or changing the doctrine. In particular, the reference to fair use "by reproduction in copies or phonorecords or by any other means" should not be interpreted as sanctioning any reproduction beyond the normal and reasonable limits of fair use. The clause was added in response to arguments by educators that, since the case law on fair use has not yet dealt with photocopying and analogous forms of reproduction, section 107 should contain language making clear that the doctrine has as much application in those areas as in any others. In making separate mention of "reproduction in copies or phonorecords" in the section, the committee does not intend to give this kind of use any special or preferred status as compared with other kinds of uses. In any event, whether a use referred to in the first sentence of section 107 is a fair use in a particular case will depend upon the application of the determinative factors, including those mentioned in the second sentence.

Intention of the committee

In general.—The expanded statement of the fair use doctrine in amended section 107 offers some guidance to users in determining when the principles of the doctrine apply. However, the endless variety of situations and combinations of circumstances that can arise in particular cases precludes the formulation of exact rules in the statute. We endorse the purpose and general scope of the judicial doctrine of fair use, as outlined earlier in this report, but there is no disposition to freeze the doctrine in the statute, especially during a period of rapid technological change. Beyond a very broad statutory explanation of what fair use is and some of the criteria applicable to it, the courts must be free to adapt the doctrine to particular situations on a case-by-case basis.

Section 107, as revised by the committee, is intended to restate the present judicial doctrine of fair use, not to change, narrow, or enlarge it in any way. However, since this section will represent the first statutory recognition of the doctrine in our copyright law, some explanation of the considerations behind the language used in the list of four criteria is advisable. This is particularly true as to cases of copying by teachers, since in this area there are few if any judicial guidelines.

The committee emphasizes that its statements with respect to each of the criteria of fair use are necessarily subject to qualifications, because they must be applied in combination with the circumstances pertaining to other criteria, and because new conditions arising in the future may alter the balance of equities. It is also important to emphasize that, by singling out some instances to discuss in the context of fair use, we do not intend to indicate that other activities would or would not be beyond fair use. Since most of the testimony before the committee involved teaching activities, the following discussion is related specifically to them, but is should not be inferred that uses of copyrighted material for instructional purposes are subject to different criteria from uses for other purposes.

Reproductions by teachers for classroom purposes.—For the reasons already discussed, the committee does not favor a statutory provision specifying educational uses of copyrighted material that would be free from copyright control. On the other hand, the doctrine of fair use, as properly applied, is broad enough to permit reasonable educational use, and education has something to gain in the enactment of a bill that clarifies what may now be a problematical situation. The committee sympathizes with the argument that a teacher should not be prevented by uncertainty from doing things that he is legally entitled to do and that improve the quality of his teaching. It is therefore important that some ground rules be provided for the application of fair use in particular situations.

The following discussion reflects the considerations lying behind the four criteria listed in the amended section 107, in the context of typical classroom situations arising today. It must necessarily be broad and illustrative rather than detailed and conclusive, but it may provide educators with the basis for establishing workable practices and policies. Recognizing that our discussion in this report is no final answer to a problem of shifting dimensions, we urge that those affected join together in an effort to establish a continuing understanding as to what constitutes mutually acceptable practices, and to work out means by which permissions for uses beyond fair use can be obtained easily, quickly, and at reasonable fees. Various proposals for some type of Government regulation over fair use and educational reproductions have been discussed since the hearings, but the committee believes that workable voluntary arrangements are distinctly preferable.

The purpose and nature of the use

Copying recognized.—In view of the lack of any judicial precedent establishing that the making of copies by a teacher for classroom purposes can, under appropriate circumstances, constitute a fair use, the educators urged that this general principle be recognized in the statute.   The new language of section 107 makes it clear that, assuming the applicable criteria are met, fair use can extend to the reproduction of copyrighted material for purposes of classroom teaching.

Nonprofit element.—Although it is possible to imagine situations in which use by a teacher in an educational organization operated for profit (day camps, language schools, business schools, dance studios, et cetera) would constitute a fair use, the nonprofit character of the school in which the teacher works should be one factor to consider in determining fair use.   Another factor would be whether any charge is made for the copies distributed.

Spontaneity.—The fair use doctrine in the case of classroom copying would apply primarily to the situation of a teacher who, acting individually and at his own volition, makes one or more copies for temporary use by himself or his pupils in the classroom.   A different result is indicated where the copying was done by the educational institution, school system, or larger unit or where copying was required or suggested by the school administration, either in special instances or as part of a general plan.

Single and multiple copying.—Depending upon the nature of the work and other criteria, the fair use doctrine should differentiate between the amount of a work that can be reproduced by a teacher for his own classroom use (for example, for reading or projecting a copy or for playing a tape recording), and the amount that can be reproduced for distribution to pupils.   In the case of multiple copies, other factors would be whether the number reproduced were limited to the size of the class, whether circulation beyond the classroom was permitted, and whether the copies were recalled or destroyed after temporary use.   For example, the complete reproduction of a fairly long poem in examination questions distributed to all members of a class might be fair use, while the distribution of separate copies of the poem without restrictions might not be.

Collections and anthologies.—Spontaneous copying of an isolated extract by a teacher, which may be a fair use under appropriate circumstances, could turn into an infringement if the copies were accumulated over a period of time with other parts of the same work, or were collected with other material from various works so as to constitute an anthology.

Special uses.—There are certain classroom uses which, because of their special nature, would not be considered an infringement in the ordinary case.   For example, copying of extracts by pupils as exercises in a shorthand or typing class or for foreign language study, or recordings of performances by music students for purposes of analysis and criticism, would normally be regarded as a fair use unless the copies or phonorecords were retained or duplicated.

The nature of the copyrighted work

Character of the work.—The character and purpose of the work will have a lot to do with whether its reproduction for classroom purposes is fair use or infringement. For example, in determining whether a teacher could make one or more copies without permission, a news article from the daily press would be judged differently from a full orchestral score of a musical composition. In general terms, it could be expected that the doctrine of fair use would be applied strictly to the classroom reproduction of entire works, such as musical compositions, dramas, and audiovisual works including motion pictures, which by their nature are intended for performance or public exhibition.

Similarly, where the copyrighted work is intended to be "consumable" in the course of classroom activities—workbooks, exercises, standardized tests, and answer sheets are examples—the privilege of fair use by teachers or pupils would have little if any application. Textbooks and other material prepared primarily for the school market would be less susceptible to reproduction for classroom use than material prepared for general public distribution. With respect to material in newspapers and periodicals the doctrine of fair use should be liberally applied to allow copying of items of current interest to supplement and update the students' textbooks, but this would not extend to copying from periodicals published primarily for student use.

Availability of the work.—A key, though not necessarily determinative, factor in fair use is whether or not the work is available to the potential user. If the work is "out of print" and unavailable for purchase through normal channels, the user may have more justification for reproducing it than in the ordinary case, but the existence of organizations licensed to provide photocopies of out-of-print works at reasonable cost is a factor to be considered. The applicability of the fair use doctrine to unpublished works is narrowly limited since, although the work is unavailable, this is the result of a deliberate choice on the part of the copyright owner. Under ordinary circumstances the copyright owner's "right of first publication" would outweigh any needs of reproduction for classroom purposes.

The amount and substantiality of the material used

Single copies of "entire" works.—In the various discussions of educational copying at the hearings and thereafter, a question that has never been resolved involves the difference between an "entire work" and an "excerpt." The educators have sought a limited right for a teacher to make a single copy of an "entire" work for classroom purposes. The committee understands that this was not generally intended to extend beyond a "separately cognizable" or "self-contained" portion (for example, a single poem, story, or article) in a collective work, and that no privilege is sought to reproduce an entire collective work (for example, an encyclopedia volume, a periodical issue) or a sizable integrated work published as an entity (a novel, treatise, monograph, and so forth). With this limitation, and subject to the other relevant criteria, the requested privilege of making a single copy appears appropriately to be within the scope of fair use.

Multiple copies of "excerpts."—The educators also sought statutory authority for the privilege of making "a reasonable number of copies or phonorecords for excerpts or quotations * * *, provided such excerpts or quotations are not substantial in length in proportion to their source."   In general, and assuming the other necessary factors are present, the committee agrees that the copying for classroom purposes of extracts or portions, which are not self-contained and which are relatively "not substantial in length" when compared to the larger, self-contained work from which they are taken, should be considered fair use.   Depending on the circumstances, the same may also be true of very short self-contained works such as a four-line poem, a map in a newspaper, a one-half page "vocabulary builder" from a monthly magazine, and so forth.

Effect of use on potential market for or value of work.—This factor, while often the most important of the criteria of fair use, must almost always be judged in conjunction with the other three criteria.   With certain special exceptions (use in parodies or as evidence in court proceedings might be examples) a use which supplants any part of the normal market for a copyrighted work would ordinarily be considered an infringement.   As in any other case, whether this would be the result of reproduction by a teacher for classroom purposes requires an evaluation of the nature and purpose of the use, the type of work involved, and the size and relative importance of the portion taken. Fair use in essentially supplementary by nature, and classroom copying that exceeds the legitimate teaching aims such as filling in missing information or bringing a subject up to date would go beyond the proper bounds of fair use.   Where the unauthorized copying displaces what realistically might have been a sale, no matter how minor the amount of money involved, the interests of the copyright owner need protection.   Isolated instances of minor infringements, when multiplied many times, become in the aggregate a major inroad on copyright that must be prevented.

Reproductions and uses for other purposes.—The concentrated attention given the fair use provision in the context of classroom teaching activities should not obscure its application in other areas.   The committee emphasizes again that the same general standards of fair use are applicable to all kinds of uses of copyrighted material, although the relative weight to be given them will differ from case to case.

For example, the doctrine of fair use would apply to all stages in the operations of information storage and retrieval systems, including input, and output in the form of visual images or hard copies.   Reproduction of small excerpts or key words for purposes of input, and output of bibliographic lists or short summaries, might be examples of fair use in this area.   On the other hand, because the potential capabilities of a computer system are vastly different from those of a mimeograph or photocopying machine, the factors to be considered in determining fair use would have to be weighed differently in each situation.   For reasons already explained, the committee does not favor any statutory provision that would exempt computer uses specially from copyright control or that would specify that certain computer uses constitute fair use.

Similarly, the fair use doctrine would be relevant to the use of excerpts from copyrighted works in educational broadcasting activities not exempted under sections 110(2) or 112. In these cases there would be other special factors to weigh: whether the performers, producers, directors, and others responsible for the broadcast were paid, the size and nature of the audience, the size and number of excerpts taken and, in the case of recordings made for broadcast, the number of copies reproduced and the extent of their reuse or exchange. The availability of the fair use doctrine to educational broadcasters would be narrowly circumscribed in the case of motion pictures and other audiovisual works, but under appropriate circumstances it could apply to the non-sequential showing of an individual still or slide, or to the performance of a short excerpt from a motion picture for criticism or comment.

As explained at pages 26 and 27 of the Register's Supplementary Report, an earlier effort to specify limited conditions under which libraries could supply photocopies of material was strongly criticized by both librarians and copyright owners, though for opposing reasons. The effort was dropped, and at the hearings representatives of librarians urged that it not be revived; their position was that statutory provisions codifying or limiting present library practices in this area would crystallize a subject better left to flexible adjustment. On the other hand, both the American Council of Learned Societies and the Department of Health, Education, and Welfare argued that the problem is too important to be left uncertain, and proposed adoption of a statutory provision allowing libraries to supply single photocopies of material under limited conditions.

As in the case of reproduction of copyrighted material by teachers for classroom use, the committee does not favor a specific provision dealing with library photocopying.

Unauthorized library copying, like everything else, must be judged a fair use or an infringement on the basis of all of the applicable criteria and the facts of the particular case. Despite past efforts, reasonable arrangements involving a mutual understanding of what generally constitutes acceptable library practices, and providing workable clearance and licensing conditions, have not been achieved and are overdue. The committee urges all concerned to resume their efforts to reach an accommodation under which the needs of scholarship and the rights of authors would both be respected.

A question that came up several times during the hearings was whether the specific exemptions for certain uses, such as those provided by sections 110 and 112, should be in addition to or instead of fair use. In other words, if an educational broadcaster failed to qualify for the exemption in section 110(2) because a particular program was not instructional, could he still claim that his use of excerpts from a copyrighted work was "fair" and therefore exempt? It is the committee's intention that the fair use principle provide a potential limitation on all of the copyright owner's exclusive rights, whether they are subject to other, specific limitations or not. Thus, while some of the exemptions in sections 108 through 116 may overlap the fair use doctrine, they are not intended to supersede it.

Proposals for presumptions as to fair use

The representatives of various educational organizations proposed that, in infringement cases involving nonprofit uses for educational purposes, the use be presumed to be "fair" and the burden of proving otherwise be placed on the copyright owner. The representatives of authors and book publishers objected strenuously to this proposal, arguing that it would transform the doctrine of fair use into a blanket exemption in these cases.

The committee believes that any special statutory provision placing the burden of proving fair use on one side or the other would be unfair and undesirable. It has, however, added a provision to section 504(c), allowing minimum statutory damages to be reduced in those cases if the teacher proves that he acted in the reasonable belief that his reproduction constituted a fair use rather than an infringement.

SECTION 108. REPRODUCTION OF WORKS IN ARCHIVAL COLLECTIONS

Although the committee does not favor special fair use provisions dealing with the problems of library photocopying, it was impressed with the need for a specific exemption permitting reproduction of manuscript collections under certain conditions. Arguments were made by representatives of archivists and historians, the General Services Administration, and the American Council on Education for a statutory provision that would authorize archival institutions to make facsimiles of unpublished works in order to deposit copies in other manuscript collections. They emphasized that the unpublished material in archival collections, which the bill gives statutory protection for the first time, is of little interest to copyright owners but of great historical and scholarly value. They urged that a limited right to duplicate archival collections would not harm the copyright owners' interests but would aid scholarship and enable the storage of security copies at a distance from the originals.

The response to these recommendations was generally sympathetic, and there was little or no opposition to them. The committee has therefore adopted a new provision, section 108, under which a "nonprofit institution, having archival custody over collections of manuscripts, documents, or other unpublished works of value to scholarly research," would be entitled to reproduce "any such work in its collections" under certain circumstances. Only unpublished works could be reproduced under this exemption, but the privilege would extend to any type of work, including photographs, motion pictures, and sound recordings.

The archival reproduction privilege accorded by section 108 would be available only where there was no "purpose of direct or indirect commercial advantage," and where the copies or phonorecords are reproduced in "facsimile." Under the exemption, for example, a repository could make photocopies of manuscripts by microfilm or electrostatic process, but could not reproduce the work in "machine-readable" language for storage in an information system.

The purposes of the reproduction must either be "preservation and security" or "deposit for research use in any other such institution." Thus, no facsimile copies or phonorecords made under this section can be distributed to scholars or the public; if they leave the institution that reproduced them, they must be deposited for research purposes in another "nonprofit institution" that has "archival custody over collections of manuscripts, documents, or other unpublished works of value to scholarly research."

This section is not intended to override any contractual arrangements under which the manuscript material was deposited in the institution. For example, if there is an express contractual prohibition against reproduction for any purpose, section 108 could not be construed as justifying a violation of the contract.

SECTION 109. EFFECT OF TRANSFER OF PARTICULAR COPY OR PHONORECORD

Effect on further disposition of copy or phonorecord

Section 109(a) restates and confirms the principle that, where the copyright owner has transferred ownership of a particular copy or phonorecord of his work, the person to whom the copy or phonorecord is transferred is entitled to dispose of it by sale, rental, or any other means. Under this principle, which has been established by the court decisions and section 27 of the present law, the copyright owner's exclusive right of public distribution would have no effect upon anyone who owns "a particular copy or phonorecord lawfully made under this title" and who wishes to transfer it to someone else or to destroy it.

Thus, for example, the outright sale of an authorized copy of a book frees it from any copyright control over its resale price or other conditions of its future disposition. A library that has acquired ownership of a copy is entitled to lend it under any conditions it chooses to impose. This does not mean that conditions on future disposition of copies or phonorecords, imposed by a contract between their buyer and seller, would be unenforceable between the parties as a breach of contract, but it does mean that they could not be enforced by an action for infringement of copyright. Under section 202, however, the owner of the physical copy or phonorecord cannot reproduce or perform the copyrighted work publicly without the copyright owner's consent.

To come within the scope of section 109(a), a copy or phonorecord must have been "lawfully made under this title," though not necessarily with the copyright owner's authorization. For example, any resale of an illegally "counterfeited" phonorecord would be an infringement, but the disposition of a phonorecord made under the compulsory licensing provisions of section 115 would not.

Effect on display of copy

Subsection (b) of section 109 deals with the scope of the copyright owner's exclusive right to control the public display of a particular "copy" of his work (including the original or prototype copy in which the work was first fixed). Assuming, for example, that a painter has sold his only copy of an original work of art without restrictions, would he be able to restrain the new owner from displaying it publicly in galleries, shop windows, on a projector, or on television?

Section 109(b) adopts the general principle that the lawful owner of a copy of a work should be able to put his copy on public display without the consent of the copyright owner. The exclusive right of public display granted by section 106(5) would not apply where the owner of a copy wishes to show it directly to the public, as in a gallery or display case, or indirectly, as through an opaque projector. Where the copy itself is intended for projection, as in the case of a photographic slide, negative, or transparency, the public projection of a single image would be permitted as long as the viewers are "present at the place where the copy is located."

On the other hand, section 109(b) takes account of the potentialities of the new communications media, notably television and information storage and retrieval devices, for replacing printed copies with visual images. Under the 1965 bill, the public display of an image of a copyrighted work would not be exempted from copyright control if the copy from which the image was derived were outside the presence of the viewers. In other words, the display of a visual image of a copyrighted work would be an infringement if the image were transmitted by any method (by closed or open circuit television, for example, or by a computer system) from one place to members of the public located elsewhere.

The committee adopted this provision and carried it a step further as a needed safeguard to copyright owners: as amended, the exemption would extend only to public displays that are made "either directly or by the projection of no more than one image at a time." Thus, even where the copy and the viewers are located at the same place, the simultaneous projection of multiple images of the work would not be exempted. For example, where each person in a lecture hall has his own viewing apparatus in front of him, the copyright owner's permission would generally be required in order to project an image of a work on each individual screen at the same time.

The committee's intention is to preserve the traditional privilege of the owner of a copy to display it directly, but to place reasonable restrictions on his ability to display it indirectly in such a way that the copyright owner's market for reproduction and distribution of copies would be affected. Unless it constitutes a fair use under section 107, or unless one of the special provisions of sections 110 or 111 is applicable, projection of more than one image at a time, or transmission of an image to the public over television or other communications channels, would be an infringement for the same reasons that reproduction in copies would be. The committee regards as too inflexible a suggestion for defining "the place where the copy is located" as "a room or limited outdoor area," but the concept is generally intended to mean that the viewers are present in the same physical surroundings as the copy, even though they cannot see the copy directly.

Effect of mere possession of copy or phonorecord

Subsection (c) of section 109 qualifies the privileges specified in subsections (a) and (b) by making clear that they do not apply to someone who merely possesses a copy or phonorecord without having acquired ownership of it. Acquisition of an object embodying a copyrighted work by rental, lease, loan, or bailment carries with it no privilege to dispose of the copy under section 109(a) or to display it publicly under section 109(b). To cite a familiar example, a person who has rented a print of a motion picture from the copyright owner would have no right to rent it to someone else without the owner's permission.

SECTION 110. EXEMPTION OF CERTAIN PERFORMANCES AND DISPLAYS

In H.R. 4347 as originally introduced, section 110 (which was then section 109) contained seven clauses. Clauses (1) through (4) dealt with performances and exhibitions that are now generally exempt under the "for profit" limitation or other provisions of the copyright law, and that would be specifically exempted under the bill. Clauses (5) and (6) provided exemptions for certain secondary transmissions, specifically nonprofit "boosters" or translators and relays of broadcasts to hotel rooms. The seventh clause dealt with the mere reception of broadcasts in a public place. The section did not contain any provision covering the operations of commercial community antenna systems, since they were intended to be fully liable for copyright infringement under that bill.

For the reasons explained below, the committee has decided to give special treatment to the entire problem of secondary transmissions, including community antenna systems. Clauses (5) and (6) in the 1965 bill have therefore been taken out of what is now section 110 and have been incorporated with some amendments in section 111. Since it does not involve a secondary transmission, clause (7) has been retained in section 110, and becomes clause (5) of that provision.

In addition to the performances and displays exempted from copyright control under section 110, the committee considered the proposal of the Department of Defense to exempt transmissions "made by the United States Government primarily for reception by United States Government employees, including military personnel, and their families." A new provision has been added to section 110(2) exempting certain instructional transmissions to Government personnel; but, with respect to transmission of programs intended for general entertainment, the committee does not believe the Government should be placed in any preferred position.

Face-to-face teaching activities

Clause (1) of section 110 is generally intended to set out the conditions under which performances or displays, in the course of instructional activities other than educational broadcasting, are to be exempted from copyright control. As amended, the clause covers all types of copyrighted works, and exempts their performance or display "by instructors or pupils in the course of face-to-face teaching activities of a nonprofit educational institution," where the activities take place "in a classroom or similar place devoted to instruction." The committee does not regard a statutory definition of "face-to-face teaching activities" as necessary to clarify the scope of the provision, but will explain what the clause is intended to cover in some detail here.

Works affected.—Since there is no limitation on the types of works covered by the exemption, a teacher or student would be free to perform or display anything in class as long as the other conditions of the clause are met. He could read aloud from copyrighted text ma-

terial, act out a drama, play or sing a musical work, perform a motion
picture or filmstrip, or display text or pictorial material to the class
by means of a projector. However, nothing in this provision is intended to sanction the unauthorized reproduction of copies or phonorecords for the purpose of classroom performance or display, and the
amended clause contains a special exception dealing with performances from unlawfully made copies of motion pictures and other audiovisual works, to be discussed below.

Instructors or pupils.—To come within clause (1), the performance or display must be "by instructors or pupils," thus ruling out
performances by actors, singers, or instrumentalists brought in from
outside the school to put on a program. However, the term "instructors" would be broad enough to include guest lecturers if their instructional activities remain confined to a classroom situation. In general,
the term "pupils" refers to the enrolled members of a class.

Face-to-face teaching activities.—Use of the phrase "in the course
of face-to-face teaching activities" is intended to exclude broadcasting or other transmissions into a classroom, whether radio or television and whether open or closed circuit. However, as long as the
instructor and pupils are in the same classroom or similar place, the
exemption would extend to the use of devices for amplifying or reproducing sound and for projecting visual images. The "teaching activities" exempted by the clause encompass systematic instruction of a
very wide variety of subjects, but they do not include performances
or displays, whatever their cultural value or intellectual appeal, that
are given for the recreation or entertainment of any part of their
audience.

Nonprofit educational institution.—The committee has amended
clause (1) to make clear that it applies only to the teaching activities "of a nonprofit educational institution," thus excluding from the
exemption performances or displays in profit-making institutions such
as dance studios and language schools.

Classroom or similar place.—The teaching activities exempted by
the clause must take place "in a classroom or similar place devoted to
instruction." For example, performances in an auditorium or stadium
during a school assembly, graduation ceremony, class play, or sporting event, where the audience is not confined to the members of a
particular class, would fall outside the scope of clause (1), although
in some cases they might be exempted by clause (4) of section 110.
The "similar place" referred to in clause (1) is a place which is "devoted to instruction" in the same way a classroom is; common examples would include a studio, a workshop, a gymnasium, a training
field, a library, the stage of an auditorium, or the auditorium itself
if it is actually used as a classroom for systematic instructional
activities.

Motion pictures and other audiovisual works.—The committee has
added a new provision to clause (1) to deal with the special problem
of performances from unlawfully made copies of motion pictures and
other audiovisual works. The exemption is lost where the copy being
used for a classroom performance was "not lawfully made under this
title" and the person responsible for the performance knew or had
reason to suspect as much. This special exception to the exemption

would not apply to performances from lawfully made copies, even if the copies were acquired from someone who had stolen or converted them, or if the performances were in violation of an agreement. However, though the performances would be exempt under section 110(1) in such cases, the copyright owner might have a cause of action against the unauthorized distributor under section 106(3), or against the person responsible for the performance for breach of contract.

Projection devices.—As long as there is no transmission beyond the place where where the copy is located, both section 109(b) and section 110(1) would permit the classroom display of a work by means of any sort of projection device or process. The committee recognizes the legitimate concern of book publishers and others with respect to the use of visual images in education to supplant the need for printed copies, but believes that the real problem is met by its amendments of section 110(2).

Instructional broadcasting

Together with those of section 112, the amended provisions of section 110(2) represent the committee's answer to one of the major issues in copyright law revision: "the extent to which educational and other nonprofit broadcasting should be exempted from copyright control." The bill as originally introduced dropped the existing general exemption for all transmissions that are not "for profit," and in clause (2) drew a line between instructional broadcasting that is an adjunct to the actual classwork of educational institutions, and "educational broadcasting" intended for the enlightenment, cultural enrichment, or instruction of the public at large. The Register's Supplementary Report, at page 35, explains this distinction as follows:

> Here is a case where balancing the scales is a delicate undertaking. Fully acknowledging the unique public value of educational broadcasting and its need for financial support, we must also recognize the large public audiences it is now reaching, the vast potential audiences that are awaiting it, and the fact that, as a medium for entertainment, recreation, and communication of information, a good deal of educational programing is indistinguishable from a good deal of commercial programing. The time may come when many works will reach the public primarily through educational broadcasting. In terms of good education it is certainly true that the more people reached the better; but in terms of the author's rights it is equally true that the more people reached the more he should be compensated. It does not seem too much to ask that some of the money now going to support educational broadcasting activities be used to compensate authors and publishers whose works are essential to those activities.

At the hearings the provisions of the 1965 bill on educational broadcasting were generally supported by authors, publishers, and performing rights societies, and were opposed by educational broadcasters and other educational organizations. The basic argument on behalf of copyright owners was that, although the growth of educational broadcasting and the variety of its programing should be strongly supported, it is vital that authors and publishers be remunerated. In the view of the copyright owners, the 1965 bill gave educational broadcasters all of the privileges they reasonably should have with respect to "in-school" instructional transmissions, and they expressed serious concern about broadening these privileges. They stressed that the line between general educational programing of a cultural nature, and "sustaining" or "public service" programs on commercial stations, has broken down, and that in many cases the two are indistinguishable as to content, size of audience, use of copyrighted material, and impact on the copyright owner.

In support of their position, the representatives of authors and publishers argued that educational broadcasting is growing, and that it already reaches huge audiences and is highly subsidized from both government and private commercial sources. They attacked as illogical and unfair a situation where performers are paid but an author's work can be freely used and his market ruined without compensation. It was pointed out, in this connection, that educational broadcasting is a principal user of serious music, and yet is asking the serious composer, its "worst victim," to subsidize it involuntarily. The copyright owners asserted that in other countries, where most or all broadcasting is "nonprofit," it would be inconceivable for authors not to be paid, and they undertook to work toward licensing arrangements at reasonable fees.

For their part, the educational interests stressed the great national importance of educational broadcasting, not only as an adjunct to the schools but also in providing adult education, promoting general cultural interests, combating illiteracy, and supporting the anti-poverty program through vocational rehabilitation classes. They argued that the 1965 bill would severely reduce the educational potential of radio and television, and would thus run counter to the expressed policies of Congress and the administration.

The educational groups felt that, by confining the exemption to "in-school" transmissions, the 1965 bill would thwart a basic function of educational broadcasting: its unparalleled capacity for reaching students widely separated geographically and economically. They urged that educational broadcasting needs maximum access with a minimum of restrictions, and that its tiny budgets cannot support the costs and uncertainties of expensive clearances and royalties. Asserting that their activities are truly nonprofit and dedicated to public service, the educational broadcasters pointed out that they compete with commercial television only in the sense that they are seeking more viewers; use of copyrighted material on television has been shown to stimulate an interest in particular copyrighted works, and to create a cultural atmosphere in which the demand for copies of works increases.

The arguments on both sides, while advanced in support of opposite positions, struck the committee as fundamentally valid and as pointing the way toward a middle course. Following the hearings, representatives of the various interests affected met together to discuss the problem and, though no definite agreements emerged from the meetings, certain areas of possible accommodation were suggested. Very recently, proposals for a nationwide communications satellite system that would directly benefit educational broadcasting have underlined the need for copyright solutions that will preserve the rights of copyright owners, but without impairing the growth of educational broadcasting or the important services it performs for the Nation. Acting on this premise, the committee broadened the exemptions in clause (2) in some respects and narrowed them somewhat in others. cordance with the other conditions of section 110(2), in the course of instructional transmissions to Government personnel who are receiving training "as a part of their official duties or employment."

Control of time and content.—A point of serious concern to authors and book publishers, among others, has been the possible danger that in the future, section 110(2) would be construed to exempt transmissions of visual images from a computer or "memory bank" to individual students in classrooms, and that such transmissions would displace the market for textbooks, workbooks, tests, answer sheets, and other instructional material. Recent developments in teaching indicate that these fears may be justifiable. Clause (2) of section 110 was intended to deal primarily with instructional broadcasting as it is now understood, and was not intended to exempt the transmission of visual images to individual students at their control, thereby substituting for copies. The committee has therefore adopted subclause (D) to confine the exemption to what was intended. Under the new subclause, the exemption would not apply if "the time and content of the transmission," rather than being controlled by the transmitting organization, "depend on a choice by individual recipients in activating transmission from an information storage and retrieval system or any similar device, machine, or process."

Religious services

The exemption in clause (3) of section 110 covers performances of a nondramatic literary or musical work "or of a dramatico-musical work of a religious nature," and displays of works of all kinds, "in the course of services at a place of worship or other religious assembly." The scope of the clause does not cover the sequential showing of motion pictures and other audiovisual works. The exemption, which to some extent has its counterpart in sections 1 and 104 of the present law, was amended by the committee to add the phrase "of a religious nature" qualifying the term "dramatico-musical work." The purpose here is to exempt certain performances of sacred music that might be regarded as "dramatic" in nature, such as oratorios, cantatas, musical settings of the mass, choral services, and the like. The exemption is not intended to cover performances of secular operas, musical plays, motion pictures, and the like, even if they have an underlying religious or philosophical theme and take place "in the course of [religious] services."

To be exempted under section 110(3) a performance or display must be "in the course of services," thus excluding activities at a place of worship that are for social, educational, fund raising, or entertainment purposes. Some performances of these kinds could be covered by the exemption in section 110(4), discussed next. Since the performance or display must also occur "at a place of worship or other religious assembly," the exemption would not extend to religious broadcasts or other transmissions to the public at large, even where the transmissions were sent from the place of worship. On the other hand, as long as services are being conducted before a religious gathering, the exemption would apply if they were conducted in places such as auditoriums, outdoor theaters, and the like.

Certain other nonprofit performances

In addition to the educational and religious exemptions provided by clauses (1) through (3) of section 110, clause (4) contains a general exception to the exclusive right of public performance that would cover some, though not all, of the same ground as the present "for profit" limitation. The following is a summary of the clause as amended by the committee.

Scope of exemption.—The exemption in clause (4) applies to the same general activities and subject matter as those covered by the "for profit" limitation today: public performances of nondramatic literary and musical works. However, the exemption would be limited to public performances given directly in the presence of an audience whether by means of living performers, the playing of phonorecords, or the operation of a receiving apparatus, and would not include a "transmission to the public." Although educational broadcasters sought a blanket exemption under clause (4) in cases where none of the performers was paid, the committee decided that the exemption of educational broadcasting activities should be confined within the scope of section 110(2). Unlike the other clauses of section 110, clause (4) applies only to performing rights in certain works and does not affect the exclusive right to display a work in public.

No profit motive.—In addition to the other conditions specified by the clause, the performance must be "without any purpose of direct or indirect commercial advantage." This provision expressly adopts the principle established by the court decisions construing the "for profit" limitation: that public performances given or sponsored in connection with any commercial or profit-making enterprises are subject to the exclusive rights of the copyright owner even though the public is not charged for seeing or hearing the performance.

No payment for performance.—An important condition for this exemption is that the performance be given "without payment of any fee or other compensation for the performance to any of its performers, promoters, or organizers." The basic purpose of this requirement is to prevent the free use of copyrighted material under the guise of charity where fees or percentages are paid to performers, promoters, producers, and the like. However, the exemption would not be lost if the performers, directors, or producers of the performance, instead of being paid directly "for the performance," are paid a salary for duties encompassing the performance. Examples are performances by a school orchestra conducted by a music teacher who receives an annual salary, or by a service band whose members and conductors perform as part of their assigned duties and who receive military pay. The committee believes that performances of this type should be exempt, assuming the other conditions in clause (4) are met, and has not adopted the suggestion that the word "salary" be added to the phrase referring to the "payment of any fee or other compensation."

Admission charge.—Assuming that the performance involves no profit motive and no one responsible for it gets paid a fee, it must still meet one of two alternative conditions to be exempt. As specified in subclauses (A) and (B) of section 110(4), these conditions are: (1) that no direct or indirect admission charge is made, or (2) that the net proceeds are "used exclusively for educational, religious, or charitable purposes and not for private financial gain."

Under the second of these conditions, a performance meeting the other conditions of clause (4) would be exempt even if an admission fee is charged, provided any amounts left "after deducting the reasonable costs of producing the performance" are used solely for bona fide educational, religious, or charitable purposes. In connection with subclause (B), the committee was impressed by the argument that, if there is an admission charge, the copyright owner should have the right to decide whether and under what conditions his work should be performed, since otherwise he could be compelled to make an involuntary donation to the fund-raising activities of causes to which he is opposed. An amendment to the subclause would thus permit a copyright owner to prevent a public performance of his work under section 110(4)(B) by serving a notice stating his objections at least 7 days in advance.

Mere reception in public

Unlike the other clauses of section 110, clause (5) is not to any extent a counterpart of the "for profit" limitation of the present statute. It applies to performances and displays of all types of works, and its purpose is to exempt from copyright liability anyone who merely turns on, in a public place, an ordinary radio or television receiving apparatus of a kind commonly sold to members of the public for private use. The main effect of this exemption would be to allow the use of ordinary radios and television sets for the incidental entertainment of patrons in small business or professional establishments such as taverns, lunch counters, hairdressers, dry cleaners, doctors' offices, and the like. The clause has nothing to do with community antenna operations, and there is no intention to exempt performances in large commercial establishments, such as bus terminals, supermarkets, factories, or department stores, where broadcasts are transmitted to substantial audiences by means of loudspeakers covering a wide area. The exemption would also be denied in any case where the audience is charged directly to see or hear the transmission.

The basic rationale of this clause is that the secondary use of the transmission by turning on an ordinary receiver in public is so remote and minimal that no further liability should be imposed. In the vast majority of these cases no royalties are collected today, and the committee believes that the exemption should be made explicit in the statute. Some fears have been expressed that technical improvements in a "single receiving apparatus of a kind commonly used in private homes" might some day lead to abuse of this exemption, but the committee does not feel that this remote possibility justifies making vast numbers of small business and professional people guilty of technical infringements.

SENATE REPORTS

NATIONAL COMMISSION ON NEW TECHNOLOGICAL USES OF COPYRIGHTED WORKS

Mr. McClellan, from the Committee on the Judiciary, submitted the
following

REPORT

[To accompany S. 2216]

The Committee on the Judiciary, to which was referred the bill
(S. 2216) to establish a National Commission on New Technological
Uses of Copyrighted Works, having considered the same, reports
favorably thereon, with amendments, and recommends that the bill,
as amended, do pass.

AMENDMENTS

1. On page 2, lines 16 and 17, strike out "representing" and insert
in lieu thereof "selected from".
2. On page 2, lines 19 and 20, strike out "representing" and insert
in lieu thereof "selected from".
3. On page 2, line 23, strike out "representing" and insert in lieu
thereof "selected from".
4. On page 5, line 5, after the word "any" insert "three or more".

PURPOSE OF AMENDMENTS

The purpose of the first three amendments is to clarify the intent
of the bill that although members of the Commission are to be chosen
from certain categories, they are to function on the Commission as
individuals and not as representatives of a particular viewpoint.
The purpose of the fourth amendment is to provide that the participation of at least three members of the Commission is required for the
conduct of hearings.

PURPOSE

The purpose of the proposed legislation, as amended, is to establish a National Commission to study and compile data on the reproduction and use of copyrighted works of authorship (1) in automatic

systems capable of storing, processing, retrieving, and transferring information, and (2) by various forms of machine reproduction. The Commission is directed to make recommendations to the President and the Congress concerning such changes as may be necessary to assure for such purposes access to copyrighted works and to provide recognition of the rights of copyright owners.

STATEMENT

The Subcommittee on Patents, Trademarks, and Copyrights of this committee has conducted 17 days of hearings on the general revision of the copyright law. Testimony was received from 150 witnesses, and a number of statements were submitted for inclusion in the hearing record.

Prior to the introduction of copyright revision legislation in the Congress, exhaustive study was given by the Copyright Office and various interested groups to those issues that it was anticipated would require attention by the Congress during the revision program. The current or potential impact of computers and other information storage and retrieval systems on the copyright revision effort was not foreseen and consequently the bill submitted to the Congress did not take into account the significance of this new technology.

The first extensive consideration of these matters in the Congress occurred during the hearings of this committee's Subcommittee on Patents, Trademarks, and Copyrights on S. 597, the general copyright revision bill. At the same time within the executive branch the Committee on Scientific and Technological Information of the Federal Council of Science and Technology was also exploring these problems. It became apparent during the subcommittee examination of this subject that if the Congress were to undertake at this time to make a final determination concerning the possible necessity of modifications in the copyright law, because of various technological advances, it would delay for at least several years the enactment of a general copyright revision bill. Such a delay would be extremely undesirable in view of the obvious need for revision of the copyright statute, which is essentially that enacted in 1909. More importantly, sufficient information is currently not available to provide the foundation for a sound judgment concerning the future development of the technology and the necessity for modification of the copyright statute.

Another important copyright issue arising from technological developments is the reproduction of copyrighted material by the use of various machines. Photocopying in all its forms presents significant questions of public policy, extending well beyond that of copyright law. No satisfactory solutions have emerged in the limited consideration devoted to this problem during the current revision effort.

Therefore, the establishment of some type of study commission appeared to be both necessary and desirable. On July 25, 1967, under the auspices of the Subcommittee, a meeting to discuss a draft bill to establish a national study commission was attended by approximately 150 representatives of authors, publishers, educators, librarians, computer users and the executive agencies. Unanimous support was expressed for the establishment of the Commission. On August 2, 1967, Senator John L. McClellan, Chairman of the Subcommittee, introduced S. 2216.

VIEWS OF GOVERNMENT AGENCIES

The Library of Congress, in its report dated September 5, 1967, endorsed S. 2216.

ANALYSIS OF LEGISLATION

An analysis of the provisions of S. 2216 follows:

Section 1(a) establishes the Commission in the Library of Congress. Section 1(b) defines the purpose of the Commission as the study and compilation of data on the reproduction and use of copyrighted works in automatic systems capable of storing, processing. retrieving, and transferring information, and by various forms of machine reproduction. It is further provided that the Commission shall make recommendations as to such changes in copyright law or procedures that may be necessary to assure for such purposes access to copyr ghted works, and to provide recognition of the rights of copyright owners.

Section 2(a) provides that the Commission shall be composed of 23 members, consisting of a Chairman who shall be the Librarian of Congress, two Members of the Senate, two Members of the House of Representatives, seven members appointed by the President selected from authors and other copyright owners, seven members appointed by the President selected from users of copyrighted works, and four nongovernmental members appointed by the President selected from the public generally. It is provided that the Senate must advise and consent to the nominations of the 18 members selected by the President. Section 2(b) provides for the selection by the Commission of one of its members as Vice-Chairman, and specifies that the Register of Copyrights shall serve as an ex officio member of the Commission. Section 2(c) defines a quorum. Section 2(d) provides for the filling of vacancies on the Commission.

Section 3(a) specifies the compensation to be received by members of the Commission. Section 3(b) provides that officers or employees of the Federal Government shall serve on the Commission without compensation, other than expenses.

Section 4(a) authorizes the Commission to appoint a staff which shall be an administrative part of the Library of Congress. Section 4(b) authorizes the Commission to procure certain temporary and intermittent services.

Section 5 authorizes the appropriation of such sums as may be necessary to carry out the provisions of this legislation.

Section 6(a) requires that the Commission shall submit to the President and the Congress within 1 year of its first meeting a preliminary report on its activities. Section 6(b) directs the Commission to submit a final report within 3 years after the effective date of this legislation. Section 6(c) authorizes the Commission to publish certain interim reports.

Section 7(a) authorizes the Commission to hold hearings, administer oaths and require, by subpena or otherwise, the attendance of witnesses and the production of documents. Section 7(b) provides authorization for various meetings, seminars or conferences.

Section 8 provides that the Commission shall terminate 60 days after the submission of its final report.

COMMITTEE CONCLUSION

The committee believes that the membership of the Commission should provide a balanced representation of all interested viewpoints, in addition to representation of the public generally. The work and recommendations of the Commission will be of the greatest significance to future uses of intellectual property. It is, therefore, imperative that those selected to serve on the Commission should, through knowledge and experience, be qualified to evaluate the social and economic implications of the new technologies.

A major factor leading to this legislation has been the use of information storage systems for educational purposes. Since it is anticipated that these systems will use copyrighted textbooks and other educational materials, it is the view of the committee that in selecting Commission members from the category of copyright owners priority should be accorded to the representatives of the creators and copyright owners of textbooks and other educational materials.

In selecting members of the Commission in the classification of users of copyrighted works, it is the intent of the committee that consideration be given to including members selected from educational institutions, librarians, manufacturers, or suppliers of computer machinery and governmental users, at the State and local level as well as the Federal Government.

It is not the intent of the committee that the Commission should undertake to reopen the examination of those copyright issues which have received detailed consideration during the current revision effort, and concerning which satisfactory solutions appear to have been achieved.

After a study of this bill, the committee recommends that the legislation, as amended, be favorably considered.

Attached, hereto, and made a part hereof is the report of the Librarian of Congress dated September 5, 1967:

THE LIBRARIAN OF CONGRESS,
Washington, D.C., September 5, 1967.

Hon. JAMES O. EASTLAND,
Chairman, Committee on the Judiciary,
U.S. Senate, Washington, D.C.

DEAR SENATOR EASTLAND: This is in response to your letter of August 10, 1967, requesting my comments on S. 2216, a bill to establish a National Commission on New Technological Uses of Copyrighted Works. I have discussed your request with the Register of Copyrights, and this letter incorporates his views as well as my own.

S. 2216, which was introduced by Senator McClellan on August 2, 1967, would establish in the Library of Congress a Commission aimed at studying and compiling information on the use of copyrighted works in information storage and retrieval devices and by "various forms of machine reproduction." Section 1 of the bill also charges the Commission with the responsibility for making "recommendations at to such changes in copyright law or procedures that may be necessary to assure for such purposes access to copyrighted works, and to provide recognition of the rights of copyright owners."

The membership of the Commission, which is set out in section 2, would total 23. The chairman would be the Librarian of Congress, and there would be four congressional members. The remaining 18 members, who would be appointed by the President with the advice and consent of the Senate, would include seven representatives of "authors and other copyright owners," seven representatives of "users of copyrighted works," and four nongovernmental members "representing the public generally."

Sections 3, 4, and 5 of the bill deal with the compensation, staffing, and expenses of the Commission. Section 4 authorizes the appointment of a staff, which would be an administrative part of the Library of Congress and would be headed by an Executive Director.

The reporting obligations and powers of the Commission are set out in sections 6 and 7. A preliminary report to the President would be required within 1 year of the Commission's first meeting, and a final report with recommendations and proposals for legislation and administrative action would be due at the end of 3 years. The Commission would be authorized to hold hearings and other meetings and conferences, and would be given subpena power. Under section 8, the Commission would terminate 60 days after submission of its final report.

I strongly support S. 2216 and its objectives. The need for a national commission to collect and evaluate information concerning the use of copyrighted works in computer systems has become increasingly apparent during the past year. Proposals for study commissions have been advanced by representatives of most of the major groups affected by the problem, including witnesses testifying at the hearings on general revision of the copyright law held before the Senate Judiciary Subcommittee on Patents, Trademarks, and Copyrights earlier this year. I believe there is strong and widespread support for legislation that will provide an effective method for assembling all of the background information Congress will need to come to grips with this rapidly evolving and vitally important issue.

At present, although we can all foresee various benefits and problems in the increasing use of copyrighted materials in information storage and retrieval systems, we have no real data on which to base firm predictions, much less detailed legislative proposals. It is clear that carefully considered statutory provisions on this subject in the copyright law will be needed by the end of the next decade, and that they should be based on as thorough an understanding of all facets of this complex problem as possible. This knowledge cannot be acquired now, when we have nothing to go on but predictions and uncertainties. It can only be achieved by concentrated study, under objective auspices, of the developing patterns over the next few years.

On the whole I believe S. 2216 is admirably suited to achieving this purpose. The scope of the Commission's aims and duties is stated in a way that is broad enough to cover a wide range of significant uses of copyrighted material by automatic data transfer systems and reproduction devices, but not to include review of problems that have been the subject of extensive separate study, such as uses by community antenna television systems or typical educational broadcasting stations.

I feel that the decisions to place the Commission under the administrative jurisdiction of the Library and to place the chairmanship in the hands of the Librarian are basically wise ones. As an arm of the legislative branch, the Library of Congress is fully capable of carrying out the administrative details necessary to implement the Commission's work; as both the national library and as the home of the Copyright Office the Library has a deeply established background in a wide range of the theoretical and practical problems the Commission will encounter. The dual purposes of the Commission's work as stated in section 1 of the bill—"To assure for such purposes access to copyrighted works, and to provide recognition of the rights of copyright owners"—reflect exactly my own view of what the Commission should aim to accomplish.

It has been suggested that a total membership of 23 is rather large and unwieldy, but I seriously doubt whether the roster could be reduced substantially in size and still produce results that would ultimately be effective. I favor the proposal to have four nongovernmental members representing the public generally. However, I think the use of the term "representing" in clauses 4, 5, and 6 of section 2(a) could produce problems. The intent appears to be to insure that the Commission's membership will be truly representative and balanced, not to suggest that the National Commissioners be bound to act within the Commission in any particular representative capacity. The staffing, reporting, and other provisions of the bill strike me as well calculated to accomplish its purposes.

A crucial issue underlying S. 2216 in its relationship to S. 597, the bill for general revision of the copyright law. As you know, the House has already passed the counterpart of the general revision bill, and the 1967 hearings before Senator McClellan's subcommittee have been completed. In contrast to most of the other issues involved in the revision bill, the problem of computer uses of copyrighted material arose as a full-scale issue less than 2 years ago. The committee report on the House bill pointed to the dangers of legislating prematurely in this area of exploding technology and, after mentioning the proposals for a study commission, the committee expressed the hope that the interests involved will work together toward an ultimate solution of this problem in the light of experience (H. Rept. No. 83, 90th Cong., first sess., pp. 24–25). The record of the Senate hearings this year contains considerable abstract speculation about the potential problems in this area, but no hard facts to support any kind of concrete legislative solutions. More experience is obviously needed before these facts can be found.

I believe very strongly that the badly needed general revision of the copyright law should not be delayed beyond the next session of Congress, and that no effort should be made to tie the provisions of the general revision bill to the Commission's recommendations for legislation. General copyright revision is critically important to all producers and users of intellectual property, and the amendments necessary to implement the Commission's report can readily be made to the revised statute. Copyright legislation directed specifically to the problems of computer uses can safely be deferred until the necessary studies have been made, because the problems that are being posed and discussed are not today's but tomorrow's.

There have been suggestions that the bill establishing a study commission should also contain provisions regulating the copyright liability of computer uses during an interim period while the studies are being made, but I believe that this would be a mistake. It may well be that temporary moratorium arrangements can and should be worked out during the period when the use of copyrighted materials in computer systems is in its formative, experimental period, but proposals along this line should be considered in the context of the general revision bill.

As I see it, the goals of the National Commission should be to seek and find genuine answers to what now promises to develop into one of the most significant problems in the history of copyright law. As Librarian of Congress, I am committed to contributing everything in my power to the achievement of the goals of S. 2216.

Sincerely yours,

L. QUINCY MUMFORD, *Librarian of Congress.*

Copyright Law Revision Hearings, 1967 Part 1

STATEMENT OF HERMAN WOUK, AUTHORS LEAGUE OF AMERICA

Mr. WOUK. Mr. Chairman—an your distinguished colleagues—my responsibility is to discuss two main topics, the doctrine of fair use and the problem of the new copying devices. These subjects are covered in our report, between pages 16 and 27.

Accepting your suggestion, Mr. Chairman, I shall speak informally, and when I occasionally quote our report, I shall give you the page number.

First. About the fair-use doctrine, I speak as a layman. But as a member of the Authors League, and a former officer on the board, I have acquired some background in this topic. Fair use is the legal doctrine which, in special instances, limits the authors otherwise exclusive right to copy; for example, use of excerpts from his work in reviews, in scholarly discussion, in criticism, in parody, and satire. Until this bill was drawn up, fair use, as I understand it, remained a doctrine of the courts. The courts had repeatedly defined it, circumscribed it, redefined it, so that there was a general understanding of what was and what was not fair use. But it was the idea of the Registrar of Copyrights and his office—and that idea apparently was picked up and endorsed by the House committee—that with the proliferation of copying devices and with the general increasing complexity of the intellectual community, it would be useful to confirm the doctrine of fair use in this legislation. So this bill now contains a brief and clear statement of criteria of fair use; that is to say, use of copyrighted material in the occasional casual ways that I have mentioned without compensating the author.

We authors accept this statement of fair use in legislation. We consider the phrasing in the bill to be good; a phrasing that we can live with.

Beyond that, sir, I want to say—and this is a personal note—the discussion of the subject in the House's report, particularly the spelling out of the House's understanding of principles of fair use, struck me as a singularly responsible and thorough examination of this difficult, vexing point which touches the lives and the livelihood of all authors. These may be a historic few pages in the life of the intellectual community, because the report does lay down guidelines and the background and the implications of fair use so well. We support it as a body. I certainly support it as an individual.

The House report—here I refer to page 16, sir—the report "also dispels the confusion surrounding claims made by educational representatives for new privileges to reproduce copyrighted material. The House report makes it clear that the bill does not deprived education of any of the rights to use copyrighted material which it now possesses: 'any educational uses that are "fair use" today would be "fair use" under the bill.' The committee's discussion also makes it clear that certain teaching practices which educational representatives had claimed the revision bill would ban, are within the area of 'fair use' and would continue to be permissible."

Here I depart to say the House report spells out these instances of educational use very helpfully, sir.

Senator McCLELLAN. May I ask if you think the House bill now clears it up so that both the educational interest and the author's interest are clearly understood and each is satisfied with it?

Mr. WOUK. I can only speak for authors, sir. We will be satisfied with this definition of it. Of course, sir, as you know, both the phrasing in the bill and the discussion in the House report are the outcome of many meetings with both sides. Great consideration is given to the educator, so on the face of it, the educators should be as happy as we are with it. But I can only speak for us.

Senator McCLELLAN. I understand that we will hear them during this series of hearings, but I would hope the two interests would resolve the difficulty and save us a headache.

Mr. WOUK. I guess and I hope that that has happened, sir. I am sure at any rate that the areas of disagreement have been so significantly narrowed down that the back of the job has been broken, sir.

Senator McCLELLAN. I am very glad to hear it and very gratified. I hope you will have no problem with it.

Mr. WOUK. I now proceed, if I may, sir, to the second topic I have to discuss. That is the question of the reproduction devices that are proliferating at the present time.

Here let me refer to page 17 and to read briefly.

As the House Committee indicates on page 60, there has been an ever increasing development of new machines and devices which reproduce copyrighted works from the printed books in which they were first made available. The new methods include devices ranging from direct copying machines (like the Xerox) to innumerable offset printing devices (which often use masters, produced by Xerox or similar machines, directly from the book being copied) to a variety of photographic and microphotographic processes which reproduce the pages of a book on microfilm, micro-cards and other forms.

Let me depart from the text and bring in a personal note here. It is my privilege to serve as a member of the Board of Trustees of a college in the Virgin Islands, where I live. We are building a library for the college, which is only 5 years old. The problem of storage space arises. Of course, you know you pay by the square foot for building a library or any other building. The question of how many volumes you need and how many you can accommodate is vital. What turned up in the course of this policy debate was that in effect, all the old calculations for building a library were dissolving. A colleague of mine, brought to a trustees' meeting excerpts from the Wall Street Journal so pertinent to the livelihood of authors that I asked him for them. I went through my files this morning and with your permission, I would like to submit them here.

Senator McCLELLAN. You wish to submit them for the record?

Mr. WOUK. Yes, I would.

Senator McCLELLAN. Very well, they may be received as an exhibit and if we conclude that they should go into the record later, we will have them printed. Let them be received as an exhibit to your testimony.

(The documents referred to were made an exhibit and may be found in the files of the committee.)

Mr. WOUK. I don't think these are significant documents, rather they are illustrative.

Wall Street Journal, Thursday, December 1:

Breakthrough! National Cash Register introduces practical paperless publishing! A microform system that·lets you publish 3200 pages on a four by six transparency, send it anywhere for a nickel, and read it full size when it gets there, again and again.

Then the advertisement goes on to say that the card is indestructible, that it can be easily read, that this will reduce the amount of space needed for books and so on. This revolutionary system is on its way.

What struck me is that 3,200 pages represents more than my life work as an author to date. It can be reduced to a four by six inch transparency and be available to readers everywhere, instantly, through electronic communications.

Sir, this is the end of copyright as we know it, as it classically exists. Copyright dissolves, if copyright is payment for the reproduction of a book. Gutenberg's invention has had its run of 400 or 500 years, and now we are going to have this.

What remains, then, if the book, as the essential vehicle of copyright, dissolves. Only the principle is left; the principle that the right to copy is reserved to the author and his heirs for a term of years. This is his compensation for his precarious, often pioneering work, in the community. This is all he has to look to.

And, sir, the restriction of the right to copy creates a free intellectual community. Before copyright existed, the writer, the intellectual, the thinker was at the beck of a patron; or he was the sevrant of the theological system, or he was an embittered starveling. The restriction of the right to copy makes the intellectual, the scholar, the poet, a free man, able to live by his own efforts.

Sir, this legislation has come at a very lucky time, at a sort of watershed in the history of publishing and of creative life. Now, just now, these devices are coming to the fore as the chief communication systems of the future.

Senator McCLELLAN. As I understand you, you said there was some provisions restricting the right to copy and use, did you not?

Mr. WOUK. Yes, sir. The discussion of this problem in the House report we consider useful and illuminating, and in general we are satisfied with the conclusions of the House report. I refer now to page 18, sir.

The House report notes that the use of this new technology to make unauthorized reproductions of copyright material threatens the potential destruction of incentives to authorship. It represents a serious danger.

We go on and say that—

The cumulative effect of making innumerable small, unauthorized editions of a piece of copyrighted material is as injurious to its author and publisher as if all the copies had been produced by a single infringer and distributed to many readers.

I skip to the bottom of the page, sir:

Some authors, for example, poets and essayists, actually derive the greater portions of their income from authorizing reproduction of small portions of their work in anthologies and other collections, rather than from the sale of the original things from which they are reproduced.

And, sir, right now a small book can be assembled through these reproductive devices, made of a snatch here from one author and a snatch here from another author. It can all be done on these machines. There is no end to the possibilities in the computer use of books, where they can store on a computer the life works of all living authors and have them for distribution in one library, or in a network of libraries all over, at the press of a button.

In meeting this challenge, and in defining the limits of the use of reproductive devices, we support the language of the bill and we appreciate and are grateful for the discussion in the House report. In general, this language and this discussion answer our needs.

Beyond that, sir, I shall be glad to answer any questions on these topics.

STATEMENT OF THE AUTHORS LEAGUE OF AMERICA

My name is Elizabeth Janeway. I am a member of the Authors League of America, the national society of professional writers and dramatists. With me are Mr. Herman Wouk, Mr. John Dos Passos, and the League's Counsel, Mr. Irwin Karp. We appear on behalf of the Authors League to present its views on S. 597.

The Bill would rewrite the laws of literary property in the United States. Not only does it provide basic changes in the Copyright Act, it also abolishes the author's extensive rights in his work under common law. The Authors League strongly supports the Revision Bill. There are a few provisions which we believe should be modified. There are others which we think should have been written differently--but to which we do not object. The Revision Bill is a complex law which affects many interests; and in the arduous process of bringing it to its present form, adjustments and compromises have been made on several provisions. We recognize this and are willing to accept many of them.

During these hearings your Committee will hear testimony from various organizations and groups which publish, produce, disseminate, program or otherwise use the writings of authors. The Authors League speaks for the self-employed authors who create much of this material: novels, plays, poems, histories, biography and similar works. As in the House hearings, some witnesses representing users, rather than creators, of copyrighted works will probably oppose provisions which preserve the author's right to be paid for the uses of his work they happen to make. As in the past, they may see in these provisions, threats to "the public interest." However, we submit that the public interest is best served, as the House Committee's Report frequently demonstrates, by a copyright law that recognizes the author's right to be compensated for the various uses that are made of the works he creates.

The ultimate public interest in copyright is to aid, stimulate and encourage the production of literature and art—and in this country the great creative accomplishments have been made in these fields by the individual author, working alone. A sound and adequate copyright law is by far the most important action our nation can take to further this important, indeed indispensable, creative activity; important, and indispensable to those who exploit the author's work commercially, and to the educators, librarians and others who need and use it.

Copyright is the legal foundation on which rests the author's right to earn his living. He must, for a reasonable time, possess the exclusive rights to publish, perform, broadcast and otherwise present his work in order to obtain compensation for the time and effort which he has invested in it. These are fundamental rights to which he is entitled under the Constitution and at common law. If these rights are diminished by exceptions to his copyright, so is his livelihood. And so is the public interest in maintaining a free flow of ideas and of independent thought.

What is at stake here is the rights of an author in something he created, something which would not have existed without him. He is not asking for special privileges in already existing public resources or facilities. Rather, he *is* a public resource, if you want to put it that way. The best way to keep him productive and to ensure his contribution to the public welfare is to let him receive a return on the values he produces. Under the protection of copyright, authors have freed themselves from dependence on patrons and subsidies and from subservience to interests other than those of the general public.

Both the Copyright Office, in preparation of this Bill, and the Judiciary Committee of the House in its hearings, listened carefully to arguments which seek to dilute the right of an author to receive a proper return on the work he creates. (That return, incidentally, is not large. A study done for the Authors League in the not too distant past reported that the average income of professional writers is about $3000 a year.) In each case, these arguments to dilute copyright were rejected. But it is probable that they will once again be brought up in these sessions, and I would like now to explain briefly why it seems to authors right that they should be rejected.

The Monopoly Argument: The first argument of this kind advances the theory that copyright is a monopoly. But copyright does not give an author control over anything except the property he has created. He can sell it or lease it, but if he holds it off the market no one is hurt except himself.

He is no more a monopolist in the antitrust sense than millions of other Americans who own land or buildings, businesses, securities, natural resources, or any other kind of property. Each one possesses the exclusive rights to use that which he has created, purchased or inherited. It is not "monopoly" as the term is used under the Sherman Act.

A monopoly exists when someone owns enough property or has enough economic power to control an industry or to prevent the free play of competition. If I write a novel (and I have written six) I can't control the market for novels or the price of novels. I can't tell people to read my novel instead of someone else's. My publisher can advertise it—and I certainly hope he will!—but he must sell it in a free and competitive marketplace.

The Patent Argument: Another argument for diluting the rights of authors draws an analogy between copyright and patents. A copyright differs from a patent because patent protects an idea and can prevent public use of that idea,[1] while a copyright protects only the author's expression of an idea. Any other writer is free to use the same idea and to express it in his own way.

Let me give you an example of this that is rather close to my own heart. My last novel appeared under the title ACCIDENT. It begins with a car crash on a highway in which two young men are hurt. The book then goes on to investigate and evaluate the events following this accident and to attempt to discover why it took place in terms of how life went with these young men and their families afterward.

My book was published also in England, but it appeared under a slightly different title because another novel entitled ACCIDENT, by a writer named Nicholas Mosely, appeared in England two months before mine did. Mr. Mosely's novel begins with a car crash, and it goes on to investigate and evaluate the reasons leading up to the crash, and what happened afterward.

Neither Mr. Mosely nor I have the faintest claim against each other. We each hit on the same idea, but we produced different expressions of it, and both books were published here and in England, bought and read, in competition with each other.

The same situation exists in the field of nonfiction. In 1963, two excellent biographies of the poet John Keats were published, and each was considered for the National Book Award. Aileen Ward's received the prize, but some experts preferred, and recommended, Walter Jackson's. In 1957, Houghton Mifflin published a biography of Bernard Baruch by Margaret Coit, the Pulitzer Prize biographer. Mr. Baruch had authorized Miss Coit's book, but while she was still at work he took exception to her approach, and went at the job himself.

Holt published his autobiography at about the same time Miss Coit's book came out, and the two volumes certainly competed for sales. I need hardly remind you of the number of cookbooks on the market, or the different dictionaries and encyclopedias which can be purchased. Professional writers and the publishing

---

[1] It even prevents use by other inventors who discover the same thing independently and without copying from the patent owner.

industry are prepared for—perhaps I should say resigned to—such coincidences. They emphasize the point that ideas are not subject to copyright, but only the specific language which a writer uses to embody his idea.

The *"Special Privilege" Argument:* Another argument advanced to dilute the author's hold on his properties is that copyright is merely a special privilege granted by Congress to authors. I realize that writers may be prejudiced in feeling that this is an argument which doesn't stand up very well, but it is as difficult for me to understand as if you told me that my children weren't mine.

We do create these books and stories and poems, and they would not exist without us. True, we create them because we hope other people will be moved by them, or amused, excited, interested, informed. They are not made for ourselves alone, but they are made by us.

The common law at present recognizes this right of creation. In Ferris v. Frohman the Supreme Court of Illinois said:

"At common law the author of a literary composition has an absolute property right in his production which he could not be deprived of so long as it remained unpublished, nor could he be compelled to publish it. This right of property exists at common law in all productions of literature, drama, music, art, and so on."

That decision was affirmed by the Supreme Court of the United States in 1912 after the passage of the copyright legislation which is now in effect, and it has been ratified by other decisions in other courts. As the Register's 1961 Report reminds us, these "exclusive rights under the common law" in unpublished works "continue with no limit even though the work is used commercially and widely disseminated." Under the proposed Copyright Revision Bill, the author will surrender his common law right. How vital, then, is his interest and how urgent his plea that his property rights should now be firmly protected by statute!

Our American society is founded on the principle that the one who creates something of value is entitled to enjoy the fruits of his labor. If that labor is in the public interest, surely the laborer is more than ever worthy of his hire.

The gist of arguments to dilute the property right of the author, his copyright, comes down to this: "We admit the work of the author is in the public interest. In fact, it is so important, so vital, so useful to the public interest that—it should be taken away from the author without payment to him! It is so valuable that the people who create it should not receive recompense for their labors!"

I believe the Senate will reject the obvious paradox of this absurd argument.

"Fair Use"—Section 107: The House Committee's Report explains how the "fair use" doctrine applies in determining whether various types of copying by educational institutions and others constitute "fair use" (and are therefore permissible) or exceed its limits. The House Report demonstrates that the doctrine of "fair use" can be used to make these determinations; and the Report itself helps provide workable guidelines for educators, authors and publishers. (H. Rept., pp. 58–66).

The Report also dispels the confusion that, during the House hearings, surrounded claims by educational representatives for new privileges to reproduce copyrighted material. The House Report makes it clear that the Bill does not deprive education of any of the rights to use copyrighted material which it now possesses: "any educational uses that are 'fair use' today would be 'fair use' under the Bill" (p. 60). The Committee's discussion also makes it clear that certain teaching practices, which educational representatives had claimed the Revision Bill would ban, are within the area of "fair use" and would continue to be permissible.

Finally, the House Report emphasizes that there is no such thing as a "nonprofit" exemption which permits educators to reproduce copyrighted materials beyond the limits of "fair use"—and that no such limitation should be written into the law.

Reprography, Computers and Copyright: As the House Committee indicates (p. 60), there has been an ever increasing development of new machines and devices which reproduce copyrighted works from the printed books in which they were first made available. The new methods include devices ranging from direct copying machines (like the Xerox) to innumerable offset printing devices (which often use masters, produced by Xerox or similar machines, directly from the book being copied) to a variety of photographic and microphotographic processes which reproduce the pages of a book on microfilm, micro-cards, and other forms.

These many new techniques (sometimes labelled "reprography") have created a new medium for disseminating an author's work. Some experts describe it as "demand publishing" or "one-at-a-time publishing"—i.e., the reproduction of a single copy or several copies of a book, or portions of it, as needed. Even today, copies can be made at costs lower than the price of some books; and the costs are continually dropping.

The House Report notes that the use of this new technology to make unauthorized reproductions of copyrighted material threatens "the potential destruction of incentives to authorship . . . . it represents a serious danger" (p. 60). The cumulative effect of making innumerable small unauthorized "editions" of a piece of copyrighted material is as injurious to its author and publisher as if all of the copies had been produced by a single infringer and then distributed to many readers. Such unauthorized reproductions reduce the sale of copies of the book. Where an institution might have purchased several copies, one can now suffice—from it copies of portions can be reproduced as readers order them. And these practices will sharply diminish the income which authors now receive from licensing the right to *reproduce* portions or abridgments of their work in anthologies, textbooks, magazines, newspapers and other forms. Indeed, some authors (e.g., poets and essayists) actually derive a greater portion of their income from authorizing the reproduction of portions of a work in anthologies and other collections, rather than from the sale of the original edition from which the portions are reproduced.

Moreover, without adequate copyright protection, competition from unauthorized reproductions would reduce the royalties paid to the author by those publishers and other concerns who, under license, are supplying materials in these new forms. For example, University Microfilms produces copies of articles and books to order by Xerography and allied methods of "reprography." It does so by permission of the original authors and publishers and it pays them royalties. In fact, it now provides most of the out-of-print books ordered from publishers.

Other publishers are providing reprints of articles on demand; and are using the new methods of reprography to prepare anthologies and teaching materials custom-tailored to the specifications of individual teachers and educational institutions—again by authorization of the authors and publishers of the material, and on payment of royalties.

Actually, these organizations function as clearing houses as well as publishers. They secure permission from large numbers of authors to allow portions of their work to be reproduced in various quantities, even single copies, upon demand. This enables users to obtain authorized material from a single source. They also serve as clearing houses to collect and distribute to authors royalties for each such use of their work.

Of course, publishers themselves have served as clearing houses for their authors for many years. Each major publisher maintains a permissions department which, over the course of a year, grants many non-exclusive licenses to reproduce portions of an author's work in anthologies, textbooks, magazines and newspapers; and also to educational institutions and individual teachers who wish to reproduce portions of these works. Such permissions are granted upon payment of reasonable royalties; and the publisher distributes them to the authors.

As the House Report suggests (p. 65), it seems likely that new methods of ganting clearances and permissions, and collecting royalties, should be developed. We believe that they can; and we will participate in a continuing effort by all those concerned to develop such procedures.

"Reprography" is not the only new medium for communicating the work of authors. It is clear that computers and computer networks will soon become a principal means of disseminating much that authors write. One study, Copyright and Intellectual Property, by Professor Julius J. Marke (January 1967, published by the Fund for Advancement of Education), describes the manner in which computers are being used to store, retrieve and disseminate books and other writings; and the manner in which systems (some existing, some in process) will function in the next few years.

Professor Marke and experts whose views he reports (pp. 88–105) make it clear that "by providing copies of works stored in the computer, these systems will become publishers." They point out that the computer will store vast quantities of books and other written materials; it will reproduce them in full-sized printed copies; display their contents on television screens; and communicate them in other forms.

A computerized library center, and systems of such centers linked together, will serve thousands upon thousands of users—located great distances from the center. As the Register of Copyrights testified before your Committee last year, the new technology will permit "instant communications and reproduction of an author's work throughout the world." Professor Marke says:

". . . the computer in essence, assumes the role of a duplicating rather than a circulating library. One copy of a book fed into such a system can service all simultaneous demands for it; of course, this substitution for additional copies will vitally affect publishers, the traditional market" (pp. 92–93).

Needless to say, it will also vitally affect the author's royalty income.

As the House Report indicates (p. 54) there have been proposals to create partial exemptions to the author's right to require authorization and payment for the use of his work in computer systems. The House Judiciary Committee rejected these proposals, stating:

"Recognizing the proven impact that information storage and retrieval devices seem destined to have on authorship, communication, and human life itself, the committee is also aware of the dangers of *legislating prematurely in this area of exploding technology.* . . . The committee believes that, instead of trying to deal explicitly with computer uses, the statute should be general in terms and broad enough to allow for adjustment to future changes in patterns of reproduction and other uses of an author's works." (Italic supplied.)

We believe the House Committee's conclusion is sound and we respectfully urge your Committee to adopt the same approach. It would be premature—at this point—to legislate restrictions on the author's basic rights over the use of his work in a medium that might well become the principal means of communicating it. Without adequate experience and understanding of the problems, needs and arrangements (for authorization and payment), Congress could freeze into the copyright law for years to come an exemption that might seriously impair, if not destroy, the author's opportunity to be compensated for these uses of his work.

Previous experience with technological explosions in other copyright fields indicate how dangerous that could be. Radio and television were not envisioned when the 1909 Act was written. As they came into being they represented as radical a departure from the then conventional means of disseminating music and dramatic works, as the computer now represents vis-a-vis publishing. Had exemptions been written into the law for these new media, composers would have been deprived of the greater part of their livelihood—for in a few years radio completely displaced the sale of published music as the source of the composer's income. And radio, the talking picture, and television each in its turn became a vital medium for the presentation of dramatic works—although in 1909 the living stage was the only practical means of doing so.

In all of these instances, the Copyright Law had preserved, in broad terms, the author's right to require permission and payment for the use of his work, and authors and publishers did work out arrangements under which their works were used, and paid for, in these new media.

In its Report, the House Committee

". . . expresses the hope that the interests involved will work together toward an ultimate solution of this problem in the *light of experience*" (p. 54). (Italic supplied.)

We agree that this must be done and authors will do so.

The Committee's Report continues:

"Toward this end the Register of Copyrights may find it appropriate to hold further meetings on this subject after the passage of the new law. In the meantime, however, Section 106 preserves the exclusive rights of the copyright owner with respect to reproductions of his work for input or storage in an information system" (p. 54).

In fact, the Register of Copyrights is now holding such meetings with the groups interested in, and vitally affected by, the new computer medium. We believe the meetings should continue while the Bill is being acted on by the Congress and after it is passed. However, for the reasons indicated by the House Committee, we do not believe that its enactment should be delayed until the parties involved reach a satisfactory accommodation. It is obvious that all sides require further study, knowledge and experience to determine what copyrighted materials the new computer systems will require, what uses they will make of them, what will be the most feasible and efficient methods by which the creators of these copyrighted works can authorize their uses by the new systems, and the most practical methods for determining and paying compensation to copyright owners for such uses.

We think that with a determined and continuing effort the groups involved will be able to formulate the necessary arrangements. Moreover, we believe their efforts can be aided by an intensive and continuing study of the problems involved. We suggest, as have others, that the study be conducted by a panel of experts appointed by the Register of copyrights, or by your Committee and the House Judiciary Committee; that it be authorized to study the various factors and problems; and that it report its findings and recommendations to Congress within a specified period of time. We believe that the Panel's study, and the continuing meetings of the interested groups (held under the auspices of the Copyright Office), should within the next two to four years develop the information and experience necessary to reach an informed and equitable arrangement that will serve the best interests of all concerned—the creators of copyrighted works, those who operate and use the computer systems, and the public.

While study and investigation are required to determine how compensation for the uses of copyrighted works by computer systems should be measured, and how it should be paid, one thing is obvious at the outset. Computer systems can afford to pay for the uses of this material. We are concerned with systems that cost vast sums of money to create and operate. Those who build and sell the computers, programs and other materials will all be paid. Educational and other institutions, which will operate these facilities, will expend great sums to acquire the machines and materials, and run them. Reporting on IBM's entry into the "education market," Forbes magazine (Sept. 15, 1966, p. 60) said:

"Even IBM speaks with awe of the vast size of the market. Total expenditures on education in this country reached about $45 billion in 1965, and federal government expenditures in this area, which are currently running at $8.4 billion, are expected to rise significantly by 1971."

And, as FORBES reported:

"RCA, General Electric, Raytheon and Xerox—makers of computers or related gear—[have] followed IBM's lead."

The author's ambitions are far more modest than those of IBM or others involved in the production or management of computer systems—educational or otherwise. All that he asks is that the Copyright Law preserve his rights in the works he creates—so that he will be fairly compensated when they are used in this vast, and well-financed, new medium.

The Exceptions to the Right of Performance: Section 110.—In place of the present "for profit" exception to the right of public performance of musical and non-dramatic literary works, the Revision Bill specifically defines the exceptions under which performance and display of copyrighted works could be made without the author's consent and compensation.

Classroom Teaching: Section 110(1).—Allows the "free" performance or exhibition of any work in the course of face-to-face classroom teaching in nonprofit educational institutions, as under the present law. We believe this exemption, together with the analysis in the House Report (pp. 66–71), is reasonable and that authors could live with it.

Protection of Dramatic Works: It is particularly important that the unauthorized use of dramatic and dramatico-musical works should not be permitted beyond the scope of such face-to-face teaching activities. The Bill preserves the dramatist's essential exclusive right over all public performances of his work, whether for profit or not, whether by schools, commercial theatres, or "open" or "closed circuit" educational television.

As the Copyright Office has noted, the "for profit" exception has never applied to any public performances of plays and dramatico-musical works because of the serious damage that such performances would cause dramatists. A public performance of a play or musical, whether or not for profit, diminishes the potential audience for other performances. In this respect these works are far more vulnerable to unauthorized performances than are musical and non-dramatic literary works. The dramatist must retain the right to determine who can publicly perform his play, and when and where it may be performed. Unauthorized performances, by one class of users, whether or not for profit, can destroy valuable opportunities to have the work performed elsewhere for profit—by professional theatres in various parts of the country, in motion pictures or on television.

Moreover, public performance of his work—whether or not for profit—is the primary, and usually the only, source of income for the dramatist. For many dramatists, the modest fees they receive from performances of their plays in schools, colleges and universities are a principal means of compensation for their work, often the only income from plays of merit that are never performed profitably, or at all, in the professional theatre. Some dramatists write plays intended solely for production in educational institutions.

Any further exception which permitted the unathorized performance of dramatic or dramatical-musical works by educational closed circuit television or any other means [beyond the face-to-face teaching exception of section 110 (1)] would be severely damaging to American dramatists.

We strongly urge your committee to preserve this aspect of the Revision Bill in its present form and to reject any proposals to dilute the protection which it gives to the dramatist's indispensable right of public performance.

STATEMENT OF JESSE W. MARKHAM, PROFESSOR OF ECONOMICS AT PRINCETON UNIVERSITY

I am Jesse W. Markham, Professor of Economics at Princeton University. For the past ten years I have devoted considerable research and study to economic issues involving intellecutal property, especially the economics of patents and copyrights. Since its beginning, I have been a member of the research staff of the Patent, Trademark and Copyright Institute of George Washington University. Since 1961, I have been Economic editorial advisor to one of the better known publishing houses. I have written, and hold copyrights to a few books myself. Let me add in all candor, however, that the issues of copyright are complex and there is a good deal about them I do not know.

I appear here today on behalf of the membership of the American Book Publishers Council and the American Textbook Institute. My reason for appearing is that I acted as coordinator and economic advisor to both of these organizations in a comprehensive study of the present and future effects of information-transfer technology on book publishing.

The findings of these studies appear in *An Economic-Media Study of Book Publishing* and are pertinent to copyright law, the matter before this committee. Since copies of this study have been sent to this committee, I do not plan to present all the findings here; I will discuss the more important ones.

Much of what I shall say centers on the implications the vast strides in the new information technologies hold for copyright. There is no question but that the new technologies create important problems for the institution of copyright; however, I wish to make it clear at the outset that the remedy is not to hold back technical progress but to adapt our legal institutions to better accommodate it. The social benefits of the more efficient methods of creating, packaging, storing and disseminating knowledge and information are immense. It is clearly not in the best interests of a democratic society that the use of these new and more efficient information technologies in any way be frustrated or retarded by institutional obstacles. On the contrary, in this area perhaps more than any other technical progress should be given all the encouragement our legal institutions can provide.

In the simplest possible terms, the economic function of copyright is the incentive it provides those with the requisite ability to create intellectual property and the incentive it provides publishers, recording firms, and similar enterprises to package and distribute these intellectual creations. This statement puts the case for copyright much too simply, so I would like to elaborate and clarify what it means.

First, I do not wish to imply that the creation of all intellectual property depends upon the existence of copyright protection. Clearly it does not. Some of the classics of literature, science, and music to which each generation has access as a cultural inheritance were created with little if any consideration for copyright protection. However, the public would surely be less familiar with these creations if it were not possible to copyright certain versions of them, and treatises on them. Second, the many scholars, scientists, and artists who may not be stimulated directly by the financial incentive afforded by copyright are very often stimulated by the incentive of publication; the copyright, in providing publishers the incentive to publish, indirectly provides scholars the incentive to create.

Finally, in the case of textbooks and similar instructional material, it is reasonably safe to assume that both author and publisher are motivated by the prospects of financial reward. The writing of textbooks is generally considered to be more a matter of creatively assembling existing knowledge for purposes of effective instruction than as a matter of creating new knowledge. Those who write them may sometimes do so for purely professional reasons but income from royalties is their principal incentive, and profit rather than prestige generally provides the publisher with the incentive to publish. The financial regard of both author and publisher is greatly dependent on copyright.

In sum then, while all intellectual creations do not come about because of copyright, it is clear that copyright plays a very important role in stimulating creative activities and in the packaging, publication and wide distribution of the results that follow from it.

I have asserted that copyright protection is essential for the publication and distribution of scholarly works; I now wish to demonstrate why this is so. The necessity for copyright protection arises from the substantial differences in costs incurred by the original publisher and by those who copy or imitate the original publication. (Hereafter, I shall use the word publication to include all creations subject to copyright.) This difference in costs is attributable to 1) the risks attending the publication of a manuscript that has not yet undergone the commercial test of the marketplace, and 2) certain prepublication costs incurred only by original publishers assuming these risks.

The original publisher incurs risks because the commercial value of an untested manuscript when carried through to a salable manufactured copy can be predicted only in terms of broad ranges. It is therefore inevitable that while some books turn out to be best sellers, some barely break even, and some lose money. In the absence of copyright protection other publishers and copiers could avoid such risks by confining their copying to books that turned out to be commercially successful. In avoiding the risks they would avoid the attending costs of bearing them.

There are also prepublication costs that fall exclusively on publishers assuming the risks of first publication. Data supplied by the ATPI to Subcommittee Number 3 of the House Judiciary Committee on May 26, 1965, show that "a single high school textbook will require on investment of $50,000 before the first copy is available for sale." This investment includes such items as advance to authors, editorial and contractual costs, book design, galley and page proofs, and initial inventory. In addition, original publishers must pay royalties to the author. An essential economic justification for copyright, therefore, is that it provides publishers with an incentive to publish original material by providing an opportunity to recover the additional costs it entails.

It follows from this that the greater the amount of the difference in costs between original publications and copying, the greater is the need for copyright. Stated another way, the lower the cost of copying an original work, the greater is the incentive to circumvent the copyright. It is fairly clear from the detailed information developed in the studies I helped coordinate for the ABPC and the ATPI that the giant technological strides in copying machines and in information storage and retrieval systems built upon the electronic computer have created strong incentives to circumvent copyright. There is every reason to believe that future technological strides will be equally as impressive, and bring with them corresponding incentives to circumvent copyright.

A study carried out by Arthur D. Little, Inc., shows that over the past two decades, copying costs per page have declined dramatically as copying technology has advanced. It is now possible, where a modest sacrifice in quality is acceptable and where no binding is required, to copy on common offset paper twenty or more copies of a standard text book at a cost per copy measurably below the price of the textbook. Studies carried out by the National Opinion Research Center of the University of Chicago show that in elementary and secondary schools and in colleges, copying machines are used with considerable frequency in copying such copyright material as textbooks, tests and answer sheets, and music scores, although copying is generally limited to several pages.

Recent and projected advances in copying technology pose immediate problems for public policy toward copyright in that they dramatically reduce the cost and effort of reproducing copyrighted printed material. For the more distant future, however, the larger problems will be posed by the application of computers and micro images and their technological decendents to the process of information storage, retrieval and dissemination. While all of their potential uses obviously cannot now be foreseen, the high speed digital computer already has important implications for authors and publishers and for public policy toward copyright.

The present state of technology suggests that the computer will affect conventional publishing in two distinct ways: 1) the initial version of some types of information that are now reduced to writing, copyrighted and published will very likely be computerized, thus bypassing conventional publishing altogether; and 2) the contents of published works will be stored in computers and, once stored, serve as a substitute for additional printed copies. Examples of the former are the innumerable pieces of scientific analysis now going initially into computers and computer networks which formerly were published in journals and as scientific tracts. An example of the latter is the eastern universities medical school network of computers and telephone lines reported in the *New York Times* on March 5, 1965. The network, when completed, will merge the information resources of the participating medical schools. It is anticipated that, as technology matures, it will become increasingly practical for networks such as this to purchase a single tape rather than copies of books for deposit in each local library or information center. The contents of "books" stored on computer tape can then be obtained by any member of the network in the form of printed copy, film, visual display on closed circuit television, or some other output.

The reduction of literary and scientific creations to computer tape for dissemination by networks carries with it the risk of dulling the incentive copyright now affords author and publisher. Under the conventional system of publishing the author and publisher are rewarded in accordance with the actual number of copies sold, and there is no problem in accounting for the copies. But as computer systems take over the function of "satellite" publishers, accounting for the number of copies becomes much more complex. Unless a system is created for the purpose there will be no accounting control even for the printed copy output of books, and it will be even more difficult to account for intangible copy "printouts" over closed-circuit television, as microfilm, and in other visual forms. This possibility of leakage may reduce the incentive of authors to create and of publishers to publish.

While the computer "revolution" may reduce some of the incentives to create intellectual property, it may also provide something in the way of a new incentive that, at least in part, offsets the reduction. If computerized forms of the contents of books will be substituted for conventional copies now purchased, then the decreased demand for the latter will in part be offset by an increase in demand for tapes or other forms of computerized copies. In a market economy, it can generally be assumed that the substitution of one form of good or service for another occurs because the price of the good being substituted has undergone a relative price decline. Accordingly, the computer may make it economically feasible to publish certain intellectual creations that might otherwise have gone unpublished. It follows, of course, that the resulting increases in effective demand for such output will be translated into incentives for author and publisher only if some means are provided for remunerating both, irrespective of whether copies are marketed as conventional printed volumes, computer tape, or tangible or visual display copies obtained from computer tape.

A likely development related to the above is that computer manufacturers themselves will increase their demand for intellectual property.

The demand for computers will increase as the volume and variety of services the computer can satisfactorily perform increases. In the past, success in the computer manufacturing industry has depended largely upon the computer manufacturer's ability to provide the requisite servicing, including programming.

This raises the very important question of how computer manufacturers, some of whom have already acquired publishing houses, will obtain the intellectual property they program. Will they enter into agreement with authors who retain copyright, or will they employ authors as they now employ programming and systems specialists so that the author's creations are considered work made for hire? Were the latter to materialize, it would pose an important issue of concentration of control over the creation, storage and dissemination of knowledge and information. Under the present system of copyright, control is dispersed over tens of thousands authors and about nine hundred publishing houses. Almost the entire output of high-speed digital computers is in the hands of about eight companies.

In summary, the essential thrust of my analysis is that the technological revolution in information storage and dissemination is apparently upon us. It brings with it both great opportunity and great challenge. The spectacular advances in copying machines have made it possible to reproduce excellent copy almost instantly and at a cost per page of a few cents—or in sufficient volume, of a fraction of a cent. The benefits of this to society, especially to the process of instruction in schools and colleges, are enormous.

The new advances in the technology of reprography establish strong economic incentives to infringe the copyright or to argue for its modification to permit freer use of copyrighted material. The surveys cited in this analysis indicate that the incentives to infringe and circumvent the copyright are already at work in the schools and colleges and will very likely become stronger as new technological advances occur.

Before summing up the economic forces that bear on this issue a word probably should be said on the moral and legal question. Reduced to its simplest terms the question is whether any individual's property right should become less secure or less viable simply because the property has become more desirable and more readily accessible to others. By analogy, if my neighbor constructs a pathway to his rose garden, thereby easing my access to it, does this bestow on me any new-born legal or moral right to take his roses? In a private property society the answer is clearly "No."

The question cannot be answered so simply in terms of economic welfare, but there are economic solutions to the problem. Under the new technology the incentive to use selections from textbooks, reference works, and other instructional material has greatly increased because the cost of reproducing them for classroom distribution has been substantially reduced. This implies that the demand for parts of books has increased, possibly but not certainly at the expense of demand for additional copies of the entire book. If this is in fact the economic issue posed by the new technology in reprography, there is little reason to suppose that the market mechanism cannot resolve this supply-demand problem. Suppliers of books—authors and publishers—must design some method whereby parts of books or, more practicably, the rights to reproduce parts of the books, may be sold. Unless they do this, either present methods of selling books and the copyright will frustrate the new technology, or the incentive to circumvent the copyright will lead to unlawful reproduction or legal reproduction through copyright revision. Not only is neither of these solutions socially desirable but, in addition, neither is likely to produce an optimum allocation of our resources to the production of knowledge or optimum patterns of use of such knowledge. In brief, the copyright to a book should not obstruct extraction of the maximum use of a book, but neither should the increased incentives to use books in ways different from past patterns lead to emasculation of the property right. The conflict of seller and buyer can be resolved here, as can most other buyer-seller conflicts, through the pricing system.

The economic issues posed by the electronic computer are more complex and less definable; the observable trends have been too short in duration and the technological possibilities too much a matter for speculation to point with certainty to what the future might bring. But two developments appear reasonably certain: there will be an increasing demand for "publishing" the contents of such intellectual creations as books in the form of computer tape, and for this reason the contents will increasingly be "read" from visual-image substitutes for the present printed page. It is possible also that copies printed out from computer tape will be substituted for both visual-image computer output and conventional published copies.

While these problems are, as has already been indicated, more complex than those posed by the new means of reprography, they are not fundamentally different. Nor do they appear to require radical solutions. The new technology in information storage and retrieval, as in the case of all other innovations in history, requires market and institutional adjustments. As the demand for "books" in the form of tape increases, publishers, at least at present, are in the best position to fulfill it and should do so. Otherwise, effective use of the new technology will be hampered. But there appears to be no fundamental difference between the social necessity of protecting intellectual property rights in film and tape and that of protecting such rights in visible and tangible printed books. Similarly, there is no fundamental distinction to be drawn between reproducing copyrighted material on a Xerox machine and reproducing it from tape or film as visual images or printed copy. If one violates our laws of private property and dulls the incentive to create, so does the other. There is, therefore, a need to clear up any uncertainties that may still exist about whether intellectual property created, stored, and retrieved in one form is on legal parity with that created, stored, and retrieved in other forms. If the copyright is economically justifiable for one, it surely should be justifiable for the other. In any case, the *form* the property takes should have relatively little bearing on the copyright principle.

There would still remain complex problems, however, even if these uncertainties were clarified. When publishers sell books in the form of tape to computer centers, the computer center becomes in effect a "satellite" publisher, capable of producing copies in a variety of ways. There then arises the problem of counting copies—the customary basis for determining the revenues of author and initial publisher. It has been suggested that a solution to this problem may be to charge a lump-sum fee at time of storage and to develop accounting control systems that reveal the volume of use and printout. Payments may then be made to publisher and author on a per "copy" basis. Similarly, as technological developments make it increasingly practicable to print out copies of books from tape, the computer may become analogous to copying machines, except that it may be more capable of reproducing whole volumes. Again, it would seem that the market might provide clues to the socially optimum solution to this problem. The basic guidelines to policy that envisage the optimum solution are the same as those invoked in the case of copying technology: while it is apparent that the copyright should not obstruct the economical use of the new technology, it is equally apparent that the new technology should not be made the means of riding roughshod over the rights of authors and publishers in the intellectual property they create and prepare for use by the public.

STATEMENT OF LEE C. DEIGHTON

Mr. Chairman, I am Lee Deighton, chairman of The Macmillan Company. I appear on behalf of the American Textbook Publishers Institute, a trade association of 125 firms engaged in publishing reference books, maps, tests, textbooks, and other materials of instruction. These firms account for 95% of the sales of such materials to the schools and colleges of the country.

It is a highly competitive industry in which no single firm commands more than 10 per cent of the market. We believe that this is as it should be in a political democracy and a free enterprise economy.

We live in a very close relationship of interdependence with the schools and colleges we supply. They are the only market for our products. We could not survive without them. More than this, the teachers in the schools and colleges are the authors of our products. At the same time, the schools of the nation rely heavily upon the instructional materials we produce.

This is in no sense a reflection upon the quality of the schools. It is in part an outcome of the extraordinary growth of enrollments and the difficulty of securing and holding enough good teachers to do the job. There is a turnover of one third of the teaching staff every year. Approximately 7 per cent of our teachers this year hold only temporary certificates. One third of the teaching staff has had less than three years of experience. They have a real and practical need for the materials of instruction that we provide.

Because instructional materials are so important in training the minds of our young people, the publishers of these materials have a very great responsibility to society. We believe that this responsibility can be best discharged by private, commercial publishers whose independence of action is guaranteed by the society they serve. The most important guarantee in our society is the copyright law, which is the legal foundation of our business. Incidentally, in every advanced nation of the free world instructional materials are provided by private, commercial publishers.

It is clear from the testimony of this morning that authors are the primary creators and proprietors whose work is encouraged and protected by copyright law. It is quite natural to wonder therefore what is the interest of publishers in copyright.

The scholars, teachers, and creative artists who write manuscripts do not have the means of turning them into printed books and of distributing them to the nation's book buyers. They present their manuscripts to private publishers who do have these means. The author contracts with the publisher to publish and distribute his works, and assigns certain rights of copyright to the publisher in consideration of grants, royalties, and advance payments against future royalties.

It is by this route that the publisher enters the copyright picture. He is required by contract to commit his capital to publication. He commits himself to expenditures *on risk* because for most books there is no certainty prior to publication that a book will sell. Since books are not usually purchased sight unseen, we must have a book in hand in order to sell it.

Professor Markham has clearly described the prepublication costs to which the publisher commits himself. Quite apart from fixed costs such as rent and taxes, he must pay the salaries of editors. He must buy and pay for photographs, maps, and artist's illustrations. He must pay for typesetting and the making of printing plates. For a single high school textbook, these prepublication costs may amount to $50,000.

For an elementary school textbook series, they are often as high as $750,000. For a new 20-volume encyclopedia which my company is publishing this year, they will be slightly more than $7,000,000. These are out-of-pocket costs before the first copy of a new book appears. If there were no copyright law to protect the publisher against piracy and misappropriation, he could not risk his capital in prepublication costs.

Now, suppose a situation in which there is no copyright protection. By means of quite simple technology, a pirate may photograph, print, bind the entire work and sell it at a cut-rate price because he does not have the prepublication costs of the original publisher. He has no editors. He buys no artwork. He pays nothing for typesetting. The interest of publishers in a strong copyright law becomes self-evident.

The function of the publisher is to create, package, and distribute. Our product is primarily the book, but we are not limited to this form. We can package and distribute our materials just as well on microfilm or on magnetic tape and will do so when a demand for these forms develops, provided they are protected by copyright. We can and do produce film, filmstrips, transparencies, and other audio-visual products, and because they are peculiarly vulnerable to misappropriation, they require the special protection which the bill before you provides.

The current study of copyright which began 12 years ago was not started at the behest of book publishers. Nor have book publishers come forth strongly at any time to request a new law. Nonetheless, we have followed the discussions closely and have participated in them eagerly. The bill before you is the result of many compromises arrived at through many hours of conference and efforts in good faith to develop a law fair to all parties of interest. Book publishers still believe that section 601, the manufacturing clause, is essentially a tariff provision that has no place in a copyright law. Yet, as written, it is a compromise that most publishers are willing to try. In the same way, we have reached an accommodation with users on fair use. Similarly, the provisions for free use of copyrighted material in educational television, for reversion of rights to authors, and many other particulars in the bill represent compromises between publishers and other parties of interest.

We respectfully request now that you examine the bill and any amendments that may be suggested to make sure that copyright does not become a hollow shell through grant of further exemptions.

We have looked at copyright legislation not only as publishers but as citizens of a free economic society. We have observed a central thread running through the dialogue of the past three years. It is quite simply a demand for free use of copyrighted material through the grant of special exemptions. It is our position equally with authors, composers, artists, and other creative talents that the product of a man's mind and imagination is property just as much as the product of his hands or machines. Every exemption granted is an abridgement of the creator's rights to enjoy the fruits of his labor. As citizens, we are concerned lest the granting of exemptions proceed so far as to hinder the flow of created materials.

Among the exemptions that have been sought in this copyright dialogue are these:

(1) the making of copies without permission or payment for use in educational institutions.

(2) the making of copies without permission or payment for instructional purposes in governmental agencies and institutions.

(3) performance and display of copyrighted material without permission or payment in educational television.

(4) input, manipulation, and display of copyrighted material in computers without permission or payment.

It is our position that the bill before you, S. 597, meets these demands in a manner fair to all parties, and in a manner that will not impede the use of new technology.

Appearing at this early point in the proceedings of your Committee, we are uncertain whether the parties of interest are still at odds concerning the uses of copyrighted material in this technology.

Book publishers have been anxious throughout the copyright study period because the drafting of a new copyright law has run simultaneously with a technological revolution in the means of duplicating and displaying copyrighted material.

Only the outlines of this revolution have so far emerged. We are well aware of the advances in photo-copying, but the development of computer networks, library networks, facsimile transmission, computer-assisted-instruction, and earth satellites is in the planning and experimental stage. It is the position of book publishers that no law written at this time can deal fairly and justly with specific devices and specific situations arising from the communications revolution. Neither the devices nor their effects upon copyright can be wholly foreseen.

The hazards of legislation made too explicit with respect to technology are noted at page 53 of the Committee Report to accompany H.R. 4347: "Although it was touched on rather lightly at the hearings, the problem of computer uses of copyrighted material has attracted increasing attention and controversy in recent months. Recognizing the profound impact that information storage and retrieval devices seem destined to have on authorship, communications, and human life itself, the committee is also aware of the dangers of legislation prematurely in this area of exploding technology.

"In the context of section 106, the committee believes that, instead of trying to deal explicitly with computer uses, the statute should be general in terms and broad enough to allow for adjustment to future changes in patterns of reproduction and other uses of authors' works."

It is precisely because the bill before you is in fact "general in terms and broad enough to allow for future changes" that book publishers can lend it their support. We would view with alarm any amendment which would permit the further encroachment by devices, machines, or processes—to use the language of the bill before you—"now known or later to be developed."

The use of copyrighted material without permission and without payment in transmission by television or computer as previously proposed constitutes a serious threat to authors and publishers.

The threat is precisely that technology of transmission and display will make one copy of a book do where hundreds or thousands have been used and purchased before. The disappearance of a market will make it impossible to publish books in quantity sufficient to return the required investment. We can adjust to the technology itself by new kinds of publications and new price structures. What we cannot adjust to is *unpaid for* use of these new materials. Unpaid use by depriving us of income would make it impossible for us to adjust.

The threat I am describing is not immediate but lies in an unknown future. The threat of use without payment in closed-circuit transmission is not immediate only because this transmission is ineffective. We may note in passing the comment in the 1967 Carnegie Report on Educational Television: "With minor exceptions, the total disappearance of instructional television would leave the educational system fundamentally unchanged." Or we may note the 1967 comment of Dr. Conant in a report of a study sponsored by the National Association of Secondary School Principals: "Only 10.9 per cent of the principals replying to the inquiry indicated that television was a major teaching device in one or more subjects in their schools."

We cannot suppose that these conditions will continue for long. The educators engaged in instructional television are a devoted and committed group. The foundations have recently offered millions of dollars of their own funds for program development and have proposed systems which would provide far greater funds to support noncommercial television. A recent Presidential message calls far additional support of educational television and exploring the use of earth satellites.

Nothing so dramatically forecasts the future as the possibility of earth satellite systems of broadcast. Earth-satellite transmission will permit simultaneous viewing throughout the country. New recording devices now available will permit viewers to record and store the transmitted program for use on classroom television sets over and over again.

Suppose now a closed-circuit program transmitted via satellite to educational institutions. Suppose that on this program the pages of a copyrighted work are displayed for reading and that in thousands of these institutions recording devices fix the program on film. In these circumstances, who would buy the books?

I have been describing the future of closed-circuit television. The same kind of transmission is now technologically possible in computer network systems. It is contemplated that in these systems, a central computer will store copyrighted works, and that they will be transmitted by wire to hundreds of individual console screens upon demand. In a system of this kind, the only copy exists in the computer. It is merely displayed on the console screen to be read at leisure by the user. The computer in effect becomes the library.

At the moment, no such network exists in educational institutions. We are still in the experimental stage in a relatively few colleges and schools across the country. Like television transmission, computer transmission is a future, not a present, threat to authors and publishers.

With this background, we may now consider the force of the exemptions from copyright previously proposed for transmission by television or computer. Use of copyrighted material without permission or payment would permit display of this material for as long as desired, as many times as desired, to as many individuals simultaneously as may be placed before cathode ray tubes. It would cover all kinds of copyrighted material from *Winnie the Pooh* to mathematical treatises.

It should be noted that the bill before you for the first time in American copyright law extends copyright to include the right to display a work publicly. (Clause 6 of section 106) This is clear and explicit recognition that methods and devices for display currently available and in growing use have the potential of destroying the market for copyrighted works. In this connection, the Committee Report to accompany H.R. 4347 says at page 55: "With the growing use of projection equipment, closed and open circuit television and computers for displaying images of textual and graphic material to 'audiences' or 'readers' this right is certain to assume great importance to copyright owners........ The committee is aware that in the future, electronic images may take the place of printed copies in some situations, and has dealt with the problem by amendments in sections 109 and 110........"

This atatement presents the heart of the problem. We are faced with a loss of market when a machine can make one copy of a work do where hundreds have been used before.

Unrestricted use in closed-circuit transmission would be damaging to all kinds of copyrighted material. To certain kinds, it might well prove fatal. Closed-circuit television is linked to educational institutions. Textbooks, workbooks, laboratory manuals, and stadardized tests are produced for this market. They can be sold nowhere else. If unlimited use destroys the market for them, private commercial publishers will find it impossible to risk the capital required for new texts and nstructional materials.

These materials are designed for sale in quantity in large markets. There are other publications of a scholarly or technical nature with total markets of only a few thousand copies. If these markets are reduced by as much as 10 per cent, the books in question cannot be published. Unrestricted use in this case, permitting one copy to serve where hundreds have served before, would quite literally dry up the sources of publication. To be quite specific, if an advanced scholarly or scientific work were encoded without permission or payment into a computer, and if this computer were part of a wide-ranging network, no scholar or scientist with access to the network would buy the book. No library associated with the network would buy the book. It would be difficult to find a publisher for another book of the same sort.

Under the present law, nonprofit television and radio are granted the right to use nondramatic literary material for performance only. This means that no copy may be made of the performance for future use. The bill before you continues this basic exemption from copyright, but authorizes the making of two copies for instructional television performance. The first copy may be held indefinitely for archival purposes; the second may be held and used without limit to the number of uses for more than a year.

This provision represents a compromise on the part of book publishers. It is their majority view that a one-time performance on educational television cannot disturb the market for a work. It is their unanimous view that repeated performances without restriction would remove any reason for purchase of the work and thus damage its market. The right to make a copy of a transmission for repeated use during the course of one year represents hazard enough. It was not objected to by publishers on the plea that a recording would permit exchange of programs between one local area and another. We would regard any extension in the number of permitted recordings as a serious erosion of basic copyright.

On page 73 of the Committee Report to accompany H.R. 4347, there appears a statement applying to radio and television transmission but not to computer transmission: "Subclause B of section 110(2) which was added by the committee, confines the exemption to transmissions normally encompassing an area whose radius is not over 100 miles. The basic theory of the instructional broadcasting exemption in clause (2) is that the permitted uses of copyrighted material are made through local transmitting organizations and are generally part of the instructional activities of local educational institutions. This theoretical base would be eroded or destroyed if, as now seems entirely possible through the use of communication satellites, for example, a nation-wide network of simultaneous educational transmissions were established and if teaching methods based on visual images rather than printed copies continued to evolve. The prospects of very serious damage to copyright owners if this happened impressed the committee as real. A radius of 100 miles is substantially larger than the areas normally encompassed by existing educational transmitters. . . ."

Our main concern is limitation to the normal radius of transmission of a single station and avoidance of earth satellite use and unlimited simultaneous transmission by other stations.

It will be alleged that in opposing the extension of free use of copyrighted material in the new educational technology book publishers are trying to prevent the growth and use of these marvellous devices. This is not the case. We are interested in the advancement of education or we would not be in book publishing. We believe that the new technology has great potential. We believe it will require new kinds of instructional materials, and we want to be in business to provide them.

We do not believe that the development of instructional television or computer-assisted-instruction requires the expropriation of our current product. It is estimated by Professor Patrick Suppes of Stanford, the leading authority in the field, that computer-assisted-instruction will cost $2 billion to install and that this money will be forthcoming. It is estimated that a satellite-based transmission program will cost $30 or $40 million per year and that this money will be forthcoming. With figures of this size in view, it is ironic indeed that authors and publishers should be asked to provide their work without payment.

We cannot understand why we are singled out. Those who make this demand fully expect to pay for equipment, for use of cables and telephone lines, for electric power, and for salaries.

It will be asserted that free use of copyrighted material is essential for educational transmission because publishers are slow and reluctant to answer requests for use of their materials. No one will deny that some publishers have been slow and inefficient in handling permission requests. On the other hand, thousands of requests are handled promptly and reasonably every month. At the Macmillan Company alone, we receive 8,000 requests a year, and we are in a current study of the feasibility of handling these requests via computer.

You may wonder why responses are not immediate and automatic. There are several interesting and important reasons why not. The basic principle is that publishers stand in a fiduciary relationship to their authors. They cannot permit uses of material which distort the intent of the author. They cannot approve quotations out of context or quotations which are in effect an abridgment or caricature of the author's work.

Two examples will illustrate the problem. We recently received at the Macmillan Company a three page letter requesting permission to use some 30 disconnected sentences and paragraphs ranging over 279 pages of an author's work. It was necessary to go to the pages of the work to discover what the effect of this kind of skip-quotation would be. It was clear, upon inspection, that the effect would have been gross distortion and the request was declined.

As a second example, we are often asked for permission to quote portions of a poem. If the request is for alternate stanzas or for a passage from which lines are omitted, we cannot in good faith grant the permission, for the result would be a distortion of the poem. If we granted permission, we would be in violation of our obligation to protect the integrity of the author's work.

Clearly, then, we cannot grant all requests for all uses of an author's work. The handling of permission requests cannot be automatic since it requires the exercise of judgment. On the other hand once user needs are made clear, it is possible that certain of them can be handled in bulk.

There is no question that applying for permission to use copyrighted material is an inconvenience. So is the paying of taxes. So is the respect for parking ordinances, and for legally posted "No Trespassing" signs. It is also an inconvenience in the schools to live with a budget system which requires planning in one year for purchase of Xerox machines and duplicating paper in another. So is the necessity which teachers must observe of filling out requisitions for pencils and erasers.

It is undeniably an inconvenience to respect copyright to the extent of applying for permission to use material that someone else has created. To overcome this inconvenience, two suggestions have been advanced by users. The first is to permit free use of copyrighted material so that no permission need be sought. The second is to set up a clearing house to which users can apply and from which they can secure permissions quickly

Book publishers are quite willing to undertake feasibility studies for methods of handling copyright commissions. We would observe, however, first that we must be protected from antitrust prosecution and second, that the complexity of the problem permits no quick and easy solution. It would be necessary to collate information from book publishing alone for some half-million titles. Information of this order can be handled only by computers. But no computer can be programmed to exercise the judgment that is required if the integrity of an author's work is to be respected.

This offer to study the means of clearing copyright permissions is genuine. On Monday of this week, book publishers were in conference with the Office of Education on this very problem. We are seeking a means to clear permissions for educational research information to be stored on microfilm and in computers for Project ERIC. The directors of this project do not yet know what kinds of copyrighted materials will be required. They do not know whether they will want entire books, or passages, or abstracts. They have no idea how many uses will be made of material stored in computers. Neither do we, but both parties intend to work together within the framework of the present copyright law to find out. For we are persuaded that the orderly process of the marketplace is the proper means for solving our problems.

Mr. Chairman, may I express the appreciation of American Textbook Publishers Institute for the opportunity you have given us to state our position.

STATEMENT OF MRS. BELLA L. LINDEN, COUNSEL, THE AMERICAN TEXTBOOK PUBLISHERS INSTITUTE, NEW YORK

Mrs. LINDEN. Mr. Chairman, may I ask your indulgence? I worked awfully hard to condence into as brief sentences as possible an overview of computer technology as a lawyer and as a representative of the American Textbook Publishers Institute sees it. I am afraid if I speak extemporaneously, I may speak twice as long.

Senator BURDICK. Then, by all means, read it.

Mrs. LINDEN. Mr. Chairman and member of the committee, I am Mrs. Bella Linden, attorney, of the New York firm of Linden & Deutsch. I am copyright counsel for the American Textbook Publishers Institute, and am appearing on their behalf.

One of the principal unresolved issues in copyright law revision is how should the copyright law deal with the new mechanized technology of handling information. The fantastic capacities, present and prospective, of computerized information networks to deal with the information explosion have so captured our imagination that there are some who insist that social progress demands that all information and copyrighted works be made available for computerized uses with minimal or no interference from the authors or publishers.

One of the purposes for my appearance here is to reiterate for the record that publishers do not wish to impede the accessibility of copyrighted material to the educational community, nor to the libraries, nor to the population at large. Making textbooks, reference works, and all other forms of creative writing available to the community has been and continues to be the publishers' main function.

What is troublesome at this time is whether all men of good will will recognize that ready access and availability to copyrighted material is not the same as free unpaid for use of such works—whether all men of social responsibility recognize that computer, or computerized information systems, are still only pieces of machinery, hardware—and they are socially useful only if and to the extent that authors and publishers provide these marvelous machines with product, with literary material, with knowledge and material to store, put into them, and to make available.

I am here to urge that information storage and retrieval is not a new concept—it was invented by the cavemen—and that the needs for legal accommodation to this new technology we urge should be examined in the context of its historical development and the historical development of our country's response to the care, preservation and enhancement of its intellectual gross product.

I would ask your indulgence so that I could trace in a couple of moments, perhaps all too briefly and too superficially, the origin and development of the body of law referred to as copyright law in response to society's recognition of its—society's—welfare.

The first forms of human communication were gestures and cries which could not be called speech—since they transmitted signs rather than symbols. Then came speech itself, that is, language, in contrast to the mere gestures of articulated sounds which accompanied emotional states. Actually perhaps even prior to speech, the first information storage and retrieval system was created by the caveman who scratched and later painted signs on the walls of his cave, thus storing information for later transmission of information forward in time. The transmission of information and ideas to distant people was later made possible by writing on clay tablets, and still later on parchment. Thus, information was stored by the caveman and later by early man as well as on clay tablets, on the walls of his cave, so he could retrieve this information at a later date.

The storage and transmission functions of the written word were enormously enhanced by the invention of moveable type which permitted the printing of books. However, the use of a printing press meant that the author no longer had possession of the single manuscript which could be read or laboriously hand copied by others. There developed a need to protect the copying (or printing) right. Thus, the generic term became the label for a newly emerging body of rights—"copyrights".

The mass distribution of books which later resulted, created the first real difficulties for an author in attempting to achieve recognition as the author of a work and in his ability to control and preserve the contents from distortions and further, his ability to achieve economic reward to the extent available in those days to authorship.

The British Parliament responded with the world's first copyright statute, known as the Statute of Anne (8 Anne c. 19 1710). This statute is the base upon which all subsequent legislation with respect to copyright, both here and abroad, have been enacted.

It may be safely assumed that the colonial lawyers participating in the Continental Congress were familiar with English law, including the law of copyright. There is evidence that at least one lawyer of the time, Noah Webster, was actively concerned in the authors' problems and with attempts to attain legislative solutions to them.

Exercising the power granted by article 1, section 8 of the Federal Constitution, the First Congress enacted the first Federal copyright statute in 1790.

"Books" as such, were not defined in the act, and coverage of the act was potentially limited only by the constitutional term "writings." Of course, a literal interpretation of "writings" would have excluded maps and charts from protection. There is no material available concerning the drafting of the bill or debate in Congress, but it would seem clear from the inclusion of maps and charts in the scope of protection that even at the birth of Federal copyright legislation in the United States it was found necessary to forcibly expand the meaning of language in a manner that would reflect the practical realities of the need for protection and the technology of that time.

Although there were innovations and improvements in the printing processes, the first significant technological breakthrough in the methods of storing and distributing information since the innovation of the printing press was the development of computerized information networks.

The information explosion and its related and yet independent phenomenon, the rapid obsolescence of information, which followed World War II, stimulated the development of computers to afford more efficient access to the intellectual gross product of our society. To the extent that computerized information storage and retrieval systems are merely more efficient performers of the same functions as clay tablets and books, that is, they fulfill the function of storage and transmission of information through time and space, the problems of protecting authors' right and incentives and at the same time affording rapid access to copyrighted material to computers instead of printing presses are, we submit, less foreboding and much less revolutionary than a technical dissertation on electronic equipment would lead one to believe.

The new science of documentation has already produced a highly technical vocabulary, but the meanings of the words are fairly clear. The steps in the process of computerized information handling are as follows—I refer now to what we call input, the various techniques whereby material, text material, written word, is translated or transformed from verbal symbols of the English language into machine readable form. In other words, the computers are not able at this juncture yet to read, to scan a page—at least, it is not economically feasible at this juncture. They do not read the words of the English language. They are transformed by an electric typewriter that translates these verbal symbols, these words of the English language, shall we say, into symbols and signs that the electronic equipment can appropriately store.

The next word of art, so to speak, that is commonly used is storage. This is the next process. First, the material is converted into machine readable form, and then it is stored in what we call the memory core of the computer.

The next process the computer is capable of is manipulating and handling all of the information within the memory core of the computer system for subsequent retrieval.

Then, in response to an inquiry, the material is made available; in other words, is retrieved. Then it is ready for output.

What happens then is that either the material is displayed or a hard copy printout of a portion or a section of the text material that has been translated into the memory core of the computer system is made available.

This is the technology, these are the techniques of activity that are now being accomplished and will increasingly be accomplished more efficiently by computerized information networks. I keep referring to computerized information storage and retrieval systems, because information storage and retrieval systems, as I am urging so strongly, conceptually are books, manuscripts, journals, clay tablets, pictures—any item on which man has been able to store his information so that he does not have to rely on his own memory.

Senator BURDICK. What you are saying, then, is that this computer is merely a 1967 clay tablet.

Mrs. LINDEN. Precisely. Of course, I think there are those hardware manufacturers who would not equate the places. But the conceptual function, the purpose is the same.

Through the generations, mankind has learned how more efficiently and in a more sophisticated manner to accomplish the same things. Just as mankind first walked, then rode a horse, then had a horse and buggy, then a train, then an airplane, then the supersonic jets. Actually, the purpose was the same. The purpose was to transport himself or possessions from one spot, geographic location, to another more efficiently. That is what computerized information storage and retrieval networks are intended to do. They achieve by a sophisticated electronic means what mankind has attempted to do and has done within a more primitive fashion via printing presses, via books, and via clay tablets.

An evaluation of the proposed copyright law relative to existing and prospective computer technology will, we submit, offer the answer to contentions that S. 597 does not appropriately respond to the new technology. Perhaps a brief overview of computer operation would help us at this point to get some notion of what the future may bring. Since the computer operates essentially with two digits, zero and one, it cannot, as I suggested earlier, operate directly with the characters of the alphabet. To store words in a computer, they must be translated into the binary numbers which constitute computer language. Presently this is accomplished by operators who use electric typewriters to copy the text, which is then internally translated into binary numbers. This translation is accomplished today by keypunch operators who create a deck of cards on which the words appear as holes punched into numbered columns. Automatic reading devices cannot read letterpress. They cannot read the printed page. The commercial production of these automatic scanning devices in quantity is 5 to 10 years down the road. At this moment, the input of printed material is an expensive and time-consuming exercise that is not lightly entered into.

The storage capacity of today's computers is enormous and is developing rapidly. It is logically possible but at this time it is not economically practical to store all of the world's knowledge in a computer memory system.

Returning to the case of printed materials, what uses can be made of them by the computer? The reason I ask the question at this juncture is to suggest that this may not be the time to reach definitive language in legislation with respect to computer technology.

I am urging the consideration of the present state of the art as a background against which the proposed copyright law ought to be evaluated.

At the present time, the actual use of copyrighted material in computers is extremely limited. A survey undertaken in January showed that during the preceding six months 167 book publishers had received only 22 requests for permission to use copyrighted material in computers. During the same period, they had received and processed thousands of permission requests for other kinds of uses.

For economic reasons the computer uses of copyrighted material lie years in the future. We can only begin at this moment to consider what they may be. We know of three potential uses: (1) scholarly study, (2) information storage and retrieval uses generally, and (3) computer-assisted instruction. I should like to describe the present state of the art so that we may better be able to evaluate whether it is advisable, no, possible at this time to draft legislation regulating computerized uses of copyrighted materials.

In scholarly study, the whole of an author's works may be read into a computer and stored in its memory. The works may then be subjected to analysis to reveal characteristics of style, or sources of information. One author's work may be compared to another's. Stylistic analysis of this sort has apparently revealed that eight out of 12 of the Federalist Papers whose authorship had been in dispute were written by Madison.

The second potential computer use of copyrighted material is the storage of books or indeed of libraries in computers for indexing and abstracting and for printout or display of appropriate portions of text. Once again, for reasons of expense and practical utility, this use is also currently minimal.

Within the Federal Government, several agencies are using computers to cope with the flow of reports generated by Government funded research. Two aspects of those attempts by governmental agencies to deal with information flow are specially pertinent. First, the computers are now used not to store printed text but simply a bibliography of titles of the reports. Second, the materials referred to by title are not copyrighted materials. That is not to say that storing of entire texts will not be practical and commercially feasible in the next decade.

Closely related to these Government agency networks, are the slowly developing library networks such as the medical library network proposed 2 years ago by a group of eastern universities and the New York State library network announced a couple of months ago. So far as we know, these networks use or will use computers only for bibliographic control. The exchange of copies of the texts will be by facsimile transmission.

In other words, it will be by some kind of photographic or what we call copying process. It will not be part of the output, so to speak, of the information stored in the computer mechanism of the network.

We are here concerned with computer storage of copyrighted materials, and it appears that at the present there is little evidence of immediate need for this kind of use except for indexing.

The third potential area of computer use of copyrighted materials is in computer-assisted instruction. This use also is in the most preliminary stages. The recent Presidential message on education proposed an experimental program for developing the potential of computers in education. It observed that computers are now used in educational institutions primarily for advanced research but can be used for other purposes "if we find ways to employ it effectively and economically and if we develop practical courses to teach students how to use it."

In other words, it is not happening yet. It undoubtedly will, it undoubtedly should but it is not something that is presently in existence and can presently be regulated. In other words, it is a prospective use.

Furthermore, there is another point that ought to be borne in mind. That is that the materials used in individualized computer instructions bear no relationship whatsoever to existing copyrighted works.

When IBM began pioneering in this field, it created its own materials for calculus and German. It did not translate any existing textbooks into computer language for display on the student's screen. In short, there appears to be no present visible demand for the input of existing copyright materials into computers for computer-assisted instruction.

The conclusion is inescapable that before computer-assisted instruction can succeed, special materials must be created for it. But if these materials are to be denied the protection of copyright, who will spend the time and money required to produce them? The demand that has been made for unpaid, free input, manipulation, and display of copyrighted materials for closed-circuit transmission would forestall the creators of the very materials that are needed to make computers the great tool they can become in the future of American education.

To summarize the publishers' position briefly: the use of copyrighted materials in computers for scholarship, library interchange, and instruction is minimal at this moment. The requirements for such use in the future are still speculative. The demand for exemption from copyright for computer use is predicated upon speculative and prospective needs. I must emphasize that furthermore, it assumes that contrary to all previous experience, publishers would not be willing to deal with customers. It seeks regulatory legislation for something that barely exists. The normal pattern of legislation in this country is to provide rules of action in situations where private parties have failed to come to agreement and the interests of society are jeopardized by this failure.

At the moment, there is no practical collision of interests between copyright proprietor and computer users. The means of conference and private negotiation have not been exhausted. They have barely been tried. Publishers are currently working out modes of action with the Office of Education.

We hope that this will be a prototype for negotiations with any and all others who seek to use copyrighted material.

We believe that this method of negotiation will produce required computer access to copyrighted materials at reasonable fees for all users.

S. 597 makes no reference to computers, but the committee report which accompanied H.R. 4347 made specific applications of the language of the bill to computer usage. The report specifically recommended that the Register of Copyrights bring together in conferences the parties of interest in this usage after passage of the bill to work out their problems with a view to further legislation if that should prove necessary.

Book publishers are prepared to go further. They would endorse provision in the bill or in your committee report for a study panel required to report within a fixed period of time to the proper committees of the Congress on the state of the computer art then prevailing, the needs for use of copyrighted materials and what legislation, if any, is needed. The requirements of computer usage are at present so little known that legislation now could be only a stab in the dark. But the art of computer use is growing so rapidly that a continuing study is essential.

Mr. Chairman, I appreciate the opportunity of appearing here to present the point of view of the American Textbook Publishers Institute.

Senator BURDICK. Thank you, Counsel.

Am I correct in believing that the language in the House bill will be sufficient for the time?

Mrs. LINDEN. Yes, Senator Burdick, because at this time the House bill merely reiterates the concept of copyright and private proprietary rights in the framework of information storage and retrieval, and the pieces of hardware known as computers are not specifically referred to, nor should they be, just as the first copyright bill did not refer to movable type as such.

Senator BURDICK. Then you agree with the House bill?

Mrs. LINDEN. I do.

Senator BURDICK. And it is your thesis that it might be premature to legislate further at this time?

Mrs. LINDEN. Yes, it is, because legislation usually is undertaken after mankind has had experience in a certain field and problems have arisen which require regulation and policing. We do not know quite yet what will be commercially feasible and what material will be used and the best manner in which it will be used. We can hardly regulate and police what we are not yet certain of.

In other words, we all agree, and this is more than merely an amorphous feeling, that computer technology is real, it exists, and is extremely useful and fascinating and worthwhile. The question as to how soon various uses will be made have not yet been answered. As recently as last week I spoke to representatives, executives of two of our major computer manufacturers. I used this analogy, and if you will bear with me, I would like to use it again. I have used it actually twice before, not only with them. I said, "Look, let us say we own a restaurant. Our catalog of copyrighted material is our menu. You come in, you are a computer user and manufacturer, or both. We are the restaurant owner and you want to eat. We say, 'Sure, we have a restaurant, here is our menu.' We say, 'What do you want to eat?'"

Well, he does not know yet. Until he knows what he wants to eat, until he tells us what he is ready to pay for, how much he is willing to spend on eating, we can respond only very piously that we believe that it is a matter of public policy that all men who are hungry ought to be allowed to eat and that all restaurants ought to be available to feed them. But we cannot feed them until we know what they want. There can be no breakdown in our relationship until they tell us what they want and until and unless we refuse to supply the demand.

In other words, it is premature for either side to be accusatory or to predict the failure either of negotiations or of responsibility in their relationship. It is something that is in the offing and it will have to be handled.

I believe that just as in our society, in our economy, we have been resourceful enough to adapt to new technology in the marketplace, we will adapt to these pieces of hardware also; that after a study based on actual experience is in the hands of your committee, you would then be able to evaluate whether legislation or governmental interference of any kind is necessary, or whether abrasions of the marketplace have functioned appropriately again in our society.

Senator Burdick. I am somewhat impressed with your statement here that you are willing to continue the discussion with the people who might be using your materials after this bill becomes law

Mrs. Linden. Well, Senator Burdick, these are not mere pious statements. They are not even altruistic. They are practical. These people are our only customers. We deal with the educational community. They are the ones we sell our textbooks to; they are the ones who buy our reference books. It is not as though one morning in 1975 or 1980 the book printing business will stop entirely. There will be a new product line, computer input, but we will still be dealing with the same customers.

The likelihood of our refusing to deal with them is very, very remote indeed. I do think that historically authors and publishers have shown suficient responsibility, with the pressure and push of the economic marketplace, so that schools have gotten books. Every now and then there is a breakdown in the problem and there is a slight collision, and there is in every industry. But somwhow, they wear each other down and it works out.

I urge, certainly that at this juncture there has not been such a crisis, a breakdown in the needs of society to get copyrighted material that requires active legislation. In fact, I urge to the contrary, that it would be dangerous. It would fix positions, jell in the law, something that the law is not ready for, that society and the educational community and publishers and authors cannot take a stand on. They will all go out on a limb, no matter what we all say we want at this moment. We cannot be sure.

Senator Burdick. Senator McClellan?

Senator McClellan. I wish to compliment the lady for her presentation. I think it is very informative.

As I understand it, you feel that it is too early for us to undertake to legislate because we would not know what we are legislating about? You believe, that your two interests are so common and you have such a mutual anticipation of future relationships and profits that it will be almost compelling that you work out your own solution, is that correct?

Mrs. Linden. That is exactly correct.

Senator McClellan. Let us hope so. We would much rather have you do it than have us do it.

Senator Burdick. Senator Fong.

Senator Fong. Am I correct that in the House bill there are provisions dealing with copyright material as far as computer use is concerned?

Mrs. Linden. Well, in the sense that the uses that are protected by copyright are protected under the proposed bill. Whether such uses are via computerized system or printing presses or Xerox machines—in other words, the law as proposed does not treat one piece of hardware as though it required very special treatment. The law deals conceptually with the idea that the author has certain rights. Whether an information network acts as a publisher or a reprint publishing house, the author's rights are the same.

Senator FONG. Using your analogy of the customer walking into a restaurant, you say you cannot give him what he wants until he tells you what he wants, does this provision charge the customer when he walks into the restaurant and picks up the menu?

Mrs. LINDEN. I am sorry, does it change?

Senator FONG. You say you do not know enough of the situation to really legislate on it. Yet it seems to me that the analogy that you presented to us of a man walking into the restaurant and you are not able to give him what he wants to eat until he knows what he wants to eat—it seems to me that you are charging him for walking in the restaurant.

Mrs. LINDEN. We are not charging him anything, because until he orders something, he does not have to pay.

Senator FONG. When the man uses the computer and puts copyrighted material into the computer he has not used it yet?

Mrs. LINDEN. He is where he is using something. Actually, what happens when you put material into a computer, educational material, which I am most familiar with, a reading textbook, a third-grade reader—no one sits down and reads it cover to cover. A chemistry textbook is not read cover to cover. You use snips and pieces at a time. That is the way it is used.

A computer output, in our lifetimes at least, is most unlikely to give to a user entire reference books or entire works. In fact, that would defeat the very purpose of the technology. It gives us little pieces and bits.

If there is no system of licensing or controlling the input, the little bits and pieces would not be sufficiently subject to control of the author or publisher to amount to very much. In other words, one cannot say that just because the restaurant owner bought a cow, until he cuts off pieces, the farmer is not hurt yet. There is a cow available in the restaurant. The computer user does not go out and buy a book because he can go and knows that he can get his slice via the computer network. He does not have to buy the whole cow. The farmer is hardly comforted by that. Authors and publishers find little comfort in this kind of argument.

Senator FONG. I think your point is well taken. Thank you.

Senator BURDICK. Let us hope that no one starves to death in this cafe. Thank you very much.

Mrs. LINDEN. Thank you.

Senator BURDICK. The next witness is Mrs. Gladys Barnette, of Learning Through Seeing, Inc., to be introduced by Congressman Reinecke, of California.

STATEMENT OF HON. ED REINECKE, A REPRESENTATIVE IN CONGRESS FROM THE 27th CONGRESSIONAL DISTRICT OF CALIFORNIA

Mr. REINECKE. Good afternoon, Mr. Chairman, gentlemen.

It is a pleasure for me to appear before this committee this afternoon. I represent part of the San Fernando Valley in California, which is very vitally interested in the proper protection of the originators of various creative works, both from the artists' and the creators' points of view, and from the technicians' and the businessman's point of view in producing this in order that these original creators and the businessmen themselves might be properly protected throughout the year.

I think I can safely say that many thousands of people who live in the San Fernando Valley are vitally dependent upon their rights being adequately protected, because this is the center of a great deal of creative activity.

With that in mind, I have read Mrs. Barnette's statement; it is pertinent and I am sure it will be interesting to you gentlemen.

I am happy to present my constituent and friend, Mrs. Gladys Barnette.

Senator BURDICK. First of all, Mrs. Barnette, your statement will be made a part of the record, without objection. If you care to summarize it, it will be appreciated.

STATEMENT OF MRS. GLADYS J. BARNETTE, EXECUTIVE AND FIRST VICE PRESIDENT, LEARNING THROUGH SEEING, INC., SUNLAND, CALIF.

Mrs. BARNETTE. I think it would be, perhaps, easier for me to read it if you do not mind, Mr. Chairman.

I may interpolate and summarize, perhaps, where possible.

Senator BURDICK. Very well.

Mrs. BARNETTE. Mr. Chairman, esteemed gentlemen of the Senate committee, a request to testify before the Committee on the Judiciary of the Senate regarding Senate bill No. S. 597 was made by our company, Learning Through Seeing, Inc., solely for the purpose of asking the committee to define in a very specific and positive way exactly what would be "fair use" when the materials in question are produced exclusively for educational purposes and have no possible sales other than to institutions of education.

To clarify the reasons why the "fair use" section of a revised copyright law should be stated in specifics, it seems best to present some background information regarding educational materials which are produced for no other purpose than helping all students to learn more effectively and to keep pace with the knowledge explosion.

Learning Through Seeing, Inc. is a small business. Its principals have long been active in the generation of educational materials exclusively for classroom use. Many years have been spent in the development of teaching techniques and programs. During these years a substantial number of copyrighted programs have been developed and more are in preparation, including auditory materials. The materials developed so far provide an integrated, sequential succession of film frames which together constitute carefully prepared and highly sophisticated lessons in a course of study having a specific purpose, such as the teaching of mathematics, English, vocabulary, language arts skills, and the improvement of reading. In order to prepare complete programs, authorities in a given field are employed or affiliated and the necessary creative and testing work is done to insure that the programs accomplish the purposes for which they are intended. The programs are then sold at prices scaled to the budget of school districts. Profits are such that a considerable number of programs must be sold to recover basic cost.

The Learning Through Seeing, Inc., organization and its programs have now engendered a justified confidence within the educational market. This confidence has not been easily earned since it has required constant effort at refinement and extension of basic techniques, continued maintenance of the highest standards and complete professional and financial commitment on the part of the principals.

It now appears that efforts, such as these, which have been entirely independent and have involved great risk with no substantial profit, and which have contributed greatly to the full effective use of educational budgets, are in danger of becoming economically unsupportable under the "fair use" provision in the new copyright bill.

The danger stems from the apparent license given to those in the educational field to utilize materials of this nature with impunity, and of course from the widespread and increasing availability of data reproduction equipment and services. The "fair use" provision contains no exception as to the use of materials prepared directly for the educational market. The usual example given in support of the provision is that of the educator who desires to copy excerpts for class study and analysis and the rationale is that the cause of education will be furthered by releasing such educators from theoretical damages for copyright infringement. This view does not, however, consider the basic fact that the entire tenor of the usage is changed when the materials have themselves been prepared expressly for educational purposes. Under such circumstances, copying can only be intended to employ the materials in whole or in part for the specific objectives for which they were prepared. The copying of such materials should not be excused either under the "fair use" provision or under a compulsory licensing provision because copying of this nature constitutes deliberate infringement.

Consultation with the Learning Through Seeing, Inc. copyright attorneys suggests that it may be contended that the "fair use" provison of paragraph 107 sets forth four standards that would preclude damage to the portion of publishing and creative industries

STATEMENT OF COMMITTEE TO INVESTIGATE COPYRIGHT PROBLEMS AFFECTING COMMUNICATION IN SCIENCE AND EDUCATION

My name is Howard A. Meyerhoff and I am President of the Committee to Investigate Copyright Problems.

The goal of CICP is to find a way to protect the "exclusive Right" of an author to his "Writings," while permitting the advantages of modern information dissemination systems to become as useful as they may without threatening or weakening the economic urge and the need to create.

We are testifying today because since 1959 we have been concerned how the full benefits of modern information dissemination systems could be obtained, without harming the basic structure of incentive and rewards on which these systems and earlier systems are based.

I am a geologist by profession. I am also a researcher and an author. At an earlier time, I was editor and publisher of two publications of the American Association for the Advancement of Science. The publications were the weekly journal "Science" and the "Scientific Monthly," now absorbed into "Science." And I also have been the Executive Director of the Scientific Manpower Commission.

CICP was organized with the thought that it was better to consider a problem at a point between gestation and emergence, than to wait for it to hatch. We felt that a mechanism to control the problem and reduce its adverse impacts should be designed early and that adjustments and improvements could be made, in the light of future insight and experience. We are not so sure now that this is true. Very possibly we would be just as far along today toward a solution to the copyright and information dissemination problem if we had not had this foresight.

It was decided at our first informal meetings that CICP had to represent all interests affected by copyright law. I believe I was elected president because I had had as many different and direct kinds of experience with all aspects of the problem as one man could reasonably be expected to have.

Since then, I and my Board of Directors have made every effort to assure CICP's continued existence as a broadly representative organization focusing on a single definable problem.

I shall return later to further detail on the history of CICP, our philosophy, some of the work we have done, some insight into the nature of the problem, and why we think it can be solved within the framework of S. 597.

CICP supports S. 597 in its present form. We think it clearly outlines the rights of the author and the rights of the user. It is precise where precision is possible and allows for negotiation between author and user where definition is not possible. For example, we have evaluated section 107, Limitations on Exclusive Rights: Fair Use. We feel that the original statement, as introduced into the House, would have been satisfactory as a basis for developing some kind of clearance system. By providing guidelines, as in the current bill, the Congress warns the user that he cannot stretch the concept too far. At the same time the provision prevents the author from restraining the user from reasonable pursuit of his work because of trivial reasons.

There has been much uncertainty recently by computer-oriented researchers as to how far they can go in their experimental work of storing, retrieving, and disseminating copyrighted information. Again, it seems that S. 597 leaves them reasonably free to experiment as they wish without fear of suit for infringement. This is implied by the words: "Notwithstanding the provisions of section 106, the fair use of a copyrighted work, including such use by . . . any other means specified by that section, for purposes such as . . . teaching, scholarship, or research is not an infringement of copyright."

Section 107 goes on to outline four (4) factors which will be used to consider whether a particular case is fair use:

"1. The purpose and the character of the use;
"2. The nature of the copyrighted word;
"3. The amount and substantiality of the portion used in relation to the copyrighted work as a whole; and
"4. The effect of the use upon the potential market for or value of the copyrighted work."

It will not be particularly difficult to determine in the light of the enumerated factors, especially 1 and 4, when a particular computer-based research information, storage, retrieval, and disseminating program moves from the experimental to the operational stage, unless one is interested in quibbling. On the other hand, if it appears necessary to field test a system by storage and transmission of large quantities of information, or by the allowance of independent, "choice by individual quantities of information, or by the allowance of independent, "choice by in-recipients in activating transmission from an information storage and retrieval system or any device, machine or process," (Sec. 110(1), D), such testing can certainly be done with noncopyrighted material.

Any other needs of the user can be negotiated with the copyright holder. If the user feels separate negotiation is too cumbersome, he should support the development of a clearinghouse system.

Simply put, we see no way by which the author can eliminate the technological capability of the user to reproduce his information at will, nor why the user should want to further reduce the rights of the author. Continuing efforts in this direction will harm both parties. They should turn their combined energies toward accommodation now.

"Fair use" is at best inconclusive. If some clearance system is not established, it will serve as a temporary guideline to the user and eventually to the courts. It does not solve the real problems, which are two: the increasing need of education, science, government, and business for multiple copies of documents; and the fact that since the copyright owner's compensation is the total return from the use of his work—the loss through "fair use" of his work cannot be measured in terms of any individual use, but only in terms of the total use and total copying.

Therefore, we fell that the present provision for fair use, while making possible some types of research use of copyrighted material in computer and microfilm storage devices, cannot solve the "computer problem," let alone the direct copying problem. At best, it serves as a temporary safety valve, until some clearinghouse system is established. At that time, the concept of fair use should lose its importance and die off as some form of vestigial tail.

I would like to continue my remarks with a brief quote from an invitation dated April 9, 1959, sent to a representative group of individuals considered interested in those aspects of the copyright law which affect communication in scientific and educational information:

"The present copyright system presents an increasingly serious problem because of the tremendous need for reproduction and dissemination of scientific and educational information. The communication of this information is unduly restricted under the overall copyright system. . . .

"New methods, inventions and techniques may solve many of the physical and intellectual problems of handling and disseminating information. The copyright system, as it now works in practice, does not permit the unrestricted circulation of information. It is felt that a more efficient way must be sought to administer the system either through changes in the law or through some structure which will permit the fullest utilization of the present law.

"It is felt that the interests of our country can best be served through the fullest interchange of scientific and educational information. With this objective in mind, we are interested in investigating how the free flow of information can be maintained and advanced on an ethical, legal and efficient basis without depriving the copyright proprietor of his rights."

This invitation was the result of a prior informal meeting of seven individuals at the office of Mr. Horace Hart, then Director of the Printing and Publishing Industries Division of the Department of Commerce. Thirty-three carefully selected individuals were invited to the conference. The criteria were that they must represent an organization, Government agency, or corporation vitally interested in copyright law and that they have a position of authority in their respective organizations.

No attempt was made to invite a representative from every organization that might be interested; this would have been impossible. Instead, we reasoned that representatives from the American Institute of Biological Sciences, the American Institute of Physics, the American Chemical Society, and the American Association for the Advancement of Science could adequately represent the problems, viewpoints, and interests of science and society publication; the McGraw-Hill Publishing Company, the American Textbook Publishers Institute, and the American Book Publishers Council could do the same for the commercial publishers. (The original invitation and the list of individuals invited are attached as Appendix A.) Most organizations invited to the conference were represented.

During the conference held on May 19, 1959, discussions demonstrated that indeed very little thought had been given to the real meaning of the newest methods of reproduction, transmission, and storage and retrieval as they were bound to affect the copyright law and the copyright owner, or to how these methods and devices could be used efficiently, if the law were to be strictly adhered to. It was equally evident that while there had been occasional consideration of the copyright problem within a variety of organizations, it had always, of necessity, been from the viewpoint and needs of the particular group.

CICP is the first group to approach the problem from a total national viewpoint. The conference voted to continue the Committee for another year and elected me to serve as Chairman until the next meeting: Mr. Joseph McDonald was elected Vice Chairman, and Mr. Gerald J. Sophar Secretary. Dr. Laurence B. Heilprin was appointed Chairman of a Study Group which was charged with defining the problem and proposing various solutions to it. A report was due the following year, prior to the second annual meeting of the Committee.

The Study Group took its job very seriously, attempting to represent all viewpoints. The second annual meeting of CICP was held May 18, 1960. I introduced the report with these remarks:

"We do not wish to leave this room this afternoon until we have determined what is next on the program, because I think we face a very cold and sober fact—that in the course of time there will be trouble, there is bound to be trouble from the multiple copying that has to be done for the dissemination of the work of authors, particularly scientific authors, and educators. And yet many of us here have a definite interest, strong perhaps in the sense of financial interest, and there are other interests, too, in seeing that this material is protected for your authors, or for yourself as a business enterprise."

The Heilprin report is as fresh today as it was in 1960. Its evaluations, conclusions, and recommendations have never been seriously challenged as to substance. The report was criticized as based too much on conjecture about what had occurred, what was occurring, and what might occur should the situation continue.

The intervening seven years have, we feel, clearly demonstrated that the Study Group's analysis was correct. (This report is attached as Appendix B.)

Regarding the criticism of conjecture, it should be stated that the Study Group actually did consider gathering data through questionnaires, but decided the timing was inappropriate for the following reasons:

1. CICP was not financed.

2. The problems were incipient ones, and the value judgments of the Study Group members—carefully chosen as to experience and access to early knowledge of the developing problem—were considered more important at that time than a conglomeration of data as to how much microfilming and photocopying of copyrighted material was going on at that early stage.

3. A forecast cannot be proven by data at the time it is made. Only after passage of time can a forecast be evaluated. It was the judgment of the Study Group that the only factual evidence consisted of such things as: the existence of microfilm and microcards, of a variety of photocopying devices, and of the ambitious experiments going on such as those in information storage and in the software and hardware of computer technology. In our judgment more could be gained at that time by trying to understand what was happening because of new technology, than by trying to determine how much. After all, the main components in the situation were well known: authors, publishers, books, readers, and copyright. Both the components and their relationship to one another had remained essentially the same for many decades, except for slight improvements in their methods of functioning and relating to one another. Suddenly basic new technological breakthroughs such as microfilm, xerography, computers, and computer programs were available. Although their effect was still minimal, to those who were perceptive it was obvious the new technology would inexorably change the nature and function of some parts of the process. Recording, duplicating, and transmission methods rapidly were changing the way information travelled from the author to the user and the rate of change was bound to accelerate. However, two essential elements would remain: the author-creator represented by the publisher, and the user represented by the librarian.

The legal relationship between these two groups was clearly established by the Constitution. It was inconceivable that the Congress would ever consider changing this basic relationship by amendment. Thus the Study Group concluded that the wisest thing to be done would be development of an accommodation which would operate under the law.

The Study Group also kept constantly in mind that the only struggle is not between the authors and the users but within the individual according to the role he is playing. To quote from the First Annual Report:

"It is important to see that the conflict is not between publishers, on the one hand, and scientists on the other. It is an internal conflict, between the scientist-user, and the scientist-publisher or his agent who is supplying the scientist-user with publications. On the surface they are not struggling for the same things. The scientist-publisher struggles to retain his grip on revenue through copyright. The scientist-user struggles for freedom to create and teach. With his advancing copying techniques he is slowly breaking the grip of the publisher. Neither is the gainer, for both serve science."

In spite of these insights testimony during the House Hearings on H. R. 4347 give little support to the above premise. Each element of the process has coalesced around its own particular function in pleading its case. The authors, publishers, educators, and librarians were represented by strong associations whose basic purpose must be the apparent ultimate good of that particular group. This testimony was sincere, but reflects the group's viewpoint rather than the entire citizenry.

CICP has defined the national problem and a goal. The problem is that the "exclusive Right" (granted an author by the Constitution and the Congress) to his "Writings," is being threatened by modern information dissemination systems. But our society clearly accepts the idea that it is beneficial to obtain as wide a dissemination of information as possible, by the most efficient means. Publishing, once a simple process (writing, editing, typesetting, printing, and distributing), permitted the author and publisher to police their own works and enforce their rights because they controlled the plates from which publication was produced. Today the author and the publisher have control only of the original dissemination, and because of new duplication and new dissemination methods have virtually lost control of secondary dissemination which can become large itself—even larger than the primary. Therefore the value of exercising their constitutional and statutory rights, as they see fit, has diminished.

Two clear rights exist: the right of the author and the right of the user. One might think from much of the testimony on HR4347 that the user feels the publisher wants to surround himself and his product with a wall of copyright monopoly to impede all progress in science and education, and that the author and publisher feel, on the other hand, that the user is interested only in getting all information free of charge from some bottomless well. These may only be expressions of frustration. However, both sides are as dependent upon one another as man is upon his environment, though he constantly fights it. The only eventual solution is found in accommodation.

The copyright law gives a right—effectively an economic or what may be called a negotiable property right—to authors and publishers. The negotiable instrument in this case—a close, though not precise, analogy—is the copyrighted message itself. Because of modern technology, the negotiable instrument might be considered subject to "counterfeiting." As the appearance of the "counterfeit" has little to do with its uniqueness and, therefore, its value, the user is usually quite satisfied with the substitute, be it a photocopy, computer print-out, or any acceptable "tangible means of expression." Though an alchemy of the message occurs and the source and origin of the message may no longer even be identifiable, the uniqueness of the message remains.

It is easy to see that the effect of the new technology is to remove from the control of the issuer the quantity of the original instruments that is printed and the price he chooses to charge. With the quantity in circulation increased, the total value may well be decreased. The fact that "counterfeits" are made in large quantity, or will be made, is bound to affect the return which can be obtained from the original investment.

The considerable discussions as to whether easy copying increases or decreases the sale of periodicals and textbooks evade the main issue. The point is that no one has the right to duplicate the message, beyond what Congress and the courts choose to call "fair use," now or in the future.

On the other hand, the publishers—especially, scientific, educational, and textbook publishers—provide a most essential part of the educational complex. Thus, they cannot ignore the utility of the new technology and deny the use of their published works for duplication or conversion. In recognition of this fact, CICP is examining what may be called a conversion contract. This will allow the copyrighted message to be stored, processed, and republished in other than its original form. This manipulation and alteration of a copyrighted work should not change the originality of the copyrighted message or "Writing."

For the administration of such extended types of use contract under the copyright law, CICP has proposed since 1960 a voluntary copyright clearinghouse. The clearinghouse would act as a marketing device, or as a switching point at which user and author can meet and negotiate the value and method of payment for reproduction or conversion rights to the copyrighted message.

CICP is not the original proponent of this idea, but has been its most consistent advocate. The late Arthur Fisher, former Register of Copyrights, stated at the Conference on the Arts, Publishing, and the Law, in May 1952:

". . . These problems are accentuated by the invention of modern devices of many kinds facilitating the reproduction and transmission of knowledge . . . .

"It has been suggested that these undertakings might be expanded by the organization of a society somewhat similar to the American Society of Composers, Authors and Publishers (ASCAP) which in the field of music licenses performance rights in the use of musical compositions. Such a society might solicit blanket authorizations to add an overriding charge to the present costs of microfilm and other reproduction of scientific articles, the charge either to be paid over to the proprietor of the works or donated to scientific development and related purposes.

"For certain types of use where the commercial and monetary aspects appear least significant, a series of calculated risks could be taken without involvement in efforts to secure specific consents. Such risks might be covered by some coinsurance device shared by a group of participating institutions or organizations."

Even Arthur Fisher indicates that a previous source generated the copyright clearance idea. In any event the genesis of the copyright clearinghouse is less important than the fact that it has the virtue of age. CICP is pleased that a number of other groups are now advocating the idea.

While we do not suggest that the voluntary copyright clearinghouse is the only solution to the problem, our studies do indicate that it is probably the solution most likely to gain wide acceptance and therefore to succeed.

Criticisms of the clearinghouse idea fall roughly into the following pattern:

1. It will be too costly.
2. Dollars cannot be spent to collect pennies.
3. It is not manageable.
4. Compliance cannot be enforced.
5. The owners of a copyright cannot be expected to let customers have any voice in the disposal of their property (although the customers are doing so right now).
6. There are not enough facts about the situation.
7. It will be impossible to devise a method for assessing or collecting payments for copying or conversion rights and equally impossible to redistribute equitably the net income to the copyright owners.

To these and similar statements CICP replies that American technology seems fully equal to the task. If we were to publish in an early issue of the "Commerce Business Daily" the following Request for Proposals or Invitation for Bid:

"RESEARCH AND DEVELOPMENT SOURCES SOUGHT

"Firms having capabilities for Studying, Designing, and Operating a switching system, which will assure the collection of fees for the copying or conversion of copyrighted material from organizations servicing the user of such material and the redistribution of the net income to the owners of the copyright, are invited to submit a Statement of Capability. Respondents to this synopsis will be evaluated on the basis of their submission of information and data relating to the following: (a) Experience and background in economic statistics; (b) Past or current experience in developing complex switching systems and obtaining maximum cost effectiveness from the systems; (c) Simulation of models which project the volume, kind, and rate of activity with the switching system for the next decade; and (d) Ability to develop model contracts which will support the system. In addition, evidence is required of the availability of an effective operating organization capable of implementing the system."

we venture the opinion that the above announcement might produce one hundred responses. The final competition for the contract might well be between ten to twenty firms. CICP does not underestimate the problem of developing a copyright clearinghouse. However, because of our national technological capabilities we feel the concept reasonable from the viewpoint of systems requirements and accounting. Any defects will be found in the legal, social, and organizational and economic aspects of the problem.

CICP supports S. 597 as an extremely well considered bill. However, since solutions to problems related to the dissemination of copyrighted scientific and educational communication appear to be partly uncontrollable, we feel that an additional device must be introduced into the process. The law states the rights of all elements involved in the process of transfer of a copyrighted message, and the rules under which the copyright owner and the user can operate. The proposed clearinghouse would establish a practical means for copyright owner and user to comply with the rules and accommodate one another. We support the bill, in the firm belief that once it becomes law, authors, publishers, scientists, educators, and other concerned parties will turn their energies to the important matter of negotiating and developing a system, rather than arguing for the most favorable position. We urge the same points previously made by us before the House Committee on HR4347 (attached Appendix C).

CICP is now conducting a small study to devise a sampling method for fairly estimating the amount of copying of copyrighted material done during any time period. Six cooperating libraries are recording each copy of copyrighted material made, by publisher, during a one-month period. The effort has two purposes: to assist in the design of a sophisticated sampling formula for a larger test, and to find out if the sampling technique can be refined to a satisfactory degree of accuracy for determination of the amount of copying of any publisher's works in a particular library. At the moment funds are not available for the larger effort.

Another study will be done by CICP to determine: (a) the knowledge and understanding of copyright law by information clearinghouse managers and their legal counsellors, and (b) their attitudes toward the copyright problem. At the same time information will be obtained on programs which have been aborted, curtailed, or suspended because of copyright. A concurrent investigation will be made to find guideposts for evaluating the quality, quantity, and economic value of copyrighted messages, duplicated or transmitted and displayed outside of the control of the copyright owner.

Support for this study is from the U.S. Office of Education and our informal contacts tell us that the contract should be signed in time for this effort to start sometime in April.

In sum, we urge that the Congress should express its desire that a solution be developed according to the goal of CICP: that "a way be found to protect the 'exclusive Right' of an author to his 'Writings,' while permitting the advantages of modern information dissemination systems to become as useful as they may without weakening or threatening the economic urge and the need to create."

CICP was created for this purpose and it desires to carry out such an assignment. We are certain that a system, plan, and organizational outline of a clearinghouse can be developed, if sufficient funds are made available.

STATEMENT OF AD HOC COMMITTEE (OF EDUCATIONAL INSTITUTIONS AND ORGANIZATIONS) ON COPYRIGHT LAW REVISION BY HAROLD E. WIGREN

Mr. Chairman and members of the subcommittee, I am Harold E. Wigren, chairman of the Ad Hoc Committee (of educational institutions and organizations) on Copyright Law Revision. I am the educational television consultant for the National Education Association and the associate director of the NEA's Division of Educational Technology. My personal description is already a matter of record in the proceedings of this committee, inasmuch as I testified before you in August of 1965 with respect to S. 1006. Today I appear before you again in my capacity as the elected chairman of the Ad Hoc Committee on Copyright Law Revision to present the consensus of the Committee's views on S. 597, which is identical with H.R. 4347 reported by the House Judiciary Committee last year. My comments will also include the provisions of the House Committee Report on H.R. 4347.

Our Ad Hoc Committee on Copyright Law Revision has 34 constituent members. (See list at end of appendix.) We have asked time to testify again because the bill on which you are holding hearings is, of course, not the same bill on which we testified previously. Further, the report on the former House bill has been released in the interim by the House Judiciary Committee. Therefore, we would like to let you know how we feel about the new bill and the report.

The new bill contains some marked improvements for education. These we appreciate. There are also some areas about which we very frankly are dubious and other areas about which we are keenly disappointed. We should like to delineate each of these in the testimony which you will hear today. This morning I am joined at this table by six individuals, whose organizations are constituent members of the Ad Hoc Committee on Copyright Law Revision, who have been chosen to testify because they represent specific areas of major concern within the Committee's membership—elementary and secondary school teachers and college instructors in both public and parochial schools, in the fields of English, foreign languages, and music. This afternoon our Ad Hoc Committee testimony continues with additional experts. You will hear testimony from representatives of educational media specialists, educational users of computers, and educational broadcasters. May I add that we are most grateful to you and your committee for this opportunity to testify.

In the Library of Congress display case exhibiting the Gutenberg Bible, the label under the Bible reads as follows:

"Through the invention of printing, it became possible for the accumulated knowledge of the human race to become the common property of every man who knew how to read—an immense forward step in the emancipation of the human mind."

This sums up in a succinct way the point of view and the concern which our Ad Hoc Committee wishes to express to the Congress in regard to revision of the copyright law. Our committee is speaking on behalf of the public interest—the right of every man to share in the accumulated knowledge of the human race, and the rights and responsibilities of teachers to make this knowledge available in the public interest.

In keeping with this point of view, we should like to reiterate that there are certain fundamental needs of education which must be protected in any revision of the copyright law. These might best be summarized in this manner: the need to make limited copies of materials for classroom use; the need to have "fair use" extended to include educational broadcasting and educational uses of computers; the need for reasonable certainty that a given use of copyrighted materials is permissible; the need for protection in the event teachers and librarians innocently infringe the law; the need to meet future instructional requirements by utilizing the new educational technology now being made available to schools; and the need to have ready access to materials. I am briefly delineating herewith the extent to which education fared in each of these areas of need under the proposed Bill and the House Committee Report. My colleagues this morning and this afternoon will speak on these matters, and others, more fully in their statements.

1. The need of teachers to make limited copies of materials for classroom use

The Ad Hoc Committee regards Section 107—the fair use provision of the Bill and the House Committee Report—as a marked improvement for classroom teachers over the previous draft. As we interpret it, Section 107 in S. 597 gives classroom teachers the right to make limited copies of copyrighted materials for purposes such as "criticism, comment, news reporting, teaching, scholarship, or research." We appreciate the addition to Section 107 in the new bill of the word "including such use by reproduction in copies or phonorecords." This will write into law for the first time that fair use of a copyrighted work includes copying to some degree. We are grateful that the House Committee Report enumerated at some length examples of reproductions by teachers for classroom purposes of single and multiple copying of materials in the course of teaching which would be considered as "fair" under the provisions of Section 107. This is in keeping with certain agreements we reached with the publishers and authors last June at the office of the Register of Copyrights.

In our original testimony before your committee, you will recall, we had requested a statutory limited copying exemption for education—a new Section 111—which we believed then, and we still believe, provides the simplest and easiest way to give the teacher the certainty he needs in his use of materials. As a result of the summit conferences held with the publishing industry representatives at the Register's office, the present wording of Section 107 was agreed upon by both groups as a compromise position, and we are willing to abide by this agreement as a means of reaching an accommodation between the two opposing positions. In so doing, however, we recognize that we have sacrificed a general exemption for certain much-needed educational uses of materials and have substituted in its stead a categorical exemption for specific types of uses which are spelled out in the House Report. We must emphasize that our acceptance of this compromise is dependent upon retention in the bill of the words "including its reproduction in copies or phonorecords" and of the full listing of examples of reproductions which would be considered "fair" now included in the Report. Anything less than this will be totally unacceptable to the Ad Hoc Committee.

2. The need to have "fair use" extended to include educational broadcasting and educational uses of computers

The wording of the House Report would appear to add restrictions for educational broadcasting which seem uncalled for by the statutory language in Section 107—restrictions which, as a matter of fact, could very well negate altogether the application of the doctrine to educational radio and television.

The Ad Hoc Committee sees no reason for this discrimination against educational broadcasting; the "fair use" needs of teaching are the same whether over the air or in the classroom.

The Ad Hoc Committee holds that the same considerations of fair use should equally apply with respect to educational uses of computers.

You will be hearing more from our committee members who will testify this afternoon on educational broadcasting and computer uses.

3. The need for reasonable certainty that a given use of copyrighted materials is permissible

In our previous testimony before your committee, we pointed out that teachers want and need the certainty of knowing when a given use of copyrighted material in the course of teaching is legitimate. We pointed out that teachers do not want to condone under-the-table uses. While the new Section 107 and the House Report are helpful in making determinations as to what might be used and what should not be allowed, there is nevertheless widespread disagreement still between publishers and educators, despite several summit conferences to resolve our differences, as to what constitutes "fair use" of a work. Teachers still will have no positive assurance that a given use of a work is a fair or permissible use. It is argued in some quarters that it is impossible to guarantee such certainty. Yet, if the experts cannot agree as to what constitutes "the fair use" of a work, how can a teacher in Pocatello, Idaho, know the answer?

Section 107 sets forth four criteria by which teachers may judge whether a given use of a work is a fair use. The Ad Hoc Committee is greatly concerned about Criterion No. 4 in this section which is "the effect of the use on the potential market for or value of the work." The House Committee Report goes on to explain this criterion by stating "where the unauthorized copying displaces what realistically might have been a sale, *no matter how minor the amount of money involved*, the interests of the copyright owner need protection." There are already those who argue that *any* given use of a copyrighted work would in effect be ruled out by this last criterion, particularly when followed by the clause "no matter how minor the amount of money involved." We implore the Senate, at the very least, to strike this explanation from the Report. It will cause apprehension and concern on the part of teachers nationwide.

4. *The need for protection in the event teachers and librarians innocently infringe the law*

The Ad Hoc Committee commends the Congress for making provisions for the waiver of statutory damages for innocent classroom teacher infringers but urges that the Senate give the same remission of damages for certain infringements for librarians and teachers on television and radio whose work is also a vital and essential part of education. Authors are protected under the bill; teachers who teach on educational television and librarians whose business it is to make the rich depositories of information available to students and teachers are *not* protected.

5. *The need to meet future instructional requirements by utilizing the new educational technology now being made available to schools*

The Ad Hoc Committee, while applauding the action of Congress to update teaching from 1909 to 1960 in the new bill, feels that the most serious handicap education faces in the new bill is that teaching has been frozen at the 1960 level. Teaching as it will become in the 1970s and 1980s has been ignored. The bill makes no provision for the new technology in teaching and learning; in fact, under the present paragraph D of Section 110, entitled "Time and content," the uses of copyrighted materials—without clearance or payment of royalties—on dial access retrieval systems or in computer assisted instruction, closed-circuit television, 2500 megahertz, or on most audiovisual devices designed for individualized and independent learning, are virtually eliminated.

American education is moving more and more toward individualized learning and independent study activities. The focus is increasingly on *learning* and less and less on *teaching*. The concept of teaching as a "stuffing" operation is gradually being dropped in favor of more dynamic inductive approaches to learning, including the examination of raw data material from which the student can make his own generalizations without mediation by the teacher at every step of the educative process. Paragraph D of Section 110 flies in the face of the future and relegates education to a horse and buggy period rather than to the jet age. It is difficult for us to understand why using machine aids to facilitate human use of copyrighted materials is considered an infringement, whereas similar but unaided use would not be an infringement. In our judgment, if copying with a pen or pencil is legitimate, then copying, reading, or analyzing with the aid of a machine should be considered legal. During the extensive debate on the copyright revision bill, much has been said about the need to protect publishers in the new technologies, but the teachers of America look to Congress to protect them when they use these new technologies for nonprofit purposes.

Unquestionably, the bill poses serious problems for educational computer users of copyrighted materials. The bill makes no mention of computers, nor does it provide language applicable to computers and computer uses; yet computers are one of the fastest growing technological advances in American education. Some of my colleagues will speak in detail with regard to this matter during the afternoon session today. The section of the Report commenting on this paragraph is equally damaging to education and makes the statutory provisions air-tight, to the detriment of education. The Ad Hoc Committee has three recommendations to make in this regard. Our committee has ready specific language for Section 110, covering these recommendations. I have included this language in the supplement to this testimony. (See Appendix.)

Surveys have shown that the alleged instructional television exemption in Section 110(2) in practice would mean an exemption for less than 1 percent of all instructional television programs due to the added restrictions in the statute on broadcast interconnections and recordings. As the result, the educational broadcasters have a new legislative proposal to present to you. It has been endorsed by the Ad Hoc Committee and is attached to my testimony. It appears to us to offer a reasonable compromise between the proprietary and educational broadcasting interests, and a workable means of insuring reasonable clearances for use of published materials on educational radio and television. (See Appendix.)

6. *The need to have ready access to materials*

Education needs a copyright law which will enable teachers and professors, as well as scholars and students, to have maximum reasonable access to a wide variety of resources for teaching and learning. The Ad Hoc Committee feels that S. 597 would seriously handicap education's uses of copyrighted materials because it substitutes for the present duration period of 28 years plus 28 years a new copyright period measured by the life of the author plus 50 years. The Ad Hoc Committee urges now, as it did in its previous testimony, the retention of the present renewal provision of the law: a 28-year initial term of copyright plus a 28-year renewal period or even a 48-year renewal period. The present renewal provision enables teacher and students to use the non-renewed 85 percent of all registered copyrights from the 29th year because the owners in such cases have allowed the work to go into the public domain. Under the new bill it could be one hundred years or more before this very same kind of material goes into the public domain and becomes useable by education. This is neither necessary nor advisable for all works. The present renewal provision in the law is simple and readily enables teachers to know when a copyrighted work is in the public domain. We urge its retention.

IN SUMMARY

Areas Which Represent Improvements for Education

1. The statutory "fair use" provision of the proposed bill and the House report as they apply to classroom teaching.
2. The waiver of statutory damages for classroom teachers who innocently infringe.

Areas Which Are Uncertain

Whether in-school telecasts on closed circuit and 2500-megahertz (megacycle) installations are limited by the same restrictions as instructional broadcasts on educational television and radio stations. (Our committee strongly feels that closed circuit and 2500-megahertz operations are simply extensions of the classroom and that teachers on these facilities should have the same statutory treatment as classroom teachers.)

Areas Which Are Definitely Damaging to Education

1. The severe limitations put on the use of the newer educational technology in the classroom, especially for individualized uses and for independent learning activities.
2. Severe limitations on the use of materials on instructional broadcasting, especially in the prescribing of the one-year limitation, the two copies, and the 100-mile radius.
3. Undue restrictions on fair use of materials for instructional radio and television broadcasts.
4. Lack of any mention whatsoever in the bill as to instructional uses of computers.
5. Duration of copyright for a period of life plus 50 years.

IN CONCLUSION

The Ad Hoc committee, in presenting its case to your committee today, asks the Congress to enact a law which will support rather than undermine or vitiate good teaching and learning practices. The Ad Hoc committee wants a reasonable and just law which is fair to both authors and users—one that can be enforced by the profession itself. It desires a new law that will provide adequately for the present and for the future both in the classroom and on educational broadcasting, that will enhance rather than inhibit the uses of materials, that recognizes the primacy of the public interest, and that enables teachers to do the job for which our nation employs them.

In conclusion, the Ad Hoc committee would like to commend both the House and the Senate committees, and the Register of Copyrights and his staff, for their diligent work and competent scholarship in spearheading this revision program. We are mindful and appreciative of their recognition and consideration of education's needs in the revision of the law. Thank you.

APPENDIX

Section 110. Limitations on exclusive rights: Exemption of certain performances and displays

Notwithstanding the provisions of section 106, the following are not infringements of copyright:

"(1) * * *

"(1A) *performance or display of a work by instructors or pupils by or in the course of a closed transmission by a governmental body or other nonprofit organization if such performance or display is in the course of the teaching (or research?) activities of a nonprofit educational institution.*

"(2) * * *"

(NOTE.—Italic matter is new.)

(It was the intent of the Ad Hoc committee on Copyright Law Revision that 110(1A) refer to controlled or closed transmissions and that 110(2) refer to uncontrolled or open transmissions.)

PROPOSED NEW SECTION ON EDUCATIONAL BROADCASTING TO BE SUBSTITUTED FOR SECTIONS 110(2) AND 112(B)

Section —. Limitations on Exclusive Rights: Educational Transmissions

(a) CERTAIN EDUCATIONAL TRANSMISSIONS EXEMPTED.—An educational transmission embodying the performance or display of a non-dramatic musical, literary, pictorial, graphic or sculptured work is not an infringement of copyright if—

(1) the content of the transmission is a regular part of the systematic instructional activities of a governmental body or non-profit educational institution;

(2) the performance or display of the copyrighted work is directly related to the teaching content of the transmission and is of material assistance to the instruction encompassed thereby; and

(3) the transmission is primarily for—

(A) reception in classrooms or similar places normally devoted to instruction, or

(B) reception by students regularly enrolled in non-profit educational institutions, or

(C) reception by persons other than regularly enrolled students to whom the transmission is directed because their disabilities or other special circumstances prevent their attendance in classrooms or similar places similarly devoted to instruction, or

(D) reception by governmental officials or employees in connection with their official duties or employment.

(b) CERTAIN EDUCATIONAL TRANSMISSIONS FULLY ACTIONABLE.—An educational transmission embodying the performance or display of a dramatic or choreographic work, pantomine, motion picture or continuous audio-visual work is actionable as an act of infringement under Section 501 and is fully subject to the remedies provided by Sections 502 through 506.

(c) LIMITATION OF LIABILITY FOR CERTAIN EDUCATIONAL TRANSMISSIONS.—
With respect to an educational transmission embodying the performance or display of a copyrighted work outside the scope of subsection (a) or (b), liability
for infringement under Section 501 does not include the remedies provided
in Section 502, 503, and 506, and the remedies included in Section 504 and 505
are limited to recovery of a reasonable license fee as found by the court under
the circumstances of the case, except as follows:

(1) Where the court finds that the infringer either has failed to make a
timely request for a license or has not accepted a timely offer of a license for
a reasonable fee, it shall award as statutory damages under Section 504(c) the
sum of not less than $100 nor more than three times the amount of a reasonable
license fee as the court considers just, to which may be added a discretionary
award of costs and attorneys' fees under Section 505;

(2) Where the court finds that the copyright owner either has failed to make
a timely reply to a request for a license or has not made a timely offer of a
license for a reasonable fee, it may reduce or withhold any award of damages
under Section 504 and may, in its discretion, award to the infringer costs and
attorneys' fees under Section 505.

(d) DEFINITIONS.—As used in this section:
   (1) "Educational tranmissions" shall mean public broadcasts over non-
   commercial educational television and radio stations operated by non-profit
   educational organizations under license by the Federal Communications
   Commission or other appropriate agency;
   (2) "Educational transmissions" shall not be precluded from the provisions of this Section — by virtue of being:
      (A) relayed from, forwarded to, converted into or otherwise inter-
      connected with other educational transmissions or re-transmissions by
      wire, radio or other communication device; or
      (B) fixed on film, tape, disc and/or other copying devices for trans-
      mission or re-transmission purposes;
and said interconnection and fixation processes shall be deemed integral parts
of the educational transmissions subject to subsections (a), (b), and (c)
respectively.

AD HOC COMMITTEE ON COPYRIGHT LAW REVISION (EDUCATIONAL ORGANIZATIONS
AND INSTITUTIONS)

1. American Association of Colleges for Teacher Education.
2. American Association of Junior Colleges.
3. American Association of School Administrators.
4. American Association of Teachers of Chinese Language and Culture.
5. American Association of Teachers of French.
6. American Association of Teachers of Spanish and Portuguese.
7. American Association of University Women.
8. American Council on Education.
9. American Educational Theatre Association, Inc.
10. Association for Childhood Education International.
11. Association for Higher Education.
12. College English Association.
13. Council of Chief State School Officers.
14. Department of Audiovisual Instruction, NEA.
15. Department of Classroom Teachers, NEA.
16. Department of Foreign Languages, NEA.
17. Department of Rural Education, NEA.
18. International Reading Association.
19. Midwest Program on Airborne Television Instruction, Inc.
20. Modern Language Association.
21. Music Educators National Conference.
22. National Art Education Association.
23. National Association of Educational Broadcasters.
24. National Catholic Educational Association.
25. National Catholic Theatre Conference.
26. National Catholic Welfare Conference.
27. National Commission on Professional Rights and Responsibilities, NEA.
28. National Council for the Social Studies.

29. National Council of Teachers of English.
30. National Education Association of the United States.
31. National Educational Television and Affiliated Stations.
32. National School Boards Association.
33. New Jersey Art Education Association.
34. Speech Association of America.

STATEMENT FOR THE NATIONAL EDUCATION ASSOCIATION OF THE UNITED STATES BY LOIS V. EDINGER

Mr. Chairman and members of the subcommittee, I am Lois V. Edinger, past president of the National Education Association of the United States. I have served as a classroom teacher of history in the high schools of Thomasville, North Wilkesboro, and Whiteville, North Carolina. I have served as a studio teacher of U.S. history on the North Carolina In-School Television Project, which is part of the North Carolina Educational Television Network. I am an associate professor of education at the University of North Carolina in Greensboro.

Today I appear before you in my capacity as a member of the Board of Trustee of the National Education Association, the largest professional organization in America, consisting of 994,000 members, which represents the broad spectrum of American education. Its membership ranges from kindergarten teachers to college professors. It includes administrators, supervisors, school principals, county and state superintendents of public instruction and their staffs, and other individuals. Approximately 90 per cent of the NEA members are classroom teachers.

Why the NEA Is Interested in Copyright Law Revision

NEA has two primary interests: the improvement of instruction in the nation's schools and the protection of the rights of teachers and their welfare. Both of these interests are affected by any revision of the copyright law.

Improvement of Instruction

Education is in the midst of a revolution—both in the content areas and in methodology. There are new curriculum developments in the major disciplines which are based on widespread change in curriculum materials. With the curriculum explosion facing us in every area and at every level in public education, close examination of all types and kinds of materials is a necessity if change is to occur at the practical level of classroom application. At best this is a difficult and complex enough problem. There is little to be gained in working out new curriculum developments, if in the end teachers, who would otherwise strengthen and improve their teaching through uses of new materials, are only to be frustrated because of artificial and inflexible restrictions which in the long run will not really protect the rights of originators or producers, but will be a severe detriment to improving instruction. NEA has a deep interest in the widespread use of many materials of instruction to strengthen and enrich the efforts of classroom teachers in all subject areas. The teacher must be free to teach and must have access to materials to do his job.

Rights and Responsibilities of Teachers

Teachers are both authors and users of materials. They want a law which will be fair and just to all concerned. We wish to see proper protection of the interests of those persons whose creative abilities produce fine instructional materials so as to stimulate the continued flow of such materials. At the same time, there is an over-riding public interest to be met also—that of flexible availability of materials for instructional purposes. Teachers and students must be able to use copyrighted materials with a minimum of time and effort devoted to making such materials available in their day to day classroom activities and on educational radio and television.

Once a reasonable law is obtained the profession will itself be in a position to aid in enforcement of the law. But as long as arbitrary and impractical barriers to materials' usage exist, teachers will be reluctant to use materials, particularly when there is a possibility that such use constitutes an infringement.

Today's Teacher

The teacher in today's schools is almost unrecognizable from the teacher in the schools which you and I attended. Whereas our teacher used the same textbook for each pupil, today's teacher uses many resources in his teaching. He has a varity of texts and supplementary materials, including trade and reference books, newspapers and magazines, educational motion pictures, filmstrips, overhead transparency projectors, opaque projectors, language laboratories, audio tape recorders, record players, slides, educational radio and television, teaching machines and programmed learning materials, and he uses these in orchestration to do specific jobs. The teacher selects resources to fit particular student needs so that certain tools are used with some students and other tools with other students.

Education is no longer the very simple process Mark Hopkins talked about—with the teacher on one end of the log and the learned on the other—but an increasingly complex and intricate one. Even before Sputnik, burgeoning enrollments and an explosion in the content areas made it imperative that the teacher enlist the power tools of educational technology to help him to do his job. Never has there been so much to teach to so many in so short a time. Never has there been such an urgent need for more effective quality instruction. Time is at a premium; ideas must be communicated with dispatch.

NEA's Position on Copyright Law Revision

Because education has a substantial interest in the copyright law, the NEA through its Division of Audiovisual Instructional Service and its National Commission on Professional Rights and Responsibilities, in July 1963, called a national conference of representatives of major educational organizations to discuss both the present copyright law and the proposals which were made for revision of the law; to canvass education's needs in a new copyright law; and to determine what steps, if any, the profession should take to deal with the situation. As a result of this conference, the widely-representative *Ad Hoc* Committee on Copyright Law Revision was formed, and the NEA has been a member of this Committee since its formation.

At its annual meeting in Miami Beach, Florida, July 1966, the NEA Representative Assembly reaffirmed its previous stand on copyright law revision by adopting unanimously the following resolution:

"RESOLUTION 14

"Maximum access to teaching materials is of vital concern to every teacher. The National Education Association recognizes that the present copyright law provides for two parallel sets of rights, the rights of those who create such materials to profit from their efforts through copyright, and the rights of education to use certain copyrighted materials in teaching. A revision of the existing law is now being considered. The National Education Association insists that the public interest requires that the copyright law provide special recognition for education which guarantees a legal right for teachers and educational institutions to make use of copyrighted materials, recognizing a limited right to copy and record such materials for nonprofit educational purposes, including educational broadcasting, as proposed by the Ad Hoc Committee (of educational institutions) on Copyright Law Revision."

The NEA feels that the *Ad Hoc* Committee's proposals are essential; and it strongly urges that the Congress not diminish its own great achievements in educational legislation by enacting a copyright bill which is not in harmony with the best interests of education and which would, in fact, inhibit the uses of materials which recent federal enactments provide.

I should like to state for the record that the NEA has philosophical objections to any statutory licensing system, or clearinghouse, proposal. Our objections are these:

1. There has long been a recognition in the copyright act of a vital distinction between commercial and non-commercial uses of copyrighted materials. We believe that this distinction, at least for education, should be continued in the new copyright law. Further, we believe that, as a matter of public policy, education should be authorized to use and to make limited copies of copyrighted materials without clearances or royalties.

2. On the basis of the clearinghouse proposals we have heard thus far, a statutory licensing system would require continuous monitoring of classrooms to know the extent and nature of the use of being made of materials in order to determine the fees to be charged to the schools and the distribution of the income among producers of the materials used. It is quite obvious that classroom monitoring of teacher uses of materials could lead to an unhealthy policing

of materials' usage in the schools with acompanying pressure by publishing groups on teachers to use their materials in order that they might obtain a larger portion of the income received by any clearinghouse.

3. The problems of imposing a rigid system of clearances on top of an informal and "fair use" arrangement would, we believe, unduly restrict practices that would be considered legitimate under the "fair use" section of the law.

4. The problems of administering a clearinghouse system would be many, and it is likely that the overhead cost required to administer such a clearinghouse would far exceed the revenues received therefrom. Educators might in all seriousness ask several other pertinent questions:

Would the clearinghouse cover all types of materials usage—textbooks, trade books, newspapers, magazines, educational films, maps, charts, flat pictures, recordings, transparencies, musical selections, etc.? Or would several different clearinghouse systems need to be developed for different types of materials—one for newspapers, one for magazines, one for educational films, one for educational television clearances, one for music? If a multiplicity of such clearinghouses were to be initiated, then would it not be necessary to institute a clearinghouse for clearinghouses?

The situation becomes enormously complex and intricate, and rather than make arrangements with several clearinghouses the teacher would instead forego using materials at all and avoid being involved in this network of red tape. Therefore, the clearinghouse would have an effect opposite to that desired by the publishers and would inhibit rather than facilitate access to materials. There is some reason to believe also that several clearinghouses within the publishing industry itself would be needed. In discussions our Association has had with the publishers at various meetings, we learned that not all materials of a given publishing house would be released to the clearinghouse. How would the teacher know which materials were a part of the clearinghouse arrangement and which were not?

Conclusion

The National Education Association applauds the Congress for its great concern for education in the historic legislation which has been enacted to date. It is our sincere hope that the Congress will continue its concern for education as it enacts significant new copyright legislation.

There are certain fundamental needs of education which must be insured in the revision of the copyright law:

1. The need of teachers to make limited copies of materials for classroom use.

2. The need to have "fair use" extended to include educational broadcasting and educational use of computers.

3. The need for reasonable certainty that a given use of copyrighted material is permissible.

4. The need for protection in the event teachers and librarians innocently infringe the law.

5. The need to meet future instructional requirements by utilizing the new educational technology now being made available to schools.

6. The need to have ready access to materials.

We ask that the Congress enact a new law we can grow with—one that fosters and encourages promising approaches to teaching; one that is responsive to the emerging frontiers of the information revolution and the new educational technology; one that is flexible, not rigid; and one that will help us meet the challenges of a clearly emerging new day in education.

We congratulate the distinguished Chairman of the Subcommittee for his sponsorship of S. 597 which meets the needs of education far better than S. 1006 introduced in the 89th Congress.

TESTIMONY ON S. 597 FOR GENERAL REVISION OF THE COPYRIGHT LAW BEFORE THE SUBCOMMITTEE ON PATENTS, TRADEMARKS, AND COPYRIGHTS, OF THE SENATE JUDICIARY COMMITTEE IN BEHALF OF THE DEPARTMENT OF CLASSROOM TEACHERS, NEA, PRESENTED BY MISS TAIMI LAHTI, ASSISTANT EXECUTIVE SECRETARY, DCT

I am Taimi Lahti, Assistant Executive Secretary of the Department of Classroom Teachers of the National Education Association. I am representing approximately 900,000 classroom teachers. Having served as a social studies teacher in rural and urban schools of my home state prior to coming to NEA, and working directly with teachers in schools over the nation, I am intensely aware that the measure under consideration here affects not only members of this NEA Department, but also every teacher and child, in every classroom, in every school in the nation.

The classroom teacher's interest in a new copyright law is primarily that of the user rather than the producer of materials. However, teachers have always been producers or co-producers of some materials, and are increasingly producing materials specifically tailored to the needs of their own classrooms.

The official position of the Department is stated in the following resolution, adopted in Miami, in July 1965:

"The Department believes that, if educators are to serve American society and if the youth of this nation are to receive high-quality instruction, maximum access to all sources of knowledge, teaching materials, and resources must be preserved. It notes with dismay the current drive to diminish or eliminate from the Copyright Law the protection for educational use of materials. It maintains that present rights must be preserved and expanded to ensure (a) right of teachers to make one copy or phonorecord of a copyrighted work and a reasonable number of copies or phonorecords of excerpts or quotations for the purpose of teaching or for course work study in connection with teaching, (b) security from harassment of placing the burden of proof in testing fair use on publishers rather than teachers, (c) exemption of noncommercial educational users who are innocent infringers from any minimum statutory damage when no actual damage to author or publisher is shown, (d) retention of present renewal provision for 28 years plus 28, and (e) right to meet future instructional needs by having reasonable access to new educational materials to be used with new education technology.

"The Department strongly urges all classroom teachers to work diligently through all channels available to ensure the inclusion of an educational exemption ensuring the rights listed above in the bills currently in Congress."

May I point out that this Resolution was drafted and adopted before the introduction of S. 597 in the 90th Congress. We congratulate the distinguished chairman of this Subcommittee for his sponsorship of S. 597 which is a far better proposal than we anticipated last July.

Most teachers, until after mid-century, relied on textbooks and standard works for their instructional materials. Use of supplementary materials was not as widespread as in recent years. The change is due in part to the better qualified, more creative teachers we have today, but more directly to the availability of new kinds of materials made possible by advances in printing and educational technology.

With the explosion of knowledge since World Wor II, and with the development of new technology, the issue of copyright infringement becomes more important to teachers who want to give their pupils the latest and best information from a variety of sources. A good teacher, for example, may use a poem from the *Atlantic*, a tape recording of Maurice Evans in a scene from *Hamlet*, a clipping from the previous day's *New York Times* all within one class period—and be in danger of violating the law three times without knowing it.

STATEMENT OF ARTHUR R. MILLER, PROFESSOR OF LAW, UNIVERSITY OF MICHIGAN

The bill currently before the Senate (S. 597) to revise the copyright laws of the United States contains a number of provisions relating to computer programs and the use of copyrighted material in computer operations. The Ad Hoc Committee on Copyright Revision, whose members represent a broad cross section of disciplines, academic institutions, and all levels of American education, has studied this bill intensively and has come to the conclusion that several of its provisions touching on computer use and computer programs may seriously hamper the educational and technological progress of the nation.

I. COMPUTERS AND EDUCATIONAL USES

The statement of Dean Fred S. Siebert of the College of Communication Arts of Michigan State University has shown the impact of the revision bill on the use of computers in instruction and research and suggested an amendment to the current bill on behalf of the Ad Hoc Committee. Although my statement will deal primarily with the question of copyrightability of computer programs and the need for some type of corrective device in the new copyright act that would prevent it from being rendered obsolete by the movement of computer technology, a brief recapitulation of the weaknesses of the bill's exemption provision (section 110) insofar as computer uses by education are concerned seems appropriate.

The basic difficulty with section 110 of the revision bill as it now stands is that it eleminates the traditional exemption for schools and libraries and substitutes exemptions for computer operations with copyrighted works that are nominal rather than real. The "face-to-face" exemption in section 110(1) does not seem to apply to computer-assisted classroom performances or displays at all. The "transmission" exemption in section 110(2) permits the performance of a non-dramatic literary or musical work or the display of a work by means of a transmission by an educational organization but only if (1) the performance or display is part of the school's systematic instruction, (2) the radius of the transmission is not more than 100 miles, (3) the transmission is made primarily for reception in classrooms, and (4) the time and content of the transmission are controlled by the transmitting organization and "do not depend on a choice by individual recipients in activating transmission from an information storage and retrieval system or similar device, machine, or process." The practical effect of section 110(2) is to destroy any exemption for computer-assisted instruction. It prevents individualization—use of the computer by schoolchildren at their own speeds—which is of the essence of computer instruction and may be its primary advantage. Secondly, the restriction to use in a classroom runs contrary to the healthy trend of modern education to eliminate the confining limitations imposed by classroom walls. Finally, the 100 mile radius is arbitrary and apparently intended to destroy the viability of computer "networks"—a bias that is unexplained by the House Report and difficult to justify. The amendment to section 110 proposed by the Ad Hoc Committee and the codification of the principle that an injunction should not be available against educational users should strike a more reasonable and socially desirable balance between copyright proprietors and educational users than does the revision bill.

II. COMPUTER PROGRAMS

The revision bill's expansive definition of copyrightable matter, which includes practically everything that is an original work of authorship and "fixed in any tangible medium of expression" (section 102) appears to extend copyright protection to the broad range of computer instruction and command devices that fall within the rubric "computer programs." As an original proposition, it seems highly dubious that computer programs should be accorded copyright protection. Programs are algorithmic plans for guiding the activities of machines to achieve functional results—operating printing presses, manipulating inventory, and recording payroll data—and are thus clearly distinguishable from the traditional subject matter of copyright protection—books, plays, and works of art. Moreover, there has yet to be any penetrating discussion of the implications of extending copyright protection to computer programs, as is evident upon examining the transcripts of the meetings held by the Copyright Office and the hearings held by the House subcommittee. Nor has there been any serious effort to determine whether programming economics need the stimulus of an artificial monopoly or whether the advantage secured by staying ahead of competition and keeping a program "private" is a sufficient incentive to continue the tremendous growth of the computer industry. For these reasons the Ad Hoc Committee adopted a resolution stating: "That a computer program (i.e., the instruction to the computer as distinguished from the substantive data stored in the computer) should not be subject to copyright."

If any copyright monopoly is to be extended to computer programs, the key question is whether the copyright should protect against the use of the program in conjunction with the computer to achieve the functional goal for which the program was designed. The question must be answered in the negative. Copyright should not embrace the process or scheme embodied in the program but must be limited to a prohibition against the program's duplication. A firm holding a copyright on a program ought not to have a "property" right in the mathematical, logical, or manipulative algorithms in the program that achieve a practical objective, such as operating and monitoring a printing press. Yet the broad definition of the proprietor's exclusive rights in section 106 of the bill could be read to extend protection to the process embodied in the program.

The vice of granting a copyright to computer programs that would cover the process is that its effect would be to give programs a level of protection similar to that accorded by patent, but without the safeguards and limitations that surround a patent grant. Traditionally, monopoly of systems, schemes, and processes has been granted only under patent, and only after proof to the Patent Office that there has been real "invention." Moreover, the monopoly lasts only 17 years. Copyright of a computer program would be available without regard to true inventiveness, without advance examination by a governmental agency, and, under the revision bill, the protection would run for approximately 75 years. This type of protection for computer programs might well tie up and inhibit the development of the computer program field. To some degree every program developed today is a "derivative" of the programs written for the first computers made in this country. Thus, had there been copyright protection for programs in the past, had programming been carried out under the constant threat of actions charging infringement of existing copyrighted programs, it is doubtful whether the recent growth of programs and in programming techniques would have been possible.

The revision bill should be adjusted to make it clear that copyright does not extend to the process embodied in or the use of computer programs.* If any copyright on computer programs is to be recognized, it must only give the proprietors the right to duplicate the instructions in the program themselves and the right to prevent others from doing so. Even this right of reproduction must be carefully restricted, however, in order that the public's ability to employ the process contained in the program is not compromised. The power to control or bar duplication of the program cannot be allowed to prevent the use of the program in a computer.

III. THE NEED FOR A CORRECTIVE MECHANISM IN THE ACT

Probably no industry in the United States is undergoing as radical and rapid a change as is the computer industry. In the future, the computer will yield startlingly unique developments in education, library science, behavioral research, the various biological and natural sciences, and numerous other fields. Almost certainly, statutory regulations adopted today that purport to strike permanent balances between creators and computer users will be rendered obsolete or function in a negative or socially undesirable manner tomorrow. Despite these risks and despite the admission in the Report accompanying the House revision bill that "the problem of computer uses of copyright material" was "touched on rather lightly at the hearings," the bill sets out comprehensive and restrictive provisions on computer uses without providing any mechanism for future revision. The infrequency of copyright revision and its consequences are well known. One merely has to examine the experience under a number of the provisions in the Copyright Act of 1909 to see how illusory the hope of revision is and how useless ancient provisions can become.

Some procedural device should be inserted in the revision bill to supply an element of self-correction; otherwise the new statute will be obsolete on the day it is enacted. There are a number of possible mechanisms: (1) the establishment of an administrative body with appropriate delegated power; (2) the creation of a body authorized to amend or add to the legislation subject to Congressional veto; (3) the establishment of an advisory council or, as recommended by the Ad Hoc Committee, a Federal study commission directed to keep the subject of copyright under consideration, study the problems as they appear, and report to a Joint Congressional Committee, with the Committee then making proposals to Congress. Any of these devices also would be useful for purposes beyond that of accommodating the copyright law to the changing panorama of the computer. For example, an internal correction mechanism could be used from time to time to promulgate definite rules for photocopying on the basis of actual experience. In any event, some type of statutory procedure is urgently needed for the periodic reassessment of the copyright questions generated by the computer.

---

*If *any* statutory monopoly on a program's process is deemed necessary to encourage the programming fraternity, patent appears to be the appropriate vehicle. The question of patent protection for computer programs is being studied by the Patent Office, which recently published a set of "guidelines" for passing on applications for computer-program patents under the existing Patent Act. However, the *Report of the President's Commission on the Patent System*, p. 13 (November 17, 1966), recommends against patent protection.

Copyright Law Revision
Hearings, 1967
Part 2

THE COPYRIGHT REVISION BILL IN RELATION TO COMPUTERS

(Statement approved by the Board of Trustees and the Task Force on Legal and Related Matters of the Interuniversity Communications Council)

S. 597, which would generally revise the copyright law of the United States, contains provisions relating to the copyright protection of computer programs and to the utilization of copyrighted works in computer operations conducted by nonprofit educational, research, and library institutions. It is submitted that these provisions in their present form will seriously hamper the educational programs of the nation. The following statement examines the impact of the bill upon the development of the use of computers in instruction and research and suggests measures and means which will fairly protect authors and publishers and which will at the same time permit the full application of the genius of the computer to the advancement of the nation's educational program.

I. COMPUTER PROGRAMS

For the purpose of this discussion, a "program" can be defined as a series of instructions which control or condition the operation of a data processing machine ("computer").[1] Typically a program aims to solve a problem; the formula or logical structure underlying the attempt to reach a solution—the rationale of the program—is the program's algorithm. A program should be visualized as distinct from the data supplied to or stored in the machine; it may be thought of as setting and operating the "switches" of the machine, which manipulate the data. When a program operates through the machine upon the data, it can bring about practical results of widely varying types, depending upon the nature of the program, the data, the capacities of the computer, and miscellaneous other factors, including the possible intermediation of other machinery. The results may range from running a factory, to managing an inventory, to preparing a concordance of the poetry of Keats.

That computer programs should be able to claim protection through copyright is on its face a strange proposition. As the programs represent algorithmic plans for using machines to achieve practical results, they are poles apart from the conventional subject matter of copyright which has historically covered such works as novels, plays, music, and pictures. There was in fact very little cogent discussion of the computer program question at the various meetings under the auspices of the Copyright Office preceding the submission of draft bills; the same also was true of the Hearings before the subcommittee which advised the House

---

[1] This description or definition is taken from the *Report of the President's Commission on the Patent System,* November 17, 1966, p. 12 (GPO 1966).

Judiciary Committee to report a Revision Bill with amendments.[2]

Despite the dearth of discussion or analysis, the present Revision Bill, nominally at least, appears to have taken the step of covering computer programs, in all their variety, as subjects of copyright. For programs, whether set out on punch cards or tapes or other forms, seem to fit under the Revision Bill's broad definition of copyrightable matter, a definition which includes nearly everything that is associated with authorship and reduced to some fixed memorial.[3]

Inclusion of computer programs as possible subjects of copyright immediately raises the all-important question of the proper scope of protection to the accorded programs by virtue of copyright. Is it intended that the copyright monopoly shall extend to the use of the program in combination with the computer to attain the result at which the program is aimed? For example, it is proposed that the plan or scheme of running a steel mill or handling payrolls by computer shall become the property of the person who holds the copyright of the program tapes or punch cards which direct the computer, which in turn directs and monitors the operation?

The revision Bill does not specifically address itself to this problem, but again we are met with broad statutory language defining the proprietor's exclusive rights.[4] The language could conceivably be read as going the whole length of giving an affirmative answer to the foregoing questions—of giving the copyright proprietor of a program ownership of the process, so to speak, which the program embodies. It is submitted in section (A) below that this possible interpretation should be clearly disavowed. In section (B) we shall go on to inquire whether any narrower kind of copyright protection of a computer program is feasible or socially desirable.

The Copyright Office decided in 1964 to receive computer programs for registration under general language of the present Copyright Act, but it freely conceded that the question of copyrightability under that statute was debatable.

(A) *Broad Copyright Protection for Programs Is Unwise and Improper.* No basis has been laid for legislation which would take the drastic step of granting monopoly protection to computer programs extending to computer processes. There has been virtually no attempt to examine into the economics of the creation or distribution of computer programs, starting with the question of the practical headstart or time advantage that a program-maker may now enjoy without statutory protection—the advantage he may secure by staying abreast or ahead of competition and keeping the program "private" through contract or other arrangements. In fact the industry has been burgeoning without the artificial stimulus of the extensive protection of programs that may be contemplated by the Revision Bill.

On principle, the vice in granting copyright to computer programs in the sense of the process is that it would amount to giving programs a breadth of protection similar to that accorded by patent, but without the safeguards and limitations that rightly surround the grant of a patent. Monopoly of systems, schemes, and the like has been granted by our law in the past only under patent,[5] and only upon proof satisfactory to a governmental agency that there has been real "invention"—a discovery marking a material advance over the prior knowledge. Such a monopoly may last only 17 years. Copyright of a computer program, on the other hand, would be available on the basis of "originality," that is, merely an absence of copying without regard to true inventiveness; there would be no serious governmental scrutiny in advance; and the protection would run for a lengthly period of time (the present period is 56 years, and the Revision Bill proposes 75 years). This kind of easy and broad protection for computer programs would threaten to tie up the computer program field and inhibit its progressive development. Had there been such a copyright regime for programs, had programming been constantly carried out under the threat of infringement actions charging plagiarism of existing copyrighted programs, it is doubtful whether the growth of programs

---

[2] References will be to S. 597, 90th Congress, 1st Sess. This Bill, except for formal matters, is the same as H.R. 4347, 89th Cong., as reported with amendments by the House Judiciary Committee on October 12, 1966 in Report No. 2237, 89th Cong., 2d Sess. The Hearings are printed as Copyright Law Revision, Hearings before Subcomm. No. 3 of House Committee on the Judiciary, 89th Cong., 1st Sess. on H.R. 4347, etc., Ser. 8, Pts. 1–3.

[3] See S. 597, & 102 (text in Appendix A). See also House Report No. 2237, p. 44.

[4] See § 106 (text in Appendix A).

[5] In an opaque passage. House Report 2237 itself suggests that "plans, methods, systems, mathematical principles" do not belong in copyright. See p. 44, n. 1.

and programming techniques of recent years would have been possible. Imagine the condition today if any sizable fraction of the thousands of existing computer programs were held in copyright and copying the processes involved were civilly actionable and even criminally punishable.

The argument has been made in support of, or at least in apology for, copyright for computer programs covering the processes, that infringement could be avoided simply by changing in some degree the sequence of steps or the problem-solving algorithm of the program. On this view, the presence of a copyright would merely compel an outsider to do some slight work of his own in order to stay out of trouble. The answer to this suggestion is: if copyright of process were accepted, (i) it would make no sense to permit escape from it by trivial variation; (ii) it is very doubtful that courts would take so lighthearted or permissive an attitude toward the infringement question. The tendency of the courts in recent years has been to enlarge rather than to contract the range of actionable plagiarism. Surely it would be most imprudent to assume that courts would be especially gingerly about finding infringement of computer programs, once the basis of protection was established.[6]

We should add here that the question of patent protection for computer programs is being studied by the Patent Office. That Office recently published and invited comments upon a set of "Guidelines" tentatively proposed by it for passing on applications for computer-program patents under the present Patent Act.[7] The "Guidelines" have ben criticized as awkward in that the text of the present Act does not envisage computer programs and the "Guidelines" cannot overcome this textual inadequacy. It may be that the Patent Act would have to be amended to deal more directly with programs. In any event, something on the order of patent appears to be the right legal vehicle for programs if it is believed that the public interest requires that further encouragement be given to programing by holding out the prospect of a substantial monopoly.[8]

(B) *Possible Limited Scope of Protection for Programs.* If the process embodied in a computer program ought not to be aggrandized through copyright, it might still seem plausible to allow a narrower copyright of a program—one that would confer upon the copyright proprietor the exclusive right to replicate the instructions themselves, the content of the punch cards, tapes, etc., and the right to bar others from making that replication, thereby compelling those others to buy the punch cards, tapes, etc. from the copyright proprietor. But it becomes evident that this right must be carefully circumscribed. For if, as we urge in section (A) above, the outsider is to be assured full access to the process—full right to practice the art comprised in the computer program—then he must be given the accompanying privilege to replicate the program in order to carry out the process or practice the art.[9] Put another way, were the copyright owner of the program empowered to bar the outsider from replicating the program even for the purpose of practicing the art, he would effectively have denied the outsider the ability to practice the art, for the outsider needs to replicate the program or something akin to it in order to instruct his own computer.

On the other hand, the copyright owner of the program might be given the right to prevent others from replicating the content of the punch cards, tapes, etc. simply for the purpose of selling the program on the market or, reproducing it in a book on programing. In general, it might not be socially harmful to permit copyright of computer programs limited in scope to replications for purposes other than carrying out the process or practicing the arts contained in the programs. Concretely: X prepares a computer program for controlling the production of steel. A copyright of the program by X (obtained on the basis of "originality") should in no event bar Y, an outsider, from producing steel in the same way, and to that end Y, if he chooses, should be at liberty to replicate X's program exactly. (Of course, Y may prefer to buy the punch cards or tapes from X.) On the other hand Y would not be at liberty to replicate X's program simply to sell copies of it to Z; he would not be permitted to enter into a competition with X in any market that may exist for selling the relevant punch cards, tapes, etc.

---

[6] In this connection, see the definition of "derivative work" in § 101 (text in Appendix A).
[7] The "Guidelines" are published in 829 *Official Gazette of U.S. Pat. Off.*, No. 1, p. 2 (August 2, 1966).
[8] See *Report of the President's Commission on the Patent System*, note 1 above, p. 13, advising against patentability. The Report adds that programs are now accepted for copyright, see note 3 above, but no argument is made that they should be copyrightable.
[9] See Baker v. Selden. 101 U.S. 99 (1879).

We imagine this sort of limited copyright in X would not be socially hurtful, although we frankly do not know whether it would be necessary or useful.

In the foregoing discussion it has not been necessary to distinguish the position of nonprofit educational or research institutions or libraries, as producers and users of programs, from that of commercial organizations. The issue is one of general principle. For the reasons developed in Part II below, however, we suggest that so far as the new legislation allows computer programs to hold copyright, educational and similar organizations deserve special privileges or exemptions on liberal lines. And in no event should those institutions be subject to *injunction* for infringement of programs. In other words, so far as the institutions are not given exempt status, they should have the equivalent of a compulsory license on terms of compensation reasonable for institutions of their kind.[10]

II. USE OF COPYRIGHTED MATERIALS BY MEANS OF COMPUTERS

We now turn to the use of "data" as distinguished from programs. As the familiar titles "information storage and retrieval" and "data processing" indicate, information or data can be introduced into computers by being placed in machine-readable form or by some more direct scanning process, can be manipulated in the computer, and can be retrieved in their original, or altered, form as hard copies or as transitory images or sounds. What if the material is under copyright?

The question centers upon the participation by computers in usages of copyrighted works by way of reproduction, performance, and so forth; and our particular interest is to consider what the Revision Bill ought to provide with respect to such computer-operations when conducted by nonprofit schools or similar institutions for their usual educational or related purposes. It should be noted that up to the present time there has been comparatively little experience with or practical application of these computer uses, and the range of eventual uses as well as the technology for accomplishing them are still largely question marks.

The traditional policy of our Copyright Act has been to exempt the public performance of nondramatic literary and musical works from copyright restrictions when the performance is carried on without a motive of profit.[11] By interpretation, it is likely that the present Act exempts the nonprofit public display of works also.[12] These exemptions given by our present Act—which for convenience we shall hereafter call the "traditional exemptions"—are of course intended to benefit educational and other like eleemosynary institutions.

Two points need stress here. First, the existence of the traditional exemptions does not mean that educational institutions or libraries are relieved of all copyright tolls. In fact these establishments are paying vast and ever growing sums yearly for copyrighted works—consider, for example, the size of the expenditure for copyrighted books. Regardless of the final fate of the computer, there is no prospect of any slackening of such financial contributions in the foreseeable future; on the contrary, education and associated endeavors will be paying more, not less, for the copyrighted works required to carry out their characteristic functions.

Second, the traditional exemptions, so far as they favor education and similar undertakings, are not a sentimental or quixotic or irrational kind of largesse which the law unjustly forces copyright proprietors to bestow on these beneficiaries. Rather the exemptions are grounded in enlightened policy. The copyright law helps to assure an adequate and lively production and distribution of intellectual works by enhancing artificially the returns from distribution. But it serves no public purpose, and is indeed pernicious, to attempt undue enhancement of those returns. Thus the monopoly rights conferred by the copyright law should be held in reasonable check both as to scope and duration. It is peculiarly fitting that the outerlimits of the copyright monopoly should be drawn with a view to

---

[10] There is precedent for this no-injunction treatment in certain provisions of the Revision Bill on the use of copyrighted works by CATV systems. See § 111.

[11] Present Copyright Act § 1(c), (e).

[12] The claim occasionally made by educators that some sort of exemption exists under the present Act for nonprofit reproduction and distribution of hard copies of nondramatic literary works, seems overdrawn; but also overdrawn is the claim sometimes made by publishers that under the present Act the exemption for nonprofit displays, etc. would be lost where the computer plays a part because some kind of reproduction is required to get the copyrighted works into the machine.

benefiting education and libraries, since the educational effort is not only intrinsically worthy of encouragement but creates and constantly enlarges the very audience upon which the copyright industries depend for their market, besides helping to generate the authors who furnish the basic material for those industries.[13]

The copyright industries—the "publishers" in the broad sense—seem to have gotten along rather well under the longstanding statutory arrangements granting the traditional exemptions. Nevertheless, the publishers have insisted throughout the evolution of the Revision Bill on rubbing out the line of the traditional exemptions. Sometimes this insistence has been so strident as to disregard the plain fact that the publishers are themselves the beneficiaries of like preferences, whether these take the form of postal subsidies, or appear in the guise of public funds appropriated directly or indirectly for the purchase or licensing of copyrighted works, or take the shape of the copyright statute which confers on them the basic monopoly. When the revision effort began, the Register of Copyrights advised that the traditional exemptions be continued. But, amid a great welter of propaganda, the Register has gradually swung around, and the result in the Revision Bill is the abandonment of the old line and the substitution of particularistic exemptions of narrower scope. As we shall soon see in more detail, the cutting down of the traditional exemptions operates with special strictness and with serious effect on schools and libraries desiring to use the advanced technology represented by the computer.

(A) *Possibility of Retaining Traditional Exemptions Subject to Future Change.* The publishers are understandably concerned that computer-operations by schools and libraries may radically change the impact of the traditional exemptions. For example, if "displays" by computers became eventually so facile as to reduce the need for purchase of books, the book publishers might be seriously affected by the operation of the relevant traditional exemption, at least until they could adjust themselves and find a place in the setting of the new technology. But the future of computer uses of copyrighted works by schools and the like is uncertain, and is likely to remain so for some time; a repressive attitude toward computer uses, written into permanent legislation, might prove thoroughly stultifying. Moreover, the narrowing or elimination of the traditional exemptions, forcing schools and libraries to seek "clearance" of rights on payment of fees, is and must for some time remain impracticable in the absence of clearing-house devices (apart from those available for music) for negotiation of permissions and fees. In these circumstances, it would have seemed advisable for the Revision Bill to hew to the line of the traditional exemptions, as the Register of Copyrights first proposed, but to establish in the Bill a procedure for reviewing and resolving the question when the shape of the future could be better discerned. This might have involved the establishment under the new law of an administrative body with appropriate delegated power, or some other self-corrective mechanism.[14] The Revision Bill does not adopt this approach.

(B) *Urgent Need to Reexamine Revision Bill's Treatment of Computer Usages.* If firm decisions are to be made now in the new legislation, then the particular dispositions of the computer questions appearing in the Revision Bill should be thoroughly reconsidered. They were little debated before they emerged in the Revision Bill, and were reached by guess and by hunch. They seem to eliminate virtually all preference for educational and related institutions utilizing copyrighted works by means of computers. Assuming that the exact line of the traditional exemptions is to be abandoned and concessions made to publishers, it still appears that the Revision Bill in its present version goes too far and makes undue concessions. In effect the Revision Bill would give the publishers full economic benefits deriving from the progressive facilitation and expansion of the use of copyrighted works promised by the future improvement of computer technology. Plainly those economic benefits should be equitably shared, not delivered over to the publishers alone. Especially is this one-sided appropriation seen to be unfair when it is realized that publishers as a group are no more to be credited with the creation of the technological improvements than schools and libraries are.

---

[13] It may also be observed that as funds for education are always running short, schools would tend, if the traditional exemptions were withdrawn, to avoid the performance and display of copyrighted works to the extent possible and turn to works which could be used without compensation. This factor would tend both to affect undesirably the selection of works for these utilizations, and to reduce the profits that the publishers would hope to achieve through withdrawal of the traditional exemptions.

[14] The administrative question is renewed in Part III below.

Examining the Revision Bill in detail, we find that the exemptions granted to schools and libraries for computer operations with copyrighted works have been reduced to the point where they are nominal rather than real.

(1) *The "face-to-face exemption."* The Revision Bill would allow an exemption for "performance" or "display" of copyrighted works by instructors or pupils in face-to-face teaching activities of nonprofit schools carried out in classrooms or similar places devoted to instruction. (We shall call this the "face-to-face exemption.") [15]

The meaning of this exemption is not clear. The text of the section, the commentary in the House Report, and the history of the provision suggest that the draftsmen had in mind only performances and displays by means of the projections long familiar in American classrooms, and did not have in mind computer-assisted classroom performances or displays. A question is also raised whether the exemption, if applicable to computer-assisted instruction at all, covers only cases where the images and sounds are delivered simultaneously to all the students in a classroom, and is inapplicable to cases where the signals are called forth by individual students in the classroom at their own rates of speed. Loss of the face-to-face exemption where there is individualized activation of the machine would be unfortunate, for this element of individualization is often of the essence of instruction by computer and may be its cardinal advantage. [16] The confinement to the "classroom" and the requirement of the actual presence of an instructor run against the healthy trend of the new educational methods designed to break out of the stultifying limitations imposed by classroom walls. Finally—and very important—is the point that the face-to-face exemption is rendered largely nugatory if a "transmission" is involved, i.e. if the images or sounds are received beyond the "place" from which they are sent. [17] Thus if the computer is located outside the "place" in which the classroom is housed—and why should it not be?—there is presumptively an infringement, subject, however, to the possibility that the very narrow "transmission exemption" (discussed in (2) immediately below) may be applicable.

(2) *The "transmission exemption."* The "transmission exemption" covers the performance of nondramatic literary or musical works or display of works by means of a transmission by a nonprofit organization, if the performance or display is part of the systematic instruction of a nonprofit school, the radius of the transmission is not more than 100 miles, the transmission is made primarily for reception in classrooms or similar places, and the time and content of the transmission are controlled by the transmitting organization and "do not depend on a choice by individual recipients in activating transmission from an information storage and retrieval system or any similar device, machine, or process." [18]

This exemption was plainly drafted with ETV in mind; the reference to computers, with the provision against individual activation, appears to have been thrown into the latest version of the Revision Bill as a kind of appendage. The effect of the appendage, however, is virtually to read this exemption out of the Bill to the extent it applies to computerized instruction. Reflexively it also does great damage to the face-to-face exemption when the computer is at a distance from the classroom. For, as already noted, individualization—activation by recipients at their own speeds—is vitally important to computerized instruction, and this falls outside the exemption. Again the reference to classrooms is too confining. Finally, it is arbitrary to speak of a fixed radius of transmission (presumably to be measured as the distance between the computer proper and its console or terminal facility). The exemption's evident bias against computer "networks" is unexplained and hard to justify.

(3) *Absence of a library exemption.* It will be noted that the two exemptions so far considered relate to teaching activities or instruction. There is no specific exemption for research or library activities by means of the computer. This omission would have drastic effects. Take the library question. Today a library of course pays for the books that are found on its shelves, but neither the library nor the readers are required to make any additional copyright payment for use of the books in the course of ordinary library operations, whether the use is in the form of simple perusal on the premises, or of lending-out. (It will be recalled that the

---

[15] § 110(1) (text in Appendix A).
[16] Cf. Licklider, "Televistas: Looking Ahead Through Side Windows," in *Public Television, A Program for Action* (Report of the Carnegie Commission on ETV) 201 (1967).
[17] See the § 101 definition of "transmission" (text in Appendix A).
[18] § 110(2) (text in Appendix A).

Register of Copyrights has in fact refused to give his support to any proposal for exacting a toll for lending-out.) The Revision Bill would introduce a diametrically opposite principle by which even intermittent displays of books through machines in libraries might be infringements.[19]

This 180-degree turn of position is, in our view, not defensible. The indeterminate "fair use" provision is not an acceptable substitute for the clear-out and reasonable delimited exemption that the situation requires.

(4) *The special problem of computer input.* Such narrow benefits as the exemptions would otherwise confer appear to be frustrated by the proposition, advanced in the House Report, that the "input" of a copyrighted work into the computer—involving its translation into machine-readable form—is itself an infringing reproduction without regard to the manner of the input or the further utilization of the work by the machine.[20] Thus an infringement may occur at the moment when a copyrighted work is introduced into the computer even if the only utilization later made of it falls squarely within one of the exemptions. So the Revision Bill, having ceremoniously conferred the alleged exemptions with one hand, brusquely takes them back with the other; indeed, takes them before then they are really given. For the performances and displays of copyrighted works as described in the exemptions are not free as far as computer operations are concerned—not truly exempted—when payment can be exacted at the threshold or access to the copyrighted works can be denied altogether by the copyright proprietors.[21]

It has been suggested that the copyright proprietor must be able to control the introduction of the work into the computer because the computer has great flexibility; while the work is "in" the computer, there is no assurance of its being availed of only in the exempted ways. But it is surely a novel prescription to block off access in order to prevent possible future theft. Moreover, the protection is illusory since anyone who intends to infringe a work by nonexempt uses without payment, would not hesitate to make the input without notice or payment to the proprietor of the work. We should add that the computer can be set up to keep records for billing purposes of the manipulation of a copyrighted work by the machine all the way from input to output.[22]

It has also been argued that the owner of the copyright is entitled to the exclusive right to translate the work into machine-readable form. If, indeed, the copyright owner has prepared the work in a form capable of being used directly by the computer, the chances are very good that the school or other institution will buy that product rather than itself go to the expense of putting the work in the required form. But there will be cases where the proprietor is not interested in making the needed transformation and the institutions must have access to the work in order to take the benefit of the exemption.

Of course, any exemption of the input as such should be lost if the work is thereafter used without consent in excess of the applicable statutory exemptions on use. So also, in revising the current bill technical advice might be sought on the feasibility of prescribing that after a work is inputted and used for exempt purposes, it must be removed from the machine and not permitted to remain there indefinitely. At some stage of technical development, it may become possible to require that inputs, even if themselves exempt, shall be reported to an official register. The important point is that input should not constitute an infringing act when the uses made are exempt—otherwise the exemptions, so-called, are completely aborted.

To sum up. We have shown the serious inadequacies of the exemptions related to computer operations. Understandably concerned about the potentialities of

---

[19] See § 109(b) (text in Appendix A), and House Report 2237, pp. 67–68.

[20] See House Report 2237, p. 54. There is an ambiguous reference here to the "fair use" provision, but this does not seem to affect the statement made in the text, assuming that the input is of all or a material part of a copyrighted work.

[21] With respect to the input question, the Revision Bill is harsher toward computers used for educational purposes than it is toward educational broadcasting in the familiar forms of radio and TV. For in the case of educational broadcasting, use of the transmission exemption is positively facilitated by the inclusion of an additional exemption allowing the broadcasters to make ephemeral recordings" of "transmission programs" embodying the performances and displays of the copyrighted works. See § 112.

[22] We should also note that our objection to making input an infringement without regard to the nature of the subsequent utilizations, does not mean that we would oppose a practice of blanket licensing of works for all-purpose computer utilizations. In cases where any non-exempt utilization of the work is contemplated, the practice may well become the regular mode.

computer uses of copyrighted works, the draftsmen of the Revision Bill have, in practical effect, gone to the extreme of shutting off nearly all substantial preferences in such uses for educational, research, and library purposes. A more equitable line must be found. Consideration should probably start by seeing how far it is fair and feasible to hold to the general line of exempting performances or displays of works for teaching, research, or library purposes in face-to-face situations and in closed transmissions controlled by nonprofit educational and similar organizations. The line of the exemption should not be twisted by harassing or frustrating limitations, such as an insistence that to retain exemption, transmissions must be activated by the transmitting organization rather than the recipients. This is nearly to deny the genius of the computer.

We repeat that in all events the remedy of injunction should not be available against educational or other like users. In case of dispute over terms as to a nonexempt use, a reasonable rate should be paid, as determined in the last event by a court, taking into account, among other relevant factors, the eleemosynary nature of the using institution. Such a provision will serve, collaterally, the benevolent purpose of encouraging the creation of satisfactory clearinghouse arrangements for licensing copyrighted works.

In recognition of the fact that the entire situation is fluid and that the lines drawn in the statute may turn out to be wrong—either too favorable to education and similar interests, or not favorable enough—the new statute should contain internal machinery for correction. To that vital subject we now turn.

III. INTERNAL MACHINERY FOR CORRECTION OF STATUTORY PROVISIONS LATER FOUND TO BE UNWISE

The House Report candidly admits that *"the problem of computer uses of copyrighted material"* was *"touched on rather lightly at the hearings."* [23] Nevertheless the subcommittee and later the full committee went on to lay down comprehensive restrictive provisions on computer uses, and all this without creating internal statutory machinery for correction over a period of time. [24] With deference, we say that this was a mistake.

It must be conceded on all hands that the computer field is subject to rapid change, that regulations now adopted may, and indeed very likely will, prove later to be foolish. The entire environment is changing.

It is hazardous to rely on the usual process of formal legislative amendment of the statute to correct abuses as they arise. Experience with a number of provisions in the present Copyright Act has definitely shown that such reliance is illusory. For in the copyright field abuses are advantages seen from the other side; they are fiercely defended by the favored groups and become extremely hard to dislodge.

Some procedural device should be found to supply the element of self-correction: otherwise the Revision Bill will be obsolete on the day it is enacted. Any one of a number of devices could be adopted. The device could consist of the establishment under the new law of an administrative body with appropriate delegated power. It could consist of creating a body authorized to amend or add to the legislation subject to Congressional veto. It could consist of establishing an Advisory Council directed to keep the subject under consideration, study the problems as they come up, and report to a Joint Congressional Committee, with the Committee then making proposals for consideration by Congress.

One or another of the described devices may be useful for purposes beyond that of accommodating the law to the changing panorama of the computer. For example, the Revision Bill relegates the problem of photocopying to the general language of the section on "fair use." Greater clarity should be sought. Thus it may be well to provide for the possibility of laying down from time to time, on the basis of experience, definite rules-of-thumb for photocopying.

But whatever may be the need in that quarter, an adjunct to the statute is clearly and urgently needed for the solution over a period of time of the copyright questions generated by the computer.

---

[23] House Report 2237, p. 53.
[24] The House Report does not go further than to recognize that the absence of any going clearance systems outside the music field is serious, but as to that it makes only the weak proposal that the interested parties should try to reach some accommodation *after* the Bill is enacted into law (p. 54). Even here it does not draw the obvious inference: provision against injunctive relief is indispensable as long as a viable clearance system does not exist.

§ 101 Definitions

As used in this title, the following terms and their variant forms mean the following:

A "derivative work" is a work based upon one or more pre-existing works, such as a translation, musical arrangement, dramatization, fictionalization, motion picture version, sound recording, art reproduction, abridgment, condensation, or any other form in which a work may be recast, transformed, or adapted. A work consisting of editorial revisions, annotations, elaborations, or other modifications which, as a whole, represent an original work of authorship, is a "derivative work."

To "transmit" a performance or display is to communicate it by any device or process whereby images or sounds are received beyond the place from which they are sent.

§ 102. Subject matter of copyright: In general

Copyright protection subsists, in accordance with this title, in original works of authorship fixed in any tangible medium of expression, now known or later developed, from which they can be perceived, reproduced, or otherwise communicated, either directly or with the aid of a machine or device. Works of authorship include the following categories:

    (1) literary works;

    (2) musical works, including any accompanying words;

    (3) dramatic works, including any accompanying music;

    (4) pantomimes and choreographic works;

    (5) pictorial, graphic, and sculptural works;

    (6) motion pictures and other audiovisual works;

    (7) sound recordings.

§ 106. Exclusive rights in copyrighted works

Subject to sections 107 through 116, the owner of copyright under this title has the exclusive rights to do and to authorize any of the following:

    (1) to reproduce the copyrighted work in copies or phonorecords;

    (2) to prepare derivative works based upon the copyrighted work;

    (3) to distribute copies or phonorecords of the copyrighted work to the public by sale or other transfer of ownership, or by rental, lease, or lending;

    (4) in the case of literary, musical, dramatic, and choreographic works, pantomimes, and motion pictures and other audiovisual works, to perform the copyrighted work publicly;

    (5) in the case of literary, musical, dramatic, and choreographic works, pantomimes, and pictorial, graphic, or sculptural works, to display the copyrighted work publicly.

§ 109. Limitations on exclusive rights: Effect of transfer of particular copy or phonorecord

(b) Notwithstanding the provisions of section 106(5), the owner of a particular copy lawfully made under this title, or any person authorized by him, is entitled, without the authority of the copyright owner, to display that copy publicly, either directly or by the projection of no more than one image at a time, to viewers present at the place where the copy is located.

§ 110. Limitations on exclusive rights: Exemption of certain performances and displays

Notwithstanding the provisions of section 106, the following are not infringements of copyright:

    (1) performance or display of a work by instructors or pupils in the course of face-to-face teaching activities of a nonprofit educational institution, in a classroom or similar place devoted to instruction, unless, in the case of a motion picture or other audiovisual work, the performance is given by means of a copy that was not lawfully made under this title and that the person responsible for the performance knew or had reason to believe was not lawfully made;

(2) performance of a nondramtic literary or musical work, or display of a work, by or in the course of a transmission by a governmental body or other nonprofit organization, if :

(A) the performance or display is a regular part of the systematic instructional activities of a governmental body or a nonprofit educational institution ; and

(B) the radius of the area normally encompassed by the transmission is no more than 100 miles ; and

(C) the transmission is made primarily for :

(i) reception in classrooms or similar places normally devoted to instruction, or

(ii) reception by persons to whom the transmission is directed because their disabilities or other special circumstances prevent their attendance in classrooms or similar places normally devoted to instruction, or

(iii) reception by officers or employees of governmental bodies as a part of their official duties or employment ; and

(D) the time and content of the transmission are controlled by the transmitting organization and do not depend on a choice by individual recipients in activating transmission from an information storage and retrieval system or any similar device, machine or process ;

[Copyright Act Revision, S. 597]

STATEMENT BY BENJAMIN KAPLAN OF HARVARD LAW SCHOOL, PRESENTED TO THE SUBCOMMITTEE ON PATENTS, TRADEMARKS, AND COPYRIGHTS OF THE SENATE COMMITTEE ON THE JUDICIARY, APRIL 4, 1967

I am Royall Professor of Law at Harvard Law School and have taught the law of copyright for many years. In January of this year I published a book on copyright comprising a series of James S. Carpentier Lectures which I delivered at Columbia Law School.

My book deals with the Copyright Revision Bill at some length.* I shall not recanvass the whole field here, but shall rather speak very briefly to the computer question.

At the invitation of the Interuniversity Communications Council (Educom), I have served as chairman of their Task Force on Law. After deliberation, our Task Force drew up a statement analyzing the Copyright Revision Bill in relation to the computer. This statement was approved by the Board of Trustees of Educom, and the conclusions have been adopted in the form of resolutions by the Council of Educom consisting of representatives of member colleges and universities. The statement and resolutions are being submitted at these hearings by Mr. W. Brown Morton, Jr., on behalf of Educom.

Subscribing fully to the statement and resolutions, I wish to make a few supplementary points.

1. The view taken by Educom is not partisan in the sense of coming from a single cohesive group with a particular axe to grind. Those associated with Educom realize that utilization of copyright works is indissolubly connected with authorship, production, and ownership of such works, for without production there can be no utilization. Moreover individual educators are themselves often authors as well as users.

Educom has sought to speak for the public interest and not for the benefit of any narrow group. In debates over Copyright Revision it has been customary to speak of issues existing between producers or proprietors, on the one side, and users, on the other. The mental picture of a tug of war is unfortunate, for it suggests that all that is at stake is the private advantage of one group over the other. The real problem is to design the legislation for the common good, and this is the objective to which the Educom statement is directed.

2. It has been apparent from the outset of the study conducted on behalf of Educom that the faults in the Copyright Revision Bill with regard to computer operations—faults which are documented in the Educom statement—derived from the fact that knowledge about the relation of the new and growing tech-

---

An Unhurried View of Copyright (1967: Columbia University Press), chapter III.

nology to education, research, and libraries was not generally available when the Bill was first formulated. Those in possession of the facts—including educators, scientists and technicians—were not aware until very recently that copyright figured at all in the future of the computer, and therefore they did not come forward until a late date with any comprehensive statement of their views or proposals. The relevant parts of the Revision Bill, drafted without adequate information, accordingly have the look of ill-considered improvisations. It is hoped that the Educom statement, together with statements and testimony offered by others, will repair the omissions and furnish a basis for the prompt interpolation in the Bill of more satisfactory provisions.

3. As the deficiencies in the present Bill in respect to computer operations have become evident in recent months or weeks, it has been suggested in some quarters that the provisions of the Bill that are objected to should be enacted as they now stand, but on some understanding that thereafter (a) the problems would be studied by the interested groups and supplemental legislation proposed, or (b) the interested groups would work toward creating a "clearing house" through which permission to use copyrighted works could be more readily obtained and payments more easily channeled, thus helping somewhat to overcome the defects of the Bill.

As to suggestion (a), I would like to urge in the strongest terms that the defects in the Bill be eliminated before the Bill is recommended to Congress and that the Bill be not recommended in its present form on any assumption that it can be brought up to the level of adequacy by amendments after enactment. The procedure of relying on later amendment would be a sad conclusion to a decade of effort bent on securing modernized legislation. More than that, it would be a highly dangerous expedient. In all likelihood it would result in inadequate legislation for the indefinite future. For it can hardly be believed that settlements that could not be obtained when the entire revision legislation hung in balance, would be obtained as more-or-less voluntary concessions when all the pressure for mutual adjustment was removed.

As to suggestion (b), the possibility of perfecting a clearing house in the reasonable future is highly problematical. In any case, the creation of a clearing house even in a thoroughly viable form would be merely a minor palliative for the defects in the Bill to which the Educom statement is addressed; it would not cure those defects. A clearing house arrangement, in facilitating transactions with copyrighted works, including permissions and payments, may be independently desirable, but it scarcely meets our contention that certain circumscribed computer utilizations for educational, research, and library purposes should be exempted from copyright restrictions and thus freed of the need for permission or payment.

4. A Bill should not be recommended unless it appears adequate in itself to cover needs as they are seen at present; but a Bill satisfactory in that sense should still contain administrative or other machinery by which selected provisions of the Bill can be rapidly adjusted to future developments. This proposal makes plain sense in the light of past copyright history which shows the enormous difficulty of trying, by application of the ordinary process of legislative amendment, to get rid of provisions of the Act of 1909 that turned out to be foolishly anachronistic. That the proposal for including such forward-looking machinery was not earlier formulated or more vigorously pressed was due to a failure—again a quite understandable one—to appreciate the weight of the changes that may come about through scientific developments over the next decade and to which we must be prepared to make rapid responses.

In conclusion, I express the hope that this subcommittee will seize the opportunity to sponsor improvements in the Revision Bill for submission to the full Committee.

STATEMENT OF ANTHONY G. OETTINGER

Mr. Chairman, may I first thank you for the invitation to appear before your Subcommittee and for the opportunity to express my views on a matter which is of deep concern to me not only as a college teacher, as President of the Association for Computing Machinery (ACM) and as a member of the Board of Governors of the American Federation of Information Processing Societies (AFIPS) (but also as a scientist and engineer directly involved in research on information processing and more specifically on technological aids to creative thought and on the impact of technology on education both in the school and in professional life. Like many of my colleagues, I am also an author drawing revenues from copyrighted works.

The Association for Computing Machinery is the professional society for individuals who apply, develop, design, and theorize about computers and computer programs; it currently numbers 20,000 members, the majority of whom are in the United States. Although I am speaking today as an individual, I have discussed my testimony with the other members of the ACM Executive Committee, Dr. Bernard Galler, Professor of Mathematics and Communication Science, University of Michigan and Mr. Donn Parker, Staff Specialist, Control Data Corporation, Palo Alto. They are in substantial agreement with what I have to say.

My academic title reflects a traditional labeling of disciplines but I prefer to describe myself as a computer scientist and engineer concerned with both the theory and the practice of information processing by all the various means afforded to us by ancient and modern technology. The variance between my labels and my self-image reflects the one basic truth about the computing and information processing field today; it is growing and changing at a tremendous rate. This can scarcely be news to this committee since the report of the House Judiciary Committee [1] clearly pointed out that "recognizing the profound import that information storage and retrieval systems seem destined to have on authorship, communications, and human life itself, the committee is also aware of the dangers of legislating prematurely in this area of exploding technology."

Some of those who have preceded me have pointed out with great force and clarity the legal implications of the Copyright Revision Bill S. 597 as presently drafted. I wish particularly to express my wholehearted agreement with the perceptive analysis of the problem provided in the statement submitted by the Interuniversity Communications Council (EDUCOM). I do not wish to repeat arguments that have already been well made by others, particularly since I am not a lawyer. I should rather like to paint for you a picture of what the pertinent sections of this bill look like to someone who, like myself, would be directly affected by the consequences.

For a couple of years now, with the support of the Advanced Research Projects Agency of the Department of Defense, I have been experimenting with the classroom use of terminals linked up via 3,000 miles of New England Telephone. Western Union, and Pacific Telephone lines to a computer system devised by my friend and colleague, Professor Glen Culler, at the University of California at Santa Barbara. Students in several Harvard courses have used this terminal to solve problems in mathematics and statistics as well as to experiment on the design of the system itself with an eye toward producing a more advanced system.

Several facts immediately stand out: transmission is clearly over more than 100 miles! The time and content of the transmission very clearly and necessarily "depend on a choice by individual recipients in activating transmission." I have therefore already run afoul of two of the conditions by which exemption is limited under Section 110 (2) of the proposed bill. It would, moreover, be very difficult for me to know whether or not the system my colleague operates 3,000 miles away had or had not incorporated in its programs that were themselves copyrighted or data that were copyrighted and which, under the spirit of the bill, had in the first place been illegally introduced into the computer.

I am now planning additional experiments over the next three years in which I expect to combine our new computer system with a variety of films, videotapes, audiotapes and other technical devices as well as the more conventional devices such as chalk and blackboard, books, technical journals, etc. In the course of these experiments I expect to peruse, display, copy, and enter into computers or other files a great variety of materials in various media. I have as yet no idea how much of what I buy, rent, borrow or produce myself I will eventually keep and either use in my classroom, publish conventionally or disseminate by less conventional means now still in the experimental stage.

Under the provisions of the bill as now conceived, I would have not only to acquire and evaluate materials but, in each instance, *before* experimenting with them, seek out the owner of a copyright, if any, make formal requests for permission to use the material, pay royalties if any are due, etc. All this before any material could actually be used and, in fact, before I could find out whether or not the material was useful! The delays, the frustrations and the chaos inherent in such a process now seem so formidable that if the bill were passed

---

[1] Report No. 2237 89th Congress, 2nd Session, October 12, 1966.

in its present form I would be tempted to return to the safer occupation of copying out manuscripts with a goose quill pen.

I am interested in the free development of the science and the engineering of both computer hardware and computer software but, as an author, I am not unmindful of the protection afforded by copyright. Yet, the logic of permitting someone to cut up his legally purchased copy of a book I have written, paste pieces on file cards and sort these by hand while precluding him from doing the same job by machine escapes me. I *am* concerned if he makes illegal use of the *end-product*, but surely as I have as little right to tell him not to use the labor-saving assistance of a computer as I have to forbid him to delegate work to a research assistant or a secretary.

The foregoing was all stated in the first person and with very specific reference to my own interests. Nevertheless I am familiar enough with the work of my colleagues in computing, libraries, and information retrieval to believe that I could quite safely have said "we", substituted innumerable variations on the general theme of educational technology or switched altogether to the broader problem of library modernization. What I have said would still remain true.

Beyond my immediate personal concerns, I can see other curious and perhaps earlier unforeseen consequences of the limitations of Section 110 (2). One could argue, for example, that programmed instruction of the linear kind where each student is presented with precisely the same sequence of questions as every other, could legitimately take place if time and content of transmissions were controlled by the transmitting organization. However, the use of branching instructional programs where the future course of instruction, the nature of questions and so on depends on prior responses by the student might well constitute "a choice by individual recipients in activating transmission" and therefore an infringement! There is still considerable controversy among investigators of these modes of programmed instruction as to which is more effective and in what circumstances. It would be a rather curious precedent in our society and I need hardly say an unfortunate one, to have scientific questions decided *a priori* by legislation. However unintentional, this would surely be a return to the Dark Ages.

A look slightly ahead of us may further help in seeing the relevant provisions of the bill in some perspective. There now exist machines that can scan printed material of limited type fonts, and convert it into machine readable form. There also exist experimental means for taking words stored in a computer and converting these into the sounds that would be heard if a person were to pronounce the words. If such processes were perfected and extended even in limited form, one could visualize a prosthetic device which would enable a blind man to turn any book into a talking book without the delays and difficulties attendant on conversion into Braille or on recording by a volunteer reader.

We would then face the anomaly that a normal man who has purchased a book in a bookstore or borrowed it from a library would be within his full rights in reading this book anytime and anywhere he pleased; but, if I read the provisions of the bill correctly, that a blind man using his prosthetic machine might well be infringing a copyright:

(a) by causing his prosthetic machine to translate print into machine readable form, whether or not transmission to a remote computer is required. If transmission were necessary, as is much more likely initially, then there might be further infringement;

(b) by his exceeding the capricious 100-mile limit (Section 110 (2)B), which would be probable since the necessary computers most likely could be provided economically only at a limited number of regional centers.

(c) through his exercising his choice as an individual recipient "in activating transmission from an information storage and retrieval system" or, as the bill goes on, "*any similar device, machine, or process*" (Section 110 (2)D—my underline).

The problems which my colleagues and I are trying to solve range in their interest and applicability from the purest of theoretical investigations to the most immediately applicable design and engineering work. In nearly every case there is strong interest on the part of various branches of the federal government and of the public at large in the solution of the problems we are attacking.

The Library of Congress has studied various approaches to automation. The Department of Health, Education and Welfare is sponsoring, through its Office of Education, numerous studies of computer-aided teaching and other technological aids to instruction. The Congress itself, the Bureau of the Budget, the Vice-President of the United States, both now and as senator, the Committee on

Scientific and Technical Information (COSATI) of the Federal Council on Science and Technology, various branches of the Department of Defense, and numerous other bodies have expressed deep concern over the information handling problems of the federal government in every sphere of its activities, and they are seeking solutions through major programs now at varying stages from the operational through the experimental to the projected. I am sure that the computing profession and the computing industry share with the publishing industry a deep concern for the fruition of these efforts.

In a sense, however, we are the victims of our own rosy predictions. The proposed bill drastically limits traditional exemptions although there is no clear and present danger of infringements, which are possible now only on the most limited and commercially uninteresting scale; in so doing, it threatens to cripple severely the very research and the very teaching necessary in order that the "information and retrieval system or any similar device, machine, or process" *materialize fully, be understood, and be controllable.*

In closing, may I address one remark to the question of copyright of programs, to cover a point which I think has been ignored in previous testimony. The statement by the Interuniversity Communications Council (EDUCOM), with which I am in agreement, objects to "the argument . . . in support of . . . copyright for computer programs covering the processes, that infringement could be avoided simply by changing in some degree the sequence of steps . . . of the program" and also rejects the corollary that "On this view, the presence of a copyright would merely compel an outsider to do some slight work of his own in order to stay out of trouble". The rejection of these views should include taking notice of the disastrous consequences that encouraging minor variations to "stay out of trouble" would have on standardization in electronic data processing, which is a subject of major interest to many members of both the Legislative and the Executive branches. Moreover, whatever one's views of the merits of standardization may be, the *deliberate* introduction of hosts of minor variations into a profession struggling to keep its head barely above a swarm of program "bugs" (or *accidental* and *unwanted* minor variations!) can only be viewed as a very grim practical joke on every taxpayer.

STATEMENT OF DR. CHARLES F. GOSNELL, CHAIRMAN, COMMITTEE ON COPYRIGHT ISSUES, AMERICAN LIBRARY ASSOCIATION

Mr. GOSNELL. Mr. Chairman, my name is Charles F. Gosnell. I am director of the libraries of New York University (NYU), and until recently was assistant commissioner of education in New York State, and State librarian. I am here today as chairman of the Committee on Copyright Issues of the American Library Association, a professional nonprofit organization of some 35,000 members, which has been working for nearly a century to advance the development of school, college, university, research, State, and public libraries, as essential foundations for a sound educational program for the Nation, and as basic institutions in the American way of life.

It was my honor to be scheduled as a witness at the hearing held by this committee on August 18, 1965. Because the Senate was heavily engaged on that day, it was not possible for me to testify, and answer your questions. I did, however, leave a statement which you graciously printed in the record.

At this time, I should like to comment particularly on substantial changes made in the amended version of S. 1006 of the first session of the 89th Congress, and which are now contained in S. 597, at present under consideration by this committee. I shall point out some startling changes implied in the fundamental philosophy of copyright. As a consequence, we should like to propose some amendments to S. 597, which we believe will help restore balance to what now constitutes a serious threat to the future of our library services for readers and researchers throughout the Nation.

First, I must compliment the committee on many aspects of the bill, which, if enacted, will be great improvements over the present statute. I know that the Register of Copyrights and his staff have worked with you, and they deserve the thanks of all of us for their keen understanding and long patience in dealing with this important problem.

One of the great improvements is that you are establishing one system of copyright under the Federal statute, which will include both published and unpublished works. We welcome also the greater clarity and precision in many parts of the bill.

Now for a review in more detail: The American Library Association in 1964 expressed by formal resolution its position on eight major issues. There are listed on page 138 of your 1965 hearings on S. 1006, and a copy is appended to this testimony so I shall not repeat them at this time.

We are fully in accord on four of these, where provisions in the present law are retained in the bill, specifically; resolution No. 2, printing of notice and date of copyright; No. 4, exemption from import restrictions; No. 5, noncopyright of Government-created material; and No. 6, no reversion of copyright to the Federal Government. On the requirements of American manufacture, resolution No. 7, a reasonable compromise has been presented. The remaining three issues, however, are of major concern to us: Nos. 1, 3, and 8.

Of utmost importance to us is the issue of fair use, resolution No. 1. We are pleased that this ancient and widely accepted doctrine of fair use is now to be incorporated into the statute, but we are profoundly disturbed by the restrictions with which it seems to be hedged, both in the law and in the interpretive report issued by the House Committee on the Judiciary (Copyright Law Revision, 90th Cong., first sess. H. Rept. No. 83). We hope that your committee will issue a report which will clarify some of the points and remove the objectionable passages. I shall comment on this later, in detail. Certainly, 'various studies have shown that publishers are not suffering from fair use.

On the matter of duration, resolution No. 3, we will be seriously affected in two ways. Duration in the bill is for an indefinite term—life of the author plus 50 years—and for an extraordinary increase in the number of years. In effect, for 85 percent of copyrights under the present system it will multiply the duration by 3 or 4 times. For the 15 percent which are now renewed, according to the Copyright Office, the effect will be to double the term for many.

We are seriously concerned that the philosophy embodied in the phrase "not for profit," resolution No. 8, has been thrown overboard altogether. This is a very serious matter. We heartily endorse the statements of such education groups as the Ad Hoc Committee on Copyright Law Revision; and the Interuniversity Communications Council, Educom, on this issue.

It appears to us that we are faced with a basic change in the fundamental philosophy and purpose of copyright, and that this will have a very heavy impact on the financial structure of the free library system of the United States and its millions of users.

Copyright in the past and present has been the right to make a profit by producing and selling copies of a literary or art work in quantity. Once the individual or the library bought a copy, he was free to bind it, rebind it, take notes from it, count the words in it, look at it through a magnifying glass or microscope, and apply the facts or fancies contained in its text as he chose. Once you bought a book you really owned it.

We librarians do not want to go into the publishing business. We insist upon the right to bind a book if we want, and lots of books come out now with a copyright notice that says you do not have the right to bind it or rebind it. There are lots of restrictions which the publishers put on. They do not mean anything under the present law, but they may mean something under the revised statute.

Authors and publishers are now seeking the right to control use of their written words by leasing or licensing, and limited sale. They seek recompense not so much for the copies sold, but payment for the number of times the copy sold may later be used and the ways in which it may be used. They seek to impose upon libraries the double burden of continuous acounting for uses of what we may have acquired, plus continuous charges as the material is used by readers.

This idea is nothing new, the authors and publishers tell us—it is practiced in Denmark and Sweden now. It was discussed at a meeting of the American Book Publishers Council at Skytop, Pa., on May 20, 1964.

A recent article in the Times Literary Supplement [1] reports on efforts in Britain to get Parliament to approve "a scheme for an extra financial return to authors and * * * publishers, on books bought and loaned by public libraries." Sooner or later, the proponents of this system admit, the taxpayer will be required to provide a substantial subsidy to the authors and publishers. A brief news item on this subject appeared in the Library Journal of New York for January 1, 1967, page 44.

This philosophy of license for use is stated in terms of modern technology, the computer, and so forth, by Laurence Heilprin, who writes:

A copyrighted work is essentially a message. A copyright is a legal privilege to attempt to control part of a communication system. * * * It is the right to derive economic benefit from the market value of a message. [2]

If that is not a new interpretation of copyright, I do not know one.

Federal assistance in public, school, and college libraries is bringing about a revolution in cooperation among libraries. They are growing with great rapidity, and at the same time they are sharing their resources with each other to a marvelous extent. Library users of all ages are benefiting. The expanding needs of readers and researchers are being met on higher and higher levels. Sales of books and other materials to libraries are booming. The next step, now beginning to be taken, is the development of communications networks. Six years ago I helped to plan such a network, which has just been started by the New York State Library.

A year ago, I served briefly as a consultant to the State Library in Hawaii, which has already established such a State network. I believe it is functioning very well and not cutting in on the sale of books.

[1] Edmund Penning-Rowsell, "Sale or Return," the Times Literary Supplement, 1967, March 9, pp. 185–186.
[2] Laurence B. Heilprin, "Technology and the Future of the Copyright Principle," Phi Delta Kappa, January 1967, vol. 48, No. 5, pp. 220–225.

All this seems to be perfectly lawful now, but would be seriously threatened by the new legislation. Some authors and publishers want to collect a tax or royalty on the benefits of cooperation. Some are opposed to cooperation in the mistaken belief that if libraries do not cooperate, they will somehow have to find more money to buy more books.

Some of the restrictions on library networks in the present bill are written in the language of radio and television broadcasting, an entirely different process. I believe in the attempts of some of those interests to shoot down the community antenna, they may destroy an innocent bystander, the library and educational information network.

Reference has been made this morning by others to several sections in the bill. It seems perfectly clear to me that the 100-mile limitation was designed for community antenna rather than for library networks, but somehow, the language moved over.

The Interuniversity Communications Council, known as Educom, has prepared a comprehensive statement on this subject, which the ALA Committee on Copyright Issues endorses completely. I quote a brief section, pages 10 and 11, from the report which was approved by Educom on March 16, 1967, which was not quoted by the Educom people this morning:

Absence of a library exemption. It will be noted that the two exemptions so far considered relate to teaching activities or instruction. There is no specific exemption for research or library activities by means of the computer. This omission would have drastic effects. Take the library question. Today a library of course pays for the books that are found on its shelves, but neither the library nor the readers are required to make any additional copyright payment for use of the books in the course of ordinary library operations, whether the use is in the form of simple perusal on the premises, or of lending-out. (It will be recalled that the Register of Copyrights has in fact refused to give his support to any proposal for exacting a toll for lending out.)

The Revision Bill would introduce a diametrically opposite principle by which even intermittent displays of books through machines in libraries might be infringements. (Bill, section 109–b, and House Report No. 83, pages 38 and 39.)

This 180-degree turn of position is, in our view, not defensible. The indeterminate "fair use" provision is not an acceptable substitute for the clearcut and reasonable delimited exemption that the situation requires.

Such narrow benefits as the exemptions would otherwise confer appear to be frustrated by the proposition, advanced in the House Report, that the "input" of a copyrighted work into the computer—involving its translation into machine-readable form—is itself an infringing reproduction without regard to the manner of the input or the further utilization of the work by the machine. Thus an infringement may occur at the moment when a copyrighted work is introduced into the computer even if the only utilization later made of it falls squarely within one of the exemptions. So the Revision Bill, having ceremoniously conferred the alleged exemptions with one hand, brusquely takes them back with the other; indeed, takes them before they are really given. For the performances and displays of copyrighted works as described in the exemptions are not free as far as computer operations are concerned—not truly exempted—when payment can be exacted at the threshold or access to the copyrighted works can be denied altogether by the copyright proprietors.

With respect to the input question, the Revised Bill is harsher toward computers used for educational purposes than it is toward educational broadcasting in the familiar forms of radio and TV. For in the case of educational broadcasting, use of the transmission exemption is positively facilitated by the inclusion of an additional exemption allowing the broadcasters to make "ephemeral recordings" of "transmission programs" embodying the performances and displays of copyrighted works.

To remedy this difficulty, the following amendments are urged for your consideration and action.

We have come up with some specific recommendations, Mr. Chairman. I have summarized them and put them in the hands of the subcommittee, and I will refer to some of them briefly.

We propose in section 110 a subsection to be added to the present sections 1 and 2, which we will for the moment call 1–A :

Performance or display of a work in the course of a closed transmission by a governmental body or other nonprofit organization if such performance or display is in the course of the teaching or research activities of a nonprofit educational institution or library.

We believe that this would cover the needs of libraries, and I believe it would cover the needs of the Educom, and I submit that to them for their consideration also.

I recommend also that sections A, B, C, and D, which were referred to, of section 110, be dropped out entirely.

In the interest of the users of libraries, we are deeply concerned also over what seems to have been an oversight in amending the bill. Apparently, due to the shift from protection under the "not-for-profit" principle, classroom teachers have given a special subsection in the bill (504(c)(2)) permitting the court to remit statutory damages when a teacher is convicted of infringement, but shows that he had reasonable ground for believing that what he had done was "fair use." We believe the same benefit should be available for librarians in nonprofit libraries, and urge strongly that they be included in this provision, and I have submitted prepared wording for this. We think librarians and teachers should be in the same boat.

In the matter of duration, we urge a return to the present system of 28 plus 28 years, over three times as long as a patent.

The duration of the term of copyright has had continuous growth over the years, outstripping patents by a large proportion, according to Mr. Verner Clapp, president of the Council on Library Resources, in an unpublished talk before the Ad Hoc Committee of Educational Organizations on Copyright Law Revision at a meeting in Washington on March 1. This withholding from the public domain is even less tolerable when it is accompanied by tightened restrictions on "fair use." Hitherto, if we had the privilege of making fair use, the matter of extent of domain was not a primary consideration. But if fair use is to be so restricted and then so much more is to be put under the restriction, we certainly object.

The extension is posited on the arguments that it would conform to European practice, and would compensate for increased life expectancy of authors. If European practice is the criterion for copyright law and they start putting the taxes on the library lending because it is European practice, we certainly will be in serious difficulty.

A study by the Copyright Office showed that at the expiration of the present 28-year term only 15 percent are renewed for the second 28-year term. Obviously, the change of term to life of the author plus 50 years, throws a blanket over everybody for the benefit of a very few.

In any event it leaves to the would-be readers and users the almost impossible task of running down death dates of obscure authors through uncooperative or defunct publishers.

It is ironic that the proposed term would extend far beyond the physical life of the paper on which most books are published nowadays.

I would propose that, under the law, libraries be given the same right to reproduce books on deteriorating paper as they have manuscripts on deteriorating paper.

The bill provides for the reproduction of works in archival collections for preservation and security. When the paper is crumbling, we would be permitted to make copies to preserve what otherwise would disappear. If the duration of copyright in published works is to extend to 75 or 100 years, which is far beyond the physical endurance of printing papers now in current use, published works must also be explicitly included in section 108. Here again I must repeat that this is an age of mass production. Single, one-at-a-time copies cannot be made and I don't believe can ever be made as cheaply as copies produced in quantity. No library is going to make copies whenever originals can be obtained. But when the publisher ceases to supply original copies, or supplies them in forms that keep deteriorating every year, the very needs of the future require us to make security copies in permanent form.

PROPOSALS FOR A CLEARINGHOUSE AND A REGULATORY COMMISSION

To our protests made in congressional hearings that the new bill is unduly restrictive we have received replies that what is needed is a clearinghouse and a continuing regulatory commission to help "work things out."

Presumably a clearinghouse, such as ASCAP, could license libraries for a modest fee. But there should be no need for libraries to have such licenses. I believe there should be no fee. There is no guarantee that a fee would remain modest. No workable proposal on such a clearinghouse has even been advanced. The task of equitable collection and distribution of fees would be a stupendous one, costing far more to operate than the fees collected.

To those who would be affected by the new restrictions, especially on computer uses and facsimile transmissions, the suggestion has been made that the bill should include provision for setting up a continuing commission to issue appropriate regulations, and resolve some of the conflicting interests after the law is passed.

STATEMENT OF PROF. ERWIN C. SURRENCY, CHAIRMAN, JOINT LIBRARIES COMMITTEE ON COPYRIGHT OF THE AMERICAN LIBRARIES ASSOCIATION, SPECIAL LIBRARIES ASSOCIATION, MUSIC LIBRARY ASSOCIATION, AND AMERICAN ASSOCIATION OF LAW LIBRARIES

Mr. SURRENCY. Mr. Chairman, I am Prof. Erwin C. Surrency. I am professor of law and law librarian at Temple University, Philadelphia, Pa. I represent the Joint Libraries Committee on Copyright.

The Joint Libraries Committee on Copyright has developed, by stages, from a committee established in 1956 by the Association of Research Libraries to survey library practices with respect to photocopying. When the revision of the copyright law came before Congress, this committee's terms of reference were expanded by their constituent organizations to study the proposed bill and represent the interests of libraries. The committee has representatives from the American Library Association, Special Libraries Association, Music Library Association, and the American Association of Law Libraries. A representative of this committee, Mr. Rutherford D. Rogers, testified before the Committee on the Judiciary of the House of Representatives. As the present chairman, I am here today to represent these organizations and to urge certain modifications of the copyright bill as it now exists.

This committee feels that it is in a unique position to testify on the behalf of users of copyright materials for only in libraries do we bring the users of the copyrighted materials and the written materials together. The libraries constitute a large segment of the publishers' market. For the advancement of ideas and knowledge, the copyright bill ought to give the users a few more privileges than that of merely buying books. Librarians feel that having bought a book, their expenditures entitle them to use that material. We are not interested in taking away any of the remunerations enjoyed by authors for we feel that libraries and schools have contributed greatly to the financial well-being of both groups. We do feel that the objective of any printed work is to inform. Hence, any interference with this process should be seriously considered by your committee before it is enacted into law. We do not subscribe to the Register of Copyright's views that the rights of authors should be stated in the statute in broad terms for, if an exclusive right exists under the statute, a reasonable bargain will be made for its use.

We feel that the fallacy of this argument is clearly demonstrated by the licensing practices of those agencies from whom one must obtain permission to perform musical and dramatic pieces. Their fees are generally a set amount, and are not based upon such factors as anticipated attendance or the type of audience. You pay the fee or you do not obtain permission to perform the piece. These fees are often beyond the budget of music departments of schools.

The joint library committee is interested in the duration of copyright, in single copying of copyright works, in overstated copyright claims, and in giving librarians the same relief as that accorded to teachers.

Duration: The first problem is the matter of duration. My committee realizes that the fundamental assumption that ran through the testimony of many of the individuals who testified before the House was the fact that the present provision of life plus 50 years would be enacted. Further, this committee was advised that it should not attempt to raise this question. However, the committee considers this matter of vital importance and feels that it should express its views on this subject.

The committee recommends that Congress enact a single period of copyright duration. We emphasize that we do not want to specify any particular period. However, we do feel that the life plus 50 years formula has many disadvantages in administering the copyright laws.

The Copyright Office has testified that there are basically two reasons for this provision. First, this is the standard provision in the laws of other countries. Because of instantaneous communications today, the Register feels that this country must come into line. Two, authors live for a longer period today than they did when the present law was adopted and hence, should be protected for a longer period of time. It is significant that originally the Copyright Office favored a fixed period. We can only speculate as to the reasons for the change.

We would like to call to the attention of the committee that nowhere has anyone presented any empirical data on the administration of the Copyright Act in these countries, and neither has anyone presented any data to show that a fixed term has any disadvantages in administration. In fact, very little is known on the actual administration of the Copyright Acts because most of our knowledge is based upon court decisions, and I might add, administrative actions of the Register's Office, which as lawyers all know, does not represent the broad view of the operation of any particular area of law. From my experience, I would say that threatening letters—and here I think this is a matter of degree, the word "threatening," but certainly when someone sends me a letter saying he is going to take me into court, I consider that a threatening letter—are sent without just cause. Because of the unfamiliarity of the bar generally with copyright problems, a practice claimed by the publishers to be an infringement is discontinued in our schools, colleges, and libraries on the mere basis of these letters. No public institution can afford a lawsuit to substantiate its legal position in an area which it feels, wrongly, I want to add, is unimportant. Boards of trustees, school boards, library boards, all feel they have far more important matters to consider than a single alleged infringement of the Copyright Act. The fixed term has been a part of our law since the first Copyright Act and before it is changed, I would like to be sure that the provision we are getting works better than the one we are giving up.

It is submitted that anyone in the United States ought to be able to look at copyright notice and from that information alone know whether the copyright is still valid or whether it has expired. However, the user is put on notice as to the publication date and in the event that he is interested in pursuing it further, he can then make a definite request from the copyright holder. Under the present life-plus-50-years formula, the user must look up biographical sources to determine the author's death date. Libraries are asked information daily about copyrights—in some types of libraries more than in others.

Many individuals have argued before other committees and in print that there is no problem in determining whether a particular author is dead. In fact, one author indicates that she had no problem with this for all she did was call up the New York Public Library for a definitive answer. Unfortunately, we are not all near the New York Public Library for this free service.

In effect, the present bill does provide for a fixed period. Section 302(e) provides that after 75 years from the year of the first publication of a work, anyone who writes to the Copyright Office and obtains a certificate to the effect that there is nothing in the records of that Office to indicate that the author is living, the writer is entitled to the benefit of presumption that the author has been dead for at least 50 years. "Reliance and good faith upon this presumption shall be a complete defense to any action for infringement under this title." It is submitted that this provision, in effect, adopts a fixed term. If a fixed term was adopted in the bill, this would relieve the necessity of the Copyright Office becoming a place for the registeration of vital statistics.

This committee was informed that it had not made out a case for a fixed period when it testified previously before the House. The majority of librarians feel very strongly that such a fixed period would make the administration of law far easier than the present formula. How we can make views stronger, or how we can impress this committee has been debated among ourselves, and my appearance here is our solution. We strongly urge our views upon this committee in the strongest possible way and we sincerely hope that the committee will consider our arguments in any deliberation on the copyright bill.

The next most important factor in a library is the problem of single copying.

In reading the testimony presented before this committee, and the committee of the House of Representatives, it becomes apparent that the chief fear of the writers and publishers is the new devices coming on the market which make copying of materials relatively easy. Granted that there are new copying machinnes which make single copies easily, there are certain factors which limit their use in a library.

The first of these limitations is economics. Single copying of books will never be as inexpensive as purchasing the original copy. None of the machines which I have seen, can copy for less than 4½ cents per page and this figure does not include the labor involved, and neither is this 4½ cents per page figure accurate for it does not include the materials for the machine; paper, fluids, and so forth. A 200-page book, using the 4½-cent figure would cost $9 to reproduce and all you would have is 200 loose pages that must be held together. A good notebook cost $1.50 or a binding job would be $4; hence, the cost to the user is nearly double the cost of the book of this size. Those of us in libraries prefer to order a book rather than reproduce the book in this fashion.

A second factor is that rarely do any of the copies made by these machines become a part of any permanent collection of books. These copies are generally used by students or scholars and then discarded when their need has passed. In other words, single copying in a library is a simplified form of note taking.

The limits of copying within the concept of fair use is a matter of uncertainty, even for the Copyright Office. The committee urges that a provision under section 107 be included which states that making a single copy within libraries for the use of scholars is within the concept of fair use.

We are told that photocopying in lieu of note taking in libraries is now recognized as fair use without objection being voiced by the publishers. We are warned that—

It has become clear * * * that the unrestrained use of photocopying * * * going far beyond the recognized limits of fair use, may severely curtail the copyright owner's market for copies of his work.

As a librarian, I can assure you that I have had publishers come into my library to investigate what materials we were photocopying and try to encourage us to stop all activity in this field. The mere enactment of the present bill will encourage threats of lawsuits over this matter. I cannot see institutions litigating this matter to establish the practice under the doctrine of fair use. Librarians feel that we would like to have some protection and not be forced to negotiate from a weak position.

Another question that has been raised is what constitutes single copying. I have known occasions where in the course of the day, several users have copied the same material without being aware that anyone else in the library has done so. I cannot control what the users in my library are willing to pay 10 cents per page to copy during the day. I submit and argue strongly that these practices are certainly within the concept of fair use.

These single copying machines have been beneficial to librarians in a number of ways. It has cut down on the number of volumes which have been mutilated in our libraries by users taking excerpts by the use of a knife. If for no other reason, I encourage the use of single copying machines.

I do not think that anyone can substantiate the claim that such copying diminished the sales of any publication. A recent sampling of users of the photocopy machine in my library indicated that none of the users of the photocopy machine would have bought the item if the machine had not been available. They were merely using the machine to take notes and have this material to use in their work. The students I questioned in this survey had a twinkle in their eyes which led me to be concerned for the library books if this machine had not been available.

There is one final reason why single copying should be recognized under this present bill. The Constitution grants Congress the power to pass copyright and patent bills to "promote progress of science and the useful arts." Certainly, to carry forward this purpose, authors and scholars must be encouraged to write, without needing advice on whether to copy or how much to copy. And neither should undue economic burdens, as the proposed fee per page, be placed upon this use. It must be recognized that writers of fiction get their ideas from observation and create a novel in the quiet of their apartments. For all nonfictional writing, the author must have access to the works of others and must have this material with him when he begins the actual process of writing. Instead of requiring him to laboriously write out his notes in longhand, why not recognize the easier way of allowing him to make copies of the pages or material he wants to use later in his writing. This can be done without economic harm.

The original purpose of this committee which I represent was to study the matter of photocopying in libraries in relation to the Copyright Act. The committee had some conferences with the publishers and was unable to reach a satisfactory agreement. We have been urged by the Copyright Office to continue our dialog with the publishers in the hope of reaching an agreement, and we will do so. I do not believe that an agreement will be possible, as it has not been possible over the years that it has been discussed.

This committee made the following findings and recommendations concerning single-copy photocopying which has been adopted by several library associations and libraries as a policy:

Recommendations:
The Committee recommends that it be library policy to fill an order for a single photocopy of any published work or any part thereof. Before making a copy of an entire work, a library should make an effort by consulting standard sources to determine whether or not a copy is available through normal trade channels.

Our committee strongly urges that the facts of life concerning single copying be recognized in this bill. We do not believe that recognition of this practice would in any way adversely affect the publishers or writers, but would go a long way in making clear the necessity for this practice and its acceptability.

The present bill in section 504(c) (2) provides that—

Where an instructor in a nonprofit educational institution who infringed by reproducing a copyrighted work in copies or photorecords for use in the course of face-to-face teaching activities in a classroom or similar place normally devoted to instruction, sustains the burden of proving that he believed and had reasonable grounds for believing that the reproduction was a fair use under Section 107 the court in its discretion may remit the statutory damages in whole or in part.

The librarians feel that they should be given this same exemption for they are as much involved in the educational process as teachers. This committee urges that librarians be included in this exemption along with educators.

DETERIORATING MATERIAL

One critic of modern civilization has observed that few things are built or made to last. This is certainly true of books which are often printed on papers which will not last 100 years. Very often, these books are not available in any reprint form because their demand does not justify the expenditure of reprinting. For this reason, the Joint Committee on Copyright requests that Congress grant to librarians the same privilege allowed archivists in section 108 to reproduce entire works for the purposes of preservation without infringement. This protection is certainly needed by libraries who are faced with the problem of preserving books for the use of future scholars.

Librarians are and have been concerned with copyright problems. During the course of their normal working day, they are often asked questions involving uses of copyright and materials, especially those librarians who are heads of libraries attached in institutions of learning and public libraries. Librarians who are heads of music departments which loan music for public performances are often queried whether an item is within the public domain. Many of the problems which we face are not discussed and determinable from this act under consideration.

There is little doubt that the novels of Scott, Dickens, and the other novelists of the 19th century, are now within the public domain, yet anyone who enters a bookstore and buys a copy of the reprint edition of these novels clearly sees a copyright notice inserted by the publisher. A new sheet of Beethoven's music that you could buy in any music store bears a copyright notice. But what this copyright covers has always been a confusing matter among librarians and, I am certain, among users. The only practical solution that a librarian can give is to advise the user to make certain that he uses the original version which is clearly within the public domain. However, if such an original copy is not available—for very few libraries have first editions of novels and other writings and sheets of original music—then such a course of action is impossible.

Therefore it is seriously urged that the committee consider inserting a provision into the copyright act requiring that the copyright notice give a general idea of what materials are claimed to be covered by the registered copyright. Our committee does not think that this is a burdensome requirement as this should not take any more than a couple of sentences. We are not urging that the copyright be voided or that the copyright holder lose any rights that he may obtain because of the failure of the notice to be technically accurate. We are merely asking that a notice be inserted to give us, the user, an idea of what materials are claimed protected under the Copyright Act. Scholars would like to know to whom credit for an idea should be given. The registration form should include a more extensive description than should the printed notice.

It is the feeling of our committee that such a requirement is not a burdensome one. If we accept the idea that the copyright bill should protect the public as well as the copyright owner, it is inconceivable that one could object to such a requirement. You will note that the request is limited only to those works which are known to be within the public domain.

CONCLUSIONS

Librarians in a sense are salesmen of the published work, whether it be books, magazines, maps, photographed records, et cetera. All libraries have an interest in promoting literary works by use of displays, bringing libraries closer to the user, advising readers on materials to read, and my indexing and preserving our literary heritage. In fact, some studies show that such programs are successful in increasing the use of books. This often results in the readers buying some books for their own use. We are informed by the register of copyrights that displays of books and other copyrighted materials are protected by section 109(b) which permits libraries to display copyright materials in exhibit cases. For this, we are grateful.

The whole problem of copyright would be obliviated, if an invention which a publisher friend of mine suggested, was ever perfected. His idea was that there should be an ink that would automatically disappear as the reader read.

In conclusion, I would like to stress that our committee feels that a change should be made in the duration of the copyright under this bill, a provision should be included to accept the idea of single copying of items within a library, the bill should recognize the rights of libraries to single copy an entire work for preservation, and finally, that librarians be included in the exemption now afforded the teacher. The librarians of this country are engaged in preserving all forms of printed materials and recordings of every description for future generations of scholars, and these activities are supported by public funds. It is not our purpose to injure financially the writers of these works, but rather it is our business to see that the materials are used and used according to the laws of this country. We have nothing to gain, but plenty to lose if the copyright bill in any way limits or discourages the freedom of use of the printed thoughts of mankind. We have no other way to make our wants and our feelings known to Congress other than by our appearance here at this hearing. We know of no other way to make our points emphatic. We rest assured that our statements will be taken into consideration by this committee in its deliberations in finally framing a copyright bill, which weighs the needs of the publisher and writer and includes protection to those who seek to educate and encourage the use of materials.

Mr. SURRENCY. Mr. Chairman, I have attached three forms for proposed language to incorporate the material which we have suggested.

Senator MCCLELLAN (presiding). These are suggested amendments.

Mr. SURRENCY. Yes, sir.

Senator MCCLELLAN. Very well. They may be received and printed in the record.

(The documents referred to follow:)

PROPOSED AMENDMENT TO SECTION 108, S. 597, GRANTING TO LIBRARIES PERMISSION TO REPRODUCE BOOKS FOR PRESERVATION

Notwithstanding the provisions of section 106, it is not an infringement of copyright for a nonprofit institution, having custody of books of value to scholarly research, which have deteriorated and cannot be used in their present condition without further mutilation, to reproduce, without any purpose of direct or indirect commercial advantage, for purposes of preservation and security.

PROPOSED AMENDMENT TO SECTION 504 (2) GRANTING EXEMPTION TO LIBRARIES

504 (c) (3) Where a library in a nonprofit institution, infringed by reproducing a copyrighted work for use in the library or elsewhere for one of its users, or for its own purposes, believing that this reproduction was within fair use under section 107, or any other provision of this act, the court will remit all damages.

PROPOSED NEW SECTION TO S. 597 TO REQUIRE NOTICE OF NEW MATERIALS IN WORKS WITHIN THE PUBLIC DOMAIN FOR WHICH A COPYRIGHT NOTICE HAS BEEN INSERTED

401 (d) A notice affixed to a work which is within the public domain and which is not subject to be registered under this act either by the author or the owner of the copyright, shall contain a statement of the subject matter for which the benefits of this act are claimed.

Copyright Law Revision
Hearings, 1967
Part 3

STATEMENT OF NORTON GOODWIN, ATTORNEY

Mr. Goodwin. Mr. Chairman and members of the committee:

My name is Norton Goodwin. I am an attorney but do not come here representing the views of any group with an interest in copyright law revision. In the interests of time I shall read my statement. In the course of my remarks I shall ask leave to have inserted in the record certain documents, copies of which I have submitted to the committee staff.

I find it encouraging that within the past few months, the question of clearinghouse systems for the right to reproduce and distribute copies of text has been the subject of increasing concern among members of the American Patent Law Association's Information Retrieval Committee, and members of subcommittee 5 of committee 304 of the American Bar Association. There is growing evidence of a concensus in some sort of a system of permissions and payments, with accounting features, analogous to the licensing for phonograph records.

The statement on the use of copyright materials by means of computers presented on Tuesday by Mr. Brown Morton on behalf of the Board of the Interuniversity Communications Council (EDUCOM) indicates a willingness on the part of educational institutions or libraries to continue to pay for the copyrighted works required to carry out their characteristic functions.

Even more encouraging is the fact that EDUCOM is seeking exempt access to copyrighted materials only "in the absence of clearinghouse devices." In earlier testimony before the subcommittee, a question has been raised as to whether there is a need at this time for specific legislation for the right to reproduce and distribute copies of text registered under a clearinghouse system. The question raised by these previous witnesses is directed, not to the need for a clearinghouse system, but to the ability of the Congress to define the operation of the system in such a way that it will be adequate to take care of needs of present technology and also for computer technologies which may arise.

I take the view that there is a present need and that a system of longstanding validity can be implemented. I submit for your consideration at this time such a statutory provision creating such a system. It is drafted to secure the right to reproduce and distribute copies of copyrighted material in technologies requiring copies to be made by third parties beyond the control of the copyright owner if, as, and when required. I submit the proposed amendment as an additional section 117 amending S. 597, to be appended at the end of my remarks as appendix A.

I submit comment on the operation of the proposed section 117 as appendix B and request the inclusion of both in the record at the end of my remarks.

In the kind of made-to-order copymaking technology that would result from the kind of clearinghouse legislation I am proposing, libraries and information retrieval centers would be in a position to respond to telephone requests for copies of specific text. They could furnish what the user really is looking for in an inexpensive airmail duplicate microform. They could also, in appropriate cases, transmit the text electronically. They could transmit a picture of the text as a facsimile or send an encodement for printout on a teletype machine.

Up to now, book publishers—people who publish in the form of legible text on paper—have enjoyed an effective monopoly in assuring copyright protection for the written word. Copyright legislation that would provide effective protection of proprietary rights in a made-to-order copy technology could create important competition. Another way of describing this kind of competition is paperless publishing. It is so described in the following advertising headline that appeared in a full-page ad in the Wall Street Journal, Thursday, December 1, 1966:

Break through! National Cash Register introduces practical paperless publication! A microform system that lets you publish 3,200 pages on a 4-by-6-inch transparency, send it anywhere for a nickel and read it full size when it gets there, again and again.

National Cash Register now quotes "made-to-order" duplicates of transparencies of this kind at about $1. At this rate, the cost advantage of large press runs for books is undercut by a factor of at least 10 to 1.

The subcommittee should bear in mind that witnesses who take a position that the time is not yet ripe for legislation that will permit the public to enjoy made-to-order copying of copyrighted materials may be strongly motivated to forestall what clearly represents a serious economic threat.

The effect of statutory provisions for a clearinghouse system for licensing the right to reproduce and distribute copies of text need not adversely affect the interest of publishers who wish to participate. One of the important benefits of enrolling text in the system is the effect this would have on exposure to fair-use copymaking activity. I have explained why such a system should be attractive to book publishers in a paper entitled: "Automated information storage and retrieval—Permissions and payments", which I presented on January 16, 1967, at an American University Institute on Printing and Publishing—Management of automation. I ask permission to have the text of that talk printed in the record at the end of my statement as exhibit 1.

Some witnesses, speaking on behalf of book publishers, have contended that the Congress must wait to see how computers are used before it can draft legislation regulating computer uses of copyrighted matter. My position has always been the exact opposite. I have had 10 years' experience in using computers for the purpose of processing data to appear in the form of printed text. I have always contended that the relationship between the computer and the meaning of human communications is fortuitous and that the relationship between words and the forms in which they are recorded and transferred inside the computer is trivial. I have always maintained that copyright rules must first be spelled out before it becomes economical to attempt to use electronics for the distribution of copyrighted matter.

With the consent of the committtee, I herewith submit as exhibit 2, to be reproduced at the end of my remarks a letter on this very point which I wrote on April 13, 1965, to the then U.S. Commissioner of Education, Mr. Francis Keppel.

At that time I was aware of vast sums of Federal money being poured into educational research. I was concerned lest the taxpayers' money be spent on hardware for computer-assisted education before copyright rules needed to protect proprietary interests in the necessary program material were first clearly defined.

It was my position then, and it is my position now, that "we have no way of knowing at this time what kind of 'hardware' will be appropriate until the Congress enacts legislation that will permit the producers of information in magnetic tape, graphic film, or other technical format to receive compensation based on a measure of the use of their publications. Money poured into hardware at this point is sheer waste. When we are assured of lawful access to information stored in technical format, and when we see in what format the information appears in the marketplace, we can then spend money on equipment."

One of the tactics that has been used to divert this subcommittee's attention from the fundamental question of clearinghouse licensing has been to attempt to explain digital computer technology. In my opinion, a discussion on digital computer technology is irrelevant to the question of providing public access to text enrolled in a clearinghouse system or of made-to-order reproduction rights for libraries and other information centers.

I know of no plans at the National Bureau of Standard's clearinghouse for Federal scientific and technical information to use computers to provide access to the technical report literature it disseminates. I checked this out last Thursday with Mr. Peter Urbach, the clearinghouse deputy chief of systems. He confirmed my impression and stated that he knew of no such plans in the Defense Department's Defense Documentation Center, either.

Both the Clearinghouse for Federal Scientific and Technical information and the comparable Defense Documentation Center are thoroughly committed to programs for making copies of technical documents on a made-to-order basis. There are detailed Federal standards to make this kind of reproduction and distribution of copies fast, effective, and cheap.

One such set of standards relates to microfiche. A microfiche is a particular kind of microform in which the images of about 60 pages of text can be recorded on a 4- by 6-inch area of film. The Federal microfiche standards to which I refer are on this particular mircofiche I hold in my hand. To read it, I simply place it in a standard viewer and move it to the first page. There is the title page. The viewer is not a computer. As you can see, it permits me to view text that is in a form I could not otherwise read. The retail price of this particular viewer is about $125. It is estimated that in volume production, it can be marketed for about $35. Similar viewers are being made by National Cash Register that permit viewing microimages at a reduction of 150 to 1 and are leased from NCR at $10 per month.

You see before you elements of a fully developed system for storing and communicating text that is presently denied to the public as a means for gaining access to copyrighted information. It has nothing to do with computers. In it, images of text are stored in a form requiring the use of a device to be legible. The current cost to the Federal Clearinghouse of making a diazo duplicate is between 8 and 10 cents. The cost is the same whether the 4- by 6-inch microfiche contains 60 pages or 2,000 pages of text.

I cannot accept the conclusion that has been urged upon you that "the first significant technological break-through in the methods for storing and distributing information since the innovation of the printing press was development of computerized information networks." You see before you a technology currently being used in commerce in which the cost per page of text in a made-to-order reproduction can range from one-tenth to one one-hundredth the cost at which the same text can be manufactured in mass production on the most advanced presses of the day.

There is at present no copyright provision adequate to secure property rights in this existing technology. The form in which the text is stored is not legible without the use of a machine or device and when in such forms, text is peculiarly vulnerable to unauthorized copymaking. Systematic identification of authorized copies is needed to deter piracy.

One witness has undertaken to describe the state of the art of computer uses of copyrighted materials in an effort to demonstrate that it is not possible at this time to draft legislation regulating computerized uses of copyrighted materials. The witness suggests as an example an application involving word recognition. The frequency with which an author uses particular words in a particular order can sometimes be associated with the characteristic literary style of that author. The use of a computer to count word frequency is a trivial application. It does not represent scholarly application, or even a true analysis, since the computer does not understand the meaning of the text.

The truth of the matter is that computers have thus far failed in every application where it has been necessary to understand the meaning of text. It was for this reason that the Automatic Language Processing Advisory Committee of the National Academy of Sciences-National Research Council, in its 1966 Report No. 1416, advised against spending further Federal funds in an effort to secure fully automatic machine translation from one human language to another. Permit me to incorporate, by reference, the text of that report, entitled: "Language and Machines," to document my conclusion that scholarly analysis is not a practical computerized use of copyrighted materials.

Indexing and abstracting were included in the second category of potential computer uses of copyrighted text, along with printout of text. As a member of the publication board of a scientific abstracting journal, I have considerable knowledge in this area and suggest that there is no evidence that a computer can do any better at producing acceptable abstracts than at fully automatic translation.

Competent abstracts require expert understanding of the subject matter under discussion and a familiarity with all the bibliographic references. Computer abstracting faces the same semantic barrier that fully automatic language translation does. It is doubtful if computers will ever be competitive with human abstractors. In any event, I have never heard of any proposal to draft legislation regulating human abstracting of copyrighted materials. I see no need for concern for computerized abstracting of copyrighted materials.

Computers cannot efficiently store text in legible form, neither can information centers in which human operators make copies for either mail or wire transmission. If we define the prerequisite that brings text within a statutory licensing system in terms of distributing copies to the public in forms that cannot be read without the aid of a machine or device, we bring within the control of the system, not only present technology for making microfiche duplicates, for transmitting text over the telephone by facsimile, and for transmitting text over communication lines in code, but we also control all computer applications for the reproduction and distribution of copies of text now known or later to be developed.

The third computer application category that the witness suggested as a matter for copyright concern was computer-assisted education. A computer-assisted program consists in a collection of text responses which the computer files and stores by number and, in addition, a small operating program. The student is instructed to select and push the right keys in response to the text he has before him. The operating program then decides mechanically which of the stored text selections should be printed out in response to this key signal. There is nothing new about text that contains material from which selected portions are to be read in accordance with operating instructions. The Book of Common Prayer is an excellent example. The particular selections of text that are appointed to be read under particular circumstances are controlled by rubrics written in italics. In the "Order of Morning Prayer," according to the use of the Protestant Episcopal Church, the following is a typical rubric:

Here, if it hath not already been said, shall follow the Lord's Prayer.

In exactly the same way, a computer-assisted educational program will mechanically produce printout No. 87 in response to a signal from the student console, if the operating program calls for this response.

I regard operational computer programs as being subject to copyright protection only as text or the equivalent of text. Such is the view advanced by the Inter-university Council on Communications—EDUCOM—last Tuesday. I see no difference between the copyright problem of text and rubrics in a computer-assisted program and the problem of controlling the printout of any text.

I want to emphasize here that the proposed licensing system is restricted to the right to reproduce and distribute appropriately registered works. The reasons why no system for clearinghouse licensing for the ephemeral display of text is proposed at this time are based on significant communications cost differences. This is explained in greater detail in a paper on "Intellectual Property in Automated Information Systems" which I presented on March 14, 1967, to the Patent and Proprietary Information Committee, Electronic Industries Association, which I offer as exhibit 3 to be printed in the record at the end of my remarks.

Although I am not urging specific legislation on behalf of any body or group, I do have colleagues in the Society of Photographic Scientists and Engineers who share a responsibility I have in assuring subscriber revenue for the publication of a technical journal. They also share my concern for the need to control and to account for automated dissemination of proprietary text. I request inclusion in the record as exhibit 4 at the end of my remarks a letter of March 21, 1967, from Dr. Deane R. White of E. I. du Pont de Nemours & Co., Inc., Photo Products Department, expressing that concern as chairman of the publications board, "Abstracts of Photographic Science and Engineering Literature."

On April 20, 21, and 22 of this year, American University is conducting a Seminar on Intellectual Property in Automated Systems: Permissions and Payments. I am looking forward to the opportunity of listening to and participating in the dialog at that seminar.

I request leave to file a further statement for the record after that meeting. I understand that the record will be kept open until at least the first day of May.

I have come to the end of my prepared statement. It was scheduled for presentation last Tuesday. On listening to the various witnesses on Tuesday, I found many of the witnesses seeking special exemptions appeared to be poorly informed as to the cost of disseminating knowledge. Some witnesses have erroneously assumed that the cost of mass-produced printed text is lower than the cost of made-to-order copies of equivalent text in graphic microforms.

Other witnesses have appeared seeking special exemptions for computer applications without any supporting evidence on the economic feasibility of such applications or the cost of computer time. No testimony has been introduced concerning the economics of transmitting knowledge at a distance by means of electronics.

For the purpose of documenting the cost of electronic library networks, I would like to incorporate by reference in the record of this hearing a paper on "Library Communications" by J. W. Emling and J. R. Harris, of the Bell Telephone Laboratories, Inc., and H. M. McMains, of the American Telephone & Telegraph Co., that appears on page 203 and following, of the proceedings of the 1963 Conference on Libraries and Automation, published in 1964 by the Library of Congress as "Libraries and Automation."

I offer in evidence a number of microfiche copies of the paper on "Library Communications." They were made to order by the Defense Documentation Center. They were made by the low-cost diazo duplicating process. It is increasingly apparent that some sort of a system of permissions and payments, with accounting features, must be provided if the public is to benefit from low-cost, made-to-order copying technologies now being used by Government agencies for disseminating knowledge.

It is impossible to evaluate the cost of operating a particular clearinghouse system except in terms of its own operating specifications. One of Tuesday's witnesses, speaking on behalf of libraries, said, and I quote:

No workable proposal on such a clearinghouse system has ever been advanced. The task of equitable collection and distribution of fees would be a stupendous one, costing far more to operate than the fees collected.

In rebuttal, I would like to offer for the record, as exhibit 5 to appear at the end of my remarks, an excerpt from a paper on "Statutory Licensing of Literary Works," which I presented at the 1965 Symposium on Photography in Information Storage and Retrieval, sponsored by the Society of Photographic Scientists & Engineers and the Office of the Chief of Research and Development, Department of the Army.

In this excerpt, I estimated a 2½-cent operating cost per 10-cent fee collected. Last December, I referred this question of operating costs to Harvey J. McMains, one of the authors of the paper on "Library Communications," referred to above, and to his associate, Dr. Milton E. Terry, and found them to be in substantial agreement.

It seems to me that the public interest in getting cheap efficient access to copyrighted knowledge via electronics and graphic microform is so great that the committee may wish to call in expert testimony on specific proposals for clearinghouse systems such as the one defined in proposed section 117. The leading authorities on information clearinghouse systems are here in Washington in the Defense Documentation Center, the Federal Clearinghouse for Technical and Scientific Information, the Atomic Energy Commission, and the National Aeronautics and Space Administration. I will be happy to furnish the committee with the names and telephone numbers of the clearinghouse systems specialists in these agencies.

In closing, I would like to point out some patent and antitrust consequences of letting the present bill go through as it is without providing for compulsory licensing for nonlegible forms of literary works. The March 10, 1967, issue of Time magazine, on page 85, documents the recent acquisition of Holt, Rinehart, & Winston, a publishing house, for an estimated $275 million of CBS stock. Other acquisitions and mergers calculated to put the control of copyrighted knowledge into the hands of electronics firms are documented in the story.

If these firms are not compelled to license the right to reproduce and distribute copies of their copyrighted holdings stored in the computer, or in graphic microform, they will be in a position to selectively license those customers who favor their patented hardware.

They will, in effect, be in a position to use their lawful copyright monopolies to unlawfully extend the period in which they are entitled to enjoy patent monopolies.

I urge upon you the public interest in forestalling such a possibility by enacting at this time some sort of statutory clearinghouse system, along the lines of the proposed section 117.

I thank you for your courtesy and patience.

AMERICAN ASSOCIATION OF UNIVERSITY PROFESSORS

Professor John O. Stedman, of the law school at the University of Wisconsin and Chairman of the Special Committee on Copyright Law Revision of the

80,000 member American Association of University Professors, testified to a Senate subcommittee today that efforts to revise the Copyright Law should take into account current political, technological, and methodological developments that are altering the scope and character of higher education.

"Our educational system," he asserted, "is on the verge of—indeed, in the midst of—a virtual revolution in terms of its methodology, the scope of its activities, and public commitment to its broad and effective support." His statement emphasized that these unique developments made it imperative that legal rights relating to the production and use of knowledge be closely examined and imaginatively defined to promote modern educational objectives.

As a temporary measure, he recommended that the proposed revison of the Copyright Law provide maximum flexibility and freedom for adjustment, thus promoting the public interest in effective education, providing the necessary stimulus to educational writing and publication, and achieving equity between competing interests. College professors, he noted, often serve as both producers and users of knowledge and have a special stake in a balanced, "public interest" approach.

Professor Stedman indicated that the AAUP believes that, pending the development of more specific rules, the public interest will most likely be promoted by primary reliance upon a broadly conceived and liberally applied "fair use" yardstick. The AAUP statement also advocated immediate, thorough and continuing study of the special relationship between educational activities and copyright requirements, in order to keep the law abreast of the ever-changing public needs and innovations in education.

STATEMENT FOR AMERICAN ASSOCIATION OF UNIVERSITY PROFESSORS BY JOHN C. STEDMAN

My name is John C. Stedman. I am a Professor of Law, University of Wisconsin, and Chairman of the Special Committee on Copyright Law Revision of the American Association of University Professors. This Association is the largest organization of college and university teachers in the United States, with approximately 82,000 members, over 1,000 active chapters, and 49 state or regional segments. The Association was founded in 1915. It has been especially active in dealing with matters involving academic freedom. Funds for the operation of the Association are derived from membership dues and voluntary contributions.

The other members of our Copyright Law Revision Committee are Ralph S. Brown, Jr., Professor of Law, Yale University; Fritz Machlup, Professor of Economics, Princeton University; James E. Miller, Professor of English, University of Chicago; and Glen E. Weston, Professor of Law, George Washington University. Our report, as embodied in my statement today, has been approved by the Executive Committee of the Association's governing body, the Council, a thirty-member, nationally-elected group.

Let me say at the outset that our approach to S. 597 has been not solely that of the educator, but also that of the author and publisher. University professors are primarily teachers, but they also provide a substantial share of the writings used in teaching and extensively contribute to, and participate in the publication of, educational journals. So, we see the picture from both sides—at least we try to.

Without further ado, let me turn to S. 597 and our comments concerning it. Some preliminary observations are in order: Our specific recommendations are a response to the dramatic changes, as we see them, that are occurring in both the methods of teaching and the make-up of the student body. Our concern is whether S. 597 adequately takes these changes into account. Consequently, we deem it necessary, first, to explore briefly these modern developments that threaten the traditional balance between education interests and copyright interests; then to sketch, even more briefly, the provisions in S. 597 affecting this relationship, and finally to examine critically some of the premises and assumptions that seem to underlie these provisions. Against this background, our comments and suggestions will, we hope, make sense to your Committee.

A. TRADITIONAL EDUCATION-COPYRIGHT RELATIONSHIP, AND MODERN DEVELOPMENTS AFFECTING THIS RELATIONSHIP

Traditionally, the educational process has relied primarily upon classroom instruction—what the bill refers to as "face-to-face" teaching—using textbooks and supplemental reference books located in school libraries as the teaching materials. Students buy the textbooks and libraries buy the reference books. Both presumably pay a price sufficient to enable both the author and the publisher to reap a profit. Where profits are not forthcoming, as is often the case, the authors and publishers may receive their reward and stimulus from other sources, such as grants or subsidies, or in other forms, such as increased prestige and the satisfaction of contributing to knowledge.

There are shortcomings: The Procrustean approach makes things hard for the too-fast or too-slow student. Deprivation, in the educational sense, sometimes results where neither the individual nor his community can afford the materials needed for an adequate education. There are also safety valves: Note-taking and copying, some of it conceivably quite extensive, goes either undetected or overlooked, or is condoned through application of the "fair use" doctrine. Supplemental activities, especially in the area of music, are permitted under the not-for-profit exemption. On the whole, the system seems to have worked. At least, educational materials do get written and published—and copyrighted—and students and libraries do buy them and use them.

Modern developments have thrown the old balance out of order—or the old order out of balance. The traditional classroom, textbook approach still persists, of course, and will continue to do so. But it has been supplemented by developments that can only be described as revolutionary and whose ultimate posture, extent and significance we can perceive only dimly. Our teaching methods are changing. We are moving extensively and rapidly into "remote" instruction, mass instruction, individualized instruction, emphasis upon *learning* instead of *teaching*. Our student body is changing. It includes and will include more and more adult students, drop-outs, both shut-ins and shut-outs, retrainees, pre-school children, continuing education, specially constituted bodies of "exceptional" students (either exceptionally bright or exceptionally dull), and so on. Our teaching technology is changing. It includes, among other things, radio, television, computers, teaching machines, projectors with their variety of movie films, microfilm, etc., and remarkable facilities for copying and replicating. We even seem to be on the way to making education an entertaining and enjoyable experience.

The economics of teaching, as well as of preparing materials for use in teaching, are also changing. The amounts that governmental bodies, foundations and other public or quasi-public entities are spending on teaching and teaching materials, especially in the innovative areas referred to above, are many times the expenditures of the past, however niggardly they may be compared to expenditures in less important or constructive fields. With the increasing interest shown by the Federal Government, the dramatic proposals of the Ford Foundation and the Killian Committee, and so on, we may expect this growth to continue. The materials and equipment needed for such expanded activities, again especially in the new fields and with the new methods, are unbelievably voluminous and expensive as compared to the past. In other words, the preparation and production of the materials and equipment needed for modern education has become a big, fast-growing and presumably profitable business in the economic sense. Some of our largest, most-forward-looking corporations have recognized this by jumping with all four feet into the middle of a movement that they have ignored in the past.

It is against this backdrop that we must view the present struggles over the terms and policies of the new copyright law. There is the struggle between the producers who understandably wish to share in the profits, whatever they may be, resulting from these increased, innovative and better-supported activities, and the educators who, equally understandably, seek maximum freedom and flexibility in the use of these new materials, methods and approaches. There is also the struggle of this committee and the Kastenmeier committee in the House, to come up with a final version that satisfies the legitimate interests of both these groups and at the same time satisfies the overriding *public* interest in encouraging and improving these expanded educational activities. Achievement of this public objective, I should add, connotes skillfully steering between Scylla and Charybdis—the Scylla of overburdening education with unwarranted obstructions and expenses, and the Charybdis of treating the producers so ungenerously as to destroy or seriously damp their incentive to create and produce.

In the extensive hearings before both committees, the interests of both the educators and of the producers of material and equipment, have been ably presented and extensively explored. It is less clear that the broad public interest—an interest that must reflect a genuine *accommodation* of both these interests, and not just a mere *compromise* between them—has been as adequately presented to the committees or been adequately reflected in the bill as it now reads. The basis for our misgivings in this respect will become clear from a brief summary of the provisions of the bill affecting education and a critique of what we deem to be the premises and assumptions that underlie these provisions. To these, we now turn.

B. PROVISIONS OF S. 597 RELATING TO EDUCATION—AND THE PREMISES THAT UNDERLIE THEM

The broadest and most significant provision, from the educator's standpoint, is section 107, the "fair use" provision. It is a general catch-all, "rule of reason" type of provision, designed to permit a reasonable use and copying of protected works "for purposes such as criticism, comment, news reporting, teaching, scholarship, or research." "Reasonableness" is to be determined by looking to the purpose and character of the use, the nature of the work, how much of the protected work is used, and the effect upon the market for the work. The House Report (p. 32) makes clear its intent to incorporate unchanged the present judicial doctrine into the statute, at the same time keeping it sufficiently flexible to cope with the changing methods and technology to which I have previously referred.

Closely related to section 107, is section 504(c), which permits a court to relieve a teacher who reproduces copyrighted material for classroom instruction from liability for *statutory* damages upon proof that he reasonable believes such reproduction to be a "fair use." The section is quite limited in its application: It applies only to reproduction of materials, to teachers in non-profit educational institutions, and to face-to-face classroom teaching. The burden of proof rests upon the teacher and his belief must be "reasonable." Only statutory damages, not actual damages, are susceptible to remission, and whether there shall be any remission at all is up to the judge.

Four other sections are of direct relevance to educational activity. All of them, as we see it, are glosses upon the "fair use" concept, and supplemental to section 107—the enumeration, so to speak, of certain acts that are deemed to be a "fair use" *per se*.

Thus, section 108 permits the reproduction, within limits, of unpublished works in order to preserve them and to make them available for research.

Section 109(b) and (c) permit display of owned copies of copyrighted materials, but again within limits.

Section 110 is limited to performance and display, and does not extend to copying. It contains three subsections of relevance to us. Subsection (1) permits performance or display sharply limited to face-to-face classroom educational activity. Subsection (2) permits broadcasts, again strictly for educational purposes. Furthermore, a 100-mile-radius limit is imposed, making it unavailable for network broadcasting and certain computer uses; and the broadcaster must control the time, content and selection of the transmission, thus denying the benefits of the section to the computerized "teaching machine" and comparable approaches that are providing significant advances today in our educational methods. Subsection (4) permits non-profit face-to-face performances of non-dramatic materials.

Section 112 permits two ephemeral recordings of transmissions authorized by section 110(2), but only one of such recordings can be put to actual use and it must be destroyed within a year.

There are other provisions in the bill, such as sections 601 and 602, that have direct relevance to education, but the foregoing are the important ones and we limit our discussion to them.

What are we to make of the foregoing provisions? The bill, as drafted, makes some concessions to education. Its wording may cover some activities going beyond the limited rights that education now enjoys under the "fair use" doctrine of the present law, notwithstanding the House Report's explicit statement of intent *not* to go beyond existing "fair use" law. To the extent, however, that it opens the gates to the significant modern developments in education—library photocopying, TV, computers, general educational broadcasting, selective and individualized instruction in lieu of mass instruction, and so on—the bill moves hesitantly, gingerly and reluctantly, if it moves at all. This approach, let me emphasize, does not stem from any lack of understanding of these significant educational developments or lack of appreciation of their importance. On the contrary, in the hearings conducted by both committees and in the Report of the House Committee, a high degree of sensitivity to these matters is shown.

Rather, a perusal of the bill itself, together with the extensive, detailed and thoughtful commentary contained in the House Report, suggests that the bill is largely bottomed upon the following premises:

(1) The exclusive privilege of copying and using a creation belongs to the author or his assignee (typically, his publisher) as a matter of right—and any exception of educational usage constitutes an impairment of this right.

(2) Except as the salutary nature of educational activity may warrant some limited concessions, education should be treated the same, in applying the copyright law, as any other activity.

(3) Preservation of the traditional rights and limitations with respect to the use of copyrighted materials in traditional ways, with minimal concessions to the new methodology, will sufficiently meet the needs of modern educational activity.

(4) Where gaps still exist as between the conflicting interests, it is both feasible and consonant with public interest to rely upon voluntary compliance, voluntary settlement, and compromise.

There is nothing startling about these propositions. All of them have their proper place in proper circumstances. Their adoption is understandable, especially within the context of the hearings that were conducted and the preliminary background studies that were made. But are they fully tenable within the present framework? And do they provide a proper basis for a sound copyright law as it applies to educational activity? I will try to state, as briefly as I can, why we think the answer to both questions is "no."

1. THE "RIGHTS" OF THE COPYRIGHT OWNER

It is natural to think of the author as possessing "rights" in his creation. The very term "copyright" connotes such status and, *once Congress has spoken*, such "rights" do, indeed, exist. But use of the term is misleading and mischievous in the present context. It begs the very question that is at issue. Basic social philosophy recognizes no inherent *rights* as such in ideas or their expression. As one of our great jurists put it:

"Ideas, . . . though upon them all civilization is built, may never be 'owned.' The law does not protect them at all, but only their expression; and how far that protection shall go is a question of more or less." (Judge Learned Hand in RCA Mfg. Co. v. Whiteman, 114 F.2d 86, 90, 2nd Cir. 1940).

It is the policy question of "more or less," not the legal question of what *are* the author's rights *vis a vis* educational activity, that is now before your committee—and this is just as true when deciding how far the "fair use" doctrine shall go as in deciding how long the copyright term should be. And the matter is to be resolved, *and under the constitutional provision can only be resolved*, in terms of the following question:

"How much is it necessary and desirable to give to the author (and those in privity with him) in order to stimulate and encourage him to write and publish in the educational field?"

This is to be determined, not by generalized references to the "interests" of the author, or of the publisher, or of the teacher, but by a hard-headed look at the *effects* of granting or denying copyright protection of varying scope to the varying types of educational "writing." Since we do not find in the record any clear evidence on this point, we do not know what the answer is. We do suggest, however, that one cannot safely rely upon analogy to either non-educational activities or to the traditional educational activities of the past in arriving at an answer. Our reason for believing this to be so are indicated below.

2. *Difference between educational and other activities in relation to copyright*

It is easy and natural to assume that a book is a book, a sale is a sale, whether one is talking about Kaplan & Brown's *Cases on Copyright* or Jacquelin Susann's *Valley of the Dolls*. But there are many good reasons, both in terms of practical effect and in terms of public interest, for distinguishing educational activity from other activities when it comes to determining how far the copyright protection should be extended. There is a strong public purpose behind educational activity. It is also predominantly supported by public or quasi-public funds. To the extent, then, that copyright obstruction or the copyright levy prevents or decreases the usage of the more desirable materials, adds to the public cost of their usage, or prices given individuals out of the educational market, the public suffers. Worse still, it may suffer without the copyright owner enjoying any compensating gain, since the educational system, traditionally hard-up as it is and possessed of large discretion in deciding whether or not to use a given material, *may* simply respond to the assertion of a copyright toll by foregoing use of the material. Granted that this does not always happen in the educational arena, and also granted that these same reactions my occur in other areas, they seem more likely to occur in education than elsewhere.

And in any event, economic-induced deprivation of the opportunity to get the best education possible, whatever the subject or whatever the level, is likely to be a matter of greater legitimate concern than denial of access to copyright material in most other fields. Finally, the education process being what it, exposure of the public to given educational materials may often stimulate increased usage, and sales, of copyrighted materials generally—frequently, of the very materials to which the student has been exposed.

The distinctions we have here suggested have not, of course, gone unrecognized. We acknowledge them, without labeling them, in our present "fair use" doctrine which has provided an important safety valve for the educational process (p. 32), in our "not-for-profit" exemption of most performances and displays, and in our relaxed attitude toward library usages and practices. For that matter, the distinction is recognized in the present S. 597 but, in our opinion, insufficiently and haphazardly.

We are not suggesting, of course, that copyright protection may not be a useful and sometimes essential stimulus to educational writing and publication. Often it is, for instance, for the educational writer or publisher who is motivated by commercial considerations, and for the scholarly journals (even though non-profit oriented) whose only source of income may be their copyright-protected publication. These journals must be protected in their economic struggles to survive. So must be the University Presses whose contributions to education, research and scholarship are matched only by their financial stringencies. What bothers us is the tendency to lump all the varied categories into one indistinguishable mass and treat them all alike from the standpoint of copyright stimulus, whether they are educational materials that must depend upon income from sales, educational materials that do not depend upon such income, materials directed primarily to other markets but useful in education as well, or materials that have no relevance at all to education and educational activities.

3. *Application of copyright to modern teaching activities*

It is understandable and tempting simply to assume that a system that has worked reasonably well in the past will continue to work as well in the future. But for reasons we have already mentioned, the educational system of the future, in many of its aspects, is likely to bear little resemblance to that of the past. Nor, in many areas, are they any more similar in terms of the motivations, the stimuli and their economics.

The process of book publication and marketing is relatively simple, as compared to some of the modern activities. The publisher publishes what the author writes and tries to sell as many copies as he can. The access to a given copy is relatively limited, thus fostering the sale of multiple copies. Each item stands pretty much on its own feet and neither aids, nor is aided by, the sale of other copies or other writings. The price is moderate with the copyright providing protection against excessive copying and competing publication, but not against competitve substitutes.

The picture with respect to TV, computers, teaching machines and the like tends to be entirely different. High production costs, mass usage, the tie-in of hardware and software, manipulation of successive improvements to maintain a head start and competitive advantage far beyond the protected life of any single creation, the use of control over one product to promote the sale of another, possible refusals to sell, limitations upon production, and resort to leasing and service-for-a-fee instead of selling—all of these and more may introduce into this field problems not usually encountered in copyright, and more akin to those that arise in the patent area.

The complexities and varieties in this area, in terms of the ways in which the materials are used, how they are merchandized, what the stimuli for creating and producing them may be, and the difficulties involved in anticipating the unforeseeable developments in the future, are dramatically posed by the advent of the modern computer. The current developments in that complex field and the inadequacy of the present bill to cope with these developments have been extensively and competently presented to you by the EDUCOM representatives and related groups. Consequently, I will forgo further discussion of this subject, other than to say that we share their concern over the injection, without further thorough investigation, of copyright protection of indeterminate scope into the computer field and their objections to treating computer in-put as, in itself, constituting an actionable infringement of copyright.

It would be most unfortunate to freeze into law rules which, however adaptable to the past, are inappropriate to the future. In the very field at hand, the juke-box exemption and the manufacturing clause serve as a warning against such impetuousness. Given the unique nature and uncertain future of the new technology in the educational field, a heavy responsibility devolves upon the Congress. Insistently pressed upon it are such questions as the following:

(1) If broad copyright protection were granted, to what extent and under what circumstances would educators simply by-pass copyrighted material?

(2) To what extent and under what circumstances would they refrain from engaging in salutary activities, rather than sustain the burden and obstructions of copyright demand?

(3) To the extent that copyright levies were imposed, who would bear the brunt of them?

(4) In what circumstances and to what extent would the returns to authors and publishers be reduced if educational usages were more generously allowed—and in what circumstances might they actually be increased?

(5) What effect would the allowance or rejection of copyright in the new technology have upon the incentives, the structure, competitive relationships, and marketing practices of the industries that supply such technology?

(6) To the extent that returns were reduced, would the incentive to write and publish be lessened or destroyed, keeping in mind the kinds of materials involved?

(7) Where copyright protection does not adequately do the job what alternative stimuli may be available to encourage writing and publication? (We suggest the possibility that much of our modern educational writing and publishing probably depends upon motives and stimuli other than copyright protection.)

There is no *single* answer to these questions. Some writers and publishers, and their writings and publications, will be both benefited and motivated-greatly by copyright. Others will not. In some circumstances, copyright protection may be the best way to stimulate and compensate. In others, subsidy or some other means may be preferable. Some educators may find themselves blocked or discouraged by the copyright barriers. Others will take the hurdle in stride.

Let me emphasize that, in posing these questions, I am not suggesting that this committee answer them, here and now. This would be asking the impossible. My purpose, rather, is to underline (1) the fact that these *are* the kinds of issues that provide the policy base for what the committee must ultimately propose, (2) the need for providing mechanism of sufficient flexibility to deal effectively and wisely with these infinitely varied circumstances, and (3) the desirability of providing some means for tending the machine, to see whether it is doing the job and to put it in shape when it is not. Here, again, the EDUCOM recommendation favoring some sort of continuing advisory and reviewing Council warrants and receives our support.

4. *Resolution of conflicts by voluntary compliance, voluntary agreement, and compromise*

Reading the House Report, one is struck by the numerous instances in which opposing interests simply could find no common ground for agreement. Whatever the reasons—and some of them are suggested by my foregoing discussion—the lack of accord leads to compromise, to putting upon the parties the resolution of their own conflicts, and, in some cases, to undue reliance upon voluntary compliance. Examples of all of these are to be found in S.597. All have their proper place in the resolution of conflicts. But they also have shortcomings from the standpoint of effective rule-making. They are a poor substitute for genuine resolution of conflicts and mutually satisfactory accommodation of opposing positions. Resort to these approaches is, we suggest, premature in the present instance.

C. SUMMARY AND CONCLUSIONS

Let me summarize as follows:

1. Our educational system is on the verge of—indeed, in the midst of a virtual revolution in terms of its methodology, the scope of its activities, and public commitment to its broad and effective support.

2. In many respects, the copyright law may affect these new developments quite differently than it does traditional educational activities—and vice versa.

3. Similarly, the copyright law may affect educational activities, new and old, that make use of copyrighted materials differently than it affects non-educational activities that make use of such materials—and vice versa.

4. It is imperative that these unique developments and relationships be defined closely, intensely, imaginatively, and in terms of promoting our modern educational objectives and stimulating the authorship and publication of materials useful in achieving these objectives. In this context, it is essential to recognize that the copyright law can and does, in some circumstances, provide a highly salutary stimulus and incentive to educational writing and publishing, but in other circumstances may prove an impediment and barrier to desirable educational activity. In short, copyright *has* an important place in our changing educational society, but so do other incentives and stimuli. It develops upon the Congress to develop a set of rules that will enable the copyright system to operate to the best public advantage and at the same time to see to it that it does not operate as an obstructive force. In the former case, the copyright interests call for protection whether the educators like it or not; in the latter case, educational activities call for protection whether the copyrighters like it or not.

5. Pending resolution and clarification of the issues and relationships referred to in the preceding paragraph—and it is our belief that they have *not* been adequately explored despite the exhaustive and competent efforts that have been expended by both Congressional committees, their staffs, and interested groups and individuals outside the Congress—it would be premature and unfortunate to lay down a hard-and-fast, difficult-to-dislodge-and-change set of rules that might distort and frustrate desirable activities on the part of *both* the educational system and the educational writers and publishers.

6. In terms of the present Revision, the following appears to us a desirable course to follow:

a. Take *immediate* steps—either directly, by setting up in the present Revision an advisory and reviewing organization charged with the necessary responsibility, or both—to study thoroughly the relationship between the copyright law and educational activity, with especial attention to such matters as have been set forth herein, looking to further legislation dealing with this relationship as concretely as the circumstances permit.

b. In the interim and as a temporary measure (and in deference to the view that it is desirable to bring the present revision effort to fruition), preserve in the Revision maximum flexibility and freedom for adjustment of the respective interests in terms of what (1) best promotes the public interest in effective education, (2) best provides the necessary stimulus to educational writing and publication, and (3) achieves "equity" as between the conflicting parties.

To accomplish these objectives, we favor reliance primarily upon a "fair use" approach, broadly enough conceived to provide the kinds of accommodations and adjustments that we have discussed herein. Within this broad framework, however, we recognize the desirability of the S. 597 approach, to wit, of spelling out certain activities that the Congress feels should be *per se* exemptions. Such spelling out, *provided it is not interpreted as limiting the scope of the "fair use" doctrine*, is desirable as a means of reducing uncertainty, controversy and resort to litigation. We emphasize, however, that primary reliance upon the "fair use" doctrine should be viewed as a temporary stop-gap measure. Although there will always be marginal areas in which it will be useful, the aim should be to supplant it, as far as possible and as soon as possible, with more specific and concrete provisions.

D. SPECIFIC RECOMMENDATIONS

1. Section 107. Fair use.

We favor retention of Section 107 unchanged, believing that the present language is sufficiently broad, as written, to permit a satisfactory adjustment between educational activities and copyright interests. We emphasize, however, the need for a *broad* approach that takes appropriate cognizance of current educational practice, if the doctrine is to work satisfactorily in the light of modern conditions. To this end, we offer two specific comments.

First, we reiterate what the House Report points out: namely the "fair use" provision stands on its own feet and is *not* limited by the more specific, but narrower, provisions of sections 108-116. In other words, activities that are not specifically listed in those sections as being *per se* a "fair use" and therefore exempt, may still be exempt under the general "fair use" provisions of section 107 where the circumstances warrant.

Second, some of the explanatory comment in House Report No. 83 concerning section 107 seems unnecessarily narrow—narrower than the section is as written and narrower than is desirable in the public interest. While we recognize that this Committee expresses only its own views and not those of the House Committee, we strongly urge its adoption of explanatory comment that is more consistent with the true spirit of the "fair use" doctrine as it has been traditionally applied. For example, the "non-profit" nature of the usage, although not a *text* of "fair use," may be a very important factor in the determination. "Instructional uses" *may* be treated differently than other uses in determining fairness. Copying by school authorities other than the immediate user may be "fair use" in many circumstances. In some cases, reproduction of works "prepared primarily for the school market" may be fair, and so may be the reproduction of an entire work. Minor displacement of a particular sale may not necessarily bar the application of the "fair use" doctrine. In some circumstances, the doctrine may properly receive as broad application to motion pictures as to other types of copyrighted materials. Finally, reference to its application in the computer field seems gratuitous and premature, pending a much harder look at how the copyright law will operate in this complex field. Indeed, as we have mentioned above and as the EDUCOM representatives have presuasively pointed out, the application of copyright protection to computer programs calls for much closer scrutiny than it has thus far received.

2. Section 504(c)(2). *Remission of statutory damages*

We recommend that the last sentence of section 504(c)(2) be amended to read as follows:

"In a case where an infringer sustains the burden of proving (i) that such infringement consisted of nonprofit educational activities and (ii) that he believed, and had reasonable grounds for believing, that his act of infringement constituted a fair use under section 107, the court in its discretion may remit statutory damages in whole or in part."

With this change, the defense would extend to all legitimate nonprofit educational activities, and get away from the narrowly-circumscribed provisions in the bill which presently limit its application to (1) instructors, (2) reproduction and (3) face-to-face classroom teaching activities. So revised, infringers would still have to sustain the burden of proof, liability for actual damages would remain intact, and the final determination whether to waive statutory damages would rest with the judge. Retention of these limitations would, we believe, amply protect the legitimate interests of the copyright owner. For that matter, your Committee may wish to consider whether judges might be given the discretion to limit recovery to the damages actually incurred, in *any* case where infringement was shown to have occurred in the good-faith belief that the usage was "fair."

3. Four other sections call for comment. Section 108 relates to archival collections; section 109(b) permits certain displays of owned copies; section 110 provides exemptions for certain types of performances and displays; and section 112(b) relates to ephemeral recordings of the educational transmissions covered by section 110(2). All four of these sections specify that certain copying and usages connected with the educational activities described therein shall be exempt from liability for infringement. The exemptions, in effect, constitute a declaration that the activities described are a *per se* "fair use" of the copyrighted matter. For reasons that we have previously stated, we deem it salutary to designate specified conduct as unequivocally fair, to the extent that this can be done. Hence, we approve of these sections, *as far as they go.* All of them, however, are extremely limited in their scope. Standing alone, they would be totally inadequate to meet the legitimate needs of modern education for a certain amount of flexibility and freedom from copyright liability.

In view of our position that the education-copyright conflict can be adequately resolved, on a temporary basis, through a proper application of the "fair use" doctrine as expressed above, and that sections 108-116 do *not* limit in any way the application of section 107 to activities that do not come within these sections, we do not presently deem essential any extension of the express exemptions set forth in sections 108, 109, 110 and 112.

If, however, the Committee should be disposed either to give section 107 an interpretation narrower than that which we have proposed, or to treat sections 108, 109, 110 and 112 as limiting in any way the scope and application of section 107, we would appreciate the opportunity to supplement our present statement with a discussion of why we feel that these sections are more circumscribed than they should be, and the respects in which we feel their scope should be enlarged.

STATEMENT OF WILLIAM M. PASSANO, PRESIDENT, THE WILLIAMS & WILKINS CO.

Mr. PASSANO. Mr. Chairman, I am William Passano, the president of The Williams & Wilkins Co. and director of Waverly Press, Inc., and with me is Mr. Lyle Lodwick, who is the director of marketing for our company, and Miss Andrea Wilderman, associate director of marketing.

The Williams & Wilkins Co. and the Waverly Press are jointly owned and affiliated companies. We are publishers and printers of scientific books, medical and scientific journals, and medical books. We have over 800 employees in Baltimore and Easton, Md. The company was founded in 1890.

While our business is not small, our markets for our products are very small—so small, in fact, that the loss of two or three sales for some of our books and journals—in each of the few hundred major markets for our products around the world—can make their publication unprofitable.

I have four compelling reasons for asking to be allowed to testify before your committee. The first is that we are a major publisher of scientific periodicals and we believe that they are particularly vulnerable to photocopying, and we do not believe that there has been very much testimony on this subject.

The second reason is that we wish to concentrate attention on the threat from photocopying rather than the threat from the computer. It is true that the computer may prove to be in the near future a real threat to owners of copyrighted material, but the threat from photocopying is here and now. It is a known, tangible matter and could and should be dealt with now, before it is too late.

Our third reason is that we are not in a position which requires that we pull our punches for fear of offending our good customers. It is true that most of our customers are in education, but they are in higher education. The great majority of those we have talked with are of the opinion that uncontrolled photocopying—for all of its immediate advantages to the educator—poses a most serious and immediate threat to scientific publishing, and therefore, to the scientific world in general.

Our final reason for wishing to testify today is that we are an independent publishing house in no way owned by or connected with a manufacturer of computers, copying machines, or any other electronic devices. Therefore, what we have to say need in no way be diluted by the necessity of "listening to his master's voice."

Let me deal with the threat of photocopying to the average scientific periodical. We know that photocopying has already seriously reduced the income of most of the 39 periodicals which we publish. Incidentally, of this number 25 are published by us for scientific societies, such as this journal, "Journal of Pharmacology and Experimental Therapeutics," which we have published since 1909, and 14 are owned by our company outright, such as this one, "Medicine," which has been published for almost 50 years.

It is easy to visualize how this erosion of income takes place. An individual scientist, instead of subscribing to a journal in his field, will go to a library and look over the table of contents of the most recent issue and get photocopies of these articles which interest him or which he would like to file away for future reference.

The research laboratory or other institution, instead of subscribing to several copies of the periodical appropriate to its work, will subscribe to one copy and make photocopies of it to distribute amongst the persons working in the laboratory.

A research worker wanting to collect copies of articles which apply to his particular research project, rather than writing the authors of these articles and asking them to supply reprints, which we as publishers have previously supplied to the authors, will photocopy the articles in question instead.

An individual or institution, instead of purchasing from us back numbers or back volumes of a periodical which have appeared prior to the current subscription to it, will go to the library and make photocopies of those articles or perhaps even of complete issues which are his special interest.

You may ask, Mr. Chairman, how do we know that this takes place?

In the first place, we have talked to librarians and scientists all around the country and they tell us that it does, in fact, take place and in great quantities. Some of our periodicals and photocopied more violently than others, but none escape. This journal, "Medicine," Senator, is one of the most photocopied journals that we publish, and sometimes there are only one or two articles in any one issue. It is a monograph-type journal and, therefore, when you photocopy one article you sometimes have photocopied the whole issue.

In the second place, the growth of our subscription business in these boom times of the 1960's lagged behind the growth of the market. It seems to us that the handwriting is obviously on the wall.

Three years ago we started four new journals. Before doing so we were very confident that the editorial content of these periodicals was excellent and filled a longfelt need. We, of course, expected these new journals to lose money at the start, but they not only did this, but are continuing to lose money today when they should, by all rights, have been on a self-supporting basis. We have been told by librarians and others that these journals are in considerable demand for photocopying. It seems obvious to us that the failure of their subscription lists to grow to a point where they would be self-supporting is due to the fact that persons who otherwise would subscribe are depending on photocopying to supply their needs.

We as a medical publisher are not the only loser in this situation. The profit shown by the 25 periodicals that we publish for scientific societies, such as this one, the "Journal of Pharmacology and Experimental Therapeutics," is shared with the scientific societies for whom we publish.

As uncontrolled photocopying reduces the income of these periodicals, the society's income is reduced as well as our own. When the circulation is curtailed to the point that income fails to cover expenses, then of course the periodicals either go out of existence or must be kept alive by subsidy either from the Government or from, in some cases, drug manufacturers.

Now, it is well known, I think, to all of us that this photocopying is illegal under the present copyright law. The difficulty is that the term "fair use" sort of eases the conscience of anyone who wants to make a copy of an article appearing in one of our journals. It is a little bit like the use of alcoholic beverages in prohibition days. A man who wanted to take a drink was going to do so regardless of what the law said in the matter, and the man who wants to make a photocopy is going to do so as long as nobody is looking over his shoulder to tell him no.

In our opinion it is unrealistic to think otherwise and to believe that examples of what might be considered "fair use" in the House report are in any way going to cut down on the billions of photocopies which are made annually today of copyrighted material.

In our opinion there are only two roads to follow if there is a serious intention to protect the rights of the copyright owner against the economic competition of the copying machine. One is to ban the use of photocopying machines unless they are operated by institutions who are charged with the responsibility of seeing that no copyrighted material is copied without the permission of the copyright owner.

We feel that it is unrealistic and not in the public interest to consider restricting in any way the use of photocopying devices. They serve a very useful purpose in the dissemination of knowledge. Since we, as publishers, are in that business, we certainly don't want to see the spread of knowledge curtailed.

To us the only solution to the problem is a simple system of royalty payments with a minimum of redtape. At this point I want to turn the floor over to Mr. Lyle Lodwick, director of marketing of my organization, who will explain to you how and why we arrived at this conclusion and how such a system will work in actual practice.

This morning, Senator, you said that you wanted answers, not questions, and we think we are in a position to give you an answer here as to how a system of royalty payments for the privilege of photocopying can be set up and made to work. It may not be the only system—I am sure it is not—and it probably is not even the best, but at least we have thought it through to the point where it can be made the beginning of a practical, workable, simple system.

Before turning the floor over to Mr. Lodwick, I would like to read you a 4-line poem written by James Russell Lowell in 1885 entitled "International Copyright." It seems to me that it is just as germane to piracy by photocopying today as it was to the type of piracy that took place when James Russell Lowell wrote it. This is the poem:

In vain we call old notions fudge
And bend our conscience to our dealings
The Ten Commandments will not budge
And stealing will continue stealing.

Thank you, sir.

STATEMENT OF LYLE LODWICK FOR THE WILLIAMS & WILKINS CO.—BALTIMORE, MD

Mr. Chairman and members of the subcommittee, two typical advertisements of copying machine manufacturers illustrate very clearly that independent publishers and their authors cannot survive much longer the economic competition of over 800,000 copying machines, which last year ground out over 14-billion copies and, with the addition of 200,000 more machines by 1970, will produce close to 30-billion pages of material, much of it of copyrighted works.

Says one advertisement:

"Look what happens when you put a coin-operated . . . copier in your library. Your readers make their own copies at the push of a button *and you keep all the money* . . .".

The happy librarian with her hands full of money tells the reader: *"It's amazing how those coins add up.".* Amazing, indeed.

Says another advertisement by another company:

"Anyone who comes into your library can walk up to a . . . copier and make a copy. That's how easy it is. It is easy for you too, because you don't have to collect coins, keep records, or share income. . . . Makes positive copies of articles or pages from newspapers, magazines, encyclopedias, reference books. . . . Makes scarce source material more readily available to more users. Discourages mutilation. . . . *All collected coins belong to you."*.

*   *   *   *   *   *   *

Mr. Chairman, S. 597 is a great bill, a "glorious" compromise, and an historic tribute to the dedicated work of your and Mr. Celler's committees and your staffs—to Mr. Kaminstein and his colleagues—to the copyright bar in its entirety—and to many in government, in the "not-for-profit" industries, and in private enterprise who know that "give-and-take" makes this great country work.

In theory, at least, and as a basis for possible future litigation, we feel that we do have protection in the 4th standard of "Fair Use" that considers the *"effect of the use upon the potential market for or value of the copyrighted work"*, and in the House Committee's now-famous two sentences:

". . . *Where the unauthorized copying displaces what realistically might have been a sale, no matter how minor the amount of money involved, the interests of the copyright owner need protection. Isolated instances of minor infringements, when multiplied many times, become in the aggregate a major inroad on copyright that must be prevented."*.

The House Committee's observation, of course, merely restates in modern and crystal-clear terms a state of affairs that existed in principle in the 1790's, when Mr. Madison and his friends recognized that many small printers scattered all over the 13 colonies could play large havoc with the country's creative authorship and with the risk-enterprise of the day.

Today, thanks to brilliant technology, effective merchandising, and well-conceived "public-image" promotion, *Everyman* can be, and is, his own "do-it-yourself" printer.

And so, we find the copying machine to be a new breed of "Juke-Box", with the capability of smothering our national resources of creativity and ingenuity, and of wiping out hundreds of publishers such as ourselves around the world. "Instant copying" has begotten "instant rationalization" in a casuistic, LSD-kind of dream world where "Free Use" double thinks into "Fair Use".

The cold, hard fact is that "Fair Use", when applied to photocopying, is dead as a door nail as a practical, workable doctrine for our day.

The cold hard fact is that we are, right now, making business decisions to phase out of publishing certain kinds of scientific books and journals most vulnerable to photocopying. *This means that many authors, and their ideas, are being—and will be increasingly—denied entry into this classic kind of "information network."*

We submit that it is *not* in the interest of science and of this country for people like ourselves to have to make these decisions in order to insure survival.

And, certainly, litigation will come too late, and prove nothing.

It seems fairly certain that if we all do not face up to *the 1967-reality of the copying machine*, some 21st-century historian is going to look back and ask *"Who Killed Cock Robin?"* in the limbo-years between the copying machine of the mid-1960's and the promises of the new computer- and "imaging-technologies" of the mid-1970's.

Mr. Chairman, the great A. North Whitehead said:

"*A clash of doctrines is not a disaster—it is an opportunity.*"

There is a very great opportunity for all of us involved in this complex dialogue to come quickly to a practical, realistic solution to the problem of directly or indirectly compensating authors and publishers for the manufacture of facsimiles of their copyrighted works by any mechanical or electronic device.

It is to deal with the copying machine, by itself, as a current problem.

If we cannot now work out a reasonable, simple accommodation to the present impact on creativity and enterprise of the copying machine—a relatively unsophisticated and definable device—how on earth can we ever face up to the more complex problems of the very near, very sophisticated future imposed upon us by the computer and its related, more sophisticated technologies?

To put it more positively, doesn't the copying machine and its copyright implications give us an easy "*pilot-plant*" opportunity and challenge to sweat out the principles and mechanisms which can be later applied to all other *imaging* processes of the "communications revolution"?

"*Control of the image*" is, after all, at the heart of all we are debating about.

In pointing out the necessity for compensation to authors and publishers, Mr. Herbert S. Bailey, Jr., of the Princeton University Press, has aptly stated (in "Saturday Review", June 11, 1966):

> "The new technologies make it clear that *what a publisher sells is not a book but the image of a book.* The author writes the manuscript; then the publisher selects it for publication, edits it, *and gives it a suitable typographic dress—an image.* Currently he sells his image as printed on paper and bound in cloth or paper at a single manufacturing establishment; in the future he will usually sell the image as reproduced on copying machines at many locations, by remote or local control, on demand . . ."

Mr. Chairman, the atmosphere is right and ready for immediate statutory recognition in S. 597 of a copying-machine royalty system on a par with the recognition accorded juke-boxes, CATV and the like.

Many scientists we have talked with recognize the ultimate implications of uncompensated copying.

Many librarians we have talked with are sympathetic to a *simple* solution for indirectly compensating authors and publishers.

In a recent editorial, "*Piracy by Photocopy*", which appeared in the October 1966 issue of Bulletin of the Medical Library Association, a national leader in library science and member of the President's "National Advisory Commission on Libraries", Dr. Estelle Brodman, points out:

> "Although the technological form might differ, the basic problems of copyright infringement and the basic arguments for copyright protection remain the same. They consist, essentially, of the ethical requirement that a person get an equitable return for his endeavors. An author should be compensated for the toil of producing a work—book, journal, article, picture, computer program—and a publisher for the risk to his capital . . .".

> "The questions involved in solving the copyright problem of the midtwentieth century have excited more heat than light . . . What is needed is for sympathetic publishers, librarians, scholars, lawyers and accounting experts to sit down together in calm and quiet and debate this question on an intellectual plane, instead of an emotional one. *Surely a society which can bring forth a computer and an understanding of the mechanisms of the genetic code can figure out a system of copyright protection which is not burdensome to any group.* Librarians have a particular interest in seeing this happen".

We would like to offer *a* solution. We believe it is simple in principle, practical in application, painless to all. and—paradoxically, it will probably cause an even bigger boom in the use of copying machines.

It is to impose a flat, nominal, non-punitive tax on copying machines and their entire output:

(1) to fund certain information activities of the government operated for the particular benefit of business, scientific and educational organizations;

(2) to fund the collection, accounting and distribution of copying royalties to participating copyright owners.

The rationale behind the first objective is that those of us in business and industry, in the sciences, and in education who benefit the most from specialized governmental information services (the National Library of Medicine, the National Agricultural Library, the Clearinghouse for Federal Scientific and Technical Information, services of the Departments of Commerce and Defense, the National Referral Center for Science and Technology, ERIC, etc.) should directly support these necessary and socially-desirable functions in direct proportion to our own information and communication needs and activities—for which copying machine usage and volume is as good and as reasonable a barometer as any. And, since many other sectors of government benefit from publication activities of both the specialized government information services and of the "private sector", the copying machine output of government agencies themselves would help fund, through royalty credits, distribution of earned royalties to owners of copyrighted material that is reproduced by the government itself.

The rationale behind the second objective is self-explanatory: to have one central location from which earned royalties from photocopying can be determined and periodically distributed to participating copyright holders.

Underlying both objectives is a basic assumption that in general, copyrighted work can be copied without the necessity for the copier to get advance permission of the participating copyright holder.

Just what is involved?

In the words of Eliot Morison in a great book, "Men, Machines, and Modern Times":

"The problem presented (is) one filled with measurable, quantifiable data susceptible of analysis and the drawing of reasonable conclusions".

Defining just what is "a copying machine" is the first problem, and collection the corollary.

Let us assume 800,000 "copying machines" by generally accepted trade definitions. This excludes higher-volume duplicators, over ½-million in number, and producing, by some estimates, over 25 times the number of copies that are produced by the newer "convenience-copiers"! Some copying machines are "infringing" into the market traditionally held by duplicators. Should duplicating devices be included in the excise-tax plan? We think not—the traditional ground rules of copyright and copyright infringement can apply here, as always.

Since the market-erosion of "copying machines" is primarily in the 1 to 100 copies-per-page area, the liability for paying the tax could be limited to owners or lessees of most machines with this economic capability.

Assuming that a reasonable, workable definition of a "copying machine" can be hammered out—by parsing prose, by actual definition by manufacturer and model, by volume considerations, by compromise—should an excise tax on *output* be applied to the vast majority of copying machines—the small, desk models so useful in businesses and in offices?

We think not—they are, by and large, self-limiting in their effect on copyright owners: there would be too much red-tape in accounting internally for what was copied; and, what is copied in the privacy of an office is nobody else's business anyway. A flat $50/year tax would seem to be reasonable, and would yield revenues and credits (from governmental installations) of about $25,000,000 a year.

With "duplicating" arbitrarily excluded, and the smaller copying machines taken care of by a simple, flat-sum tax, *where is the primary source of revenues necessary to finance the information-dissemination and copying-royalty distribution activities of the government?*

It mainly lies in those machines which, on a normal 8-hour-a-day basis, produce from about 1,000 to about 25,000 copies a month, and account for about 90% of all page-images copied—over 12-billion copies last year. Practically all have metered output, and most are leased. In the case of the latter, all that is necessary is for the copying-machine manufacturer to collect monthly from his lessees the tax on the output and turn it over to the government.

At ½-cent a page tax, a 10,000/month machine would yield $50 a month; at 2-cents a page tax, the *national* output in 1966 would have yielded $240-million. ("It's amazing how those coins add up.")!

Whatever rate established—*and it should be only enough to cover minimal needs and not be a deterrent to legitimate copying*—the collection mechanism involves no more than adding an additional amount to the usual rental charge. "On-premises" owners would merely remit directly to the U. S. Treasury.

Now, if the collection problem is "susceptible of analysis and the drawing of reasonable conclusions", so is the determination of actually how many pages of the 14-million currently photocopied were from copyrighted sources.

First, we propose that publicly-supported, "not-for-profit", libraries be required, in this public interest, to keep track of the number of pages photocopied from each work bearing a copyright notice in their collections, and report this information periodically to whatever copyright-royalty clearing house facility is established to handle the situation. (This does not apply to coin-operated copying machines furnished by commercial operators where the librarian has no control over the operation by patrons of the library—these are subject to the excise tax on their metered-output, but no reports are required).

We would like to emphasize that the librarians' responsibility for copying machine usage does not require any more bookkeeping than logging and accumulating the amount of pages copied by users of the copying machines under the library's control, and identifying the source-items bearing a copyright notice and the quantities copies therefrom. *It is reportable if it bears a copyright notice (from 1910 on)*—as pointed out later, royalty distribution will be made only (by the Clearing House) if the copyright is valid and the owner requests participation.

We would also like to re-emphasize that this is no more than a straight, simple record-keeping operation, much of the labor of which can be handed over to the patron desiring photocopies.

What would this information, reported by all publicly-supported libraries yield?

A national picture of hom many times each copyrighted work was copied—a national sum of just how much copying of copyrighted works is done by patrons of "not-for-profit" libraries—a national sample of the relative copying-popularity of copyrighted works that can be a reasonable basis for extrapolating the total copying of *each* copyrighted work.

Again, common-sense and reasonable accommodation must play a role.

If, from this "quantifiable" procedure we find out:

(1) what percentage of the total of last year's 14-billion photocopies were processed by "not-for-profit" libraries serving all types of patrons in government, in all types of business, commerce industry, and in science, technology and education, and

(2) the frequency to which each copyrighted book and journal was copied, we at least have the beginnings of a basis for distributing royalties to the copied copyright owners. In short, we now know that (for purposes of illustration) say, 500-million out of the 14-billion photocopies made can be accounted for by "not-for-profit" libraries.

What more is copied of copyrighted works by those other than publicly-supported libraries?

Plenty, we believe.

We are now close to both the heart of the problem, and the means of solution

And, we are coming close to determining how much copying royalty should be distributed to the copyright owner. Just how much is left of the 14-billion photocopies that will determine what *final* percentage of it is of copyrighted works, irrespective of an identification of which works were photocopied?

Therefore, our second proposal is to have an appropriate governmental agency determine (1) how many pages are photocopied and what is the *percentage* of copying machine output *by the government itself* of copyrighted works, and (2) what is the copying machine output and what is the *percentage* of total output,—off-premises of their libraries, but *on*-premises of *academic, "not-for-profit" institutions* of copyrighted works? If administrators of the former do not know, perhaps the taxpayers ought to. Administrators of the latter certainly ought to be in a position to know how many copying machines are owned and/or leased "on campus" and in the schools and what their total annual output is of copyrighted works versus administrative forms, theses and the like. Rough-heft and ball-park estimates will do.

Summing up so far, we now have the *total quantities* of photocopies of copyrighted material made by *publicly-attended libraries* of all types, *governmental institutions*, and *educational institutions*. For purposes of illustration only it might break down like this:

Type of institution:	Number of pages photocopied annually of copyrighted works
Libraries, all classes	500,000,000
Educational institutions	1,500,000,000
Government, Federal, State, local	750,000,000
Subtotal	2,750,000,000

What about photocopying by business and industry, and by commercial photo-copying services?

Here, all we need are total quantities. Since the machines are taxed on an entire output basis, there would be no advantage in reporting anything but a reasonable, accurate estimate, perhaps once a year, to the copying machine manufacturer. Thus, a company liable for the excise tax on, say 1,000,000 photo-copies a year, could report that approximately 10%, or whatever, was from material bearing a copyright notice. Again, ball-park estimates will do.

Let us assume that business and industry account for 250,000,000 photocopies of copyrighted material. We now have a grand total of 3-billion copies as a base for redistributing copyright royalties.

Now, only libraries have to identify what copyright sources were actually copied from.

Can we assume that a frequency distribution of copying based on library experience only can be applied to all copying of copyrighted works? We think so. Libraries serve all segments of the American public—all types of students, scholars, and businesses.

There is a big enough mix of needs mirrored in library photocopying traffic to justify it as a giant and valid sample for determining copying royal distribution.

Thus, if library photocopying were 500-million of the 3-billion, it would be a fair assumption that any royalty page rate established for a copyrighted work should be multiplied by a factor of 6 to reflect the total effect of all copying on that work.

Here's how it might work with a typical scientific journal. Most of ours average 2¢-a-page as a pro-rata of their subscription price. If library experience indicated that all libraries made 50,000 copies of pages from a particular journal, then the royalty distribution would be $6,000 ($.02 x 50,000 x 6). If this particular journal had a subscription rate of $30/year, the $6,000 copying royalty payment would reimburse the scientific society and its publisher for the loss of income from only 200 potential subscribers lost to "convenience copying."

Mr. Chairman, all of what we have said is only a start toward a solution. We strongly believe that reasonable people could constructively work out better prin-ciples of analysis, clearer details of execution, more realistic "balancing of equi-ties" than we have sketched above. And, quite obviously, there are plenty of "ifs, ands and buts" which would have to be hashed out. For instance, the above, we believe, would be entirely acceptable to us as a publisher of scientific journals—we would definitely participate. But, as also a publisher of textbooks more and more subject to anthologizing, we probably would elect not to participate in roy-alty distribution for those particular copyrighted works.

This is basically a "no-tickee, no-washee" system for authors and publishers. If they elect to participate in copying-royalty distributions for any particular copy-righted work, they waive the right to require advance permissions for non-com-mercial copying. Quite obviously, as this system develops, copyrighted works will, in the future, have to bear both permissive and limitative conditions as a guide to the copiers. And the transition into this "way of life" will involve many head-aches which reasonable people will have to live with.

Thanks to computer and systems technologies, the copying-royalty clearing house facility need not be much more than a modern, sophisticated accounting operation. It will have core storage of all active copyright owners; their names and addresses, their royalty rate per page (based on pro-rata of list price): whether or not they are participating in copying-royalty distributions. It will re-ceive as "input" the reports from the libraries showing how much each copy-righted work was copied. It will pay out, say once a year, earned royalties above a reasonable minimum level.

We believe the copying-royalty clearing house should be under the jurisdiction of the Congress, and under the supervision of the Library of Congress.

Mr. Chairman, we do not have the competence to draft the specific legislative language that would carry out the objective of our recommendation that *a nomi-nal tax finance selected information-dissemination activities of the government, establish a copying-royalty clearing house facility, and fund copying-royalty payments.*

We do feel, however, that S. 597 should give some broad, statutory recogni-tion of the concept.

And, since "the way to begin is to begin," there is no reason a reasonable time-table could not be set up along the lines of the following: (1) develop and enact the necessary tax legislation, to be effective January 1, 1968; (2) authorize the Library of Congress to establish a *Copying-Royalty Clearance Facility* to be operational for the distribution of royalties by January 1, 1969.

We fully appreciate the complexities involved, but we are completely convinced that the effect of the copying machine on independent publishing must be faced up to now.

In summary, if all of us can only work out together a reasonable accommodation to the photocopying problem in the context of the basic principles of copyright, living with the computer age will come a lot easier.

What a wonderful and challenging opportunity!

We appreciate the opportunity to appear before you, and will welcome any questions.

Copyright Law Revision
Hearings, 1967
Part 4

STATEMENT ON S. 597 BY HARRY N. ROSENFIELD, ESQ., FOR AD HOC COMMITTEE (OF EDUCATIONAL INSTITUTIONS AND ORGANIZATIONS) ON COPYRIGHT LAW REVISIONS

The Ad Hoc Committee appreciates this opportunity to deal with certain matters raised in, or resulting from, the recent hearings before this Committee. Time will not permit me to cover all such questions. However, we are deeply concerned about four particular matters as follows:

    (1) the efforts of some witnesses to erode fair use into meaninglessness so far as education is concerned;

    (2) S. 597's virtual elimination of individualized instruction through modern technology;

    (3) the failure to distinguish between closed circuit and open broadcast channels in instructional broadcasting; and

    (4) amendments proposed by the publishers.

We take heart in Senator McClellan's opening statement in these hearings that there are certain provisions of S. 597 which he may not be able to support in their present form. We earnestly hope that among these provisions are the ones which cause us so much concern.

I. FAIR USE

The Ad Hoc Committee's basic position urged the Congress to enact both a fair use section and a special statutory authorization for limited copying rights for educational uses as a means of preserving and expanding the "not for profit" concept. We still believe this original proposal is the simplest and best way of dealing with education's needs under the copyright law. However, we agreed to a compromise position which would achieve approximately the same result in a different way, involving both important new language in § 107 and a legislative history.

I should like to comment on both aspects of this agreement (1) § 107. The *sine qua non* of our agreement is the present language of § 107, unchanged. Although this section represents a compromise in which we sacrificed certainty and a specific statutory exemption, we intend to honor our agreement. If others fail to honor theirs, or if the agreement is abridged by changes in § 107, the Ad Hoc Committee will regard the whole agreement as dishonored and will feel free to return to its original proposals and requests.

The book publishers and music interests have urged amendments to the language of § 107 which the Ad Hoc Committee opposes.

Either these changes are unimportant—and therefore unnecessary—or important and therefore abridge the agreement. In either event, we vigorously urge this Committee to reject *all* efforts to amend the text of § 107 as it now appears in S. 597. Anything less than the present text could mean complete reassessment by the Ad Hoc Committee of its position on § 107.

(2) *The legislative history.*—The essence of the total agreement reached on fair use, which is embodied in the language of § 107, is virtually negated by several statements in the House Committee's Report (House Rep. No. 83, 90th Cong., 1st Sess., on H.R. 2512):

    (a) Our basic understanding of the agreement is correctly stated in that Report's comments that the fourth criterion of § 107 "must always be judged in conjunction with the other three criteria" (p. 35, 2nd full paragraph, 1st sentence) and that the four criteria "must be applied in combination with the circumstances pertaining to other criteria" (p. 32, 3rd full paragraph). However, these statements—and the essence of our agreement—are, we fear, wholly vitiated by another statement in the House Report dealing with the fourth criterion, as follows:

"Where the unauthorized copying displaces what realistically might have been a sale, *no matter how minor the amount of money involved*, the interests of the copyright owner need protection" (p. 35, 2nd full paragraph, next to last sentence). [Emphasis added.]

The language "no matter how minor the amount of money involved" flies in the face of the combined consideration of all four criteria and prevents dealing with all four criteria in conjunction with each other. It is a categorical assertion which, in effect, wipes out the other three criteria. At the very least, it creates such uncertainty as to endanger the meaningfulness of the entire section as it was intended to authorize limited copying for educational purposes.

As I have stated, while § 107 (and its legislative history in the House Report) is not what we really want, we shall live by our agreement to accept it—*provided* it is the agreement we made. And we did *not* make any agreement which includes the language "no matter how minor the amount involved." Therefore, we urgently request the Senate Judiciary Committee that the concept embodied in this quoted sentence be specifically and categorically rejected as part of the legislative history of § 107.

Lest there be any misunderstanding as to some comments that have been made by various witnesses in the course of these hearings, we wish to make crystal clear *our* understanding of the fundamental nature of fair use as it is encompassed in S. 597:

(i) Fair use, and the limited educational copying it specifically authorizes, is not an occasional or only casual right, as one witness stated. For us, "fair use" is a fundamental statutory charter. Such use is not given by leave of the copyright owner, but is specifically reserved for education by Congress out of the copyright monopoly. Otherwise, teachers are prevented from creative teaching and effective use of available resources.

In our agreement on fair use, there is nothing occasional or casual about education's right of fair use. Instead of occasional, it is a constant right; instead of casual, it is a continuing right. Anything less is a perversion of our agreement and would be, for us, automatic breach of the agreement. Therefore, we urgently appeal to the Committee to make this matter absolutely clear in its report.

(ii) Another witness was candid enough to state that he regarded fair use "as a temporary safety valve" after which "the concept of fair use should lose its importance and die off as some form of vestigial tail." If this be true, we want nothing of § 107 and S. 597.

Education proposed a two-prong approach, retention of the "not for profit" concept plus a statutory authorization for limited copying for educational purposes. We receded from this position and accepted a compromise involving a rewritten fair use provision and a clear legislative history, only upon the basis of the iron-bound assurance that—

"the doctrine of fair use, as properly applied, is broad enough to permit reasonable educational use" (House Rep. No. 83, p. 32).

The compromise was based on the assurance of a lasting charter in the fair use provisions and legislative history protecting the right of teachers to teach effectively.

If these assurances are not valid, either because of an alleged "casual" or "occasional" applicability of "fair use," or because educators have been tricked into a short-term life for fair use, then our agreement has been broken and we shall not feel bound by it. We are certain that such abridgements were not intended by the House Judiciary Committee. We hope that this Committee's report will plainly, clearly, and positively reject such unauthorized and unacceptable glosses upon the legislative history of § 107.

If there is a breech in the agreement as the Ad Hoc Committee understands it, either in terms of the statutory language or the legislative history, the Ad Hoc Committee's position remains as stated in the first round of hearings before this subcommittee on April 5, 1965. We then testified in behalf of—

"(1) the retention of the 'for profit' concept for nonprofit educational organizations and institutions; and

"(2) its application both to performance and restricted copying for nonprofit educational purposes."

For the Committee's convenience, I attach as *Appendix 1* an excerpt of the pertinent position of my earlier statement, which includes proposed language designed to meet education's needs.

(b) In still another aspect, the Report of the House Committee on fair use is unsatisfactory and unwise. This arises out of the language in the House Report (p. 36) unduly restricting fair use by educational broadcasts. Both classroom and broadcast teachers should have the same right of fair use under § 107 and the same opportunity for waiver of minimum statutory damages under § 504(c) (2). We recommend that the Senate report affirmatively reject any unjustified unfairness to educational broadcasts.

II. INDIVIDUALIZED INSTRUCTION, § 110(2)(D)

The second major issue I wish to mention arises out of § 110(2)(D). This section virtually bars individualized uses of the newer education classroom technology whose purpose is to encourage independent learning activities. This provision is highly deleterious to effective teaching as we now know it, and we urge its complete deletion.

Take for example the foreign language laboratory. Schools buy tape-recorded speech patterns for students to imitate. When the tape is used on a machine in the room where the student is located so that transmission is unnecessary, § 110 (2)(D) does not apply. Where the tape is used by means of a machine which transmits the sounds at a teacher's activation, § 110(2)(D) does not apply. But where the identical tape is used in the identical machine, but is activated by a student, even if he be in the same room with the teacher this is forbidden by § 110(2)(D). Or if the student was ill and absent, and tries to make up the lesson later on the very same system, it is barred. Please bear in mind that we are *not* here necessarily talking of copies—we are using mostly tape we bought and paid for, and for the very purpose for which it was purchased, *e.g.*, to be heard by the student in order that he might learn by imitating the purchased tape.

Nor are we here dealing with the computer problems of input and output and their statuts under copyright law.[1]

In the language laboratory we use the very copy we bought for the only purpose for which it was bought. There is an internal inconsistency in the bill: if a teacher pushes the button, so to speak, the use of copyrighted material on such a transmission is permissible; if a student does, it is impermissible.

Education is increasingly moving in the direction of individualized learning. It is becoming less and less teacher-oriented and more and more student-oriented. The trend is for the student to take greater responsibility for his learning through self-directed *learning* activities instead of formal *teaching* activities. Section 110(2)(D) is a body-blow to all this—it is wholly unjustified on any responsible basis.

With all the persuasiveness at our command, we plead with this Committee to eliminate § 110(2)(D) from the bill, as indicated in *Appendix 2.*

III. THE FAILURE TO DISTINGUISH CLOSED CIRCUIT FROM OPEN CHANNEL INSTRUCTIONAL BROADCASTS

S. 597, and the House Report on the similar provisions of H.R. 2512 (see p. 41, 2nd full paragraph), do not distinguish between closed circuit or point-to-point instructional broadcasting, on the one hand, and open channel broadcasting, on the other. This is based upon an error of fact. Closed circuit transmissions consist of limited, controlled, and non-public systems *within* the schools; they are controlled or closed transmissions not available to the public. It is unrealistic and unreasonable to treat them just like open channel broadcasts which can be picked up by anyone who tunes in.

Consequently, we believe that closed circuit or controlled transmissions should not be under the provisions of § 110(2), but under a new provision which we have proposed, § 110(1A). The text of this proposal is in *Appendix 3*, attached hereto.

---

[1] The Ad Hoc Committee believes that computer input should not be an infringement, and the testimony of Professor Siebert and Professor Miller on March 16, 1967, clearly states the Ad Hoc Committee's views on this matter. Since this subject has been assigned to others in this hearing, however, no further comment will be made at this time.

IV. AMENDMENTS PROPOSED BY PUBLISHERS

Our fourth point relates to the changes proposed jointly by the American Book Publishers Council, Inc. and the American Textbook Publishers Institute on March 15, 1967. The Ad Hoc Committee objects to five of these proposals, accepts one, and makes no comment about another.

(1) § *101, p. 6, lines 5–6.*—We see neither need nor justification for this proposal, and object to it.

(2) § *101, p. 6, line 7.*—We accept this as reasonable.

(3) § *107, p. 8, line 34.*—We vigorously object to tampering with the fair use section. If this section is to be tinkered with, our "agreement" is breached, as stated previously.

(4) § *110(1), p. 10, line 3.*—We vigorously object to limitations on classroom teaching. This proposal would, for practical purposes, bar all of the most useful forms of modern technology in face-to-face classroom teaching.

(5) § *110(4), p. 10, line 31.*—We vigorously object to this proposal. It would be a serious and heavy blow especially to musical education. It would hamper schools by requiring a 20-day advance notice and really seems designed merely as a statutory first step toward a compulsory license for every school in America. This step should be brought out in the open, and debated as such, rather than being concealed behind a seemingly innocuous, but actually devastating, requirement.

(6) § *112(b), p. 16, line 25.*—We vigorously object to this proposal, in part for the same reasons stated in ¶ 5, *supra.*

(7) § *304(F), p. 34, line 3.*—No comment.

In conclusion, we respectfully suggest that there are some fundamental principles that should be determinative in consideration of copyright legislation.

First, former Attorney General Katzenbach stated to the Congress that "Copyrights are forms of monopolies." (House Rep. No. 1742, 87th Cong., 2d Sess., p. 6) It is of utmost importance to realize that—

"Even at its best, copyright necessarily involves the right to restrict as well as to monopolize the diffusion of knowledge," Hudon, 49 *Amer. Bar Assn. Journal* 759 (1963).

Second, the Congress, the Supreme Court and the Register of Copyrights have all affirmed the primacy of the public interest over the copyright proprietor's interest:

(1) The House Report on the Present law stated that copyright was given— "not primarily for the benefit of the author, but primarily for the benefit of the public," House Rept. No. 2222, 60th Cong., 2d Sess., p. 7.

(2) The Supreme Court has said:

". . . the copyright law . . . makes a reward to the owner of secondary consideration," *U.S. v. Paramount Pictures, Inc.*, 334 U.S. 131, 158 (1948).

(3) And the Register of Copyrights said, in his 1961 Report to the Congress: "Within limits the author's interests coincide with those of the public. Where they conflict the public interest must prevail. . . . And the interests of authors must yield to the public welfare where they conflict." (p. 6)

Elsewhere this Report also says:

"The needs of all groups must be taken into account. But these needs must also be weighed in the light of the paramount public interest." (p. xi)

We respectfully suggest that "the paramount public interest" in the U.S. is its system of public and private schools which reaches into every home in every corner of the nation.

STATEMENT OF MRS. BELLA L. LINDEN, FOR THE AMERICAN TEXTBOOK PUBLISHERS INSTITUTE

Mrs. LINDEN. Mr. Senator, ladies and gentlemen, I listened very carefully indeed to Mr. Harry Rosenfield's comments and prayer for relief. The fact is that with respect to fair use, the agreement reached between the publishers and the educators has not in any fashion to any degree whatever been modified or abridged or retreated from by any representative of either authorship or the publishing industry.

The comment illustrative of the alleged breach, which Mr. Rosenfield adverted to, related to a comment made by an independent lawyer who had a proposal for a clearinghouse in the computer area. It was his contention that if his proposal were adopted, then fair use would become a moot question.

To say, therefore, at a hearing of the Senate that the educators feel as though, and I am quoting Mr. Rosenfield, "they were tricked into a short-term life for fair use," is a most unfortunate comment indeed. I think that I characterize it, I might submit, quite charitably.

With respect, specifically to the urging by the educational group as represented by Mr. Rosenfield this morning that section 110(2)(d) be eliminated from the law which, in the scope of the language, intends to encompass a whole area of technological uses and not, as illustrated very modestly, the kind of use where one tape purchased will be used in the fashion intended by the purchaser—that is, the school system— again, that is a most, most unfortunate oversimplification.

Section 110(2)(d) is that section which deals with computer technology, now known or hereinafter developed. It is the entire area of dialog involving so-called computerized uses of educational material to which we will address ourselves separately later.

With respect to that area of use to which the educators advert, which is known as dial access, or computer-based instruction, we submit that the books the authors write, and publishers package and distribute to the schools, are for the purpose of teaching students, not for the purpose of teaching teachers. And, therefore, the market to which these works are addressed, whether it is in hard copy form or otherwise, is the market for the pupil. If there is a technology now developed which mechanically supplants the use of hard copy instruction, which creates a different kind of environmental learning process, then we submit it is a substitute for one mechanical device, the printing presses by another mechanical device, and does not in any way result in the preemption of the private sector in the creation of educational material.

Illustrative of that point, I got permission to make known this morning an arrangement between two corporations, major corporations in this country, concluded yesterday. One of these corporations is a client of mine, and I participated in the arrangements. I would like to state as follows:

Harcourt, Brace & World, one of the five largest educational publishers in the United States, has arranged with Radio Corporation of America to create special material compatible with RCA hardware equipment for use in computer-based instruction. It should be noted that Harcourt, Brace & World is an independent publisher, neither owned nor controlled by any manufacturer of computer equipment. It is also interesting to note that Radio Corporation of America is entering into an arrangement with an unaffiliated publishing house (despite the fact that it owns a publishing house of its own) involving an exchange of views on educational goals as well as information on computer technology in the field of computer-based education. Harcourt, Brace & World intends to invest hundreds of thousands of dollars on the development of instructional material for use with these computerized systems. It is the essence of the arrangement with RCA that Harcourt, Brace & World will retain ownership of the software (i.e. the instructional material) it creates. RCA is apparently of the view that the wider the range of materials available for computer usage, the greated will be the interest of the education community in installing systems of instruction based on computers and display equipment. This is an excellent example of the way our economic system functions. The traditional incentives under our system of private ownership result in an increased improved distribution of knowledge and learning techniques for the benefit of the public at large unequalled elsewhere.

Senator McClellan. There are 3 minutes left to your side.

Mrs. Linden. I shall just finish this quickly.

Obviously, since the publisher can in no way enjoy any financial rewards from the sale by RCA of hardware equipment, the only incentive to invest the kind of time, effort and money that is essential in the development of appropriate special, novel instructional materials is the financial returns on the sale and use of its creative property. Clearly, the stimulation to proceed in this venture exists only because Harcourt, Brace & World has and envisions that it shall have appropriate copyright protection for its intellectual properties.

Senator McClellan. You have 2½ minutes left, unless you extend the time; and if the time is extended any, the other gentleman will have that much time for rebuttal.

Mr. Brennan. The next is Mr. Karp.

STATEMENT OF IRWIN KARP, AUTHOR'S LEAGUE OF AMERICA

Mr. Karp. I address myself very briefly to Mr. Rosenfield's comments on proposed section 110(1)(A), in which the educational witnesses are asking a drastic change and a broad exemption for closed circuit television. We point out first that contrary to the provisions of the present law and the provisions of the bill before your committee, this proposed exemption would cover every type of copyrighted work—not merely books and music, which for special considerations have resulted in limited exemptions—but motion pictures, plays, and other forms of work.

It means that a single performance recorded by an educational broadcaster could be multiplied and copied and broadcast not only through one school system, but through television systems of many schools throughout the country. Hundreds of thousands, and even millions of people would see one broadcast of one particular work with tremendously devastating effects for the author and publisher of that work. I would respectfully urge that this provision should not be adopted because of its dire consequences.

With the brief time remaining to me, about 30 seconds——

Senator McClellan. You have 1 minute.

Mr. Karp. Let me say that one of the basic considerations that should be kept in mind is that there cannot be a dichotomy between types of "education." We have heard much about education, and I would remind the committee that the author who writes the book that an educator reads is as much a part of the educational process as the teacher who reads it or performs it—and the author is entitled to consideration.

The author is poorly paid for his services in our society. Ironically, the few authors who write the kind of works that make a lot of money do not usually write the books that are used in schools. We would ask for the same respect for the author's services as the teacher, who organizes in a union and bargains collectively with a school system, asks for his position.

FOLLOW-UP PRESENTATION FOR EDUCOM

I am W. Brown Morton, Jr. I appeared before this Subcommittee on April 4, 1967 on behalf of EDUCOM. At that time I was accompanied by Mr. Edison Montgomery, President of EDUCOM. Dr. James G. Miller, Vice-President and Principal Scientist for EDUCOM, and Professor Arthur R. Miller of the University of

Michigan Law School, who is, with me, a member of the EDUCOM Task Force for Legal Matters, not the least of which matters is the copyright problem.

To recapitulate briefly, EDUCOM, more formally known as the Interuniversity Communications Council, is a voluntary organization founded by some eight universities in widely-scattered parts of the country and now numbering seventy member universities with about 190 campuses in 29 States and two Provinces of Canada. It was founded because it was felt that the expanding scientific capabilities for rapid data processing, information storage and retrieval electronic communication and transmission, both auditory and visual, and the consequent potential for new methods of instruction and research—in short, the "computer" revolution, compelled a joint action. Frankly, one thing the universities feared was "over-government". Now, one area of threatened over-government is copyright. S. 597, as presently phrased, would put the developing technology of our day which the higher education institutions of our country want to put to use with imagination and drive into a strait-jacket. It is suggested that higher education wants a free ride. This is not so. We want freedom to go forward, but in no sense a lack of obligation to pay proper tribute to the past. The sole argument seems to us to be about what is "proper".

In response to the request of the Subcommittee that we be specific in our attention to S. 597 and what changes require to be made in it, in EDUCOM's view to make it minimally acceptable-to EDUCOM. I set out hereinafter detailed language drafted after day-long consideration by a Drafting Subcommittee of EDUCOM's Legal Task Force consisting of Professor Benjamin Kaplan of Harvard Law School and Professor Arthur Miller of Michigan Law School and myself. I characterize the changes thus suggested as minimal simply to avoid the inference that the resulting amended bill would constitute the ideal 1967 Copyright Law that anyone of the Drafting Subcommittee would himself advance. It is, I think, a fair statement that all members of the EDUCOM Legal Task Force would prefer to see a completely fresh approach made to a copyright law for the future which wasn't an attempt at modification of a draft which had taken its principle form before the problems of modern technology had been made apparent. The reasoning which underlies EDUCOM's position seems correctly and properly stated in our April 4th presentation and I will not burden the record with a repetition.

Specific EDUCOM Minimal Changes Required to Render S. 597 Compatible With EDUCOM's Program and Objectives :

A. To deal with the limitation of copyright protection to be afforded computer programs:

Alternative 1: Add to Section 106 the following proviso:

* * * *Provided, however,* That nothing in this title shall be construed to give the owner of copyright the exclusive right to any idea, process, plan, or scheme embodied or described in the copyrighted work or the right to prevent the preparation of any copy or derivative work that is necessary to the use of any idea, process, plan, or scheme embodied or described in the copyrighted work as an incident of such use.

Alternative 2: As a separate Section :

Notwithstanding the provisions of Section 106, a work consisting of a program of instructions to cause a data processing or information storage and retrival system or any similar device, machine or process to perform selected operations is not infringed by the reproduction or other use of the work to accomplish that purpose; but subject to the provisions of this title the work may be infringed by its reproduction for sale or distribution.

B. To correct the limitation on reproduction for archival purposes which excludes many modern research and storage techniques :

Strike the word "facsimile" from Section 108.

C. To deal with the matter of computer input, EDUCOM would be satisfied with the proposal already made and identified as McGowan proposal. However, the following would also satisfy EDUCOM :

As a separate section :

Notwithstanding the provisions of Section 106, the input or introduction of a copyrighted work, whether by means of a copy or derivative work or otherwise, into a data process or information storage and retrival system or any similar device, machine, or process, such input or introduction is merely ancillary or incident to a performance or display of the work declared non-infringing by Sections 108 or 110 shall not be considered an infringement.

D. The exemption provided by Section 110(2) of S. 597 is peculiarly directed to the needs of educational television. EDUCOM does not wish to suggest modifications of exemptions satisfactory for that purpose in order to achieve exemptions satisfactory for EDUCOM'S purpose. EDUCOM, therefore, proposes an additional subsection of Section 110 as follows:

§ 110(x) performance of a nondramatic literary or musical work, or display of a work, by or in the course of a transmission by a governmental body or other nonprofit organization, if:

(a) the performance or display is a regular part of the systematic instructional, educational or research activities of a governmental body or a nonprofit educational institution; and

(b) the transmission is made for:

(i) reception in classrooms or places normally devoted to instruction, education, or research, or

(ii) reception by persons to whom the transmission is directed because their disabilities or other special circumstances prevent their attendance in classrooms or similar places normally devoted to instruction, education, or research, or

(iii) reception by officers or employees of governmental bodies as a part of their official duties or employment; and

(c) when the transmission emanates from a data processing or information storage and retrieval system or any similar device, machine or process, and the transmission is carried on a closed system and received by persons engaged in instructional, educational, or research activities at a nonprofit organization or officers or employees of governmental bodies as a part of their official duties or employment;

E. EDUCOM recommends that the Copyright Act include provision for the creation of an Advisory Council or other regularly established and funded body for the continued review and improvement of the workings of copyright. A model for such a Council which would be acceptable to EDUCOM can be found in the proposal of Section 15 of the proposed Patent Reform Act of 1967, S. 1042, 90th Congress, First Session.

F. EDUCOM believes that there should be a specific relief of non-profit organizations from the injunctive remedy for certain otherwise infringement acts and proposes the following as an additional section:

In the case of the non-exempt use by non-profit educational institution through the medium of a data process and information storage retrieval system or any similar device or process of a work which has been published or publicly performed or displayed by or with the authority of the copyright proprietor, the institution shall not be subject to the remedies provided in Sections 502–506 but, instead, shall be liable to pay a license fee reasonable for an institution of that kind as found by the Court under the circumstances of the case.

Respectfully submitted.

W. BROWN MORTON, Jr.

Senator McCLELLAN. Thank you. You have used only 14 minutes. You yield back a minute of your time.

Mr. BRENNAN. Mrs. Linden is next.

Senator McCLELLAN. All right, Mrs. Linden. How much time do you wish to take?

STATEMENT OF MRS. BELLA L. LINDEN, THE AMERICAN TEXTBOOK PUBLISHERS INSTITUTE

Mrs. LINDEN. I should like 2 days, 2 years; but I would be satisfied with 8 or 9 minutes.

I certainly agree with Mr. Brown Morton that the educational community authorship and publishers are not truly here in an adversary position, although the express relief each side is requesting appears like an outright difference of view. I suspect—more than suspect, I am firmly convinced—that all of us, functioning in a field of intercommunication, simply have not communicated sufficiently or properly with each other.

Mr. Brown Morton and I concur. Neither of us knows what we mean when we say "computer" program. It is an imprecise word. It is a word used with respect for the present state of the art. In other words, as computer technology burgeons and develops and explodes even in the kind of arrangement between Harcourt, Brace, and RCA, what today is considered a computer program may be considered an entire new work tomorrow. Therefore, it would be most unfortunate, indeed, if we settled one way or the other on a copyright law that utilizes terms or concepts of a technology that, brilliant as its future appears to be and undoubtedly will be, is still in its relative infancy.

Secondly, with respect to computer input, I have not heard Mr. Brown Morton say it this morning, but I have heard his colleagues readily agree, and I have heard all people who have addressed themselves to the subject in my presence, all concur, that computer technology, computer input, is not a simple process or device. It is not one kind of using of material, but various ways of using of material. Some is facsimile copy, some is the actual taking of text material and converting it via keypunch or an electric typewriter into machine-readable form.

There are undoubtedly other techniques. There are scanning devices now being developed. Therefore, any discussion today involving express language changes in the law, which take into account the present usage or the relevance of computer input, would again, I submit, be most unfortunate, indeed.

Therefore, it seems to me that—oh, I must add in addition, that all of us agree that the use, and it was so stated by the Educom representatives when they last testified here, and it is part of the record, that the use of actual total texts or textual material is not yet commercially viable. Opinion varies among the experts. All seem to place it 5 to 10 years hence, whether they are IBM representatives, RCA representatives, professors, at universities, or otherwise. Therefore, again there is no immediate—immediate—need to change the existing law, whether it is the law as it is in effect today or the law that is to be legislated if this House and Senate agree so to amend the law. There is no justification, I submit, to change the language of the law until we are all certain that we know what we are talking about.

At the time that Educom last testified, in response to Senator Burdick's direct question as to how they use today, or propose to use, because they are not using it yet, any text material, their response is, "It is all experimental; it is for experimental purposes only." The word used actually was "tinkering." We are "tinkering" with copyrighted material.

In response to a further question at that hearing where the publishers have been approached and asked whether they would give permission under existing law, not under the proposed bill, for the experimentation or tinkering, the answer was a hesitant, "Well, we have not gotten around to it yet, except with respect to one publishing organization." And that publishing organization responded, so Educom testified, affirmatively, gave all the use of the work that was required for experimental purposes.

Therefore, the question really, the essence of the dialog is not that the publishers and authors wish to stay with the Gutenberg invention.

The fact is that publishers, and we reiterate, do not own printing presses, do not own papermills, do not own binderies. They, together with authorship, create, package, promote, sell, distribute information, knowledge, text material to the educational community at large. They have no vested interest whatsoever in traditional techniques of distributing information. All they ask and all they seek is that in an economy of private enterprise, the concept of a private sector be retained, and that those people who create and package the intangible property, intellectual property, be afforded the same kind of respect, the same kind of economic incentive as those who create machinery, hardware, tables, chairs, airplanes, guns, and milk. All they seek is parity. They do not seek a superior position.

It has been urged repeatedly by some limited group that copyright is a monopoly. The word "monopoly," is an emotionally charged phrase in our country, and we respond, all of us do—I, as well as the users of this phrase—with a certain amount of abhorrence. But the fact is that the kind of monopoly granted to copyright is not the kind that our antitrust laws advert to. Copyright says to the creator of the work, first you have to make it available for everyone to read and understand your ideas, or at least the opportunity to, before you get any reward whatsoever. So that it is not a withholding of intellectual property; it is an incentive to distribute intellectual property. If we are to retain a private sector in our economy, if we are not to have a nationalized utility or a nationalized industry, either a Government-sponsored or utility-supervised information and knowledge utility, we must retain the private competitive sector. And that can only be done for the good of the public, for the good of all Americans extant, existing, and future.

If we recognize the balance and scale, and if we recognize the existence of private property in intangible things, in material as well as abstract things, in the expression of ideas as well as in the machinery, whether it is in the printing press or a radio station or sophisticated computers which accomplish the other much more effectively, we must recognize that without freedom of creation, without competitive creation, the alternatives are inimical to the American system.

We, therefore, urge that great caution be exercised before any legislation is contemplated, before there is a breakdown of negotiations between authors and publishers and users, before there has been a destruction of the normal give and take of the marketplace. We urge that a study group be organized and that the law be left alone for a 3- to 5-year period so that all of us would then knowingly understand the technology that would already be in existence before we legislate in any respect with respect to it.

Senator McCLELLAN. You used 8 minutes. There are 7 minutes left.

STATEMENT OF HORACE S. MANGES, AMERICAN BOOK PUBLISHERS COUNCIL

Mr. MANGES. Mr. Chairman, from both copyright owners and users, we hear a plea for further study of this problem. We think well of Educom's alternative suggestion of an advisory council to report to a congressional committee. This study after the law is passed, the council being built into the law, I take it, is what Educom would like. The main question at issue is what should be the law pending completion and availability of the study. With respect to mechanized informational systems, should copyrighted material be subject to control of the copyright owner at input or output, subject, of course, to the application of the doctrine of fair use? I do not believe that this approach can be fairly criticized as Gutenbergian.

We submit that under the present law, input is simultaneously a translation, a new version and a copy of the original work—and, on all of these counts, is an infringement. We urge that such law be not changed unless and until a thorough study of the problem establishes the fairness of any such radical move.

One of the witnesses for the Ad Hoc Committee on Educational Institutions testified last month before this subcommittee that during any study interval we should "maintain the traditional exemptions." Certainly the rights to translate, to make new versions and to copy have always belonged to the copyright owner.

The same witness then said, "We would like to tinker. We would like to see the capacity of these devices. Let us do so while this study is going on."

In reply, we say we have no desire to thwart scholarship. By all means, let technology be advanced. Experiment, yes; tinker, yes. But do so, either with the vast amount of material in the public domain or with copyrighted material as to which permission has been obtained.

We believe that many publishers would issue licenses for experimental use, and some have already done so when requested. We contend that such permission can be obtained at reasonable cost and within a reasonable time. Until the results of a study are available, let us not risk applying a drastic remedy to other peoples' property which may destroy an entire market of theirs. Such market may develop into one of their most important substantial sources of revenue. We contend that a likelihood exists that the mere presence of an electronic reproduction in a machine could deprive a publisher of a substantial market for printed copies, and that if input were exempted, there would likewise be no market for machine-readable copies.

We also urge that control at input is essential. We contend that it is most inequitable to base control on output, which does not clearly reflect the value of the function which the copyrighted work performs. Manipulation within the system by computation, analysis, comparison, or combination with other data may well play a role which is of great value to the computer owner, yet there would be no adequate compensation for the creative efforts of the author.

Moreover, it would seem likely that if copyrighted instructional materials are to be put into computerized informational systems without payment or permission, the creation of such materials will be severely discouraged.

Moreover, we contend that it would be exceedingly difficult for a copyright owner to protect his work against distortion, mutilation, or other misuses if he has no control over input.

We submit that there is greater danger of injustice in legislating prematurely in an area of new and fast-developing technology. Accordingly, we urge that in those sections of the bill where the rights of the parties are affected by scientific progress, the bill should be sufficiently

general to permit study while still protecting the rights of authors
and publishers.

Senator McCLELLAN. Thank you very much.

Mr. Karp has 3 minutes.

STATEMENT OF IRWIN KARP, AUTHOR'S LEAGUE OF AMERICA

Mr. KARP. Mr. Chairman, it is obvious from the testimony before
your committee and from discussion in other forums that the only
thing that is certain is that there is great uncertainty about what a
computer is, what a storage and retrieval system is, and great uncertainty as to what impact they will have upon the creative work of
authors and publishers. The proposal by Educom, for example, with
reference to data process or information storage and retrieval system
is broad enough to cover not only what some of us think of as a computer (a shiny new IBM) machine—it would cover a system as simple
as a drawer full of microfilm cards or as complex as a nationwide
"bookless" library. There are many kinds of storage systems and information retrieval systems.

Secondly, no matter in what shape or direction the new technology
goes, it is creating a whole new medium for communicating creative
and intellectual production. It is not a matter of whether it is comparable to the book. We are creating whole new systems which will reproduce and disseminate the book, and we are asked today to freeze
out authors.

We cannot blindly assume on the basis of the incomplete information available that input alone is no problem and that to allow an
exemption to these vast new systems, these possibly nationwide public
utilities of knowledge, we are harming no one. On the contrary, there is
much concrete evidence already that the insertion of certain types of
information into computers ends forever their usefulness in any other
form, because they will never be printed out again. Their great value
is as reference material, and the reference will be made in the future,
perhaps, to one volume in one national computer system, rather than
to thousands of copies of that same book on a library shelf. It is obvious that until this problem is studied, no intelligent exclusion can
be formulated.

SUPPLEMENTAL STATEMENT OF AMERICAN BOOK PUBLISHERS COUNCIL, INC.

The Council limits itself herein to such rebuttal material which it was unable
to include in the oral presentation on April 28th because of lack of time or
because the material was published thereafter or which embraces subjects not
selected by the Chairman for oral argument.

AD HOC COMMITTEE'S STATUTORY PROPOSALS OF MARCH 16, 1967

The Council vigorously opposes the amendments proposed in the appendix to
the statement dated March 16, 1967 of Dr. Harold E. Wigren, Chairman of the
Ad Hoc Committee on Educational Institutions and Organizations. These proposals seek to broaden what the Council deems already too broad exemptions set
forth in Sections 110(2) and 112(b).

Sections 106, 108, 110, 502–506

It is the Council's position that none of the foregoing proposals should be favorably acted upon except that portion of "E" which recommends that the Bill should include provision for the creation of an Advisory Council for the continued review and improvement of the workings of copyright, such Advisory Council to report to the Congress.

The Council submits that in order to prevent the likelihood of substantial damage to the rights of authors and publishers without proof of valid reason therefor, all the other Educom proposals should await the proposed study and recommendations thereon except that in the Council's view no further study is required to decide that Section 110 is already too broad and should not be extended beyond instruction, to education or research.

FAIR USE

Section 107

The seriousness of the photocopying problem to authors and publishers is vividly pointed up in an article in the Wall Street Journal of May 2, 1967 entitled "Copiers & Copyrights". An example of present practice, which is likely to be extended substantially in the future, is there described as follows:

"Copying has spread well beyond libraries, of course. One disgruntled publisher cites Massachusetts Avenue in Cambridge, Mass., as 'the Sunset Strip of copying.' The street goes through Harvard Square, home of Harvard University, and some dozen local shops offer copying facilities to the students thronging the area.

"A Cambridge men's clothing store, J. August Co., has a Xerox 2400, the company's biggest and fastest model, installed near the neckties. It's 'used steadily, nine solid hours a day,' says the store's president, James M. Jacobs. He's planning to install a second machine.

"'This is an aid to education,' says Mr. Jacobs. The students dash in and Xerox chapters of books in short supply at the library or articles from scholarly journals they have smuggled out, he says."

Especially in the light of warnings like the foregoing (aside from the reasons presented orally) the Council urges this Subcommittee to adopt the interpretation of the House Committee Report as to the fourth criterion governing fair use (H.R. Committee Report, p. 35).

THE CONSTITUTIONAL QUESTION

The Constitution in Article I, Section 8, provides that Congress "shall have the power to promote the Progress of Science and Useful Arts by securing for limited Times to Authors and Inventors the exclusive Right to their respective Writings and Discoveries."

The recorded material (generally music) contained on records is written and composed by *authors*. Those who perform the music and those who record it are not authors but merely performers and recorders; their contribution, though of importance, is not *authorship*. Additionally, *writings* can only mean something readable or visually perceptible and cannot be stretched to mean sounds recorded on cylinders or disks. It is true the courts have interpreted the Constitutional provision liberally. Photographs, motion pictures and statuary have received judicial protection as writings. But however much the term "writings" is stretched, it certainly cannot encompass what is not visually perceptible and what cannot be made visually perceptible in any meaningful way even with the aid of a machine or device.

That there is a limit to *"writings-*stretching" has been made clear by the Supreme Court. In the landmark *Trade-Mark Cases 100 U.S. 82 (1879)* the Court held that the Congress does not have the power under Article I, Section 8 to protect trade-marks because trade-marks lack originality and creativity and are not the writings of authors. In the course of so deciding the Court said that the "ordinary trade-mark has no necessary relation to invention or discovery . . . If we should endeavor to classify it under the heading of 'writings of authors,' the objections are equally strong. In this as in regard to invention, originality is required. And while the word 'writings' may be liberally construed, as it has been, to include original designs for engraving, prints, etc., it is only such as are *original*, and are founded in the creative powers of the mind."

The Supreme Court, having thus noted in the *Trade-Mark Cases* that it is liberal to construe "writings" to include engravings and prints, in *Burrow-Giles Lith. Co. v. Sarony, 111 U.S. 53, 58, 4 Sup. Ct. 279, 281 (1884)*, held "writings" to include a photograph. The court on this occasion said the word was not intended to be restricted to books only but "By writings in that clause is meant the literary productions of those authors, and congress very properly has declared these to include all forms of writing, printing, engravings, etchings, etc., by which the ideas in the mind of the author are given *visible expression.*" (emphasis supplied) In 1908 in *White-Smith Music Pub. Co. v. Apollo Co. 209 U.S. 1, 28 Sup. Ct. 319 (1908)* the Court had before it the question whether perforated rolls of music to be used in connection with the defendant's player pianos were copies" of the plaintiff's music and consequently, under the statute then in effect, an infringement of the copyright in the plaintiff's music compositions. Under the pre-1909 statute if the rolls were not copies of the musical notation of the plaintiff, that is the "writing," then they would not infringe. The Court held that "When the combination of musical sounds is reproduced to the ear it is the original tune as conceived by the author which is heard. These musical tones are not a copy which appeals to the eye. In no sense can musical sounds which reach us through the sense of hearing be said to be copies as that term is generally understood, and as we believe it was intended to be understood in the statutes under consideration." (p. 323 of 28 Sup. Ct.) The Court held that "These perforated rolls are parts of a machine which, when duly applied and properly operated in connection with the mechanism to which they are adapted, produce musical tones in harmonious combination. But we cannot think they are copies within the meaning of the copyright act." (p 323 of 28 Sup. Ct.)

In *Mazer v. Stein, 347 U.S. 201 (1954)* the Supreme Court held that since the parties in that case had not properly raised the question of the Constitutional power of Congress to confer copyright protection on works of art or their reproduction the Court would not consider the question. Justices Douglas and Black disagreed with the majority about considering the question and said "It is time that we came to the problem full face." They asked, "Is a sculptor an 'author' and is his statue a 'writing' within the meaning of the Constitution? We have never decided the question."

If there is a serious question about whether the Constitutional term "writings" is broad enough to include statuettes and if sound recordings are merely "parts of a machine which . . . produce musical Tones in harmonious combination" and are "not intended to be read" and not "copies" of musical writing and certainly not visually perceptible, with or without the aid of a machine or device, can it be doubted that they are not "writings," in the Constitutional sense, even when the word is construed liberally? We respectfully submit to you that whatever else they may be and whatever merit they may have, phonograph records or sound recordings are not "writings" and are not within the Constitutional power of the Congress to protect under the copyright statute.

In conclusion, Gentlemen, we believe that it is unnecessary, undesirable and unconstitutional to extend copyright performing rights protection to records.

Thank you very much.

———

AMERICAN CHEMICAL SOCIETY,
Ann Arbor, Mich., May 5, 1967.

Hon. JOHN L. McCLELLAN,
Chairman, Senate Judiciary Subcommittee on Patents, Trademarks and Copyright, Senate Office Building, Washington, D.C.

DEAR MR. CHAIRMAN: The American Chemical Society is the largest membership organization devoted to a single science in the entire world. Membership consists of more than 106,000 chemists and chemical engineers. The Society is a non-profit organization originally incorporated in New York State in 1876 and reincorporated by an Act of Congress in 1937.

It should be noted that the American Chemical Society was chartered by the Congress of the United States under Public Law No. 358, 75th Congress, Chapter 762, 1st Session, which was signed into law by President Franklin D. Roosevelt on August 25, 1937. Our interest in S. 597, a bill providing for the general revision of the copyright laws, Title 17, United States Code, which is now being considered by the Subcommittee is self-evident from a reading of the objects of the Society, as set forth in Sec. 2 of its Congressional charter which provides as follows:

SEC. 2. That the objects of the incorporation shall be to encourage in the broadest and most liberal manner the advancement of chemistry in all its branches; the promotion of research in chemical science and industry; the improvement of the qualifications and usefulness of chemists through high standards of professional ethics, education, and attainments; the increase and diffusion of chemical knowledge; and by its meetings, professional contacts, reports, papers, discussions, and publications, to promote scientific interests and inquiry, thereby fostering public welfare and education, aiding the development of our country's industries, and adding to the material prosperity and happiness of our people.

A vital part of the Society's activities by which it seeks to realize its purpose to encourage in the broadest and most liberal manner the advancement of chemistry in all its branches is its publications program, the largest of its kind in the world. The Society's publications program now includes 18 journals varying from scholarly journals containing reports of original research from such fields as medicinal chemistry, biochemistry, and agricultural and food chemistry, to a weekly newsmagazine designed to keep chemists and chemical engineers abreast of the latest developments affecting their science and related industries. In addition, the Society is the publisher of CHEMICAL ABSTRACTS, one of the world's most comprehensive abstracting and indexing services.

In its 1966 budget the Society provided $16 million in support of its publications program. This money will be derived chiefly from subscriptions. The journals and other published writings of the Society serve two important functions, namely: First, they accomplish the increase and diffusion of chemical knowledge and related purposes of the Society. Secondly, they generate revenue, without which the Society could not support and continue its publications program in furtherance of its Congressional charter. The protection of copyright has proved an important factor in the growth and development of the scientific publishing program of the Society.

For these and related reasons, the Society has followed with great interest the studies and activities of the Copyright Office of the Library of Congress and of the committees of the House and Senate which have now culminated in your Subcommittee's consideration of S. 597 relative to the general revision of the present copyright laws set forth in Title 17, United States Code.

Although we have noted with great interest the many substantial changes in the copyright law which will result from the enactment of S. 597, we will limit our comment at this time to the deeply troublesome issues related to the doctrine of "fair use," and the photocopying or other means by which machines are being widely used today to reproduce written and printed matter of every description. Section 107 of the pending bill mentions what lawyers refer to as the doctrine of fair use and defines it in part. Under this doctrine, which we are informed is merely a codification of what is in all likelihood the present law in the United States, it is not an infringement of copyright to reproduce excerpts of a copyrighted work for certain restricted and qualified purposes such as criticism, comment, news reporting, teaching, scholarship, or research.

Looking elsewhere in the Bill we note other limitations imposed upon the otherwise exclusive rights of a copyright proprietor to reporduce or copy his copyrighted material, and to permit or deny that privilege to others. We are also aware that certain interests have been quite active in their efforts to persuade the Copyright Office and the Congress that still other uses should be permitted without the necessity for securing the permission of the copyright proprietor. These provisions of the Bill and the pressures being exerted to secure still further concessions which will further limit the right of copyright proprietors to protect their material against unauthorized uses are of genuine concern to the American Chemical Society.

The American Chemical Society disseminates more scientific information in the field of chemistry than any other organization. Our accomplishments in area have been recognized both by Congress and by other branches of Government. Our accomplishments in this area have been recognized both by Congress and by other branches of Government. Our investments are great from the standpoint of both manpower and dollars. We believe that our service program is a vital service which must be continued. The Society is deeply concerned, however, that the unauthorized use of materials under an increasingly liberalized "fair use" doctrine could impair or even destroy our ability to generate, publish and disseminate such scientific information in the future. While the Society in no way seeks to hamper or restrict either the learning process or the use of technological developments and equipment needed to improve the exchange of information, it cannot be oblivious to the effects of these developments on the essential financial support needed to continue the publishing function which generates the basic materials. Accordingly, we would urge that this Subcommittee weigh carefully the wisdom of adopting any new proposals which are either designed to permit, or will necessarily result in the further impairment or destruction of these sources of scientific writings.

The Society conducts research and experimentation on the use of computers and allied electronic devices for the handling and dissemination of scientific information. Based on our own experience and observations of the work of others doing research in this area, we see that such developments are leading us toward systems where a single original work will be used to disseminate multiple copies as well as a variety of sub-collections of information derived from the original work. In effect, we are in the process of enhancing the distribution of an author's works by replacing the printing plate with the capability of electronic processing. We urge that the proposed bill be aware of the impact of such developments on the role of copyright protection and follow a course which will in no way prove confining in terms of future technological progress.

If the present Bill is enacted, it will be the first time the United States statutes on copyright laws have ever mentioned the doctrine of fair use. While the purposes of doing so are laudatory, we are concerned that the language in Section 107 will be misinterpreted by some and deliberately distorted by others for the purpose of making unauthorized uses of copyrighted material not intended by the Congress. For these reasons, we think it would be wiser to delete Section 107 from the Bill in its entirety so that persons will be encouraged to inquire before reproducing copyrighted materials.

The American Chemical Society is actively engaged in a continuing program of development and study relative to the photocopying problem, the use of computerized technology and the question of fair use, in an effort to find solutions which are compatible with the best interests of both copyright producers and users. We are vigorously pursuing a long-standing program to provide interested persons with copies of materials copyrighted by the Society at the lowest possible cost, and to license others to reproduce such materials.

Despite these efforts, it is an accepted fact that photocopying of complete articles and other copyrighted materials is a widely practiced among scientists as in other lines of endeavor. Although we have no figures to indicate precisely the volume of such copying, in terms of subscription losses, it does appear that the amount of photocopying of chemical publications is considerably higher than in other fields of science. In a study of the copying of technical journals from the New York Public Library, five American Chemical Society journals appeared on the list of 22 most copied journals, and ranked 2, 3, 5, 12, and 13, respectively. Bonn, George S., "Science Technology Periodicals," *Library Journal*, 88(5), 951–8, March 1, 1963.

The American Chemical Society will continue to explore these problems in an effort to find solutions on a private level and we are willing to participate with others in any studies concerning this general problem. While these efforts are being made by private interests, we urge that this Subcommittee carefully scrutinize any proposals it may receive relative to the imposition of further limitations upon the rights of copyright proprietors.

Respectfully submitted.

C. G. OVERBERGER.

PATENTS, TRADEMARKS, AND COPYRIGHTS

Mr. McCLELLAN, from the Committee on the Judiciary, submitted the following

REPORT

OF THE

COMMITTEE ON THE JUDICIARY
UNITED STATES SENATE

MADE BY ITS

SUBCOMMITTEE ON
PATENTS, TRADEMARKS, AND COPYRIGHTS

[Pursuant to S. Res. 49, 91st Cong., first sess., as extended]

INTRODUCTION

During the first session of the 91st Congress, pursuant to Senate Resolution 49, which was approved on February 7, 1969, the Standing Subcommittee on Patents, Trademarks and Copyrights was authorized to "conduct a full and complete examination and review of the administration of the Patent Office and a complete examination and review of the statutes relating to patents, trademarks, and copyrights." To enable the subcommittee to carry out its duties under the resolution, the Senate authorized expenditures of $105,000 for the period between February 1, 1969 and January 31, 1970. By a careful handling of the monies appropriated, the subcommittee was not required to seek additional funds from the Senate last year to cover the increased salaries authorized by the July pay bill and was able to return approximately $1,000 to the contingent fund of the Senate at the expiration of the resolution.

The Judiciary Committee in 1969 referred to the subcommittee twenty-three bills in which the subject matter thereof pertained to patents, trademarks or copyrights. The activities of the subcommittee last year included the study of and evaluation of these measures. Among the legislation referred to the subcommittee were bills to provide for the general revision of both the copyright law and patent law, private relief measures in the field of patent law, bills to amend the trademark statutes to provide for a Federal law of unfair competition and legislation to extend the duration of copyright protection in certain cases. Several of these measures were acted upon by the subcommittee during the first session of this Congress. The activities of the subcommittee also included the providing of assistance by the staff to Members of the Senate on matters relating to patents, trademarks and copyrights.

COPYRIGHT LAW REVISION

The most significant development in 1969 in the field of copyright law revision was the approval of legislation by the subcommittee to provide for the first general revision of the copyright laws and procedures since 1909. As the subcommittee had concluded its extensive hearings on this subject in the 90th Congress, it was able last year to complete action on S. 543, the current copyright revision legislation. The subcommittee reported S. 543 with amendments to the full Judiciary Committee on December 10th with a recommendation that it be approved. It is anticipated that the Judiciary Committee will consider the bill in early 1970.

Senator John L. McClellan, Chairman of the Subcommittee, introduced S. 543 on January 22, 1969. Other than for necessary technical amendments, relating principally to the effective dates of certain provisions, this bill is identical to S. 597 which Senator McClellan introduced in the 90th Congress at the request of the Librarian of Congress. The bill, as introduced, contained two titles. Title I provides for the general revision of the copyright statutes and procedures and contains the vast majority of the bill's many complicated and controversial provisions. Title II provides for the establishment in the Library of Congress of a National Commission on New Technological Uses of Copyrighted Works. During consideration of the bill, the subcommittee amended it to provide for title III. Title III provides for the Protection of Ornamental Designs of Useful Articles. A brief summary of the major provisions contained in each of the bill's three titles is included in this report.

TITLE I
REVISION OF COPYRIGHT STATUTES AND PROCEDURES

1. Subject matter of copyright

Under the bill, the subject matter of copyright is original works of authorship fixed in any tangible medium of expression, now known or later developed, from which they can be preceived, reproduced, or otherwise communicated, either directly or with the aid of a machine or device. The measure retains the present categories of copyrightable works and includes protection for the first time to sound recordings. S. 543 also specifies that the United States Government is prohibited from securing a copyright in any of its publications.

2. Single system of copyright protection

The bill abolishes the present dual system of common law protection for unpublished works and the Federal law protection for published works. The measure establishes a single system of Federal statutory protection for all works covered by the bill regardless of whether they are published or unpublished. S. 543 does not, however, abolish or limit any rights or remedies under the common law or statutes of any State with respect to unpublished works not protected by the bill, or any cause of action arising from undertakings commenced before January 1, 1971, or any activities violating rights that are not equivalent to any of the exclusive rights within the general scope of copyright as specified by the legislation.

3. Duration of copyright

Under the current law, the term of copyright is twenty-eight years from first publication or registration plus another twenty-eight years if the copyright is renewed. The bill changes this term of protection and provides in general that works created after the effective date of this legislation shall endure for a term consisting of the life of the author and fifty years after his death. With respect to joint works, the fifty years is computed from the death of the last surviving author. In the case of anonymous works, pseudonymous works, or works made for hire, the measure specifies that the term shall consist of seventy-five years from the year of its first publication, or a term of one hundred years from the year of its creation, whichever expires first. Regarding works now protected, the legislation provides that copyrights subsisting in their first term shall endure for twenty-eight years from the date it was originally secured with renewal rights for a further term of forty-seven years. For copyrights in their renewal term, the bill extends the duration of protection to seventy-five years from the date the copyright was originally secured.

4. Exclusive rights in copyrighted works

The bill provides the owner of a copyrighted work five exclusive rights. Under the measure, a copyright owner is given the exclusive right to, (1) reproduce the work in copies or phonorecords, (2) prepare derivative works based upon the work, (3) distribute copies or phonorecords of the work, (4) perform the work publicly, and (5) display the work publicly. The bill specifies, however, that certain limitations shall apply to these rights.

5. Fair use

The doctrine of fair use is one of the most important limitations on the copyright owners' exclusive rights. The fair-use limitation, which is a judicially developed doctrine, permits a limited amount of copying without it being an infringement of copyright. The bill provides for the first statutory recognition of the doctrine and specifies that the fair use of a copyrighted work, including the reproduction of copies for purposes of teaching or research is not a copyright infringement. In determining whether the doctrine applies to a particular case, the bill specifies that four factors are to be considered. These factors are the purpose and character of the use, the nature of the work, the amount of the work used and the effect of the use upon the potential market or value of the copyrighted work.

6. Reproduction by libraries and archives

Another of the limitations on a copyright owners' exclusive rights is the reproduction of copyrighted works by libraries and archives. The bill provides that under certain conditions it is not an infringement of copyright for a library or archives to reproduce or distribute no more than one copy or phonorecord of a work. The reproduction or distribution must not be for any commercial advantage and the collections of the library or archives must be available to the public or to other persons doing research in a specialized field. The measure also specifies that the reproduction or distribution of an unpublished work must be for the purpose of preservation and security, or for deposit for research use in another library or archives. The bill further provides that the reproduction of a published work must be for the purposes of replacement of a copy that is damaged, deteriorating, lost, or stolen, and that the library or archives has determined that an unused replacement cannot be obtained at a normal price from commonly-known trade sources in the United States. The rights given to the libraries and archives by this provision of the bill are in addition to those granted under the fair-use doctrine.

TITLE II

NATIONAL COMMISSION ESTABLISHED

The language in Title II, as introduced, is identical to that contained in S. 2216 approved by the Senate in the first session of the 90th Congress. The provisions of Title II establishes in the Library of Congress a National Commission on New Technological Uses of Copyrighted Works to study and compile data on the reproduction and use of copyrighted works of authorship (1) in automatic systems capable of storing, processing, retrieving, and transferring information, and (2) by various forms of machine reproduction. The measure further provides that the Commission shall make recommendations as to such changes in copyrighted law or procedures that may be necessary to assure for such purposes access to copyrighted works, and to provide recognition of the rights of the copyright owners.

Title II, as introduced, also specified that the Commission shall be composed of 23 members, consisting of a Chairman who shall be the Librarian of Congress, two Members of the Senate, two Members of the House of Representatives, seven members appointed by the President selected from authors and other copyright owners, seven members appointed by the President selected from users of copyrighted works, and four nongovernmental members appointed by the President selected from the public generally. It further required that the Senate must advise and consent to the nominations of the 18 members selected by the President. The measure also provided for the selection by the Commission of one of its members as Vice Chairman and specified that the Register of Copyrights shall serve as an ex officio member of the Commission.

During the subcommittee's consideration of Title II, concern was expressed over the scope of the Commission's study. In order to clarify the intent of the subcommittee, the measure was amended to provide that the study of the reproduction of copyrighted works by various forms of machine reproduction did not include reproduction by or at the request of instructors for use in face-to-face teaching activities. Title II was also amended to assure that the Commission's study was to include the creating of new works by the application or intervention of such automatic systems or machine reproduction.

The Subcommittee also amended Title II to provide that the Commission shall be composed of thirteen members consisting of the Librarian of Congress and twelve members appointed by the President without the advice and consent of the Senate. The twelve members appointed by the President shall consist of four selected from authors and other copyright owners; four selected from users of copyrighted works and four nongovernmental members selected from the public generally. The measure was further amended to provide that the President shall appoint the Chairman and Vice Chairman and that seven members of the Commission shall constitute a quorum. The remaining provisions of Title II are miscellaneous in nature and relate to such functions as the financing of the Commission, the filling of vacancies on the Commission, and its term which is 3 years from the effective date of the legislation.

Annual Report of the Librarian of Congress
June 30, 1969

Program for General Revision of the Copyright Law

The general revision program, which for more than a decade has been the focal point of intensive effort by the Copyright Office, was stalled throughout fiscal 1969. The substantial momentum achieved by House passage of the bill on April 11, 1967, gradually dwindled and it became apparent that Senate action would not be forthcoming before the end of the 90th Congress. This disappointing delay was the result of a complex combination of circumstances and conflicts but there is no question that the root problem was the issue of cable television. In the history of American copyright law it is hard to think of an issue that has occasioned more widespread, intense, and highly publicized controversy.

Last year's report reviewed the decision of the Supreme Court in *United Artists Television, Inc.* v. *Fortnightly Corp.*, 255 F. Supp. 177 (S.D.N.Y. 1966), *aff'd*, 377 F. 2d 872 (2d Cir. 1967), *rev'd*, 392 U.S. 390 (1968), in which at least certain kinds of cable television systems were held free of liability for copyright infringement. This decision was handed down just before the beginning of the fiscal year, but it had become clear even earlier that, whatever conclusion the Court reached, legislative progress on the general revision bill could not be expected until the impact of the ruling upon various industries had been absorbed and evaluated. It was perhaps a hopeful sign that negotiations of any sort continued, and that the whole revision program did not collapse.

Recognizing the inevitability of carrying the revision bill over into the 91st Congress, both Houses passed the fourth of a series of joint resolutions extending the duration of expiring second-term copyrights. The new law, which was signed by President Johnson on July 23, 1968, extended through December 31, 1969, copyrights that were due to lapse at the end of 1968. The program for general revision entered the 91st Congress with a noise that, if not exactly a whimper, was certainly far from a bang.

On January 22, 1969, Senator John L. McClellan, chairman of the Subcommittee on Patents, Trademarks, and Copyrights of the Senate Judiciary Committee, introduced a new revision bill S. 543. This version was essentially the same as the 1967 bill, not including the amendments added on the House floor. An innovation was a new title II, establishing a National Commission on New Technological Uses of Copyrighted Works. This measure, in the form of a separate bill, had been passed by the Senate in October 1967 but had not been acted upon by the House.

In a statement accompanying the new bill Senator McClellan explained that the text of the 1967 version had been retained in order to permit the subcommittee to resume its consideration of general revision at the point where it had been suspended by adjournment of the 90th Congress. At the same time, he reaffirmed his intention to seek affirmative subcommittee action on the bill as soon as possible in the 91st Congress.

The remainder of the fiscal year was spent in continuous meetings, discussions, and maneuvering on the cable television problem. The issues were clarified and areas of possible future compromise were suggested, but as the year ended it was obvious that agreement was a long way off. A series of meetings and drafts on the issue of library photocopying proved equally unsuccessful in resolving that issue.

On April 3, 1969, Senator Harrison A. Williams, Jr., introduced a proposed amendment to S. 543 which, among other things, was intended to give performers and record producers a right to royalties for the public performance and broadcasting of sound recordings. The new proposal, which was a substantially revised version of an earlier amendment introduced by Senator Williams in 1967, was cosponsored by Senators George Murphy, Edward W. Brooke, Thomas Dodd, Vance Hartke, Stephen M. Young, and Hugh Scott. Like its predecessor, the amendment proved controversial.

Viewing the situation of general revision as

of July 1, 1969, an objective observer could construe the frustrations of the preceding year as either a process necessary to finding solutions or as the beginning of a process of disintegration. It is too soon to predict which path the present revision program will take, but two conclusions seem clear. First, the events of the year dramatized more effectively than ever the inadequacies of the 1909 statute to deal with the copyright problems of today. Moreover, unless the present revision package succeeds in the 91st Congress, it will be necessary to reevaluate the entire legislative program and adopt new approaches.

Annual Report of the Librarian of Congress
June 30, 1970

General Revision of the Copyright Law

In this 15th year since the inauguration of the program for general revision of the copyright law, hope sprang anew when, on December 10, 1969, the Subcommittee on Patents, Trademarks, and Copyrights of the Senate Judiciary Committee approved the comprehensive revision bill, S. 543, with a number of amendments made by the subcommittee. And on December 16, 1969, in anticipation of enactment of the revision bill during 1970, Public Law 91-147 was enacted, extending until December 31, 1970, all renewal copyrights that would otherwise expire before that date.

But once again, hope dissolved into disappointment during the second session of the 91st Congress as it became evident that there would be no resolution of the tangled issue of cable television (CATV), which has recently been the main setback to general revision. On August 17, 1970, after the close of the fiscal year, Senator John L. McClellan, chairman of the subcommittee, announced that no further action on the bill would be taken in the Senate during the current session.

The revision bill as approved by the Senate subcommittee on December 10, 1969, made a number of amendments to S. 543 as it had been introduced on January 22, 1969, in the early days of the 91st Congress. Among the several major changes was a completely rewritten section 111 dealing with secondary transmissions by cable television of broadcasts of copyright material. Some of the major changes were provisions requiring payment of royalty fees for use of copyrighted sound recordings in broadcasts and other public performances, the fees to be divided between the record producers and the performers; provisions for photocopying by libraries, supplementing the general stipulations on fair use; a chapter providing for a tribunal, to be appointed as needed, for the two purposes of reviewing periodically the various compulsory license rates fixed in the bill and of determining the distribution of royalty fees paid for compulsory licenses, when claims are in dispute; and the addition, as a separate title III, of the text of the

bill previously passed by the Senate for the protection of ornamental designs of useful articles.

On the crucial issue of cable television, the new section 111 provided basically for a compulsory license permitting cable television systems to carry the signals of all local broadcast stations and a specified number, varying in different circumstances, of distant broadcast stations. The application of the license to distant stations would be subject to certain limitations, designed to preserve, to a stated extent, the exclusive rights of local broadcasters in particular programs and to maintain the blackouts imposed on local televising of professional sports events. For the compulsory license, the cable system would pay a total fee under a schedule of rates based on specified percentages of its revenue from subscribers.

In commenting on the new section 111, the Federal Communications Commission expressed its desire that the copyright revision bill do nothing more than provide for a compulsory license and fix the license fees including the method of their collection and distribution, leaving to FCC regulations the determination of which broadcast signals should be carried by cable systems under the compulsory license and the conditions and limitations on such carriage. At the same time, the Commission proposed separate legislation, introduced by Senator John O. Pastore on request on March 23, 1970, as S. 3635, which would authorize the Commission in broad terms to regulate cable (community antenna) systems.

On June 24, 1970, the FCC adopted a set of proposed rules on the carriage of broadcast signals by cable systems (35 Fed. Reg. 11045). Its proposals, which differ in several material respects from the provisions in section 111 of S. 543, were held open for comments until November 23, 1970. The Commission stated that its proposed rules would not become effective until Congress had enacted legislation to provide for payments to copyright owners.

Senator McClellan on August 17, 1970, announced that the subcommittee would not seek further action on S. 543 in the Senate during the current session. In the statement quoted in the *Congressional Record*, he said:

Accordingly, it is anticipated that by the time the 92d Congress convenes the FCC will have promulgated the necessary rules relating to the carriage of broadcast signals by cable systems and associated matters. This should facilitate action by the next Congress on the CATV provisions of the copyright bill.

He added that he intended to introduce a successor to the revision bill in the next Congress and hoped that its consideration could "resume in the Committee on the Judiciary at the point where proceedings are now being suspended."

On the same day, in conjunction with this statement, Senator McClellan introduced for himself and the other four members of the subcommittee, S. J. Res. 230, extending until December 31, 1971, all renewal copyrights that would otherwise expire before that date. This joint resolution was passed immediately by the Senate. Its effect, together with the five earlier extensions of a similar character, would be to

continue until December 31, 1971, all renewal copyrights in which the total term of 56 years would have expired between September 19, 1962, and December 31, 1971.

Annual Report of the Librarian of Congress
June 30, 1971

GENERAL REVISION OF THE COPYRIGHT LAW

At the beginning of the new fiscal year, S. 543, 91st Congress, as approved by the Subcommittee on Patents, Trademarks, and Copyrights of the Senate Judiciary Committee on December 10, 1969, was pending before the full committee. As mentioned in last year's report, Senator John L. McClellan, chairman of the subcommittee, announced on August 17, 1970, that no further action on the bill would be taken in the Senate during the remainder of that session, chiefly because of unresolved problems relating to the carriage of broadcast signals by cable systems.

On February 8, 1971, Senator McClellan reintroduced the revision bill in the 92nd Congress as S. 644, which is substantially identical to S. 543 as approved by the subcommittee in the preceding Congress. In introducing the new bill, Senator McClellan indicated that he expected the Federal Communications Commission to reach a conclusion before long on the rules it proposed to issue concerning cable system carriage of broadcast signals, after which the Senate committee could proceed with its consideration of the revision bill.

The Federal Communications Commission conducted a thorough set of hearings on various problems associated with cable television during the month of April 1971 and later indicated that it expected to decide on its rules for cable system carriage of broadcast signals by the first week in August.

A tentative agreement in principle between representatives of the cable television industry and the major producers of copyrighted motion picture television programs was announced on June 14, 1971, after a long period of negotiations. Shortly thereafter, the television broadcasters declared their strong opposition to the terms of this agreement.

On July 15, 1971, as another new fiscal year began, Senator McClellan introduced S.J. Res. 132 to extend until December 31, 1972, the duration of subsisting copyrights that had been renewed but would otherwise expire before that date. In introducing this bill, Senator McClellan summarized the situation regarding the revision bill as follows:

It is apparent that the Congress cannot complete action during this session on the legislation for general revision of the copyright law. The copyright revision bill has been delayed for several years principally because of the cable television controversy. More recently the Congress has been awaiting action by the Federal Communications Commission on the necessarily related communications aspects of CATV. The Congress has now been advised by the Chairman of the Federal Communications Commission that the Commission anticipates completing its current CATV rule-making proceedings before the start of the summer recess of the Congress. Clearly, however, adequate time will not remain for action on the revision bill and, therefore, it is necessary to consider another temporary extension of copyrights.

Annual Report of the Librarian of Congress
June 30, 1972

Fiscal 1972 was a year of renewed hope and several important developments in copyright. Hope for passage of the copyright revision bill was spurred by assurances of further action in the next Congress. A significant enactment added a new class of copyrightable material—sound recordings—to the present law.

GENERAL REVISION OF THE COPYRIGHT LAW

The bill for the general revision of the copyright law, which was passed by the House of Representatives five years ago and has been pending in the Senate since then, received a boost when Senator John L. McClellan, chairman of the Subcommittee on Patents, Trademarks, and Copyrights of the Senate Judiciary Committee, indicated on June 20, 1972, that he knew of no reason why the Subcommittee could not promptly report a revised bill in the next Congress. Senator McClellan made the statement on introducing a new measure, S.J. Res. 247, to extend for two more years the duration of certain renewed copyrights. He pointed out that progress by the Congress on the revision bill has been delayed by the copyright and regulation ramifications of the cable television controversy pending before the Federal Communications Commission, but that completion of the commission's proceedings and its recent adoption of new rules had opened the way for the copyright bill. He stated that a modified version of the bill would be introduced in the 93d Congress and that he intended to bring the bill to the floor of the Senate at the earliest feasible time.

Copyright for Sound Recordings

On October 15, 1971, President Richard M. Nixon approved a measure amending the copyright law by making published sound recordings copyrightable under certain conditions, and by providing additional sanctions for infringement—including criminal prosecution in certain cases—where copyrighted musical works are unlawfully used on sound recordings.

By the terms of this enactment, Public Law 92-140, a sound recording may be subject to statutory copyright protection if the sounds constituting the recording as published were first fixed on or after February 15, 1972, and if the sound recording is published with a notice of copyright in the form prescribed by the law. This act, whose provisions were taken in substance from the general revision bill, was enacted to combat the widespread and systematic piracy that had seriously jeopardized the market for legitimate tapes and discs. It provides for the protection of sound recordings against their unauthorized duplication and distribution to the public. To be subject to protection under this enactment, the recording must have been published with a special form of copyright notice, consisting of the symbol ℗, the year of its first publication, and the name of the copyright owner of the sound recording.

This measure, which adds a new category of copyrightable material to the statute for the first time in half a century, required considerable preparation by the Copyright Office. The Regulations of the Copyright Office were amended; a new application, Form N, was printed and copies distributed for use in making registrations; printed information circulars and announcements were issued; and physical facilities for the handling and examination of the applications and deposits were prepared.

The new law became effective on February 15, 1972. During the remainder of the fiscal year, registrations were made for 1,141 sound recordings, and it is expected that an appreciably larger number will be registered in the next fiscal year. Among the inquiries and legal problems generated by the law are the scope of the sound recording copyright, the relationship of that copyright to the underlying musical, literary, or dramatic work, and the copyrightability of various "new versions" of previous recordings.

When registration has been made and processing in the Copyright Office completed, the deposit copies of the recordings are transferred to other departments of the Library of Congress, where they are available for addition to the collections.

Annual Report of the Librarian of Congress
June 30, 1973

Some activity on the bill for the revision of the copyright law, a general increase in the workload, significant administrative changes in the Copyright Office, and important progress on the international scene—these were the major developments in the copyright field during fiscal 1973.

GENERAL REVISION OF THE COPYRIGHT LAW

The bill for the general revision of the copyright law was put before the 93d Congress with the introduction of S. 1361 on March 26, 1973, by Senator John L. McClellan, chairman of the Subcommittee on Patents, Trademarks, and Copyrights of the Senate Judiciary Committee. Except for certain technical changes, the new bill was identical with the measure introduced in the 92d Congress and was similar, other than for some few amendments, to the bill in the 91st Congress that was approved by the subcommittee in December 1969. A similar bill had been passed by the House of Representatives in April 1967.

Senator McClellan stated, in introducing the new bill, that the cable television issue had precluded progress on general revision and that another major issue, the photocopying of copyrighted works, was at present the subject of considerable attention. While expressing reservations about the value of further hearings, he indicated that the subcommittee would hear supplementary presentations on issues that might have been affected by recent developments. And, as the fiscal year ended, hearings were announced for July 31 and August 1, 1973, on library photocopying, general educational exemptions, the cable television royalty schedule, carriage of sporting events by cable television, and an exemption for recording religious music for broadcasts.

H.R. 8186, a bill for the general revision of the copyright law, identical with its Senate counterpart, was introduced on May 29, 1973, by Representative Bertram L. Podell. No action was taken by the House on this bill during the fiscal year.

The Williams & Wilkins Case:
The Williams & Wilkins Company
v.
The United States

IN THE

United States Court of Claims

No. 73–68

THE WILLIAMS & WILKINS COMPANY,

Plaintiff,

—against—

THE UNITED STATES,

Defendant.

PLAINTIFF'S BRIEF

ALAN LATMAN
COWAN, LIEBOWITZ & LATMAN
Attorney for Plaintiff
200 East 42nd Street
New York, New York 10017

ARTHUR J. GREENBAUM,
of Counsel

STATEMENT OF THE CASE

Introduction

This is an action for copyright infringement under 28 U.S.C. §1498 (b). The action is based on the photocopying of articles from plaintiff's copyrighted journals by defendant through its National Institutes of Health ("NIH") and National Library of Medicine ("NLM"). The photocopying is part of a comprehensive system whereby the libraries routinely fill requests for journal articles by photocopying them. Under this system, several million pages per year are copied.

There has never been any controversy as to the following facts: (a) plaintiff is the proprietor of record of copyrights covering the journals in question; (b) defendant copied directly from plaintiff's journals, thereby physically producing facsimiles; and (c) such copying reproduced the *entire* articles in question. As a result, it is submitted that plaintiff has established a *prima facie* case of infringement of its rights under Section 1 (a) of the Copyright Act.*

The key inquiry is whether defendant has rebutted plaintiff's *prima facie* case by establishing any of its defenses. Commissioner Davis correctly found that defendant had not done so, issuing a 32-page Opinion

_____
* 17 U.S.C. § 1(a) provides: "Any person entitled thereto, upon complying with the provisions of this title, shall have the exclusive right: (a) To print, reprint, publish, copy, and vend the copyrighted work;"

together with 45 Findings of Fact and a recommended Conclusion of Law "that plaintiff is entitled to recover reasonable and entire compensation for infringement of copyright". Only defendant has filed exceptions to the Commissioner's Report.

The Court has before it three *amicus* briefs in support of defendant totaling 219 pages. Consent of the parties has already been given to the filing of several *amicus* briefs in favor of plaintiff. It is recognized that neither the number of pages nor number or identity* of *amici* is significant in this appeal. Rather, there is only one appropriate basis for determination of this appeal: the full record of evidence actually offered and admitted. as governed by the law to be discussed below. The result should be this Court's conclusion that the considered and comprehensive findings and opinion and recommended conclusion of law of the Commissioner are eminently well-reasoned. well-documented and correct.

Accordingly, we submit that determination of the appeal is not aided by references to the partiality or

_____
* Distinguished societies such as the American Chemical Society, American Institute of Physics, National Council of Teachers of Mathematics, Authors League of America, Association of American Publishers, Association of American University Presses, and American Society for Testing and Materials are filing briefs in support of the Commissioner's Report, following the filing in support of defendant of *amicus* briefs by equally distinguished groups, including the American Library Association ("ALA"), Association of Research Libraries ("ARL") and the National Education Association of the United States ("NEA").

"predisposition" or "subjectivity" of the Commissioner (Deft. Brief, pp. 6, 54 n. 1; ALA Brief, p. 5); reliance on material either expressly excluded from evidence (Deft. Brief p. 26, see n. 2) or never offered (e.g., *Id.*, pp. 58–59; ARL Brief, pp. 53–60); selectively appending letters written by or to the plaintiff after the trial of this case (ALA Brief, Appendix); practices followed by one or more *amici* in situations not fully explained to the Court (ARL Brief, p. 4)* nor to editorials by interested parties commenting on Commissioner Davis' Opinion (See Deft. Brief, p. 26, n. 1).

We also submit that determination of this case is not materially aided by the mass of data concerning the mission of NIH and NLM and the purposes for which the articles in question were photocopied. (See, *e.g.*, Deft. Brief, pp. 30–33; ARL Brief, p. 76, ff.; ALA Brief pp. 16–19). There is no disagreement between the parties on these matters, but they beg the question. In

_____
* The practices of the American Medical Association with regard to its journal are referred to by defendant (Brief 26, 49). If these practices were relevant and had been admitted in evidence at the trial, they would have been subjected to cross examination, as a result of which the differences between the Journal of the American Medical Association and the journals in suit would have been revealed. For example, JAMA is distributed free of charge to all members of the AMA, is heavily supported by advertising, and is immune to the effects of photocopying because members receive the Journal free, whether they want it or not. Thus, it operates in a different economic context from that of plaintiff's journals, and accordingly is not at all "... susceptible to the harmful effects of photocopying." See Deft. Brief, p. 49. In any event, it is absurd to suggest that AMA's decisions should bind plaintiff and all other publishers and authors.

other words, "to further medical research or to improve medical treatment" (Deft. Brief, p. 30) may have been the purpose of the photocopying and indeed the mission of NIH and NLM. But it is also the purpose for which the articles were published, since the parties are also in agreement that publication in recognized private journals, such as the ones in question, is essential to research.

Plaintiff's activities contribute to research, education and biomedical communications. Thus, plaintiff as a leading medical publisher shares with others, including NIH and NLM, the task of improving public health by the dissemination of medical information.

In light of the foregoing, the beneficial purposes of defendant's library operations are no more relevant than the other socially useful activities of defendant for which compensation is regularly sought in this Court.

With these points of clarification, the correctness of the Commissioner's Findings of Fact emerges more sharply. As will be noted in detail in the Appendix, defendant actually attacks as unsupported by the record only five of the Commissioner's sixty-eight subfindings. These findings are summarized in Part I of his Opinion in a manner which, it is believed, furnishes all the necessary facts material to the consideration of the questions presented. Plaintiff will now attempt to highlight these facts.

Facts

Plaintiff, though a relatively small company, is one of the major publishers of medical journals in the United

5

States (F-1; 202).* It publishes a number of its journals in conjunction with non-profit medical and scientific societies. In such cases, the society gets from 50% to 90% of the net profits (F-9(b)).

Four journals are directly involved in this suit. Three of these have for many years been published in conjunction with societies. The journals, while prestigious, have a small number of subscriptions and sell at a moderate price. These facts may be summarized in the following table.

---

* Numbers preceded by "F." refer to the Commissioner's findings; numbers without any other abbreviation refer to transcript pages.

Journal	Society	First Published By Plaintiff With Society	1969 Approx. No. of Subscriptions	1969 Price
Medicine	—	—	5,400	$12
Pharmacological Reviews	American Society of Pharmacology and Experimental Therapeutics	1909	3,100	$15
Journal of Immunology	American Association of Immunologists	1920	4,700	$22 (society members) $44 (non-members)
Gastroenterology	American Gastroenterological Association	1946	7,000	$12.50 (society members) $25 (non-members)

5

These four journals are among the leading journals in their respective fields. For example, *Gastroenterology* is far and away the outstanding journal in the specialty of gastroenterology in the United States and probably in the world (F-9; 908). *Medicine* publishes comprehensive, definitive articles and is well-disseminated (F-9(a); 544).

Plaintiff has established a licensing program to cover various forms of exploitation of its medical journals. As summarized in Finding 36, this program includes the following:

(i) Reproduction of articles as part of a new book, particularly for use by educational institutions.

(ii) Reproduction, for a payment, of multiple copies by Government agencies and others.

(iii) Sale of microfilm editions.

(iv) Authorization of reprint houses.

(v) Royalty-bearing license to the Institute of Scientific Information to provide requesters with copies.

(vi) Licenses to libraries, including Government libraries, to make copies for users at 5 cents per page.

In 1967 and 1968, defendant concededly made at least one copy of various complete articles from the four journals mentioned above. These articles are respectively set forth in the eight counts of the complaint and are referred to by the count number in which they are alleged. In fact, the Count I work was copied three times, twice for the same user. The Count IV, Count V

7

and Count VIII works were each copied twice (F-6(b); Pltf. Ex. 11-A; 1213).

This copying was done under the comprehensive system of providing photocopies of articles in scientific journals which is an integral part of NIH library and NLM operations. Photocopying under this system is basically performed by the making of a photographic copy of the article on microfilm and by using the microfilm for further photocopying (203; 724; 751).

The NIH library photocopying service employs two Xerox copying machines and two Recordac microfilm cameras in conjunction with a Xerox Copyflo printer to provide the 12,000 NIH employees (F-12(a)) with permanent copies of journal articles (Pltf. Ex. 14, p. 15; 173–174). Four employees operate this equipment (607; 1270) and filled over 85,000 requests for photocopies of journal articles in fiscal year 1970, representing the photocopying of almost 1,000,000 pages (F-15; 621–622; 783).

NLM is a library furnishing material generally to other libraries and institutions, giving the same service to commercial interests as it does to medical schools, hospitals, foundations and government institutions (463). Requests by commercial companies, particularly drug companies, account for about 12% of NLM's services (F-21(a); Pltf. Ex. 29, p. 13; 469).

This service is referred to as "interlibrary loans"— a euphemism as applied to journal articles which are photocopied and never returned (F-21(a)). NLM, rather than the user, determines whether to make interlibrary

8

"loans" in the original or as photocopies (F-23(a); 204; 472–473).

NLM's microfilm technique uses mobile 35mm. cameras which have an electrical power line overhead and can move up and down the aisles of the library to film material which is brought to the end of the stack range (F-21(b); 724). As a result of NLM's comprehensive system of "loaning" journals by permanently furnishing photocopies of journal articles, NLM filled more than 120,000 requests, representing about 1.2 million pages of photocopies in fiscal 1968 (F-21(b)).

In performing its photocopying, defendant leases its copying machines from Xerox Corporation, whom it pays according to the number of pages photocopied (F-15; 175; 495).

The libraries in question purport to follow various limitations on their photocopying by reason, *inter alia*, of the danger of infringing copyrights (F-17(a) and (b); cf. 22; 23). Indeed, other libraries of defendant, such as the Library of Congress, in making interlibrary loans, actually lend the original volume and do not make photocopies without the authorization of the copyright proprietor (F-44; 772; Pltf. Ex. 46). Notwithstanding these purported limitations, it is impossible to enforce them (F-17(b); 1322). In any event, there is nothing in the policy of either the NIH library or NLM to prevent co-workers on the same project from each receiving copies; users from returning to secure additional copies; or other requests resulting in the making of many copies (F-17(a); F-22(a); 1256; 1320-21; 778; 806). As a result, users sometimes order a photocopy for themselves and later re-order for a colleague (F-17(b); 1355-56) or make

9

further photocopies obtained from the library to distribute to colleagues or otherwise (F-17(b); 547).

This suit for reasonable compensation was not brought to halt photocopying. The Commissioner's Opinion notes:

"Plaintiff does not seek to enjoin the photocopying of its journals. Rather, it merely seeks a reasonable royalty therefor. Its licensing program would so indicate for, as far as the record shows, plaintiff will grant licenses to anyone at a reasonable royalty" (Opinion, pp. 28-29).

The suit was undertaken to insure the survival of private, limited circulation, scientific journals (1142; 436) which all agree serve a vital national purpose (273; 489).

Questions Involved

I. Did the Commissioner err in finding that plaintiff's certificates of copyright registration establish, as a matter of law, that plaintiff has standing to bring this action?

Even if plaintiff's standing were not established as a matter of law, did the Commissioner err in finding facts establishing that plaintiff is the proper party to bring this action?

II. Did the Commissioner err in finding defendant failed to establish that its comprehensive system of copying complete articles constitutes fair use?

  A. Can copying of complete journal articles ever be fair use?

10

  B. Does the law consider the number of unauthorized copies made at one time a determinant of whether infringement has taken place?

  C. Does the fair use doctrine apply to the comprehensive system of copying utilized by the Government libraries involved in this suit?

  D. Does the general economic health of plaintiff debar it from establishing copyright infringement in this action?

I

PLAINTIFF IS THE PROPER PARTY TO BRING THIS SUIT BECAUSE IT IS THE OWNER OF COPYRIGHTS COVERING THE EIGHT ARTICLES COPIED BY DEFENDANT.

A. Plaintiff's record ownership is sufficient

Defendant concedes that plaintiff is the *record* owner of the copyrights covering the journals in question. This concession, without more, precludes defendant's argument that plaintiff is not an "owner" of copyrights entitled to sue in this court under 28 U.S.C. §1498 (b).

This Court has examined the effect of record ownership on the right to sue under the analogous patent provision, now 28 U.S.C. §1498 (a). In *N. V. Montan* v. *United States*, 102 F. Supp. 1016 (Ct. Cl. 1952), plaintiff was the assignee of a patent, but its assignment had not been recorded in the Patent Office. The Court deemed crucial the *record title* as shown in the Patent Office records and dismissed the petition.

11

Dorr-Oliver, Inc. v. *United States*, 432 F.2d 447 (Ct. Cl. 1970), applied this rule to the present situation where the plaintiff *is* the record owner. It holds that equitable ownership rights of strangers to the suit cannot be raised as defenses against the legal title holder.

Defendant nevertheless argues (Brief, p. 14) that *Dorr-Oliver* does not rule out an attack on the standing of the record title holder. But that is precisely the thrust of *Dorr-Oliver*. The Court noted there that, except for the possible impact of the anti-assignment statute (not here involved), defendant's attempt to pierce record ownership "would be dismissed without fanfare" 432 F.2d at 451.*

Similarly unsuccessful is defendant's attempt to minimize the impact of *Widenski* v. *Shapiro, Bernstein & Co.*, 147 F.2d 909 (1st Cir. 1945), with the comment that "this case simply held that the legal copyright owner was a proper and indispensable party to a suit for copyright infringement." This is precisely what the case held. And under the above precedents in this Court, plaintiff here is the "legal copyright owner" and thus the "proper . . . party" to bring this suit.

Accordingly, the precedents relied upon by the Commissioner do indeed establish the propositions for which they are cited in his Opinion.

Defendant attempts to distinguish these precedents on the ground that "the defense of nonownership as

---

* Commissioner Davis' opinion in *Dorr-Oliver* was adopted by the Court, 432 F. 2d at 449.

12

raised here by defendant is not an equitable defense, but rather a legal defense." (Brief, p. 14). If such a distinction were relevant, defendant belies this assertion on the very next page of its Brief. When one has gone through the permutations set forth on page 15 of Defendant's Brief, it appears that defendant must be arguing that plaintiff holds the copyrights as trustee. Cf. *Geisel v. Poynter Products, Inc.*, 295 F. Supp. 331 (S.D.N.Y. 1968). Such a relationship, of course, creates the classic example of an *equitable* claim by beneficiaries which would in no way affect the right of plaintiff as trustee to sue third parties.

Plaintiff has standing to bring this suit *solely* on the basis of its *record* ownership. Plaintiff needs nothing else—by way of evidentiary presumptions or supplementary evidence—to sue in this Court. As will appear below, however, plaintiff here also enjoys the benefit of both a statutory presumption of ownership and corroborative evidence.

B. The Statutory Presumption of Ownership

Defendant reiterates at page 16 of its Brief its further concession that "plaintiff's certificate of registration entitled plaintiff to a presumption that it is the owner of the individual articles in the journals published by it." Such a presumption, emanating from the copyright statute itself, 17 USC §209, is well recognized. See, *e.g.*, *Hedeman Products Corp. v. Tap-Rite Products Corp.*, 228 F. Supp. 630 (D.N.J. 1964). Cf. *Tennessee Fabricating Co. v. Moultrie Mfg. Co.*, 421 F.2d 279 (5th Cir. 1970); *Wihtol v. Wells*, 231 F.2d 550, 553 (7th Cir. 1956).

13

Defendant's concession of a presumption of ownership is followed by an incredible argument as to how the presumption has allegedly been rebutted:

> "Since plaintiff does not have a written assignment granting to it ownership rights in the articles involved, defendant submits that any presumption in plaintiff's favor has been rebutted, and it is his burden to affirmatively establish ownership." (Brief. p. 16).

A presumption is designed to avoid the necessity of supporting evidence, not to require such evidence. The presumption of innocence in criminal cases is not rebutted by the defendant's failure to offer proof, documentary or otherwise. The presumption of corporate capacity to sue or be sued, cf. Rule 33 (a) of this Court, is not rebutted by the failure to offer in evidence the corporate charter. Similarly, the absence of proof of an assignment, written or otherwise, does not rebut the presumption of title; on the contrary, such evidence is rendered unnecessary by the presumption.

To rebut the presumption of title, defendant must come forward with evidence that title is in someone else. Cf. *Universal Athletic Sales Co. v. Salkeld*, 340 F. Supp. 899 (W.D. Pa. 1972). Defendant has failed to do so. Indeed, defendant apparently is of the view that such failure on its part is of some benefit to defendant, as reflected in the cheerful assertion that *none of the authors who testified "were asked either by the defendant, plaintiff or the Commissioner if they asserted any interest in the articles which they wrote."* (Brief. p. 17) [Emphasis added]

14

Defendant accurately refers to this as "nontestimony" (*Id*). Nontestimony is no testimony—it is in no sense a rebuttal of a statutory presumption.

C. Testimony Supporting Plaintiff's Record Ownership and Statutory Presumption

The foregoing furnishes the context for the testimony, accepted by the Commissioner, that authors by custom assigned their ownership rights to plaintiff. As indicated above, such testimony was offered not to substitute for plaintiff's record title and presumption of ownership, but to supplement it. The Commissioner's finding of fact in this regard, presumed to be correct by Rule 147 (b), need be reviewed by the Court only if the Court were to find that record title is insufficient *and* the statutory presumption has been rebutted. As indicated above, it is submitted that record title is sufficient and, even if it were not, plaintiff's statutory presumption stands unrebutted. For this reason, the entire discussion in Point II of Defendant's Brief and Point IV of the *amicus curiae* brief of ARL is distorted. Plaintiff did not have the burden of proving an assignment; defendant had the burden of disproving title in plaintiff and, relying on nontestimony, failed to do so.

Turning to the arguments attacking the Commissioner's findings of fact on this point, the following may be noted:

(1) Defendant has twitted plaintiff's witnesses throughout with metaphysical questions as to how a custom is "observed"; this pre-occupation continues

15

unabated (e.g. Brief, p. 19). The custom is, in fact, clearly observed from uncontroverted evidence in the present case. This shows that: (a) plaintiff published the journals in question with a copyright notice in plaintiff's name; (b) plaintiff regularly secured copyright registrations in its name in the Copyright Office; (c) plaintiff proceeded to grant various licenses for certain uses of the journals; (d) plaintiff sells reprints, even to the authors of the articles themselves.* All of the foregoing objective facts reflect a pattern of doing business over a long period of time properly characterized by the Commissioner as a custom. Thus, the recognition of ownership in plaintiff can be "observed" in this course of conduct.

(2) Defendant and ARL argue that the Commissioner must somehow recognize and enforce the inchoate and unexpressed desires of some authors as to how the copyright owned by plaintiff should be administered. Doubtless many authors have many ideas in this respect,** without consequences on copyright ownership. Defendant and ARL emphasize an interest in the authors to achieve "the widest dissemination possible." But such an interest is entirely consistent with copyright protection, including compensation for photocopying.

---

* On page 19 of its Brief, defendant concedes that "authors sometimes seek permission to reprint their own articles."

** It would appear more appropriate in this respect to credit the views of the Authors League which is filing its own *amicus* brief, than to rely on the ARL for the articulation of "the interests and objectives of the authors of these articles." See ARL Brief, p. 30.

16

Most instructive in this connection is the experience of the Office of Education ("OE"), a sister agency of NIH and NLM within the Department of Health, Education and Welfare. In funding the research and development of educational materials, OE was naturally interested in "the widest dissemination possible." The Office initially sought to achieve this result by prohibiting copyright protection for materials developed with its funds. This was the so-called "public domain" policy of 1965. See 30 F. R. 9408 (July 12, 1965). It turned out that this policy discouraged the kind of investment that private publishers would have to make in order to publish. The result was no dissemination. The policy was accordingly modified in 1968 to permit exceptions to the public domain policy. See 33 F. R. 3653 (March 1, 1968).

OE found that this modification was still insufficient and in 1970 even further liberalization took place. This change made a limited term of copyright protection available even without a special showing of necessity. 35 F. R. 7317 (May 9, 1970). It was thus recognized, through experience not through speculation, that without the exclusivity offered by copyright there would be *no* dissemination.

What the foregoing means is that an author's desire to achieve wide dissemination—an interest shared by his publisher—tells us absolutely nothing about how such dissemination is to be achieved. Nor, even more clearly, does it tell us who owns the copyright and can sue in this case.

(3) In the absence of any stated conditions, the law implies a complete transfer of rights. *Best Medium*

17

Publishing Co. v. *The National Insider, Inc.*, 259 F. Supp. 433 (N.D. Ill. 1966), *aff'd*, 385 F.2d 384 (7th Cir. 1967), *cert. denied*, 390 U.S. 955 (1968); Cf. *Pushman* v. *New York Graphic Society*, 287 N. Y. 302 (1942); *Geisel* v. *Poynter Products, Inc.*, 295 F. Supp. 331 (S.D.N.Y. 1968). Defendant neither undertook nor sustained its burden of proving any condition.

Accordingly, the argument that authors want wide dissemination is no substitute for *proof* by defendant that a particular agreement was made by the authors when they submitted their manuscript to plaintiff.

On pages 20-21 of its brief defendant attempts to brush aside the *Best Medium* and *Geisel* cases on the erroneous ground that the works there involved were not a "contribution" to a periodical, as is here involved, but rather involved "a sale for a monetary consideration". Defendant misreads the word "contribution" as implying "gift". A contribution is a term of art in the periodical field meaning the individual piece submitted by an author not on the staff of the periodical. It has nothing to do with whether compensation, direct or indirect, is involved. The word is used in this sense in the copyright statute itself. See 17 U.S.C. §24; 37 CFR §§202.3 (c) and 202.5.

The Commissioner correctly found that the cases were *not* distinguishable. Indeed, if a consideration were needed, the Commissioner found that "publication of research by medical journals though not perhaps of immediate monetary benefit to the researchers, nevertheless enhances, and may even be crucial to, their long term professional and economic opportunities". (Opinion, p. 9). Moreover, even the non-

18

monetary rewards enjoyed by these authors are sufficiently significant to constitute "consideration".

(4) Defendant's reliance at page 23 on *Brattleboro Publishing Co.* v. *Winmill Publishing Corp.*, 250 F. Supp. 255 (D. Vt.), *aff'd*, 369 F.2d 565 (2d Cir. 1966) is misplaced. That case focused on the circumstances of the creation of an advertisement to determine who in the first instance owned rights.* In its inquiry the Court considered the "works for hire" doctrine and other questions foreign to our case and concluded that the rights to the advertisements were owned by the advertisers. In the present case, the authors concededly created the articles but, unlike the advertisers in *Brattleboro*, impliedly assigned their rights to plaintiff. Indeed the advertisers *could not* have assigned their rights since they ran their ads in a number of newspapers at the same time. Under such circumstances it would be impossible for any one of the publishers to be the copyright proprietor. Here, of course, the articles were published only in plaintiff's journals.

Equally unavailing is defendant's reliance on *Kinelow Publishing Co.* v. *Photography in Business, Inc.*, 270 F. Supp. 851 (S.D.N.Y. 1967).** This case involved a corporate author, Western Electric. The evidence dem-

---

* Expense was perhaps a proper factor to be considered. However, in considering all ramifications of the expense factor, one should note the Commissioner's findings that authors "look to medical journals to bear the expenses of editing, publishing and disseminating" and that any contributions made by authors were not shown to be substantial compared with the total cost of publication (Opinion, p. 9).

** Defendant argues that *Kinelow* is the only cited case dealing specifically with contributions to scientific periodicals

19

onstrated a clear corporate policy, before the first publication, that the article was to be published not only in the plaintiff's publication, but in numerous other publications as well, presumably to reach different readerships. Accordingly, there could not be an implied transfer of copyright from this corporate author to any one publisher because Western Electric wished to have its works published in the first instance in more than one journal. Indeed Western Electric turned over its manuscript material to the other publishers, including defendant, which knew the article was being published in other publications.

In contrast, the conceded evidence in the present case is that authors request permission to reprint their own articles (Deft. Brief, p. 19). *A fortiori*, the authors did not regard themselves as being entitled to authorize publication in more than one journal. There is no evidence here of any such multiple publication.

In fact, the evidence shows that the selection of a single journal in which an article should be published is crucial because in the words of one author, "the acceptance of an article by one of the leading journals . . . stamps it as having a certain quality." (F-9(a); 909).

Finally, the Commissioner's ruling is firmly supported by the authoritative decision in *Alexander* v. *Irving Trust Co.*, 132 F. Supp. 364 (S.D.N.Y.), *aff'd*, 228 F. 2d

(Footnote continued)
and implied assignment of rights. As will be seen, in *Alexander* v. *Irving Trust Co.*, 228 F.2d 221 (2d Cir. 1955), the Court of Appeals for the Second Circuit affirmed a decision recognizing that the copyright in a contribution to *a medical journal* is owned by the publisher, rather than the contributor.

20

221 (2d Cir. 1955), *cert. denied*, 350 U.S. 996 (1956) where an article was submitted for exclusive publication in the "Medical Journal". The court held that "in the absence of proof to the contrary it must be presumed that plaintiff [author] transferred her work without any reservation whatever and that The Medical Journal and Record Publishing Company, Inc. became the absolute proprietor of the copyright."

II

DEFENDANT HAS FAILED TO ESTABLISH THAT ITS COMPREHENSIVE SYSTEM OF COPYING COMPLETE ARTICLES CONSTITUTED FAIR USE

A. The Doctrine of Fair Use is Completely Inapplicable to Defendant's Copying of Entire Works: The Amount and Substantiality of the Taking

The doctrine of fair use has been described as simply an attempt by the courts "to bring some order out of the confusion surrounding the question of how much can be copied". Note, 14 *Notre Dame Lawyer* 443, 449 (1939). Perhaps this is why fair use is sometimes akin to the doctrine of *de minimis non curat lex*. Cf. *Toulmin* v. *Rike-Kumler Co.*, 137 USPQ 533 (S.D. Ohio 1962), *aff'd*, 316 F. 2d 232 (6th Cir.), *cert. denied*, 375 US. 825 (1963). Defendant urges that the millions of pages of photocopies ground out by its microfilm cameras, Copyflo attachments and Xerox machines represents "a fair and insubstantial amount" of copying (Brief p. 34). Apparently, this argument is made be-

---

21

cause defendant recognizes that fair use comes into play only when a relatively small amount of copying takes place. In such a situation, a number of factors may be considered to determine whether what was copied amounts to a "fair" or "unfair" use. On the other hand, it is well established that where substantial or wholesale copying takes place, no such weighing of factors is permissible.

The rule was aptly summarized in 1937 by the U.S. Court of Appeals for the Ninth Circuit, as follows:

"Counsel have not disclosed a single authority, nor have we been able to find one, which lends any support to the proposition that wholesale copying and publication of copyrighted material can ever be fair use." *Leon* v. *Pacific Telephone & Telegraph Co.*, 91 F.2d 484, 486 (9th Cir. 1937)

Neither defendant nor its *amici* have been able to cite any such case;[*] indeed, the authorities uniformly support the proposition that unauthorized wholesale copying (i.e., copying all or most of a work) can *never* be fair use, regardless of extenuating circumstances.

For example, in *Wihtol* v. *Crow*, 309 F. 2d 777 (8th Cir. 1962), a high school choral instructor and church choir director innocently rearranged a copyrighted choral work to make it practicable for his choirs to sing. He then reproduced copies of this new arrangement and performed it once with his high school chorus and on one Sunday with his church choir—all for an educational purpose and without profit.

[*] Neither the characterization of the statement in *Leon* as dictum (which it of necessity is) nor the other bewildering references on page 35 of Defendant's Brief (e.g., footnote 1) obscures this lack of authority.

22

The Court held for plaintiff, finding infringement because defendant copied "all, or substantially all of a copyrighted song" and because such wholesale copying could not conceivably be considered fair use merely because the infringer had an innocent intent.

The more celebrated "Jack Benny" case involved a humorous parody of a melodrama. The defendant there argued that the change in treatment made defendant's version a fair use and presented a number of creative contentions to support its defense. These included Mr. Benny's "custom" over 25 years to present such parodies and the fact that burlesque of a work is in effect literary criticism. The Court held that "there is only a single decisive point in the case: one cannot copy the substance of another's work without infringement of his copyright." *Benny* v. *Loew's, Inc.*, 239 F.2d. 532 (9th Cir. 1956), *aff'd*, 356 U.S. 43 (1958). *Accord: Walt Disney Productions* v. *Air Pirates*, 345 F. Supp. 108 (N.D. Cal. 1972). It is also noteworthy that *Holdredge* v. *Knight Publishing Corp.*, 214 F. Supp. 921 (S.D. Cal. 1963) cited several times by defendant (Brief p. 29 and 53) actually held for the plaintiff, finding there "an extensive use . . . well outside the scope of the concept of 'fair use'."

Public Affairs Associates, Inc. v. *Rickover*, 284 F. 2d 262 (D.C. Cir. 1960), *judgment vacated*, 369 U.S. 111 (1962) applied the foregoing rule in a dramatic fashion. That case was a declaratory judgment action seeking to establish the right of plaintiff to use certain speeches by Admiral Rickover on the ground, *inter alia*, of fair use. The Court recognized the various factors that might come into play "if less than the whole text of

---

23

the speeches is taken" and held that a decision as to the legal effect of such use was premature. The Court held, however, that where verbatim copies of speeches are taken, the Court was able at the threshold to rule out even the possibility of the defense of fair use.

Defendant presumably has not questioned the foregoing rule. It argues the inapplicability of the rule because articles, rather than complete issues of periodicals, are copied verbatim. Thus, if an entire issue or a substantial part of an entire issue were photocopied, there would apparently be agreement between the parties that the fair use defense is not applicable. Such agreement is supported by defendant's long standing stated policy to refrain from copying an entire, or substantially entire, issue (F. 17(b): 22(c)).* Therefore, the entire issue of fair use can, it is submitted, be disposed of if it is determined that an article from a periodical issue, rather than the issue itself, is to be viewed as the "work" in question.

The beginning and end of this inquiry would seem to be furnished by the clear words of the statute itself. Section 3 provides:

"The copyright provided by this title shall protect all the copyrightable components of the work copyrighted.... The copyright upon composite works or periodicals shall give to the proprietor thereof all the rights in respect thereto which he would

---

* It is unnecessary to determine whether copying a 30-page (Count VII and VIII Works), 40-page (Count I Work is 38 pages) or a 50-page (Count II Work) article amounts to copying substantially the entire issue in which such articles appear.

24

have if each part were individually copyrighted under this title." (17 U.S.C. §3)

The present case, of course, involves periodicals which are expressly mentioned in this section. An article is the pertinent "part" of the periodical referred to in the statute. Accordingly, plaintiff's copyrights in its journals cover each and every article contained in the journals as fully as if each article "were individually copyrighted." See, e.g., Advertisers Exchange, Inc., v. Laufe, 29 F. Supp. 1 (W.D. Pa. 1939); King Features Syndicate v. Fleischer, 299 Fed. 533 (2d Cir. 1924). cf. Phillips v. The Constitution Publishing Co., 72 USPQ 69 (N.D. Ga. 1947).

It follows from the foregoing that defendant's copying of complete articles constitutes copying entire separate copyrighted works—a situation which under the authorities discussed above precludes applicability of fair use. This result is supported by a long line of cases expressly holding that the test of infringement—whether a taking is substantial and material—is to be applied to each copyrightable component, and not to the entire work covered by the copyright. E.g., Markham v. A. E. Borden Co., 206 F.2d 199 (1st Cir. 1953); Hedeman Products Corp. v. Tap-Rite Products Corp., 228 F. Supp. 630 (D.N.J. 1964).

In the Markham case, the defendant copied 9 items from hundreds of items covered in plaintiff's copyrighted catalogs. The Court of Appeals for the First Circuit held that Section 3 of the Copyright Act was applicable and required protection for each of the 9 component parts. The Court made clear that protection for each of the component parts was necessary "in order for the protection to be meaningful." 206 F.2d at 202.

25

This reasoning is fully applicable to the periodicals published by plaintiff and the articles contained in each issue. The articles individually must be protected in order for protection to be meaningful. Each article stands on its own feet; its significance is normally unrelated to other articles which happen to be included in the same issue of a periodical.* It is clear that copyright protection for such a self-contained article cannot be made to depend on the happenstance of whether it was published together with few or many other articles.

Defendant's attempt to meet the logic and force of this solid line of authority utterly fails. First, defendant misstates the case of Mathews Conveyor Co. v. Palmer-Bee, Co., 135 F.2d 73 (6th Cir. 1943) which held that defendant's sketches were not sufficiently similar to plaintiff's photographs to constitute "copies."**

Defendant relies heavily on New York Tribune v. Otis & Co., 39 F. Supp. 67 (S.D.N.Y. 1941) as "perhaps

---

* Since a book or "monograph" is not generally a "composite work" and a chapter is usually an integral part of what precedes and follows it, the stated policy of defendant to refrain from copying a monograph chapter, while freely copying a periodical article, is but one of the illogical consequences of defendant's photocopying practices.

** The Markham court, supra, noted possible confusion in the Mathews opinion. Moreover, Markham cited Henry Holt & Co. v. Liggett & Myers, 23 F. Supp. 302 (E.D. Pa. 1938), where the use of only three sentences from a scientific treatise in an advertisement was held to be infringement and not fair use.

26

the closest case to the present case" (Brief, p. 37). But aside from other differences, that case involved a motion for summary judgment by defendant, arguing that fair use must be applied and infringement rejected. The motion was denied. Thus, the case simply stands for the proposition that a portion of the editorial section of a newspaper may not be copied without the risk of infringement.

Accordingly, the "material and substantial" test is not to be applied to each issue of plaintiff's periodicals, but to each component article. See Hedeman Products Corp. v. Tap-Rite Products Corp., supra, 228 F. Supp. at 634, n. 2. When so applied, defendant cannot begin to invoke the doctrine of fair use, because it is guilty of copying complete works considered to be individually copyrighted. As noted above, such wholesale copying can never be condoned.

B. The "Single Copy" Fallacy: The Law

It is deemed unnecessary in this brief to deal with all of defendant's stated limitations regulating its comprehensive system of photocopying. Indeed the testimony actually shows very little observance of these policies.* However, the very cornerstone of defendant's

---

* For example, a key limitation in the photocopying policy of NLM is stated to be refusal to furnish photocopies of articles appearing within the last five years in periodicals included on a list of available journals (F-22(b)). The deviations from this policy are so substantial as to lead to the conclusion that this "limitation" is virtually ignored (179-B-179 F). Plaintiff's four journals in question are all on this list (203) and most of the articles had been published within five years of their being photocopied.

27

position (and apparently something that it considers indispensible to its fair use argument) is the stated policy of defendant to furnish only one copy of an article to a single user at one time. It will be shown below that such a limitation is, in point of fact, meaningless, unenforceable and indeed not enforced. But even if defendant at all times made truly single copies, it could not, as a matter of law, sanctify such a system of copying.

Thus, the Commissioner did not, as stated by defendant at page 10 of its Brief, reject the single copy argument of defendant *solely* because factually defendant makes more than a single copy of an article; he also held, quite properly, that "there is nothing in the copyright statute* or the case law to distinguish, in principle, the making of a single copy of a copyrighted work from the making of multiple copies". (Opinion, page 14).

The only case found in which the question was expressly raised is *Chappell & Co., Ltd.* v. *Columbia Graphophone Co.*, [1914] 2 Chancery Div. 745. Defendants there argued that the making of a single phonograph record was not an infringement "because

---

* ALA discusses at p. 22 of its brief the exceptions to the requirement of domestic printing and manufacture found in 17 USC § 107. This tariff-type provision has universally been recognized as "an anomaly in our copyright law" embodying policies "beyond the province of copyright". See *Report of Register of Copyrights on the General Revision of the U.S. Copyright Law*, 87th Cong. 1st Sess. 122-123 (1961). To borrow from this provision in order to construe basic provisions of the Copyright Law is another example of distortion of policy found in the *amicus* briefs supporting defendant.

28

there was only this one (1) copy made." The Court held that under the applicable British statutes "there is no foundation for the argument . . . that it was not an infringement of the copyright . . . to make one copy only of the work." Although we are, of course, dealing with a different statute, there would appear to be no call for different logic from that involved in the *Chappell* case.

A case closer to home strongly supports this result, although the issue was apparently not directly raised. In *Shapiro, Bernstein & Co.* v. *4636 S. Vermont Avenue, Inc.*, 367 F.2d 236 (9th Cir. 1966) the defendant was held liable for the sale of a single copy of a music book. This is not surprising since the Supreme Court has noted, in the context of the minimum statutory damages provided in section 101 (b), the Congressional declaration that "just damages, *even for the circulation of a single copy*, cannot be less than $250. . . ." *Douglas* v. *Cunningham*, 294 U.S. 207, 210 (1935) [Emphasis added]

In addition to the foregoing, a number of cases clearly show that only one item of infringement was involved, although no comment on this fact was made in the opinion. This is particularly true in the case of infringement of the right to perform music publicly for profit. In virtually every case, the courts are dealing with a single performance but this fact has never precluded relief. See, *e.g., Chappell & Co.* v. *Middletown*

Farmers Market, 334 F. 2d 303 (3rd Cir. 1964); *Leo Feist, Inc.* v. *Lew Tendler Tavern, Inc.*, 267 F.2d 494 (3rd Cir. 1959); *Buck* v. *Crescent Gardens Operating Co.*, 28 F. Supp. 576 (D. Mass. 1939). See *Associated*

29

Music Publishers, Inc. v. *Debs Memorial Radio Fund*, 141 F. 2d 852 (2d Cir. 1944).

Indicative of the importance of even a single copy in the electronic era is *Walt Disney Productions* v. *Alaska Television Network*, 310 F. Supp. 1073 (W. D. Wash. 1969). It there appears that a single unauthorized videotape of a television broadcast was made and later transmitted over cable television. The Court found liability without, however, specifically mentioning the "single copy" point. This case reminds one that a "single copy" of a journal might some day be stationed in a single location, with images of articles transmitted electronically nationwide. One "single copy" so transmitted would be an infringement as are the "single copies" being furnished here.

The entire Point II of the ARL brief (pages 33 through 66) and Appendix rely on the proposition that the word 'copy' as used in defining the 'exclusive right' of an author in Section 1 of the Copyright Act has to be understood in a special and limited sense. The special and limited sense being sought is to treat Section 1 as if the word "copy" were not present.

But the House Patent Committee in reporting on the 1909 Act (as quoted in pertinent part at page 47 of the ARL Brief) expressly notes that the word "copy" was *added* to the statute.*

---

* ARL's reliance on other props must also fail. It is noteworthy that in *Harper* v. *Shoppell*, 26 Fed. 519 (S.D.N.Y. 1886), a cornerstone of the ARL Brief, the plaintiff secured a new trial and was ultimately successful, 28 Fed. 613 (S.D.N.Y. 1886) in a case involving the copying of but a single illustration from a weekly newspaper.

30

The "Single Copy" Fallacy: The Facts

When one analyzes the "single copy" service offered by a library, it becomes apparent that one is not talking about a single copy at all. In other words, the result of a multiplication of single copies is a multitude of copies even though they are furnished one at a time to individual scientists.

Professor Nimmer has aptly noted that "there would appear to be a qualitative difference between each individual scholar performing the task of reproduction for himself, and the library or other institution performing the task on a wholesale basis* for all scholars. If the latter is fair use, then must not the same be said for a non-profit publishing house that distributes to scholars unauthorized copies of scientific and educational works on a national or international basis?" *Nimmer on Copyright* 654 (1972)

The foregoing analysis is supported by evidence of what actually takes place at NIH Library and at NLM. The supposed magic of the single copy limitation is destroyed by the following:

---

* The facts concerning the enormous scope of photocopying by defendant need not be reiterated here in detail. The

Government itself noted in 1966 its installation of 55,000 machines at a yearly cost of 80 million dollars (Pltf. Ex. 32), and the serious effect of widespread copying on the sale of technical articles (Id., p. 6). The use of a system of photocopying by the two libraries in question, as a central, as opposed to casual, part of their operations, pervades the record (e.g. F-15; 178; 203; 467; 484-85; Pltf. Ex. 33, p. 36). And it has been conceded that more people secure photocopies from NIH than would copy substantial portions by hand (F-17(b); 175).

31

(1) The libraries have no way to enforce their stated one-copy-per-user limitation inasmuch as there is no procedure to check whether the same user has requested a copy earlier (F-17(b); 1322). Defendant's own witness testified that he has reordered copies of the same article (1355). Indeed there are at least four instances in the record of *the same individual's having ordered two copies of the same article on the same day* (Pltf. Ex. 11-A, pp. 25, 30, 31 and 34). The duplication of "particular articles over and over" found by the Commissioner do not, as stated on page 12 of Defendant's Brief, refer solely to these four dramatic instances; the record reveals many others, as noted in (2) below.

(2) Both libraries will frequently furnish simultaneously two copies of the same article to different users. Indeed, usually NIH will make four copies inasmuch as it will shoot two different microfilmings of the article and produce separate copies from each (1326). This process can go on indefinitely since NLM will furnish any number of libraries with copies of the same article (F-22 (a)) and the record shows numerous cases where different individuals have in fact ordered copies of the same articles.

(3) The Count III, Count IV, Count V and Count VI works were all copied from the same issue of the same periodical by the same user on the same day (Pltf. Ex. 11-A, pp. 2, 3).

These examples can be supplemented *ad nauseam* to demonstrate that the concept of a single copy limitation in library photocopying is an illusion.

32

C. No Special Fair Use Doctrine for Defendant in this Action: The Purpose of the Use

It has been demonstrated above, in such cases as *Wihtol v. Crow, Jack Benny,* and *Admiral Rickover* that fair use may be unavailable even when defendants argue that one or more of the factors traditionally relevant are in their favor. Based on the facts in this case, however, defendant cannot, in any event, benefit from the fair use factors it discusses.

This case does not involve the utilization of extracts from a work in the course of creating a new work; rather, it represents a bare verbatim reproduction. This distinction is fully conceded by defendant and its *amici* (See, e.g. ALA Brief, p. 14). What they apparently do not realize, however, is that the entire concept of fair use is based on the necessity to comment on and discuss earlier works either by way of criticism or

simply by another author in the same field. To accomplish this purpose, the precise words of the earlier work must often be copied or paraphrased. This kind of creative development is in no way reflected in the photocopying performed here. As but an example, a reviewer or an author would never reproduce verbatim a forty-page article in the course of a review or a subsequent work.

It follows from the foregoing that the many quotations (e.g., ALA Brief, pp. 16-17) contained in the briefs of defendant and its *amici* concerning the relationship between fair use and science must be read in the con-

33

text of *new* authors creating new publications. The crucial point is that there is more, rather than less, reason to justify copying in the case of a new publication than in the case of a bare verbatim reproduction.

When one looks at the purpose of the use made by defendant, we find that neither the "non-profit" character of the Government nor the scholarly purpose for which the copies were made can be of any aid to defendant. With respect to the former, it is clear that *every* use by the Government is in effect "non-profit." If this factor were to be determinative, or even significant, there would be no cases possible against the Government for copyright infringement. Yet in 1960, Congress specifically gave this Court exclusive jurisdiction to hear such cases.

What is even more striking is that before Congress passed this enabling statute, its attention had been called to the increased risks of liability caused by the development of copying machines and a special plea was made to Congress to insure that the Government, and not the employee of the Government doing the copying, be made liable. In other words, when Congress enacted 28 U.S.C. Section 1498(b) in 1960, its purpose was twofold: a) To waive sovereign immunity and make the Government liable for copyright infringement in a manner similar to its liability for patent infringement; and (b) to protect Government employees from personal liability for copyright infringement. In commenting on the latter objective, the Secretary of Commerce called

34

to the attention of Congress the fact that "the increasing use of desk photocopying machines in the routine administration of the departments make the possibility of infringement [by Government employees] an ever increasing danger." H.R. Rep. No. 624, 86th Cong. 1st Sess. 5 (1959). It was the purpose of the legislation to remove the employee from the risk of such liability and substitute the Government. This was achieved by the 1960 legislation. Thus, one of the specific reasons Congress passed the 1960 statute was to make the Government liable for infringement by photocopying as is here involved.

Indeed the fact that the Government is not insulated from liability in this situation is also reflected by the more recent efforts of the Department of Health, Education and Welfare to amend the present copyright statute so as to include express sanction for the acts complained of in this action.* *Hearings on H.R. 4347 and other bills before Subcomm. No. 3 of the House Judiciary Comm., 89th Congress, 1st Sess. 1133 (1965).* Neither the statute creating NLM in 1956, 42 U.S.C. §275, *et seq.*, nor the one providing financial assistance to regional libraries in 1965, 42 U.S.C. §280 b-1, *et seq.*, is of any help to defendant. The Register of Copyrights noted that those statutes were not "in any way in derogation of the rights granted under the Copyright Law to the proprietor of the copyright" (F-43(a)).

---

* ARL concedes at page 69 of its brief that these efforts were made "lest silence by Congress on the subject be construed as indicating an intent to disapprove this limitation on the exclusive rights of copyright holders". Congress has remained silent. See Opinion, pp. 24; 31.

35

The copyright law did not, either in 1956, 1965 or today, sanction photocopying of the type here involved. As early as 1957 the Director of NLM stated that free photocopying at that library had developed "beyond reasonable bounds"; that the copying of recent journals of wide availability is satisfying "a need which the printing press, not the camera, is designed to fill"; and that NLM should not run a copying service as such (Deft. Ex. 71, p. 490). Because of this, he recognized a number of years ago the likelihood of a test in the courts of the copyright issue posed by NLM's photocopying activities (F-43(a); Pltf. Ex. 38, p. 1375).

Turning to other aspects of the purpose of the photocopying, we agree with defendant's statement that the purpose of a use is "closely interrelated" with another criterion for fair use, the character of the work being copied (Deft. Brief, p. 30). This interrelation is emphasized by defendant presumably as the basis for defendant's statement that the photocopies were here made "for the express purpose for which the articles were created, i.e., to further medical research or to improve medical treatment." Plaintiff agrees. But the people who used photocopies of plaintiff's works are the very people plaintiff seeks to serve in its publishing activities and *for the very same purposes.*

It is thus meaningless for defendant and its *amici* to belabor the point that the purpose of photocopying was scholarly, inasmuch as every use made of plaintiff's works can be so classified. Accordingly, since everyone purchasing subscriptions, reprints and taking licenses for photocopying is doing so for a scholarly purpose, plaintiff's market is potentially affected by defendant's copying.

36

D. Defendant's "Economic" Argument: Effect on Potential Market

Defendant apparently argues that the factor of *actual* economic injury is relevant to a determination of the defense of fair use. It is conceded that some cases and commentators speak, in connection with the question of fair use, of the competitive effect of the use on the *potential* market for the original. This is often discussed in terms of whether the use could serve as a substitute for

the original. But this is universally in the context of trying to determine whether a sufficient amount of the work has been taken to constitute infringement. See p. 20, *supra.* Such a determination is sometimes very difficult because only a portion of the copyrighted work has been copied. Accordingly, as a factor in determining whether a partial copying is "fair" or "unfair," the courts sometimes assess whether the portion taken would be sufficient to serve as a substitute for the original. However, as demonstrated above, such a determination is completely unnecessary in the present case because entire articles from plaintiff's journals have been taken and each individual article is a complete "work."

Even if the competitive factor mentioned in the cases were relevant, defendant misreads this factor. As indicated above, inquiry into the effect of the use on the potential market for the original is asking whether the defendant has made the *kind* of use which *could* serve as a substitute for the original. In other words, we are speaking of "actual or *potential* consumer demand," *Nimmer on Copyright* 649. [Emphasis added].

In the present situation the Government takes the position that the libraries in question furnish users with

37

photocopies in lieu of loaning them the original (Pltf. Ex. 25; 172). Defendant and its *amici* seem to think that such a "loan" rather than a "sale" means no liability. On the contrary; in view of defendant's concession, there can absolutely be no issue as to whether or not the use here involved can serve as a substitute for the original. It concededly does.

It is thus useless to speculate as to whether a particular library or doctor would in fact subscribe to the particular issue in question (see ARL Brief, pp 73-74). As the Commissioner noted: "The photocopies are exact duplicates of the original articles; are intended to be, and serve the same purpose as the original article." (Opinion, p. 16). This ability to serve as a substitute is what the courts and commentators mean by the effect of the use on a copyright owner's potential market for his work.

Even if all of the foregoing were not the case, the economic "evidence" in the record in no way supports defendant's position. As put forward by defendant, this evidence consisted of plaintiff's income tax returns and the testimony of an economist as an expert witness presumably to show that plaintiff's overall business is healthy. It hardly seems necessary to state that this is completely beside the point.

There was no attempt to pinpoint the reasons for the economic health of the plaintiff. Moreover, it is clear that plaintiff has taken a number of steps to mitigate what it considers the potentially harmful economic effects of photocopying (1138-1139). Defendant's expert, who candidly testified that he had not addressed himself explicitly to any question relating to the photocopying of plaintiff's journals (1032-1033), doubted

38

that anyone could tell whether any particular instance or instances of photocopying would or would not result in the loss of a particular form of revenue by a publisher such as plaintiff regardless of what data was available (1107).

The testimony of defendant's expert witness confirmed plaintiff's testimony that the damage inflicted by photocopying on plaintiff cannot be measured with exactitude in dollars (72-73). Of course, there would seem to be no dispute on a number of facts from which inferences can be drawn. For example, testimony from defendant's witnesses confirmed that the consequences of extensive photocopying services may well be that the researcher finds it necessary to request fewer reprints of articles (503). Moreover, plaintiff and others ascribe losses of subscriptions (e.g., Pltf. Ex. 34) and failure of growth of subscriptions (986-987; 436) to photocopying. Accordingly, the Commissioner was justified in finding damage "from the fact that the photocopies are intended to supplant the original articles" (Opinion, p. 17).

If measurement of subscription growths were relevant, it is noted that two of the publications in question actually lost subscribers from 1968 to 1969 (F.39(a); 1091). What is more significant is the fact that plaintiff, in its normal publishing functions, has an established program of licensing derivative uses of its articles beyond merely the sale of subscriptions. Indeed, plaintiff has already embarked on a program of licensing the furnishing of single photocopies to readers (F.36; 127) and has even granted such a license to libraries (F.36 (vi); 126-127).

39

Furthermore, it is clear that the kind of photocopying here involved is directly in the mainstream of a publisher's rights under copyright. This is true whether or not sales of original subscriptions are affected. By analogy, no one would argue that a paperback or even a motion picture version of a novel must reduce the demand for the original hard cover copy (which they do not) in order for the proprietor's copyright to encompass paperback or motion picture rights. Thus, plaintiff's right to recover reasonable compensation cannot be made to depend on its general economic health or whether it can or cannot pinpoint a specific lost subscription due to defendant's photocopying.

Economics are important, but not for the reasons cited by defendant. The fundamental reason for commencing this suit was to insure the survival of private, limited circulation scholarly or technical journals (1142; 436) which, all agree, serve a vital national purpose (e.g. 273; 489).

The problem can be concisely described: It is virtually impossible to increase the number of subscribers to such journals beyond those in the discipline served by the particular journal. However, while the number of subscribers remains static, the costs of publication continually increase. At the same time photocopying technology continues to improve, enabling copies to be made more cheaply and efficiently. If subscription prices are raised to cover costs plus a reasonable profit, the point is soon reached where, instead of subscribing, some users of the material will photocopy. And every time there is a subscription price increase and the photocopying technology improves, there is a greater incentive to photocopy. Thus, raising subscription

40

prices does not solve the problem of providing sufficient income to cover cost because it simply encourages fewer subscriptions and more photocopying. Eventually, there will be so few subscribers and the prices will be so high that the journal will cease publication.

The only way to save private limited circulation technical journals from extinction is to broaden the income base.* This can only be done by spreading the cost of publication among a greater number of users, including those who use the journal through photocopying. A photocopying license will enable subscription costs to be kept at a reasonable level and place the burden of supporting the journal more equitably upon those who use it (1140-1141).

In sum, plaintiff, as it has stated many times in the record, does not wish to stop photocopying. It simply seeks a way to increase the income base on its journals so that it may recover its costs of publication and a reasonable profit. While it may not be relevant to this particular litigation, it should be noted that plaintiff has become certain that a reasonable and workable plan to collect photocopying royalties is possible.

* One alternative which has been suggested is government subsidy. However, this concept is unacceptable because it is not desirable to have the government support enterprises which can be supported privately; because government support is subject to political and budgetary considerations which makes it undependable; and finally, government payment brings with it government control. If at all possible, the government should not be involved in controlling the dissemination of scientific information. See Opinion, p. 10.

41

III

NONE OF THE MISCELLANEOUS ARGUMENTS OF DEFENDANT AND ITS AMICI DEFEAT PLAINTIFF'S RIGHT TO REASONABLE COMPENSATION

To respond to all of the arguments made throughout the briefs of defendant and its *amici* would extend this brief unduly. More importantly, such detailed response is, we submit, unnecessary because of the irrelevance of most of the arguments to the case at hand. Several will be discussed below.

1. *Some Constitutional Aspects.* With all due respect, we do not view the lengthy and citation-laden brief of NEA as helpful in the resolution of this case. The "novel" argument (see NEA Brief, p. 37) that enforcement of a copyright violates the First and Ninth Amendments of the Constitution is based on a number of faulty premises. A most significant one is discussed in the Authors League Brief: The public's right to learn is enhanced, not abridged, by the continued publication of scientific journals by plaintiff.

NEA's entire brief focuses on its version of "access." Defendant and its *amici* would have the Court believe that the *only* way users can have access to published material is by photocopying journal articles without paying the copyright owner. Among the many other fallacies in this position, exposed in the *amicus* briefs in

ort of the Commissioner's Report, is the fallacy of
ting compensated photocopying with no photo-
ing. This sleight-of-hand is often assisted by
ing only one side of a scholarly discussion of the

ect. For example, ALA quotes and italicizes at
th on pages 8 and 9 of its brief from the Varmer
ly, "Photoduplication of Copyrighted Material by
aries", to show the importance of photocopying.*
truncates this passage to avoid setting forth the
graph following the portion it quotes. The omitted
graph is:

"However, much of the materials needed for
scholarship and research is of recent date and is
under copyright, and the question arises whether
the making and furnishing of photocopies of copyrighted material without the permission of the copyright owner is a violation of his exclusive right to
copy secured by section 1(a) of the copyright law.
It is the purpose of this study to examine this question and to consider possibilities for its solution."

t is believed that the NEA Brief is refuted by the
y authorities and language on which it relies.

'or example at page 46 of its Brief, NEA quotes the
lowing language of Chief Justice Hughes in *Fox Film
rp.* v. *Doyal*, 286 U.S. 123, 127 (1932):

"The owner of the copyright, if he pleases, may
refrain from vending or licensing and content himself with simply exercising the right to exclude
others from using his property."

Access would be enormously reduced if plaintiff did
at the Supreme Court and NEA agree it can do—re-
ain from distributing any of its journals. Plaintiff does,
wever, distribute its journals, and permitting such

* The Commissioner also quotes extremely pertinent
rtions of the Varmer Study in his Opinion at pp. 22-23.

3

istribution to enjoy the protection of the copyright
w can hardly violate the First Amendment.

NEA quotes language at pages 53 and 54 pur-
orting to support the proposition that "customary
se" becomes "fair use" without regard to the various
riteria for determining whether a given use is "fair
se" (see p. 51). The five quotations on pages 53 and 54
ll define fair use as "*reasonable* and customary" Of
ourse, reasonableness is the essence of fair use; thus,
'customary" is an additional requirement, not a sub-
titute for reasonableness. And as pertinently stated in
Rosemont Enterprises v. *Random House, Inc.*, 366 F.
2d 303 (2d Cir. 1966):

"The fair use concept is based on the concept
of reasonableness and extensive verbatim copying
or paraphrasing of material set down by another
cannot satisfy that standard."

Here, the "verbatim copying" was not merely "extensive"; it was complete.

The other constitutional arguments in the briefs of
defendant and its *amici* are equally without merit.
They are circular and beg the question. This is demonstrated clearly in the *amicus* briefs supporting the

Commissioner's Report. What can be pointed out here,
however, is the strange nature of the claim that the
progress of science will be halted by compensating
plaintiff for the use of its journals through photocopying. This fallacy is demonstrated by simply considering the self-restraint of defendant and other libraries
with respect to copying as much as a chapter from a
book or "monograph". Defendant's libraries have

44

functioned and medical research has apparently proceeded apace despite the fact that libraries do not
photocopy in this area. Constitutional decisions construing the Bill of Rights cannot be made to depend on
a librarian's classification of an item as a "periodical"
or a "monograph" *

We now turn briefly to various other arguments
threading their way through the briefs of the defendant
and its *amici*:

2. *Custom.* The argument that library photocopying, as involved in this suit, takes place pursuant to a
long-standing custom falls of its own weight. Defendant
concedes that in 1958 "there was virtually no photocopying as presently practiced...." (Deft. Brief, p. 46).
This really is the beginning and end of the "custom"
argument and must be borne in mind whenever defendant or its *amici* talk of a fifty-year or even a thirty-
five year custom. Photocopying as here involved is a
relatively new phenomenon to which must be applied
the established and controlling precedents discussed
above.

It is equally clear that the so-called "custom" has
never been acquiesced in by authors, publishers and
other copyright proprietors.** Indeed, the libraries

* Defendant's witness Scott Adams, former Deputy Director of NLM, testified that where "monographs" are concerned,
there are economic consequences to the author which may
justify inhibitions on photocopying (850). Since concededly at
least publishers are involved economically with journal
publishing, Mr. Adams' explanation supports plaintiff in this
suit.
** Plaintiff's witness, Dr. Heumann, whose testimony has
been deceptively excerpted by defendant and its *amici* (see, e.g.

45

themselves were never uniform in their practices nor
confident of their position. See Opinion, page 17, n. 11.
In any event, recent photocopying has always operated
under a cloud. This was, as pointed out above, recognized by the NLM Director who stated that the issue
would have to be resolved by the courts (F-43(a)).

The cloud certainly is in no way removed by the so-
called "gentleman's agreement". This document was
written in the 1930's when "photocopying" required
darkroom facilities or other delays and expenses involved with photostats and the like; the wet and/or
odoriferous processes that followed also bore little resemblance to the rapid and convenient manner of
producing photocopies today—for the first time at prices
cheaper than printing.

In any event, the "gentleman's agreement" seems
to resemble "the emperor's new clothes". To begin
with, it speaks simply of making a photocopy "of a
part" of a copyrighted work. It does not define the

word "part", as defendant and its *amici* seem to be assuming, so as to permit the photocopying of an *entire* journal article.

Little thought was given to periodicals, a fact un-

(Footnote continued)
NEA Brief, p. 56-57) testified that "about a decade ago, when the new technology permitting rapid and convenient photocopying came in, the number and amount of photocopying increased markedly" (432) and that "there have been interminable discussions at library, medical and information meetings about the validity and propriety of doing this kind of copying" (433). Moreover, the record shows that plaintiff never acquiesced in these practices (F-41(c)).

46

doubtedly explained by the absence of periodical publishers from the groups in question. Finally, the "gentleman's agreement" speaks in terms of an "exemption from liability" and states that "legally, no individual or institution can reproduce by photography or photomechanical means, mimeograph or other methods of reproduction, a page or any part of a book without the written permission of the owner of the copyright".

This lawsuit seeks to apply this rule of law to a comprehensive system of copying entire articles from periodicals.

3. *Foreign Statutes.* The farfetched discussion of foreign copyright statutes on pages 66–68 of Defendant's Brief and Appendix serves to demonstrate the following: (a) When a special exemption from the normal liability of the Copyright Law is desired, a statute is required. See Opinion, p. 24. (b) The United States statutory law is noticeably different from foreign statutory law in many matters central to the question of copyright e.g., notice, registration, duration, renewal, etc. Indeed, the facts in this case would not exempt defendant from liability even under some of the statutes it cites.

4. *The Procedures for Compensating Plaintiff.* ALA makes the absurd argument that "the primary reason the Commissioner refused to consider the arguments put forth by defendant and its *amici* is his unfounded opinion" that library photocopying was not threatened and "that his decision would at most create only a minimal additional burden for libraries." (ALA Brief, p. 36). This is a patent distortion of the Com-

47

missioner's opinion. In any event, defendant now confirms (Brief p. 65 n. 1) the following conclusion of the Commissioner:

"...it is clear that plaintiff's right to compensation under 28 U.S.C. §1498(b) cannot depend on the burdens of compliance." (Opinion p. 29).

The foregoing furnishes the context of the Commissioner's findings that there would be in no event insuperable administrative or fiscal burdens (e.g. F-40)*. In other words, once again, defendant and its *amici* seek to shift to plaintiff an inappropriate burden of proof, this time, of a completely irrelevant set of facts.

But the evidence itself in no way established that

the payment of a royalty for photocopying will have the "deleterious" effect suggested. The question is in the words of the NIH Librarian, simply a question of "wherewithal" (174-175; Cf. Opinion p. 30). Defendant made absolutely no effort at the trial to prove its assertions in this connection; the unsupported rhetoric of the *amici* in their briefs cannot substitute for such proof.

5. *Exclusive Right to Copy Includes "Public" and "Non-Public" Copying.* A pivot of the ARL brief is that only "public" copying is actionable. It is noteworthy

* It is significant, for example, that when plaintiff first complained, NLM was quite able, as a simple administrative matter, first to cease, then to flag, the photocopying of plaintiff's journals and that the requested royalties were "surprisingly small" (F-40(b)). Moreover, it was noted a number of times during the trial that the Xerox Corporation is paid a charge for each page photocopied and that blanket licenses (with no significant administrative costs) were possible.

48

that Section 1(a) of the Copyright Law is not limited to "public" acts, as sharply contrasted with the rights provided in Sections 1(c), 1(d) and 1(e). There would have been no need for the word "public" in these latter subsections if ARL's interpretation of Section 1 rights were correct.

ARL's contention at page 77 of its brief that the case of *American Institute of Architects* v. *Fenichel,* 41 F. Supp. 146 (S.D.N.Y. 1941), "comes closer than most...decisions to the facts before this Court" merely demonstrates the bankruptcy of precedents on behalf of defendant. The Court was quite explicit in the *Fenichel* case in basing its decision on such factors as "the nature of a book of forms", and the express statement on the cover of the booklet indicating that the forms were intended by the plaintiff for the use actually made by defendant.

6. *The Role of Libraries.* ALA's argument (pp. 29 through 35 of its brief) that libraries are merely passive "agents", are fully answered by the *amicus* briefs in support of the Commissioners Report. We would only note that it is the defendant, with its comprehensive system of furnishing photocopies, which initiates and generates the photocopies rather than acting merely as a middleman for users. In other words, the libraries under their Interlibrary Loan Code, determine whether to lend the original or photocopies (e.g., F-23). Moreover, the significance of a massive library operation as opposed to a casual, spontaneous individual act, has been accurately described in *Nimmer on Copyright* 654 as discussed at page 30 above.

Libraries actually claim that their photocopying sub-

49

stitutes for their patrons' hand copying—the permissibility of which itself has never been judicially established. But such copying imposes its own physical and economic limitations, in sharp contrast to the operations of a comprehensive photocopying system. No one hand copies a forty-page article; one does, of course, take notes, but such notes do not serve as a substitute for the original article.

CONCLUSION

For all of the foregoing reasons it is respectfully submitted that the Commissioner's Findings of Fact, Opinion and recommended Conclusion of Law be adopted by the Court.

Respectfully submitted,

ALAN LATMAN,
COWAN, LIEBOWITZ AND LATMAN
Attorney for Plaintiff

ARTHUR J. GREENBAUM,
of Counsel

A1

APPENDIX

Plaintiff's Response to Defendant's Exceptions

It is submitted that the documentation for the Commissioner's findings is so clear that little comment is required on Defendant's Exceptions. Much of the documentation for a number of key findings is supplied in the cross references to the record found in the summary of facts of Plaintiff's Brief. Furthermore, defendant actually quarrels with the support for very few of the Findings.

Defendant's Exceptions may be analyzed as follows:

The forty-five Findings contain twenty-three subparagraphs and thus total sixty-eight specific findings. Defendant objects to only fifteen. Of these, seven do not question the record's support for the Commissioner's Finding or attack it as unsubstantiated, but simply ask that material be added.*

Most of this additional material consists of data, in exquisite detail, to show the purpose of the photocopying, or the mission of NIH and NLM, discussed above. What is so amazing about defendant's tedious quest for proliferation of the Findings is the fact that Commissioner has fully recognized defendant's point (just as plaintiff has conceded it) by Finding 6(b), to the effect that the persons requesting the photocopies were "all physicians or other professional medical personnel who requested from NIH or NLM copies of

* Findings 6, 13, 17, 40(a), 41(b), 43(a), and 43(b).

A2

the articles in connection with medical research work or patient care at NIH or elsehwere".

Of the eight Exceptions which do not relate to the foregoing, three are on the ground of irrelevance.* One of these will be commented upon below. Accordingly, only the five remaining Exceptions are on the ground that the Findings are unsupported by the record.

These Exceptions may be answered summarily by noting the record references supporting the Commissioner:

Commissioner's Finding	Page of Defendant's Exception	Record References Supporting Commissioner's Finding
10(a)	10	48; 908-909; 544
10(b)	12	25-26; 87; 269-270; 423
11	14.	426
39(a)	17	Deft. Ex. 102
39(b)	20	Deft. Ex. 103; Pltf. Ex. 34; 72-73; 1107; 1184

Thus, the Findings to which defendant takes exception are indeed supported by the record.

With regard to defendant's requests for amplification only one need be commented on, namely, the request that Finding 10(a) include the finding that the use of photocopies is "essential" to medical research. This same assumption underlies virtually all of the reasoning in the various *amicus* briefs. As indicated above, it is not plaintiff's intention to curtail or halt photocopying; such activity is a convenient tool in research. To state that it is "essential" is, however, an exaggeration and

* Findings 36, 42 and 44.

A3

is unsupported by the record references on which defendant relies on page 10 of its Exceptions. It should be noted that the question posed to each of the witnesses whose testimony appears respectively at the eight cited references was substantially:

"Do you think being able to obtain phocopies of journal articles enables you to perform your research work more effectively?"

This is, of course, different from proof that the use of photocopies is "essential". It is pointless to parlay adjectives because while Dr. Banks used the word "indispensable", Dr. Starr insisted on changing "effectively" to "efficiently" (714). It is submitted that, in any event, the finding of essentiality would be against the weight of the evidence offered by Doctors McKusick and Scott, both of whom eminently bespoke effective research and neither of whom do much photocopying (670; 991).

The Exception to Finding 36 on page 16 of Defendants Exceptions erroneously states that the record does not disclose whether the license to the Institute for Scientific Information is for single copies. Although the "single copy" fallacy has now been fully exposed, the record is clear that plaintiff's licensing activities does in fact include single copies. For example, in the course of questioning at page 42, it is noted:

"I am assuming for the purpose of my question, that the person is requesting only one copy. If you were to furnish him with a copy, a single copy, isn't it true that you would furnish him with a Xerox copy?"

A4

Again, at 43, the question was repeated "If you were given a request for a single copy, would you or would you not furnish a Xerox copy?" In the course of the response, Mr. Passano, Chairman of the Board of Plaintiff, testified "I would refer him to a firm in Philadelphia which is in the business of supplying copies of articles". Mrs. Albrecht later identified that organization as the Institute for Scientific Information (127). This is the "evidence of record" which defendant argues, in its objection to Finding 36, does not exist.

Docket No. 73-68

IN THE UNITED STATES COURT OF CLAIMS

THE WILLIAMS & WILKINS CO.,

Plaintiff,

v.

THE UNITED STATES,

Defendant.

BRIEF <u>AMICUS CURIAE</u> OF
THE AUTHORS LEAGE OF AMERICA, INC.

IRWIN KARP, Attorney for
THE AUTHORS LEAGUE OF AMERICA, INC.,
as <u>AMICUS CURIAE</u>
120 Broadway
New York, N.Y. 10005
(212) 349-4141

October 30, 1972

1

Interest of the Authors League

The Authors League is the national society of American writers. Its fundamental purpose is to preserve the author's rights in the works he creates. The League was the principal spokesman for authors at the House and Senate Hearings on the pending Copyright Revision Bill; and it has filed amicus curiae briefs in several cases involving construction of the Copyright Act.

Since this case poses a copyright issue of vast importance to writers, the Authors League respectfully requests permission to file this brief in support of the Commissioner's Findings and Report.

2

The Interest of Authors

This suit is brought by a publisher. But the rights at issue are those secured to authors by the Copyright Act (17 U.S.C. 9), herein called "The Act". Essentially, defendant and its principal amici, ARL, ALA and NEA*, argue that the rights granted to an author in Sec. 1 of the Act do not permit him, or a publisher who acquires these rights from him, to require libraries to compensate him when they reproduce copies of his copyrighted articles for their patrons.

Defendant and its amici challenge the fundamental right of an author - the right to derive income from the reproduction of copies of his book, article, monograph, poem or other work. The economic survival of professional authors depends on that right. The creation of a library reproduction exemption, which the defendant's amici demand here, could diminish or destroy the author's income from the medium which first disseminates his work, from other media which may subsequently reproduce and distribute it, and from the new single-copying medium created by the revolution in reproduction technology.

A library copying exemption would also damage the professional author by seriously injuring private-enterprise

* "ARL" refers collectively to the ASSOCIATION OF RESEARCH LIBRARIES and the other organizations which have filed a joint brief *amicus curiae* with it.

"ALA" refers to the AMERICAN LIBRARY ASSOCIATION

"NEA" refers to the NATIONAL EDUCATION ASSOCIATION

3

publishing which is essential to him, and to his readers. Whether the rights are held by the author, or transferred to his publisher, denial of the right to protect them against unauthorized library copying could reduce the publisher's income and prospective income. Aside from an immediate concurrent loss of income, all authors (including scientists or scholars who submit articles without direct compensation) may suffer an even more drastic injury - the ultimate discontinuance of a periodical, journal or publishing house. The list of popular magazines and literary and scholarly publications which have died in recent years makes this possibility all too much a probability.

The defendant and its library amici invoke the "public interest" to defend their efforts to diminish rights of authors and publishers who create the materials that libraries store and circulate. But their view of the "public interest" and the purposes of copyright is myopic and self-centered. The library copying exemption they seek would be harmful to the "public interest" and to the progress of science and the arts.

Summary of Argument (A)

The Ambiguous Euphemism: "Single Copying"

Defendant and its amici claim that an author has no right to be compensated when libraries reproduce single copies of

4

his article. More ambitiously, ARL also claims the privilege for books and entire periodicals. The terms "single copies" and "single copying" are ambiguous euphemisms which conceal the basic issue.

The question is not whether one copy of an author's article may be reproduced during the copyright term without his con-

sent. The issue is whether a number of copies may be reproduced without his consent; including, as here, copies that reproduce, page for page, the printed text of the article. The "single", in "single copying" and "single copies", means that one copy is distributed by the library to each user who requests one. Under the "fair use" theory urged by defendant and its amici any library could reproduce as many unauthorized copies of the article as necessary to fill the orders of users, so long as each user received one copy.*

Moreover, each of the 4,200 libraries belonging to ALA, each library belonging to the ARL group, and every other

* Presumably "single copying" also means that each copy is reproduced to fill an order, as received. And this gives defendant and its amici the benefit of the doubt. However, they are apparently employing the term to include reproducing several copies at one time, so long as one copy is distributed to a user. We submit their "single copying" theory is wrong in either version. Our discussion is directed primarily to the reproduction of one copy at a time to fill an order; obviously our arguments apply with even greater force to reproduction of several copies at one time, distributed one copy to a user.

5

library in the United States could reproduce as many unauthorized copies of the same article as it had requests from users. The alleged privilege of reproducing unauthorized copies is not claimed only for NIH and NLM.* It is claimed for all non-profit libraries. Indeed, under the defendant's fair use theory, the privilege would also apply to thousands of other non-profit institutions.

Nor is the alleged privilege limited to articles on medicine: defendant and especially its amici claim the power to reproduce articles, and other copyrighted works, in their collections on subjects of interest for their readers. At a minimum, the library amici claim the power to reproduce copies for "individual scholars and other readers" (ARL Br. p. 1); and "readers engaged in scientific or scholarly research" (ALA Br. p. 1). For scientific and scholarly publications such as plaintiff's, this means an exemption permitting libraries and others to reproduce copies of articles for all present or potential readers of the periodicals.

Summary of Argument (B)

This brief addresses itself to the copyright issues raised by defendant and its amici:

* NIH refers to National Institutes of Health and its library.
NLM refers to National Library of Medicine.

6

POINT I   The rights granted the author in Sec. 1(a) of the Act encompass the reproduction of "single copies" of his article or other work. Only ARL seriously, and erroneously, contends such reproduction is not covered by these rights. Its theory is contradictory to the claim of fair use relied on by defendant and ARL. Actually, reproduction of copies infringes the author's rights to print and reprint his work, to publish his work, and to copy his work.

POINT II   The Constitution authorizes Congress to grant authors the exclusive right to reproduce "single copies" of their works. That power is contained in the explicit language of the Constitution and is consistent with the means selected by the Constitution to promote the progress of science and the useful arts. The Court should not judicially legislate a library single copying exemption; and that is what defendant and its amici seek, under the guise of "fair use".

POINT III   Library reproduction of "single copies" of copyrighted articles or other works is not fair use. It does not meet the four basic criteria of fair use. Such naked verbatim reproduction of copies of an article or other work is not the kind of "use" which "fair use" is intended to protect; it is not a means of "promoting the progress" of science and the arts contemplated by fair use; the dangers it poses to Constitutional and statutory methods of promoting that progress

7

far outweigh any advantages it might have to librarians, or to individuals who choose to order copies of the work from libraries.

POINT IV   The First Amendment does not deny authors or publishers the right to be compensated when copies of their works are reproduced by libraries. Their right to compensation is compatible with the First Amendment; and it makes possible the independent, entrepreneurial system of authorship and publishing which the First Amendment was designed to safeguard. Protection of the author's and publisher's right to compensation is essential to provide "access" to articles and books, and preserve freedom to read.

The "Ownership" Issue

Defendant contends that plaintiff is not the owner of the articles. The Authors League does not express an opinion on this ownership issue. However, we emphasize that the basic copyright issues to be decided involve authors' rights. Defendant and its amici would still assert, under their "single-copying" theories, that NIH and NLM were entitled to reproduce copies of the articles without authorization of the copyright owner if the authors had been paid by plaintiff for the right to publish their articles, if they shared in income from subsequent uses, if they had retained all rights, if the articles had been copyrighted in their names, and if they (rather than plaintiff) had sued defendant for infringement.

8

POINT I

The Rights Granted the Author in Sec. 1(a) Encompass Reproducing "Single Copies" of His Work

(i) The ARL theory

ARL argues that unauthorized library reproduction of "single copies" of an article for readers is not within the rights granted its author in Sec. 1(a) - and therefore not an infringement. It contends that such reproduction is not embraced in the author's "exclusive right to . . . copy" his work, claiming this right is limited to the publication and sale of "editions." (ARL Br. p.38) And ARL assumes that unauthorized library "single copying" is not within the other and separate rights granted an author in Sec. 1(a).

This ARL theory is, of course, totally inconsistent with the fair use theory urged by defendant and ALA, and also invoked by ARL. Fair use is a defense claimed where the use made by defendant is an activity covered by rights granted the author where the use is "technically an infringement" (Def. Br. p. 14). ARL also argues that if the rights granted in Sec. 1(a) encompass reproduction of "single copies," the grant is unconstitutional to that extent.

We submit that the ARL theory is wrong. As plaintiff demonstrates, library reproduction of a copyrighted article

9

infringes an author's copyright. We agree with their analysis. "Single copying" infringes various of the rights granted in Sec. 1(a).

(ii) Defendant's NLM and NIH infringed Plaintiff's "exclusive right (a) to print, reprint . . . . the copyrighted work."

The exclusive rights to "print" and "reprint" the copyrighted work, in Sec. 1(a) are not confined to making copies on a printing press. They include the reproduction of copies by such means as typewriter, mimeograph or photostat. Thus, in Macmillan Co. v. King, 223 Fed 862 (D. Mass. 1914), where infringing copies were mimeographed or typed, the Court said:
" 'Printing' I must regard as including typewriting or mimeographing, for the purposes of the Act, and (defendant) has therefore 'printed' them". (p. 867).
See also: American Visuals Corporation v. Holland, 239 F. 2d 740, 745 (2d Cir. 1956); White v. Kimmell, 193 F. 2d 744 (9th Cir. 1952); NIMMER ON COPYRIGHT, Sec. 101.3.
Unquestionably the reproduction of copies of plaintiff's articles by Xerox machines constituted "printing" or "reprinting" within the meaning of Sec. 1; far more so than retyping or mimeographing them. What the NIL and NLM machines reproduced were not handwritten pages, or typewritten copies. What came out of the machines were copies of the printed text of plaintiff's

10

articles, as they appeared in plaintiff's periodicals; in the identical typeface, word for word, line for line. The result was essentially the same as if defendant's libraries had reset the same type, or

made offset plates from photographs of plaintiff's periodicals, and reproduced copies on a printing press.
Had NIH or NLM set a Xerox machine at "100" and produced 100 copies of one of the articles, in one run, perhaps even ARL would concede this was an exercise of plaintiff's exclusive right to "print" or "reprint" the work. And that unauthorized reprinting would be infringement per se, even though the libraries never disseminated the copies. American Code Co., Inc. v. Bensinger, 282 F. 829, 834 (2d Cir. 1922); Greenbie v. Noble, 151 F. Supp. 45, 63 (S.D.N.Y. 1957); NIMMER ON COPYRIGHT, Sec. 102.
The right to print is infringed whether one or several copies is reproduced, at one time, without authorization. ARL quotes language purporting to support its erroneous claim that the right to "copy" does not include making "single copies." But it does not cite any case holding (or suggesting) that the rights to "print" or "reprint" are limited by any minimum numerical qualification. There is no such case. The Copyright Act does not impose any numerical qualification on the rights to print and reprint; it does not limit these rights to the printing of

11

"editions;" and it does not limit them to making a production run of a significant number of copies for publication. These alleged conditions and limitations are figments of ARL's imagination, not requirements of the Act.
ARL quotes the comment (ARL Br. p.35) that the author has the power to "multiply" copies of his work. Obviously. Each time another copy is reproduced, copies are "multiplied." "Multiply" means "to increase in number." None of the cited decisions use the word "multiply," which does not appear in the Act, to change the absolute, unqualified right to "print." The number of copies printed was not an issue in these cases. In none, did the Court hold that the printing of one copy was not an infringement of the right to print. This is hardly surprising. At that time economic and efficient machines for one-at-a-time "printing" of a work were not available to infringers. Unauthorized reproduction of a printed work was only economically feasible if several copies were run off at one time, on a press or mimeograph machine.
But the Xerox, and comparable machines, make possible one-at-a-time reproduction of copies of a printed work. With an accumulation of these reproductions, a number of unauthorized copies can be produced without the author's consent. If each infringer could claim immunity on the theory it had made only

12

one copy, or one copy at a time, the author's fundamental rights could be seriously eroded or completely destroyed by this process of attrition, by this accumulation of unauthorized "single copies." As indicated in our discussion of fair use, there is no "single copying" immunity; and authors are protected against this process of attrition. (infra. p. 41).

(iii) Defendant's NLM and NIH Infringed Plaintiff's "exclusive right (a) to . . . publish . . . the copyrighted work . . ."

Defendant's libraries infringed plaintiff's "exclusive right (a) to publish . . . the copyrighted work(s)." Dissemination of copies without charge or payment constitutes publication. American Visuals Corporation v. Holland, 239 F. 2d 740, 742 (2d Cir. 1956); Macmillan Co. v. King, 223 Fed. 862, 867. (D.C. Mass. 1914). And even assuming that Xeroxing of copies was not "printing," publication occurs when copies reproduced in such form are disseminated. cf. American Visuals Corporation v. Holland, supra (at p. 745) (photostats of pencilled material); Macmillan Co. v. King, supra (typed or mimeographed); White v. Kimmell, 193 F. 2d 744 (9th Cir. 1952) (mimeographed).
In American Visuals Corporation v. Holland, supra

13

The Court noted that where the author was claiming protection under the statute "the requirements for publication are quite narrow." It emphasized:
"In each case the courts appear so to treat the concept of 'publication' as to prevent piracy" (p. 744)
In Macmillan Co. v. King, supra the Court held that a limited publication by an unauthorized user was infringement. There, defendant loaned infringing copies to 15 students in one term, and to 17 students in the next term. (223 Fed. at pp. 867, 868). In American Visuals Corporation v. Holland, supra the Court

noted that in two cases* Judges A. Hand and L. Hand, respectively ruled:

> "that deposit of two copies of the work with the Library of Congress in compliance with the requirements of the Copyright Act, was sufficient publication to enable plaintiff to maintain suit under the act . . ." (239 F. 2d at 743).

The Court also cited Atlantic Monthly Co. v. Post Pub. Co., 27 F. 2d 556 (D.C. Mass., 1928), "holding a single sale for 10¢ of one of three written copies, sufficient publication under the Federal Copyright Act." See also Werckmeister v. American Lithographic Company, 134 Fed. 321, 325, 326 (2d Cir. 1904) (dissemination or offer of a single copy to the public is publication).

---

* Cardinal Film Corporation v. Beck, 248 Fed. 368 (SDNY 1918); Stern v. Jerome H. Remick & Co., 175 Fed. 282 (SDNY 1915).

14

Defendant's libraries disseminated one, two or three copies of plaintiff's articles in the test periods sampled. This, per se was a publication. Moreover, these copies were distributed pursuant to a system which constituted publication. Under this system, defendant's libraries furnished copies of the articles to scientists, doctors and other patrons who requested them, and was prepared to furnish additional copies to other patrons who asked for them. The procedures were known to the thousands of the libraries' users and prospective users; and were employed by them. NLM, for example, filled 120,000 requests for copies of journal articles and distributed 1,200,000 pages in fiscal year 1968. In effect, defendant's libraries make a continuing offer to a very substantial number of patrons to distribute copies of plaintiff's articles* (and others); that offer, coupled with the distribution of even one copy, is clearly "publication." NIMMER ON COPYRIGHT, Sec. 104; Werckmeister v. American Lithographic Company, supra; American Visuals Corporation v. Holland, supra (at p. 745).

Had the defendant's libraries filled their patrons' requests for copies of plaintiff's articles from stocks of 100 or 200 copies per article, prepared at one time for that purpose,

---

* The privilege claimed by ARL and ALA for libraries necessarily implies that each library may offer to furnish copies of plaintiff's articles to each patron who requests one.

15

they would have "published." Here the copies were distributed from a potentially greater number of Xerox copies of the articles the libraries could produce, on demand, to fill requests made under their rights.

The fact that each copy is distributed on order, one copy to a user, does not obviate "publication." That is the essence of most publication. The book store is a principal medium by which books are distributed to the public -- i.e. published. The typical method of book store distribution is one copy to a user, to fill user's order. The mail order publisher and book club, who distribute directly to users, publish by disseminating one copy to each patron, when his request is received -- as does the defendant's NLM when it receives a request for one of the plaintiff's articles by mail and ships back a copy to fill the order.

Finally, defendant and its amici ignore the fact that printing and publishing are done on a "single-copy" basis; i.e., there are commercial reprint publishers who fill each customer's order for a book or other work by reproducing a single copy of the work, by the Xerox process, and sending it to the customer. One of the major "one-at-a-time" (i.e. "single-copy"), commercial reprint publishers is the Xerox subsidiary, University Microfilms. It reproduces such copies of copyrighted works under licenses from the copyright owners to whom it pays a royalty.

16

(iv) Defendant's NLM and NIH Infringed Plaintiff's "exclusive right (a) to . . . copy . . . the copyrighted work."

As Professor Nimmer points out, the exclusive right "to copy' his work is the most fundamental right granted an author by the Act (NIMMER ON COPYRIGHT, Sec. 101); and it encompasses the reproduction of "single copies" (ibid, Sec. 101.3). Indeed, the controversy over library copying has proceeded from the universal assumption that it is an activity encompassed by the rights granted the author in Sec. 1(a). The issue has been whether any library "single copying" is fair use; and if so, to

what extent. cf. Borge Varmer, PHOTODUPLICATION OF COPYRIGHTED MATERIALS (Study No. 15, 86th Cong., 2d Sess. pp 49-50): NIMMER ON COPYRIGHT, Sec. 145.

ARL's argument that reproduction of "single copies" is not a use within the right "to copy" is based, in part, in culling phrases from opinions that have nothing to do with this issue. ARL also purports to find support for its theory in Harper v. Shoppell, 26 Fed. 519 (C.C.S.D.N.Y. 1886). The support is not there.

In Harper, defendant had purchased a cut -- an illustration -- which had appeared in HARPER'S WEEKLY. He then made an "electrotype plate" of the illustration and sold it; the acts which plaintiff claimed infringed its copyright in HARPER'S WEEKLY. Until the 1870 Copyright Act, "copying" was

17

one of the rights granted by the copyright in a cut, but not by the copyright in a book or periodical. Plaintiff had copyrighted its periodical, but not the cut.

However, the Court attached quite a different significance to the word "copying" than ARL now does. It said:

> "It would not be an infringement of a book . . . to prepare and arrange the type in exact imitation of the original, so that a copy of the book might be reproduced by printing; nor would it be to sell the means of making such a copy to another." (P. 520) (Emphasis supplied)

The Court interpreted "copying" as producing the means by which copies of a work were reproduced. The unauthorized creation of type to be used for reproducing a book was not infringement of a book copyright; the unauthorized reproduction of a plate to be used for reproducing an etching, engraving or cut was infringement of the copyright in such works.

This is underlined by the Court's comment:

> "The question here is. . . . whether the defendant has infringed plaintiff's copyright in their book by making a plate from which a copy of a portion of their book could be produced . . . ." (p. 520) (Emphasis supplied)

Here, defendants, NIH and NLM did not make plates from which copies could be reproduced - they reproduced copies. Indeed, the Harper v. Shoppell Court would have held

18

the NIH and NLM copying was infringement for it did not subscribe to the ARL "single copying" theory. The Court said:

> "A book is infringed by printing, publishing, importing, selling, or exposing for sale of any copy of the book." (p. 520)

In any event, this Court need not decide that question, since this distinction between copyrights in cuts and copyrights in books and journals was eliminated by the 1909 Act. The right "to copy" was granted to authors of books and periodicals as well as creators of cuts and illustrations. Thus, bringing Harper v. Shoppell up to date, since 1909 the copyright in a book or periodical is infringed "by copying" . . . . "by making any copy of the book."

As the Supreme Court emphasized, "Congress declar(ed), however, that just damages, even for the circulation of a single copy, cannot be less than $250." Douglas v. Cunningham, 294 U.S. 207, 210 (1935) (emphasis supplied)

POINT II

The Author's Right to be Paid for Library Reproduction of his Work is Constitutional

Defendant and its amici argue that the Copyright clause of the Constitution requires the Court to grant defendant's libraries, and all non-profit libraries, the privilege of reproducing copies of plaintiff's copyrighted articles for their clients, and other readers and users. ARL argues that the Constitution prohibits Congress from granting authors the right to be paid for such reproduction, if indeed the rights secured by

19

Sec. 1(a) do encompass library single-copying. Defendant and its amici also contend that Constitutional policy of copyright - as they see it - requires the Court to sustain unauthorized library copying as fair use. Not surprisingly, we disagree.

(i) The Constitution and the "Purpose" of Copyright

The Constitution authorizes Congress to secure to authors "the exclusive right in their respective writings" (Art. I, Sec. 8). The power is not merely discretionary. The words "Congress shall have the power" do not precede the Copyright clause; they preface all the powers granted Congress in Sec. 8, including the powers "to lay and collect taxes .... to borrow money .... to regulate commerce ...." (etc.). Indeed the power to secure copyright to authors precedes the powers "to declare war .... to raise and support armies .... to provide and maintain a navy ..." Obviously the authors of the Constitution considered the enactment of copyright laws a fundamental responsibility of Congress; and no more discretionary than levying taxes, borrowing money or maintaining armed forces.

The Constitution states that the purpose of Federal copyright laws is to "promote the progress of science and useful arts." But defendant and its amici completely fail to understand how the purpose is to be accomplished. They assume that it is by denying the author his "exclusive rights" whenever unauthorized

20

reproduction might, in their view, also promote that progress. True it is that the primary purpose of Federal Copyright legislation is to promote the progress of science and the arts; that is why reward to authors is said to be "secondary." But the Constitution makes it crystal clear how that progress is to be promoted - namely, "by securing for limited times to authors .... the exclusive rights to their respective writings ..." The protection of those exclusive rights was chosen by the Constitution as the means of promoting the progress.

Thus in Mazer v. Stein, 347 U.S. 201 (1954) after quoting the comment that the Copyright Act "makes reward to the owner a secondary consideration," the Court went on to state (p. 219):

"However, it is 'intended definitely to grant valuable, enforceable rights to authors, publishers, etc., without burdensome requirements; 'to afford greater encouragement to the production of literary [or artistic] works of lasting benefit to the world.' " Washingtonian Co. v. Pearson, 306 U.S. 30, 36"

The Court then emphasized how the Constitutional purpose is promoted:

"The economic philosophy behind the clause empowering Congress to grant patents and copyrights is the conviction that encouragement of individual effort by personal gain is the best way to advance public welfare through the talents of authors and inventors in 'Science and useful Arts'."

21

Professor Nimmer says: "We may assume that the men who wrote the Constitution regarded the system of private property per se as in the public interest. In according a property status to copyright they merely extended a recognition of this interest into a new sector." (Sec. 3.1) As he correctly observes, the Constitutional provision for granting "exclusive rights" to authors was a provision for according property status for their works. "Property" says BLACK'S LAW DICTIONERY "is, in the strict legal sense, an aggregate of rights which are guaranteed and protected by government."

Thus the Constitution provides that the public interest in having literary and scientific works created be promoted by having authors and publishers depend on a private enterprise - property rights system: i.e., property rights in their work, dependence on "personal gain" from individual efforts for reward and compensation. The other consequence of this "economic philosophy behind the clause" is that "sacrificial hours devoted to such activities" may result in losses, rather than gains.

It is apparent that ARL, ALA and NEA do not understand, or reject, the "economic philosophy behind the (Copyright) clause." NEA, for example, repeatedly invokes the dread and insidious "copyright monopoly" (NEA Br. pp46-49); urging that a free copying license must be granted libraries to avoid extending that "monopoly." An author's copyright in his article or novel

22

does not give him control over the market for books; only over specified uses of his work, which must compete in the marketplace with thousands of others. It is not a grant by the State of the exclusive right to engage in the printing or publishing business; it only gives the author the exclusive right to print, publish, copy or sell copies of the work he creates.* See: U.S. v. Dubilier Condenser Corp, 289 U.S. 178, 186 (1933); Rohmer v Commissioner of Internal Revenue, 153 F. 2d 61, 63 (n.9) (2d Cir. 1946).

* Whether an author has a "moral" or "natural" claim to rights in his work is irrelevant in light of the Constitutional grant of exclusive rights to him. But the following quotation may be enlightening to ALA, ARL and NEA:

"Copyright .... does not prevent any one from using for himself the facts, the knowledge, the laws or combinations for a similar production, but only from using the identical form of the particular book or other production - the actual labor which has in short been expended in producing it. It rests therefore upon the natural, moral right of each one to enjoy the products of his own exertion, and involves no interference with the similar right of any one else to do likewise ....

"The Copyright is therefore in accordance with the moral law - it gives to the man who has expended the intangible labor required to write a particular book or paint a picture security against the copying of that identical thing." Henry George, PROGRESS AND POVERTY, P. 411.

23

Copyright is a "monopoly" only in the sense that any property is; its owner has exclusive rights to use it. In Interstate Circuit v. United States, 306 U.S. 208 (1939), Mr. Justice Roberts, dissenting on other grounds, said:

"I agree that while the Copyright Act gives a distributor a so-called monopoly, that monopoly cannot be made the cover for a conspiracy to restrain trade or commerce. But I think it obscures the issue to use the phrase "monopoly."

* * * *

"All the Copyright Act does is create a form of property in the literary or artistic production of the author or artists."

* * * *

"The monopoly, so called, amounts to no more than the attachment to the work of an author or composer or producer of motion pictures the same rights as inhere in other property under common law." (at pp. 235-236)

It obscures the issue to argue, as the library amici do, that because the author's rights are granted by Federal Statute, libraries are entitled to a free, broad license to use it - a "single copying" right, under the guise of fair use. The principle is well established that (all) property is a creature and creation of law ..." (73 C.J.S. PROPERTY Sec. 1, p. 145). All bundles of exclusive rights ("property") are granted by the State, through legislation or Court decision.

24

Property rights in billions of dollars of property have been created dolely by Acts of Congress; exclusive rights in land, oil and other natural resources.*

There is, of course, one distinction between the Copyright Act and these other statutes conferring property rights on individuals. The other statutes grant exclusive rights in resources that previously belonged to the Nation, that were part of the public domain. The Copyright Act grants the author exclusive rights in something that he created and that previously belonged to him. At common law, the author's work is his "absolute property ... protected like other personal property." (Copyright Revision Study No. 29, p. 3.) Common law rights in unpublished works "continue with no limit even though the work is used commercially and widely disseminated." COPYRIGHT LAW REVISION, Report of the Register of Copyrights, p. 40 (87th Cong., 1st Sess.); Ferris v. Frohman, 223 U.S. 424 (1912); 17 USC 2.

(ii) Sec. 1(a)'s prohibitions against unauthorized Library copying are Constitutional

ARL, supported by defendant, argues that Congress

* e.g. Homestead Acts, (1862, 12 Stat. 392; 1891, 26 Stat. 1097; 1908, 35 Stat. 6); Morrill Acts, (1862, 12 Stat. 503; 1883, 22 Stat. 484; 1890, 26 Stat. 417); Pacific Railroad Acts, (1961, 12 Stat. 489; 1864, 13 Stat. 356; 1866, 14 Stat. 79); Act of May 10, 1872 (Mineral Resources) (17 Stat. 91)

25

cannot Constitutionally grant an author rights to be compensated for library reproduction of copies of his work. ARL argues that library copying promotes the progress of science and the arts, and therefore it cannot be prohibited under Article I, Sec. 8.

But, as we noted, ARL and its cohorts ignore the means by which the Constitution intended to promote the progress of science and the arts. It did not say Congress should secure for authors only those rights which Congress thought would promote science and the arts; certainly it did not limit Congress to granting only those rights which the ARL or ALA or NIH and NLM or the Courts thought would promote that progress. On the contrary, the Constitution made a threshold value judgment

- it said, explicitly, that the progress of science and the arts should be promoted by "securing to authors . . . the exclusive rights in their respective writings." It does not add any limitations, qualifications or exemptions. As Professor Nimmer says, "the phrase 'to promote the progress of science and the useful arts . . .' must be read largely as in the nature of a preamble, indicating the purpose of the power but not in limitation of its exercise." (Sec. 3.1)

The grant of exclusive rights may not be the only way to promote science and the arts; but it is the Constitutional way. Congress could have enacted a Copyright Act in haec verba,

---

26

stating in Sec. 1(a) that an author shall have "the exclusive rights" in his work for the copyright term. It has spelled out those rights in the subdivisions of Sec. 1. It added "not-for-profit" limitations on certain of the performing rights. But it did not grant the author the "exclusive rights" to print, publish and make copies of his work, without limitation or exception. We respectfully submit that with such a broad (indeed absolute) Constitutional mandate to Congress, the Court could not hold that it was unconstitutional for Congress to grant authors rights which entitle them to payment for library reproduction of their works.

(iii) The Court Should Not Judicially Legislate
a Library Copying Exemption

Actually defendant and its amici ask the Court to engraft a broad and sweeping library-copying exemption on Sec. 1(a). The exemption they claim goes far beyond the most liberal application of the fair use doctrine; it cannot be justified under the guise of fair use, as we demonstrate in Point III. Defendant, ARL and ALA claim a library copying exemption is necessary to promote the progress of science and the arts. We disagree. We think it will stifle that progress. But the decision is neither ours, nor theirs; nor, we respectfully submit, is it the Court's. Only Congress can decide whether such an exemption would promote the progress of science and the arts more effectively than the present statute, which it has adopted in keeping with the very

---

27

words of the Constitutional mandate.

POINT III

Defendant's Copying of Plaintiff's
Copyrighted Articles Was Not Fair Use

Defendant and its amici contend that the NIH and NLM reproduction of copies of the entire text of plaintiff's copyrighted articles is "fair use," and therefore did not infringe plaintiff's copyrights. We wholeheartedly agree with plaintiff that the doctrine of fair use does not apply to this naked reproduction of verbatim copies of an entire work, or of a substantial portion of a work. Leon v. Pacific Tel. and Tel. Co., 91 F. 2d 484, 486 (9th Cir. 1937); Wihtol v. Crow, 309 F. 2d 777 (8th Cir. 1962); Public Affairs Associates, Inc. v. Rickover, 284 F. 2d 262, 272 (D.C. Cir. 1960); Judgment vacated, 309 U.S. 111 (1962); Rosemont Enterprises v. Random House, Inc., 366 F. 2c 303, 310 (2d Cir. 1966).

(i) "The Amount Used" was excessive

As Commissioner Davis noted in his opinion, there are four standards which courts consider in determining whether a particular use is a "fair use." One standard is the "amount and substantiality of the portion used in relation to the copyrighted work as a whole." Clearly, if the "amount . . . . of the portion used" is an essential criterion, then a

---

28

reproduction of an entire work cannot be a fair use. Defendant concedes this. But it claims that each article was not "an entire work" but rather a portion of the Journal in which it appeared - and that the Journal was the "entire work." Plaintiff contends that each article is an entire work. We agree.

Plaintiff notes that under Sec. 3 of the Act, the copyright on a composite work or periodical gives the proprietor "all rights

in respect thereto which he would have if each part were individually copyrighted under this title." The purpose of the Section was stated in the Report on the 1909 Act which said the Section "does away with the necessity of taking a copyright on the contributions of different persons included in a single publication." (H.R. Rep. No. 2222, 60th Cong. 2d Sess., P. 9.) Sec. 3 simply allows each separate contribution to a periodical to be copyrighted under the one notice of the proprietor; although each contribution could also be copyrighted under a separate notice.

Furthermore, Sec. 24 of the Act provides that each article contributed to plaintiff's journals is a separate work. Section 24 states:

". . . . That in the case of any other copyrighted work, including a contribution by an individual author to a periodical . . . . or other composite work, the author of such work . . . . shall be entitled to a renewal and extension of the copyright in such work . . . ." *(Emphasis added)*

29

Here then are self-contained, separate, 30, 40 and 50 page articles; having no relation with the other articles in the same periodical. Each by definition of Sec. 24 is a separate copyrighted work. (Indeed, defendant contends that each is a separate work, still owned by its author.) But whether an author retains his rights in an article or conveys them to the publisher of the periodical, the article's character as a separate work does not change.

The defendant claims that one copyright notice makes a periodical the "work" for testing "fair use." But if plaintiff hereafter places a separate copyright notice in each contribution, each would be copyrighted separately, whether in plaintiff's name or the author's (Copyright Office Form BB - "Contribution to a Periodical Manufactured in the United States"). Then, even defendant and its amici could not bring themselves to contend the article was not a separate "work." Certainly the unauthorized library reproduction of an article copyrighted under a separate notice would be a use of the entire work, and hence not a fair use under the criterion which presupposes that only a portion - not unfair in amount or substantiality "in relation to the copyrighted work as a whole" - can be appropriated under "fair use." Of course, where the author retains rights in his contribution, as professional authors sometimes do, the article must be considered "the copyrighted work as a whole" for fair use purposes.

30

Moreover, even assuming the periodical is "the copyrighted work as a whole" the unauthorized reproduction of an entire article, ranging from 30 to 50 pages in length, far exceeds the amount and substantiality, in relation to the entire "work," which may be reproduced under the guise of fair use.

(ii) The Bare, Verbatim Reproduction of a Copyrighted Work
is Not a "purpose" Intended by Fair Use

Another criterion of fair use is "the purpose of the use." Essentially, defendant and its amici argue that making copies of plaintiff's articles for scientists or other readers helps promote progress, and that this is a purpose intended by "fair use." Not so.

In case after case the claim of fair use arises where the defendant author (or his publisher) has incorporated into his work, material from a prior work by the plaintiff author (or publisher). Where "fair use" is sustained, it is because the portion taken for use in the separate work the defendant created is not unreasonably large in amount, or substantiality, and the use of the material in defendant's work does not affect the market for the plaintiff.

"Fair use" is consistent with the basic purpose of the Copyright Clause: "to afford greater encouragement to the production of literary (or artistic) works of lasting benefit

---

31

to the world." (Washingtonian Co. v. Pearson, 306 U.S. 30, 36) (emphasis added); quoted with approval in Mazer v. Stein, 347 U.S. 201, 219, the Court again emphasizing that the purpose was "encouragement of individual effort" and "sacrificial days devoted to such creative activities. . . ." (emphasis added). Its purpose is to aid a second author in the production of his literary or artistic work; by permitting him to make limited use, in it, of material from another author's prior work. Thus, the "production of" new "literary (or artistic) works" is encouraged.

The point is brought home in Rosemont Enterprises, Inc. v.

Random House, Inc., 366 F. 2d 303 (2d Cir. 1966). The Court said:

> "We, however, cannot subscribe to the view that an <u>author</u> is absolutely precluded from saving time and effort by referring to and relying upon prior published material . . . . It is just such wasted effort that the proscription against the copyright on ideas and facts, and to a lesser extent the privilege of fair use, are designed to prevent." (at p. 310) (emphasis supplied)

As the Court said, whether "the privilege may justifiably be applied" to defendant's work depends, <u>inter alia</u>, on "whether their preparation requires some use of (plaintiff's) prior materials dealing with the same subject matter." (at p. 307)

In <u>Rosemont</u>, as in other "fair use" cases, the issue is whether the author of a second work may use in it, material

32

from another author's work. It involves use in "production" of new works, "creative activities."

Fair use does not apply, as defendant, ARL and ALA assume, to the bare verbatim reproduction of the plaintiff author's work. NIH and NLM did not use material from plaintiff's articles in the creation of a new article or book. What NIH and NLM did, and what ARL and ALA ask that all libraries be allowed to do, is simply reproduce copies of the plaintiff's works and disseminate them. This is not what the doctrine of "fair use" intends. In <u>Rosemont</u>, material that had appeared in LOOK articles on Howard Hughes were used in defendant's new work, a biography of Hughes. Had Random House merely reprinted the LOOK articles, for libraries to distribute free to historians and scholars requesting copies, that could not be fair use.

As Mr. Justice Reed said in Public Affairs Associates, Inc. v. Rickover, 284 F. 2d 262 (D.C. Cir. 1960), judgment vacated 369 U.S. 111 (1962):

> "The publication of a work consisting in substantial part of quotations from copyrighted works is not permitted under the theory of fair use." (at p. 272)

And in <u>Rosemont</u>, the Court said "extensive verbatim

33

copying . . . of material set down by another cannot satisfy (the) standard" of fair use. 366 F. 2d at p. 310.

(iii) The Effect on the Plaintiff's "Potential Market"

Another criterion of fair use is "the effect of the use on the copyright owner's <u>potential</u> market for his work." (emphasis added) Actually the test does not apply here since the naked verbatim reproduction of copies of a work, or a substantial part of a work, is not "fair use," for the reasons indicated above.

In any event, the unauthorized reproduction of copies of plaintiff's articles has a harmful effect on plaintiff's potential market for its journals, and for the individual articles. That effect precludes fair use. The "<u>potential</u> market" effect includes the effect in the future, not merely the number of those previously lost sales or dollar damages it can prove at the trial.

In every true fair use case, a Court must decide at the time of trial that no matter how many copies of the defendant's work are sold in the future, or how many

34

performances are later given, plaintiff's <u>potential</u> market will not be harmed.

Undoubtedly copies of the articles in suit will continue to be reproduced in the future, without plaintiff's authorization - - if the Court adopts the defendant-ARL-ALA theory that library "single copying" is fair use. Defendant and its amici do not merely claim the making of the copies proven at the trial is fair use. They argue that the reproduction of single copies of articles by NIH and NLM in the future will be fair use; and that the reproduction, in the future, of single copies of the articles by any non-profit library for scholars, researchers, etc. will be fair use. Their briefs make it clear they seek the right to continue reproducing the articles in suit and other articles now or hereafter published by plaintiff (or any other publisher); and that if the Court adopts their theory, NIH, NLM and libraries will continue to reproduce single copies.

Therefore, the Court could not conclude that the continued reproduction of unauthorized verbatim copies of plaintiff's articles would not damage plaintiff's

35

potential market for the articles, for its journals, or for individual articles published in the future.

Unauthorized library copying will reduce library purchases of journals. If a library can reproduce copies of articles then, as ALA admitted in its prior brief, one subscription will substitute for the additional subscriptions that would otherwise be required to meet users' requests for a valuable journal. Moreover, as ALA admitted, unauthorized library copying would reduce library purchases of journals even more drastically. If one library, such as NIH or NLM, can reproduce copies for the patrons of other libraries, then the other libraries do not have to buy subscriptions themselves, and the supplying library needs only one subscription, not the additional ones previously required to make "library loans." Under the single copying exemption sought by library amici, <u>one</u> subscription copy of any journal could literally satisfy the needs of patrons of libraries all over the United States.*

---

* Individual subscriptions to journals would also be diminished under a library copying exemption. Each individual subscriber is not interested in every article published in a journal. If he can select those that interest him from INDEX MEDICUS, or some similar abstract, and obtain copies from a library, he is likely to cancel his subscription to one or more of the technical journals he subscribes to.

36

Unauthorized reproduction of copies, under a library copying exemption, would also diminish the plaintiff's income from other sources. And it would also deprive thousands of authors and publishers of such income; for ALA and ARL do not limit their claim of fair use to library copying of plaintiff's articles. They assert it applies to all works of interest to library patrons.

As Professor Nimmer pointed out, the determination of effect on "potential sale of plaintiff's work" must be considered with respect to all media in which it could be disseminated (Sec. 145). Articles, novels, poetry and other works which are first published in periodicals are subsequently disseminated by reproduction in anthologies, paperback editions, textbooks, other periodicals and newspapers, and in customized anthologies. Income from these subsequent reproductions is a significant source of revenue to authors and publishers; sometimes more significant than income derived from the initial publication. Unauthorized library copying of articles and other works would substantially diminish their income from these sources.

An author's income is an accretion of small payments: a royalty on each copy sold, a fee or royalty for each subsequent reproduction of his work. Therefore no payment is

37

"unimportant" to him. Each contributes to the gradual accumulation of an amount which someday, hopefully, will compensate him for the labor, time and talent he invests in creating the work. The publisher's income is also derived by the same process, and investment.

Moreover, unauthorized reproduction of copies, under a library copying exemption, would diminish the income derived by plaintiff (and other authors and publishers) from the sale of single copies by reproduction services and some libraries it has licensed to reproduce copies of its articles on a royalty basis. In recent years, a new source of income for authors and publishers has been the royalties paid on single copies of articles and entire books reproduced, under license, by companies such as University Microfilm, Inc. The advances in reproduction technology have created a new medium in which books and articles may produce additional income for their authors and publisher - the sale of single copies.

This is a familiar occurrence in copyright. For years the works of composers were disseminated by live public performances and sheet music; then by records, then by radio, then by talking pictures, and then by television. Not every new medium reduced the composer's income from existing media; in fact, some new media (e.g. radio, talking pictures) actually increased his income from other media (e.g., records). No Court has ever

38

held that, because a use in a new medium did not diminish the author's income from the use of his music in existing media, it would be fair use for others to use his work without permission in the new medium. Emergence of mass-circulation paperback books in the 1950's did not diminish the author's income from the sale of hardcover copies; it often augmented that income. But no library or university press is entitled to reproduce paperback copies of a book on the theory that this is fair use because it does not diminish income from hardcover sales.

Defendant argues that plaintiff has not proven any substantial loss to this time from the unauthorized copies of its articles, and that this therefore permits its libraries to continue reproducing copies of plaintiff's articles. ALA and ARL claim the alleged lack of proof of damage entitles all libraries to copy plaintiff's articles, and everyone else's articles, now and forever.*

But, as we have noted, the "potential market" standard in a true fair use situation involves the effect in the future on the copyright owner's potential market. And

---

* Actually proof of damage is irrelevant to the theory of fair use asserted by defendant and its library amici. It is clear from their briefs that they would assert the theory even if more positive proof of past damage could have been adduced.

39

the determination of that future effect is not limited to (i) damages inflicted by the particular defendant, or (ii) damages which plaintiff can prove.

The dangerous potential market effect of unauthorized single copying is that an accumulation of such copies produced by defendant and others (sheltering under ALA-ARL's proposed exemption) would damage plaintiff, and countless other authors and publishers. In an era when technology has created a new medium of one-at-a-time reproduction, it would be disastrous if each unauthorized reproducer of copies could claim "fair use" on the theory that it had made only one, or a few copies. The author's fundamental rights could be eroded by this process of attrition.

A basic purpose of awarding damages in a copyright suit is to prevent others, not only defendant, from infringing and thus contributing to this process of attrition. Thus, in F. W. Woolworth Co. v. Contemporary Arts, Inc., 344 U.S. 228, the Supreme Court said:

" * * * The statutory rule, formulated after long experience, not merely compels restitution of profit and reparation for injury but also is designed to discourage wrongful conduct. The discretion of the court is wide enough to permit a resort to statutory damages for such purposes. Even for uninjurious and unprofitable invasions of copyright the court may, if it deems it just, impose a liability within statutory limits to sanction and vindicate the statutory policy." (at p. 233)

40

An award of damages to plaintiff is essential to enforce the "copyright policy" and prevent continued reproduction of its articles by defendant and others in the future. And, as we have noted, here there is no doubt that there will be such infringement if an award is denied; defendant and its amici concede that libraries will do so.

Defendant argues that plaintiff has not presented proof of "substantial damage" in the past. But this is commonplace in infringement situations; it is the reason for the statutory damages provisions of Section 101. In Brady v. Daly, 175 U.S. 148 (1899), the Court said:

" * * * It is evident that in many cases it would be quite difficult to prove the exact amount of damages which the proprietor of a copyrighted dramatic composition suffered by reason of its unlawful production by another, and yet it is also evident that the statute seeks to provide a remedy for such a wrong and to grant to the proprietor the right to recover the damages which he has sustained therefrom.

＊ ＊ ＊ ＊ ＊

" * * * In the face of the difficulty of determining the amount of such damage in all cases, the statute provides a minimum sum for a recovery in any case, leaving it open for a larger recovery upon proof of greater damages in those cases where such proof can be made. * * *"

(at p. 154)

In F. W. Woolworth & Co. v. Contemporary Arts, Inc., 344 U.S. 228 (1952), the Court quoted the following from Douglas v. Cunningham, 294 U.S. 207, 209:

41

"The phraseology of the section was adopted to avoid the strictness of construction incident to a law imposing penalties, and to give the owner of a copyright some recompense for injury done him, in a case where the rules of law render difficult or impossible proof of

damages or discovery of profits."

The difficulty of proving damages is compounded where "single copying" is involved. Plaintiff sampled NIH and NLM records for selected test periods and determined the number of copies made in those periods. Additional copies undoubtedly were made by NIH and NLM in other time periods not surveyed. And additional copies undoubtedly were made by other libraries, research centers, and similar institutions. It would be an impossible burden for an author or publisher to prove the number of unauthorized copies of an article already reproduced by a defendant and by others throughout the United States, or the precise impact of that copying on past subscriptions and single copy sales. It would be even more difficult for the plaintiff to prove how many unauthorized copies will be reproduced in the future; or to prove how much income will be lost in the future, if unauthorized single copying continues. This is why the "potential market" test in a true fair use case deals with the "potential" effect of future reproduction of the work. This is why courts award damages even for "uninjurious and unprofitable invasions of copyright." (F. W. Woolworth & Co. v. Contemporary Arts, Inc., supra,

42

at P. 233) This is why courts award damages for one infringing performance or the sale of a single copy. (See cases cited at Point IIB, Plaintiff's Brief.)

ALA argues that plaintiff should not be allowed to "maximize" its profits. Apparently ALA has somehow concluded that plaintiff has earned "enough." But the Copyright Act does not place a limit on the amount of "personal gain" a copyright owner should derive from his work. Indeed, it does not guarantee him any gain; nor does it guarantee him against loss. The bizarre philosophy of the ALA also ignores the fact that the publisher's income from one work helps underwrite the publication of other works, frequently unprofitable ones. Certainly ALA does not concede that if plaintiff could later demonstrate that its losses from library copying reached the amount which ALA or ARL considered "significant," continued library copying would cease to be fair use under their theory. On the contrary, under their theory, they would still argue that library copying is fair use.

43

(iv) There is no "For-Profit" Limit on Section 1(a) Rights

NIH and NLM do not charge for the copies they reproduce for patrons. But this does not make their infringement fair use. Where Congress wanted to place a "for-profit" limit on a right granted to authors, it did so explicitly. For example, the right to publicly perform music is limited to performances "for profit." Non-profit performances may be presented without his consent.

But Section 1(a) does not place a "for-profit" limit on the author's exclusive rights to print, reprint, publish, copy, or sell his work. The reason is obvious. We listen to many performances of the same composition. The more we hear it, the more we appreciate and enjoy. Therefore, non-profit performances do not diminish the for-profit performances for which the composer is paid. But we need only one copy of a book or periodical or article. If a library or school can reproduce it without permission or payment, the author loses the income from that prospective source forever.

Unauthorized reproduction of copies of copyrighted works is completely prohibited to "non-profit" copyists - libraries who do the copying without charge, or others. The House Judiciary Committee said:

"As shown by a Copyright Office study dated July 22, 1966, the educational groups are mistaken

44

in their argument that a for profit limitation is applicable to educational copying under the present law."

(H.R. Rep. No. 83; 90th Cong., 1st Sess.)

(v) Unauthorized "single copying" is not "note taking"

It is also suggested that library single copying is justified as a "substitute" for "note taking." This is nonsense. If I copy a 30 or 40 page article, I produce 60 or 80 pages of handwritten script. What comes out of the NIH and NLM Xerox machines are reproductions of the printed text of plaintiff's articles. These copies were substitutes for the journals, or for reprints on the articles, which plaintiff or its licensees could sell.

The printed text of one of plaintiff's articles is more legible, more compact, than a handwritten copy. More important, copying the article by hand is slow and tiresome. It would take several hours to reproduce a 30 or 40 page article (Copyright Law Revision, Hearings before Subc. No. 3, House Jud. Comm., 89th Cong. 1st Sess., p. 1756). The user avoids wasting time and energy if he buys a copy of plaintiff's article from plaintiff or its licensees, or if he acquires a Xerox copy of the printed text. That is the reason why scholars, researchers, and other readers buy or borrow a printed copy of a book or article when it contains a substantial amount of material they require. The

45

Xerox copy is a substitute for the copy sold to the user or sold to the library which lends it to him.

(vi) Articles "Contributed" by Authors may not be
Reproduced without the Copyright Owner's Consent

The articles in suit were "contributed" by their authors without compensation. Defendant and its amici assert that this justifies unauthorized "single copying." We disagree.

First of all, defendant, ARL and ALA do not take the claim seriously. They do not concede that where authors are paid, unauthorized single copying is infringement. They claim the same privilege to reproduce articles by authors who are paid for the right to publish them in periodicals and who share (usually 50% or more) in all income from subsequent uses, including income from the sale of single copies.

Second, the authors of articles have received what they sought - publication of the articles in the journals. Had they wished to permit free single copying after publication, they could have insisted on it as a condition to allowing plaintiff to publish their articles; or they could have chosen other methods of dissemination if plaintiff refused to accept the condition. After a publisher acquires rights, an author obviously cannot authorize others to make uses which infringe those rights. And, as we have indicated, if

46

we are to have a free enterprise publishing system, publishers cannot be denied the right to derive income from copyrighted works they have risked capital, and invested effort, to print and disseminate.

(vii) Unauthorized Library Copying for
Library Patrons is Infringement

Defendant says NIH and NLM were agents for their patrons. Agents are also liable for copyright infringement. But actually the libraries were not agents. They made the copies at their own expense; they had no agency relationship with users; they did what they did because they chose to do it.

There is no similarity to the situation in Fortnightly Corp. v. United Artists Television, 392 U.S. 390 (1968). CATV systems were held not to infringe copyrights in television programs because their acts were not "public performances" of the programs, the right alleged to be infringed, but merely an incident to the customer's reception of the performance by the broadcaster. Here libraries reproduced copies of the plaintiff's articles, an act clearly within the ambit of "print(ing)", "publish(ing)" and "copy(ing)" under Sec. 1(a).*

It is unnecessary to decide whether a reproduction made by the user would be an infringement; although we submit

* See Point I, supra

47

it is.* (We also submit that users would not make copies if the NIH and NLM, under license from plaintiff, furnished the copies.) Defendant's libraries reproduced the copies. It cannot escape liability on the ground the act might not have been infringement if performed by someone else.

It is specious to argue that library copying is fair use because the use which the patron makes of the copy is a "fair use." The patron reads or studies the copy. That is not a "right" secured to the author under the Copyright Act. It does not even involve "fair use." Moreover, books and periodicals sold by publishers and bookstores are employed by their purchasers ("users") for study, reference, scholarship and the other purposes for which NIH and NLM's patrons use the copies of plaintiff's articles reproduced by the libraries. That is the purpose for which books and journals are created and disseminated. But the ulti-

mate use by the user does not permit a bookstore, or library, to reproduce copies for the user without permissions.

* Certain of the rights granted in Sec. 1(a) are limited by the qualification "public." For example, the right to perform "publicly" a dramatic work [1(d)] or a musical composition [1(e)]. However, there is no "public" limitation on the rights to print, publish or copy a copyrighted work. Anyone who reproduces a copy of a copyrighted work has infringed these unqualified rights. Obviously if 200 individuals each produce a Xerox copy of an article, 200 unauthorized copies have been created and placed in the hands of 200 users with no less effect on the author's rights than if the 200 copies were reproduced by one copyist, and distributed (one copy per person) to the 200 users. See also Nimmer on Copyright, Sec. 101.3.

48

Nor is it any defense that defendant's libraries reproduced copies for scientists, doctors and similar users. These are the very readers for whom the journals are published.

(viii) The "Gentlemen's Agreement"

The "Gentlemen's Agreement" was not signed by plaintiff. It was not signed by any author. It was not signed by any association representing authors. In any event, such a document would not permit a Court to rule that fundamental rights granted to authors under the Copyright Act could be surrendered for all time, for all authors and publishers. Even "Gentlemen" don't have that power; the Constitution gave it to Congress. Certainly a document prepared by two trade associations in 1935 could not establish a "custom" binding on individuals and organizations who were not represented, three decades later when technology had radically changed media of communication and created new ones. Indeed, "custom" cannot be legislated into existence by contract. If these associations or publishers and librarians had combined or contracted to restrain individual authors or publishers from enforcing their rights under the Copyright Act, that combined action or such contract would violate the Sherman Act and would be illegal and unenforceable. A court should not permit these two associations or their members to achieve the same forbidden result by judicially approving a so-called "custom" which they sought to establish through an "agreement."

49

The Authors League, and authors, have never recognized any custom which permitted unauthorized single copying by libraries. On the contrary, they have taken the opposite position for many years, publicly and before the Congress. Moreover, the "Gentlemen's Agreement" specifically states that "legally no individual or institution can reproduce by photography or photomechanical means, or mimeograph or other methods of reproduction, a page or any part of a book without the written permission of the owner of the copyright."

(ix) The "Public Interest"

Defendant and its amici claim that library single copying is fair use because it is in the public interest that they distribute unauthorized copies to their users. But the public interest served by fair use and by copyright is to encourage the production of new works of literature and art.

Unauthorized library reproduction, sanctioned under a broad, free exemption misnamed "fair use," would drastically curtail the exclusive rights Congress granted to authors "to encourage the production of literary . . . works." It would diminish their "personal gain (which) is the best way to advance the public welfare through the talents of authors." Once plaintiff's articles are published, it may serve the short-term interests of some libraries, or users, for libraries to

50

reproduce copies because either they, or users, do not wish to buy copies from the plaintiff or its licensees, or take a license to reproduce copies. But that short term interest is served at the expense of the basic "underlying philosophy" and interest of the Copyright Act - to secure exclusive rights to authors as the best method of encouraging the production of new works.

Neither libraries, their associations, nor the Courts should substitute their judgment that the policy is wrong, or that unauthorized reproduction and dissemination of copies is more important than the creation and publication of the work being copied. That is a judgment which only Congress could make; and any form of library copying license would require a change in the present Copyright Act.

Defendant and the library amici suggest that the dissemination of copies of plaintiff's articles would be choked off unless libraries are held to have a single copying privilege under the guise of fair use. The threat is grossly exaggerated. Plaintiff has authorized various licensees and other libraries to make single copies of its articles, on a royalty basis. (125-127). It has offered to license defendant's libraries

51

to reproduce copies, on a royalty basis.* None of this interests defendant, ALA or ARL. And they would press for a free privilege in any case where single copies were available from a copyright owner or its licensee. They do not limit their claim to situations where copies are not available from the copyright owner or his licensees.

In truth, the controversy between defendant's libraries and plaintiff, and between the library amici and all authors and publishers, really involves one basic issue - money. Defendant's libraries, ARL and ALA have decided - in their wisdom - that it is inconvenient and unnecessary to pay royalties to authors and publishers for library reproduction of copies of copyrighted works. Even though, as here, the amount would be modest, the library amici have made the final judgment - no royalties for authors and publishers. But it is not their decision to make. Any change in the Copyright Act can only be made by Congress.

---

* If defendant's libraries or ARL and ALA believe that the private enterprise-copyright system of publishing "inhibits" the dissemination of certain articles, there are of course other alternatives available to them. For example, NIH or NLM (or other non-profit institutions) could publish the articles without seeking copyright protection. Or, defendant's libraries could have indexed the articles in the INDEX MEDICUS and then reproduced copies for their patrons, by the same Xerox process, from the typewritten manuscript, or from a text they printed.

52

The fact is that the only obstacles to library reproduction of copies of plaintiff's articles for NIH and NLM users are the libraries and their associations. If they recognized plaintiff's rights under the Copyright Act, they could obtain a license to reproduce copies of its copyrighted articles. Or if they preferred to get out of the reprint publishing business, they could obtain copies for their users from the plaintiff or the reproduction service that plaintiff had authorized to provide reprints.

53

POINT IV

Plaintiff's Right, Under the Copyright Act, to be Compensated for Library Photocopying is not barred by the First Amendment

(i) The NEA "Theory"

The National Education Association has submitted a brief supporting the defendant. It is a potpourri of quotations from First Amendment opinions, none relevant to the issues of this case, interspersed with a rambling discussion which seems directed to the conclusion that the First Amendment somehow bars publishers of journals from receiving compensation when libraries reproduce copies of their copyrighted works.

Then, after 40-plus pages of vague discourse suggesting this, NEA says " . . . we have here merely a question of determining the meaning and scope of the judicial doctrine of 'fair use'." (emphasis supplied) (Br. p.50)

This is practically the only statement in the NEA brief with which we can agree. "Fair use" is a judicial

54

doctrine; and the basic issue here is whether the NIH-NLM reproduction and distribution of copies of plaintiff's copyrighted articles is or is not fair use, under the standards developed by the Courts in the cases which established this judicial adjunct to the Copyright Act. There is nothing in the fair use decisions which supports the NEA argument that fair use is a doctrine designed or necessary to protect First Amendment rights. There is nothing in these cases which supports the NEA claim that the NLM-NIH practices must be held fair use to avoid a violation of the First Amendment. And there is nothing in the First Amendment which requires the Court to write a new limitation on authors' and publishers' rights into the Copyright Act; although that is what the NEA is actually asking the Court to do.

(ii) "Freedom to Read" does not Mean Denial of the Copyright Owner's Right to be Compensated When Copies of his Work are Reproduced

There is no conflict between the First Amendment and the author's or publisher's right, under the Copyright Act, to be compensated when copies of his work are reproduced. This and the other rights under the Act which permit them to be paid for uses of their works are compatible with the First Amendment. Indeed these rights make possible the independent, entrepreneurial system of authorship and publishing whose "freedoms" the First Amendment protects. Both the First Amendment and the Copyright Act work in harmony for a common

55

purpose: to enable a diversity of privately operated media of communication to function, free of government control and free of government subsidy. Weakening the right of authors and publishers to the be compensated for uses of their works increases the reliance on government subsidy and support. Increased government financing of the media inevitably produces increased government control over content - as great a threat to freedom to write, publish and read as direct restraint. Thus the NEA's demand that the Court write a new restriction on the author's and publisher's right to be compensated for library reprinting of their works will damage, not protect, freedom to read.

Undoubtedly the First Amendment protects freedom to read. The Authors League has fought vigorously for this principle in several cases where it has filed amicus curiae briefs, including some of those cited by the NEA: e.g. Times Film Corp. v. Chicago, 365 U.S. 43, 856 (1961); Butler v. Michigan, 352 U.S. 380 (1957); and Winters v. New York, 333 U.S. 505 (1948). But it is perfectly clear that these opinions, and the others quoted at random by NEA, offer no support for its last-minute theory that Commissioner Davis' opinion infringes First Amendment rights.

Essentially NEA argues that unless libraries can make copies of copyrighted works without paying compensation to the publisher or author, "freedom" to read is curtailed. This is a "novel"*, but completely erroneous, theory. The Courts have never interpreted the word "freedom" in the First Amendment

---

* NEA Br,p.37

56

to mean "gratis" or "free of charge." The Supreme Court knows that publishers charge money for their books and periodicals, and it has frequently emphasized that there is no conflict between their profit motive and the First Amendment. Time, Inc. v Hill, 385 U.S. 374, 397 (1967); New York Times Co. v. Sullivan, 376 U.S. 254, 266 (1964); Bantam Books v. Sullivan, 272 U.S. 58, 65 (1963); Smith v. California, 361 U.S. 147, 150 (1959); Burstyn v. Wilson, 343 U.S. 495, 501 (1952).

Indeed, the Court has recognized that the profit motive encourages both the dissemination of information, which the First Amendment is designed to foster, and the protection of First Amendment freedoms. In Smith v. Sullivan, holding that "dissemination (which) takes place under commercial auspices" is protected by the First Amendment, the Court noted "Certainly a retail bookseller plays a most significant role in the process of distribution of books." (361 U.S. at 150) And in Bantam Books v. Sullivan, the Court said: "The publisher has the greater economic stake, because suppression of a particular book prevents him from recouping his investment in publishing it. Unless he is permitted to sue, infringements of freedom of the press may too often go unremedied." (376 U.S. at 65) (emphasis supplied).

Thus, the publisher's right to recoup his investment and to be compensated for uses of his work is an ally, not an enemy, of First Amendment freedoms. And no Court has ever

57

held that a bookseller, or printer or library was permitted by the First Amendment to infringe an author's copyright by reproducing copies which were distributed "free" or at a lower price than the publisher charged. The First Amendment does not deny the publisher or author the right to be compensated for uses of their work, just as it does not deny the State the right to tax the income they derive from those uses. Arizona Publishing Co. v. O'Neil et al, 304 U.S. 543 (1938); Steinbeck v. Gerosa, 4 N.Y. 2d 302, 151 N.E. 2d 170; appeal dism. 358 U.S. 39 (1958).

As the Supreme Court noted in New York Times Co. v. Sullivan, 376 U.S. 254, 269, the First Amendment "was fashioned to assure unfettered interchange of ideas for the bringing about of political and social changes desired by the people" (quoting Roth v. United States, 354 U.S. 476, 484). It is, of course, axiomatic that an author's copyright does not prevent anyone from discussing or repeating his ideas. Rosemont Enterprises, Inc. v. Random House, Inc., 366 F. 2d 303. Thus, there is no conflict between the First Amendment objective and the limited protection which copyright gives to the author's expression. Anyone is free to circulate his ideas; but they are not free to make copies of the work without his consent.

58

See: Rosemont Enterprises, Inc. v. Random House, Inc., supra ("The fair use concept is based on the concept of reasonableness and extensive verbatim copying or paraphrasing of material set down by another cannot satisfy that standard;" 366 F. 2d at p. 310); Walt Disney Productions v. Air Pirates, 345 F. Supp. 108 (1972).

Thus, the NEA, the ARL or any of the ARL co-amici were free to communicate the ideas contained in plaintiff's copyrighted articles to the public. The plaintiff's copyrights did not interfere with their First Amendment Freedom to discuss or disseminate these ideas. Actually NEA is making a complaint which has no basis in the First Amendment or the Copyright Act.

Plaintiff is willing to make additional copies of the articles available; in fact it is making them available. It has authorized various licensees and libraries to make and distribute copies of the articles, on a royalty basis. It has offered to license defendant's libraries to reproduce copies, on a royalty basis. NEA's complaint is not that plaintiff is attempting to prevent people from reading the articles; but rather that plaintiff is asking to be compensated when copies are reproduced. But, as we have noted, a publisher's request that he be compensated for reproductions of his work does not infringe the First Amendment; and "fredom to read" does not mean that an infringer is entitled to produce "free" copies.

59

In reality, the NIH-NLM copies were not "free." The public, via the income tax, pays the substantial direct and indirect costs the libraries incur in producing these reprints of plaintiff's articles. Neither defendant, the various library amici or NEA has suggested that the Xerox corporation or other suppliers interfere with "freedom to read" because they make NIH and NLM pay for the goods and services required in the making of the reprints. Nor have the amici requested that library personnel work without salary while producing the reprints, to preclude their compensation from being a restraint on the library customer's "freedom to read."

Indeed, it is strange that the NEA should, of all organizations, argue that the payment of compensation is a violation of the First Amendment freedom to read. NEA members have always insisted on their right to be adequately compensated for their services in making published materials and information available to readers. NEA members by the thousands, each year, deny students access to articles, books and other materials for prolonged periods of time; teacher strikes shut down school rooms, school libraries and entire school systems. No reasonable person would contend that these concerted denials of access were an interference with the First Amendment "freedom to read;" although they certainly would be under the NEA's "theory." On the other hand, plaintiff has not sought to stop any library from making reprints of its articles (no less shut down a library). It has only asked to be paid a royalty when NIH-NLM make reprints of its articles; and

60

it continues to make copies available through other libraries and licensees.

(iii) Protection of the Copyright Owner's Rights is Essential to Provide "Access" to Books and Articles and Preserve Freedom to Read

At the core of the NEA, ARL and ALA briefs is the incredible assumption that librarians and teachers alone provide "access"

to articles and books, and that publishers are greedy interlopers who interfere with the good works of these public servants by demanding compensation when reprints of their copyrighted works are produced. In reality, it is the publishers who perform the indispensible and primary tasks of providing "access;" without them, the librarian and teacher could not perform their secondary functions, in this process.

Nothing in the Copyright Act would have prevented NIH or NLM from performing the primary access-providing function with respect to articles such as plaintiff published. Nor does the Act prevent any of the other amici, some with far greater resources than plaintiff, from providing that primary function. Any of them could have used their Xerox machines and money to produce and distribute copies of the typed manuscripts of articles such as plaintiff publishes.

Here, however, the library amici, NEA and defendant would prefer an arrangement more convenient to them, albeit disastrous to plaintiff and other publishers of technical and scientific journals such as the American Chemical Society, the

61

American Institute of Physics and ASTM. Defendant's amici are really arguing that these publishers should be willing to provide the money, skills and services required to select and edit the manuscripts of articles, to set them in type, print and bind them, and distribute them throughout the country.* When these preliminary formalities are completed, say defendant's amici, they will provide "access" to the public (something the publishers presumably failed to do) by using the new printing technology of the Xerox process to run off reprints of the articles. Making these reprints, say defendant's amici, is "fair use" and (according to the NEA) an activity protected by the First Amendment.

It does not occur to the defendant's amici that NIH, NLM and other libraries are satellites revolving around the publisher's sun. If he did not print the articles and distribute them, the libraries would not be able to reprint them on their Xerox machines. It is the publisher, not the library, which does the tough, hard, risky work of providing primary access.

Nor does it occur to the defendant's amici that the Xerox machine, like its predecessor the offset press, is still a machine for turning out printed copies of a work; but that it now makes possible, literally, one-at-a-time publishing. Just as the libraries run off copies one-at-a-time, a single copy for a user, so do commercial publishers such as Xerox's University Microfilms. (See p. 15, supra)

* In addition, these activities mark the articles with the "stamp of quality" which leads scientists to read them.

62

The printing of single copies of articles and books, to fill single orders, is now a technical and economic reality, thanks to the Xerox machine.

The new exemption which defendant and its amici ask this Court to carve out of the rights now granted authors and publishers under Section 1 of the Act would allow libraries to reprint and distribute plaintiff's articles, and articles by any publisher, without compensation. The inevitable result will be to drive such publishers out of business. The ultimate triumph for the ARL, ALA and NEA will be that neither they nor the publishers will then be providing "access," and "freedom to read" such materials will really have been diminished. To argue that the Xerox machine has not made one-at-a-time publishing a reality is to ignore reality; and to ignore this reality is to repeat the errors of those pedants who scorned the juke-box, the record, the radio, the motion picture and the television set as gadgets - and who argued that each could never create a new medium for disseminating copyrighted materials.

Conclusion

It is respectfully submitted that defendant's exceptions should be denied; and that the Court should adopt the opinion, findings of fact and recommended conclusions of law contained in the Report of Commissioner Davis.

Respectfully Submitted,

Irwin Karp
    Attorney for The Authors League
    of America, Inc., Amicus Curiae
120 Broadway
New York, New York 10005

October 30, 1972

In the

United States Court of Claims

No. 73-68

THE WILLIAMS & WILKINS CO.,

Plaintiff,

v.

THE UNITED STATES,

Defendant.

BRIEF AMICUS CURIAE OF ASSOCIATION OF AMERICAN PUBLISHERS, INC.

AND

THE ASSOCIATION OF AMERICAN UNIVERSITY PRESSES, INCORPORATED

Charles H. Lieb
*Attorney for
Association of American
Publishers, Inc. and
The Association of American
University Presses, Incorporated
Amicus Curiae*
733 Third Avenue
New York, N. Y. 10017

(212) TN 7-3800

1

This brief is submitted in behalf of Association of American Publishers, Inc., and The Association of American University Presses, Incorporated, (hereinafter referred to as "AAP" and as "AAUP," respectively) as amicus curiae.

AAP is a trade association of book publishers in the United States. Its 280 member companies and subsidiaries are believed to produce 80% or more of the dollar volume of books published in the United States. Some of its members also publish scientific and technical journals. The Williams & Wilkins Company is not an AAP member.

AAUP is a not-for-profit educational membership corporation. Its 69 regular and 7 international members are scholarly publishing divisions of colleges and universities and certain other educational institutions located primarily in North and South America.

2

The Interest of AAP and AAUP

The membership of AAP and of AAUP, non-profit and for-profit alike, have a vital interest in the library photocopying issues presented in this case. Library photocopying as practiced by NIH and NLM[1] today is intended to supplant the published work, and if permitted to continue will erode the economic base upon which most publishing is structured. This will be as true for journals and books published by professional or religious societies and not-for-profit organizations as for those published by companies organized for profit.

Most authors write for financial reward but some do not. One can be an author and not look for direct economic return. Some authors publish to advance their prestige, others to further research, and still others because of the "publish or perish" imperative.

This is not so with a publisher, however, whether for-profit or not-for-profit.[2] Publishing requires a capital investment. At the minimum, there must be an organization to review and select manuscripts for publication. In many cases royalties must be advanced to the author during the pre-publication period. In most cases the publisher must edit for substance and expression. He must pay for paper, printing and binding, for advertising and for promotion including in some cases generous sampling. He must, in many cases, support a corps of salesmen and facilities for warehousing and shipping. His sales are not certain since frequently they are made on a sale and return basis, his annual inventory turnover is small and his investment to produce the first dollar of sales is large. Publishing is not a large industry and its profits, either on an invested capi-

[1] NIH refers to National Institute of Health and NLM refers to National Library of Medicine.

[2] Other than a professional society such as American Medical Association which supplies the journal to its members without a special charge.

3

tal basis or as a percentage of sales, are less than average. Publishers, whether in the profit or non-profit sector, in the long run must bring in enough income from sales and licensing to cover the cost of production and sale and to pay the cost of the required capital.

Publishers recognize the interplay between the copyright grant of exclusivity and the rights of others including authors, scholars and teachers to make fair use of their copyrighted material. But they know too that they cannot continue to function as publishers if by a mistaken application of the doctrine of fair use an unauthorized copy is permitted to displace the sale of the original or to pre-

empt its other markets.

The interest of AAP and of AAUP therefore is to preserve a balance between the rights of publishers and their authors and the rights of users.

It is in this context that we address ourselves to the arguments advanced by the defendant and its amici.

Preliminary Statement

The term "interlibrary loan" as used in this case refers not to the lending by one library to another of the journal in which the requested article is published, but to the delivery, on a non-return basis, of a photocopy of the journal article which the lending library produces for that purpose.

The interlibrary loan program is the system which has been established by the library community to facilitate these procedures and has been most recently codified in the 1970 edition of Interlibrary Loan Procedure Manual.[1]

The words, "photocopying" and "photocopies," as used in this case are used generically, and refer not only to

[1] S. Thomson, Interlibrary Loan Procedure Manual (1970).

4

conventional photocopying but to the whole range of image making processes.

As practiced by NIH and NLM, photocopying involves the use of Recordac[1]-microfilm cameras capable of producing images in reduced size of 8½" x 11" original documents at the rate of approximately 300 pages per minute and of Xerox Copyflo printers which can enlarge and print from microfilm at the rate of 20 feet equal to approximately 26 pages per minute.[2]

NIH and NLM either hand-deliver or mail the photocopies requested of them. But equipment on the market today permits photocopied images to be transmitted almost instantaneously for thousands of miles by telephone line, cable or over the air.

NIH operates a central library, serving ten institutes employing 4,000 professionals and 8,000 others. But the issues presented in this case would be the same if the defendant were an industrial giant operating a central library for tens of thousands of its employees.

NLM is a national as well as a regional medical library administering an interlibrary loan system serving the mid-Atlantic region, although at times extending its services beyond that area. But the issues here would be the same if the defendant were a library system spanning the country, or like the British Central Library[3] or the proposed

[1] Recordac is manufactured by Eastman Kodak Company.

[2] Xerox Corporation describes its Xerox Copyflo 11 Continuous Printer, Model No. 1-20 as follows: "The Copyflo 11 Model No. 1-20 produces quality . . . prints on a continuous roll of ordinary paper. . . . It reproduces from 16 mm to 35 mm positive or negative roll microfilm. . . . Sharp, dry, ready-to-use prints emerge at the rate of 20 feet a minute."

[3] According to Lord Eccles, who has responsibility for the system, the National Central Library in 1970 made loans to or bor-

(footnote continued on following page)

5

UNISIST[1] system, crossing national frontiers to form part of world wide networks.

Central libraries and library systems whether organized along geographical or specialty lines exist because of the value of "sharing rather than duplicating library resources."[2] "Sharing" is a euphemism which translated into the economics of library management means that by the systematic use of photocopies or facsimile transmissions one published copy of a work can take the place of many.

Library sharing undoubtedly is socially desirable. But unless the publisher is otherwise compensated, the "sharing" principle discourages or inhibits the publication of the very works which the library will want to acquire and share with others.

True library lending in its original form—the actual delivery on loan of the published work itself, does not appreciably limit the anticipated publishing income.³ Library photocopying as practiced by NIH and NLM creates an open-end drain on the prospective market for the works, tending to make economically marginal works unpublishable and some otherwise economically sound works marginal.

(footnote continued from preceding page)

rowed from 70 different countries. "The National Lending Library at Boston Spa received 54,000 requests of which, in part, thanks to improvements in photocopying, 90 percent were satisfied. The National Reference Library of Science and Invention issued 17 percent, of all their photocopies in response to requests from overseas." THE BOOKSELLER, September 4, 1971.

¹ UNISIST STUDY REPORT ON THE FEASIBILITY OF A WORLD SCIENCE INFORMATION SYSTEM (Unesco, Paris 1971).

² R. HAYES & J. BECKER, HANDBOOK OF DATA PROCESSING FOR LIBRARIES, at 7 (1970).

³ Because of the time interval between the borrowing and the return of the loaned books the number of loans is necessarily limited, and loaned copies deteriorate and require replacement.

6

In our view, the photocopying practices of NIH and NLM exceed the most generous interpretation of fair use. This does not mean, as suggested by the defendant and its amici, that photocopying should be discontinued. It means instead that as in the case of tables, chairs, brick and mortar, the use of copyrighted material in such manner should be paid for.

Indeed, one of the ironies of this case is that although the libraries so fiercely oppose payment for photocopying copyrighted material for interlibrary loan purposes, many of them make interlibrary charges among themselves for expenses incurred in fulfilling loan requests, and all pay for the use of copying equipment and paper.

POINT I

Library copying is *prima facie* infringement.

The statute, 17 U.S.C. § 1, gives the copyright owner the exclusive right:

"to print, reprint, publish, copy, and vend the copyrighted work."

These are repetitive terms, conferring the twofold right to make copies and to publish copies;—printing and reprinting being "modes of copying," and vending "a mode of publishing."¹

Abe A. Goldman recently wrote:

"Of the uses to which the author (or his successor as the copyright owner) is given the exclusive rights,

¹ REPORT OF THE REGISTER OF COPYRIGHTS ON THE GENERAL REVISION OF THE UNITED STATES COPYRIGHT LAW, HOUSE COMMITTEE ON THE JUDICIARY, 87th Cong., 1st Sess., 21 (July 1961).

7

the most basic are the making and distribution of copies of the work.'"¹

NIH and NLM without permission copy and distribute material copyrighted by Williams & Wilkins and others. NIH in fiscal 1970 filled 85,744 requests for photocopies of journal articles.² NLM in fiscal 1968 filled about 120,000 requests with photocopies of original articles. About 12% of the latter were requests by drug and other commercial companies. Report at 45. NLM sells its catalogue of acquisitions, *Index Medicus*, to medical practitioners to help them keep abreast of current medical literature and to enable them to order photocopies of the listed material. Report at 45.

Defendant and Association of Research Libraries, *et al.* (hereinafter referred to as "ARL"), insist that NIH's and NLM's copying and distribution practices do not infringe Williams & Wilkins' exclusive right to make copies of and to distribute their copyrighted works.

Defendant argues that NIH and NLM make only "single copies," that is, one copy at a time on demand, and that the term "copy" as used in 17 U.S.C. § 1(a) "is equivalent to multiplication and does not encompass the making of a single copy."³ ARL argues that copying to be actionable "must include 'printing' (or 'reprinting')

¹ *Copyright as It Affects Libraries: Legal Implications*, COPYRIGHT, CURRENT VIEWPOINTS ON HISTORY, LAWS, LEGISLATION at 38, (A. Kent & H. Lancour eds. 1972). Mr. Goldman is General Counsel to the Copyright Office. The views he expressed are his own and do not necessarily reflect those of the Copyright Office.

² *Commissioner's Report and Opinion* (hereinafter cited as "Report") at 41.

³ Brief for Defendant to the Court of Claims (hereinafter cited as "Defendant's Brief") at 13.

8

and 'publishing' of copies of copyrighted material,'" and that NIH and NLM neither print nor publish.

Neither contention has merit. Each is supported by resort to the language of copyright statutes prior to the current act. The short answer to both is that the current act specifically makes copying an exclusive right of the copyright owner and it is this act which governs this case.

To state the defendant's argument is to disprove it. To make a "single copy" of an original is to multiply the original. One plus one is the equivalent of two times one.

ARL's argument is likewise self-defeating. Defendant's copying *is* accompanied by printing and by publishing. To print is "to make an image of;"² to publish is "to issue . . . for distribution to the public."³ NIH and NLM reproduce and make images of copyrighted material for distribution. They copy, they print and they publish.

ARL quotes Nimmer to support its argument that mere "copying" is not infringement. ARL Brief at 33-46. But it fails to quote the portion of his statement that is relevant to this case, that except for a musical work, the right to copy is the most fundamental of the copyright owner's rights and is subject only to two limitations—namely, that the copy must be tangible and that it must be visually perceptible.⁴

The microfilm and xerographic copies which NIH and NLM make are tangible and visually perceptible and therefore, *prima facie*, infringe plaintiff's copyrights.

¹ Brief for ARL as Amicus Curiae to the Court of Claims (hereinafter cited as "ARL Brief") at 33.

² RANDOM HOUSE DICTIONARY OF THE ENGLISH LANGUAGE at 1144 (Unabridged Edition 1966).

³ *Id.* at 1162.

⁴ M. NIMMER ON COPYRIGHT, § 101.1 at 377 (1972 ed.).

9

POINT II

The fair use doctrine does not justify defendant's copying.

Fair use developed as an author's right to borrow from or build upon or to criticize previously published works. It is in this context that Mr. Justice Story in *Folsom* v. *Marsh*[1] enumerated what have become the four classic tests to determine whether the borrowing is fair or unfair. As most recently restated in S.644,[2] the proposed Copyright Revision Bill, they are:

"i) The purpose and character of the use;

ii) The nature of the copyrighted work;

iii) The amount and substantiality of the portion used in relation to the copyrighted work as a whole; and

iv) The effect of the use upon the potential market for or value of the copyrighted work."

Each is inter-related but it is uniformly recognized that the effect of the copying upon the copyright owner's potential market for the copyrighted work is of prime importance.[3]

Borrowing for the purpose of authorship or criticism is not to be confused with the scholar's right to make notes for his own use. Some justify this kind of copying as a *de minimis* infringement and therefore not actionable. Others claim it as a right of the reader specifically reserved from the exclusive rights granted to the author. It is a

---

[1] *Folsom* v. *Marsh*, 9 Fed. Cas. 342, No. 4901 (D.Mass. 1841).

[2] S. 644, 92d Cong., 1st Sess. § 107 (1971).

[3] NIMMER, *supra*, § 145 at 646.

10

matter of little but academic interest here and is moot insofar as the issues in this case are concerned.

The *library* is a new party in the dichotomy. It neither copies for authorship nor for its own use. It copies to serve its own purposes and on demand for others. Some library photocopying may qualify as fair use. NIH's and NLM's systematic large-scale photocopying cannot.

"In essence," the Commissioner said, NIH and NLM provide "a reprint service *which supplants the need for journal subscriptions*". Report at 14 (emphasis supplied). This is the very kind of copying which the House Judiciary Committee condemned. "Where the unauthorized copying displaces what realistically might have been a sale . . . the interests of the copyright owner need protection."[1]

Nimmer puts it this way:

"One who creates a work for educational purposes may not suffer greatly by an occasional unauthorized reproduction. But if every schoolroom or library may by purchasing a single copy supply a demand for numerous copies through photocopying, mimeographing or similar devices, the market for copyrighted educational materials would be almost completely obliterated. This could well discourage authors from creating works of a scientific or educational nature. If the 'progress of science and useful arts' is promoted by granting copyright protection to authors, such progress may well be impeded if copyright protection is largely undercut in the name of fair use."[2]

The refusal on the part of the defendant to recognize this leads it to self-defeating extremities.

---

[1] H.R. REP. No. 83, 90th Cong., 1st Sess. 35 (1967).

[2] NIMMER, *supra*, § 145 at 653.

11

Defendant says that although NIH and NLM "make a lot" of fair use copies it is an "unproved and erroneous premise that a lot of fair use is an unfair use." Defendant's Brief at 40. It says that although NIH's and NLM's

photocopying practices are extensive "this fact alone will not make defendant's photocopying practices an unfair use." Defendant's Brief at 41. It says that if the making of any single photocopy can be justified under the first three criteria of fair use[1] then the making of "*all* photocopies" no matter how "widespread" can be justified. Defendant's Brief at 41-42 (emphasis supplied).

Defendant and its amici confuse the "occasional unauthorized" reproduction to which Nimmer refers[2] with the "comprehensive system," Report at 40, which defendant's libraries operate to deliver large numbers of copies to large numbers of people. The fallacy on which they premise their argument was well described in the Sophar and Heilprin Report as follows:

"The conundrum of fair use is that the wider its area of application, the less fair and the less useful it becomes as a valid legal doctrine, and the more likely it becomes that the copier, researcher, educator and general user of copyrighted material, whether individual or institution, is an infringer."[3]

---

[1] The purpose and character of the use, the nature of the work, and the amount used.

[2] NIMMER, *supra*, § 145 at 653.

[3] G. Sophar and L. Heilprin, The Determination of Legal Facts and Economic Guideposts with Respect to the Dissemination of Scientific and Educational Information as it is Affected by Copyright—A Status Report, Final Report, Prepared by The Committee to Investigate Copyright Problems Affecting Communication in Science and Education, Inc., for the U. S. Department of Health, Education and Welfare, Project No. 70793 (hereinafter cited as "Sophar and Heilprin Report") at 17 (1967).

12

Fair use is "essentially supplementary" by nature[1] and was developed for trivial situations.[2] Its rationale is that copying will be consistent and compatible with the publisher's right and need to preserve the potential market for his work. NIH's and NLM's use is a *group* or *system* or *network* use—not an occasional or spontaneous use. It is a use which *erodes* the market for the work and thus is the very antithesis of fair use.

POINT III

The library cannot shield itself by claiming the scholar's fair use privilege. It acts for itself and not as the scholar's agent.

ARL argues that to make a single copy for one's *personal* use is not in itself an infringement of copyright; that the right of the reader to make the copy for his own use encompasses the right to request that a library make the copy for him, and therefore when the library makes the copy at the request of the individual reader it does so without liability for infringement. ARL Brief at 33-34.

American Library Association (hereinafter referred to as "ALA") makes the same argument but in a different manner. It does so by posing two questions:

"Question 1: Is it fair use for a scientist, researcher or scholar to make a single copy of an article in a copyrighted journal for use in research or study?

"Question 2: Assuming the answer to Question 1 is in the affirmative, is the fair use privilege of the scientist, researcher or scholar destroyed if the *library*

---

[1] H.R. REP. No. 83, *supra*, 35.

[2] Cf. Sophar and Heilprin Report, *supra*, at iii.

13

acting as his agent, makes the photocopy for him at his request?"[1]

Viewed in this light, says ALA, only Question 1 is of

first impression. Question 2, it says, is not novel, and agency law and the *Fortnightly* case[2] require a ruling that the library patron's privilege of fair use is not destroyed by the mere fact that the *library* makes photocopies for him at his request. ALA Brief at 6.

We differ.

The library, when it makes and delivers to its patrons a photocopy of a work which it owns, is no more an agent of the patron than the vendor from whom the patron buys a newspaper or book or food or clothing.

True, as ALA says, the library serves as intermediary or middleman between the publisher and the reader but so does the printer, the wholesaler and everyone else who fulfills a function in the distribution system.

It is no answer to say that NIH and NLM make no charge for the photocopy and therefore cannot be likened to a vendor. Many libraries do charge their patrons for the photocopying expenses involved in fulfilling the request. And many libraries in the Interlibrary Loan Program charge the requesting library for their expense and overhead. But the presence or absence of a charge is immaterial. One does not become an agent because he delivers a product gratis, nor a principal merely because he accepts compensation.

ALA says that it is illogical and a semantic nicety to suggest that because a library rather than a reader makes

---

[1] Brief for ALA to the Court of Claims (hereinafter cited as "ALA Brief") at 5 (emphasis supplied).

[2] *Fortnightly Corp. v. United Artists Television, Inc.,* 392 U.S. 390 (1968).

14

the photocopy, what might have been fair use on the reader's part becomes infringement on the library's part. ALA Brief at 31.

The argument overreaches itself. For a reader to copy from his own book, he must have purchased the book. For a reader to make a copy from the book which he borrows from the library, the library will have had to purchase a sufficient number of copies of the book to satisfy the needs of all of its patrons.

But if NIH purchases one book[1] to serve the needs of 4,000 professionals and 8,000 others, it obviously is using its microfilm and xerographic equipment to produce multiple photocopies of the work in lieu of purchasing additional copies of the work in the original form.

And if NLM purchases one copy of a work, listing it in *Index Medicus* to make it known that photocopies are available, it is obviously using that equipment to displace the purchase by NLM and by others of additional copies of the work.

What ALA and its fellow amici and defendant overlook is the drastic difference, insofar as the economic viability of publishing is concerned—between copying for personal use by a reader who has the book in his possession, and by an NIH or NLM which through its photocopying service obviates the need of the reader or the requesting library to buy or borrow the book.

The argument that the library is merely an "agent" for the patron and therefore, should not be exposed to liability for merely doing what its patron asks it to do is shallow. A printer who as an "agent" for another prints an infringing work, even though innocent of intent to infringe, is himself guilty of infringement.[2]

---

[1] In some cases two books.

[2] NIMMER, *supra,* § 102 at 384.

15

But the analogy is misleading. The library is neither agent nor contractor for anyone. It acquires and catal-

ogues and lends works in its own behalf, thereby fulfilling its societal function. When it photocopies a copyrighted work, it does so as an institution and not as an individual. And because it *is* an institution, the photocopying it does is of a different level and quality than that done by an individual.

This "qualitative difference" as Nimmer calls it[1] is the very thing that distinguishes the library from the scholar. And this distinction was pinpointed in the following passage from the 1967 House Judiciary Committee Report on Copyright Revision:

"Isolated instances of minor infringements, when multiplied many times, become in the aggregate a major inroad on copyright that must be prevented."[2]

The *Fortnightly* case, *supra,* is of no aid to ALA either. ALA analogizes the position of the library to that of the CATV operator in *Fortnightly* and concludes that because the operator was held to be more a viewer than a performer, and therefore not a copyright infringer, so the library here should be considered more a researcher or scholar than a publisher, and therefore not an infringer. ALA Brief at 33.

There are basic differences of course.

The statutory term "performance," the meaning of which was the issue in *Fortnightly* is a term which is difficult to apply to the broadcaster—CATV operator—viewer relationship, but the statutory terms to "print," "publish" and to "copy" are readily related to the publisher-library-reader relationship involved here. *Fortnightly, supra,* at 398.

---

[1] NIMMER, *supra,* § 145 at 653-654.

[2] HOUSE REP. No. 83, *supra,* 35.

16

The CATV equipment in *Fortnightly* was "little different" from that used by the television viewer, and therefore in the Court's view, it "no more than enhances" the viewer's capacity to receive the broadcaster's signal, *Fortnightly, supra,* at 399.

NIH and NLM "enhance" the scholar's access to published works when they provide reading facilities in their libraries or when they lend the work in its published form to its patrons. But when NIH and NLM use xerographic printers and microfilm cameras to make and deliver copies of copyrighted material to their patrons they reprint and publish the work and clearly infringe upon the copyright owner's exclusive rights.

The Commissioner correctly so found, Report at 13-14, and in so finding followed the relevant teaching of *Fortnightly:*

"§ 1 of the Act enumerates several 'rights' that are made 'exclusive' to the holder of the copyright. [to print, reprint, publish, copy, and vend the copyrighted material]. If a person, without authorization from the copyright holder, puts a copyrighted work to a use within the scope of one of these 'exclusive rights' he infringes the copyright."[1]

POINT IV

The "custom" and the "Gentlemen's Agreement" argument.

Defendant seems to suggest that fair use aside, custom and the so-called 1935 Gentlemen's Agreement justify NIH's and NLM's photocopying practices.

It is not necessary to discuss the legal theories which are advanced with respect to the interplay between custom and

---

[1] *Fortnightly, supra,* at 394-395.

17

fair use because there is no factual justification for the argument.

There is, in fact, no "custom" to justify NIH's and NLM's photocopying. If "custom" means a practice acceded to by all interested parties, which would be its only relevant meaning here, there has never been agreement by affected publishers or authors that their works might be copied and distributed in the wholesale manner shown to exist here. And if "custom" connotes an acceptance of a practice over a period of time, the "network" and "system" concept of library sharing which NIH and NLM have adopted is too recent—and indeed as yet too undeveloped, for "custom" to have any meaning.

The fact is that librarians have never relied on existing custom. If anything they have attempted *unilaterally* to create a custom; but the caveats and cautions which they have expressed within their community indicate their concern that their practices are not legally justified and this is clearly indicated in the outstanding work on the subject, the Saunders monograph, *Origin of The "Gentlemen's Agreement" of 1935*.[1] Saunders states:

> "As early as 1933, Binkley, [Chairman of Joint Committee on Materials for Research] had asked for an opinion from the Library of Congress and had received a memorandum to the effect that 'copying of copyrighted periodicals by the film method would appear to be prohibited.' The originator of the memorandum, Mr. William Brown, Acting Register of Copyrights, based his opinion on the assumption that the copies would be made for rather general use in libraries or elsewhere and would be used in such a

---

[1] This document was prepared in 1963 partly for a Master's degree at the American University and is reproduced in REPROGRAPHY AND COPYRIGHT LAW, Appendix B at 159, (L. Hattery & G. Bush eds. 1964).

18

way as to diminish sales of the original. He went on to say, however, that 'doubtless the making of extracts from a copyrighted work for one's own private reference or study, would come within the limits of so-called fair use'."[1]

According to Saunders, Binkley in 1933 thought it necessary to draft a form of legal order for photocopying that will "adequately distribute the risk of copyright infringement" and in this connection stated "that the legal advisor at the Library of Congress is taking the copyright holders' side."[2]

In 1934 after further discussions with an attorney familiar with copyright matters, Binkley's next step, according to Saunders, was to build a "dossier on copyright" so that the Joint Committee could "step in the right direction" when technological progress in microfilming methods had fully developed. In September of the same year conversations and correspondence were initiated with the National Association of Book Publishers (now extinct) which resulted in the so-called 1935 Gentlemen's Agreement.[3]

That document specifically stated that mechanical reproductions from copyrighted material are presumably intended to take the place of hand transcriptions and are to be governed by the same principles which govern hand transcriptions, and that it would be unfair to the author or publisher to make possible "the substitution of the photostats for the purchase of a copy of the book itself either for an individual library or for any permanent collection in a public or research library."

---

[1] REPROGRAPHY AND COPYRIGHT LAW, *supra*, at 162.

[1] *Id.* at 163.

[2] Reproduced in Report at 56-57 and in REPROGRAPHY AND COPYRIGHT LAW, *supra*, Appendix A at 157-158.

19

The Gentlemen's Agreement never became an effective instrument, not only because the organizations which signed it disappeared but because by 1956 the *library community itself rejected it*. Verner W. Clapp in his monograph, *Copyright—A Librarian's View* published by the Association of Research Libraries (August 1968) had this to say at 22:

> "But by 1956 there was considerable dissatisfaction [within the American library world] with [the Gentlemen's Agreement]. It was objected that the 'exemption from liability' which it granted implied an admission of wrong-doing which libraries were not prepared to concede. Furthermore, the organizations which made the agreement in 1935 and confirmed it in 1939 had gone out of existence without leaving successors to their commitments; and even had this not been the case, it is very dubious what value the 'exemption from liability' would possess at the later date. Accordingly, at the same time the Association of Research Libraries appointed the committee which eventually produced the Single Copy Policy mentioned below."

The Single Copy Policy to which Mr. Clapp refers had its genesis in a 1961 recommendation to the Joint Libraries Committee[2] and forms the basis for the National Interlibrary Loan Code[3]

Nimmer makes this comment about the Code:

> "In an attempt to establish a concept of fair use by force of custom, the American Library Association has adopted a 'Reproduction of Materials Code' . . . It would seem that this practice is no more entitled to the

---

[1] Prepared for the National Advisory Commission on Libraries.

[2] REPROGRAPHY AND COPYRIGHT LAW, *supra*, at 169.

[3] S. THOMSON, INTERLIBRARY LOAN PROCEDURE MANUAL, *supra*, at 1.

20

claim of fair use than is the practice of teachers in making such material available for their students.'"[1]

The fact is that despite the reliance by defendant and its *amici* upon "established" library photocopying practices there is no general agreement as to what these practices are or should be.

Borge Varmer in his study, *Photoduplication of Copyrighted Material by Libraries*,[2] prepared for the Senate Committee on the Judiciary, 86th Congress, 2d Session (1960) said at 53:

> "There is little valuable information as to current practices of libraries generally in making and supplying photocopies. Perhaps this much can be said: that libraries differ widely in their practices, and that many of them feel that the present uncertainty as to permissible scope of photocopying hampers their services to researchers and needs to be resolved."

The difference in library practices and the uncertainty as to their permissible scope to which Varmer referred persists to this day. See, for example, the August 1971 second printing of the Thomson *Interlibrary Loan Procedure Manual, supra*, in which it is stated:

> "Interpretation of copyright law is in continuous process of revision, particularly in the light of Congressional hearings on pending legislation and of court decisions. *Each library should determine its own*

policy in the context of current law and precedent, including the concept of 'fair use'."[1] (Emphasis supplied.)

[1] NIMMER, *supra*, § 145 at 653.

[2] STUDY No. 15, COPYRIGHT LAW REVISION.

[3] Chapter 5 at 49.

21

There is no support for NIH's and NLM's photocopying practices either in "custom" or the 1935 Gentlemen's Agreement, and it is clear that the Interlibrary Loan Code does not even purport to state a uniform copying practice.

POINT V

The constitutional argument.

Article 1, Section 8 of the United States Constitution authorizes Congress to enact a copyright statute to "promote the Progress of Science and useful Arts."

Congress has enacted a copyright statute under which although reward to the owner is a secondary consideration, it is "intended definitely to grant valuable, enforceable rights to authors, publishers, . . . to afford greater encouragement"[1] to them to produce literary works.

The economic philosophy underlying the statute is "the conviction that encouragement of individual effort by personal gain is the best way to advance public welfare through the talents of authors and inventors in 'Science and useful Arts'."[2]

Defendant differs. In its judgment progress in science can be furthered without encouraging personal gain. According to defendant, photocopying by NIH and NLM promotes medical research,[3] but to require defendant to pay plaintiff a royalty for the photocopying privilege would "serve only to enrich the plaintiff without resulting in any concomitant public goods." Defendant's Brief at 64.

Defendant says therefore that it is not urging that library photocopying "*should* be excused from the opera-

[1] *Washingtonian Co.* v. *Pearson*, 306 U.S. 30, 36 (1939).

[2] *Mazer* v. *Stein*, 347 U.S. 201, 219 (1954).

[3] with which we entirely agree.

22

tions of the copyright statute." It says instead "that such photocopying *must* be exempt from copyright restrictions if copyright in this case is to be constitutionally valid." Defendant's Brief at 65 (emphasis in original).

The flaw in defendant's argument is that it seeks to substitute its judgment and conviction for the judgment and conviction expressed by Congress.

Defendant would jeopardize plaintiff's right to maintain economic viability for its publications by permitting NIH and NLM to continue to photocopy as they do now, without license from or payment to the plaintiff. ARL and ALA would do likewise. National Education Association of the United States (hereinafter referred to as "NEA") finds further support for photocopying without payment in the First and Ninth Amendments.

Defendant and its amici misunderstand the issue. The issue here is not whether the scientific community and the public in general are to be *allowed* access to Williams & Wilkins journal articles. Access is available to all, either through direct subscription, purchase of reprints from plaintiffs' licensees,[1] or by true library borrowing. The issue is whether NIH and NLM may as a matter of policy systematically supply photocopies of plaintiff's copyrighted material to all who request them without suitably compensating the plaintiff.

The arguments advanced by defendant and its amici are reminiscent of the fabled blind men and the elephant. It is true that photocopying of the articles without payment will give the scientific community access to these articles. But it is also true that the scientific community will have access to these articles even though NIH and NLM produce the photocopies under license from Williams & Wilkins.

Defendant and its amici seem to suggest that NIH and NLM could better serve the community if no payment is

[1] Report at 39, 53.

23

required to be made to Williams & Wilkins. This may be true in the short run but it is equally true that future publication by Williams & Wilkins will be endangered by the resulting diminution of revenues from its present publications.

More bread would be available today if we mill the seed corn stored for tomorrow. But there will be less bread tomorrow. This is the philosophy expressed by the copyright statute and it is consistent with and not repugnant to the philosophy of the Constitution.

Conclusion

Defendant fears dire results if NIH and NLM are held to be infringers. The consequences are not so drastic. NIH and NLM can accept photocopying licenses from Williams & Wilkins which are and have been available to them, and as the Commissioner notes, they may make photocopies of material published from and after July 1, 1965, under the NIH policy revised as of that date.[1]

Defendant's amici's concerns that research, scholarship and teaching will be irreparably damaged by judgment for Williams & Wilkins are likewise not justified. The fair use rights of libraries in general will not necessarily be affected by denial to NIH and NLM of the right to operate

[1] As published in 35 F. R. 5470. The Commissioner said: "It is pertinent to note that resolution of this issue in plaintiff's favor should be of minor practical consequence to the Government's future copying of articles stemming from Public Health Service-funded research. The Sophar and Heilprin report found that 85 percent of the material photocopied by U.S. libraries is less than 5 years old, and 90 percent is less than 10 years old. Since the Public Health Service's express license policy is nearly 7 years old, most of the Government's prospective copying (as well as its copying for the past year or so) of articles stemming from grant-funded research, will be of articles which resulted from grants awarded subsequent to July 1, 1965, and will therefore be royalty free." Report at 27-28.

24

a large-scale reprint service without permission from the owners of the copyrighted material. Nor will a decision adverse to the defendant in this case determine the limits of fair use copying by scholars, researchers and teachers.

NEA in addition expresses concern that the finding of infringement will in some manner undercut or vitiate or negate the Congressional intent as expressed in the proposed copyright revision bill.[1] This too is not justified. Senator McClellan recently indicated that the Subcommittee on Patents, Trademarks and Copyrights, of which he is Chairman, is very much aware of the Commissioner's decision and he stated on the Senate floor that his Subcommittee had "anticipated this problem and had consequently added a special library photocopying section to the revision bill.'"[1]

It is clear that widespread copying without permission—the kind of copying that is done by NIH and NLM—cannot be justified either under the statute or as a fair use exemption. It cannot be justified philosophically either. Marsh Jeanneret, Director of University of Toronto Press, recently had this to say:

"There can be no right to the use of literary copyrights without fee simply in the name of education, any more than an institution can demand the right to video-tape the best lectures of its most popular instructors for free (and economical) replaying to classes in the future. The public which insists on either privilege without compensation will succeed merely in stultifying further creativity.'"[3]

[1] S.644, 92d Cong., 1st Sess. (1971). Brief for NEA as Amicus Curiae to the Court of Claims at 9-10.
[2] 118 Cong. Rec. S9772 (daily ed. June 20, 1972). Senator McClellan refers to § 108 of S.644, 92d Cong. 1st Sess.
[3] Marsh Jeanneret, Editorial, *Copyright and the Scholar* in Scholarly Publishing, Vol. 1, No. 3, at 227 (April 1970).

25

The photocopying done by defendant's libraries is without legal justification and the finding of infringement should be affirmed.

Respectfully submitted,

CHARLES H. LIEB
Attorney for
Association of American
 Publishers, Inc. and
The Association of American
 University Presses, Incorporated
Amicus Curiae
733 Third Avenue
New York, N.Y. 10017

(212) TN 7-3800

PASKUS, GORDON & HYMAN
 Elizabeth Barad
 of Counsel

November 3, 1972

No. 73-68

IN THE UNITED STATES COURT OF CLAIMS

THE WILLIAMS & WILKINS COMPANY,
Plaintiff,

v.

THE UNITED STATES,
Defendant.

DEFENDANT'S BRIEF

HARLINGTON WOOD, JR.
Assistant Attorney General

THOMAS J. BYRNES
Attorney
Department of Justice

1

This is an action for copyright infringement brought under the provisions of 28 U.S.C. § 1498(b). The plaintiff, Williams & Wilkins Company, a publisher of medical journals and books, is located in Baltimore, Maryland. The defendant is the United States Department of Health, Education, and Welfare, and, more particularly, the National Institutes of Health and the National Library of Medicine. In a report filed February 16, 1972, the Commissioner determined that defendant has infringed plaintiff's copyrights. Defendant has excepted to certain findings of fact made by the Commissioner and to the conclusion of law recommended by the Commissioner. This brief is in support of these exceptions. Defendant urges the Court to adopt defendant's exceptions in making its finding of fact, to reject the conclusion of law recommended by the Commissioner and to dismiss the plaintiff's petition.

2

QUESTIONS PRESENTED

1. Did the Commissioner err in finding that plaintiff was the owner of the journal articles involved herein and, thus, entitled to copyright such articles?

2. Did the Commissioner err in holding that the exclusive right to "copy" granted a copyright proprietor by 17 U.S.C. § 1(a), prohibits libraries from furnishing their patrons with a single photocopy of a journal article?

3. Did the Commissioner err in holding that the defendant's libraries, in furnishing single photocopies of journal articles to their patrons, did not make a fair use of plaintiff's copyrighted journals, and thus, infringed plaintiff's copyrights?

3

STATEMENT OF THE CASE

The conduct of defendant alleged by plaintiff to be copyright infringement is the practice of the library at NIH and NLM of furnishing to the users of these libraries, upon written request, a single photocopy of a journal article. In the case of the NIH library, the users are employees of NIH. NLM is a librarian's library, and its users are other libraries. These user libraries ultimately forward the photocopies provided by NLM to physicians and medical researchers. A more complete description of the activities of NIH and NLM appear later in this brief in Part III, section A-1.

In the complaint, as amended, eight specific instances of infringement are charged. In each of these, defendant is alleged to have made a copy of a single specified journal article. The articles involved in this suit are fully identified in the Commissioner's findings. For purposes of this brief, it is sufficient to state that the articles involved herein were published in various issues of journals entitled Medicine, Pharmacological Reviews, Journal of Immunology and Gastroenterology, and that the latter three journals are published by plaintiff in association with and for the benefit of certain professional societies. For

4

purposes of liability only, defendant has admitted that either NLM or the NIH library has made at least one photocopy of each of the articles involved herein.

As indicated above, filed concurrently herewith are exceptions to certain findings made by the Commissioner. In addition, some exceptions have been provided with comments which explain more fully the reasons for the exception and the evidence in support thereof. Both the exceptions and the comments thereon have been extensively annotated with references to the trial record. Consequently, a reference to the record will be supplied here only to avoid ambiguity. In general, the plan of this brief follows the plan adopted by the Commissioner in this report.

Since the filing of the Commissioner's report, the Association of Research Libraries (ARL) and the American Library Association (ALA), who filed briefs amicus curiae before the Commissioner, have again indicated to defendant their intention to file briefs amicus curiae before this Court. Defendant has been advised that the American Medical Association, the largest national organization of physicians and health practitioners, intends to join in the ARL brief. In addition, the National Education Association (NEA) has indicated its intention to file a brief amicus curiae. Because these organizations and defendant represent different interests, it is to be expected that in the

briefs of defendant and the amici curiae differing weights and differing modes of treatment will be accorded to the points in issue. Defendant urges that no argument be rejected

5

simply because it appears in the briefs of the amici but not in defendant's brief or in defendant's bried but not in the brief of the amici.

To explain his findings of fact and to support his recommended conclusion of law, the Commissioner appended thereto an extensive opinion. In this opinion, the Commissioner referred to this case as one of first impression, which, indeed, it is. Moreover, this case is one which has far reaching consequences for the entire medical profession. It involves not merely the question of the legitimacy of the photocopying practices of the NIH library and NLM, but also the much broader question of whether private copyright interests are to be permitted to interfere with and control the application of modern technological innovations such as photocopying to the advancement of medical care and medical research and education. It was perhaps in recognition of the widespread importance of the issues raised in this case that the Commissioner declared that resolution of these issues required the "judgment of Solomon" combined with the "dexterity of Houdini." It is unfortunate that in reaching his conclusions the Commissioner employed more "dexterity" than "judgment."

6

The Commissioner's opinion is clearly not a reasoned decision based upon an impartial consideration of all the facts. It is instead an argument based upon unproven assumptions, untenable inferences and logical fallacies. Further, those facts unfavorable to the conclusion reached are not distinguished or refuted, but are simply ignored. In the exceptions filed with this brief, defendant presents, with supporting citations to the record, those facts ignored by the Commissioner. In this brief, defendant will expose the weaknesses of the Commissioner's argument and demonstrate that there is no foundation for plaintiff's claim in fact or law.

STATUTES INVOLVED

The following statute is involved in this suit. 28 U.S.C. § 1498(b) states:

Hereafter, whenever the copyright in any work protected under the copyright laws of the United States shall be infringed by the United States, by a corporation owned or controlled by the United States, or by a contractor, subcontractor, or any person, firm, or corporation acting for the Government and with the authorization or consent of the Government, the exclusive remedy of the owner of such copyright shall be by action against the United States in the Court of Claims for the recovery of his reasonable and entire compensation as damages for such infringement, including the minimum statutory damages as set forth in section 101(b) of title 17, United States Code: Provided, That a Government employee shall have a right of action against the Government under this subsection

7

except where he was in a position to order, influence, or induce use of the copyrighted work by the Government: Provided, however, That this subsection shall not confer a right of action on any copyright owner or any assignee of such owner with respect to any copyrighted work prepared by a person while in the employment or service of the United States, where the copyrighted work was prepared as part of the official functions of the employee, or in the preparation of which Government time, material, or facilities were used: And provided further, That before such action against the United States has been instituted the appropriate corporation owned or controlled by the United States or the head of the appropriate department or agency of the Government, as the case may be, is authorized to enter into an agreement with the copyright owner in full settlement and compromise for the damages accruing to him by reason of such infringement and to settle the claim administratively out of available appropriations.

Except as otherwise provided by law, no recovery shall be had for any infringement of a copyright covered by this subsection committed more than three years prior to the filing of the complaint or counterclaim for infringement in the action, except that the period between the date of receipt of a written claim for compensation by the Department or agency of the Government or corporation owned or controlled by the United States, as the case may be, having authority to settle such claim and the date of mailing by the Government of a notice to the claimant that his claim has been denied shall not be counted as a part of the three years, unless suit is brought before the last-mentioned date.

Other statutes referred to in this brief are reproduced in relevant part in the appendix.

8

SUMMARY OF ARGUMENT

In this brief, defendant will set out three major defenses. These are (1) non-infringement, (2) non-ownership, and (3) fair use.

The defense of non-infringement is based on the proposition that the exclusive right "to copy" provided in 17 U.S.C. § 1(a) does not prohibit the NIH library or NLM from furnishing single copies of medical journal articles to physicians and other qualified health scientists.

The defense of non-ownership is bottomed on the fact that plaintiff has not acquired either expressly or by custom any ownership rights in any of the articles involved herein and, thus, not entitled to copyright said articles.

Affirmatively, defendant contends that photocopying, as practiced by the NIH and NLM, comes within the exception to plaintiff's exclusive rights, if any, provided by the doctrine of fair use. Defendant will establish that making single copies of medical and scientific journal articles is a reasonable, fair, and customary use of plaintiff's journals, and that such copying serves the constitutional purpose of copyrights, that is, to promote the arts and sciences.

During trial and before the Commissioner, defendant urged two additional defenses. These were (1) implied

9

license to copy with respect to Counts IV, V and VI, and (2) lack of a real party in interest as plaintiff with respect to Counts II, III, IV, V and VI. Defendant does not concede that the Commissioner's rulings on these issues are correct. However, as these defenses have a limited impact, defendant will not pursue them further in order not to obscure the major issues before this Court.

ARGUMENT

I. Defendant Has Not Infringed Any Copyrights Owned by Plaintiff

In its brief on this point before the Commissioner, defendant adopted the arguments and conclusions presented in the brief *amicus curiae* filed on behalf of the Association of Research Libraries (ARL). As stated above, defendant has been advised by the counsel for the ARL that they intend to again file a brief *amicus curiae* before this Court; defendant has also been advised by counsel for the plaintiff that no objection to the filing of this brief would be made by plaintiff. No useful purpose would now be served by including in this brief a detailed repetition of the arguments and conclusions set forth in the ARL brief and defendant again adopts and incorporates by reference the ARL position with respect to this point. In summary form, the ARL position is that an examination of the prior

10

copyright acts, the legislative history of the present copyright act, the contemporaneous interpretation given the present copyright act by the Library of Congress, and the relevant court decisions establishes that the exclusive right to copy provided in 17 U.S.C. § 1(a) was neither intended nor has it been construed to prohibit the making of single photocopies by libraries. It is, of course, elementary that plaintiff cannot recover unless defendant has violated an exclusive right granted to it by the copyright law.

The principal factual error made by the Commissioner in rejecting the ARL position is his adoption of plaintiff's invention of the "single copy fallacy." The Commissioner's discussion of defendant's photocopying operations and the restrictions im-

posed thereon is not only meager, but highly distorted. To sustain his adoption of the "single copy fallacy," the Commissioner relies upon the fact that on occasion more than one copy of a given journal article is made by defendant's libraries either for the same requester or for different requesters. While not referred to by the Commissioner, the record establishes that where an individual was shown to have ordered or received more than one photocopy, the second copy was either for the use of a colleague or for the replacement of an illegible or undelivered copy (R. 568, 1356). The functions of the libraries involved here in this

11

suit are to provide scientific and medical information and not to act as policemen. While it is true that the libraries have no way of absolutely enforcing the single copy policy, it does not follow that the libraries would not or do not enforce the single copy policy when it is known that it is being violated. The situation referred to by the Commissioner of NLM furnishing a photocopy of the same article on consecutive days is a hypothetical one and not shown in the record to have ever actually occurred. The record does disclose that all limitations imposed by these libraries are rigidly adhered to. Exceptions to the page limit are permitted only on approval of the Assistant Chief, Library Branch, NIH, and NIH photocopy equipment operators are instructed to bring to the attention of their supervisor attempts to copy substantial portions of journals. NLM employs several layers of review to ensure compliance with its policy. The single copy per request is enforced. It is possible for a library user to obtain more than one copy of a journal article by submitting at different times more than one request. But this can happen, as plaintiff concedes, only because NLM and NIH are not aware that a violation is occurring.[1]

[1] During discovery, plaintiff took the deposition of the photocopy equipment personnel, portions of which are included in the present record (R. 1165-1176, 1256-60, 1322-26). Each of these employees was fully conversant with the limitations of the NIH policy.

12

In describing the practices of defendant's libraries, the Commissioner unfairly and incorrectly characterizes these practices by stating that ' the libraries duplicate particular articles over and over" and that "many [photocopies] are copies of the same article." What the record actually discloses is that some duplication takes place. For example, plaintiff survey of NIH operations shows only four instances of duplication in over 200 requests. PX-29, which is a copy of a speech given by Mr. Scott Adams in 1964 (at that time Mr. Adams was deputy director of NLM) discloses that at NLM duplication occurs at a rate of 10% in the 102 most heavily used journals which constitute only one third of the total requests. If all requests were considered, the duplication rate would be considerably reduced, since a given journal *title* is copied on the average only 2.7 times each year. The Sophar report[1] so often cited by the Commissioner in other connections, shows that for libraries in general the duplication rate is negligible - about 3% (p. iii). Thus while duplication occurs, its magnitude is nowhere near as great as suggested by the Commissioner.

[1] Sophar & Heilprin. "The Determination of Legal Facts and Economic Guideposts with Respect to the Dissemination of Scientific and Educational Information as Affected by Copyright Status Report," Final Report Cont. No. OEC-1-7-070793-3559, U.S.D. HEW, Dec. 1967.

13

The Commissioner, also following the plaintiff's lead, contends that the courts have held that making a single copy can be an infringement, citing cases. The Commissioner's view of these cases is erroneous, for none are concerned with the issue at hand. These cases involve music rolls,[1] movie films,[2] and book publishing.[3] The holdings of these cases cannot be expanded to the extent of making a single photocopy of a medical journal article an infringement of copyright.

In summary, defendant submits that the term "copy" as used in 17 U.S.C. § 1(a) and as interpreted in light of previous statutes, its legislative history, and the administrative regulations adopted under it, is equivalent to multiplication and does not encompass the making of a single copy. Since no right granted plaintiff under the copyright statute has been violated, its petition should be dismissed.

II. Plaintiff Is Not the Owner of the Journal Articles Involved Herein

Before proceeding with the merits of this issue,

---

[1] White Smith Music Pub. Co. v. Apollo Co., 209 U.S. 1 (1908), in which the Supreme Court held that a music roll for a player piano was not a copy of a musical composition.

[2] Patterson v. Century Productions, Inc., 93 F. 2d 489, 35 U.S.P.Q. 471 (C.A. 2, 1937) in which the court held movie film to be a copy of a movie film.

[3] Greenbie v. Noble, 151 F. Supp. 45, 113 U.S.P.Q. 115 (S.D.N.Y., 1957) in which the court used the terms printing and copying interchangably.

14

defendant wishes to dispose of a preliminary objection made by the Commissioner in his opinion. This objection is that in a suit under 28 U.S.C. § 1498 equitable rights of ownership of strangers to the suit cannot be raised as defenses against the legal title holder. This objection is without merit for two reasons. First, the cases cited by the Commissioner do not establish the proposition for which they are cited. In Dorr-Oliver, Inc. v. United States, 193 Ct. Cl. 187, 432 F. 2d 447, 167 U.S.P.Q. 474, defendant claimed that the record title holder of the patent was not the actual owner of the patent. This Court did not rule such a defense was improper, rather it held that the facts pleaded by defendant were insufficient to establish the defense relied upon. Further, Widenski v. Shapiro Bernstein & Co., 147 F. 2d 909, 64 U.S.P.Q. 448 (C.A. 1, 1945) does not support the Commissioner's objection. This case simply held that the legal copyright owner was a proper and indispensable party to the suit for copyright infringement.

Secondly, the defense of nonownership as raised here by defendant is not an equitable defense, but rather a legal defense. The Commissioner's objection evinces a serious misunderstanding as to the actual nature of a copyright certificate. A copyright certificate, unlike a patent, does

15

not disclose on its face what it covers. Only an examination of the copyrighted work and the factors surrounding its creation and publication can reveal what is included within the scope of the copyright protection evidenced by the copyright certificate. Cf. Eggers v. Sun Sales Corp., 263 Fed. 373 (C.C.A. 2, 1920). A periodical may include many diverse types of works, some of which may be copyrightable by the periodical publisher and others not copyrightable. For example, a periodical can include works in the public domain, works copyrighted by another which are reproduced with permission, works owned by the periodical publisher as a trustee, and, finally, works owned outright by the periodical publisher. The publisher of a periodical including works of these various types would be entitled to receive a copyright certificate naming the periodical as the work covered by the certificate. However, the scope of protection provided by this copyright certificate is limited to material copyrightable to the periodical publisher, 17 U.S.C. § 3. Furthermore, under the terms of the copyright law, only the author or the proprietor of a literary work can obtain a copyright thereon, 17 U.S.C. § 9. The general copyright issued to the publisher of a periodical does not cover the individual articles therein unless the publisher is the proprietor of each of such individual

16

articles. Morse v. Fields, 127 F. Supp. 63, 104 U.S.P.Q. 54 (S.D.N.Y., 1954). The Commissioner's objection as stated above would preclude defendant from showing that the material for which copyright infringement is claimed was in the public domain. Clearly then, the Commissioner's objection is without merit, and defendant is entitled to raise the nonownership defense.

While it may be that plaintiff's certificate of registration entitled plaintiff to a presumption that it is the owner of the individual articles in the journals published by it, defendant contends that any such presumption has been here effectively rebutted. Once the presumption has been rebutted, the burden is on the copyright proprietor to show that he is the owner of the work for which he claims copyright. Van Cleef & Arpels, Inc. v. Schechter, 308 F. Supp. 674, 164 U.S.P.Q. 540 (S.D.N.Y. 1969). Plaintiff, through two of its officers, has admitted that it did not obtain a written assignment transferring title of the articles involved herein from the authors thereof to plaintiff. Since plaintiff does not have a written assignment granting to it ownership rights in the articles involved, defendant submits that any presumption in plaintiff's favor has been rebutted, and it is his burden to affirmatively establish ownership. As the following discussion shows, plaintiff has failed to sustain this burden.

17

Lacking a written assignment, plaintiff and the Commissioner rely upon what they claim is a prevailing custom in the scientific journal publishing field, that is, an author by submitting an article to a journal publisher assigns completely his rights therein to said publisher. The Commissioner, in his opinion, states that the evidence of record supports this finding of such a custom. Exactly what evidence the Commissioner relies upon is not stated unless it is the conclusion that authors do not claim an interest in their published works or have not questioned the existence of this custom. In his opinion, the Commissioner states:

Authors of two of the articles in suit testified at trial, and neither asserted an interest (legal or equitable) in their respective articles. It is reasonable to infer that testimony from other authors would be the same . . . .

This statement is a gross distortion of the record, and no finding of fact is made in support of this statement.

In actual fact, authors of three of the articles in suit testified at trial. None were asked either by defendant, plaintiff or the Commissioner if they asserted any interest in the articles which they wrote. The inference drawn by the Commissioner from this nontestimony as to what the testimony of other authors would be on this point is incredible, especially in view of the fact that one of the authors did

18

state in response to a question about the existence of the custom referred to above that he "presumed a shadow of ownership remained in the author." (R. 672). Moreover, the authors testified that in publishing articles they intended to achieve the widest dissemination possible. They considered that publication of the findings and the results of research was an essential part of the research and that the use of photocopies was essential to the efficient conduct of medical research. Authors prefer to have their articles published in journals which do not restrict the access thereto by imposing a royalty upon photocopying by scientists, are aware that photocopies of journal articles are made and even use photocopies in their own research work, and have no objection to photocopying but consider it essential to the efficient conduct of medical research. Furthermore, any transfer of ownership rights from authors to publishers could well be limited by the condition that photocopying by scientists is not restricted.

While the Commissioner states that the evidence of record supports the finding that a custom exists whereby authors in submitting articles to journal publishers impliedly assign their rights in such articles to the periodical publisher, a more accurate review of the record would disclose that the evidence in the record is not sufficient to support such a

19

finding. The most favorable testimony for plaintiff is that of its Chairman of the Board and its President. Both of these gentlemen testified as to the existence of such custom. Neither could accurately describe it or say where he had learned it. Both claimed to have observed it in practice, but the President admitted that he had never actually observed it. A witness called specifically by plaintiff for the purpose of establishing the existence of this custom could only testify that he "assumed" that title was transferred from the author to the publisher upon submission of the article (R. 424).

The evidence opposed to this custom contended for by plaintiff and the Commissioner is much stronger. An author of over 300 journal articles stated that he had never heard of such a custom until plaintiff's Chairman of the Board told him of it two weeks before trial. Furthermore, this same author stated that he presumed some shadow of ownership remained with the author. While it is true that the authors sometimes seek permission from the publisher to reprint their own articles, it is also true that authors wishing to use published material from another author obtained permission from both the other author and his publisher. While plaintiff's witnesses testified that permission from an author is done as a matter of courtesy and permission from

20

the publisher is done because he is the copyright proprietor, such testimony is a gratuitous characterization which has no basis in fact and is not supported by any facts of record. The following testimony by Dr. McKusick, one of the authors of the Count I article in suit, at page 672 of the record, is relevant on this point.

... I recall the fact that if anyone produces a significant amount -- of -- a couple of paragraphs from your article or reproduces a picture, a chart, or table that your -- the author's permission is obtained for that.
Is that merely courtesy, or is that copyright?
COMMISSIONER DAVIS: That is the $64,000 question.
In support of his conclusion of the existence of a custom whereby authors impliedly assign to the publisher their rights in an article by submitting the article to the publisher, the Commissioner cited several cases. These are Giesel v. Poynter Products, Inc., 295 F. Supp. 331, 160 U.S.P.Q. 590 (S.D.N.Y. 1968) and Best Medium Publishing Co. v. National Insider, Inc., 259 F. Supp. 433, 152 U.S.P.Q. 56 (N.D. Ill. 1966), aff'd. 385 F. 2d 384, 155 U.S.P.Q. 550 (C.A. 7, 1967), cert. denied, 390 U.S. 955. As defendant pointed out in its brief before the Commissioner, these

21

cases involved a sale for a monetary consideration of the work to the publisher. They do not involve as, as is at issue here, whether a contribution of an article to a periodical results in an assignment of rights in the article to the periodical publisher. In its brief, defendant cited Kinelow Publishing Co., Inc. v. Photography In Business, 270 F. Supp. 851, 155 U.S.P.Q. 342 (S.D. N.Y. 1967) in support of its argument that the record here does not support the finding of the custom contended for by plaintiff and the Commissioner. The Commissioner in his opinion characterized the Kinelow case as "not apposite." In view of the fact that this case is the only case cited by either party which deals specifically with the contribution of a scientific article to a periodical and whether by custom such articles are assigned to the publisher, the Commissioner's characterization of this case is erroneous to say the least. In Kinelow, the publisher, like plaintiff here, lacked a written assignment by which title to the article was transferred to it, and again, like plaintiff here, attempted to rely upon a custom to the effect that a contributed article is impliedly assigned to the publisher when the publisher agrees to publish the contribution. The court in Kinelow rejected the publisher's contention that such a custom existed. An important factor in reaching this decision

22

was the fact that the authors never intended to convey exclusive rights, but rather intended to achieve wide dissemination of the article contributed. Defendant submits that the present case is governed by the Kinelow case. The record herein clearly establishes that the authors of medical articles published in plaintiff's journals never intended to convey exclusive rights to plaintiff for the simple reason that copyright and its ramifications are never considered by authors in connection with the publication of journal articles.[1] Further, the record herein clearly establishes that the scientists and physicians who wrote the articles involved herein intended to achieve the widest dissemination possible of their articles. Again, the following testimony from Dr. McKusick is highly appropriate (at R. 669-670):
COMMISSIONER DAVIS: Well, is it fair to say that your interest is as I understand your testimony is dissemination of this article in whatever form? Is that it?
THE WITNESS (Dr. McKusick): Indeed. Yes. Yes, Sir.
Moreover, in view of the attitude that authors of the articles involved herein have towards photocopying of their articles by other medical scientists and practitioners,

---
[1] In connection with the publication of books, authors are fully aware of copyright and of the importance of a written assignment which includes the conventional author's royalty (R. 671).

23

it cannot be contended that the authors herein intended the plaintiff publisher to be the sole publisher of their articles.
The Commissioner in his opinion considers the fact that authors contributed their articles to plaintiff rather than selling them to plaintiff in return for a monetary consideration to be of little significance. He finds that plaintiff publisher provided consideration to the authors of the articles herein involved by publishing their work because such publication results in an enhancement of the professional and economic opportunities of such authors. Defendant submits that the characterization by the Commissioner of the publication of authors' articles as a consideration is illusory. Any enhancement of the professional and economic opportunities of authors which result from the publication of their articles do not result from the publication

of the article per se. Rather, any such enhancement results from the intrinsic merit of the articles themselves to which plaintiff has contributed nothing.
One further consideration that should be borne in mind in resolving this question is the principle enunciated in Brattleboro Publishing Co. v. Winmill Publishing Corp., 250 F. Supp. 255, 149 U.S.P.Q. 41 (D. Ver. 1966), aff'd, 369 F. 2d 565, 151 U.S.P.Q. 666 (C.A. 2, 1966). The court

24

in this case held that in the absence of a contrary agreement, it is presumed that title to a copyrighted work belongs to the party at whose expense the work was created and not to the periodical publisher who published the work, even though the publisher obtained a general copyright on the periodical. The articles involved herein were created at the expense of the authors thereof.[1] Plaintiff contributed editorial services only. And for the six articles published in professional society journals, the editorial services were of a minimal nature. Under the principle enunciated in Brattleboro, title to the articles involved herein remains in the authors thereof, and was not transferred to plaintiff.
In his opinion, the Commissioner states that it is implicit in defendant's arguments on this issue that it is unfair for plaintiff to derive a monetary profit from the work of medical researchers who do not share in that profit directly with the plaintiff, and that defendant's position

---
[1] For articles published in JI, the authors are required to pay plaintiff pages charges of $44 for each page in excess of six (6). (R 46, 1319). Dr. McKusick, a co-author of the Count I article made plaintiff $800 in order to have color photographs included in his article (R. 668).

25

thus overlooks the fact that with respect to most of plaintiff's journals any profits derived therefrom are shared with the professional societies for which the journals are published. The Commissioner's argument on this point amounts to no more than the erection of a straw man which the Commissioner conveniently knocks down. Defendant has no objection whatsoever to the plaintiff making a fair profit on the publication of its journals. In fact, defendant proved that plaintiff did in fact make such a profit with respect to the journals involved herein. No one disputes that plaintiff performs a useful function in publishing medical journals, a function which entails entreprenurial risks. Defendant's position is simply that plaintiff is adequately compensated for these risks by the profits earned by it on the original sale of its journals and that a royalty on photocopying by the NIH library and NLM is not necessary to enable plaintiff to profitably survive as a medical journal publisher. The Commissioner also states that most of plaintiff's journals operate for the benefit of the medical profession itself and, thus, for the benefit of the public, because the professional societies share in the journal income derived from the journals published by plaintiff. This argument by the Commissioner seems to imply that professional societies agree with the position taken by plaintiff with respect to this suit. The facts are

26

otherwise. Several professional societies including the American Medical Association, have indicated their belief that the practice of the libraries here involved of making available to qualified medical practitioners and researchers a single copy of journal articles is not objectionable and have consented to this practice.[1] Moreover, the record in this case discloses that the past president, the president and president-elect of the American Gastroenterological Association (AGA) also did not object to this practice by defendant's libraries.[2]
The Commissioner concludes his argument by stating that 95% of current medical literature is published by private publishers and that in the absence of such private publishers, publication of medical literature would devolve upon other organizations such as the Government. In the first place, there is no basis in the record stating that 95% of medical literature is published by private publishers and

---
[1] Editorial, Journal of the American Medical Assoc., 220 1357-8 (June 5, 1972), Copyright notice, Journal of Medical Education 47 (May 1972).
[2] These views of the officers of the AGA were contained in a letter (DX 115) which defendant offered in evidence. While the Commissioner sustained plaintiff's objection, this letter was referred to in defendant's findings. It is certainly not proper for the Commissioner to reach a conclusion directly contrary to the only evidence offered, whether such evidence is legally admissible or not.

27

the facts are otherwise.[1] In a footnote on this point (p. 10), the Commissioner raises the spectre of Government censorship, partially quoting from the UCLA Project to support his contention. The full discussion of Government censorship in UCLA Project[2] at p. 956-957 is as follows:

> But if a government agency could effectively replace private organizations for selecting and marketing written material, a second and probably more crucial problem would be raised: government influence over the content of writings. The direction of scientific and technical research in the United States, including research in the social sciences, is now greatly influenced by the need for institutional funding. The federal government funds the vast majority of research work, and is consequently influencing the initial planning of research. Within the limits of research which he has had to design with an eye to obtaining federal funding, the researcher is today free to reach whatever conclusions his data and his personal predispositions indicate. But if the government becomes the only publisher of research, it may be that the Government Printing Office will have the final say over whether his results are worth publishing. Most scholars simply do not have the money to pay for publication. Even if they could finance the publication of their works, the lack of professional journals may sufficiently deter the publication of research found objectionable or unworthy by the government. As a practical matter, it might be impossible for an author out of favor with government officials to publish his work at

[1] Cf. PX 29 (pp. 13, 14) where it is stated that of the 63 American journals from the list of 100 most heavily photocopied journals, only seven (7) are sponsored by commercial publishers.

[2] Project - New Technology and the Law of Copyright: Reprography and Computers, 15 UCLA L. Rev. 931 (1968).

28

> all. The loss of private markets might thus create complete governmental control over what is written and published and the consequent dangers of even well-meaning censorship.
>
> The danger of government censorship need not be great in the scientific field. Many scientific journal articles are presently subjected to scrutiny by panels of scientists who determine "publishability" independently of the editors of journals. Retaining such an evaluative process would allow professional scientists in the author's field, rather than bureaucrats, to decide what is published. *(Emphasis added and indicates portions omitted by the Commissioner.)*

The real import of this discussion is that while the problem of government censorship might theoretically arise if private medical publishers disappeared, the problem is readily solvable and the means for doing so already exist. This is quite different from the effect that the Commissioner intended to achieve. Argument by innuendo has no place in a decision of a court of law.

In conclusion, defendant submits that the evidence of record and applicable law clearly demonstrate that plaintiff does not own any interest in the articles involved herein sufficient to permit it to validly copyright such articles and that any such presumption in plaintiff's favor has been conclusively rebutted. Plaintiff's petition should therefore be dismissed.

29

III. Photocopying of Medical Journal Articles As Practiced by NIH and NLM Is a Fair Use

Fair use is a privilege of persons other than the owner of the copyright to use the copyrighted material in a reasonable manner without the consent of the copyright owner. Technically an infringement, it is allowed on the ground that the appropriation is reasonable and customary. Holdredge v. Knight Publishing Corp., 214 F. Supp. 921, 136 U.S.P.Q. 615 (S.D. Cal. 1963). It is defendant's intention to compare the photocopying practices of the NIH library and NLM with the factors considered by the courts in determining what is a fair use and to show that such photocopying meets the underlying policy reasons for the application of fair use. In addition, defendant will refute the arguments made by the Commissioner in his opinion against the application of fair use in this case.

A. The Factors Considered By the Courts In Determining What Is Fair Use

Fair use is a doctrine that has been said to virtually defy definition, and each case must be decided upon its own facts. Time, Inc. v. Bernard Geis Associates, 293 F. Supp. 130, 159 U.S.P.Q. 663 (S.D.N.Y. 1968). Nevertheless, as good a description as any of the factors considered in the application of fair use may be found in the Report of the Register of Copyrights On the General Revision of the U.S.

30

Copyright Law, Committee on the Judiciary, U.S. House of Representatives, 87th Congress, 1st Session, July, 1961. The Register of Copyrights stated as follows at pages 24-25:

> Whether any particular use of a copyrighted work constitutes a fair use rather than infringement of copyright has been said to depend upon (1) the purpose of the use, (2) the nature of the copyrighted work, (3) the amount and substantiality of the material used in relation to the copyrighted work as a whole, and (4) the effect of the use on the copyright owner's potential market for his work. These criteria are interrelated and their relative significance may vary, but the fourth one -- the competitive character of the use -- is often the most decisive.

Each of these factors will be examined in relationship to the facts of this case. From this examination, it will be clear that fair use is properly applicable in this case.

1. The Purpose of the Use and the Character of the Work

These two factors in this case are interrelated. Photocopies of the articles involved herein were made for the express purpose for which the articles were created, i.e., to further medical research or to improve medical treatment.

The photocopies involved herein were made by the NIH library and NLM. Those made by the NIH library were made at the request of certain of its employees, while NLM furnished photocopies to other medical libraries who in turn furnished them to physicians or other medical researchers.

31

The basic mission of NIH is to advance health and well being through the promotion of research, the training of medical personnel and the development of medical institutions, and the improvement of biomedical communications. The research function of NIH is carried on either intramurally or by way of grants. Intramural research is carried on by various specialized institutes on the campus at Bethesda, Maryland. NIH employs over 12,000 persons of whom over 2,000 have advanced professional degrees. The research conducted by NIH employees results in the publication of over 2,000 technical and scientific journal articles each year. Grant research is conducted by various individuals and organizations and institutions throughout the country which receive funds awarded by NIH. These funds are used to pay the salaries of the investigators, the cost of equipment, supplies, and publications, the fees necessary to have research results published, and various other incidental expenses. Four employees or former employees of NIH who actually requested photocopies of certain of the articles involved herein from the NIH library, testified during the trial. Each explained in detail the purpose for which the photocopy was obtained and the relevance of the article photocopied to that purpose. Each explained how he used the photocopy obtained and what was done with it. (Three still have the photocopy and use it in their work.)

32

NLM is a unique institution which was statutorily created in 1956 for the express purpose of disseminating medical information. It originated in 1836 as the Surgeon General's Library. NLM contains one of the world's largest collections of medical literature. Its collection of medical material is available without charge to physicians and other scientists all over the world through the means of interlibrary loans of journal material and through direct loan for book material. In addition, NLM publishes the Index Medicus, which abstracts the world's medical literature, provides special bibliographic services, and conducts research into improved methods of library science and communication of medical information. The physician who requested and ultimately received the photocopy of the Count VIII article made by NLM testified. The actual interlibrary loan form used is in evidence. This physician was stationed in Japan in an Army hospital and obtained the photocopy of the Count VIII article in order to treat a particular patient. This physician has also retained the photocopy obtained from NLM and, in fact, exhibited it to the Court.

Defendant submits that the foregoing evidence which was not contradicted, impeached, or rebutted, establishes beyond question that the photocopies made by NIH and NLM are carried on for a serious and legitimate purpose and that the specific articles involved were directly related to these

33

purposes. Further, these purposes are vital to the health and well being of this nation.

2. The Amount and Substantiality of the Use

While the users of the NIH library and NLM are somewhat different, the photocopy operations of each are operated on similar basic principles. Each library has adopted a policy designed for two purposes: (1) to prevent abuse of the library's facilities, and (2) to protect the legitimate interests of copyright holders as such interests have been established by custom. The policies of NIH and NLM impose several requirements and restrictions on obtaining photocopies from these libraries which include: (1) a written request must be submitted, (2) only a single copy will be furnished, (3) only a limited number of pages will be furnished, generally 40 or 50, and (4) excessive copying from a single issue or a single volume of the journal will not be permitted. In addition, NLM will not furnish photocopies of articles published within the preceding five years in journals appearing on the widely available list. Such journals are presumed to be available locally and libraries requesting photocopies of articles from such journals are directed to local sources. It is clear that the policies outlined above were expressly designed to bring the photocopying operations of these libraries within what has been traditionally regarded

34

as a fair and insubstantial amount. [1]

One of the grounds upon which the Commissioner rejected the application of fair use in this case was that he considered photocopying by defendant's libraries to be "wholesale copying [which] meets none of the criteria for fair use." (p. 16).

Exactly what the Commissioner meant when he characterized defendant's photocopying as wholesale was not stated. Three meanings are possible: (1) defendant copies entire articles, (2) defendant makes more than one copy of some articles, or (3) defendant simply does a lot of copying. Whatever meaning the Commissioner intended, his conclusion that defendant's photocopying is not fair use is erroneous.

The proposition that wholesale copying can never be a fair use is derived from Leon v. Pacific Telephone & Telegraph Co., 91 F. 2d 484, 34 U.S.P.Q. 237 (C.A. 9, 1937). In Leon the infringement complained of was the publication for sale of an inverted telephone directory which had been

---

[1] For further detail on this point, see Part III, Section B-1, of this brief, infra.

35

wholly copied from plaintiff's copyright directory in the normal form. These facts sufficiently distinguish the Leon case from the present case so that the purported wholesale copying rule of Leon cannot be blindly applied to this case. This holding of the Leon case has been characterized as dictum. Latman, Fair Use of Copyrighted Works, Study No. 14, Prepared for the Subcommittee on Patents, Trademarks and Copyrights of the Committee on the Judiciary, United States Senate, 86th Congress, 2d Session (1960).[1] The Leon dictum was relied on by the Court in Benny v. Loews, 239 F. 2d 532, 112 U.S.P.Q. 11 (C.A. 9, 1956). The Benny case is of doubtful precedential value inasmuch as it was affirmed only by an evenly divided Supreme Court. Wihtol v. Crow, 309 F. 2d 777, 135 U.S.P.Q. 385 (C.A. 8, 1962) and Public Affairs Associates, Inc. v. Rickover, 284 F. 2d 262, 127 U.S.P.Q. 231 (C.A.D.C. 1960) are distinguishable on their facts from the present case; both involved multiple publications of the copyrighted work.

In its brief before the Commissioner, the plaintiff argued that its view with respect to wholesale copying was

---

[1] In citing this work by plaintiff's attorney, defendant is neither intending to embarrass nor to impugn the integrity of plaintiff's attorney. Defendant recognizes the right and, indeed, the duty of plaintiff's attorney to take positions which are or may appear to be inconsistent with positions taken earlier. Defendant is citing this work because it

---

is a study prepared for the Senate Committee on the Judiciary under the supervision of the Register of Copyrights.

36

supported by 17 U.S.C. § 3. This argument appears to have been accepted by the Commissioner in Footnote 5 on page 6. Plaintiff contended that in accordance with 17 U.S.C. § 3 each article in its journal should be treated as a separate copyrighted work. This argument in this respect is erroneous for two reasons.

The first is that it ignores the facts. Plaintiff's journals are not sold by the article. They are sold by the volume and, in rare circumstances, by the issue. Plaintiff keeps no stock of reprints on hand. The second is that the applicable law does not support the conclusion that is drawn, viz., that the substantiality test must be applied to the article rather than the journal.

The principal case relied upon by plaintiff in its brief before the Commissioner was Markham v. A. E. Borden, 206 F. 2d 199, 98 U.S.P.Q. 346 (C.A. 1, 1953). Both Unistrut Corp. v. Power, 175 F. Supp. 294, 121 U.S.P.Q. 381 (D. Mass. 1958) and Hedeman Products Corp. v. Tap-Rite Products Corp., 228 F. Supp. 630, 141 U.S.P.Q. 381 (D.N.J. 1964) rely on and cite Markham. The Court in Markham did in fact apply 17 U.S.C. § 3 to nine items in plaintiff's advertising catalog and found infringement. To reach this result, however, it was necessary for the Court in Markham to distinguish Mathews Conveyor Co. v. Palmer-Bee Co.,

37

135 F. 2d 73, 57 U.S.P.Q. 219 (C.A. 6, 1943) in which an exactly contrary result was reached. The ground upon which Markham distinguished Mathews Conveyor is especially significant, i.e., Mathews Conveyor was stated to have indiscriminately applied the rule which has its "chief utility in protecting literature and scientific endeavors." Thus, Markham did not say that materiality and substantiality in determining fair use of scientific and technical works is to be determined by a routine and mechanical application of 17 U.S.C. § 3.

In Mathews Conveyor, the Court cited New York Tribune, Inc. v. Otis & Co., 39 F. Supp. 67, 49 U.S.P.Q. 361 (S.D.N.Y. 1941). The New York Tribune case is perhaps the closest case to the present case yet found. There, the defendant photostated an editorial from plaintiff's newspaper and sent copies of it, together with an explanatory letter, to selected public officials and the like. The defense of fair use was made by motion for summary judgment. The Court expressly considered 17 U.S.C. § 3, but yet it did not reject defendant's defense of fair use on that ground. Defendant's motion for summary judgment was rejected to permit the plaintiff to discover whether defendant's motive was commercial and to determine the exact number of copies made, both of which factors the Court considered to be relevant to the issue of fair use. The New York Tribune

38

case clearly demonstrates that plaintiff's argument that copying an entire article cannot be a fair use is erroneous.

This principle that copying an entire journal article is permissible under the doctrine of fair use was also recognized by the Committee on the Judiciary of the House of Representatives in its report on the copyright revision bill.[1] In its discussion of fair use provisions of the revision bill (H.R. 2512) in the context of educational and classroom uses, the Committee states at pp. 34, 35:

> Single copies of "entire" works. -- In the various discussions of educational copying at the hearings and thereafter, a question that has never been resolved involves the difference between an "entire work" and an "excerpt." The educators have sought a limited right for a teacher to make a single copy of an ' entire" work for classroom purposes. The committee understands that this was not generally intended to extend beyond a "separately cognizable" or "self-contained" portion (for example, a single poem, story, or article) in a collective work, and that no privilege is sought to reproduce an entire collective work (for example, an encyclopedia volume, a periodical issue) or a sizable integrated work published as an entity (a novel, treatise, monograph, and so forth). With this limitation, and subject to the other relevant criteria, the requested privilege of making a single copy appears appropriately to ' e within the scope of fair use.

---

[1] H.R. Rep. No. 83, 90th Cong., 1st Session (Copyright Law Revision) (1967).

39

The Committee also made plain its belief that this statement regarding fair use was generally applicable to all types of uses stating at p. 35:

> Reproductions and uses for other purposes.--The concentrated attention given the fair use provision in the context of classroom teaching activities should not obscure its application in other areas. The committee emphasizes again that the same general standards of fair use are applicable to all kinds of uses of copyrighted material, although the relative weight to be given them will differ from case to case.

Thus, there is no basis in fact or law for the Commissioner's holding that defendant's photocopying practices are not a fair use simply because entire journal articles are copied.

The second possible meaning for the term wholesale copying is that defendant makes more than one copy of some articles. The facts with respect to this point have been set forth and discussed in Part I of this brief. As shown above, multiple copies of the same article are very rarely made, and then only in response to a second request from a user whose first request was not filled or from a second user. In any event, the Commissioner's opinion does not explain why making multiple photocopies of some articles should subject defendant to liability for all photocopies made.

The third meaning for wholesale copying possibly

40

intended by the Commissioner is that defendant's libraries make a lot of copies. If this is the meaning intended by the Commissioner, then finding such use to be an unfair use results from the application of the unstated, unproved and erroneous premise that a lot of fair use is an unfair use.

As shown in the exceptions submitted concurrently with this brief, five (5) of the persons identified as having requested photocopies of the articles specified in the counts testified. Each of these requesters explained in detail the work in which they were engaged and of the relationship of the article photocopied to this work. Further, each of these requesters stated in detail how the photocopies made permitted them to carry on their work more effectively. It cannot be doubted that Dr. Gabore when confronted with the interpretation of the electro-encephalogram of a child afflicted with a mucopolysaccharidose would have been fully justified if he had personally made a photocopy of the Count I article. [1] Likewise, it cannot be disputed that

---

[1] The importance of the Count I article to the medical profession is shown by the fact that the National Foundation reprinted with permission 5,000 copies of the Count I article for distribution to physicians in connection with its programs. Inasmuch as the National Foundation paid no royalty to plaintiff, it is difficult to perceive why plaintiff is seeking compensation from defendant for using the Count I article in precisely the same way as the National Foundation.

41

Dr. Pitcher when treating a patient with liver complications would have been fully justified if he had personally made a photocopy of the Count VIII article. [1] Defendant, who employed Drs. Gabore and Pitcher, cannot be held liable for providing to these physicians what they had a right to obtain. Behind each of the many photocopies of journal articles that defendant's libraries have provided lies a request from a physician or scientist who has a need for a photocopy of the particular journal article requested. In fact, plaintiff has conceded the articles published in journals are such that they would only be copied for scholarly purposes.

If in describing defendant's photocopying practices as "wholesale," the Commissioner intended to mean simply that defendant's practices are extensive, this fact alone will not make defendant's photocopying practices an unfair use. Insofar as the first three criteria for judging fair use are concerned, i.e., the purpose of the use, the character of the work, and the amount and substantiality of the use are concerned, no significant distinction can be made because defendant's photocopying practices are widespread. If the making of any single photocopy of a journal article can be

---

[1] It is interesting to note that Dr. Pitcher's need for the Count VIII article arose nine (9) years after the publication of this article.

42

justified as fair use under these three criteria, then all photocopies made by defendant's libraries can be so justified. Defendant submits that the evidence of record amply supports the finding that the photocopying practices of defendant's library are in fact justified under these three criteria.

There remains for consideration the fourth criterion for determining whether a given use is a fair use, i.e., does the use have an adverse effect on plaintiff's actual or potential market for the copyrighted work. The question to be determined then is simply whether defendant's photocopying practices are so extensive and widespread that they have caused economic harm to plaintiff? The Commissioner has concluded that they do and, in so holding, the Commissioner has made his most grievous error, for he has accepted at face value the myth that widespread photocopying causes journal publishers to lose revenue because of the loss of subscription sales, reprint sales and the like.

3. The Adverse Effect on Plaintiff's Potential or Actual Market

The Commissioner found in effect that the photocopying practices of the NIH library and NLM have in fact adversely affected the actual or potential market for plaintiff's journal. During the trial, defendant presented a considerable body of evidence which established that plaintiff's journals

43

were not adversely affected by defendant's photocopying. The Commissioner ignored this evidence but instead relied on questionable inferences, a misapprehension as to the requirements of the law, and the thoroughly unconvincing and self-serving statements of plaintiff's witnesses. Before considering in detail the evidence presented by defendant in this regard (which is for the most part included in the exceptions to the Commissioner's findings), several preliminary observations made by the Commissioner should be answered.

The Commissioner at page 16 of his opinion states:

> The photocopies are exact duplicates of the original articles; are intended to be substitutes for, and serve the same purpose as, the original articles; and serve to diminish plaintiff's potential market for the original articles since the photocopies are made at the request of, and for the benefit of, the very persons who constitute plaintiff's market.

This statement is erroneous in several respects. Defendant's libraries do not make photocopies to serve as substitutes for the original journal but rather make photocopies to serve as a substitute for the loan of the original journal (See for example legend affixed to all NLM photocopies, Commissioner's Finding 24). Moreover the persons who request and obtain photocopies from defendant's libraries are not members of plaintiff's potential market. The medical personnel requesting photocopies of the articles specified

44

in the counts stated that they already personally subscribed to four to ten journals. These persons have not used photocopies as a substitute for a subscription (R. 574). It should be obvious that no one can subscribe to all medical journals even if it were economically possible (R. 715). Moreover, both NIH and NLM, which subscribe to at least two copies of the journals involved herein, have found from experience that as photocopying increases, subscriptions also increase.

The Commissioner has also stated at page 16:

> Plaintiff need not prove actual damages to make out its case for infringement.

The Commissioner appears to have confused defendant's claim of fair use, which has historically permitted an accused infringer to show, inter alia, that the copyright proprietor has not been economically harmed by the alleged infringement, thus, avoiding a finding of infringement, and a copyright proprietor's privilege of relying on the statutory minimum damage provisions instead of proving actual damages after an infringement has actually been found. The cases cited by the Commissioner do not sustain his assertion. In fact, Macmillian Co. v. King, 223 Fed. 862 (D. Mass. 1914) held precisely the opposite (at 868):

> Proof of actual damage is not necessary for the issuance of an injunction if infringement appears and damage may probably follow from its continuance.
> (Emphasis added)

45

The other cases [1] cited by the Commissioner are merely concerned with the operation of the minimum damage provisions of the Copyright Act.

Defendant has maintained since the inception of this suit that the financial performance of plaintiff's journals and business as a whole is relevant to determine if photocopying by defendant has had an adverse effect on plaintiff's potential or actual market. Plaintiff, of course, has denied the relevance of such evidence and, judging from the fact that the Commissioner totally ignored defendant's evidence on this point, the Commissioner agrees with plaintiff.

In order to determine if a photocopy has had an adverse effect on the actual or potential market for a copyrighted work, it is not enough to say that the photocopy is a facsimile of the original or that the photocopy is furnished in lieu of lending the original. What must be determined is this: does the photocopy serve as a substitute for a subscription to the journal? Selling subscriptions is the major means by which plaintiff earns income from its copyrighted property. [2] It is

---

[1] Brady v. Daly, 175 U.S. 148 (1899); F. W. Woolworth & Co. v. Contemporary Arts, Inc., 344 U.S. 228 (1952).
[2] Defendant realizes that plaintiff also earns income from the sale of reprints and back volumes. However, reprint sales account for generally less than 20% of subscription sales, and back volume sales are generally considerably less than reprint sales. In any event, the evidence is clear that in the past 10 years, there has been no diminishing of the number of reprints sold to authors.

46

by this time evident that it is impossible to prove whether any given photocopy displaced a subscription sale. The Commissioner would appear to agree with defendant on this point.

Since direct evidence is impossible, resort must be had to indirect evidence. The indirect evidence in the record consists of the financial statements for the period 1958 through 1969 for the journals involved and the income tax returns filed by plaintiff for the period 1959 through 1968. The financial statement for PR for 1958-1964 were unavailable, and could not be analyzed by defendant's expert. In any event, other factors, not the least of which is the failure of PR to publish the full number of text pages agreed upon could explain the erratic performance of PR. Moreover, plaintiff has earned or could have earned substantial interest on the surplus funds reserved for unpublished pages, thus further obscuring the actual financial performance of PR.

Because of the period covered by these financial statements and tax returns, they are of special relevance in determining whether plaintiff has been adversely affected by photocopying. These data begin when there was virtually no photocopying as presently practiced and end when photocopying has reached its present proportions. Thus, if photocopying was having any adverse effect on plaintiff's operations, such

47

effect would be reflected in the rate at which plaintiff's business and journals grew as was admitted by plaintiff's Chairman of the Board. Now, it is immediately evident that if plaintiff's journals were steadily losing subscriptions and plaintiff's business was steadily declining during the ten year period when photocopying grew from nearly zero to its present size, one could claim with considerable justification that photocopying was the culprit.[1] However, the facts in this case are otherwise. Plaintiff's journals and business as a whole are admittedly doing rather well. The important factor is not that they are doing well, but how well they are, in fact, doing. For every indicator where a comparison was possible, plaintiff's business is found to be growing faster than the gross national product.[2] Plaintiff's Chairman of the Board conceded that plaintiff's business

---

[1] The quality of plaintiff's journals is conceded not to have materially changed in the period 1958 through 1969. In 1968, during negotiations between plaintiff's president, Mr. Reville, and the American Gastroenterological Society (AGA) concerning the losses incurred in the operation of GA in 1967 and 1968, the possible adverse effect of photocopying was not considered nor did Mr. Reville ask anyone in plaintiff's organization to advise him of such effect (R. 97, 98).
[2] These comparisons were made by computing the ratio of the average of some indicator for a period after 1964 to the average of the same indicator for a similar period prior to 1964 and comparing this ratio with a ratio computed in a like manner for the gross national product. The indicators examined included subscription sales, number of subscriptions and total income for the journals and net sales, total income, gross profit and taxable income for plaintiff's business as a whole.

48

should grow at a rate equal to the rate of growth of manpower working in the field of science. The only evidence of record of that rate of growth is that it is about 4%.[1] The rate of growth of the gross national product, as shown on the charts prepared by defendant's expert, is greater than 4%. Thus, over the period in which plaintiff's business should have shown an increasing adverse effect from photocopying, plaintiff's business was growing at a rate greater than that which can be expected.[2] In view of this fact, plaintiff cannot claim that photocopying is causing it to lose sales of

---

[1] This rate of growth has been found to be specifically applicable to the growth of engineering and physical scientific manpower. Plaintiff's Chairman of the Board conceded that this rate could also apply to medical scientific manpower. Plaintiff offered no evidence to rebut the applicability of the 4% rate. It has been reported that for the years 1963 through 1970, the average yearly rate of growth for the number of physicians has ranged from 2.5 to 2.9 percent. A Report on Physician Manpower and Medical Education, American Medical Association, Chicago, Ill. June 1971.
[2] Defendant is aware that two of the journals involved here lost subscriptions in 1969, i.e., MED and PR. As to PR, the comments made above as to the number of pages published should suffice. As to MED, defendant's expert pointed out that MED's number of subscriptions closely tracked over the preceding ten year period NIH research appropriations, which also dropped in 1969. Further, it is a matter of common knowledge that in 1969 the economy, as a whole, suffered a recession.

49

subscriptions, sales of back volumes, and sales of reprints.[1]

In an article entitled "Why We Sue the Government," written in April 1968, plaintiff's Chairman of the Board made the following statement:

> We only wish in some manner to be paid a royalty on each copy made to offset the loss in the sale of subscriptions, reprints and back volumes which photocopying brings about. [DX 87-7]

During the trial of this case, plaintiff's Chairman of the Board was asked about this statement and the following colloquy took place:

> Q Was that statement true when you made it?
> A I thought it was.
> Q Is it true today?
> A I think it is.
> Q Do you want anything more?
> A No.

---

[1] As stated above, several journals including those published by the American Medical Association and the Journal of Medical Education have consented to the practice of providing single copies of journal articles to researchers and other qualified personnel. It would seem that these journals are at least as susceptible to the harmful effects of photocopying as are plaintiff's journals. Indeed, the action taken by these journals would seem to indicate that no such harmful effects occur.

50

Defendant submits that plaintiff should be taken at its word. . . Since the present record is devoid of any evidence showing that photocopying by the Government has caused plaintiff to lose subscription sales, reprint sales, or back volume sales, and in fact shows that such losses have not occurred, plaintiff is not entitled to recover any compensation in this lawsuit.

To support his assertion that library photocopying causes economic harm to plaintiff, the Commissioner states at page 17:

> Also, there is evidence that one subscriber canceled a subscription to one of plaintiff's journals because the subscriber believed the cost of photocopying the journal had become less than the journal's annual subscription price; and another subscriber canceled a subscription, at least in part because library photocopies were available. (See also Commissioner's finding 39(b))

The evidence relied upon by the Commissioner in this statement is extensively considered in the defendant's exceptions. To summarize briefly here, the first instance is not of record because the Commissioner sustained a hearsay objection to it. The second pertains to testimony by plaintiff's Chairman of the Board in which he described a telephone survey of 18 former subscribers to a defunct journal living in the Baltimore area. One such former subscriber, according to plaintiff's Chairman of the Board,

51

discontinued his subscription partly because of the availability of photocopies. The meagreness of this testimony when compared to the facts obtained from the financial statements and tax returns is glaringly apparent.[1] That the Commissioner would hold the defendant liable on the basis of such evidence is astounding. This is truly a case of making a mountain out of a molehill.

The Commissioner also states that photocopying is causing it to lose royalties from licenses.[2] The evidence concerning these licenses is very meager. There is no evidence to show the purpose for which the photocopies permitted under these licenses are being made, and there is no evidence to show that these licenses are for single copies of single articles as opposed to multiple copies of single articles. Moreover, it is clear that neither of the licenses referred to were in effect at the time this suit was filed (R. 76, 135) or are even now in effect (R. 130). It is highly significant that none of these licenses were offered in evidence during the trial of this case. Moreover, plaintiff itself considers these licenses unimportant. When plaintiff receives a request for a copy of a journal article, it first refers the requester to the author of the article for

[1] Plaintiff has never conducted a detailed study of the effect of photo-copying on its operations.
[2] In a statement made by plaintiff's Chairman of the Board after the filing of this suit, no mention was made of a loss of royalties (DX 87-7).

52

a free reprint.

The Commissioner's reliance on the possible loss of royalty income as a ground for denying defendant the defense of fair use is legally undefensible. The very purpose of this lawsuit is to determine if defendant's photocopying practices require a license from plaintiff. 28 U.S.C. § 1498(b), upon which plaintiff's suit is based, as its predecessor 28 U.S.C. § 1498(a) dealing with patents, is an eminent domain statute granting defendant a license. Irving Air Chute Co. v. United States, 117 Ct. Cl. 790, 93 F. Supp. 633, 87 U.S.P.Q. 246 (1950). To rely on the possible loss of royalty income as a ground for finding liability is equivalent to arguing that since plaintiff will lose money if it loses this lawsuit, and since plaintiff wins this lawsuit if it loses money, therefore plaintiff wins this lawsuit. The logical fallacy, i.e., using as a premise the conclusion to be proved, has been recognized for centuries, and has been called "begging the question." Whether plaintiff loses royalty income is the end result of this lawsuit, not the starting point for determining defendant's liability. There never would be a case of fair use if the question of whether the use adversely affected the actual or potential market for the copyrighted work could be answered simply by determining if the use could have been licensed, because all uses can be licensed. Of course, the fallacy in the Commissioner's

53

line of argument is not eliminated because plaintiff has assigned to another the right to receive the royalty income.

B. The Policies Underlying The Application of Fair Use

Three reasons have generally been advanced for the application of fair use. These are: (1) the fact that the use made of the copyrighted work is a fair, reasonable and customary use, (2) the special latitude given to scientists and scholars to use prior copyrighted works, and (3) the need to ensure that copyright serves its constitutional purpose of promoting the arts and sciences. The latter two reasons are, of course, interrelated.

1. Photocopying by NIH and NLM is a Fair, Reasonable and Customary Use

Several cases have defined a fair use as one that is fair, reasonable and customary. Holdredge v. Knight Publishing Corp., 214 F. Supp. 921, 136 U.S.P.Q. 615 (S.D. Cal. 1963); Rosemont Enterprises, Inc. v. Random House, Inc., 366 F. 2d 303, 150 U.S.P.Q. 715 (C.A. 2, 1966). The foregoing portions of this brief have set forth in detail the policies adopted by NIH and NLM to ensure that only a fair and insubstantial amount of copyrighted work is photocopied and lack of any adverse effect that such photocopying has on plaintiff's ability to sell journal subscriptions.

54

The conclusion that photocopying by NIH and NLM is a fair and reasonable use inevitably follows. Moreover, photocopying by libraries has been the custom for more than 50 years, conceded by plaintiff's own witnesses.[1]

For many years, the custom of libraries in general has been to furnish photocopies of journal articles in lieu of lending the original. This custom is clearly shown in the "Gentlemen's Agreement" and the General Interlibrary Loan Code (Revised 1956), and the long uninterrupted practice of libraries under these understandings.[2] Defendant does not claim that the "Gentlemen's Agreement" is legally binding on plaintiff, but it is to be noted that the "Gentlemen's Agreement" was accepted as a statement of principle by a group adversely affected by the practice sanctioned. The Supreme Court has stated in United States v. Midway Oil Co., 263 U.S. 459 at 475 (1915):

[1] The willingness of the Commissioner to find a custom relating to the implied assignment of the article from the author to the journal publisher on much less convincing evidence and his refusal to find a recognized custom of library photocopying from the testimony of virtually the same witnesses is a cogent illustration of the Commissioner's pre-disposition in this case.
[2] See DX 51 and DX 74.

55

... that in determining the meaning of a statute or the existence of a power, weight shall be given to the useage itself -- even when validity of a practice is the subject of investigation.

See also, Udall v. Tallman, 380 U.S. 1 (1965). Even Professor Nimmer, who is, as the Commissioner's opinion shows, no friend of library photocopying, has conceded that the force of custom can weigh in favor of fair use. Nimmer on Copyright, § 145. The policies governing the furnishing of photocopies at both NIH and NLM have been derived and adapted from the "Gentlemen's Agreement" and the General Interlibrary Loan Code.

One of the reasons given by Commissioner for refusing to give any weight to the "Gentlemen's Agreement" as evidence of a custom of library photocopying is that "no periodical publishers were represented" (at page 19) citing Varmer.[1]

The Commissioner read Varmer incorrectly; what Varmer states is that "generally" periodical publishers were not represented. Whether periodical publishers were "generally" represented or not represented at all is of no

[1] Varmer, Photoduplication of Copyrighted Material by Libraries, Study No. 15, Copyright new Revision, prepared for Senate Commissioner on the Judiciary 86th Congress 2d Session (1960).

56

moment, because defendant does not claim the "Gentlemen's Agreement" to be legally binding on anyone. What defendant does claim is the Gentlemen's Agreement and the practice of libraries under it as exemplified in the General Interlibrary Loan Code are evidence of an uninterrupted and heretofore undisputed custom of library photocopying such as is presently practiced by defendant's libraries. It can be disputed that libraries in general have since the date of the "Gentlemen's Agreement" been making photocopies of entire journal articles and have likewise consistently claimed that such photocopying was sanctioned by the "Gentlemen's Agreement."

The Commissioner also claims that by its terms the "Gentlemen's Agreement" would not permit the type of photocopying practiced by defendant's libraries. The Commissioner states at page 20

In any event, the "gentlemen's agreement" by its own terms condemned as "not * * * fair" the making of photocopies which could serve in "substitution" for the original work, and further noted that "[o] rders for photo-copying which, by reason of their extensiveness or for any other reasons" could serve as duplicates of the original copyrighted work "should not be accepted."

This is another example of misleading by the Commissioner. What the "Gentlemen's Agreement" actually said was:

57

It would not be fair to the author or publisher to make possible the substitution of the photostats for the purchase of a copy of the book itself either for an individual library or for any permanent collection in a public or research library. Orders for photo-copying which, by reason of their extensiveness or for any other reasons, violate this principle should not be accepted. In case of doubt as to whether the excerpt requested complies with this condition, the safe thing to do is to defer action until the owner of the copyright has approved the reproduction.

Thus, the Agreement condemns as unfair only those photocopies which would serve as a substitution for a book. In fact, the

Agreement expressly sanctions the practice by libraries of making photocopies of periodicals in place of loaning the original periodical. (DX 74, p. 31). As pointed out above, defendant's libraries make photocopies in lieu of lending the original journal.

The Commissioner in his opinion also distinguishes between hand copying and photocopying on the ground that the latter "poses a real and substantial threat to copyright owners' legitimate interests." He includes also extensive quotations from "authorities" which agree with, although do not prove, his contention that photocopying is a substantial threat. In this connection he also alludes to the Sophar report [1] which characterizes photocopying as "a non-violent

---

[1] Sophar & Heilprin. "The Determination of Legal Facts and Economic Guideposts with Respect to the Dissemination of Scientific and Educational Information as Affected by Copyright Status Report," Final Report Cont. No. OEC-1-7-070793-3559, U.S. D. HEW, Dec. 1967.

58

form of civil disobedience" and which is regarded as a leading exponent of the proposition that photocopying is an economic threat to periodical publishers. These authorities, including the Sophar report, all suffer from the same defect; they lack sufficient facts to support the conclusion reached. The Sophar report is typical. In its preparation, extensive surveys were conducted among libraries and other organizations making and using photocopies from which it was determined, presumably correctly, that a tremendous amount of photocopying was done annually. From the simple fact that the amount of annual photocopying was huge, the Sophar report concluded that such photocopying was harmful to publishers. No information of any kind was obtained from periodical or book publishers. The conclusion that photocopying is per se harmful is presented as a self-evident proposition needing no supporting evidence.

One report not cited by the Commissioner reached a contrary conclusion. This is the Fry report[1] which concluded:

---

[1] George Fry & Associates, "Survey of Copyrighted Material Reproduction Practices in Scientific and Technical Fields" Chicago, Illinois, March 1962.

59

The basic conclusion of this report is that at the present time, no significant damage occurs to the copyright holders in the scientific and technical fields although duplication of this material is widespread and is growing rapidly.

Authors of scientific and technical journal articles are notably unconcerned with the problem. In fact, the majority of them actually consider the copying of their material to be an advantage to them. By far, the greatest percentage of authors are not paid for their contributions to scientific and technical journals and, therefore, suffer no economic damage. In the final analysis, authors are concerned only from the standpoint of misuse or plagiarism.

Publishers of scientific and technical books are generally not concerned at present by the inroads of facsimile duplication practices because (1) the cost of copying an entire "in-print" book is excessive, and (2) they realize that researchers rely primarily on journal material in their work.

The numerical majority of scientific journal publishers are unconcerned about potential economic damage resulting from facsimile copying practices. This group takes the position that either the copying of copyrighted material is not widespread, or that it does not constitute a significant threat to the existence of their publications.

Unlike the Sophar report, the Fry report does include consultation with book and periodical publishers and its conclusions are based on these consultations. The Fry report was published in 1962, and this early date might diminish its pertinence were it not for the fact that its conclusions are amply supported by the financial data of record concerning plaintiff's journals.

60

NLM was organized in its present form by an Act of Congress, 70 Stat. 960, 42 U.S.C. §§ 275 et seq. This statute specifically provides that NLM shall make available medical information by supplying photographic reproductions thereof. 42 U.S.C. § 276(a)(4). As plaintiff has pointed out, at the time the NLM Act was passed, it was impossible to sue the federal government for copyright infringement; yet, individual Government employees were liable. No one could seriously assert that in passing the NLM Act Congress was ordering the Government

employees to commit acts of copyright infringement for which they would be personally liable. A more reasonable interpretation is that Congress was aware that fair use was considered to permit photocopying single copies of medical journal articles.[1] Thus, Congress' action in 1956 in directing NLM to make available photographic reproductions of medical information is further persuasive evidence of the existence and recognition of the custom of library photocopying.

A similar argument can be made with respect to the Medical Libraries Assistance Act of 1965 which provided grants for the establishment of regional medical libraries.

---

[1] Cf. Foti v. Immigration and Naturalization Service, 375 U.S. 217 at 223 (1963), where the Court held that the usages and procedures, actually followed at the time of enactment of a provision, must reasonably be regarded as composing the context of the legislation.

61

79 Stat. 1059; 42 U.S.C. § 280(b), et seq. The Congress specifically authorized that such grants could be used for the "acquisition of duplicating devices . . . to facilitate the use of the resources of the library by those who are served by it." 42 U.S.C. §§ 280(b)-8(b)(3). Again, it can hardly be contended that Congress was promoting copyright infringement. Again, the only reasonable interpretation is that Congress knew that fair use would exempt such libraries from copyright infringement in the established use by libraries of such equipment.

The Commissioner would refute this argument by saying at p. 28 that:

. . . it cannot be inferred that Congress intended the statutes to be in derogation of the copyright laws, absent an express indication to the contrary.
(Footnote omitted)

This is another example of the Commissioner using the conclusion to be reached as a premise. Defendant does not contend that the photocopying practices of its libraries are in derogation of the copyright statutes; defendant contends that such practices are fully consistent with these statutes. Further, defendant contends that such practices were considered to be consistent with the copyright statutes in 1956 and 1965 when the National Library of Medicine Act and the Medical Library Assistance Act were passed. These practices and the nearly universal

62

interpretation of them formed the background in which these Acts were passed. The purpose of the NLM Act was "to aid the dissemination and exchange of scientific and other information important to the progress of medicine and to the public health" (42 U.S.C. § 275) and the purpose of the Medical Library Assistance Act was to prevent the loss to the medical community of the value of the ever-increasing volume of medical literature through the lack of adequate facilities to disseminate such literature (42 U.S.C. § 280(a)). Contrary to the suggestion of the Commissioner, there is nothing in the express provisions or the stated purposes of these Acts which limits dissemination of medical literature to that literature which is in the public domain.

2. Wide Latitude Is Given to Scientists and Scholars in Copying Prior Copyrighted Works

The following statement from Sampson & Murdock Co. v. Seaver-Radford Co., 140 Fed. 539 at 541 (C.C.A. 1, 1905), is especially apropos here:

So, also, it is clear that, under some circumstances and for certain purposes, a subsequent publisher may draw from the earlier publication its identical words, and make use of them. This is peculiarly so with reference to works in regard to the arts and sciences, using those words in the broadest sense, because, with reference to them, any publication is given out as a development in the way of progress, and, to a certain extent, by common consent, including the implied consent of the first publisher, others interested in advancing the same art or science may commence where the prior author stopped. This includes medical

63

and legal publications, in which the entire community has an interest, and which the authors are supposed to give forth, not only for their own pecuniary profit, but for the advancement of science. Therefore as to copyrighted works of that character, by the common consent to which we have referred, subsequent authors are sometimes entitled, and, indeed, required, to make use of what precedes them in the precise form in which last exhibited, so that with regard to them the rules under the copyright statutes are very far from fitting a case like that we are now considering.

As has been pointed out above, NIH directly, and NLM ultimately, furnish photocopies of medical journal articles only to qualified medical researchers and practitioners. Moreover, the record amply demonstrates the close connection between the professional work of the persons requesting the photocopies and the subject matter of the article copied. Defendant submits that fair use does permit NIH and NLM to furnish medical literature to its users "in the precise form in which last exhibited."

3. The Need to Ensure that Copyright Promotes the Arts and Sciences

Among the many cases which have justified the application of fair use on the ground that copying of a copyrighted work must sometimes be allowed without liability to ensure that the copyright does in fact promote the arts and sciences are: Mathews Conveyor Co. v. Palmer-Bee Co., 135 F. 2d 73, 57 U.S.P.Q. 219 (C.C.A. 6, 1943); Berlin v. E.C. Publications, Inc., 329 F. 2d 541, 141 U.S.P.Q. 1 (C.A. 2, 1964); Rosemont Enterprises, Inc. v. Random House, Inc.,

64

366 F. 2d 303, 150 U.S.P.Q. 715 (C.A. 2, 1966); Time, Inc. v. Bernard Geis Associates, 293 F. Supp. 130, 159 U.S.P.Q. 663 (S.D.N.Y. 1968). In the Berlin case, the Court made the following observation at 543, 544 (3 in U.S.P.Q.):

In the words of Article 1, Section 8, of the Constitution, copyright protection is designed "To promote the Progress of Science and useful Arts," and the financial reward guaranteed to the copyright holder is but an incident of this general objective, rather than an end in itself. As a result, courts in passing upon particular claims of infringement must occasionally subordinate the copyright holder's interest in a maximum financial return to the greater public interest in the development of art, science and industry.

NIH and NLM are agencies specifically created by Congress to promote the public health and welfare through medical research and communication. The evidence of record clearly demonstrates that the library resources are essential to the achievement of these goals and that the use of photocopies of medical journal articles enables these goals to be accomplished more effectively. In addition, the evidence of record establishes that any restriction upon photocopying of medical journal articles, either by way of royalty or otherwise, can only have a deleterious effect on the practice of medicine and medical research. Such a royalty will serve only to enrich the plaintiff, without resulting in any concomitant public good.[1] Indeed, the facts disclose

[1] At two places in his opinion, the Commissioner refers to a scheme whereby plaintiff would be paid a royalty for each (Continued)

65

that plaintiff will be enriched at the expense of the public good.

The Commissioner's arguments with respect to this point are unpersuasive. It is not enough to say that the present copyright statute was the means selected by Congress to effectuate the constitutional power granted to it. The operation of the copyright statute in each case must be examined to determine if in that case the exercise of the power will be consistent with the constitutional objective of promoting the progress of science. Statutes constitutional in one case may be unconstitutional in others. Nashville C. & St. L. Ry. v. Walters, 294 U.S. 405 (1935).

Defendant is not urging that photocopying by its libraries should be excused from the operation of the copyright statute, but rather that such photocopying must be exempt from copyright restrictions if copyright in this case is to be constitutionally valid. It should be noted

[1] Continued
photocopy made by defendant's libraries (pp. 18, 29, 30). The Commissioner appears to have uncritically accepted the merits of such a scheme as exemplified by the ASCAP system and to have minimized the disadvantages of such a system applied to defendant's libraries. Defendant has never suggested such a system would be impossible to administer, but defendant has contended that administrative costs might be more than the royalties paid. As the Commissioner states, defendant did not press this point in its brief because it recognizes that

plaintiff's right to recover cannot be defeated by such difficulties. A fortiori plaintiff's right to recover can in no way depend on the ease with which defendant can be forced to pay.

66

that despite the admonishments of Mr. Justice Fortas set forth in his dissenting opinion in Fortnightly Corp. v. United Artists Television Inc., 392 U.S. 390 (1968), the Supreme Court held that CATV broadcasts were not copyright infringements. Defendant submits that this case is indeed a proper one for subordinating plaintiff's pecuniary interests in procuring a maximum profit to the Constitutional purpose of promoting the public health and welfare by the application of fair use to photocopying medical journal articles by NIH and NLM.

C. The Copyright Laws of Numerous Foreign Countries Permit the Reproduction of Journal Articles

The practice of making photocopies or other mechanical reproductions of copyrighted works is not unique to the United States. This practice also occurs in many foreign countries. The copyright laws of several foreign countries include specific provisions to cover the practice of library photocopying, while others have provisions which permit copying of works for the purpose of personal or individual study.[1]

[1] A complete compilation of foreign laws may be found in the treatise entitled Copyright Laws and Treaties of the World, compiled by the United Nations Educational, Scientific and Cultural Organization, which is periodically updated by the addition of supplements. Defendant will undertake to supply from this treatise copies of the statutes herein referred to, if needed. Complete citations to the foreign laws referred to herein are provided in the Appendix.

67

The copyright statute of the United Kingdom specifically provides that libraries may make available copies of single articles from journals without liability under certain conditions. These conditions are that the library must not be operated for profit, that the copies are to be provided for private study or research, that the person is furnished only one copy, that no more than a single article from a journal be copied, and that the person requesting the copy be required to pay the cost of making the copy. Similar provisions are contained in the copyright statute of New Zealand.

The copyright statutes of Denmark, Finland, Italy, Norway and Sweden specifically provide that a single copy of a disseminated work may be reproduced for private use and that a library may make available photographic reproductions of copyrighted works for the purpose of and use in their activities. France, the German Federal Republic, Liechtenstein, Mexico, the Netherlands and the U.S.S.R. provide in their copyright statutes that single copies of a disseminated work may be made for purposes of private research and study. Canada, India, Ireland and South Africa, while having no specific provisions permitting reproduction of copyrighted works for purposes of private study, do provide that fair dealing for purposes of private study of research shall not be an infringement.

68

These countries noted above represent the greater part of Western Europe and North America, and, perhaps not entirely coincidentally, that part which is the most technologically developed. Among the advanced nations, the United States stands alone as not having some kind of statutory provision which would permit library photocopying for purposes of research and study. Heretofore it has been assumed by nearly all concerned that the decisional law of fair use did permit libraries to make single copies of journal articles for purposes of study and research. It would be indeed unfortunate for this country to adopt a position so much out of step with its own past traditions and with the express statutory law of so much of the civilized world.

CONCLUSION

To plaintiff's charge of copyright infringement, defendant has presented three major defenses: non-ownership, non-infringement, and fair use. Defendant submits that each of these defenses has been established in fact and in law.

In retrospect, the following facts have been established:
  1. Plaintiff publishes in journals, articles on medical subjects written by various physicians, teachers, and researchers for which privilege plaintiff has paid nothing.

69

2. Plaintiff earns income from the sale of these journals (mainly through annual subscriptions) which income has increased steadily over the past ten years at a rate faster than that of the gross national product.

3. NIH and NLM furnish, in accordance with the traditional practice of libraries, single photocopies of medical journal articles to qualified medical researchers and practitioners for use in connection with their research and practice.

4. NIH and NLM have adopted policies on photocopying to ensure that their photocopying operations are fair, reasonable, and within the limits recognized by custom.

The law is as stated by the Supreme Court in Fortnightly Corp. v. United Television Artists, Inc., 392 U.S. 390, 158 U.S.P.Q. 1 (1968), that every use of a copyrighted work is not an infringement and that use short of infringement is to be encouraged. Under the facts stated above and the applicable law, defendant submits that photocopying by NIH and NLM is not an infringement. Defendant further submits that plaintiff is not entitled

70

to any compensation for the use that defendant has made of its copyrighted works.

Plaintiff's petition should be dismissed.

Respectfully submitted,

HARLINGTON WOOD, JR.
Assistant Attorney General

THOMAS J. BYRNES
Attorney
Department of Justice

71

APPENDIX

A. STATUTES REFERRED TO IN THIS BRIEF

17 U.S.C. § 1:

§ 1. Exclusive rights as to copyrighted works.

Any person entitled thereto, upon complying with the provisions of this title, shall have the exclusive right:
(a) To print, reprint, publish, copy and vend the copyrighted work; . . .

17 U.S.C. § 3:

§ 3. Protection of Component Parts of Work Copyrighted; Composite Works or Periodicals.

The copyright provided by this title shall protect all the copyrightable component parts of the work copyrighted, and all matter therein in which copyright is already subsisting, but without extending the duration or scope of such copyright. The copyright upon composite works or periodicals shall give to the proprietor thereof all the rights in respect thereto which he would have if each part were individually copyrighted under this title.

17 U.S.C. § 9:

§ 9. Authors or Proprietors, Entitled: Aliens.

The author or proprietor of any work made the subject of copyright by this title, or his executors, administrator, or assigns, shall have copyright for such work under the conditions and for the terms specified in this title: . . .

42 U.S.C. § 241:

§ 241. Research and investigations generally.

The Surgeon General shall conduct in the Service, and

encourage, cooperate with, and render assistance to other appropriate public authorities, scientific institutions, and scientists in the conduct of, and promote the

72

coordination of, research, investigations, experiments, demonstrations, and studies relating to the causes, diagnosis, treatment, control, and prevention of physical and mental diseases and impairments of man, including water purification, sewage treatment, and pollution of lakes and streams. In carrying out the foregoing the Surgeon General is authorized to --
(a) Collect and make available through publications and other appropriate means, information as to, and the practical application of, such research and other activities;

* * * *

(d) Make grants-in-aid to universities, hospitals, laboratories, and other public or private institutions, and to individuals for such research or research training projects as are recommended by the National Advisory Health Council, . . .

42 U.S.C. § 275:

§ 275. Congressional declaration of purpose; establishment

In order to assist the advancement of medical and related sciences, and to aid the dissemination and exchange of scientific and other information important to the progress of medicine and to the public health, there is established in the Public Health Service a National Library of Medicine (hereinafter referred to in this part as the "library").

42 U.S.C. § 276 Functions

(a) The Surgeon General, through the Library and subject to the provisions of subsection (c) of this section, shall --
(1) acquire and preserve books, periodicals, prints, films, recordings, and other library materials pertinent to medicine;

73

(2) organize the materials specified in clause (1) of this subsection by appropriate cataloging, indexing, and bibliographical listing;
(3) publish and make available the catalogs, indexes, and bibliographies referred to in clause (2) of this subsection;
(4) make available, through loans photographic or other copying procedures or otherwise, such materials in the Library as he deems appropriate;
(5) provide reference and research assistance; and
(6) engage in such other activities in furtherance of the purposes of this part as he deems appropriate and the Library's resources permit . . . .

§ 280b. Congressional findings and declaration of policy

(a) The Congress hereby finds and declares that (1) the unprecedented expansion of knowledge in the health sciences within the past two decades has brought about a massive growth in the quantity, and major changes in the nature of, biomedical information, materials, and publications; (2) there has not been a corresponding growth in the facilities and techniques necessary adequately to coordinate and disseminate among health scientists and practitioners the ever-increasing volume of knowledge and information which has been developed in the health science field; (3) much of the value of the ever-increasing volume of knowledge and information which has been, and continues to be, developed in the health science field will be lost unless proper measures are taken in the immediate future to develop facilities and techniques necessary to collect, preserve, store, process, retrieve, and facilitate the dissemination and utilization of, such knowledge and information.

74

(b) It is therefore the policy of this part to--
(1) assist in the construction of new, and the renovation, expansion, or rehabilitation of existing medical

library facilities;

(2) assist in the training of medical librarians and other information specialists in the health sciences;

(3) assist, through the awarding of special fellowships to physicians and other practitioners in the sciences related to health and scientists, in the compilation of existing, and the creation of additional, written matter which will facilitate the distribution and utilization of knowledge and information relating to scientific, social, and cultural advancements in sciences related to health;

(4) assist in the conduct of research and investigations in the field of medical library science and related activities, and in the development of new techniques, systems, and equipment for processing, storing, retrieving, and distributing information in the sciences related to health;

(5) assist in improving and expanding the basic resources of medical libraries and related facilities;

(6) assist in the development of a national system of regional medical libraries each of which would have facilities of sufficient depth and scope to supplement the services of other medical libraries within the region served by it; and

(7) provide financial support to biomedical scientific publications.

75

§ 280b-8. Grants for establishment of regional medical libraries--Appropriations

(a) In order to enable the Surgeon General to carry out the purposes of section 280b (b) (6) of this title, there are hereby authorized to be appropriated for each fiscal year, beginning with the fiscal year ending June 30, 1966, and ending with the fiscal year ending June 30, 1970, such sums, not to exceed $2,500,000 for any fiscal year, as may be necessary. Sums made available under this section shall be utilized by the Surgeon General, with the advice of the Board, to make grants to existing public or private nonprofit medical libraries so as to enable each of them to serve as the regional medical library for the geographical area in which it is located.

Uses for which grants may be employed

(b) The uses for which grants made under this section may be employed include, but are not limited to, the following--

(1) acquisition of books, journals, and other similar materials

(2) cataloging, binding, and other procedures for processing library resource materials for use by those who are served by the library;

(3) acquisition of duplicating devices and other equipment to facilitate the use of the resources of the library by those who are served by it;

(4) acquisition of mechanisms and employment of personnel for the speedy transmission of materials from the regional library to local libraries in the geographic area served by the regional library; and

76

(5) construction, renovation, rehabilitation, or expansion of physical plant considered necessary by such library to carry out its proper functions as a regional library.

* * * *

77

B. LIST OF CITATIONS TO FOREIGN LAWS

CANADA, Copyright Statute, Revised Statutes of Canada, 1952, Ch. 55, Section 17(2)(a).

DENMARK, Copyright Statute, Law No. 158 of 1961, May 31, 1961, Lovtidende A, 1961, No. XI, p. 295, Sections 11 & 12. See also, Royal Decree, July 21, 1962, L. A, 1962, No. 272, Section 3.

FINLAND, Copyright Act, Law No. 404, July 8, 1961, Suomen Asetuskikoelma, 1961, p. 799, Articles 11 & 12. See also, Decree No. 441 of 1961, August 25, 1961, S.A. 1961, p. 855, Article 3.

FRANCE, Copyright Statute, No. 57-296, March 11, 1957, Journal Officiel, March 14, 1957, p. 2723 and April 19, 1957, p. 41, 43, Article 41-2.

GERMAN FEDERAL REPUBLIC, Copyright Statute, September 1, 1965, Bundesgesetzblatt I, p. 1273, No. 51, September 16, 1965, Article 53. See also, Article 54.

INDIA, Copyright Act, 1957, June 4, 1957, effective January 21, 1958, Gazette of India, Extra, Part II, No. 15 of June 6, 1957 and No. 34 of January 21, 1958, Section 52(1)(a)(i).

IRELAND, Copyright Statute, April 8, 1963, Public General Acts No. 10, 1963, Section 12(1)(a).

ITALY, Copyright Statute, Law No. 633, April 22, 1941, as amended, August 23, 1946, Gazetta Ufficiale, July 16, 1941, No. 166 and August 23, 1946, No. 206, Article 68.

LIECHTENSTEIN, Copyright Statute, October 26, 1928, as amended August 8, 1959, Liechtensteiniches Landes-Gesetzblatt, No. 12, November 3, 1928 and No. 17, October 26, 1959, Article 22.

MEXICO, Copyright Statute, November 4, 1963, Diario Official, December 21, 1963, Article 18(e).

NETHERLANDS, Copyright Statute, September 23, 1912, as amended to May 22, 1958, Staatsblad, 1914, item 489, 1915, item 446, 1917, item 702, 1931, item 264, 1932, item 45, 1956, item 343, 1958, item 296, Article 17.

78

NEW ZEALAND, The Copyright Act 1962, December 5, 1962, Govt. Doc. 62942-62, Sections 21(1) & 21(2). See also, Section 19.

NORWAY, Copyright Statute, May 12, 1961, Norsk Lovtidende, 1961, p. 377, Articles 11 and 16.

REPUBLIC OF SOUTH AFRICA, Copyright Statute, May 19, 1965, Government Gazette, June 4, 1965, No. 1128, Section 10(1)(a).

SWEDEN, Copyright Statute, Law No. 729 of 1960, December 30, 1960, Svensk Forfattningssamling, 1960, p. 1949, Sections 11 & 12. See also, Royal Decree of June 2, 1961, No. 348, S.F. 1961, p. 827-830, Section 3.

U.S.S.R., Copyright Law, May 16, 1928, Sobranie Zakanov, No. 27, 1928, Texts 245 & 246, Section 9(o)

UNITED KINGDOM, Copyright Statute, November 5, 1956, 4 & 5 Elig. 2, Ch. 74, Section 7(1). See also Section 6.

Docket No. 73-68

IN THE UNITED STATES COURT OF CLAIMS

THE WILLIAMS & WILKINS CO.,
Plaintiff

v.

THE UNITED STATES,
Defendant

BRIEF AMICUS CURIAE OF THE NATIONAL EDUCATION ASSOCIATION OF THE UNITED STATES

Harry N. Rosenfield
1735 De Sales Street, N.W.
Washington, D.C. 20036

(202-393-0250)

1

QUESTIONS BEFORE THE COURT

"Putting the wrong questions is not likely to beget[1] right answers even in law," according to Mr. Justice Frankfurter. And Mr. Justice Rutledge once said:

"To state the question often is to decide it. And it may do this by failure to reveal fully what is at stake."[2]

Amicus respectfully suggests that the Commissioner's decision is in error because he put "the wrong questions" and therefore considered and restricted himself to answering other questions which fail "to reveal fully what is at stake."

Amicus believes that the dispositive questions, which were not considered by the Commissioner, are as follows:

1. Constitutional
   Does "fair use" have constitutional protection under the Bill of Rights? And if so, what is the relationship between such constitutional protection and the status of the copyright holder under the copyright provision of the Constitution?

---

[1] Vanston Bondholders Prot. Com. v. Green et al., 329 U.S. 156, 170 (1946) (concurring)
[2] Yakus v. U. S., 321 U.S. 414, 482 (1944) (dissenting)

2

2. Custom and "Fair Use"
   Is a customary use a "fair use," without regard to the normally applicable criteria used in the absence of such custom?

Only if the answer to both of these questions was in the negative was it appropriate for the Commissioner to embark on the consideration of the "criteria" for "fair use." Amicus respectfully suggests, as it will attempt to show hereinafter, that the answer to the proper questions here posed is as follows:

1. Constitutional
   "Fair use" has constitutional protection under both the First and Ninth Amendments. Reasonable resort to this protection has priority over the mere privilege accorded to the copyright owner by permissive and non-mandatory action of the Congress under the copyright clause of Article I, §8.

2. Custom and "Fair Use"
   A customary use is a fair use, without need for compliance with criteria which are applicable and necessary where custom is not involved.

The Commissioner's failure to pose and answer these threshold questions makes his decision fatally erroneous in law, for having failed to deal with the proper issues at stake in this case.

3

THE INTEREST OF THE NATIONAL EDUCATION ASSOCIATION

The Commissioner's decision seriously threatens adverse effects upon millions of teachers and multiple-millions of students in America's schools. If the Commissioner's decision is allowed to stand, it could well limit the capacity of the American school system to teach effectively.

The National Education Association of the United States (incorporated under a statute of the Congress) is the largest professional organization in the United States. With the combined membership of its State and local affiliates, the NEA represents some two-million of the nation's educators, with elementary and secondary classroom teachers and college professors making up about 90% of its membership.

The NEA is an independent, voluntary, nongovernmental organization that works for better schools. To further this end, it strives for the improvement of the professional status of teachers.

NEA's interest in the copyright law is of long standing. For example, in 1963, it was instrumental in creating an Ad Hoc Committee on Copyright Law Revision, which includes representatives of some 42 educational organizations covering the full-range of education in the United States. This independent committee has been chaired by an NEA staff member. The group meets regularly to study proposed copyright legislation

4

and to make recommendations to the Congress in behalf of the public interest.

The NEA's own resolution on copyright law revision, passed by its Delegate Assembly, starts with the following sentences:

"The National Education Association believes that maximum access to teaching materials is of vital concern to every teacher."

The copyright law affects the teaching process at its inner core. Formerly, teachers tended to use the same textbooks for all pupils. Today's teacher uses many resources in his teaching. He has a variety of texts and supplementary materials, including trade and reference books, newspapers and magazines, educational motion pictures, film strips, audio and video tapes and cartridges, overhead transparency projectors, record players, slides, instructional TV and radio, programmed instructional material, and computer-assisted instruction. The modern teacher uses all of these resources in orchestration to do specific jobs. He selects resources to fit particular learner needs and objectives. Those teachers are most effective who capture the mood of the moment, who use some suddenly discovered motivation of their pupils at the teachable moment. The copyrighted works most needed by teachers are recent and contemporaneous materials, not text books. Teachers want to update texts and have their classroom work relevant and meaningful to current developments. It is because of such materials and needs, and because of the newer educational technologies, that most of education's

5

copyright problems arise.

Perhaps the most dramatic example of the kind of copyright problems faced by teachers was the reading of Robert Frost's poem, "The Gift Outright," at President Kennedy's inauguration. Many English teachers used it in the immediately following days, to illustrate the value of poetry in capturing the spirit and essence of a key moment in our national consciousness. The poem was copyrighted but not available in any textbook. Should a teacher deprive his students of such a universal national experience because the poem was not in the textbook? For many younger students in American schools this might be the first introduction to one of America's outstanding poets. Obviously, teachers could not have planned ahead for this situation. The copyright problems of teachers are infrequently so dramatically illustrated as with the Frost poem but they occur daily and are critical to meeting the needs of effective teaching.

Would it advance the public interest, would it be consonant with the provisions and purpose of the copyright clause of the Constitution, to lose the teachable moment by waiting for months to get the book through purchase, for a one-time use whose timeliness would long since have disappeared?

NEA believes that immediate use of the Frost poem was a typical educational "fair use" authorized under the copyright law. Such use is consonant with the Supreme Court's concept of the importance of education today:

"Today, education is perhaps the most important function of state and local government. . .It is required in the performance of our most basic

6

responsibilities. . .It is the very foundation of good citizenship. Today it is a principal instrument for awakening. . .cultural values, in preparing. . .for later professional training and in helping. . .to adjust normally to his environment."[3]

The most seriously adverse impact of the Commissioner's decision directly upon education is his erroneous and improperly limited interpretation of "fair use." The NEA believes that the Constitution's copyright clause and the "fair use" doctrine must be interpreted so as to support, not to restrict, good teaching practices, by assuring non-profit and non-commercial educational purposes of a reasonable and ready access to teaching materials. In particular, the Commissioner's opinion threatens two aspects of "fair use" that are of utmost importance to America's pupils and teachers:

(1) the customary and long-established practice of teachers in making limited copies of copyrighted materials for classroom use and teaching purposes, and

(2) the opportunity to meet instructional requirements through access to copyrighted materials by means of the new educational technologies.

Special Problem: Legislation Under Consideration. As already indicated, this case involves more than the customary concern of an amicus. Far more is involved here. The Commissioner's decision may well decide the meaning of pending Congressional legislation for comprehensive copyright revision in a manner wholly inconsistent with the Congressional understanding of the meaning of "fair use" as interpreted by the courts.

[3] *Brown* v. *Board of Education*, 347 U.S. 483, 493 (1954).

7

For many years the Congress has been considering proposals for comprehensive revision of the current copyright law which was adopted in 1909. Extensive hearings have been completed in both the House and the Senate. Thus far, only the House has passed a bill. The House Judiciary Committee reported a bill in 1966 (H. Rep. No. 2237, 89th Con., 2d Sess); and again in 1967 (H. Rep. No. 83, 90th Cong., 1st Sess).

The report of the House Judiciary Committee clearly reflects vigorous and controversial debate, during extensive hearings, over the meaning of "fair use" for education. For the first time, the Committee proposed statutory recognition of "fair use." The House report indicated some key factors behind its judgment

    (1) There are no judicial precedents for the meaning of "fair use" in connection with nonprofit schools.[4]

    (2) In adopting statutory "fair use," the Committee "intended to restate the present judicial doctrine of fair use," neither augmenting nor constricting it.[5]

[4] "...the case law on fair use has not dealt with photocopying and the analogous forms of reproduction" for educational purposes. "...as to cases of copying by teachers...in this area there are few if any judicial guidelines,". House Rep. No. 2237, 89th Cong., 2nd Sess, on H.R. 4347, pp. 60-1. See also statement by Copyright Office's General Counsel: "...The decisions have not dealt with copying specifically for the purpose of teaching or research. The formulation in the bill does; it cites, as examples of purposes for which copying or other uses might qualify as fair use...", Goldman, *Can Copyright Law Revision Respond to the New Technology*?, 64 LAW LIBRARY J. (No. 4, Nov. 1968), 387 at 393.
[5] House Rep. No. 83, 90th Cong. 1st Sess (1967), p. 32.

8

    (3) To give some guidelines of what such statutorily-adopted judicial "fair use" means, the Committee set forth at length specific examples of school and teaching activities which in its judgment are such "fair use."

The significant fact is that in arriving at such examples, the House Judiciary Committee relied on no judicial precedents and cited none. Instead, virtually all of its examples as to legally acceptable educational "fair use" were adopted substantially, if not in *haec verbi*, from examples which a parade of educational witnesses had described as being the long-standing *custom* of schools and teachers.[6] Thus, we have here a Congressional understanding that judicial "fair use" derives from the *custom followed in schools.*

Amicus respectfully suggests that there is a fundamental inconsistency as to the origin and meaning of "fair use," between the House Judiciary Committee's Report and the Commissioner's decision, and that such difference might be crucial to the operability of America's schools. The Commissioner's view undercuts the understanding of the House Judiciary Committee as to the judicial doctrine of "fair use" and therefore vitiates the entire basis for the House's action. The Commissioner's failure to accept and give effect to customary use as "fair use" runs directly counter to the obvious intent and understanding of the House Committee in turning to educational custom to describe the judicial "fair use" which it was accepting by statute for educa-

[6] See, for example, *New Technology and the Law of Copyright: Reprography and Computers,* 15 UCLA L. REV. 939, 953 (1968).

9

tional purposes.

Briefly, the House Judiciary Committee's report is specifically designed, in part, to protect the educational community of America[7], by specifying what "fair use" means for the nation's schools. The Commissioner's decision, on the other hand, negates the substance of that legislative understanding. Amicus seeks, among other things, to vindicate the basic concept of "fair use" upon which the House Committee's report is based, and which is rejected by the Commissioner's decision, *i.e.,* that customary use is "fair use."

What is at stake here, therefore, is not only the future of judicial determinations of "fair use" under the present law but also the meaning, *in futuro,* of comprehensive copyright law revision so far as it intimately affects America's schools.

ARGUMENT

I. CONSTITUTIONAL ISSUES

At Heart of Case

Constitutional issues are at the very heart of this case - but they were ignored by the Commissioner.

Amicus respectfully suggests that "fair use" (or the right of reasonable access to copyrighted materials) has constitutional protection under the First and Ninth Amendments in the Bill of Rights.

[7] House Rep. No. 2237, 89th Cong., 2nd Sess., on H.R. 4347 at pp. 60-1.

10

Despite the Commissioner's silence on the substantial and dispositive constitutional issues, his opinion infringes heavily upon the constitutionally-protected right of reasonable access to the cultural, educational, scientific, historical, technical and intellectual heritage of the Nation.

This right has constitutional protection directly and under the penumbra of

    (a) the First Amendment (Freedom of Press), and

    (b) the Ninth Amendment.

This case involves a conflict between

    (a) the American public's *constitutional right* of reasonable access to copyrighted materials, and

    (b) the copyright owner's *statutory privilege* emanating from the copyright law. In this latter connection, as will be shown, the Constitution gives *no* constitutional *right* to copyright owners. It merely authorizes the Congress, under severe limitations, to enact copyright legislation. At most, therefore, the copyright owner has a statutory *privilege*, not a constitutional *right.*

Consequently, in the necessary "balancing" process which the Court must undertake, the "balance" must be in favor of the overriding and constitutionally-protected right of the American public to reasonable access to its national heritage, copyrighting notwithstanding. In this context, "fair use" - as a constitutionally protected right - fully sanctions the defendant's practice in the instant case.

11

Need for Constitutional Decision

The Supreme Court has said: "Federal statutes are to be so construed as to avoid serious doubt of their constitutionality."[8] Elsewhere the Supreme Court has

    "repeatedly held that as between two possible interpretations of a statute, by one of which it would be unconstitutional and by the other valid, our plain duty is to adopt that which will save the act. Even to avoid a serious doubt the rule is the same."[9]

Amicus respectfully submits that, in order to avoid an unconstitutional result as applied to the facts of this case, the proper application of the First Amendment's provision protecting Freedom of Press and the Ninth Amendment's reservation of unenumerated rights to the people requires interpreting the copyright clause of the Constitution and the term "fair use" to encompass the long-established practice followed by defendant in this case.

Even where it has not been necessary to reach constitutional issues to decide a case before it, the Supreme Court has specifically expressed its view on the constitutional questions which would have been present "if reached by the court."[10] On occasion the Supreme Court has deliberately decided to reach the

[8] *International Association of Machinists* v. *Street,* 367 U.S. 740, 749 (1961). See also *Dennis* v. *United States,* 341 U.S. 494, 501 (1951); *Communist Party* v. *Gatherwood,* 367 U.S. 389, 392 (1961).
[9] *NLRB* v. *Jones & Laughlin Steel Corp.,* 301 U.S. 1, 30 (1937). See also *United States* v. *Rumely,* 345 U.S. 41, 45 (1953) and cases therein cited.
[10] *Peters* v. *Hobby,* 349 U.S. 331 (1955); *Kent* v. *Dulles,* 357 U.S. 116, 129-130 (1958). *Semble, Rice* v. *Sioux City Cemetery,* 349 U.S. 70, 72 (1955). See also *Volanski* v. *United States,* 246 F. 2d 842, 845 (6th Cir. 1957), per Stewart, C.J.

12

constitutional issue, although the case could have been decided on other grounds, because it was necessary to solve such constitutional issue in order to avoid future difficulties.[11]

The Supreme Court has also indicated that it will delve into certain areas, albeit rarely,

"not only to make sure that substantive constitutional standards have not been thwarted, but also to provide guidance for the future to the lower courts in an area which borders so closely upon constitutionally protected rights."[12]

The instant case is peculiarly fitting, and calls out, for constitutional clarification and interpretation.

This Court may be confronted with the argument that, after all, the Constitution does authorize the Congress to enact copyright legislation. Without reference to the limited authority thus conferred, and without further reference to the amicus's illustration of the difference between a constitutional right and a statutory privilege, a recent statement of the Supreme Court is applicable:

"The existence of a permissible purpose cannot sustain an action that has an impermissible effect."[13]

In that case, the Supreme Court said it "focused upon the effect

---

[11]Youngstown Sheet and Tube Co. v. Sawyer, 343 U.S. 579, 585 (1952). Cf. United States v. U. S. Gypsum Co., 333 U.S. 364, 387 (1948) ("While this issue need not be decided to dispose of this case, it seems inadvisable to leave the decision as a precedent.")
[12]Scales v. U.S.A., 367 U.S. 203, 230 (1961).
[13]Wright v. Emporia City Council, 407 U.S.   , 40 LW 4806, 4810 (1972).

13

- not the purpose or motivation - . . ."[14]

As Justice Black declared in another context,

"Freedom of the Press from governmental interference under the First Amendment does not sanction repression of that freedom by private interests."[15]

Very recently, the Supreme Court also stated that

"A clear and precise enactment may nevertheless be 'overbroad' if in its reach it prohibits constitutionally protected conduct."[16]

The constitutional issue is clearly before the court and requires adjudication in this case.

A. The Constitution Grants No Rights to Copyright Owners

Article I, §8, of the Constitution grants no rights to authors; it merely grants power to Congress to enact copyright legislation. The Supreme Court so ruled in the very first case in which it considered this problem. There, counsel for complainants insisted that the constitutional provisions did not originate a right but merely protected one already in existence. The Supreme Court specifically rejected this argument:

"Congress then, by this act, instead of sanctioning an existing right, as contended for, created it. . . .This right, as has been shown,

---

[14]Ibid.
[15]Associated Press v. U.S., 326 U.S. 1, 20 (1945).
[16]Grayned v. City of Rockford,   U.S.   , 40 LW 4881, 4884 (1972).

14

does not exist at common law -- it originated, if at all, under the Acts of Congress."[17]

The House Report on the current Copyright Law of 1909 also made this same point crystal clear:

"The enactment of copyright legislation by Congress under the terms of the Constitution is not based upon any natural right that the author has in his writings, for the Supreme Court has held that such rights as he has are purely statutory rights. . . .The Constitution does not establish such rights, but provides that Congress shall have the power to grant such rights if it thinks best."[18]

There is a long and uninterrupted line of cases holding unequivocally that copyright protection is completely and solely a matter of statute,[19] and that copyright is only a privilege or a franchise.[20] Under Supreme Court rulings it is settled law that any copyright right is simply a creature of statute.[21] As distinguished from literary property, copyright

---

[17]Wheaton v. Peters, 8 Pet. 591, 661, 663 (1834). To the same effect, see Mazer v. Stein, 347 U.S. 201, 214 (1954); Fox Film Corp. v. Doyal, 286 U.S. 123, 127 (1932); Caliga v. Inter Ocean Newspaper Co., 215 U.S. 182, 188 (1909).
[18]House Report No. 2222, 60th Cong., 2d Sess., p. 7.
[19]Miller Music Corp. v. Daniels, Inc., 362 U.S. 373, 375 (1960); Bentley v. Tibbals, 223 F. 247, 248 (2d Cir. 1915); Grant v. Kellogg Co., 58 F. Supp. 48, 52 (S.D. N.Y. 1944), aff'd 154 F. 2d 59 (2d Cir. 1946); Bobbs-Merrill Co. v. Strauss, 210 U.S. 339, 346 (1908).
[20]Local Landmarks v. Price, 170 F.2d 715, 718 (5th Cir. 1948).

---

[21]American Tobacco Co. v. Werckmeister, 207 U.S. 284, 291 (1907); Bobbs-Merrill Co. v. Strauss, supra n. 19, at 346, White-Smith Music Pub. Co. v. Apollo, 147 F.226, 227 (2d Cir. 1906), aff'd 209 U.S. 1, 15 (1908). See also Loew's Inc. v. C.B.S., 131 F.Supp. 165, 173 (1955), aff'd 239 F.2d 532 (9th Cir. 1956), aff'd by equally divided court, 356 U.S. 43 (1958).

15

is wholly a matter of Congressional discretion to grant or to withhold.[22] The Supreme Court recently held that in connection with copyrights "the Constitution is permissive" not mandatory.[23]

The Supreme Court has also held that the conditions upon which copyright is granted are wholly within the constitutional power of Congress to prescribe.[24] The whole history of the copyright law shows that an author has no constitutional property right in or to copyright protection and that such "right" as an author obtains is a privilege to be granted or withheld by Congress in its discretion. As the House Report on the present copyright law said of copyright rights granted to authors: ". . .Congress has the power to annex to them such conditions as it deems wise and expedient."[25] The very first copyright law, enacted in 1790, 1 STAT. p. 124, c 15, gave protection only to maps, charts and books, and that only for a 14-year period plus renewal of 14 years. It did not cover periodicals, drawings, works of art, musical composition, dramatic composition -- to name but a few. And even the

---

[22]Kraft v. Cohen, 117 F.2d 579, 580 (3d Cir. 1941); Keene v. Wheatley, 14 Fed.Cas. 180, 185 #7644 (Cir.Ct.Pa. 1820).
[23]Deepsouth Packing Co., Inc. v. The Laitram Corp., 406 U.S. 518, 530 (1972).
[24]Wheaton v. Peters, supra n. 17, at 663-4 (1834). See also Application of Cooper, 254 F.2d 611, 616 (C.C.P.A. 1958), cert. denied 358 U.S. 840 (1958); Stuff v. La Budde Feed & Grain Co., 42 F. Supp. 493, 496 (E.D. Wis. 1941) (See NIMMER ON COPYRIGHTS (1972), p. 14.).
[25]Op. cit., supra n. 18, p. 9.

16

present far more extensive law of 1909 is not all-inclusive and places limits on author's copyright privileges. Congress has limited the number of years during which an author may exercise copyright privileges. Congress has limited the uses to which the copyright owner's copyright privileges attach, i.e., the "for profit" limitation on public performance rights; compulsory licenses; the non-inclusion of "rental rights," to cite but a few.

In addition to Congressional limitations of any so-called "property" rights in copyright, the courts have also developed a further limitation through the doctrine of "fair use," of which more will be said hereinafter.

Thus, it is clear that copyright is a privilege conferred by statute and not a right guaranteed by the Constitution.

B. The First Amendment Protects the American People's Right of Reasonable Access to Matter Subject to Copyright.

The Commissioner's interpretation of "fair use" under the copyright law denies defendant (and, as well, millions of teachers and students) the right of Freedom of the Press under the First Amendment, because of his limitation of defendant's right of reasonable access to the cultural heritage of the nation.

1. Constitutional Rights of the American People are at Stake Here,

The American people's rights are at stake here, although they do not appear as party to the suit. And more

---

17

particularly, the rights of America's teachers and students, as individuals and as teachers and students, are in jeopardy if the Commissioner's decision be upheld.

The Bill of Rights exemplified a clear rationale for Freedom of Press, that a free press was the only instrumentality for protecting the American people's right to know.

The Supreme Court has long recognized that a free press is essential to a free people. Mr. Justice Black wrote for the Court:

"The First Amendment. . .rests on the assumption that the widest possible dissemination of information from diverse and antagonistic sources is essential to the welfare of the public, that a free press is a condition of a free society."[26]

Mr. Justice Frankfurter said in the same case that "the business of the press. . .is the promotion of truth regarding public matters by furnishing the basis for an understanding of them," and that the basic function which a Constitutionally guaranteed free press serves in our nation "is to have the flow of news not trammeled."[27]

Throughout our national history this concept of the press as an instrumentality of the American people has been pervasive in judicial readings of the First Amendment. Mr. Justice Sutherland wrote in connection with a claim of

[26]Associated Press v. U.S., 326 U.S. 1, 20 (1945).
[27]Ibid., pp. 28, 29.

18

abridgement of freedom of press:
"The predominant purpose of the grant of immunity here invoked was to preserve an untrammelled press as a vital source of public information."[28]

Freedom of Press is a right of the American people; the press is a trustee of that right. Freedom of Press was not designed as a special privilege for the publishing business, but rather as an extension of the personal rights of each American. It is a guaranty of the individual's rights, and was thus joined in the First Amendment of the Bill of Rights with the rights of free speech, assembly and petition.

The Supreme Court has characterized "the freedom of speech and that of press as fundamental personal rights and liberties. The phrase is not an empty one and was not lightly used. It reflects the belief of the framers of the Constitution that exercise of the rights lies at the foundation of free government by free men."[29]

The Supreme Court has recognized that the First Amendment's guarantee of freedom of press is "not for the benefit of the press so much as for the benefit of us all."[30]

"Free press" is only a shorthand way of saying that the press must be free because of the right of all Americans to

[28]Grosjean v. American Press Co., 297 U.S. 233, 250 (1936).
[29]Schneider v. State, 308 U.S. 147, 161 (1939).
[30]Time, Inc. v. Hill, 385 U.S. 374, 389 (1967). See also United States v. Powell, 171 F. Supp. 202, 205 (N.D. Calif. S.D. 1959).

19

be informed. Arthur Hays Sulzberger of The New York Times addressed the Trustees of the New York Public Library on this issue:

"Perhaps we ought to ask ourselves now just what freedom of the press really is. . .Freedom of press -- or, to be more precise, the benefit of freedom of the press -- belongs to everyone, to the citizen as well as the publisher. The publisher is not granted the privilege of independence simply to provide him with a more favored position in the community than is accorded to other citizens. He enjoys an explicitly defined independence because it is the only condition under which he can fully perform his role, which is to inform fully, fairly and comprehensively. The crux is not the publisher's freedom to print; it is rather the citizen's right to know! What I would point out is that freedom of the press is your right as citizens and not mine as a publisher."[31]

Col. Robert R. McCormick of the Chicago Tribune said: "The freedom of the press is the freedom of the American people."[32]

The Editor-in-Chief of the Waterbury (Conn.) Republican American, E. R. Stevenson, wrote: "Let us consider what freedom of the press is. It is really something that belongs to all the people and is not the treasured possession of a privileged class known as Editors."[33]

[31]Nov. 13, 1956. Privately printed, p. 9. (Available at New York Public Library, 42nd Street Branch, New York City.)
[32]McCormick, THE CASE FOR FREEDOM OF THE PRESS 23 (1933).
[33]What is Freedom of the Press, SPECIAL LIBRARIES, Vol. 32, No. 6, pp. 206-08 (July-August 1941).

20

Elisha Hanson, distinguished counsel for the American Publishers Association, put it thus:
"The right to have a free press is the right of the people, not a privilege of a particular segment of our economy engaged in the business of gathering and disseminating information in printed form. Publishers are but trustees of this right."[34]

2. Right of Access

The right of access, as such, has been increasingly recognized by the Supreme Court as an integral part of the rights guaranteed by the Bill of Rights. Thus,
- the right of "suitable access to social, political, esthetic, moral and other ideas and experiences. . ."[35]
- the right to "receive information and ideas"[36]
- the right to receive printed matter[37]
- the right of access to certain religious publications[38]
- the right of access to a sufficient library to permit prisoners to prepare legal papers[39]

[34]The Two Bulwarks of Liberty: A Free Press and an Independent Judiciary, 41 A.B.A.J. 217, 218 (1955).
[35]Red Lion Broadcasting Co. v. F.C.C., 395 U.S. 367, 290 (1969).
[36]Kleindienst v. Mandel et al., 408 U.S. , 40 LW 5103 (June 29, 1972); Stanley v. Georgia, 394 U.S. 557, 564 (1969).
[37]Lamont v. Postmaster General, 381 U.S. 301 (1965).
[38]Cruz v. Beto, 405 U.S. 319 (1972).
[39]Martin v. City of Struthers, 318 U.S. 141, 143 (1943). See also Younger et al. v. Gilmore et al., 404 U.S. 15 (1971) (under equal protection clause of 14th Amendment).

21

- the right of access to the courts.[40]
Just as such rights of access are ancillary to, and come within the penumbra of, rights protected by the Bill of Rights[41] (or other provisions of the Constitution), so the right of reasonable access (through ' fair use") to copyrighted materials pertaining to the cultural, historical, educational, scientific, technical, and religious heritage of the nation comes within the penumbra of the right of Free Press guaranteed by the First Amendment.

3. The Right of Free Press Includes the RIGHT TO READ

The First Amendment would be sterile today if its sanctions were limited to the mere act of printing. The Zenger Case decided that over 200 years ago.[42] The Supreme Court has not so limited Freedom of Press:

[40]California Motor Transport Co. et al., v. Trucking Unlimited, 404 U.S. 508, 513 (1972).
[41]For the right to hear as being within the penumbra of the Freedom of Speech provision of the First Amendment, see Thomas v. Collins, 323 U.S. 516, 534 (1945). See also Molpus v. Fortune, 432 F.2d 916 (5th Cir. 1970); Picklings v. Bruce, 430 F.2d 595, 598-9 (6th Cir. 1970); Brooks v. Auburn University, 412 F.2d 1171, 1172 (5th Cir. 1969); ACLU v. Radford, 315 F. Supp. 893 (E.D. Va. 1970); Smith v. University of Tennessee, 300 F.Supp. 777 (E.D. Tenn. 1969); Snyder v. Board of Trustees, 286 F.Supp. 927 (N.D. Ill. 1968).
[42]As far back as 1644, Milton's Areopagitica was a defense of "the liberty of unlicensed printing," McKEON, MERTON & GELLHORN, THE FREEDOM TO READ 43 (1957).

22

"Liberty of circulating is as essential to that freedom as liberty of publishing; indeed, without the circulation, the publication would be of little value."[43]
The Supreme Court has ruled that Freedom of Press protects not only the publishers right to print[44] and to publish[45], and the distributor's right to circulate[46], but also the public's "right to receive information and ideas"[47] and the public's right to read, Butler v. Michigan, 352 U.S. 380 (1957), involved a state statute which made a criminal offense of the publication, sale and distribution of any literature "tending to the corruption of the morals of youth." The statute was challenged as an unconstitutional infringement of freedom of press and due process under the First and Fourteenth Amendments. The

[43]In the Matter of Jackson, 96 U.S. 727, (1878), cited with approval in Lovell v. Griffin, 303 U.S. 444, 452 (1938).
[44]Lovell v. Griffin, supra n. 43, at 452; Winters v. New York, 333 U.S. 507, 509 (1948). See also, Marsh v. Alabama, 326 U.S. 501 (1946); Martin v. City of Struthers, 319 U.S. 141 (1943).
[45]Grosjean v. American Press Co., supra n. 28, at 250; New York Times v. Sullivan, 376 U.S. 254, 270 (1964).
[46]In the Matter of Jackson, supra n. 43; Winters v. New York, supra n. 44.
[47]Kleindienst v. Mandel et al., supra n. 36; Stanley v. Georgia, supra n. 36, at 564; Red Lion Broadcasting Co. v. F.C.C., supra n. 38, at 390; Griswold v. Connecticut, 381 U.S. 479, 482 (1965); Lamont v. Postmaster General, supra n. 37, at 307-8 (Brennan, concurring). See also, New York Times Co. v. U.S., 403 U.S. 713 (1971).

23

State's Attorney General denied that the statute did violence either to the free press clause of the First Amendment or to the due process clause of the Fourteenth Amendment. And the

Attorney General of Texas, amicus curiae, claimed that the book there in question was not within the protection of the First Amendment's freedom of press.

The Court unanimously found the statute unconstitutional:
"The incidence of this enactment is to reduce the adult population of Michigan to reading only what is fit for children. It thereby arbitrarily curtails one of those liberties of the individual, now enshrined in the Due Process Clause of the Fourteenth Amendment, that history has attested as the indispensable conditions for the maintenance and progress of a free society." (384-85)

Butler was decided in 1957. Again in 1965, the Supreme Court proclaimed the right - specifically - of school teachers to read, as part of their First Amendment rights, Lamont v. Postmaster General, supra n. 37 at 307. And in 1969, a plaintiff claimed "the right to read" and the Supreme Court confirmed that right, Stanley v. Georgia, supra n. 36 at 565.

A leading scholar in this field recognized that
". . .the readers and consumers. . .have more at stake than anybody else."[48]

[48]Chafee, Reflections on the Law of Copyright: I, 45 COL. L. REV. 503, 517 (1945).

24

Thus, the Constitution protects more than freedom to print; without reading by the public "publication would be of little value."

The constitutional protection for Freedom of Press was designed to achieve an end, the right of the public to read. In order to accomplish this end -- which the Supreme Court has ruled to be included within the constitutional protection of each individual American -- it is necessary to have reasonable access. Freedom of Press must at the very least, include freedom of access to materials affecting the educational, cultural, historical, political, scientific and religious background of the nation. Anything less would hamstring the fundamental objective of the First Amendment, the people's right to read.

The applicable reach of the First Amendment is well illustrated by the recent decision of the Supreme Court in Kleindienst v. Mandel et al., supra n. 36, where both the majority and the minority agreed that the First Amendment guaranteed access to hear, to receive information, to learn, to know. Mr. Justice Powell, for the Court, said:
"In a variety of contexts this Court has referred to a First Amendment right to 'receive information and ideas.' 'It is now well established that the Constitution protects the right to receive information and ideas. This freedom [of speech and press] . . .necessarily protects the right to receive. . .' Martin v. City of Struthers, 319 U.S. 141, 143 (1943). . .Stanley v. Georgia, 394 U.S. 557, 564 (1969)."

He also cited Thomas v. Collins, supra n. 41, at 534 (1945) as protecting the right of workers "to hear what he [a labor

25

organizer] had to say." The 1972 decision also cited Red Lion Broadcasting Co. v. F.C.C., supra, at 38, where Mr. Justice White, for the unanimous Court, concerning the FCC's "fairness doctrine," stated of the First Amendment:
". . .It is the right of the public to receive suitable access to social, political, esthetic, moral and other ideas and experiences which is crucial here. That right may not be constitutionally abridged either by Congress or by the F.C.C."

The Kleindienst Case also cited Lamont v. Postmaster General, supra n. 37, upholding the right of an American citizen to receive communist political propaganda as a First Amendment right, and Mr. Justice Powell stated that "This Court has recognized that this right is 'nowhere more vital' than in our schools and universities. . ."

Mr. Justice Powell also cited with approval the following from the District Court's opinion:
"The concern of the First Amendment is. . .with the rights of the citizens of the country to have the alien enter and to hear him explain and seek to defend his views; that is of the essence of free government," 325 F.Supp., at 631.

In a comment peculiarly appropriate to the instant case, Mr. Justice Powell stated:
"The Government also suggests that the First Amendment is inapplicable because appellees have free access to Mandel's ideas through his books and speeches. . .While alternative means of access to Mandel's ideas might be a

relevant factor were we called upon to balance First Amendment rights against governmental regulatory interests -- a balance we find unnecessary here in the light of the discussion that follows. . . - we are loath to hold on this record that existence of other alternatives extinguishes

26

altogether any constitutional interest on the part of the appellees in this particular form of access." at (5106)
". . .the Court's previous decisions concerning the 'right to receive information',. . .'" (to use Powell's expression, at p. 5106) were accepted by the dissenting opinions. Mr. Justice Douglas, wrote (at page 5108):
"The First Amendment involves not only the right to speak and publish but also the right to hear, to learn, to know. Martin v. Struthers, 319 U.S. 141, 143; Stanley v. Georgia, 394 U.S. 557, 564."

And Mr. Justice Marshall's dissenting opinion, in which Mr. Justice Brennan joined, states:
"As the majority correctly demonstrates, in a variety of contexts this Court has held that the First Amendment protects the right to receive information and ideas, the freedom to hear as well as the freedom to speak. . .the right to speak and hear - including the right to inform others and be informed about public issues - are inextricably part of that process. The freedom to speak and the freedom to hear are inseparable; they are two sides of the same coin."

The comments of both majority and minority in Kleindienst, concerning the right to hear, as part of the First·Amendment, apply with equal force to the right to read, and the right of access to copyrighted reading matter.

But, it may be asked, where is there anything in the First Amendment about "the right to read?" The same sort of question was faced directly by Justice Brennan in a case where the very issue of the right to read was involved and where the Court specifically stated that the First Amendment rights of

27

school teachers protected their right to read.[49] In a concurring opinion, Mr. Justice Brennan said:
"It is true that the First Amendment contains no specific guarantee of access to publications. However, the protection of the Bill of Rights goes beyond the specific guarantees to protect from congressional abridgement those equally fundamental personal rights necessary to make the express guarantees fully meaningful. . .I think the right to receive publications is such a fundamental right. The dissemination of ideas can accomplish nothing if otherwise willing addressees are not free to receive and consider them. It would be a barren marketplace of ideas that had only sellers and no buyers." (at 308)

In a similar situation concerning the right of association, Mr. Justice Powell gave the Supreme Court's answer to this sort of inquiry:
"Among the rights protected by the First Amendment is the right of individuals to associate to further their personal beliefs. While the freedom of association is not explicitly set out in the Amendment, it has long been held to be implicit in the freedom of speech, assembly and petition."[50]

He also stated that ". . .the Constitution's protection is not limited to direct interference with fundamental rights." Mr. Justice Powell made a point that is relevant in the current case: "We are not free to disregard the practical realities."

On the facts of the instant case, defendant's

[49]Lamont v. Postmaster General, supra n. 37 at 307.
[50]Healy et al. v. James et al., 408 U.S.   , 40 LW 4887, 4891 (June 26, 1972).

28

practice is within the permissible realm of "fair use" which derives from the right of access that is constitutionally-protected by the First Amendment's Free Press clause. For the purpose of this case, it is not necessary to decide the outer reach of such right.

4. The First Amendment Protects the Student's Right to Learn

The First Amendment protects, as has already been indicated,
  - the right of "suitable access to social, political, esthetic,

moral and other ideas and experiences"
- the right to "receive information and ideas"
- the right to receive printed matter
- the right to hear
- the "right to read"

So far as the student is concerned, all of these constitutionally protected rights add up to the RIGHT TO LEARN, a right that derives directly from the First Amendment.[51]

[51] A similar protection emanates from the Fourteenth Amendment. Meyer v. Nebraska, 262 U.S. 390 (1923) ("...denotes....the right of individual to acquire useful knowledge...") See also Serrano v. Priest, 5 Cal. 3d 584, 589, 487 Pac. 2d 1241 (1971). (At 618: "...in a democratic society free public schools shall make available to all children equally the abundant gifts of learning."). See also Hobson v. Hanson, 269 F.Supp. 401, 480, 488, 492, 512-3 (1967), app. dism'd, 393 U.S. 801 (1969) where the Court struck down a school board's "track system" of assigning pupils as being contrary to their right to learn. The decision was based on the equal protection clause.

29

The Supreme Court said that the "aim" of the First Amendment "was to unlock all ideas..."[52] Mr. Justice Douglas said that

"...the First Amendment involves...the right...to learn, to know..."[53]

This constitutionally-protected right to learn requires reasonable access, through "fair use," to copyrighted materials which are basic to the learning process.

5. The First Amendment Protects the Freedom of Teachers and Students to Reasonable Access to Copyrighted Materials

The Supreme Court has said that
"The vigilant protection of constitutional freedom is nowhere more vital than in the community of American schools."[54]

This right involves not only the defendant in this case but also the teaching process in the United States, with its many million teachers and students. And, of course, children are within the protection of the Bill of Rights. "Neither the Fourteenth Amendment nor the Bill of Rights is for adults alone."[55] The Sixth Amendment protects a 12-year old,[56]

[52] Times Film Corp. v. Chicago, 365 U.S. 43, 81 (1969).
[53] Kleindienst v. Mandel et al., supra n. 36, at 5108 (dissenting). For the "right to know" under the Ninth Amendment, see infra.
[54] Shelton v. Tucker, 364 U.S. 479, 487 (1960).
[55] In re Gault, 387 U.S. 1, 13 (1967).
[56] In re Winship, 397 U.S. 358 (1970).

30

and First Amendment rights apply to teen-agers.[57] Chief Justice Warren said, for the Court, that
"Teachers and students must always remain free to inquire, to study and to evaluate..."[58]

The First Amendment is basic to effective teaching. As the Supreme Court stated:
"The First Amendment was designed to enlarge, not to limit, freedom in literature and in the arts as well as in politics, economics, law, and other fields...Its aim was to unlock all ideas for argument, debate, and dissemination."[59]

Both the teaching and the learning process require such "unlocking" of ideas through reasonable access to knowledge, which means reasonable access via "fair use" to materials subject to copyright protection. Cardozo put it well:
"There is no freedom without choice and there is no choice without knowledge...Implicit, therefore, in the very notion of liberty is the liberty of the mind to absorb and beget...At the root of all liberty is the liberty to know."[60]

As illustrated by the statement of interest, supra, we have here a situation in which, as the Supreme Court stated,

[57] Tinker v. Des Moines School District, 393 U.S. 503 (1969); Board of Education v. Barnette, 319 U.S. 624 (1943).
[58] Sweezy v. New Hampshire, 354 U.S. 234, 250 (1957).
[59] Times Film Corp. v. Chicago, 365 U.S. 43, 81 (1961).
[60] CARDOZO, PARADOXES (1928), 104.

31

the Court cannot shut its eyes to "the plainest facts of our national life."[61]

We have here far more than "harmless, empty shadows."[62] A "pragmatic assessment"[63] of the instant situation justifies the fear that by ignoring First Amendment rights the Commissioner's

opinion and holding could destroy the capacity of America's teachers to teach effectively and seriously inhibit the effectiveness of the pupils' learning process.

C. The Ninth Amendment Protects the Right of Americans to Knowledge and to Read

The Ninth Amendment to the Constitution provides as follows:
"The Enumeration in the Constitution of certain rights, shall not be construed to deny or disparage others retained by the people."

This is the reserved right of the American people to all rights not specifically granted by the Constitution, the right to all unenumerated rights.

Generally a neglected provision of the Bill of Rights, the Ninth Amendment came to life in Mr. Justice Goldberg's concurring opinion (for himself, the Chief Justice and

[61] NLRB v. Jones & Laughlin Steel Corp., supra n. 9, at 41 (1937).
[62] Poe v. Ullman, 367 U.S. 497, 508 (1961).
[63] Kingsley Books, Inc. v. Brown, 354 U.S. 436, U.S. 436, 442 (1957).

32

Mr. Justice Brennan) in Griswold v. Connecticut.[64] He said:
"The language and history of the Ninth Amendment reveal that the Framers of the Constitution believed that there are additional fundamental rights, protected from governmental infringement, which exist alongside those fundamental rights specifically mentioned in the first eight constitutional amendments..." (p. 488)

He continued:
"The Ninth Amendment simply shows that the intent of the Constitution's authors that other fundamental rights should not be denied such protection or disparaged in any other way simply because they are not specifically listed in the first eight constitutional amendments." (p. 492)

Mr. Justice Goldberg saw the following as the "fundamental rights" protected by the Ninth Amendment but not listed in the previous eight:
"In determining which rights are fundamental, judges are not left at large to decide cases in light of their personal and private notions. Rather, they must look to the 'traditions and [collective] conscience of our people' to determine whether a principle is 'so rooted [there]...as to be ranked as fundamental.' Snyder v. Massachusetts, 291 U.S. 97, 105. The inquiry is whether a right involved 'is of such a character that it cannot be denied without violating those "fundamental principles of liberty and justice which lie at the base of all our civil and political institutions"....' Powell v. Alabama, 287 U.S. 45, 67. 'Liberty' also gains content from the emanations of ... specific [constitutional] guarantees and 'from experience with the requirements of a free society.' Poe v. Ullman, 367 U.S. 497, 517 (dissenting opinion of Mr. Justice Douglas)" (p. 493-4).

[64] 381 U.S. 479 (1965).

33

There is strong historical justification for the belief that the intent of the framers of the Bill of Rights was that the Ninth Amendment should apply "where the asserted right appears to the court as fundamental to a free society but is, nevertheless, not specified in the Bill of Rights."[65]

It is the amicus's respectful position that in a democracy nothing is more fundamental than the right of the people to have reasonable access to the cultural heritage of the nation under the copyright law. This is an absolute necessity for teachers, if a democracy is to survive and protect itself as a free society.

"The Ninth Amendment is a reservoir of personal rights necessary to preserve the dignity of existence of man in a free society. The Ninth Amendment is the place to which we must turn for protection of individual liberty from infringements not enumerated and perhaps not contemplated, by the founding fathers."[66]

"The ninth amendment was intended to assert that the constitutional formulations were not to be narrowly interpreted."[67] A leading legal commentator indicates that, whatever else the Amendment may cover, it provides for "the right to have access to information...":

[65] Redlich, Are There 'Certain Rights Retained by the People'?, 37 N.Y. U.L. REV. 787, 808 (1962).

[66]State v. Abelloni, 50 Hawaii 384, 390, 393 (1968) (Levenson, J. concurring).
[67]Kutner, The Neglected Ninth Amendment: The 'Other Rights' Retained by the People, 51 MARQ. L. REV. 121, 125 (1968).

34

"Related to this right to information is the right to know as encompassed in academia and cultural freedom. A college professor or school teacher has the right to pursue knowledge. . ."[68]

Another distinguished commentator said (even before Griswold): "One of the newest of the unenumerated rights is that to knowledge. . ."[69]

If the right of young people to wear long hair in school comes within the penumbra of the First Amendment and the reach of the Ninth Amendment[70], then how much more valid is the application of the Ninth Amendment to something as fundamental to a free democratic society as the right of reasonable access, through "fair use," by those same students (and their teachers) to that free society's cultural heritage?

But what about the impact of the copyright provision in the Constitution (Article 1, Section 8) on the Ninth Amendment? In Ashwander v. TVA,[71] the Court stated:

[68]Ibid., at 139.
[69]O. John Rogge, Unenumerated Rights, 47 CAL. L. REV. 787, 811 (1959).
[70]Breen v. Kahl, 419 F.2d 1034, 1036 (7th Cir. 1969), cert. den, 398 U.S. 937 (1970). Contra, King v. Saddleback Jr. Col. Dist., 445 F.2d 932 (9th Cir. 1971), cert. den. (with 2 dissents) 404 U.S. 979 (1971).
[71]297 U.S. 288, 330-1 (1936).

35

"And the Ninth Amendment. . .does not withdraw the rights which are expressly granted to the Federal Government. The question is as to the scope of the grant and whether there are inherent limitations. . ."

The Ninth Amendment's reach starts, at least, from the limited "scope of the grant" for copyright legislation and from the "inherent limitations" so clearly illustrated by the judicial development of the doctrine of "fair use" notwithstanding the seemingly complete monopolies granted by the copyright laws.

Under the Ninth Amendment, "rights may arise or appear by reason of limitations placed upon or by limits of granted powers."[72]

"A person has the right not to have the government act where it lacks power. In addition, he has other rights, which deny government power to act where otherwise it might. For example, the government has the power to regulate bankruptcy proceedings [U.S. Constitution, Art. I, Section 8], but it lacks power to regulate them in such a way that a property owner is deprived of property without due process of law [Louisville Bank v. Reedford, 295 U.S. 555 (1935)]. The government has power to preserve its own existence [Dennis v. U.S., 341 U.S. 494, 501 (1951)], but that power is tempered by the rights guaranteed by the First and Fifth amendments [Aptheker v. Secretary of State, 378 U.W. 500 (1964)]. Similarly, where a person has an inherent right, recognized by the ninth amendment, it protects him against

[72]Kelsey, The Ninth Amendment of the Federal Constitution, 11 IND. L. J. 309, 311 (1936).

36

some exercise of power which might otherwise be proper . . .It is in areas where government has power to act that it is important to the individual to have positive rights."[73]

Amicus respectfully submits that, the copyright clause notwithstanding, the Ninth Amendment guarantees and protects the right of American citizens to read the cultural heritage of their nation, and authorizes for teachers reasonable access to such heritage for their teaching duties even when it is in copyrighted form. These rights come within what Mr. Justice Douglas, speaking for the Court in Griswold, and specifically mentioning the Ninth Amendment, called

"penumbras, formed by emanations from those [Bill of Rights] guarantees that help give them life and substance."[74]

The Ninth Amendment fully authorizes the defendant's practices in this case as constitutionally-protected "fair use."

D. The Constitution Is A Living Document.

The Constitution is a living and sensitive document which adjusts to the major needs of the American people. The Bill of Rights protects freedom of reasonable access to the nation's cultural heritage, under the copyright law, and thus sanctions defendant's practice in this case. That the

[73]Comment, G. L. Garner, The Ninth Amendment, 30 ALBANY L. REV. 89, 99 (1966).
[74]Supra n. 64, at 484.

37

articulation of the constitutional right of reasonable access might appear novel is no defense against its validity. Chief Justice Burger stated that it makes no constitution difference "that it has taken this Court nearly two centuries to 'discover' a constitutional mandate. . ."[75] In Johnson v. Louisiana[76] the Supreme Court reinterpreted a 200-year old, and admittedly settled, doctrine of American legal history. What was involved there, as well as here, is what Mr. Justice Powell called "a change in focus in the Court's approach. . ."[77] and the requirement for "a fresh look at the question. . ."[78] And only in June of 1972 did that Court find constitutional infirmity in capital punishment under the Eighth Amendment although admittedly it had "been employed throughout our history."[79]

The very fact that constitutional protection for "fair use" has not been customarily articulated is in itself an aid to this Court in the present instance. As the Supreme Court stated more than 90 years ago:

[75]Coleman v. Alabama, 399 U.S. 1, 22 (1970).
[76]406 U.S. 404 (1972).
[77]Ibid., p. 372, note 9. (concurring)
[78]Ibid., p. 376. See also Erie v. Tompkins, 304 U.S. 64 (1938); Brown v. Board of Education, supra n. 3; Cooper v. Aaron, 359 U.S. 1 (1958).
[79]Furman v. Georgia, 408 U.S.   , 40 LW 4923 (June 29, 1972).

38

"The question is now a new one in this court, and we are not fettered by an inveterate course of decision upon it. We are at liberty. . .to decide it upon reason and not by precedent."[80]

As the ancient law giver Maimonides put it, the gates of interpretation are never closed.[81]

The Supreme Court has said:
"The Constitution of the United States. . .was made for an undefined and expanding future.

"It is more consonant to the true philosophy of our historical legal institutions to say that the spirit of personal liberty and individual right, which they embodied, was preserved and developed by a progressive growth and wise adaptation to new circumstances and situations of the forms and processes found fit to give, from time to time, new expression and greater effect to modern ideas of self-government."[82]

With reference to the meaning of words in constitutional context, Mr. Justice Holmes said:
"[W]hen we are dealing with words that also are a constituent act, like the Constitution of the United States, we must realize that they have called into life a being the development of which could not have been foreseen completely by the most gifted of its begettors. . .The case before us must be considered in the light of our whole experience and not merely in that of what was said a hundred years ago."[83]

[80]Conner v. Long, 104 U.S. 228, 243 (1881).
[81]THE GUIDE FOR THE PERPLEXED (ed. S. Pines, Univ. of Chicago, 1963), 327-8.
[82]Hurtado v. California, 110 U.S. 516, 531, 530 (1884).
[83]Missouri v. Holland, 252 U.S. 416, 433 (1922).

39

The Supreme Court cited with approval another comment by Mr. Justice Holmes that is relevant:
"But as Mr. Justice Holmes once said: 'The provisions of the Constitution are not mathematical formulas having their essence in their form; they are organic living institutions transplanted from English soil. Their significance is vital not formal; it is to be gathered not simply by taking the words and a dictionary, but by considering their origin and the line of their growth.' Gompers v. United States, 233 U.S. 604, 610."[84]

The sensitivity of the Constitution to "the new circumstances and situations" constantly facing the American people, its "adaptability,"[85] is especially true of the great liberties protected by the First Amendment.

As Mr. Justice Frankfurter said: "Some words are confined to their history; some are starting points for history. Words are intellectual and moral currency. . .Like currency words sometimes appreciate or depreciate in value."[86] Cardozo said: "The great generalities of the Constitution have a content and significance that vary from age to age."[87]

[84]Konigsberg v. State Bar of California, 366 U.S. 36, 49-50, note 10 (1961).
[85]Appalachian Coals Inc. v. United States, 288 U.S. 344, 360 (1933), per Hughes, Ch. J.
[86]Frankfurter, Some Reflections on the Reading of Statutes, 47 COL. L. REV. 527, 537-38 (1947).
[87]NATURE OF THE JUDICIAL PROCESS (1921), 17.

40

Words can "import a policy that goes beyond them."[88] In constitutional interpretation it is necessary to go "far beyond the meaning of the phrase in isolation" to its "guiding history."[89]

The purpose of Constitutional provisions is the controlling feature in their application according to that Court. Mr. Justice McKenna said for the Court:

"Legislation, both statutory and constitutional, is enacted, it is true, from an experience of evils but its general language should not, therefore, be necessarily confined to the form that evil had theretofore taken. Time works changes, brings into existence new conditions and purposes. Therefore, a principle, to be vital, must be capable of wider application than the mischief which gave it birth, This is peculiarly true of constitutions. . .In the application of a constitution, therefore our contemplation cannot be only of what has been, but of what may be. Under any other rule a constitution would indeed be as easy of application as it would be deficient in efficacy and power. . .Rights declared in words might be lost in reality. And this has been recognized. The meaning and vitality of the Constitution has been developed against narrow and restrictive construction."[90]

[88]Holmes J., Olmstead v. United States, 277 U.S. 438, 469 (dissenting); majority decision overruled, Katz v. U.S., 389 U.S. 347, 352 (1967).
[89]Chapman v. United States, 365 U.S. 610, 619 (1961), per Frankfurter, J., concurring. Cf: "Reasoning which in one age would make no impression whatsoever, in the next age is received with enthusiastic applause," I Lecky, HISTORY OF THE RISE AND INFLUENCE OF THE SPIRIT OF RATIONALISM IN EUROPE, vii (1865).
[90]Weems v. United States, 217 U.S. 349, 373 (1910) (emphasis added.) Cf: Mr. Justice Harlan, dissenting, Poe v. Ullman, supra n. 62, at 544.

41

The Supreme Court has long been responsive to the special need for guarding the Bill of Rights and especially First Amendment rights "with a jealous eye."[91] A liberal interpretation of such rights has been called by the Court "the only conclusion supported by history":

"For the First Amendment does not speak equivocally. . . It must be taken as a command of the broadest scope that explicit language, read in the context of a liberty-loving society, will allow."

". . .the only conclusion supported by history is that the unqualified prohibitions laid down by the framers were intended to give to liberty of the press, as to the other liberties, the broadest scope that could be countenanced in an orderly society."[92]

First Amendment rights have been persistently protected from erosion by indirection as well as by direct act.[93] "Sophisticated as well as simple minded" evasions of Constitutional rights have been condemned.[94] "The Constitution deals with substance, not shadows. Its inhibition was levelled at

[91]AFL v. Swing, 312, 325 (1941).
[92]Bridges v. California, 314 U.S. 252, 263, 265 (1941). See also Olmstead v. United States, supra, at 471, 476.
[93]Guinn v. United States, 238 U.S. 347, 361 (1915); Grosjean v. Amer. Press Co., supra n. 28, at 250 (1936); Speiser v. Randall, 357 U.S. 513, 518 (1958). See also United States ex rel Milwaukee Publication Co. v. Burleson, 255 U.S. 407, 430-31 (1931) (Brandeis, J., dissenting); United States v. Rumely, supra n. 17 at 58 (Douglas J., concurring).
[94]See Mr. Justice Frankfurter's comment, Lane v. Wilson, 307 U.S. 268, 275 (1939). Cf: Louisiana ex rel Gremelion v. NAACP, 366 U.S. 293 (1961).

42

the thing, not the name."[95] The substance, "the thing," in Freedom of Press, is freedom of reasonable access.

The extraordinary genius of the Bill of Rights is its adapta-

bility to the problems of each successive generation of Americans. The present generation's special and urgent problem is the protection and assurance of the American people's right of reasonable access to its cultural heritage through the doctrine of "fair use" of copyrighted materials. The history of the struggle for Freedom of Press bars any notion that the Bill of Rights provides freedom to print and disseminate information but denies freedom to acquire it through reasonable access and "fair use." In the context of mid-20th century America and the present world situation, Freedom of Press must embody reasonable access, and "fair use" of, the nation's heritage.

The very nature of the Bill of Rights calls for its interpretation and reinterpretation to meet new and undecided issues. Such is this case.

E. In "Balancing" Interests Courts Must Give Priority to the Public Interest (For Reasonable Access) Over the Copyright Proprietor

"Cases such as this one inevitably call for a delicate balancing of important but conflicting interests," said Mr. Justice White in a different context. That statement is

[95]Cummings v. Missouri, 4 Wall. 277, 325 (1866).

43

completely applicable here.[96]

"When Congress' exercise of its enumerated powers clashes with those individual liberties protected by the Bill of Rights, it is our 'delicate and difficult task' to determine whether the resulting restriction on freedom can be tolerated."[97]

As Mr. Justice Marshall wrote:

"As Robel and many other cases show, all governmental power - even the war power, the power to maintain national security, or the power to conduct foreign affairs - is limited by the Bill of Rights. When individual freedoms of Americans are at stake, we do not blindly defer to broad claims of the Legislative or Executive, but rather we consider those claims in the light of the individual freedom."[98]

"Balancing" has a unique context in copyright matters. As Story said in one of the very early cases:

"Patents and copyrights approach, nearer than any other class of cases belonging to forensic discussion, to what may be called the metaphysics of the law, where the distinctions are, or at least may be, almost evanescent."[99]

And Chafee stated that

"Copyright admits of philosophic thinking more than most other parts of the law."[100]

[96]State of Wisconsin v. Yoder et al., 406 U.S. 205, 237 (1972) (concurring).
[97]U. S. v. Robel, 389 U.S. 258, 264 (1967).
[98]Kleindienst v. Mandel et al., supra n. 36, at 5112 (dissenting).
[99]Folsom et al. v. Marsh et al., 9 Fed. Cas. 342, No. 4901, at 344 (1811).
[100]Chafee, supra n. 48, at 503.

44

Holmes warned courts of this sort of special problem:

"I think that judges themselves have failed adequately to recognize their duty of weighing considerations of social advantage. The duty is inevitable, and the result of the often proclaimed judicial aversion to deal with such considerations is simply to leave the very ground and foundation of judgments inarticulate, and often unconscious . . ."[101]

1. Primacy of the Public Interest

The Congress, the Supreme Court, and the Register of Copyrights have all affirmed the primacy of the public interest over the copyright proprietor's interest:

The House Report on the present law stated that copyright was enacted

"not primarily for the benefits of the author, but primarily for the benefit of the public."[102]

The Supreme Court has said:

". . .the copyright law. . .makes a reward to the owner of secondary consideration."[103]

The Register of Copyrights stated to Congress in his 1961 Report:[104]

[101]Holmes, The Path of the Law, 10 HARV. L. REV. 458, 467 (1897).
[102]House Report No. 2222, 60th Cong., 2d Sess., p. 9.

103 Mazer v. Stein, supra n. 17, at 219 (1954). Accord.: U.S. v. Paramount Pictures, Inc., 334 U.S. 131, 158 (1948); U.S. v. Loew's Inc., 371 U.S. 38, 46 (1962).
104 COPYRIGHT LAW REVISION, Report of the Register of Copyrights, House Com. Print, 87th Cong., 1st Sess. (July 1961).

45

"Within limits the author's interests coincide with those of the public. Where they conflict the public interest must prevail. . . .And the interests of the authors must yield to the public welfare where they conflict." (p. 6)

"The needs of all groups must be taken into account. But these needs must also be weighed in the light of the paramount public interest." (p. xi)

In "balancing" between the copyright owner's mere statutory privilege and the user's constitutional rights, the decision must fall on the user's side of the line, in terms of the concept adopted by the Supreme Court in the CATV case.[105]

With particular reference to the judicial doctrine of "fair use" - the issue at stake in this very case - the courts gave as a justification for their doctrine the constitutional requirement to subordinate the interest of the copyright proprietor to the public interest.[106]

Heed to the fragility of constitutional rights was urged by the Supreme Court. The "spike mike" decision, said Mr. Justice Stewart,

"is based upon the reality of an actual intrusion into a constitutionally protected area. What

105 Fortnightly Corp. v. United Artists Television, Inc., 392 U.S. 390 (1968).
106 Berlin v. E. C. Publications Inc., 329 F.2d 541, 543-4 (2d Cir. 1961), cert. den. 379 U.S. 822; Rosemont Enterprises Inc., v. Random House, Inc., 366 F.2d 303, 309 (2d Cir. 1966), cert. den. 385 U.S. 1009; Greenbie v. Noble, 151 F. Supp. 45, 67 (D.C.N.Y. 1957).

46

the Court said long ago bears repeating now: 'It may be that it is the obnoxious thing in its mildest and least repulsive form; but illegitimate and unconstitutional practices get their first footing in that way, namely, by silent approaches and slight deviations from legal modes of procedure.' Boyd v. United States, 116 U.S. 616, 635."[107]

Inconspicuous rejection or unrecognized suppression of reasonable access (via "fair use") to materials vital to the teaching and learning of America's cultural heritage can, and often is, achieved through copyright.

The Commissioner's decision could well deprive defendant - and, by extension, millions of teachers and students in America's schools - of rights of Freedom of Press guaranteed by the First Amendment.

2. Copyright Monopoly to be Strictly Construed

The Supreme Court has indicated that copyright ownership is a monopoly. For the Court, Chief Justice Hughes said:

"The owner of the copyright, if he pleases, may refrain from vending or licensing and content himself with simply exercising the right to exclude others from using his property."[108]

"Copyrights," the Attorney General of the United States stated, "are forms of monopolies. . ."[109] "Even at its best," wrote the

107 Silverman v. U.S., 365 U.S. 505, 512 (1961).
108 Fox Film Corp. v. Doyal, supra n. 17, at 127.
109 House Rep. No. 1742, on H.J. Res. 676, 87th Cong., 2d Sess. (May 2, 1962), p. 6.

47

Assistant Librarian of the Supreme Court, "copyright necessarily involves the right to restrict as well as to monopolize the diffusion of knowledge."[110] In Fortnightly, the Supreme Court has shown its antipathy to broadening the scope of the copyright owner's monopoly:

"The Copyright Act does not give a copyright holder control over all uses of his copyrighted work. Instead, §1 of the Act enumerates several 'rights' that are made 'exclusive' to the holder of the copyright. If a person, without authorization from the copyright holder, puts a copyrighted work to a use within the scope of one of these 'exclusive rights,' he infringes the copyright. If he puts the work to a use not enumerated in §1, he does not infringe."[111]

In a patent case arising under the copyright-patent provision

of the Constitution, Mr. Justice White said for the Court:

"Moreover, we must consider petitioner's claim in the light of this Nation's historical antipathy to monopoly."[112]

110 Hudon, The Copyright Period: Weighing Personal Against Public Interest, 49 ABAJ 759 (1963).
111 Fortnightly Corp. v. United Artists Television, Inc., 392 U.S. 390, 20 L.Ed. 2d 1176, 1180 (1968). Footnote 8 of the Court's opinion reads in part, as follows:
"8. 'The fundamental [is] that "use" is not the same thing as infringement,' that use short of infringement is to be encouraged. . .,' Kaplan, An Unhurried View of Copyright 57 (1967)."
112 Deepsouth Packing Co., Inc. v. The Laitram Corp., supra n. 23, at 530. A footnote to this statement said, "See the discussion in Graham v. John Deere, 381 U.S. 1, 7ff (1966)."

48

Mr. Justice Douglas recently adverted to the relationship between monopoly and the constitutional status of copyright:

"While this Court has not had many occasions to consider the constitutional parameters of copyright power, we have indicated that the introductory clause, 'To promote the Progress of Science and useful arts," acts as a limitation on Congress' power to grant monopolies through patents. In Graham v. John Deere Co., 383 U.S. 1, 5-6, we said:

'The clause is both a grant of power and a limitation. . . The Congress in the exercise of the patent power may not overreach the restraints posed by the stated constitutional purpose. . .'

He continued:

"The framers of the Bill of Rights added the guarantees of freedom of speech and of the press because they did not feel them to be sufficiently protected by the original Constitution. This liberty is necessary if we are to have free, open, and lively debate of political and social ideas . . .We should not construe the copyright laws to conflict so patently with the values that the First Amendment was designed to protect."[113]

In passing, it is worth noting that copyright proprietors are wont to argue that whatever may have been the legal proprieties prior to xerography, when the predominant copying tool was a pencil or at most a typewriter or a mimeograph machine, the whole context has changed (to the presumed detriment of the user's rights) with the xerox machine. This is erroneous in constitutional terms. That the xerox was

113 Lee et al. v. Runge, 404 U.S. 887, 888-9, 892-3 (1971) (dissenting on denial of petition for writ of certiorari) *(emphasis added)*.

49

not contemplated in 1909, when the present copyright law was enacted, gives the copyright owner no greater monopoly than he would have had with earlier systems of reproducing copies. See, for example, U.S. et al. v. Midwest Video Corp.,[114] where the Court held that the Federal Communications Commission had jurisdiction over CATV although CATV "was developed long after enactment of the Communications Act of 1934." See also concurring opinion of Chief Justice Burger (at p. 649).

It is also relevant to note that the Copyright Office submitted a brief amicus before the Supreme Court in Mazer v. Stein, supra n. 17, signed by the present Register of Copyrights, George D. Carey, then in his role as Principal Legal Advisor to the Copyright Office. This brief makes the important point that neither the method of reproduction nor the resulting number of copies affect the copyrightability of a work. It seems an obvious and a fortiori conclusion that the same constitutionally applies to "fair use," whether the reproduction is by hand or by xerox. Mr. Carey's Brief Amicus to the Supreme Court stated:

"Literary works which in an earlier era would perhaps have been reproduced by hand on illuminated parchment or in other single copies have not become less copyrightable by virtue of their present reproduction in thousands of copies by manufacturing techniques involving the use of movable types, plates, etc. Similarly, painting masterpieces once reproduced on canvas or as murals in single copies are now frequently reproduced in color plates for distribution in thousands of individual copies or in periodical

114 406 U.S. 649, 650 (1972).

50

or book form. Neither the mechanical and manufacturing processes used in this reproduction, the number of copies . . .would appear to affect the copyrightability or essential

nature of the work itself."
      (pp. 30-1, n. 13) (underlining supplied)
Thus, in terms of "balancing" rights, the monopoly-granting
power of the copyright provision of the Constitution must be
construed in a manner consonant with two fundamental considerations:
  (1) that Congress's monopoly-granting power in copy-
       right is very limited and restricted; and
  (2) that the copyright-granting power of Congress cannot
       override rights protected by the First and Ninth
       Amendments of the Bill of Rights.
In "balancing" the interests involved, it is sufficient for this
Court to rule that in the current case the defendant acted within
its rights. It is not necessary, in this case, to reach any other
questions on the relationship of the First Amendment and the
copyright clause.[115] This is all the more true since we have here
merely a question of determining the meaning and scope of the
judicial doctrine of "fair use."

II. CUSTOMARY USE IS "FAIR USE" UNDER THE COPYRIGHT LAW

Much of the Commissioner's discussion of "fair use" is either
irrelevant or premature, because of his failure to recognize that
"customary use" becomes "fair use" without

---

[115] See Ashwander v. TVA, supra n. 71, at 347 (Brandeis, J., concurring).

51

regard to the various criteria for determining whether a given use
is fair use.
  A use that has been sanctioned by custom is " fair use,"
without regard to other criteria which may be applicable to uses
not sanctioned by custom. One a "fair use" has been moulded
by custom, it operates without regard to the four criteria used
by the Commissioner in his opinion.

A. Custom and the Common Law

"Fair use" is a common law doctrine, fashioned by the courts
themselves. The courts have rejected the purportedly "exclusive"
rights of the copyright proprietor, by developing the common
law doctrine that some uses, "fair uses," are exempted from the
copyright proprietor's monopoly.
  The history of Anglo-Saxon law teaches that common law
springs, to a large degree, out of custom. Holmes, in the opening
paragraph of THE COMMON LAW (1881), said: "The life of the
law is not logic, but experience." (p. 5).
  Elsewhere in the same classic, he speaks of a specific field of
law:
      ". . .may only mean that the custom of the realm and the
      common law are the same thing. . ." (p. 150)
Story wrote:
      "The common law is the lex non scripta, that is, the
      unwritten law,. . .composed of customs, and usages,
      and maxims."[116]

---

[116] STORY, MISCELLANEOUS WRITINGS, (1852, reprint 1969) 442.

52

Blackstone wrote:
      "The unwritten or Common Law is properly distinguish-
      able into three kinds: (1) General customs. . . (2) Particu-
      lar customs. . . (3) Certain particular laws. . ."[117]
Holland put it thus:
      "Custom exists in law in every country. . .It is known in
      England as 'the common law'. . ."[118]
Our courts have accepted this same doctrine. The Supreme
Court said in 1870:
      "Customs have sprung from the necessities and convenience
      of business and prevailed in duration and extent until they
      acquired the force of law. This mass of our jurisprudence
      has thus grown, and will continue to grow, by successive
      accretions."[119]
And similar expressions have been found in more recent Federal
decisions:
  − ". . .a lawful custom is itself part of the common
     law."[120]
  − "A lawful custom is part of the common law. . ."[121]

---

[117] COMMENTARIES, pp. 67-8.
[118] THE ELEMENTS OF JURISPRUDENCE (1910), 59.
[119] Merchants' Bank v. State Bank, 10 Wall. 604, 651 (1870).

---

[120] Nicoll v. Pittsvein Coal Co., 269 F. 968, 971 (2d Cir. 1920).
[121] U.S. Shipping Board E. F. Corp. v. Levensaler, 290 F. 297, 300
(C.A.D.C. 1923), cert. den. 266 U.S. 630 (1924).

53

B. Custom and "Fair Use"

In one of the earliest copyright cases before it, the Supreme
Court clearly indicated that "custom or usage" is a valid basis
for determining the common law of copyright.[122]
  A leading case speaks of:
      ". . .what is commonly referred to as a 'fair use' - one that
      is reasonable and customary."[123]
Another Federal Court defined "fair use" as follows:
      "Though technically an infringement of copyright, it is
      allowed by law on the ground that the appropriation is
      reasonable and customary."[124]
And a Federal Court of Appeals has stated that
      ". . .it is both reasonable and customary for biographers
      to refer to and utilize earlier works. . ."[125]
The same position had earlier been adopted by the very early
English cases. In 1761, in a case where the question was the
copying of one-tenth of a work, the court said:
      "Consider it upon the custom and usage."[126]

---

[122] Wheaton v. Peters, supra n. 17 at 659.
[123] Shapiro, Bernstein & Co. Inc. v. P. F. Collier and Son, Co., 26
U.S.P.Q. 40, 42 (S.D.N.Y. 1939).
[124] Holdredge v. Knight Pub. Corp., 214 F. Supp. 921, 924 (D.C. Calif.
1963).
[125] Rosemont Enterprises Inc. v. Random House, Inc., supra n. 103, at
308.
[126] Dodsley v. Kinnersley, 27 Eng. Rep. 270, 271 (1761).

54

In another early English case involving very substantial copying,
an injunction was denied because
      ". . .it is very important to observe that, for many years,
      such a course as I have stated has been pretty generally
      adopted. . ."[127]
Halsbury states:
      "As regards the matter to which it relates, a custom takes
      the place of the general common law."[128]
The legal commentators on copyright have also equated cus-
tom and "fair use," at least since Drone in 1879: [129]
      "simply a use which is legally permissive, either because
      of the scope of a copyright, the nature of a work, or by
      reason of the application of known commercial, social or
      professional usages, having the effect of custom, insofar
      as these do not expressly run contrary to the plain lan-
      guage of copyright legislation."[130]
De Wolf described "fair use" as
      "a use technically forbidden by the law, but allowed as
      reasonable and customary. . ."[131]
Ball writes:
      "Fair use is technically an infringement of copyright, but
      is allowed by law on the ground that the appropriation
      is reasonable and customary."[132]

---

[127] Saunders v. Smith, 40 Eng. Rep. 1100, 1107 (1838).
[128] LAWS OF ENGLAND (3rd ed. 1955).
[129] DRONE, A TREATISE ON THE LAW OF PROPERTY IN INTEL-
LECTUAL PRODUCTIONS (1879), 389.
[130] WEIL, AMERICAN COPYRIGHT LAW (1917) 429 (underlining
supplied).
[131] De WOLF, AN OUTLINE OF COPYRIGHT LAW (1925) 143
[132] BALL, THE LAW OF COPYRIGHT AND LITERARY PROPERTY
(1944) 260. Cited with approval in Loew's Inc. v. C.B.S., supra n.
21, at 175.

55

Nicholson states:
      " 'Fair use' of copyrighted material has been defined by
      the courts as that extra-legal use that is usual, reasonable
      and customary."[133]
Similar comments appear in the law reviews.[134]
  A significant comment was made by a distinguished and long-
time leader of the copyright bar, Joseph A. McDonald:
      "Non-infringing uses are either 'fair use' as recognized in
      the decided cases or uses which are sanctioned by custom
      in the trade or in the business to which they relate. It
      might be argued that uses which are sanctioned by custom
      are impliedly authorized. This is true. However, such an
      authorization springs not from the owner of the material
      or his representative but from the overall framework of
      creation, licensing or use in the field. Under such circum-
      stances the authorization, express or implied, of the indi-
      vidual owner is not needed by the user."[135]

This latter point is clear, and attested by many cases, that consent by the copyright owner is not necessary where custom has its effect:

". . .custom derives its efficacy from its adoption into law, and when once established is binding, irrespective of any manifestation of assent by parties concerned. . ."136

133 NICHOLSON, A MANUAL OF COPYRIGHT PRACTICE FOR WRITERS, PUBLISHERS AND AGENTS (2d ed. 1956) 91.
134 Comments and Notes, Copyright Fair Use - Case Law and Legislation, 1969 DUKE L. J. 73, 88; Student Comment, The Effect of the Fair Use Doctrine in Textbook Publishing and Copying, Part II, 2 AKRON L. REV. 112 (1968); Case Note, 15 SO. CALIF. L. REV. 249 (1942).
135 Jos. A. McDonald, Non-Infringing Uses, 9 BULL. OF COPYRIGHT SOCIETY OF U.S.A. 466 (Aug. 1962).
136 WILLISTON ON CONTRACTS, Section 649.

56

"Fair use" does not depend upon the consent of the copyright owner, whether it derives from various criteria or from custom independently of other criteria.

The absence of relevant cases has troubled some of the commentators. Nevertheless, Nimmer writes:

"There is no reported case on the question of whether a single handwritten copy of all or substantially all of a protected work made for the copier's own use is an infringement or fair use. If such a case were to arise the force of custom might impel a court to rule for the defendant on the ground of fair use."137

Thus, "fair use" derives from two major sources, (1) customary use, and (2) other uses meeting certain criteria established by the courts. In both instances the courts have fashioned a common law doctrine independent of - and to some extent contradictory with - the copyright statute. Custom, therefore, is a basic source of "fair use." When such customary use is established, "fair use" prevails independent of the other criteria applicable in the absence of custom.

C. The Evidence Shows Custom Prevailed Here

The undisputed evidence in the trial of this case shows a history of at least 50 years of photocopying in library systems. Plaintiff's own witness, Karl F. Heumann,

137 NIMMER ON COPYRIGHTS, Sec. 146, p. 654 (1972). Per contra: Cohen, Fair Use In the Law of Copyright, ASCAP, COPYRIGHT LAW SYMPOSIUM, No. 6 (1955), 42 at 51; Crossland, The Rise and Fall of Fair Use; The Protection of Literary Materials Against Copyright Infringement by New and Developing Media, 20 SO. CAR. L. REV. 153, 154, 166 (1968).

57

Executive Editor of the Federation of American Societies for Experimental Biology, replied to questions as follows:

"Q. Are you familiar with library photocopying?
A. Reasonably familiar.
Q. How long would you say that has been going on?
A. Fifty years.
Q. Would you say that is the custom?
A. Yes." 138

The Director of the National Library of Medicine, Dr. M. M. Cummings, testified that copying has been "going on more than 50 years."139

There is other solid documentary evidence that the Library of Congress had a custom of copying, including photocopying, dating back at least until 1901,140 and that after the enactment of the current copyright law in 1909, the Library of Congress continued and expanded this practice.141 The former Acting Librarian of Congress, Verner Clapp, wrote:

"Back in 1901, the regulations of the Library of Congress freely permitted photocopying, a room being reserved for the purpose, and this permission specifically ran to articles covered by copyright."142

138 T. 430-1.
139 T. 455. See also Defendant's Exhibits No. 51, 74, and T. 431, 836.
140 See Brief Amicus Curiae of Association of Research Libraries, et al,. before Commissioner, pp. 13-4.
141 Ibid,. pp. 21 et seq.
142 V. Clapp, Can Copyright Law Respond to the New Technology, 64 LAW LIBRARY J. 387 (No. 4, Nov. 1968).

58

Undisputed testimony in this case by the Deputy Director of the National Medical Library, Scott Adams, reaffirms this statement by Verner Clapp:

"Let me say that this code of practice -- that it is rooted in custom; it goes all the way back to the beginnings of the century, or even before the beginning of the century . . .During the intervening years this has become a well-established custom, a well-established practice."143

Apropos of this historical evidence of custom for library photocopying, it is pertinent to note that the Supreme Court has held, in another context, that where usages and procedures were in actual practice at the time legislation was enacted, it must be reasonably assumed that they became an accepted part of the legislation.144

D. Common Sense Approach

There is also a common sense approach to this whole question which seems to have been ignored by the Commissioner. ". . . common sense often makes good law," said Mr. Justice Douglas.145 After all, society's purpose in creating and fostering libraries as institutions for the preservation of culture is, at least in part, to enable successive generations to study that heritage for the advancement of science and the arts. ". . .it has been the custom from time immemorial for

143 T. 837-8
144 Foti v. Immigration and Naturalization Service, 375 U.S. 217, 223 (1963).
145 Peak v. U.S., 353 U.S. 43, 46 (1957).

59

scholars and others to hand copy."146 Verner Clapp, former Acting Librarian of Congress, looked at this whole matter in perspective:

"Now from very earliest times, this record keeping profession [librarians] has facilitated copying. It facilitated copying with cuneiform styles, with goosequill pens and fountain pens and ball-point pens, with typewriters, photostat cameras, microfilm cameras, and now with coin-operated photocopying devices. It has taken technology in its stride for at least 3,000 years. . ."147

In this connection there is significance in the so-called Gentlemen's Agreement of 1935, to which reference is made in the Commissioner's opinion. This Agreement included the following statement:

". . .a student has always been free to 'copy' by hand; and mechanical reproductions from copyrighted material are presumably intended to take place of hand transcriptions, and to be governed by the same principles governing hand transcriptions."148

It is respectfully submitted that this statement makes sense. It represented at the time not a new practice but rather a reaffirmation of an existing custom accepted by all concerned in the field of publishing and libraries.

146 Petre, Statutory Copyright Protection for Books and Magazines Against Machine Copying ASCAP, COPYRIGHT LAW SYMPOSIUM, No. 14 (1966), p. 180. (". . .it is submitted that photocopying single copies for private research is a 'fair use.' " p. 202).
147 Clapp, op. cit., supra n. 142, at 399.
148 Defendant's Exhibit 74.

60

If the law fails to accept the common sense point of view and the custom recognized in the Gentlemen's Agreement, the following comment seems appropriate:

". . .we are in the ridiculous position of insisting that the scholar has a right to make a copy for his private use only if he does so under conditions of maximum inefficiency in the use of his time and resources. . ."149

Custom is stabilized common sense, a recognition by society of a stabilized relationship between possible or actual adverse parties. As Mr. Justice Frankfurter said, ". . .words acquire scope and function from the history of events which they summarize."150

"Our concern is with realities, not nomenclature," said Mr. Justice McReynolds,151 and Mr. Justice Brewer stated that ". . .courts must recognize things as they are. . ."152

The realities of the present situation are that "fair use" includes the custom of library photocopying in this case.

149 R. Shaw, Publication and Distribution of Scientific Literature, COLLEGE AND RESEARCH LIBRARIES, Vol. XVII(4), 293 at 302 (July 1956).
150 Phelps Dodge Corp. v. N.L.R.B., 313 U.S. 177, 186 (1941).
151 Senior v. Braden, 295 U.S. 422, 429 (1935).
152 Adams Exp. Co. v. Ohio State Auditor, 166 U.S. 185, 225 (1897).

61

III. CONCLUSION

The issue before the Court is whether the judicial doctrine of "fair use" authorizes the defendant's practice in this case. *Amicus* respectfully submits that it does.

The doctrine of "fair use" is merely a shorthand way of saying that the copyright proprietor does not have complete monopoly despite the statutory language. "The Copyright Act does not give a copyright holder control over all uses of his copyrighted work."[153] "It would be idle and trite to say that no right is absolute."[154]

The judicial doctrine of "fair use," which was developed in the face of a seemingly exclusive copyrighted privilege, is a recognition of the public interest against monopoly. And with good reason, for as Drone once stated of "fair use,"
> "The recognition of this doctrine is essential to the growth of knowledge. . ."[155]

The judicial development of "fair use" is an example of what the distinguished legal philosopher Morris R. Cohen once said:

153 Fortnightly Corp. v. United Artists Television Inc., supra n. 105, at 393.
154 Orient Ins. Co. v. Daggs, 172 U.S. 557, 566 (1869). See also Dennis v. U.S., 341 U.S. 494, 508 (1951).
155 Drone, op. cit., supra n. 129, at 386-7.

62

> "If judges never make law, how could the body of rules known as the common law ever have arisen or have undergone the changes which it has."[156]

The fashioning of Federal remedies to protect Federal rights has been recognized by the Supreme Court over the years. Recently, for example, the Supreme Court said:
> "The remedy sought by Illinois is not within the precise scope of remedies prescribed by Congress. Yet the remedies which Congress provides are not necessarily the only federal remedies available. 'It is not uncommon for federal courts to fashion federal law where federal rights are involved.' Textile Workers v. Lincoln Mills, 353 U.S. 448, 457. When we deal with air and water in their ambient or interstate aspects, there is a federal common law, as Texas v. Pankey, 441 F.2d, recently held."[157]

In such instances, the Supreme Court held that "There are no fixed rules that govern; . . . ," and the Court's discretion prevails.[158]

The Supreme Court in Textile Workers said:
> "The range of judicial inventiveness will be determined by the nature of the problem."[159]

The present case calls for this same inventiveness in fashioning

a remedy for the protection of defendant's Federal constitutional and customary rights to continue the practice here involved. The doctrine of "fair use" is already in place

156 COHEN, LAW AND THE SOCIAL ORDER (1933), 112.
157 State of Illinois v. City of Milwaukee, et al., 406 U.S. 91, 103 (1972).
158 Ibid., at 106-7.
159 Textile Workers v. Lincoln Mills, 353 U.S. 448, 456-7 (1957).

63

and already codifies customary and acceptable practice. "Fair use" - as a common law doctrine - is not a static principle. It partakes of the common law's most characteristic trait, flexibility and sensitivity to changing developments, societal demands, and the public interest at any given time. As Madison once put it, "no language is so copious as to supply words and phrases for every complex idea."[160] Few ideas in the law are as complex as "fair use."

In initiating and developing the "fair use" doctrine, the Anglo-American courts have shown their ' judicial inventiveness" and their sensitivity to the need for fashioning a remedy "where federal rights are involved."

160 The Federalist, No. 37 (Cooke ed., 1961), at 236.

64

The instant case cries out for the courts, once again, to fashion the parameters of their own "fair use" doctrine so as to recognize the validity of constitutional protections, customary uses, and the public interest in the advancement of knowledge and the sciences, by protecting the practice here sub judice.

For all the foregoing reasons, the Commissioner's recommended conclusions of law should be rejected, the defendant's photocopying practice in this case should be held to be authorized, and the plaintiff's petition should be dismissed.

Respectfully submitted,

NATIONAL EDUCATION ASSOCIATION

by

Harry N. Rosenfield
1735 De Sales St., N.W.
Washington, D.C. 20036
202-393-0250

IN THE

United States Court of Claims

No. 73-68

THE WILLIAMS & WILKINS COMPANY,

Plaintiff,

vs.

UNITED STATES,

Defendant.

BRIEF AMICUS CURIAE
OF THE
AMERICAN LIBRARY ASSOCIATION

PERRY S. PATTERSON
WILLIAM D. NORTH
RONALD L. ENGEL
JAMES M. AMEND
JOHN A. WATERS
130 East Randolph Street
Chicago, Illinois 60601
(312) 726-2929

Washington Counsel:
PERRY S. PATTERSON
THOMAS B. CARR
1776 K. Street N.W.
Washington, D.C. 20006
(202) 833-8400

Of Counsel:
KIRKLAND & ELLIS
130 East Randolph Street
Chicago, Illinois 60601

I. QUESTION PRESENTED

The question to which the American Library Association ("ALA") addressed itself in its previous *amicus curiae* brief directed to Commissioner Davis was:

> Whether not-for-profit academic, research, and public libraries are liable for copyright infringement as a result of their long-standing practice of making single photocopies of portions of copyrighted works at the request and for the use of readers engaged in scientific and scholarly research.

In his Report to this Court, the Commissioner recommended that this question be answered in the affirmative, and that the plaintiff-publisher be awarded "reasonable

and entire compensation" for defendant's copyright infringement. Of course, this Court's adoption of the Commissioner's recommendation would be binding only upon the defendant United States Government. However, such a decision would constitute precedent whose potential effect transcends the interests of the instant litigants.

II. THE INTEREST OF THE ALA

The ALA is a non-profit organization which counts among its members over 4,200 academic, research, and public libraries and over 32,000 librarians located in every one of the fifty states. The interests of these members in their continuing ability to disseminate recorded knowledge to the public and this Court is immediately and vitally affected by the decision of this Court. This is acknowledged by the instant plaintiff. On April 15, 1972, shortly after the release of the Commissioner's Report, plaintiff published in the *Library Journal*, which is read by substantially all of the ALA's members, a so-called "Statement of Fact and Faith"* in which it summarizes the findings and recommendations of the Commissioner and then states:

> These are the facts of the court case, but the implications may well be causing grave concern to librarians and the users of libraries. Let us make our position clear. We are by no means going to halt the proper dissemination of medical knowledge; our ideals now are the same as formerly—to serve the medical and science communities to the best of our abilities. There will be no halt to the photocopying of material, as such a halt would indeed be harmful to the dissemination of knowledge. · · ·

---

* A copy of this "Statement" is appended hereto as Exhibit A. *(Please see page 96.)*

> Instead, we have worked out a simple plan based on the idea of a reasonable annual license fee for the right of copying our materials.

The foregoing is a bit premature, since this Court has not yet reached its decision. Nevertheless, the acknowledged grave concern and fears of ALA members are not allayed by the offer of a "simple plan based on the idea of a reasonable annual license fee" from the plaintiff.* Within this velvet glove is the iron-fisted threat of further legal action should the ALA's members find the "plan" not so reasonable and simple and hence unacceptable. And beyond this, there is no guaranty that the other thousand or so publishers will be so "cooperative" when, in reliance on a decision affirming the Commissioner, they seek similarly to tax ALA's members for a practice that has gone un-

challenged for many years.

This Court should not be misled. The adoption of the Commissioner's Report will quickly embroil libraries and librarians in negotiations, administrative matters, and legal actions, the prospects or net effect of which will force the cessation of traditional library photocopying and the consequent denial of this important means of access to recorded knowledge to scientists, researchers, and scholars.

---

* See the recent (May 5, 1972) letter from the Chairman of the Board of plaintiff to the Chief of the Order Division of the Library of Congress, appended hereto as Exhibit B.† From this letter it is apparent: 1) that plaintiff has not yet worked out the "reasonable plan" it will present to the concerned libraries; 2) that the plan, in any event, will cover only those readers presenting themselves in person at a library, but not readers who reside at great distances from libraries and would normally communicate with them by mail; and 3) that the plan would not cover inter-library requests, for example, by a library which does not have a copy of a back issue of a journal requested by one of its patrons. It is apparent, therefore, that the "Statement" (Exhibit A) is intended to lull the libraries into a false sense of complacency.   † *(Letter omitted by request.)*

III. EXCEPTIONS TO COMMISSIONER DAVIS' REPORT

A. INTRODUCTION

It is partly for the foregoing reasons that the ALA takes strong exception to the Report of Commissioner Davis. But the ALA's position is not merely a plea that it be spared from burdens which will severely impair its ability to disseminate knowledge. Much more importantly, the Commissioner's Report misapplies the copyright law to the facts concerning library photocopying.

In its previous brief the ALA explained in detail how the doctrine of fair use, viewed in the light of the standards of the Copyright clause of the Constitution and the relative interests of libraries and their users on the one hand, and those of the copyright proprietors on the other, constituted a complete defense to the charge of infringement. Rather than meet this argument head on, the Commissioner merely stated in conclusory fashion that:

> Whatever may be the bounds of "fair use" as defined and applied by the court, defendant's [traditional library photocopying] is clearly outside those bounds. (Op. 16)*

Exercising the "judgment of Solomon" and the "dexterity of Houdini" (Op. 2), the Commissioner felt that since the instant plaintiff was not seeking an injunction (Op. 18), and no great financial or administrative burdens would be placed on libraries by his decision in the interim (Op. 29-30), libraries should present their fair use arguments to Congress (Op. 24) to seek relief. Of course other copy-

---

* Commissioner Davis' Opinion shall hereinafter be referred to as "Op", and the numerals appearing thereafter will denote particular pages thereof.

---

right proprietors may well seek injunctive relief against non-government libraries based on the precedent established herein, and the premise concerning lack of burdens is totally without foundation, as will be pointed out hereinafter. In any event, the Commissioner was clearly in error in ignoring the fair use defense advanced by the ALA. His subjective and groundless feeling that little harm would be caused by such an abdication of his responsibility is no excuse.

B. THE DOCTRINE OF FAIR USE PROVIDES A COMPLETE DEFENSE FOR TRADITIONAL LIBRARY PHOTOCOPYING

It is apparent that the Commissioner failed to grasp the true dimensions of the question presented to him. For purposes of proper analysis this question, set forth at page 1 *supra*, must be broken down into two sub-questions, namely:

Question 1: Is it fair use for a scientist, researcher, or scholar to make a single photocopy of an article in a copyrighted journal for use in research or study?

Question 2: Assuming the answer to Question 1 is in the affirmative, is the fair use privilege of the scientist, researcher, or scholar destroyed if the library, acting as his agent, makes the photocopy for him at his request?

When viewed in this light, it is clear that only *Question 1* is of first impression. And the question is still one of first impression, since the Commissioner failed to consider it, let alone answer it. His only statement at all relevant to this issue is the tautology that there is no case law which would support an affirmative answer to *Question 1* (Op. 21). Of course there is no case law in support of a

6

negative answer either, since this is the first time the question has been presented for judicial determination. Should the Commissioner's Report be adopted, this dearth of case law will continue to prevail.

It is submitted that *Question 1* is the primary issue before this Court. It is further submitted that on the facts developed at trial the question demands an affirmative answer. And once this demand is satisfied, *Question 2*, which is not novel, can be placed in its proper context. Agency law and a decision of the Supreme Court in a completely analogous context will require a ruling that the libraries' patrons' privilege of fair use is not destroyed by the mere fact that libraries make photocopies for them at the patrons' request. Should this Court accept plaintiff's distorted picture of libraries as publishers competing with it, rather than as agents of their patrons, as did the Commissioner, and continue to ignore the fair use defense available to their patrons, the incongruous result will be an act being held liable for an act which his principal was free to do and the consequent destruction of the fair use defense.

In the expectation that this Court will give proper consideration to the two real questions presented herein, the facts and law relevant to each will be discussed below.

B(1) Question 1—IS IT FAIR USE FOR A SCIENTIST, RESEARCHER, OR SCHOLAR TO MAKE A SINGLE PHOTOCOPY OF AN ARTICLE IN A COPYRIGHTED JOURNAL FOR USE IN RESEARCH OR STUDY?

B(1) (a)—Facts

Most, if not all, of the facts which are relevant to a determination of the foregoing question are not in dispute. Because the question was not considered at the hearing, however, some of these facts are not contained in the Com-

7

missioner's Report, and those that are mentioned are spread throughout the Report. For this reason these facts will be marshalled and briefly summarized below.

1. Photocopying by scientists, researchers, and schol-

ars is mainly from non-profit journals published by scientific and professional societies. (Sophar and Heilprin report, pps. 67-70.)*

2. There are an overwhelming number of journals published by a multitude of publishers containing articles of interest to scientists, researchers, and scholars.

   a. In the biomedical field alone it is estimated that there are in excess of 10,000 journals published. (T. 275).**

   b. It has been estimated that about 1,000 or more publishers originate the bulk of the materials photocopied by scientists, researchers, and scholars. (Sophar and Heilprin report, pps. 58-60).

3. Library patrons request, and are given, only one photocopy of a particular article, and never a copy of a whole journal or book. (Op. 14, 46).

4. The overwhelming majority of photocopies obtained from libraries are used for purposes of research and study. (T. 189-90). There is absolutely no evidence that any scientists, researchers, or scholars who obtained photocopies from libraries have ever republished the articles or competed in any manner whatsoever with the publisher thereof.

---

* See, Op. 2, footnote 2, for a full citation to this report.

** As used herein "T" will refer to the trial transcript and the numerals appearing thereafter will denote particular pages thereof.

8

5. Absent photocopying, scientists, researchers, and scholars would be denied access to much of the work published in their fields.

   a. This has been admitted by the plaintiff. In its "Statement" (Exhibit A) plaintiff states:

   There will be no halt to the photocopying of material, as such a halt would indeed be harmful to the dissemination of knowledge.

   b. The Commissioner, in his Report, found:

   A library is essential to the conduct of medical research. A principal product of research scientists is their publications and publication of results is a vital part of research. (Op. 40).

   c. A study conducted for the Senate Subcommittee concerned with the revision of the Copyright law reported:

   The various methods of photocopying have become indispensable to persons engaged in research and scholarship, and to libraries that provide research material in their collections to such persons. Effective research requires that the researcher be informed of the findings and opinions of others and have an opportunity to study the materials written by them. These materials are often very extensive and appear in a large number of publications. It is here that the libraries provide an indispensable service to research by furnishing the individual researcher with the materials needed by him for reference and study.

   The need of researchers for ready access to a mass of materials is present in every field of scholarly investigation, but the problem is exemplified most clearly in the field of scientific and technical research. The body of scientific and technical literature has grown so rapidly during the last few decades that it would be extremely dif-

9

*ficult for the individual scholar or research-
er to gain access to the works he may need
to consult unless he can obtain copies from
a library.* This is true especially of periodical literature.

> *It would be virtually impossible for a per-
> son engaged in research to subscribe to all
> the periodicals which from time to time
> may touch upon his field of interest, and
> even the libraries where he lives may be
> unable to furnish the necessary material.
> Nor can libraries be expected to meet the
> needs of any number of researchers by loan
> of the copies in their collections.* In re-
> sponse to the needs of researchers, most
> major libraries are equipped to provide
> them with photocopies of materials in the
> library's collections. *It is invaluable to
> a researcher to be able to obtain from a
> central or specialized library photocopies
> of the various articles he needs for reference
> and study.* Varner, "Photoduplication of
> Copyrighted Material by Libraries", Copy-
> right Law Revision Study No. 15, Senate
> Subcommittee on Patents, Trademarks and
> Copyrights, 86th Cong., 1st Session. (em-
> phasis added).

d. The testimony at trial confirmed the essentiality of photocopies to access:

> Q. Am I to understand, then, that the reason
> for which photocopies were substituted for
> lending the original journal was to improve
> the scientist's accessibility to the published
> scientific record?

10

> A. Yes, I might add, there are two aspects of
> the word "access" as I would use it there
> . . . — one is the question of physical ac-
> cessibility: that is, to produce physical
> proximity, to place it immediately at an
> individual's disposal; and the other func-
> tion that Xerography or photo-duplication
> does perform is breaking up the scientific
> record into units and permitting the free
> assemblage of those units into packages
> which particularly — relate specifically to
> the scientist's own comple. interests. (T.
> 824-5).

e. The testimony at trial also indicated that a
scientist, researcher, or scholar could not afford to subscribe to specific journals which
would only occasionally contain articles relating
to his field because:

> [O]verall, there are an insufficient number
> of articles in that specific journal that are
> of specific interest or use to me . . .
> (T. 574-5).

f. Copies of many journal issues are available
only from libraries, and access to articles therein only by means of photocopies. The testimony
at trial further shows the problems which inhere in attempting to obtain reprints from authors. One doctor testified that in less than
one-third of the cases of requests for reprints
was he successful in obtaining same, and that
the fraction was even smaller for articles
appearing in older journals. (T. 559). His
testimony was confirmed by that of a research
technician employed by the National Institute
of Health, who stated that from past experience
his department did not even attempt to order
reprints of articles from journals over three
years old, since almost without exception such
orders were not filled. (T. 527).*

6. Scientists, researchers, and scholars have been ob-

11

taining photocopies of journal articles for at least
fifty years, and the practice was well established
as far back as 1935. (T. 430-1; Defendant's Exhibit
74).

7. There is absolutely no evidence that any publishers
suffer a loss in subscription, back volume, or reprint
revenue by reason of the obtaining by scientists, researchers, or scholars from libraries of single photocopies of articles appearing in the publishers'
journals. The only statements relating to any such
alleged loss at trial were:

> [From the Chairman of plaintiff's Board of
> Directors]

> Q. Is there any way to measure specifically, the
> amount of potential harm photocopying has
> done to Williams & Wilkins' journals?

> A. Only by general business common sense and
> *things that you hear* from subscribers, librari-
> ans and so forth. (T. 73; emphasis added).

> [From plaintiff's President]

> Q. Am I correct in understanding that Williams &
> Wilkins has never made a detailed study of the
> actual effect of photocopying on its business?

> A. Yes, you are correct. (T. 1300).

See, also, Finding 39 (Op. 53-4).

---

* Plaintiff's Exhibit 2 contains a notice to the effect that the publisher does not attempt to keep a stock of back issues and cannot
guarantee to supply back issues of belated renewals, and that issues
of even the current volume "may be out of print at the time the
subscription order is received".

12

The foregoing facts, provide a clear basis for a successful
fair use defense on behalf of the scientists, researchers,
and scholars who obtain single photocopies of journal
articles relating to their fields.

B(1) (b)—The Law of Fair Use Applied to the Facts

Before applying the doctrine of fair use to the facts
set forth above, it is well to have the definition of and
basis for the doctrine firmly in mind. The Copyright
Clause of the Constitution authorizes Congress:

> To promote the Progress of Science and useful Arts,
> by securing for limited Times to Authors . . . the ex-
> clusive Right to their . . . Writings. (U.S. Const. Art.
> 1, §8).

Even before the creation of our own copyright system,
the courts of England recognized the potential conflicts
inherent in a system designed to promote the dissemination of information by granting monopolies on the manner of its expression. In the case of *Sayre v. Moore*, 102
Eng. Rep. 139 (K.B. 1785), Lord Mansfield stated:

> We must take care to guard against two extremes
> equally prejudicial; the one, that men of ability, who
> have employed their time for the service of the com-
> munity, may not be deprived of their just merits and
> the reward of their ingenuity and labor; the other,
> that the world may not be deprived of improvements,
> nor the progress of the arts be retarded. (102 Eng.
> Rep. at 140).

The non-statutory doctrine of fair use has been fashioned
by the courts in this country to guard against the latter
evil referred to above.

A succinct definition of the doctrine is found in the case
of *Rosemont Enterprises, Inc. v. Random House, Inc.*, 366

13

F.2d 303 (2d Cir. 1966), wherein the Court remarked:

"Fair use" is a "privilege in others than the owner of a copyright to use the copyrighted material in a reasonable manner without his consent, notwithstanding the monopoly granted to the owner * * *" Ball, Copyright and Literary Property 260 (1944). See generally Latman, Fair Use of Coyprighted Works, Study No. 14, prepared for the Subcommittee on Patents, Trademarks and Copyrights, Senate Comm. on the Judiciary, 86th Cong., 2d Sess. (Comm. Print 1960). The fundamental justification for the privilege lies in the constitutional purpose in granting copyright protection in the first instance, to wit, "To Promote the Progress of Science and the Useful Arts." U.S. Const. Art. 1, § 8. See Mathews Conveyor Co. v. Palmer-Bee Co., 135 F.2d 73 (6th Cir. 1943); Note, 56 Colum. L. Rev. 585, 595 (1956). To serve that purpose, "courts in passing upon particular claims of infringement must occasionally subordinate the copyright holder's interest in a maximum financial return to the greater public interest in the development of art, science and industry." Berlin v. E.C. Publications Inc., 329 F.2d 541, 544 (2d Cir. 1964). Whether the privilege may justifiably be applied to particular materials turns initially on the nature of the materials, e.g., whether their distribution would serve the public interest in the free dissemination of information and whether their preparation requires some use of prior materials dealing with the same subject matter. Consequently, the privilege has been applied to works in the fields of science, law, medicine, history and biography. See Latman, supra at 10. (366 F.2d at 306-7).

It is readily apparent that the question presently under discussion poses exactly the issues referred to above—namely, should the interests of publishers in profit maximization be subordinated to the interests of scientists, re-

14

searchers, and scholars in furthering art, science, and industry, so as to permit the latter to obtain single photocopies of articles in copyrighted journals without the consent of the publisher and notwithstanding the copyright claimed by him. As mentioned hereinbefore, this question is one of first impression and was neither discussed nor answered in the Commissioner's Report.

Once the foregoing question is properly recognized as the central issue presented in this case, the ALA will agree with the Commissioner upon the criteria which are to be used in its determination. As set forth in the Commissioner's Report (Op. 15), these criteria are:

a) the purpose of the use;

b) the nature of the copyrighted work;

c) the amount or substantiality of the material used in relation to the copyrighted work as a whole; and

d) the effect of the use on a copyright owner's potential market for his work.

It must be recognized, however, that this case differs from those in which the foregoing criteria have heretofore been applied. This is not the usual situation where portions of a copyrighted work have been lifted and incorporated in another work which competes with the original. Scientists, researchers, and scholars obtain single photocopies of journal articles for purposes of research and study, and not for republication in other works. (T. 189-90). They are not authors attempting to misappropriate the work of earlier authors to their own profit-seeking ends. They seek merely *access* to the earlier work for *use* in their fields by the only means through which access

15

is available, i.e., photocopying.* The foregoing distinction between misappropriation and use is clearly recognized in the landmark case of *Baker v. Selden*, 101 U.S. 99 (1879), wherein the Supreme Court stated:

The very object of publishing a book on science or the useful arts is to communicate to the world the useful knowledge which it contains. But this object would be frustrated if the knowledge could not be used without incurring the guilt of piracy of the book. And where the art it teaches cannot be used without employing the methods and diagrams used to illustrate the book . . . such methods and diagrams are to be considered as necessary incidents to the art, and given therewith to the public; not given for the purpose of publication in other works explanatory of the art, but for the purpose of practical application.

* * *

On the other hand, the teachings of science and the rules and methods of useful art have their final end in application and use; and this application and use are what the public derive from the publication of a book which teaches them. . . . The use of the art is a totally different thing from a publication of a book explaining it. (101 U.S. at 103-4).

The Commissioner ignored the *misappropriation* versus *use* distinction as applied to scientists, researchers, and scholars and instead focused his attention solely on the ac-

---

*   It is well established that a "fair use" may be made of a copyrighted article. In that respect an owner of a copyright is in a different position than an owner of a patent.

"* * * One radical difference is that a patent confers an exclusive right to use, * * * whereas a copyright contemplates and permits fair use by all persons of the copyrighted work. * * *" 18 C.J.S., Copyright and Literary Property, § 92, p. 213.

Karll v. Curtis Pub. Co., 39 F. Supp. 836, 837 (S.D. Cal. 1941).

16

tivities of their agents—the libraries. Had the true question been recognized, it would have been clear that under the criteria set forth above a defense of fair use is established on behalf of the principals, as will be seen from the following.

1. Nature of the Use

It has been pointed out above that scientists, researchers and scholars merely *use* the single photocopies of journal articles they obtain and only for purposes of research and study. (See Fact No. 4, supra, p. 7). Such uses clearly qualify to have the appellation "fair" appended to them.

Indeed, it is to protect such *uses* against claims of copyright infringement that the doctrine of fair use was fashioned. As stated in *Loew's Inc.* v. *Columbia Broadcasting System, Inc.*, 131 F. Supp. 165 (S.D. Cal. 1955), aff'd, 239 F.2d 532 (9th Cir. 1956), aff'd, 356 U.S. 43 (1958):

Thus, in the field of science and the fine arts, we find a broad scope given to fair use. "This doctrine permits a writer of scientific, legal, medical and similar books or articles of learning to use even the identical words of earlier books or writings dealing with the same subject matter." . . . The writer of such works "invites reviews, comments and criticism" and we could add, the "use" of the books and portions and quotations therefrom for the purpose of the advancement of learning.

* * * the law permits those working in a field of science or art to make use of ideas, opinions, or theories, and in certain cases even the exact words contained in a copyrighted book in that field [citing cases]. This is permitted in order, in the language of Lord Mansfield in Sayre v. Moore, 1 East 361, 102

Eng. Reprint 139 "that the world may not be deprived of improvements, nor the progress of the arts be re-

17

tarded." In such cases the law implies the consent of the copyright owner to a fair use of his publication for the advancement of the science or art. (131 F. Supp. at 175).

See also, *Baker v. Selden* and *Rosemont Enterprises, Inc. v. Random House, Inc., supra.*

It is well recognized, then, that a scientist, researcher, or scholar can *borrow* even the exact words from an earlier copyrighted work and use them in a new work for the advancement of learning without infringing the copyright:

The latitude which is permitted a second author within the pale of "fair use" was stated in Sampson & Murdock Co. v. Seaver-Radford Co., 1 Cir., 1905, 140 F. 539, as follows:

* * * so, also, it is clear that, under some circumstances and for certain purposes, a subsequent publisher may draw from the earlier publication its identical words, and make use of them. This is peculiarly so with reference to works in regard to the arts and sciences, using those words in the broadest sense, because, within reference to them, any publication is given out as a development in the way of progress, and, to a certain extent, by common consent, including the implied consent of the first publisher, others interested in advancing the same art or science may commence where the prior author stopped. This includes medical and legal publications, in which the entire community has an interest, and which the authors are supposed to give forth, not only for their own pecuniary profit, but for the advancement of science. *Greenbie* v. *Noble,* 151 F. Supp. 45, 67-8 (S.D.N.Y. 1957).

and,

Succinctly stated, this doctrine [fair use] permits a writer of scientific, legal, medical and similar books or articles of learning to use even the identical words

18

of earlier books or writings dealing with the same subject matter. *Thompson* v. *Gernsback,* 94 F. Supp. 453, 454 (S.D.N.Y. 1950).

A totally anomalous situation would thus be presented if the Commissioner's opinion were affirmed. The result would be that a scientist, researcher, or scholar could borrow the exact words from a copyrighted journal article and use them in the publication of a new article dealing with the same subject and competing with the original. If, however, he borrowed these same words in the form of a photocopy, and did nothing with them except refer to them in his research and study, he would be guilty of copyright infringement. The law of copyright does not, and this Court should not, permit a cloak of formalism to mask such a ludicrous state of affairs. The nature of the *use* of single photocopies by scientists, researchers, and scholars clearly qualifies it for protection under the fair use doctrine.* And as has been pointed out above, photo-

---

* To the extent, if any, that some few library patrons depart from the norm in their use of photocopies, and further distribute copies thereof or use their contents in competing works, the copyright proprietors have their rights against "unfair users", and those rights are not insubstantial. If infringement is established, the copyright owner is entitled to: (1) any profits made by the infringer by reason of this infringement under 17 U.S.C. § 101; (2) damages which are set at a statutory minimum of $250 under 17 U.S.C. § 101; and (3) costs and attorneys' fees under 17 U.S.C. § 116. Thus, the copyright owner has effective ways to protect against even minimal infringements, short of mislabelling *every* scientist, researcher, and

scholar as infringers and burdening libraries with the task of exacting unwarranted tribute from them.

19

copying is essential to the access which will permit such use.* (See, Fact No. 5, *supra,* pp. 8-11).

2. *Nature of the Copyrighted Work*

Photocopying for scientists, researchers, and scholars is mainly from non-profit journals published by scientific and professional societies (Fact 1, p. 7).** Authors who

---

*As the Court remarked in *Rosemont, supra:*

We, however, cannot subscribe to the view that an author is absolutely precluded from saving time and effort by referring to and relying upon prior published material. Cf. Oxford Book Co. v. College Entrance Book Co., 98 F.2d 688 (2d Cir. 1938). It is just such wasted effort that the proscription against the copyright of ideas and facts, and to a lesser extent the privilege of fair use, are designed to prevent. (366 F.2d at 310).

** Only in rare and exceptional cases will even a portion of a monograph be photocopied (T: 600-604; 844-50; 1329). The reason for this was explained at trial by the ex-Deputy Director of the National Library of Medicine as follows:

Now, it is also the rule that an individual scientist contributes a paper without charge. There is no formal contractual relationship between either the society at whose meeting he presents this paper or the publisher and the individual scientist-author. It is "contributed", a contributed paper. He received no pecuniary reward at all for having contributed—usually; I am speaking in generalizations; this is the usual practice in the sciences—having contributed that paper.

This, therefore, is one economic system. Simultaneously the same scientist lives in another economic system, that of the publication of monographs or textbooks. These—it is the exception where a monograph is contributed. Almost universally it is the subject of a contractual relation between a publisher—and usually a commercial publisher—and the individual author, in which there is a pecuniary award to the author of the monograph. * * *

20

contribute articles to such journals typically receive no compensation from the publisher and are interested only in the widest possible dissemination of the results of their research. (T. 669-70).

And, of course, it is precisely when the copyrighted work is of the foregoing nature—relating to science and the useful arts—that the doctrine of fair use is given its broadest definition. *Rosemont, Baker,* and *Loew's, supra.* Thus, the application of the second criterion to the facts of the present situation also clearly supports a finding of fair use.

3. *The Amount and Substantiality of the Material Used in Relation to the Whole*

Whereas the Commissioner completely ignored the first two criteria discussed above, he did briefly treat this third criterion. He suggested that the *de minimis* standard was the proper basis for the doctrine of fair use. (Op. 15). This was clear error. And this error was compounded by his reliance upon inapposite precedent, which he cited for the purported proposition that wholesale copying or the copying of substantial portions of a copyrighted work is never fair use. (Op. 16).

The faults in the Commissioner's approach are easily demonstrated. First, it is clear that *de minimis* is not the basis for the doctrine of fair use. The true relationship between *de minimis* and fair use is described in Cohen, *Fair*

(Footnote continued)

All that I'm saying, and I'm making a—I'm not trying to get

into this in great depth, but all I'm saying is that the whole business of pecuniary award to the creator, and the question of property, is more cogent, is more pertinent, in the field of monographic publishing than it is in the field of scientific journal publishing. (T. 847-49).

21

Use in the Law of Copyright, ASCAP, COPYRIGHT LAW SYMPOSIUM (No. 6, 1955), p. 44, 47 as follows (footnotes omitted):

> It is only when the preliminary questions: is the material copyrightable? was it copyrighted? was it copied? and was enough copied to satisfy the "substantial appropriation" doctrine and to make the *de minimis* doctrine inapplicable? have been answered in the affirmative, that the question of whether there has been a fair use arises . . .

And *Nimmer on Copyright* also acknowledges that the fair use defense is not grounded on the *de minimis* standard:

> . . . It is certainly possible, as do the foregoing definitions in whole or in part, to employ the term fair use as a label for similarity which is not substantial. It is possible, but not very helpful since this approach merely restates the problem of determining substantial similarity, and ignores what may be regarded as the crucial problem of fair use. *That problem arises where it is established by admission or by the preponderance of the evidence that the defendant has copied sufficiently from the plaintiff so as to cross the line of substantial similarity.* The result must necessarily constitute an infringement unless the defendant is rendered immune from liability because the particular use which he made of plaintiff's material is a "fair use." In this more meaningful sense fair use is a defense not because of the absence of substantial similarity but rather despite the fact that the similarity is substantial. (*Nimmer on Copyright,* 1971 ed., p. 644-5; emphasis added).

Accordingly, even if it is conceded that a given scientist, researcher, or scholar has done more than a *de minimis* amount of copying, this does not foreclose consideration of fair use. On the contrary, it simply permits the con-

22

sideration of the numerous equitable factors, discussed above and below, which compel a finding of fair use.

Second, the photocopying done by scientists, researchers, or scholars is *not* "wholesale". Only *one* photocopy of *one* article in a journal is photocopied in the overwhelming majority of the instances of present concern.* An entire journal is never copied. (Op. 5).

---

* The Copyright Act itself recognizes both *single copies and private use* as exceptions to the limited monopoly which it grants. 17 U.S.C. § 107 states in relevant part:

During the existence of the American copyright in any book, the importation into the United States of any piratical copies thereof or of any copies thereof . . . which have not been produced in accordance with the manufacturing provisions specified in Section 16 of this title . . . is prohibited; *provided, however,* that except as regards piratical copies, such prohibition shall not apply:

* * *

(d) To any book published abroad with the authorization of the author or copyright proprietor when imported under the circumstances stated in one of the four subdivisions following, that is to say:

First. When imported, *not more than one copy at one time, for individual use and not for sale;* but such privilege of importation shall not extend to a foreign reprint of a book by an American author copyrighted in the United States.

* * *

Third. When imported, *for use and not for sale, not more*

than one copy of any such book in any one invoice, in good faith *by or for any society or institution incorporated for educational literary, philosophical, scientific or religious purposes, or for the encouragement of the fine arts, or for any college, academy, school, or seminary of learning, or for any State, school, college, university, or free public library in the United States.*

Fourth. *When such books form parts of libraries or collections purchased en bloc for the use of societies, institutions, or libraries designated in the foregoing paragraph . . . and are not intended for sale. . .* (emphasis added).

23

Third, and most importantly, this entire criterion was misapplied by the Commissioner. The amount of a work copied, if it is substantial,* has heretofore been considered only in the common situations wherein the borrowed portion has been republished in a new work by the borrower. In such situations the concern of the Courts has been that the borrower, if he borrowed too much, was taking a free ride on the coattails of the copyright owner and reaping commercial benefit where he had not sown. It is cases involving the foregoing rationale that the Commissioner turned to for the purported rule that:

> [I]t is not "fair use" to copy substantial portions of a copyrighted work when the *new work* is a substitute for, and diminishes the potential market for, the original. (Op. 16; emphasis added).

The easy answer to the foregoing is that there is no "new work" involved in the instant case, and both the "rule" and the cases from which it is derived are totally inapposite. The scientists, researchers, and scholars who obtain single photocopies of a journal article *use* them for research and study. (Op. 4). They do not republish the articles, nor do they incorporate them into new articles.**

---

* If it is not, *de minimis* standard would then be applied, and the case would be dismissed without even reaching the question of fair use.

** As reported in *National Institute, Inc.* v. *Nutt,* 28 F.2d 132, 134 (D. Conn. 1928), the case of *Nicols* v. *Pitman,* 26 L.R. Ch. Div. 374, recognized the clear distinction between use and republication. In that case the defendant took shorthand notes of a copyrighted lecture and republished the notes as an article in a periodical. The Court held that the audience at the lecture *were at liberty to take the fullest notes for their own personal use,* but not to use them afterwards for the purpose of publishing the lecture for profit.

24

The reply to the question "how much is photocopied?" is "one copy of one article", but the question itself is irrelevant as posed by the Commissioner. Professor Nimmer acknowledges that:

> It would seem, nevertheless, that there may be certain very limited situations wherein copying of the entire work for a different functional purpose may be regarded as a fair use. (Nimmer, *supra* at 651).

In the present case copying of the entire work is not involved, and moreover the different functional purpose is critical. This purpose is to provide access to articles in the only feasible manner—i.e., by photocopying them.

4. *The Effect of the Use On a Copyright Owner's Potential Market for His Work.*

Since the Commissioner found this fourth criterion to be the most important, it would be well to review the relevant evidence, findings, and law. The evidence on the question of potential market damage is clear. The plaintiff claimed to be bringing this suit only "to offset the loss in the sale of subscriptions and back volumes and reprints that each photocopy brought about".* However the plaintiff never made a study of the actual effect of photocopying on its business (T. 1300), and in support of its alleged losses cited only its own common sense and things that it had heard (T. 73, 1300). (See, Fact 7, p. 11, supra). Thus there was not one scintilla of admissible or probative evidence that photocopying had caused a loss to plaintiff. In fact, the Commissioner found that plaintiff's business was flourishing. (Finding 39, Op. 53-4). Moreover, in spite of the fact that scientists, researchers, and scholars

---

* Defendant's Exhibit No. 87-7; T. 70-71.

25

have been obtaining photocopies from libraries since as long ago as 1935, only one publisher—the instant plaintiff—has felt compelled to attempt to halt this practice.* The evidence is clear. The photocopying practices challenged herein have not been shown to diminish the potential market for the journals copied.

In spite of the evidence or lack thereof on the economic effects of photocopying, the Commissioner found:

> [D]amage may be *inferred* in this case from the fact that the photocopies are intended to supplant the original articles (Op. 17; emphasis added).

Of course, the only relevant testimony shows that photocopies do not *supplant* originals. An individual can only subscribe to so many expensive journals, and in many instances a given journal will contain an insufficient number of articles of interest to him to warrant his subscription. (T. 574-5). Thus, photocopies do not *supplant*, they *supplement*, and it does not follow that one who photocopies would otherwise be a subscriber.**

---

*As stated by William M. Passano, Chairman of the Board of Williams & Wilkins in an article entitled "How Photocopying Pollutes Sci-Tech Publishing," *Publishers Weekly*, February 2, 1970, p. 64:

> One would think that publishers would join forces against the common enemy, but such has not proved to be the case.

** On the facts of the present case it can be clearly demonstrated that photocopying does not supplant journal subscription. From the table at page 36 of the Commissioner's Report it can be seen that during the 108 day period between Sept. 27, 1967 to Jan. 12, 1968, a total of thirteen (13) copies were made of the eight (8) articles in suit by the two library defendants. The eight (8) articles which were copied appeared in five journal volumes published by

---

26

It should be further noted that the "market effect" criterion was also formulated for dealing with situations involving a *new work*, which competed with the original and could potentially diminish its sales. This is not the present situation. What is involved here is *use* of a photocopy as opposed to *use* of the original journal in which the article appeared.

And even if it were acknowledged that the use of photocopies by scientists, researchers, and scholars resulted to a limited extent in a minor loss of potential sales of original journals, this would not be fatal to the defense of fair use. Publishers can claim no inherent or natural rights in the writings of authors. *Fox Film Corp.* v. *Doyal*, 286 U.S. 123, 127 (1932). The Copyright Laws are not intended to codify any moral principle holding the financial interests of publishers inviolate. The end sought by the Copyright Laws is to promote the public interest. Financial incentives are offered only as a means to this end.

(Footnote continued)

plaintiff. Extrapolating these figures, approximately forty (40) photocopies of the articles in question would be made yearly, and adding a margin of 25%, this figure would be fifty (50). If it is assumed for convenience that the fifty (50) copies are divided equally among the five (5) journal volumes, in one year a total of ten (10) copies of articles appearing in any one volume would be made by the two library defendants. In this regard it should be noted that it is *volumes*, not articles, to which plaintiff seeks subscriptions. Further conservatively assuming that the two libraries serve 4000 scientists (this is estimated to be the size of the NLM professional staff, Op. 3, although the NLM serves the whole country), it is seen that the chances of a given scientist photocopying a portion of a given journal in any one year are about 1/400. Can it seriously be contended that given these odds the scientist would subscribe to the expensive journal if photocopies were not available? If he did, it would be on the expectation that in 400 years he would find one article which was useful to him. The question therefore answers itself. Photocopying does not supplant journal subscription.

27

The Congressional Report which accompanied the present Copyright Act recognized this objective:

> The enactment of *copyright legislation* by Congress under the terms of the Constitution *is not based on any natural right that the author has in his writings*, for the Supreme Court has held that such rights as he has are *purely statutory rights*, but upon the *ground that the welfare of the public will be served and progress of science and useful arts will be promoted by securing to authors for limited periods the exclusive right to their writings.* The Constitution does not establish copyright, but provides that Congress shall have the power to grant such rights if it thinks best. *Not primarily for the benefit of the author, but primarily for the benefit of the public, such rights are given. Not that any particular class of citizens, however worthy, may benefit, but because the policy is believed to be for the benefit of the great body of the people, in that it will stimulate writing and invention, to give some bonus to authors and inventors.* (House Report No. 2222, 60th Congress, 2d. Session, p. 6-7; emphasis added).

And in the case of *Berlin* v. *E. C. Publication, Inc.*, 329 F.2d 541 (2d Cir. 1964), the Second Circuit expressed the same views, i.e., that profit maximization must give way to the public interest in regard to the Copyright Laws, as follows:

> While indeed broad, the area in which a copyright proprietor is permitted the exclusive commercial benefits of his copyright work is clearly not without limit. In the words of Article I, Section 8, of the Constitution, copyright protection is designed "to promote the Progress of Science and useful Arts," *and the financial reward guaranteed to the copyright holder is but an incident of this general objective, rather than an end in itself. As a result, courts in passing upon particular claims of infringement must occasionally*

28

> subordinate the copyright holder's interest in a maximum financial return to the greater public interest in the development of art, science and industry. (329 F.2d at 543-4, emphasis added).

It is thus manifest that copyright infringement is *not* established simply upon a showing that the use of a copyrighted work complained of derogates from the copyright owner's goal of profit maximization. The present attack on library photocopying is based solely on a desire for profit maximization.

B(1) (o)—Question 1 Should Be Answered in the Affirmative

It will be recalled that *Question 1*, one of first impression in this Court, is:

Is it fair use for a scientist, researcher, or scholar

to make a single photocopy of an article in a copyrighted journal for use in research or study?

From the foregoing analysis of the criteria bearing on fair use in the present context, it will be seen that the "nature of the use" and the "nature of the copyrighted work" clearly dictate an affirmative answer to this question. It was further demonstrated that the amount photocopied by an individual scientist, researcher, or scholar is not substantial, and that in any event the "how much" criteria is inapplicable to a case where there is only *use* of the original material and no republication or incorporation in a competing work. Finally, the lack of evidence of photocopyings' having any adverse effect on the copyright owners' potential market was shown. The inference of any such effect, which is the only factor possibly militating against a finding of fair use, is of scant importance. The copyright owner's attempt to obtain profit maximization is more than offset by the fact that to deny scientists, researchers, and scholars their traditional right to

29

make single photocopies of journal articles is to deny them access to, and the ability to use, the recorded knowledge in their fields.

Clearly, an affirmative answer to Question 1 is warranted on the facts of this case.

B(2) Question 2—ASSUMING THE ANSWER TO QUESTION 1 IS IN THE AFFIRMATIVE, IS THE FAIR USE PRIVILEGE OF THE SCIENTIST, RESEARCHER OR SCHOLAR DESTROYED IF THE LIBRARY, ACTING AS HIS AGENT, MAKES THE PHOTOCOPY FOR HIM AT HIS REQUEST?

B(2) (a)—Facts

Once again, the facts relevant to *Question 2* are not in dispute and will be summarized below. These facts will be taken verbatim from the Opinion of the Commissioner.

1. "Usually, researchers request photocopies of articles to assist them in their on-going projects." (Op. 4)

2. "[Libraries, pursuant to the General Interlibrary Loan Code] will provide only one photocopy of a particular article, per request, and will not photocopy on any given request an entire journal issue." (Op. 5, 14).

3. "A library is essential to the conduct of medical research." (Op. 40)

The foregoing are the only facts necessary to require a negative answer to *Question 2*. Libraries merely act as agents for their patrons and do for them at their request what they themselves are privileged to do under the doctrine of fair use. Moreover, libraries exercise care so that they do not, themselves, overstep the boundaries of the fair use privilege accorded to their patrons. Thus, it

30

would be anomalous if the agent-library were held liable on a charge to which its principal-patron had a complete defense. To so hold would be to fly in the face of the law of agency.

B(2) (b)—Question 2 Should Be Answered in the Negative

It is readily apparent why the plaintiff herein seeks to impose copyright infringement liability upon libraries rather than attacking their readers directly. The reason is simply that almost all (and perhaps every one) of these readers are not infringers but rather are "fair users". What is not so apparent is why the Commissioner

accepted the plaintiff's view and totally ignored *Question 1, supra.*

The purported basis for ignoring the fact that libraries are merely agents of readers is that under the Copyright Act, 17 U.S.C. § 1(a), unauthorized "copying" purportedly constitutes the literal standard of infringement.* By

---

*In fact, Congress never intended the proscription against "copying" to apply to books or other such printed publications. And in any event, the words used in the Copyright Act are open to judicial interpretation to avoid ridiculous and unintended results. Thus, in the case of *G. Ricordi & Co.* v. *Mason,* 201 F. 184 (S.D.N.Y. 1912), the Court held that not every version of a copyrighted work is a "version" within the meaning of the Copyright Act:

Although Section 1 of the Copyright Act, which went into effect July 1, 1909 (Act March 4, 1909, c. 320,35 Stat. 1075 [U.S. Comp. St. Supp. 1911, p. 1472]), in broad terms gives complainant the exclusive right "to translate the copyrighted work into other languages or dialects, or make any other version thereof," etc., still the summing up of a libretto by merely outlining the plot or theme, detailing the incidents in such a way as to give in the fewest words possible the so-called story,

31

having library employees operate reprographic machines on behalf of readers, so the argument goes, suddenly it is the libraries and not the readers who are doing the "copying". Somehow, when the *same* reader, for the *same* purposes, asks the library to photocopy the *same* portion of a work for him, instead of loaning the work to him, the reader's fair use is deemed irrelevant. The illogic of this contention is manifest—the library acts only as the agent of the reader and its actions do not destroy the "fair use" privilege that is available to the reader. The fact that the library may be referred to as the "copier" in the latter situation is a semantic nicety of no significance.

This wholly technical approach to library photocopying ignores the true functional relationships of the parties—copyright owners as disseminators of information and readers as users thereof, with libraries serving merely as intermediaries. In *Fortnightly Corp.* v. *United Artists Television, Inc.,* 392 U.S. 390 (1968), the Supreme Court had occasion to interpret the literal language of the Copyright Act in light of present day realities:

But our inquiry cannot be limited to ordinary meaning . . . for this is a statute that was drafted long before the development of the electronic phenomena with which we deal here. (392 U.S. at 395).

(Footnote continued)

as was done by the defendant with the operas "Germania" and "Iris," does not constitute the making of such a version thereof as was in the contemplation of Congress when the copyright statute was enacted.

A literal definition of the words "make any other version thereof" would not only include the defendant's publication, but also the newspaper publication, after performance, of any reviews or criticisms, even when written by reporters invited by the owner of the play to witness the production. (201 F. at 184-5).

32

The present situation is closely analogous to that before the Supreme Court in the *Fortnightly* case. The three parties whose interests were before the Court—the copyright owners, the CATV operator, and the television viewers—were in similar positions to the plaintiff, the libraries,* and the readers herein.

The CATV operator transmitted without license broadcasts of copyrighted materials to viewers who could not otherwise receive them. The question presented was whether this constituted "performance" of the copyrighted works so as to infringe under the literal language of the copyright law. The Supreme Court answered this question as follows:

Rather, resolution of the issue before us depends upon a determination of the function that CATV plays in the total process of television broadcasting and reception.

Television viewing results from combined activity by broadcasters and viewers. Both play active and indispensable roles in the process; neither is wholly passive.

• • •

Despite these deviations from the conventional situation contemplated by the framers of the Copyright Act, broadcasters have been judicially treated as exhibitors, and viewers as members of a theater audience. Broadcasters perform. Viewers do not perform. Thus, while both broadcaster and viewer play crucial roles in the total television process, a line is drawn between them. One is treated as active performer; the other as passive beneficiary.

---

* A distinction that should be kept in mind is that the CATV operator was profiting from its activities, whereas libraries do not profit from photocopying. (Sophar and Heilprin report: p. 48).

33

When CATV is considered in this framework, we conclude that it falls on the viewer's side of the line. Essentially, a CATV system no more than enhances the viewer's capacity to receive the broadcaster's signals; it provides a well-located antenna with an efficient connection to the viewer's television set. It is true that a CATV system plays an "active" role in making reception possible in a given area, but so do ordinary television sets and antennas. CATV equipment is powerful and sophisticated, but the basic function the equipment serves is little different from that served by the equipment generally furnished by a television viewer.

• • •

. . . CATV systems receive programs that have been released to the public and carry them by private channels to additional viewers. We hold that CATV operators, like viewers and unlike broadcasters, do not perform the programs that they receive and carry. (392 U.S. at 397-401).

The CATV "middleman" was held not liable for copyright infringement because he did "no more than enhance the viewers' capacity to receive" television broadcasts. Similarly, the "middleman" in the present suit—the library—does no more by photocopying than enhance the researchers' and scholars' access to and use of printed materials, to which such readers have a right under the doctrine of fair use. A copyright owner could sue the customer of CATV, itself, if the customer were to perform the broadcast for profit (as by charging admission to a television reception of a concert of copyrighted music). Likewise, if a reader utilizes a photocopy obtained from a library for purposes outside the realm of fair use, the copyright owners' cause of action lies against the reader and not the intermediary library.

34

The following statements by the Commissioner concerning the *Fortnightly* decision and its relation to the instant case are of interest:

What defendant really appears to be arguing is that the copyright law *should* excuse libraries from liability for the kind of photocopying here in suit. That, of course, is a matter for Congress, not the

courts, to consider for it involves questions of public policy aptly suited to the legislative process. In an analogous context in *Fortnightly Corp., supra,* Justice Fortas noted at 408:

The task of caring for CATV is one for the Congress. Our ax, being a rule of law, must cut straight, sharp, and deep; and perhaps this is a situation that calls for the compromise of theory and for the architectural improvisation which only legislation can accomplish. (Op. 24).*

In saying that the only relief available to libraries and their patrons must come from Congress, the Commissioner completely ignored the judicial doctrine of fair use. And the ax that fell in *Fortnightly* struck the neck of the copyright proprietor, not that of the CATV "middleman", whose position is analogous to that of the libraries herein.

As a practical matter libraries are in no position to raise a "fair use" defense based on each particular reader's actual manner of utilizing the copied article. Thus, if it is decided that *libraries* are liable for copyright infringement in respect of photocopying, they will be faced with the Hobson's choice of either collecting copyright royalties in respect of every page photocopied for every reader regardless of "fair use" or completely discontinuing the practice of photocopying.

---

* It should be noted that this statement by Mr. Justice Fortas was made in his dissenting opinion, in which no other Justice joined.

35

The result of the first of these choices is obvious. It would deprive readers who would be "fair users" of an opportunity to raise the fair use defense in support of their right to free access to and use of works in the library's collection. The only advantage served would be to collect royalties from those very few readers (if any) who would use photocopies for infringing (i.e., non-"fair use") purposes. Discontinuance of library photocopying would be even more disastrous to the interests of readers and would be of no benefit to the copyright owners. The results would be a significant lessening in the availability of works in libraries' collections, and a replacement of library photocopying with private copying or with coin-operated copying on the library premises by readers themselves.

If reader photocopying were to be the norm, the copyright owner would be thrown back upon his remedies as against the individual reader. Those readers making a "fair use" of their photocopies would have a defense to such an action; whereas the small number of readers violating the copyright law would be liable for infringement. Since this situation prevails currently, there is absolutely no justification whatsoever for forcing libraries to discontinue their photocopying practices, which are so essential to scientists, researchers and scholars, or for depriving such readers of their right to raise the defense of fair use.

It would perhaps be more convenient for the plaintiff herein to measure and collect royalties at the library level, but the monopoly of the copyright law cannot be enforced for mere convenience. The plaintiff has its rights against the ultimate users of photocopies of its materials, and as noted hereinbefore those rights are not insubstantial. (See, footnote at p. 18, *supra*).

36

In sum, logic, policy, and precedent support a functional analysis of the parties' relationships in the library photocopying area. That analysis shows the copyright proprie-tor's position to be nothing more than a thinly veiled attack on the "fair use" defense enjoyed by scholars and researchers for the benefit of the public. Functionally, libraries do nothing more than act as agents or instru-mentalities of readers. Libraries should not face expo-sure to copyright infringement for doing merely what their readers ask them to do. *Question 2* must be an-swered in the negative.

C. PRACTICAL CONSIDERATIONS

The primary reason the Commissioner refused to con-sider the foregoing arguments, which clearly support a fair use defense for the challenged photocopying practices, is his unfounded opinion that the critically important practice itself was not threatened and that his decision would at most create only a minimal additional-burden for libraries. Thus, the Commissioner knows that "courts should be mindful of the practical consequences of their decisions" (Op. 29), yet he failed to appreciate that he was, in fact, sounding the death knell for library photocopying. In view of plaintiff's own admission that a halt to photocopying "would indeed be harmful to the dissemination of knowledge'"*, the Commissioner's mis-conceptions as to the practical effects of his recommended decision cannot be permitted to stand.

---

* See Exhibit A appended hereto.

37

C(1) LIBRARY PHOTOCOPYING IS THREATENED IN THE PRESENT SUIT

In his opening statement at trial, plaintiff's counsel said:

> This case has nothing to do with the stopping of photocopying. The Commissioner knows that an injunction is not available in *this court*, nor is plain-tiff in any case seeking to curtail this use of its articles. (Emphasis added).

And the foregoing position statement was accepted at face value by the Commissioner, and relied upon by him in support of his finding that his decision would not prohibit photocopying.

Manifestly, the plaintiff's position may be peculiar only to it, and even then intended to apply only to suits against government libraries where injunctive relief is unavail-able in any event. In extrapolating the instant Plaintiff's position to other copyright owners, the Commissioner failed to recognize that these other owners may well seek injunctive relief against non-government libraries, based on the precedent of the instant case. Such a possibility is not remote if, for example, the photocopying royalties demanded by such other proprietors are not "reasonable" and the libraries refuse to or cannot accede to their de-mands.

The Commissioner has lost sight of the fact that statu-tory copyright constitutes, by definition, *only the right to exclude others from doing certain acts*. Although the remedies available under the Copyright Act include in-junctive relief and damages*, they do not include the right to exact royalties for future use of copyrighted materials. In practice, royalties are paid merely to buy peace from

---

* 17 U.S.C. § 101.

38

the onerous burden of an injunction. A holding by this Court that library photocopying constitutes copyright in-

fringement would be precedent for a ruling that the owner of a copyright could prevent libraries from photocopy-ing in the future.

This Court must be alert to the implications of this power in the context of the Copyright Act, which contains *no provision for compulsory licensing*. Thus, the holding sought by plaintiffs would necessarily grant copyright owners absolute power either to suppress library photo-copying entirely or to extort a monopolistic price for a royalty agreement.

C(2) ROYALTIES ON LIBRARY PHOTOCOPYING WOULD IMPOSE ONEROUS ECONOMIC AND ADMINISTRA-TIVE BURDENS ON LIBRARIES

Even if every owner of a copyright in a scientific or pro-fessional journal was committed not to seek injunctive re-lief against libraries, the practical consequences of a de-termination by this Court that owners are nevertheless entitled to royalties on all photocopying would effectively halt the practice. The Commissioner acknowledged that about 1,000 publishers (who publish the journals commonly photocopied) would benefit from his decision, but found that:

> [I]t does not appear that payments of royalties to these other publishers will create an undue or oppres-sive administrative burden. (Op. 30).

Perhaps this is true for the government library-defendants in the instant case, but it is most certainly not true in re-spect of the 4,200 member libraries of the ALA. More-over, the Commissioner failed to take account of the op-pressive economic burdens which would be created in addition to the administrative burdens.

39

All monies a library may be required to spend in pay-ment for or collection of photocopying royalties must be taken from its other functions, such as acquisitions of new materials to improve its collection.* Thus, imposition of royalties on library photocopying would necessarily limit access to written works by decreasing the library's ability to acquire such works.

Moreover, to the extent that the burden of royalties would be passed on to the scientist, researcher, or scholar, such limitations would be even more direct. In this re-gard, a practicing physician testified:

> There are great variations in interest in getting an article. I mean, some you must have, and others you say you'd like to have, and so on; and I think all of us have that small germ of parsimony, or whatever you call it, and frugality. So that there, very definite-ly, when you know there is going to be a charge, you, if it is a borderline situation, say, "Well, I won't bother." (T. 922-3).

And most importantly, if the burdens were passed on, the fair use defense which is available to almost every library patron would be a nullity. The library could not deter-mine which few of its patrons were not entitled to this defense and would have to sacrifice the interests of *all* its patrons through the collection of royalties from each of them. This is what the instant plaintiff desires them to do, as it would certainly make plaintiff's life easier and result in a windfall profit to it and other publishers. Using the same rationale, however, the owner of a copy-right in a musical composition would be permitted to collect performance fee royalties from *record manufac-turers* for *every record* sold by them, regardless of the fact that 99% of such records are sold for in-home use,

---

* T. 271-20.

40

and only 1% are sold for performance in restaurants, on radio shows, etc. Somehow, the absurdity of this proposition is lost sight of in the context of the present case.

And regardless of whose pockets the royalty payments come from, the administrative costs to the libraries in merely collecting, accounting for, and distributing the royalties would be substantial and could well exceed the amount of royalties collected.* This Court should consider the practical problems which would be involved were an academic, research, or public library to attempt to secure separate royalty agreements for the literally thousands of copyrighted journal items in its collection. It should consider the problems of merely determining with whom the agreement should be negotiated and if one is necessary in respect of a given article.

An indication of the magnitude of these problems is found in the instant case. Defendants argued that the plaintiff was neither a copyright proprietor nor the real-party-in-interest and therefore did not have standing to bring the instant lawsuit. In support of its position defendant cited, for example, the agreement relating to copyright between the American Association of Immunologists and plaintiff, under which the *Journal of Immunology* is published, and which provides in relevant part:

5. PROCUREMENT OF COPYRIGHT. The Association is the owner of the periodical but for the convenience of both parties copyright shall be procured by and in the name of the Publisher, and the costs incident thereto shall be charged to the profit-and-loss account of the periodical. *The Associ-*

---

* T. 486-88, 614.

41

ation reserves the right to have the copyright assigned to the Association if at any time in the future this seems desirable. [Emphasis supplied.] (Op. 35).

The Commissioner side-stepped the issue by stating that there was a presumption that plaintiff had standing (Op. 7), and that in any event "equitable rights of ownership of strangers to the suit cannot be raised as defenses against the legal title holder" (Op. 8).* However, legal presumptions and procedural rules aside, the problems that libraries will encounter in merely determining the person or persons with whom royalty arrangements are to be negotiated for a given article or journal are obvious.**

Furthermore, many of the journals photocopied contain much uncopyrighted or uncopyrightable material such as government reports (17 U.S.C. §8) and public domain material. Of course, whatever copyrights may exist in the journal as a whole do not, and cannot, cover such material.*** *Sawyer v. Crowell Publishing Co.,* 46 F. Supp.

---

* The Commissioner was clearly in error in this regard. See, *Public Ledger v. New York Times,* 279 F. 747 (2d Cir. 1922).

** Moreover, a copyright notice only identifies the copyright proprietor as of the date of publication. If, in the meantime, the copyright is assigned to another person or if an individual copyright owner dies or if a copyright is renewed by someone other than the original owner, the copyright notice necessarily would not reflect the true identity of the copyright owner.

*** 17 U.S.C. § 3 clearly recognizes that a composite work covered by a blanket copyright may contain uncopyrighted material:
The copyright provided by this title shall protect all the *copyrightable components* of the work copyrighted. (Emphasis added)

42

471 (S.D.N.Y. 1942). However, it would be impossible for a library to determine which articles or material in a supposedly "copyrighted" journal were properly subject to a claim for photocopying royalties without an undue amount of research and dispute of the type reflected in the Commissioner's Report under the heading "The license defense". (Op. 24).* Administrative feasibility would require the libraries to pay or collect royalties on every page photocopied. The result would again be a windfall profit to publishers, and the unwarranted taxation of scientists, researchers, and scholars for access to materials which they are clearly free to use without charge.

And even if those articles in a given journal requiring royalty payments and the proper person with whom rates for that article should be negotiated could be readily identified, this Court should further consider the fact that there are thousands of journals, each containing many articles, in the collections of most of the ALA's members.** This further suggests the problems which would inhere in libraries' accounting for royalties due under each separate agreement they negotiate.

The Commissioner clearly did not consider the foregoing factors, for if he had, he would never have stated that the payment of royalties to copyright owners would not create any undue or oppressive burdens.

---

* See the enigmatic reference to "photocopyable pages" in Exhibit B. Apparently, plaintiff recognizes this problem but offers no recommendations concerning its solution.

** The administrative complexities of negotiating royalty agreements with every owner (assuming he could be identified and located) of every potentially copyrighted work in a library collection are completely beyond comprehension. According to published U.S. Government statistics, in 1969 alone the Copyright Office issued 80,706 new copyright registrations for periodicals. (*Report of the Librarian of Congress,* 1969, p. 97).

43

There is simply no question that libraries, confronted with the alternative of ceasing all photocopying or seeking royalty agreements from copyright owners, will choose the former. The above-discussed insurmountable problems associated with royalty agreements make it obvious that they really have no alternative.

C(3) THERE IS NO ASCAP-TYPE SYSTEM FOR PHOTOCOPYING ROYALTIES WHICH WILL RELIEVE THE BURDENS OCCASIONED LIBRARIES

The Commissioner appears to have ignored both the fair use defense available to scientists, researchers, and scholars, and the onerous burdens which will befall libraries if this defense is not successful, on the basis of a pie-in-the-sky hope that all the difficulties between libraries and journal publishers can be satisfactorily reconciled through the formation of an ASCAP-like licensing body. In this regard the Commissioner stated:

It has been suggested that there be established a clearing house for access, permissions and payments for photocopying of copyrighted materials. The clearinghouse would relieve institutional copiers of the burdens of royalty distribution and might also be instrumental in setting up blanket royalty arrangements, thus relieving the institutions from most recordkeeping requirements. (Op. 30).

Of course, the foregoing "suggestion" and the hope on which it is based provide no excuse for the nullification of a valid defense of fair use.

Moreover, there is no such clearinghouse system in existence, and it does not appear likely that there will be one in the near future, if at all. Such a system, in order to be workable and of value in relieving libraries' burdens,

44

would. require the cooperation of every journal publisher in the United States. They would have to agree on uniform royalty rates and further upon the proportion of the fees collected to be distributed to each. The latter determination would require a detailed statistical study of library photocopying so that an equitable distribution of proceeds could be effected, which would have to be continuously updated to take account of the plethora of new materials published every year. The possibility that such cooperation will be forthcoming is remote, and it is further doubtful that all the publishers will be willing to expend the funds necessary to establish the required administrative machinery. As stated by the instant plaintiff:

> One would think that publishers would join forces against the common enemy, but such has not proved to be the case.*

Moreover, inherent in any ASCAP-type system are legal problems, arising primarily under the antitrust laws. Since 1941, ASCAP has operated under a consent decree designed to assure, to the extent possible, that broadcasters of copyrighted music shall not be compelled to pay license fees out of proportion to the actual use they make of copyrighted music. See 1940-43 CCH Trade Cases ¶56,104 (S.D.N.Y. 1941), as amended, 1950-51 CCH Trade Cases ¶62,595 (S.D.N.Y. 1950). Although this decree allowed blanket-licensing of all ASCAP copyrighted compositions, intervening court decisions have made it clear that such blanket licenses may constitute an illegal tie-in under the Sherman Act as well as a misuse of copyright. *United States v. Paramount Pictures*, 334 U.S. 131 (1948); *United*

---

* *Publisher's Weekly*, February 2, 1970, p. 64.

45

States v. Loew's, Inc., 371 U.S. 38, 45-50 (1962). Consequently, CBS recently brought a private antitrust action against ASCAP, asserting that ASCAP's blanket and per-program licenses constituted illegal price-fixing, boycotting, and tying by forcing a broadcaster "to pay for the right to use all copyrighted music in the ASCAP pool even though it might want rights only as to some of those musical compositions." 1972 CCH Trade Cases ¶73,997, p. 92,152. (S.D.N.Y. 1972). ASCAP's motion for summary judgment was denied, and the case has been set for trial. There the issue will be whether the Sherman Act requires ASCAP to license its compositions on a "per use" basis. with the broadcaster keeping records of how many times each composition is performed. *Ibid.*, at p. 92,155.

In view of these developments, it is doubtful that the

Commissioner's dreams for an ASCAP-type system, to relieve libraries from the onerous burdens he would saddle them with, will come true. Rather, "blanket royalty arrangements" such as he suggests may well be held a violation of the Sherman Act, and any legally acceptable system will place on libraries the onerous burden of making records of all photocopying of each individual article. The Commissioner has grounded his decision on the presumed availability of a licensing procedure against which a *prima facie* showing of illegality has been made out in a federal district court. Thus, the Commissioner's proposed solution is small comfort to the ALA or, for that matter, to plaintiffs. It is to be hoped, then, that this Court will not similarly attempt to "split the baby" utilizing the "judgment of Solomon" (Op. 2) and will instead realize the true practical consequences of an affirmance of the Commissioner's opinion.

46

IV. CONCLUSION

It is submitted that, when the true questions before this Court are appreciated, it will be apparent that it is fair use for a scientist, researcher, or scholar to make a single photocopy of an article appearing in a journal and that this privilege is not destroyed when a library, as agent for such person, makes the photocopy at his request. It is further submitted that the practical consequences of a holding that this traditional practice constitutes copyright infringement would be to completely halt the practice, resulting in a denial of access to recorded knowledge to those persons who would otherwise use it to promote the progress of science and the useful arts.

Respectfully submitted,

AMERICAN LIBRARY ASSOCIATION
Amicus Curiae

By ....

Perry S. Patterson
of
KIRKLAND, ELLIS & ROWE
1776 K. Street, N.W.
Washington, D.C. 20006
(202) 833-8400

Of Counsel:
WILLIAM D. NORTH
RONALD L. ENGEL
JAMES M. AMEND
JOHN A. WATERS
of
KIRKLAND & ELLIS
2900 Prudential Plaza
Chicago, Illinois 60601
(312) 726-2929

In the United States Court of Claims

No. 73–68

(Decided November 27, 1973)

THE WILLIAMS & WILKINS COMPANY v. THE UNITED STATES

Alan Latman, attorney of record, for plaintiff. Arthur J. Greenbaum and Cowan, Liebowitz & Latman, of counsel.

Thomas J. Byrnes, with whom was Assistant Attorney General Harlington Wood, Jr., for defendant.

Irwin Karp, for The Authors League of America, Inc., amicus curiae.

Philip B. Brown, for the Association of Research Libraries, Medical Library Association, American Association of Law Libraries, American Medical Association, American Dental Association, Mayo Foundation, Robert H. Ebert, M.D. (in his capacity as Dean of the Faculty of Medicine, Harvard University), The University of Michigan Medical School, The University of Rochester, School of Medicine and Dentistry, American Sociological Association, Modern Language Association of America, and History of Science Society, amici curiae. Cox, Langford & Brown and John P. Furnan, of counsel.

Harry N. Rosenfield, for The National Education Association of the United States, amicus curiae.

William D. North, for the American Library Association, amicus curiae. Perry S. Patterson, Ronald L. Engel, James M. Amend, John A. Waters, Thomas B. Carr, and Kirkland & Ellis, of counsel.

Charles H. Lieb, for the Association of American Publishers, Inc. and The Association of American University Presses, Incorporated, amici curiae. Paskus, Gordon & Hyman, and Elizabeth Barad, of counsel.

Arthur B. Hanson, for The American Chemical Society, amicus curiae. Hanson, O'Brien, Birney, Stickle & Butler, of counsel.

Davies, Hardy, Ives & Lawther, for The American Institute of Physics Incorporated, amicus curiae. Robert E. Lawther, of counsel.

Robert B. Washburn, Virgil E. Woodcock, and Woodcock, Washburn, Kurtz & Mackiewicz, for American Society for Testing and Materials and National Council of Teachers of Mathematics, amici curiae.

Before COWEN, Chief Judge, DAVIS, SKELTON, NICHOLS, KASHIWA, KUNZIG and BENNETT, Judges.

OPINION

DAVIS, Judge, delivered the opinion of the court:

We confront a ground-breaking copyright infringement action under 28 U.S.C. § 1498(b), the statute consenting to infringement suits against the United States.[1] Plaintiff Williams & Wilkins Company, a medical publisher, charges that the Department of Health, Education, and Welfare, through the National Institutes of Health (NIH) and the National Library of Medicine (NLM), has infringed plaintiff's copyrights in certain of its medical journals by making unauthorized photocopies of articles from those periodicals. Modern photocopying in its relation to copyright spins off troublesome problems, which have been much discussed.[2] Those issues have never before been mooted or determined by a court. In this case, an extensive trial was held before former Trial Judge James F. Davis who decided that the Government was liable for infringement. On review, helped by the briefs and agreements of the parties and the amici curiae,

---

[1] Prior to 1960, § 1498 provided only for patent infringement suits against the Federal Government. In that year, Congress amended the section to make the United States liable in money for copyrighted infringement, pursuant to Title 17 of the United States Code, the general copyright statute. This is the first copyright case to reach trial in this court.

[2] We list in the Appendix, infra, several considerations to these problems.

---

we take the other position and hold the United States free of liability in the particular situation presented by this record.

I[3]

Plaintiff, though a relatively small company, is a major publisher of medical journals and books. It publishes 37 journals, dealing with various medical specialties. The four journals in suit are Medicine, Journal of Immunology, Gastroenterology, and Pharmacological Reviews. Medicine is published by plaintiff for profit and for its own benefit. The other three journals are published in conjunction with specialty medical societies which, by contract, share the journals' profits with plaintiff. The articles published in the journals stem from manuscripts submitted to plaintiff (or one of the medical societies) by physicians or other scientists engaged in medical research. The journals are widely disseminated throughout the United States (and the world) in libraries, schools, physicians' offices, and the like. Annual subscription prices range from about $12 to $44; and, due to the esoteric nature of the journals' subject matter, the number of annual subscriptions is relatively small, ranging from about 3,100 (Pharmacological Reviews) to about 7,000 (Gastroenterology). Most of the revenue derived from the journals comes from subscription sales, though a small part comes from advertising.[4] The journals are published with notice of copyright in plaintiff's name. The notice appears at the front of the journal and sometimes at the beginning of each article. After publication of each journal issue (usually monthly or bimonthly) and after compliance with the requisite statutory requirements, the Register of Copyrights issues to plaintiff certificates of copyright registration.

NIH, the Government's principal medical research organization, is a conglomerate of institutes located on a multi-acre campus at Bethesda, Maryland. Each institute is concerned with a particular medical specialty, and the insti-

---

[3] We borrow, with some modifications, the statement of facts from the opinion of Trial Judge James F. Davis.

[4] E.g., the November 1956 issue of Medicine has 86 pages, four of which carry commercial product advertising. The August 1965 issue of Journal of Immunology has 206 pages, nine of which carry commercial product advertising.

---

tutes conduct their activities by way of both intramural research and grants-in-aid to private individuals and organizations. NIH employs over 12,000 persons—4,000 are science professionals and 2,000 have doctoral degrees. To assist its intramural programs, NIH maintains a technical library. The library houses about 150,000 volumes, of which about 30,000 are books and the balance scientific (principally medical) journals. The library is open to the public, but is used mostly by NIH in-house research personnel. The library's budget for 1970 was $1.1 million; of this about $85,000 was for the purchase of journal materials.

The NIH library subscribes to about 3,000 different journal titles, four of which are the journals in suit. The library subscribes to two copies of each of the journals involved. As a general rule, one copy stays in the library reading room and the other copy circulates among interested NIH personnel. Demand by NIH research workers for access to plaintiff's journals (as well as other journals to which the library subscribes) is usually not met by in-house subscription copies. Consequently, as an integral part of its operation, the library runs a photocopy service for the benefit of its research staff. On request, a researcher can obtain a photocopy of an article from any of the journals in the library's collection. Usually, researchers request photocopies of articles to assist them in their on-going projects; sometimes photocopies are requested simply for background reading. The library does not monitor the reason for requests or the use to which the photocopies are put. The photocopies are not returned to the library; and the record shows that, in most instances, researchers keep them in their private files for future reference.

The library's policy is that, as a rule, only a single copy of a journal article will be made per request and each request is limited to about 40 to 50 pages, though exceptions may be, and have been, made in the case of long articles, upon approval of the Assistant Chief of the library branch. Also, as a general rule, requests for photocopying are limited to only a single article from a journal issue. Exceptions to this rule are routinely made, so long as substantially less than an entire journal is photocopied, *i.e.*, less than about half of the journal. Coworkers can, and frequently do, request single copies of the same article and such requests are honored.

5

Four regularly assigned employees operate the NIH photocopy equipment. The equipment consists of microfilm cameras and Xerox copying machines. In 1970, the library photocopy budget was $86,000 and the library filled 85,744 requests for photocopies of journal articles (including plaintiff's journals), constituting about 930,000 pages. On the average, a journal article is 10 pages long, so that, in 1970, the library made about 93,000 photocopies of articles.

NLM, located on the Bethesda campus of NIH, was formerly the Armed Forces Medical Library. In 1956, Congress transferred the library from the Department of Defense to the Public Health Service (renaming it the National Library of Medicine), and declared its purpose to be "* * * to aid the dissemination and exchange of scientific and other information important to the progress of medicine and to the public health * * *." 42 U.S.C. § 275 (1970). NLM is a repository of much of the world's medical literature, in essence a 'librarians' library." As part of its operation, NLM cooperates with other libraries and like research-and-education-oriented institutions (both public and private) in a so-called "interlibrary loan" program. Upon request, NLM will loan to such institutions, for a limited time, books and other materials in its collection. In the case of journals, the "loans" usually take the form of photocopies of journal articles which are supplied by NLM free of charge and on a no-return basis. NLM's "loan" policies are fashioned after the General Interlibrary Loan Code, which is a statement of self-imposed regulations to be followed by all libraries which cooperate in interlibrary loaning. The Code provides that each library, upon request for a loan of materials, shall decide whether to loan the original or provide a photoduplicate. The Code notes that photoduplication of copyrighted materials may raise copyright infringement problems, particularly with regard to "photographing *whole*

issues of periodicals or books with *current copyrights*, or in making *multiple copies* of a publication." [Emphasis in original text.] NLM, therefore, will provide only one photocopy of a particular article, per request, and will not photocopy on any given request an entire journal issue. Each photocopy

6

reproduced by NLM contains a statement in the margin. "This is a single photostatic copy made by the National Library of Medicine for purposes of study or research in lieu of lending the original."

In recent years NLM's stated policy has been not to fill requests for copies of articles from any of 104 journals which are included in a so-called "widely-available list." Rather, the requester is furnished a copy of the "widely-available list" and the names of the regional medical libraries which are presumed to have the journals listed. Exceptions are sometimes made to the policy, particularly if the requester has been unsuccessful in obtaining the journal elsewhere. The four journals involved in this suit are listed on the "widely-available list." A rejection on the basis of the "widely-available list" is made only if the article requested was published during the preceding 5 years, but requests from Government libraries are not refused on the basis of the "widely-available list."

Also, NLM's policy is not to honor an excessive number of requests from an individual or an institution. As a general rule, not more than 20 requests from an individual, or not more than 30 requests from an institution, within a month, will be honored. In 1968, NLM adopted the policy that no more than one article from a single journal issue, or three from a journal volume, would be copied. Prior to 1968, NLM had no express policy on copying limitations, but endeavored to prevent "excessive copying." Generally, requests for more than 50 pages of material will not be honored, though exceptions are sometimes made, particularly for Government institutions. Requests for more than one copy of a journal article are rejected, without exception. If NLM receives a request for more than one copy, a single copy will be furnished and the requester advised that it is NLM's policy to furnish only one copy.

In 1968, a representative year, NLM received about 127,000 requests for interlibrary loans. Requests were received, for the most part, from other libraries or Government agencies. However, about 12 percent of the requests came from private or commercial organizations, particularly drug companies. Some requests were for books, in which event the book itself was loaned. Most requests were for journals or journal arti-

7

cles; and about 120,000 of the requests were filled by photocopying single articles from journals, including plaintiff's journals. Usually, the library seeking an interlibrary loan from NLM did so at the request of one of its patrons. If the "loan" was made by photocopy, the photocopy was given to the patron who was free to dispose of it as he wished. NLM made no effort to find out the ultimate use to which the photocopies were put; and there is no evidence that borrowing libraries kept the "loan" photocopies in their permanent collections for use by other patrons.

Defendant concedes that, within the pertinent accounting period, NLM and the NIH library made at least one photocopy of each of eight articles (designated by plaintiff as the Count I-to-Count VIII articles) from one or more of the four journals in suit. These requests, as shown at the trial, were made by NIH researchers and an Army medical officer (stationed in Japan) in connection with their professional work and were used solely for those purposes. In seven of the eight counts in the petition, the article requested was more than two years old; in the eighth instance it was 21 or 22 months old.

II

We assume, for the purposes of the case, but without

deciding, that plaintiff is the proper copyright owner and entitled to sue here,[3] and we agree with plaintiff that, on that assumption, it can sue for infringement of the eight separate articles.[4] This faces us squarely with the issue of infringement.

Perhaps the main reason why determination of the question is so difficult is that the text of the Copyright Act of 1909, which governs the case, does not supply, by itself, a

[3] Defendant vigorously contests the publisher's claim to be the copyright "proprietor" and its right to sue in this court. The argument is that the individual authors of the articles are the owners and they have not assigned their rights to plaintiff.

[4] Section 3 of the copyright statute, 17 U.S.C. § 3, says that, "* * * [t]he copyright upon composite works or periodicals shall give to the proprietor thereof all the rights in respect thereto which he would have if each part were individually copyrighted under this title." This means, and was intended to provide, that each article in the journals is protected from infringement to the same extent as the entire issue. *Advertisers Exch., Inc.* v. *Laufe,* 29 F. Supp. 1 (W.D. Pa. 1939) ; *King Features Syndicate* v. *Fleischer,* 299 F. 533 (C.A. 2, 1924).

8

clear or satisfactory answer. Section 1 of the Act, 17 U.S.C. § 1, declares that the copyright owner "shall have the exclusive right: (a) To print, reprint, publish, copy, and vend the copyrighted work; * * *." Read with blinders, this language might seem on its surface to be all-comprehensive—especially the term "copy"—but we are convinced, for several reasons, that "copy" is not to be taken in its full literal sweep. In this instance, as in so many others in copyright, "[T]he statute is hardly unambiguous * * * and presents problems of interpretation not solved by literal application of words as they are 'normally' used * * *." *DeSylva* v. *Ballentine,* 351 U.S. 570, 573 (1956). *See, also, Fortnightly Corp.* v. *United Artists Television, Inc.,* 392 U.S. 390, 395–96 (1968).

The court-created doctrine of "fair use" (discussed in Part III, *infra*) is alone enough to demonstrate that Section 1 does not cover all copying (in the literal sense). Some forms of copying, at the very least of portions of a work, are universally deemed immune from liability, although the very words are reproduced in more than *de minimis* quantity. Furthermore, it is almost unanimously accepted that a scholar can make a handwritten copy of an entire copyrighted article for his own use, and in the era before photoduplication it was not uncommon (and not seriously questioned) that he could have his secretary make a typed copy for his personal use and files. These customary facts of copyright-life are among our givens. The issue we now have is the complex one of whether photocopying, in the form done by NIH and NLM, should be accorded the same treatment—not the ministerial lexicographic task of deciding that photoduplication necessarily involves "copying" (as of course it does in dictionary terms).

One aspect of the history and structure of the 1909 Act offers another reason for refusing to give "copying" in Section 1, as applied to these articles, its simplest "ordinary" reach. It is pointed out to us, on the basis of analysis of the copyright laws from 1790 to 1909,[7] that the early statutes

[7] Congress enacted the first copyright statute in 1790 (Act of May 31, 1790, ch. 15, 1 Stat. 124). Thereafter, the statute was revised from time to time, notably in 1802, 1831, 1870, and 1891. In 1909, the present statute was passed (Act of March 4, 1909, ch. 320, 35 Stat. 1075) and later was codified as 17 U.S.C. (Act of July 30, 1947, 61 Stat. 652).

9

distinguished "copying" from "printing," "reprinting," and "publishing," and provided that the copyright in books is infringed by "printing," "reprinting" and "publishing," while the copyright in other works (*e.g.*, photographs, paintings, engraving, drawings, etc.) is infringed by "copying." *Cf. Harper* v. *Shoppell,* 26 F. 519, 520 (C.C.S.D.N.Y. 1886). The 1909 Act obliterated any such distinction in its text. It provides in § 5 a list of all classes of copyrightable subject matter (including books and periodicals), and says in § 1 that the owner of copyright shall have the exclusive right

"to print, reprint, publish, copy and vend the copyrighted work." Thus, the 1909 Act, unlike the earlier statutes, does not expressly say which of the proscribed acts of § 1 apply to which classes of copyrightable subject matter of § 5. Defendant and some of the amici say that, to be consistent with the intent and purpose of earlier statutes, the "copying" proscription of § 1 should not apply to books or periodicals; rather, only the proscribed acts of "printing," "reprinting" and "publishing" control books and periodicals. The proponents of this view stress that the legislative history of the 1909 legislation does not suggest any purpose to alter the previous coverage.[8]

This is quite a serious argument. However, in view of Congress's general inclusion of the word "copy" in Section 1 and of the practice under the Act since 1909, we are not ready to accept fully this claim that infringement of periodical articles can come only through "printing," "reprinting" or "publishing." But we do believe this point—that there is a solid doubt whether and how far "copy" applies to books and journals—must be taken into account in measuring the outlines of "copying" as it involves books and articles.

Adding to this doubt that "copy" blankets such printed matter is the significant implication of a special segment of the background of the 1909 statute, a sector of history which is peripheral but revealing. The then Librarian of Congress,

[8] For instance, H.R. Rep. No. 2222, 60th Cong., 2d Sess. 4 (1909) states: "Subsection (a) of section 1 adopts without change the phraseology of section 4952 of the Revised Statutes, and this, with the insertion of the word 'copy,' practically adopts the phraseology of the first copyright act Congress ever passed—that of 1790. Many amendments of this were suggested, but the committee felt that it was safer to retain without change the old phraseology which has been so often construed by the courts."

10

Herbert Putnam, was the leading public sponsor of that Act (outside of Congress itself), and was intimately involved in its preparation from at least 1906 on. While the bill was being considered in Congress, the Library's 1908 "Rules and Practice Governing the Use and Issue of Books," p. 6, specifically provided:

"*Photographing.* Photographing is freely permitted. The permission extends to the building itself and any of its parts, including the mural decorations. *It extends to articles bearing claim of copyright,* but the Library gives no assurance that the photograph may be reproduced or republished or placed on sale. These are matters to be settled with the owner of the copyright" (emphasis added).

After the 1909 Act became law, the Library continued the same provision. The 1913 version of the "Rules and Practice"[9] added the following on "Photostat," after the above paragraph on "Photographing":

Photo-duplicates of books, newspapers, maps, etc. can be furnished at a reasonable rate by means of the photostat, installed in the Chief Clerk's Office. Apply to the Chief Clerk for a schedule of charges.

Later editions, throughout Dr. Putnam's tenure (which ended in 1939), contained the same or comparable provisions.[10] Indeed, when he left his post in 1939, he was honored by the American Council of Learned Societies because (among other things) "You have led in adapting the most modern photographic processes to the needs of the scholar, and have * * * made widely available for purposes of research copies of your collections * * *." This illuminating slice of history, covering the time of enactment and the first three decades of the 1909 Act, should not be ignored.

These are the leading reasons why we cannot stop with the dictionary or "normal" definition of "copy"—nor can we extract much affirmative help from the surficial legislative text. As for the other rights given in Section 1, "vend" is clearly irrelevant (since NIH and NLM do not sell), and the applicability to this case of "print," "reprint" and "publish" is more dubious than of "copy." The photocopy process

[9] There was an 1911 edition, but no copy has been located.

[10] The Library's current practice is described in Part III, 3, note 16, *infra.*

11

of NIH and NLM, described in Part I, *supra*, does not even amount to printing or reprinting in the strict dictionary sense; and if the words be used more broadly to include all mechanical reproduction of a number of copies, they would still not cover the making of a single copy for an individual requester. If the requester himself made a photocopy of the article for his own use on a machine made available by the library, he might conceivably be "copying" but he would not be "printing" or "reprinting." The library is in the same position when responding to the demands of individual researchers acting separately.

For similar reasons there is no "publication" by the library, a concept which invokes general distribution, or at least a supplying of the material to a fairly large group.[11] The author of an uncopyrighted manuscript does not lose his common law rights, via publication, by giving photocopies to his friends for comment or their personal use—and publication for Section 1 purposes would seem to have about the same coverage. In any event, the hitherto uncodified principles of "fair use" apply to printing, reprinting, and publishing, as well as to copying, and therefore the collocation of general words Congress chose for Section 1 is necessarily inadequate, by itself, to decide this case.

III

In the fifty-odd years since the 1909 Act, the major tool for probing what physical copying amounts to unlawful "copying" (as well as what is unlawful "printing," "reprinting" and "publishing") has been the gloss of "fair use" which the courts have put upon the words of the statute. Precisely because a determination that a use is "fair," or "unfair," depends on an evaluation of the complex of individual and varying factors bearing upon the particular use (see H.R. Rep. No. 83, 90th Cong., 1st Sess., p. 29), there has been no exact or detailed definition of the doctrine. The courts, congressional committees, and scholars have had to be content

---

[11] To the extent that *Macmillan Co.* v. *King*, 223 F. 862. (D. Mass. 1914), may possibly suggest that "publication" can occur through simple distribution to a very small restricted group, for a special purpose, we think the opinion goes too far.

12

with a general listing of the main considerations—together with the example of specific instances ruled "fair" or "unfair." These overall factors are now said to be: (a) the purpose and character of the use, (b) the nature of the copyrighted work, (c) the amount and substantiality of the material used in relation to the copyrighted work as a whole, and (d) the effect of the use on a copyright owner's potential market for and value of his work.

In addition, the development of "fair use" has been influenced by some tension between the direct aim of the copyright privilege to grant the owner a right from which he can reap financial benefit and the more fundamental purpose of the protection "To promote the Progress of Science and the useful Arts." U.S. Const., art. 1, § 8. The House committee which recommended the 1909 Act said that copyright was "[n]ot primarily for the benefit of the author, but primarily for the benefit of the public." H.R. Rep. No. 2222, 60th Cong., 2d Sess., p. 7. The Supreme Court has stated that "The copyright law, like the patent statutes, makes reward to the owner a secondary consideration." *Mazer* v. *Stein*, 347 U.S. 201, 219 (1954) ; *United States* v. *Paramount Pictures*, 334 U.S. 131, 158 (1948). *See* Breyer, *The Uneasy Case for Copyright: A study of Copyright in Books, Photocopies, and Computer Programs*, 84 Harv. L. Rev. 281 (1970). To serve the constitutional purpose, " 'courts in passing upon particular claims of infringement must occasionally subordinate the copyright holder's interest in a maximum financial return to the greater public interest in the development of art, science and industry.' *Berlin* v. *E.C. Publications, Inc.*, 329 F. 2d 541, 544 (2d Cir. 1964). Whether the privilege may justifiably be applied to particular materials turns initially

---

on the nature of the materials, e.g., whether their distribution would serve the public interest in the free dissemination of information and whether their preparation requires some use of prior materials dealing with the same subject matter. Consequently, the privilege has been applied to works in the fields of science, law, medicine, history and biography." *Rosemont Enterprises, Inc.* v. *Random House, Inc.*, 366 F. 2d 303, 307 (C.A. 2, 1966).

It has sometimes been suggested that the copying of an entire copyrighted work, any such work, cannot ever be

13

"fair use," but this is an overbroad generalization, unsupported by the decisions[12] and rejected by years of accepted practice. The handwritten or typed copy of an article, for personal use, is one illustration, let alone the thousands of copies of poems, songs, or such items which have long been made by individuals, and sometimes given to lovers and others. Trial Judge James F. Davis, who considered the use now in dispute not to be "fair," nevertheless agreed that a library could supply single photocopies of entire copyrighted works to attorneys or courts for use in litigation. It is, of course, common for courts to be given photocopies of recent decisions, with the publishing company's headnotes and arrangement, and sometimes its annotations. There are other examples from everyday legal and personal life. We cannot believe, for instance, that a judge who makes and gives to a colleague a photocopy of a law review article, in one of the smaller or less available journals, which bears directly on a problem both judges are then considering in a case before them is infringing the copyright, rather than making "fair use" of his issue of that journal. Similarly with the photocopies of particular newspaper items and articles which are frequently given or sent by one friend to another.[13]

---

[12] *Leon* v. *Pacific Tel. & Tel. Co.*, 91 F. 2d 484, 486 (C.A. 9, 1937) and *Public Affairs Associates, Inc.* v. *Rickover*, 284 F. 2d 262, 272 (C.A.D.C. 1960). vacated and remanded, 369 U.S. 111 (1962), which are often cited in this connection, both involved actual publication and distribution of many copies, not the simple making of a copy for individual personal or restricted use. In *Wihtol* v. *Crow*, 309 F. 2d 777 (C.A. 8, 1962), 48 copies of the copyrighted song were made and distributed, and there were a number of public performances using these copies. It was as if the defendant had purchased one copy of sheet music and then duplicated it for an entire chorus.

On the other hand, *New York Tribune, Inc.* v. *Otis & Co.*, 39 F. Supp. 67 (S.D.N.Y. 1941), shows that copying of an entire copyrighted item is not enough, in itself, to preclude application of "fair use." Although it was already plain that an entire copyrighted item (a newspaper editorial) had been reproduced, the court ordered further proceedings to take account of other factors.

[13] Verner Clapp, former Acting Librarian of Congress, has pointed out some of the uses of a photocopy for which the library copy original is unsuited (*Can Copyright Law Respond to the New Technology?*, 61 Law Lib. J. 387, 407 (1968) :

"I cannot submit the original conveniently in a court, in a suit of law. I cannot put the original into my filing cabinet. I can't shuffle it with notes in preparation for an address. I can't make notes on it. I can't conveniently give it to a typist. I can't use it as printer's copy. I can't send it through the mail without serious risk of loss of an original. With a photocopy I can do all these things plain and more, and this is the reason I want a copy."

14

There is, in short, no inflexible rule excluding an entire copyrighted work from the area of "fair use." Instead, the extent of the copying is one important factor, but only one, to be taken into account, along with several others.

Under these over-all standards, we have weighed the multiplicity of factors converging on the particular use of plaintiff's material made by NIH and NLM, as shown by this record. There is no prior decision which is dispositive and hardly any that can be called even close; we have had to make our own appraisal. The majority of the court has concluded that, on this record, the challenged use should be designated "fair," not "unfair." In the rest of this part of our opinion, we discuss *seriatim* the various considerations which merge to that conclusion. But we can help focus on what is probably the core of our evaluation by stating summarily, in advance, three propositions we shall consider at greater length: First, plaintiff has not in our view shown, and there is inadequate reason to believe, that it is being or will be harmed substantially by these specific practices of NIH and NLM; second, we are convinced that medicine and medical research will be injured by holding these particular practices to be an infringement; and, third, since the problem of accommodating the interests of science with those of the publishers (and authors) calls fundamentally for legislative solution or guidance, which has not yet been given, we should not, during the period before congressional action is forthcoming, place such a risk of harm upon science and medicine.

1. We start by emphasizing that (a) NIH and NLM are non-profit institutions, devoted solely to the advancement and dissemination of medical knowledge which they seek to further by the challenged practices, and are not attempting to profit or gain financially by the photocopying; (b) the medical researchers who have asked these libraries for the photocopies are in this particular case (and ordinarily) scientific researchers and practitioners who need the articles for personal use in their scientific work and have no purpose to reduplicate them for sale or other general distribution; and (c) the copied articles are scientific studies useful to the requesters in their work. On both sides—library and requester—scientific progress, untainted by any commercial

15

gain from the reproduction, is the hallmark of the whole enterprise of duplication. There has been no attempt to misappropriate the work of earlier scientific writers for forbidden ends, but rather an effort to gain easier access to the material for study and research. This is important because it is settled that, in general, the law gives copying for scientific purposes a wide scope. *See, e.g., Rosemont Enterprises, Inc.* v. *Random House, Inc., supra,* 366 F. 2d at 306–07; *Loew's, Inc.* v. *Columbia Broadcasting System, Inc.,* 131 F. Supp. 165, 175 (S.D. Cal. 1955), *aff'd,* 239 F. 2d 532 (C.A. 9, 1956), *aff'd by an equally divided Court,* 356 U.S. 43 (1958); *Greenbie* v. *Noble,* 151 F. Supp. 45, 67–68 (S.D.N.Y. 1957); *Thompson* v. *Gernsback,* 94 F. Supp. 453, 454 (S.D.N.Y. 1950); *Henry Holt & Co.* v. *Liggett & Myers Tobacco Co.,* 23 F. Supp. 302, 304 (E.D. Pa. 1938).

2. Both libraries have declared and enforced reasonably strict limitations which, to our mind, keep the duplication within appropriate confines. The details are set forth in Part I *supra,* and in our findings. Both institutions normally restrict copying on an individual request to a single copy of a single article of a journal issue, and to articles of less than 50 pages. Though exceptions are made, they do not appear to be excessive, unwarranted, or irrational. For instance, though on occasion one person was shown to have ordered or received more than one photocopy of the same article, the second copy was for a colleague's use or to replace an illegible or undelivered copy. Some care is also taken not to have excessive copying from one issue or one volume of the periodical. While a certain amount of duplication of articles does, of course, occur, it does not appear to be at all heavy.[14] There is no showing whatever that the recipients use the libraries' photocopying process to sell the copies or distribute them broadly.

NIH responds only to requests from its own personnel, so that its entire photoduplication system is strictly "in-house"—in the same way that a court's library may supply

[14] One survey of NIH operations shows only 4 instances of duplication in over 200 requests; at NLM, as of 1964, duplication occurred at a 10% rate in the 102 most heavily used journals (constituting one-third of total requests); if all requests were considered, the rate would be less. The Sophar & Heilprin report (see Appendix), which is not friendly to library photocopying, estimates that for libraries generally the duplication rate was about 8% (p. 111).

16

a judge of that court with a copy of a law journal article or a reported decision. NLM fulfills requests more generally but it has adopted the practice of not responding (outside of the Government) where the article appears in a recent (preceding 5 years) issue of a periodical on its "widely-available list". The result is that the duplication of recent issues of generally available journals is kept within the Government, and distribution to the larger medical public is limited to older, less available issues and to journals which are harder

to obtain from medical libraries. It is a fair inference, supported by this record, that at the very least in the latter classes the demand has been inadequately filled by reprints and the publisher's sale of back issues. *See, also,* Part III, 4, *infra.* In those instances not covered by "five year" policy, the impression left by the record is that, on the whole, older rather than current articles were usually requested.

Brushing aside all such breakdowns, plaintiff points to the very large number, in absolute terms, of the copies made each year by the two libraries. We do not think this decisive.[15] In view of the large numbers of scientific personnel served and the great size of the libraries—NIH has over 100,000 volumes of journal materials alone, and NLM is currently binding over 18,000 journals each year—the amount of copying does not seem to us to have been excessive or disproportionate. The important factor is not the absolute amount, but the twin elements of (i) the existence and purpose of the system of limitations imposed and enforced, and (ii) the effectiveness of that system to confine the duplication for the personal use of scientific personnel who need the material for their work, with the minimum of potential abuse or harm to the copyright owner. The practices of NIH and NLM, as shown by the record, pass both of these tests, despite the large number of copies annually sent out.

Without necessarily accepting the full sweep of the concept that the library is nothing more than the individual requester's ministerial agent, we do agree that the NIH and NLM systems, as described in the evidence, are close kin to the current Library of Congress policy, *see* note 16, *infra,*

[15] In 1970, NIH copied 85,744 and NLM 93,746 articles.

17

of maintaining machines in the library buildings so that readers can do their own copying. The principal extension by NLM and NIH is to service requesters who cannot conveniently come to the building, as well as out-of-town libraries. But the personal, individual focus is still present. The reader who himself makes a copy does so for his own personal work needs, and individual work needs are likewise dominant in the reproduction programs of the two medical libraries—programs which are reasonably policed and enforced.

3. We also think it significant, in assessing the recent and current practices of the two libraries, that library photocopying, though not of course to the extent of the modern development, has been going on ever since the 1909 Act was adopted. In Part II, *supra,* we have set forth the practice of the Library of Congress at that time and for many years thereafter.[16] In fact, photocopying seems to have been done in the Library at least from the beginning of this century. *Can Copyright Law Respond to the New Technology?* 61 Law. Lib. J. 387, 400 (1968) (comments of V. Clapp). In 1935 there was a so-called "gentlemen's agreement" between the National Association of Book Publishers (since defunct) and the Joint Committee on Materials for Research (representing the libraries), stating in part: "A library * * * owning books or periodical volumes in which copyright still subsists may make and deliver a single photographic reproduction * * * of a part thereof to a scholar representing in writing that he desires such reproduction in lieu of loan of such publication or in place of manual transcription and solely for the purposes of research * * *." Though this understanding discountenanced photoduplication of an entire book it was regularly construed as allowing copying of articles. There have been criticisms of this pact, and we cite it, not as binding in any way on plaintiff or any other pub-

[16] Currently, and for some time, the Library of Congress has said that copyright material will "ordinarily" not be photocopied by the Library "without the signed authorization of the copyright owner," but "[e]xceptions to this rule may be made in particular cases." The Library does, however, maintain machines which readers may themselves use for photocopying; these machines contain notices saying that "a single photocopy of copyrighted material may be made only for the purpose of study, scholarship, or research, and for no other purpose" and "the sale and/or further reproduction of any photocopied copyrighted materials is illegal."

18

lisher, or as showing universal recognition of "single" photocopying, but as representing a very widely held view, almost 40 years ago, of what was permissible under the 1909 statute.

There is other evidence that, until quite recently, library photocopying was carried on with apparent general acceptance. Witnesses in this case testified that such photocopying has been done for at least fifty years and is well-established. The National Library of Medicine Act, in 1956, by which NLM was created (42 U.S.C. § 275, *et seq.*), provided at § 276(4) that the Secretary of Health, Education, and Welfare, through NLM, should "make available, through loans, photographic or other copying procedures or otherwise, such materials in the Library as he deems appropriate * * *"; and the Medical Library Assistance Act of 1965 (42 U.S.C. § 280b-1, *et seq.*) provided that grants be made to medical libraries for, among other things, "acquisition of duplicating devices, facsimile equipment * * * and other equipment to facilitate the use of the resources of the library." 42 U.S.C. § 280b-7. These two pieces of legislation indicate to us that Congress knew in 1956 and 1965 of the practice of library photocopying, and assumed that it was not beyond the pale. The General Interlibrary Loan Code (revised in 1956), *see* Part I, *supra*, is a similar indication of the extent of the practice, and of the general position of the libraries (at the least) that such copying is permissible.

The fact that photocopying by libraries of entire articles was done with hardly any (and at most very minor) complaint, until about 10 or 15 years ago, goes a long way to show both that photoduplication cannot be designated as infringement *per se*, and that there was at least a time when photocopying, as then carried on, was "fair use." There have been, of course, considerable changes in the case and extent of such reproduction, and these developments bear on "fair use" as of today, but the libraries can properly stand on the proposition that they photocopied articles for many years, without significant protest, and that such copying was generally accepted until the proliferation of inexpensive and improved copying machines, less than two decades ago, led to the surge in such duplication. The question then becomes whether this

19

marked increase in volume changes a use which was generally accepted as "fair" into one which has now become "unfair."

4. There is no doubt in our minds that medical science would be seriously hurt if such library photocopying were stopped. We do not spend time and space demonstrating this proposition. It is admitted by plaintiff and conceded on all sides. *See, e.g.* Varmer, *Photoduplication of Copyrighted Material by Libraries*, Study No. 15, "Copyright Law Revision," Studies Prepared for the Subcommittee on Patents, Trademarks and Copyrights, Senate Judiciary Committee (1959), p. 49; Memorandum of General Counsel Willcox, Department of Health, Education and Welfare, June 7, 1965, Hearings before Subcommittee No. 3, Committee on the Judiciary, H. of Reps., 89th Cong., 1st Sess., on H.R. 4347, H.R. 5680, etc., "Copyright Law Revision," Part 2, 1132, 1133. The trial testimony of a number of the requesters and authors documents the point. The supply of reprints and back numbers is wholly inadequate; the evidence shows the unlikelihood of obtaining such substitutes for photocopies from publishers of medical journals or authors of journal articles, especially for articles over three years old.[17] It is, moreover, wholly unrealistic to expect scientific personnel to subscribe regularly to large numbers of journals which would only occasionally contain articles of interest to them. Nor will libraries purchase extensive numbers of whole subscriptions to all medical journals on the chance that an indeterminate number of articles in an indeterminate number of issues will be requested at indeterminate times. The result of a flat proscription on library photocopying would be, we feel sure, that medical and scientific personnel would simply do without, and have to do without, many of the articles they now desire, need, and use in their work.[18]

5. Plaintiff insists that it has been financially hurt by the photocopying practices of NLM and NIH, and of other libraries. The trial judge thought that it was reasonable to infer that the extensive photocopying has resulted in some

[17] Plaintiff itself publishes a notice to the effect that it does not attempt to keep a stock of back issues, and it refers requests for reprints to the author.
[18] We think the alternative of compulsory licensing is not open to us under the present copyright statute. *See, infra,* Parts III, 6, and IV.

20

loss of revenue to plaintiff and that plaintiff has lost, or failed to get, "some undetermined and indeterminable number of journal subscriptions (perhaps small)" by virtue of the photocopying. He thought that the persons requesting photocopies constituted plaintiff's market and that each photocopy user is a potential subscriber "or at least a potential source of royalty income for licensed copying."[19] Studies rejecting as "fair use" the kind of photocopying involved here have also assumed, without real proof, that the journal publishers have been and will be injured. *See, e.g., Project—New Technology and the Law of Copyright: Reprography and Computers*, 15 U.C.L.A. L. Rev. 931 (1968); *Sophor & Heilprin, "The Determination of Legal Facts and Economic Guideposts with Respect to the Dissemination of Scientific and Educational Information as It Is Affected by Copyright—A Status Report"* (1967).

The record made in this case does not sustain that assumption. Defendant made a thorough effort to try to ascertain, so far as possible, the effect of photoduplication on plaintiff's business, including the presentation of an expert witness. The unrefuted evidence shows that (a) between 1958 and 1969 annual subscriptions to the four medical journals involved increased substantially (for three of them, very much so), annual subscription sales likewise increased substantially, and total annual income also grew; (b) between 1959 and 1966, plaintiff's annual taxable income increased from $272,000 to $726,000, fell to $589,000 in 1967, and in 1968 to $451,000; (c) but the four journals in suit account for a relatively small percentage of plaintiff's total business and over the years each has been profitable (though 3 of them show losses in particular years and in all years the profits have not been large, varying from less than $1,000 to about $15,000, some of which has been shared with the sponsoring

[19] It is wrong to measure the detriment to plaintiff by loss of presumed royalty income—a standard which necessarily assumes that plaintiff had a right to issue licenses. That would be true, of course, only if it were first decided that the defendant's practices did not constitute "fair use." In determining whether the company has been sufficiently hurt to cause these practices to become "unfair," one cannot assume at the start the merit of the plaintiff's position, i.e., that plaintiff had the right to license. That conclusion results only if it is first determined that the photocopying is "unfair."

21

medical societies);[20] and (d) plaintiff's business appears to have been growing faster than the gross national product or of the rate of growth of manpower working in the field of science. Defendant's expert concluded that the photocopying shown here had not damaged plaintiff, and may actually have helped it.[21] The record is also barren of solid evidence that photocopying has caused economic harm to any other publisher of medical journals.

Plaintiff has never made a detailed study of the actual effect of photocopying on its business, nor has it refuted defendant's figures. It has relied for its assumption (in the words of the chairman of its board) on "general business common sense and things that you hear from subscribers, librarians and so forth." Its argument—and that of the other supporters of its position[22]—is that there "must" be an effect because photocopies supplant the original articles, and if there were no photocopying those who now get the copies would necessarily buy the journals or issues. But this untested hypothesis, reminiscent of the abstract theorems beloved of the "pure" classical economics of 70 or 80 years ago, is neither obvious nor self-proving. One need not enter the semantic debate over whether the photocopy supplants the original article itself or is merely in substitution for the library's loan of the original issue to recognize, as we have already pointed out, that there are other possibilities. If photocopying were forbidden, the researchers, instead of subscribing to more journals or trying to obtain or buy back-issues or reprints (usually unavailable), might expend extra time in note-taking or waiting

22

their turn for the library's copies of the original issues—or they might very well cut down their reading and do without much of the information they now get through NLM's and NIH's copying system. The record shows that each of the individual requesters in this case already subscribed, personally, to a number of medical journals, and it is very questionable how many more, if any, they would add. The great problems with reprints and back-issues have already been noted. In the absence of photocopying, the financial, time-wasting, and other difficulties of obtaining the material could well lead, if human experience is a guide, to a simple but drastic reduction in the use of the many articles (now sought and read) which are not absolutely crucial to the individual's work but are merely stimulating or helpful. The probable effect on scientific progress goes without saying, but for this part of our discussion the significant element is that plaintiff, as publisher and copyright owner, would not be better off. Plaintiff would merely be the dog in the manger.

Since plaintiff and those who take the same view have not attempted any hard factual study of the actual effect of photocopying, it is not surprising that others have concluded against an adverse impact. The 1962 Fry Report (George Fry & Associates, "Survey of Copyrighted Material Reproduction Practices in Scientific and Technical Fields," March 1962) states that the "basic conclusion of this report is that at the present time, no significant damage occurs to the copyright holders in the scientific and technical fields although duplication of this material is widespread and is growing rapidly." In March 1965, Dan Lacy, Managing Director, American Book Publishers Council, told a House of Representatives committee: "It has been pointed out that recent technological developments have enormously increased the amount of photocopying in libraries and technology is continuing to change rapidly. Most of this photocopying, at least at present, probably consists of excerpts and probably mostly of journal articles. *Most of it at present is probably undertaken in lieu of manual note taking, typing, or handwriting a copy, and in lieu of library loan rather than in lieu of buying a copy*" (emphasis added). Hearings before Subcommittee No. 3, Committee on the

23

Judiciary, H. of Reps., 89th Cong., 1st Sess., on H.R. 4347, H.R. 5680, etc., "Copyright Law Revision," Part 1, p. 120. The record in this case does not prove that the situation was any different at the time of the trial.

To us it is very important that plaintiff has failed to prove its assumption of economic detriment, in the past or potentially for the future. One of the factors always considered with respect to "fair use," *see supra*, is the effect of the use on the owner's potential market for the work. This record simply does not show a serious adverse impact, either on plaintiff or on medical publishers generally, from the photocopying practices of the type of NIH and NLM. In

the face of this record, we cannot mechanically assume such an effect, or hold that the amount of photoduplication proved here "must" lead to financial or economic harm. This is a matter of proof and plaintiff has not transformed its hypothetical assumption, by evidence, into a proven fact.

In this connection it is worth noting that plaintiff does not have to concern itself, with respect to these journals, with authors or medical societies who are interested in a financial return. The authors, with rare exceptions, are not paid for their contributions, and those societies which share profits do not press for greater financial benefits. Indeed, some of the authors of the copied articles involved in this case testified at the trial that they favored photocopying as an aid to the advancement of science and knowledge.

6. Added to the powerful factors we have been considering is another (already suggested by the discussion in Part II, *supra*)—the grave uncertainty of the coverage of "copy" in Section 1 of the 1909 Act and the doubt whether it relates at all to periodicals.₂₃ The latitude for "fair use" is of course lessened to the extent Congress has been explicit in spelling out protection to the copyright owner. But Congress has, up to now, left the problem of photocopying untouched by express provision and only doubtfully covered to any extent by the generalizations of Section 1. The statute must, of course, "be applied to new situations not anticipated by Congress, if, fairly construed, such situations come within its intent and meaning" (*Jerome H. Remick & Co. v. American Automobile*

24

Accessories Co., 5 F. 2d 411 (C.A. 6, 1925), *cert. denied*, 269 U.S. 556), but our problem is with the latter part of this quotation. That being so, we think that, in evaluating "fair use," we should give the benefit of the doubt—until Congress acts more specifically—to science and the libraries, rather than to the publisher and the owner.

While, as we have said, this record fails to show that plaintiff (or any other medical publisher) has been substantially harmed by the photocopying practices of NIH and NLM, it does show affirmatively that medical science will be hurt if such photocopying is stopped. Thus, the balance of risks is definitely on defendant's side—until Congress acts more specifically, the burden on medical science of a holding that the photocopying is an infringement would appear to be much greater than the present or foreseeable burden on plaintiff and other medical publishers of a ruling that these practices fall within "fair use."

Plaintiff's answer is that it is willing to license the libraries, on payment of a reasonable royalty, to continue photocopying as they have. Our difficulty with that response—in addition to the absence of proof that plaintiff has yet been hurt, and the twin doubts whether plaintiff has a viable license system and whether any satisfactory program can be created without legislation ₂₄—is that the 1909 Act does not provide for compulsory licensing in this field. All that a court can do is to determine the photocopying an infringement, leaving it to the owner to decide whether to license or to prohibit the practice. Plaintiff and other publishers cannot enjoin governmental libraries (because 28

25

U.S.C. § 1498, *supra* note 1, is the sole remedy), but if photocopying of this type is an infringement the owners are free under the law to seek to enjoin any and all nongovernmental libraries. A licensing system would be purely voluntary with the copyright proprietor. We consider it entirely beyond judicial power, under the 1909 Act,[35] to order an owner to institute such a system if he does not wish to. We think it equally outside a court's present competence to turn the determination of "fair use" on the owner's willingness to license—to hold that photocopying (without royalty payments) is not "fair use" if the owner is willing to license at reasonable rates but becomes a "fair use" if the owner is adamant and refuses all permission (or seeks to charge excessive fees).

The truth is that this is now preeminently a problem for Congress: to decide the extent photocopying should be allowed, the questions of a compulsory license and the payments (if any) to the copyright owners, the system for collecting those payments (lump-sum, clearinghouse, etc.), the special status (if any) of scientific and educational needs. Obviously there is much to be said on all sides. The choices involve economic, social, and policy factors which are far better sifted by a legislature. The possible intermediate solutions are also of the pragmatic kind legislatures, not courts, can and should fashion. But Congress does not appear to have put its mind directly to this problem in 1909, undoubtedly because the issue was not considered pressing at that time. That statute is, unfortunately, the one we must apply, and under it we have the choice only of thumb's up or thumb's down, for the photocopying practice involved in this litigation, without any real Congressional guidance. Intermediate or compromise solutions are not within our authority.[36] The theme of this subpart 6 of Part III of the opinion is that, on balance and on this record, thumb's up seems to us less dangerous to the varying interests at stake during the period which remains before Congress definitively takes hold of the subject.

[35] A court's powers under the anti-trust legislation is another matter.
[36] It has been suggested, however, that publishers now have the power to adopt the intermediate solution of charging more for subscriptions sold to libraries or other entities which engage regularly in photocopying.

26

7. The revision of the 1909 Act is now under consideration and has been for several years. The House of Representatives passed a bill in the 90th Congress (in April 1967), but the Senate has not acted.[37] In its report on the bill which the House adopted (H.R. REP. No. 83, 90th Cong., 1st Sess.), the House Committee on the Judiciary discussed the existing doctrine of "fair use" at some length (pp. 29–37). We cite these comments, not as binding on us, but as the official views on the extent of "fair use" of the committee of the House of Representatives with cognizance over copyright; as such, they are and should be influential.

The report makes it very clear that photocopying can be a "fair use," in proper circumstances; it negatives the notion that copying of a complete work can never be a "fair use"; and it obviously believes that the doctrine is flexible, depending upon the particular situation.[38] The report does not, however, express a categorical or clear view whether photocopying of the sort we have in this case is or is not a "fair use" under the doctrine as it has been developing. Rather, the committee's observations are delphic, with each side being able to quote to us one or another passage, or to argue by analogy from the specific situation (classroom teaching) considered in greatest detail in the report.

Specifically on library photocopying the committee says (p. 36) that it does not favor a specific provision dealing with that subject, and it adds: "Unauthorized library copying, like everything else, must be judged a fair use or an infringement on the basis of all of the applicable criteria and the facts of the particular case. Despite past efforts, reasonable

[37] A synopsis of the revision effort (up to 1968) is set forth in *Fortnightly*

Corp. v. *United Artists Television, Inc.*, 392 U.S. 390, 396 n. 17 (1968).
[38] The report says (p. 29) that "* * * since the doctrine is an equitable rule of reason, no generally applicable definition is possible, and each case raising the question must be decided on its own facts"; that (p. 32) the committee endorses "the purpose and general scope of the judicial doctrine of fair use, as outlined earlier in this report, but there is no disposition to freeze the doctrine in the statute, especially during a period of technological change. Beyond a very broad statutory explanation of what fair use is and some of the criteria applicable to it, the courts must be free to adapt the doctrine to particular situations on a case-by-case basis; and that (p. 32) "Section 107, as revised by the committee, is intended to restate the present judicial doctrine of fair use, not to change, narrow, or enlarge it in any way."

27

arrangements involving a mutual understanding of what generally constitutes acceptable library practices, and providing workable clearance and licensing conditions, have not been achieved and are overdue. The committee urges all concerned to resume their efforts to reach an accommodation under which the needs of scholarship and the rights of authors would both be respected."

We read this report, as a whole, as recognizing affirmatively that, under the existing law, library photocopying can be "fair use" in proper circumstances, and as leaving the determination of whether the particular circumstances are proper ones to an evaluation "of all the applicable criteria and the facts of the particular case." That is, of course, the overall standard we are using, and therefore we consider our approach to be consistent with that of the Committee. Although one cannot say that the report places its sanction directly on the photocopying practices now before us, neither does it suggest or intimate that they are "unfair." That question is left open. The report is nevertheless helpful because it indicates the correctness of our general approach, and also because it contradicts the concept, urged by plaintiff, that photocopying of an entire article is necessarily an infringement.

8. The last component we mention, as bearing on "fair use", is the practice in foreign countries. The copyright legislation of the United Kingdom, New Zealand, Denmark, Finland, Italy, Norway, Sweden, France, the German Federal Republic, Lichtenstein, Mexico, the Netherlands, and the U.S.S.R. have specific provisions which we think would cover the photocopying activities of NLM and NIH. Canada, India, Ireland and South Africa, while having no specific provisions permitting copying of copyrighted works for the purposes of private research and study, do provide, more generally, that fair dealing for purposes of private study or research shall not be an infringement.[39] These provisions in foreign countries with problems and backgrounds comparable to our own are highly persuasive that the copying done

[39] The foreign laws are compiled in *Copyright Laws and Treaties of the World*, published by UNESCO.

28

here should be considered a "fair use," not an infringement.[40] Where Congress has left such a large void to be filled entirely by the courts, it is appropriate for us to consider what other jurisdictions have done either by way of legislation or judicial decision.

IV

Fusing these elements together, we conclude that plaintiff has failed to show that the defendant's use of the copyrighted material has been "unfair," and conversely we find that these practices have up to now been "fair." There has been no infringement. As Professor (now Mr. Justice) Kaplan observed, it is "fundamental that 'use' is not the same as 'infringement' [and] that use short of infringement is to be encouraged * * *. " Kaplan, *An Unhurried View of Copyright* 57 (1967); *see Fortnightly Corp.* v. *United Artists Television, Inc.*, 392 U.S. 390, 393–95 (1968).

So as not to be misunderstood, we reemphasize four interrelated aspects of our holding. The first is that the conclusion that defendant's particular use of plaintiff's copyrighted material has been "fair" rests upon all of the elements discussed in Part III, *supra*, and not upon any one, or any combination, less than all. We do not have to, and do not, say that any particular component would be enough, either by itself or together with some of the others. Conversely, we do not have to, and do not, say that all the elements we mention are essential to a finding of "fair use." They all happen to be present here, and it is enough for this case to rule, as we do, that at least when all co-exist in combination a "fair use" is made out.

Connected with this point is the second one that our holding is restricted to the type and context of use by NIH and NLM, as shown by this record. That is all we have before us, and we do not pass on dissimilar systems or uses of copyrighted materials by other institutions or enterprises, or in other

<hr>

⁣⁣⁣ᵃ The general report of the Committee of Experts on the Photographic Reproduction of Protected Works [a joint committee of UNESCO and the United International Bureau for the Protection of Intellectual Property (BIRPI)] recommended that libraries should have the right to provide one copy free of copyright for each user provided that such copy, in the case of a periodical, shall not be more than a single article. 4 *Copyright* 195, 197 (1968).

29

fields, or as applied to items other than journal articles, or with other significant variables. We have nothing to say, in particular, about the possibilities of computer print-outs or other such products of the newer technology now being born. Especially since we believe, as stressed *infra*, that the problem of photo and mechanical reproduction calls for legislative guidance and legislative treatment, we feel a strong need to obey the canon of judicial parsimony, being stingy rather than expansive in the reach of our holding.

The third facet articulates the same general premise—our holding rests upon this record which fails to show a significant detriment to plaintiff but does demonstrate injury to medical and scientific research if photocopying of this kind is held unlawful. We leave untouched, because we do not have to reach them, the situations where the copyright owner is shown to be hurt or the recipients (or their interests) would not be significantly injured if the reproductions were ruled to infringe.

Finally, but not at all least, we underline again the need for Congressional treatment of the problems of photocopying. The 1909 Act gives almost nothing by way of directives, the judicial doctrine of "fair use" is amorphous and open-ended, and the courts are now precluded, both by the Act and by the nature of the judicial process, from contriving pragmatic or compromise solutions which would reflect the legislature's choices of policy and its mediation among the competing interests. The Supreme Court has pointed out that such a "job is for Congress" (*Fortnightly Corp.* v. *United Artists Television, Inc.*, 392 U.S. 390, 401 (1968)), and in an earlier copyright case in which it was recognized that the owner might be morally or economically entitled to protection the Court applied "the act of Congress [as it] now stands," saying that the other "considerations properly address themselves to the legislative and not to the judicial branch of the Government." *White-Smith Music Co.* v. *Apollo Co.*, 209 U.S. 1, 18 (1908). Hopefully, the result in the present case will be but a "holding operation" in the interim period before Congress enacts its preferred solution.

On this record and for these reasons, we hold the plaintiff not entitled to recover and dismiss the petition.

30

APPENDIX

SOME DISCUSSIONS OF LIBRARY PHOTOCOPYING

B. Varmer, Photoduplication of Copyrighted Material by Libraries, Study No. 15, Copyright Law Revision, Studies Prepared for Senate Comm. on the Judiciary, 86th Cong.,

2d Sess. (1960) ; G. Sophar and L. Heilprin, The Determination of Legal Facts and Economic Guideposts with Respect to the Dissemination of Scientific and Educational Information as it is Affected by Copyright—A Status Report, Final Report, Prepared by The Committee to Investigate Copyright Problems Affecting Communication in Science and Education, Inc., for the U.S. Department of Health, Education, and Welfare, Project No. 70793 (1967) ; Report of the Register of Copyrights on the General Revision of the U.S. Copyright Law to the House Comm. on the Judiciary, 87th Cong., 2d Sess. at 25–26 (1961) ; Project—New Technology and the Law of Copyright: Reprography and Computers, 15 U.C.L.A. L. Rev. 931 (1968) ; V. Clapp, Copyright—A Librarian's View, Prepared for the National Advisory Commission on Libraries, Association of American Libraries (1968) ; Schuster and Bloch, Mechanical Copyright, Copyright Law, and the Teacher, 17 Clev.-Mar. L. Rev. 299 (1968) ; "Report on Single Copies"—Joint Libraries Committee on Fair Use in Photocopying, 9 Copyright Soc'y Bull. 79 (1961–62) ; Breyer, "The Uneasy Case for Copyright: A Study of Copyright in Books, Photocopies, and Computer Programs," 84 Harv. L. Rev. 281 (1970) ; Note, "Statutory Copyright Protection for Books and Magazines Against Machine Copying," 39 Notre Dame Lawyer 161 (1964) ; Note, Education and Copyright Law: An Analysis of the Amended Copyright Revision Bill and Proposals for Statutory Licensing and a Clearinghouse System," 56 Va. L. Rev. 664 (1970) ; Hattery and Bush (ed.), Reprography and Copyright Law (1964).

COWEN, *Chief Judge*, dissenting:

It is my opinion that our former Trial Judge James F. Davis fully and correctly resolved the difficult and perplexing issues presented by this case in his scholarly and well-reasoned opinion. I would therefore adopt his opinion, findings of fact, and recommended conclusions of law as a basis for a judgment by the court in favor of the plaintiff.

In its discussion of the grounds for the decision which rejected the trial judge's conclusions, the court has, in my opinion, unduly emphasized the facts that are favorable to the defendant and has given inadequate consideration to

31

other facts which led the trial judge to reach a contrary result. For these reasons, I am incorporating in this dissent those portions of the trial judge's opinion which I think are particularly pertinent to the grounds upon which the case has been decided. In view of the court's extensive discussion of the issues and its consideration of some matters not argued to the trial judge, I am supplementing his opinion with the material that follows.

As a preface to my disagreement with the court, I think it would be helpful to point out that this is not a case involving copying of copyrighted material by a scholar or his secretary in aid of his research, nor is it a case where a teacher has reproduced such material for distribution to his class. Also, it is not a case where doctors or scientists have quoted portions of plaintiff's copyrighted articles in the course of writing other articles in the same field. We are not concerned here with a situation in which a library makes copies of ancient manuscripts or worn-out magazines in order to preserve information. What we have before us is a case of wholesale, machine copying, and distribution of copyrighted material by defendant's libraries on a scale so vast that it dwarfs the output of many small publishing companies. In order to fill requests for copies of articles in medical and scientific journals, the NIH made 86,000 Xerox copies in 1970, constituting 930,000 pages. In 1968, the NLM distributed 120,000 copies of such journal articles, totalling about 1.2 million pages. As the trial judge correctly observed, this extensive operation is not only a copying of the copyrighted articles, it is also a reprinting by modern methods and publication by a very wide distribution to requesters and users.

Photographic Reproduction of Plaintiff's Journal Articles Is An Abridgement of the Copyright Owner's Exclusive Right To Copy

The majority maintains there is a "solid doubt" whether and how far the word "copy" in Section 1(a) of the 1909 Copyright Act applies to books and journals. The argument continues that the infringement of periodical articles can come only through "printing," "reprinting," or "publishing."

32

Certainly few things in the law are beyond all doubt or qualification. I think it is apparent, however, from the wording of the 1909 Act, and from the cases interpreting that Act, that Congress intended the word "copy" to apply to books and journals as well as other copyrightable materials. Section 1(a) of the 1909 Act gives the copyright proprietor the exclusive right to "print, reprint, publish, copy, and vend the copyrighted work." 17 U.S.C. § 1 (1970). It follows that copying of a substantial portion of the copyrighted work by someone other than the copyright owner would be an infringement.

I think the trial judge correctly concluded that there is nothing in the legislative history of the 1909 Act which indicates that a restrictive definition of the word "copy" was intended. A significant change in the 1909 Act was the elimination of sections 4964 and 4965 of the prior copyright statute, which it is claimed, are the source of the distinction between the copying of books and the copying of other copyrighted material.[1] By removing those two sections and by adopting the general classification of "copyrighted works" in Section 1(a) and a general listing of all copyrightable works in Section 5 of the 1909 Act, Congress obliterated the distinction, if there ever had been one, between the copying of books and the copying of other materials.[2]

As a result of the simple clarity in the phrasing of the copyright owner's exclusive rights in the 1909 Act, it is not surprising that numerous court decisions interpreting that Act have focused on the copying of copyrighted material (including books and other items of this type) as the infringing act. *See, e.g., Harold Lloyd Corp.* v. *Witwer*, 65 F. 2d 1, 16–19 (9th Cir. 1933); *King Features Syndicate* v. *Fleischer*, 299 F. 533, 535 (2d Cir. 1924).

[1] These sections had been in the copyright law since 1831 and had been twice re-enacted. Act of February 3, 1831, ch. 16, §§ 6 and 7, 4 Stat. 436; Act of July 8, 1870, ch. 230, §§ 99 and 100, 16 Stat. 214; Act of March 3, 1891, ch. 565, §§ 4964 and 4965, 26 Stat. 1109.
[2] The trial judge observed that it was the intent of Congress in all the copyright acts to proscribe the unauthorized duplication of copyrighted works. The words used in the various statutes were simply attempts to define the then-current means by which duplication could be effected. I believe this is a fair statement, but it is not necessary to debate the statutory history in light of the changes in the 1909 Act.

33

I have not been able to find one decision since the 1909 Act which has held that the word "copy" in section 1(a) would not apply to the making of one or a number of copies of a book or other material of this type. The cases have simply not recognized the claimed distinction between copying and printing or publishing. For example, in *New York Tribune, Inc.* v. *Otis & Co.*, 39 F. Supp. 67 (S.D.N.Y. 1941), the court found the making of photostatic copies of plaintiff's newspaper editorial and masthead to be a "good cause of action on its face," and denied defendant's motion for summary judgment. *Id.* at 68. The defendant in that case had distributed the photocopies to a selected list of public officials, bankers, educators, economists and other persons. The court drew no distinction between printing, publishing, or copying. By comparison, the copying and distributing of the newspaper editorial and masthead in that case is very similar to the copying and distributing of the journal articles in the present action.[3]

Therefore, I do not think there is substantial doubt that the photocopying by defendant's libraries is a copy of the plaintiff's journal articles in violation of the copyright owner's exclusive right to copy or to multiply copies of his work under section 1(a). I can see no reason to draw a distinction between copying of "books" and copying of other materials when the distinction is expressly rejected on the face of the

copyright statute, has not been observed in numerous cases applying the 1909 Act, and has no reasonable basis in light of the purposes of copyright protection.[4]

[3] For cases involving the copying of segments from a copyrighted catalog by photographic reproduction, *see* Hedeman Products Corp. v. Tap-Rite Prods. Corp., 228 F. Supp. 630, 633–34 (D.N.J. 1964); R. R. Donnelley & Sons Co. v. Haber, 43 F. Supp. 456, 458–59 (E.D.N.Y. 1942).
[4] The fact that Dr. Putnam, the Librarian of Congress at the time of the 1909 Act, interpreted the word "copy" not to include library photoduplication is no indication that the Congress drafted the statute with this intent. The absence of any provision allowing library photoduplication in the statute or the legislative history indicates, as much as anything else, that Congress did not consider it to be exempt from the Act. The many efforts to amend the law to authorize photocopying by libraries provide a strong indication that existing law was not intended to grant this exemption to libraries. See n. 14, trial judge's opinion.

34

II

The Photocopying of Plaintiff's Copyrighted Articles Was Not Fair Use

1. Realizing the necessity for showing that the defendant's unauthorized copying of plaintiff's articles was both reasonable and insubstantial, the court relies heavily on policies which were adopted by the libraries in 1965. Although these policies were designed to limit the extent of copying that had been done in prior years, the trial judge's opinion and the findings of fact show the exceptions are routinely granted by the defendant's libraries, that there is no way to enforce most of the limitations, and that defendant is operating a reprint service which supplants the need for journal subscriptions.

In particular, the trial judge has, I think, clearly demonstrated that the claimed "single-copy-per-request" limitation is both illusory and unrealistic. He has found, and it is not disputed, that the libraries will duplicate the same article over and over again, even for the same user, within a short space of time. NLM will supply requesters photocopies of the same article, one after another, on consecutive days, even with knowledge of such facts. I find great difficulty in detecting any difference between the furnishing by defendant's libraries of ten copies of one article to one patron, which he then distributes, and giving each of ten patrons one copy of the same article. The damage to the copyright proprietor is the same in either case.

2. The law is well settled, and I believe not questioned by the court in this case, that under Section 3 of the Copyright Act, plaintiff's copyrights of the journals cover each article contained therein as fully as if each were individually copyrighted. Section 3 expressly mentions periodicals, and for the purpose of determining whether there has been infringement, each copyrightable component is to be treated as a complete work. *Markham* v. *A. E. Borden Co.*, 206 F. 2d 199, 201 (1st Cir. 1953).

It is undisputed that the photocopies in issue here were exact duplicates of the original articles; they were intended to be substitutes for and they served the same purpose as the original articles. They were copies of complete copyrighted

35

works within the meaning of Sections 3 and 5 of the Copyright Act. This is the very essence of wholesale copying and, without more, defeats the defense of fair use. The rule to be applied in such a situation was stated in *Leon V. Pacific Telephone & Telegraph Co.*, 91 F. 2d 484, 486 (9th Cir. 1937) as follows:

> Counsel have not disclosed a single authority, nor have we been able to find one, which lends any support to the proposition that wholesale copying and publication of copyrighted material can ever be fair use.

For other cases to the same effect, *see Public Affairs Associates, Inc.* v. *Rickover*, 284 F. 2d 262, 272 (D.C. Cir. 1960), *judgment vacated for insufficient record*, 369 U.S. 111 (1962); *Benny* v. *Loew's Inc.*, 239 F. 2d 532, 536 (9th Cir.

1956), *aff'd by an equally divided court sub nom., Columbia Broadcasting System, Inc.* v. *Loew's Inc.,* 356 U.S. 43 (1958); *Holdredge* v. *Knight Publishing Corp.,* 214 F. Supp. 921, 924 (S.D. Cal. 1963). *See also* M. Nimmer, *Nimmer on Copyright* § 145 at 650–51 (1973 ed.).

Although the majority states that the rule announced in the cases cited above is an "overbroad generalization, unsupported by the decisions and rejected by years of accepted practice," the court cites no decisions in support of its position.

3. I recognize that the doctrine of fair use permits writers of scholarly works to make reasonable use of previously copyrighted material by quotation or paraphrase, at least where the amount of copying is small and reliance on other sources is demonstrated. *See, e.g., Rosemont Enterprises, Inc.* v. *Random House, Inc.,* 366 F. 2d 303 (2d Cir. 1966), *cert. denied,* 385 U.S. 1009 (1967); *Simms* v. *Stanton,* 75 F. 6, 13–14 (C.C.N.D. Cal. 1896). However, I think the basic error in the court's decision is its holding that the fair use privilege usually granted to such writers should be extended to cover the massive copying and distribution operation conducted by defendant's libraries. The articles are not reproduced by the libraries to enable them to write other articles in the same field. In fact, booksellers and licensed copiers of plaintiff's journals sell copies of journal articles to the same class of users and for the same purposes as the copies reproduced by defendant's libraries.

36

I do not believe that anyone would contend that the ultimate use of the purchased articles by scientists, doctors, or drug companies would permit the commercial concerns mentioned to reproduce copies without plaintiff's permission. In an effort to overcome this obstacle, the majority relies in part on the nature and function of the NIH and the NLM and the fact that the articles are reproduced and distributed free of charge. I do not know of any case which holds that an unauthorized reproduction which is made without profit amounts to fair use by the infringer, and there are decisions to the contrary.[5]

Moreover, as plaintiff has pointed out, almost every service provided by Government agencies is financed by appropriated funds and furnished without charge to the recipient. If Congress had intended to relieve Government agencies from liability for copyright infringement whenever the material is copied or otherwise reproduced without charge to the recipient, there would have been no need for the enactment of the 1960 Amendment, now 28 U.S.C. § 1498(b), which gives us jurisdiction of this action.

Defendant also argues that its libraries are entitled to the fair use privilege of scientists, researchers, or scholars, because the libraries act as their agent in making the photocopies at their request. This argument is so far-fetched that the majority balks at embracing it completely. It collides with reality. The libraries installed and operate the reproduction and distribution operation on their own initiative and without any kind of an agreement with the ultimate users of the copies. There is no showing that these alleged—and in the case of NLM generally unknown—principals have any say in the formulation of the policies and practices of the photocopying operation. The libraries decide, without consulting or obtaining the consent of the alleged principals, whether to loan the original of the journals or to provide

to make and sell copies to doctors and scientists. The essential elements of agency are wholly lacking.

4. The trial judge found that it is reasonable to infer from the evidence that the extensive unauthorized copying of plaintiff's journal has resulted in some loss of revenue and serves to diminish plaintiff's potential market for the original articles. Since the inferences made by the trial judge may reasonably be drawn from the facts and circumstances in evidence, they are presumptively as correct as his findings of fact. *Bonnar* v. *United States,* 194 Ct. Cl. 103, 109, 438 F. 2d 540, 542 (1971). *See also Baumgartner* v. *United States,* 322 U.S. 665, 670 (1944); *Penn-Texas Corp.* v. *Morse,* 242 F. 2d 243, 247 (7th Cir. 1957). Accordingly, under the standards which we employ for reviewing the findings of our trial judges, I would adopt these findings. *Davis* v. *United States,* 164 Ct. Cl. 612, 616–17 (1964); *Wilson* v. *United States,* 151 Ct. Cl. 271, 273 (1960).

Although the court states that it rejects the trial determinations as to both actual and potential damage to plaintiff, I think the opinion shows that the court's conclusion is based primarily on its finding that plaintiff failed to prove actual damages. In so doing, the majority relies heavily on evidence that the plaintiff's profits have grown faster than the gross national product and that plaintiff's annual taxable income has increased. This evidence is irrelevant to the economic effects of photocopying the journals in this case, because these periodicals account for a relatively small percent of plaintiff's total business. Moreover, the extent of plaintiff's taxable income for the years mentioned does not reflect the effect of defendant's photocopying of plaintiff's journals, and particularly the effect it will have on the prospects for continued publication in the future.

By the very nature of an action for infringement, the copyright proprietor often has a difficult burden of proving the degree of injury. It is well established, however, that

38

proof of actual damages is not required, and the defense of fair use may be overcome where potential injury is shown. *See, e.g., Henry Holt & Co., Inc.* v. *Liggett & Myers Tobacco Co.,* 23 F. Supp. 302, 304 (E.D. Pa. 1938). As Professor Nimmer has stated, the courts look to see whether defendant's work "tends to diminish or prejudice the potential sale of the plaintiff's work." M. Nimmer, *Nimmer on Copyright* § 145 at 646 (1973 ed.).

The problem posed by library photocopying of copyrighted material has long been a subject of controversy. Several studies of this problem have pointed out that extensive photocopying by libraries is unfair because of its potential damage to the copyright owner. The trial judge has quoted from the reports of several of these studies.[6]

In a thorough and thoughtful discussion of the effects of reprography, prepared at the University of California, Los Angeles, and funded by the National Endowment for the Arts, it is stated:

> It has long been argued that copying by hand "for the purpose of private study and review" would be a fair use. Users are now asserting that machine copying is merely a substitute for hand copying and is, therefore, a fair use. But this argument ignores the economic differences between the two types of copying. Copying by hand is extremely time consuming and costly, and is not an economic threat to authors. *Viewing reprography as though it were hand copying, however, overlooks the effect of the total number of machine copies made. Few people hand copy, but millions find machine copying economical and convenient. Allowing individual users to decide that their machine copying will not injure the author and will thus be a fair use fails to take into account the true economic effect when thousands of such individual decisions are aggregated.*
> The problem is vividly presented by the practice of

---

[5] It has been held that the copying or printing of something which has been lawfully copyrighted is an infringement "without any requirement that there be a sale or that profits be made from sale of the copies." Chappell & Co., Inc. v. Costa, 45 F. Supp. 554, 556 (S.D.N.Y. 1942). In Wihtol v. Crow, 309 F. 2d 777 (8th Cir. 1962), the First Methodist Church was found to be liable for a choral instructor's copying of a copyrighted song.

[6] *See* the trial judge's opinion for quotations from B. Varmer, Photoduplication of Copyrighted Material by Libraries, Study No. 15, Copyright Law Revision, Studies Prepared for the Senate Comm. on the Judiciary, 86th Cong. 2d Sess. 62–63 (1960); Report of the Register of Copyrights on the General Revision of the U.S. Copyright Law, House Committee Print, 87th Cong., 1st Sess. 25–26 (1961). M. Nimmer, *Nimmer on Copyright* § 145 at 653–54 (1973 ed.). *See also* Crossland, *The Rise and Fall of Fair Use: The Protection of Literary Materials Against Copyright Infringement by New and Developing Media,* 20 S. Car. L. Rev. 153, 154 (1968).

photocopies. The libraries are no more the agent of the users of the material than are the venders of plaintiff's magazines and the commercial concerns which are licensed by plaintiff

39

the National Library of Medicine. The Library justifies its distribution of reprographic copies of journal articles to biomedical libraries (without permission of the copyright owner) on the basis of a 1939 understanding between publishers and libraries called the "Gentlemen's Agreement." Under this agreement photocopies are permitted whenever the user would have made a hand copy himself, the rationale being that no purchases of the author's work are displaced under these circumstances. When an individual would actually copy by hand, the theory is valid; there is no sound reason to force him to do the work. But many people obtain copies from the library who would not copy by hand, and who might in fact buy a copy of the work if they were unable to receive an inexpensive machine reproduction of it. Thus, the library interprets the Gentlemen's Agreement in its favor and thereby "justifies" a substantial amount of copying. (Emphasis supplied.) *Project, New Technology and the Law of Copyright: Reprography and Computers*, 15 U.C.L.A. L. Rev. 931, 951 (1968).

As the majority points out, one study, made in 1962, concluded that photocopying did not result in economic damage to publishers at that time: Fry & Associates, Survey of Copyrighted Material Reproduction Practices in Scientific and Technical Fields, 11 Bull. Cr. Soc. 69, 71 (1963). This study also stated:

> One situation was reported during the survey in which economic damage may occur. A prominent university library in a small town with several corporate research and development centers gives excellent service on its collection. This library felt that these corporate libraries are subscribing to only the minimum number of journals. They rely on the university to supply photocopies of other material.
>
> * * * * *
>
> This is the one clear-cut example disclosed during the survey of dilution of the publishers' circulation market. *Id.* at 119.

Indeed, this example is very nearly the situation presented by this case. Government institutions, medical schools, hospitals, research foundations, drug companies, and individual physicians are supplementing their collections, if they

40

subscribe to any journals, by acquiring free photocopies of articles from the NLM.[7]

In addition to the conclusions of those who have studied the problem extensively, there are other facts and circumstances in this record which I think amply support the views of the trial judge that the system used by defendant's libraries for distributing free copies of plaintiff's journal articles attracts some potential purchasers of plaintiff's journals.

Subscription sales provide most of the revenue derived from the marketing of plaintiff's journals. It is important to remember that each of plaintiff's journals caters to and serves a limited market. Plaintiff's share of the profits from these journals has varied from less than $1,000 to about $7,000 annually.[8] In the context of rising costs of publication, an inability to attract new customers, and the loss of even a small number of old subscribers may have a large detrimental effect on the journals. A representative of William & Wilkins Company testified that in recent years there have been journals that have failed, and in the opinion of those at Williams & Wilkins, photocopying has played a role in these failures.[9] The majority relies on the fact that subscriptions for the four journals in this case have shown a general increase over the last five years, but two of the journals, *Medicine* and *Phar-*

[7] It should be noted that the Fry survey was made when photocopying was not as prominent as it is today. Even at that time, the Fry Report notes that larger publishers (who were photocopied most heavily) complained about the effects of photocopying. Fry Report at 86–87. Secondly, the Fry Report operates on the dubious assumption that in most cases the photocopy serves as a substitute for loaning the original material and does no more damage than would loaning of the original material.

In addition to the Fry Report, the majority cites a statement by Dan Lacy, Managing Director, American Book Publisher's Council, to the effect that photocopying is undertaken in lieu of manual note taking, typing, or handwriting a copy, and in lieu of a library loan rather than in lieu of buying a copy. We can hardly expect a representative of an organization of book publishers to be an expert on the problems of journal publishers. Library photocopying of books does not pose the same threat to a book publisher as photo-

copying of journal articles does to its publisher. Rarely are books photocopied completely. At present, there appears to be no competition for the consumer market between libraries and book publishers.

[8] For example, in 1968, profit from *Pharmacological Reviews* was $1,154.44 (on sales of about $40,000). The profit was divided, $1,039 to the American Society for Pharmacology and Experimental Therapeutics and $115.44 to plaintiff. In 1969, net income from *Gastroenterology* was $21,312 (on sales of about $245,000) and $11,532.35 of that amount was offset by losses the previous year, leaving a balance of $9,779.73. The balance was split between plaintiff and the American Gastroenterological Association, plaintiff getting $4,889.86.

[9] Tr. at 73.

41

macological Reviews, have shown a slight decrease in subscriptions from 1968 to 1969. In addition, the *Journal of Immunology* showed losses in the period prior to 1961; *Gastroenterology* showed losses in 1967 and 1968; *Pharmacological Reviews* showed a loss in 1969. There is no evidence to show specifically whether any particular instance or instances of unauthorized photocopying of plaintiff's journals has or has not resulted in the loss of revenue to plaintiff. However, I think the record, as a whole, supports the determination of the trial judge that the photocopying in this case has had a tendency to diminish plaintiff's markets in the past.

The NLM publishes a monthly indexed catalog of journal articles in medicine and related sciences entitled "Index Medicus." The index is widely distributed to medical libraries, research centers, schools, hospitals, and physicians. The catalog announces its new publications and acquisitions and thus advertises to the medical and scientific community, which constitutes plaintiff's market, that certain articles are available free of charge in the form of a photocopy.

At the present time, the NIH purchases only two subscriptions to plaintiff's journals. If nothing else, it would certainly need more than the two copies to meet the requests of the large in-house staff. Although it has been argued that the photocopies are merely a substitute for the loan of an original and does no more harm than the loan of the original material, I think this argument is fallacious. One copy of the original material could not possibly be loaned to as many requesters as the numerous photocopies, the competitive effect of which is much greater. Also, the photocopies are not required to be returned and become the property of the possessor. They can be marked, cut into segments, placed in the files, and otherwise put to uses that would be impossible with a loan of the original. While the library may look at the giving of a photocopy as a substitute for a loan, the user and would be purchaser gets an exact copy of the original article which is a substitute for a purchased copy.

One of the new sources of income to publishers is the supplying of back issues or providing copies of such issues. When plaintiff receives a request for an out-of-print article, the customer is generally referred to the Institute of Scientific Information, which is licensed by plaintiff to make the photo-

42

copies. If the same articles can be obtained from the NLM without charge, it seems obvious that the supplying of free copies by the defendant's libraries will tend to diminish plaintiff's income from this source. NLM reproduces and supplies copies of journal articles to the patrons of other libraries. Therefore, the libraries who make the requests do not have to buy subscriptions for the use of their own patrons.

III

Foreign Laws Do Not Justify an Exemption From the Copyright Laws

The court relies to some extent on the copyright laws of the United Kingdom, New Zealand, Denmark, Finland, Italy, and other countries. The plaintiff says there are many differences between our copyright laws and those of other countries, and plaintiff does not agree that the defendant would be exempt from liability under the statutes of some of the countries named. However, we need not delve into the details of the copyright legislation of these foreign countries. There is a shorter answer to the court's reliance on foreign laws. Unlike the legislative bodies of these countries, the Congress has not yet changed the Copyright Act of 1909 to permit the same kind of copying by the NIH and the NLM. If the time has come when the defendant's libraries should be exempted from the provisions of the Copyright Act to the extent permitted by the court's decision, the exemption should be provided by legislative action rather than by judicial legislation.

IV

A Judgment for Plaintiff Will Not Injure Medicine and Medical Research

The court has bottomed its decision to a very large extent on its finding, which is not disputed, that medical science would be seriously hurt if the photocopying by defendant's libraries is entirely stopped. But the court goes further and concludes that a judgment for plaintiff would lead to this result. It is not altogether clear to me how the court arrives

---

43

---

at the second conclusion, and I think it is based on unwarranted assumptions.

The plaintiff does not propose to stop such photocopying and does not desire that result. What plaintiff seeks is a reasonable royalty for such photocopying and, in this case, a recovery of reasonable compensation for the infringement of its copyrights. Plaintiff has established a licensing system to cover various methods of reproducing its journal articles, including reproduction by photocopying. One of the licensees is a Government agency, and on several occasions plaintiff has granted requests from Government agencies and others for licenses to make multiple copies (Finding 36). In May 1967, the photocopying of plaintiff's journal articles was monitored by NLM for a 90-day period which was judged to be a representative sample. As the trial judge has shown, NLM found that it would have paid plaintiff from $250 to $300 if it had granted plaintiff's request for royalty payments. The Director of NLM testified that this was, in his opinion, a surprisingly small sum. He also testified (Part III, trial judge's opinion) that the payment of a royalty to plaintiff for photocopying "has nothing to do with the operation of the library in the fulfillment of * * * [its] function. It is an economic and budgetary consideration and not a service-oriented kind of thing." This is the only direct testimony that I have found on how the payment of royalties for photocopying will affect the functions of the library, and it gives no indication or intimation that the payment of royalties to plaintiff will force NLM to cease the photocopying.

The court has laid heavy emphasis on the public interest in maintaining a free flow of information to doctors and scientists, and on the injury that might result if this flow should be stopped. However, there is another facet to the public interest question which is presented in this case. The trial judge put it well in his statement:

> The issues raised by this case are but part of a larger problem which continues to plague our institutions with ever-increasing complexity—how best to reconcile, on the one hand, the rights of authors and publishers under the copyright laws with, on the other hand, the technological improvements in copying techniques and the

---

44

---

legitimate public need for rapid dissemination of scientific and technical literature. (Part III, trial judge's opinion)

In enacting the 1909 Act, the House Committee said:

> The enactment of copyright legislation by Congress under the terms of the Constitution is not based upon any natural right that the author has in his writings * * * but upon the ground that the welfare of the public will be served and progress of science and useful arts will be promoted by securing to authors for limited periods

the exclusive rights to their writings. H.R. Rep. No. 2222, 60th Cong., 2d Sess. 7 (1909).

In *Mazer* v. *Stein*, 347 U.S. 201, 219 (1954), the Supreme Court emphasized that the copyright protection given to authors and publishers is designed to advance public welfare, stating:

> "The copyright law, like the patent statutes, makes reward to the owner a secondary consideration. * * *"
> However, it is "intended definitely to grant valuable, enforceable rights to authors, publishers, etc. * * *"
> The economic philosophy behind the clause empowering Congress to grant patents and copyrights is the conviction that encouragement of individual effort by personal gain is the best way to advance public welfare through the talents of authors and inventors in "Science and useful Arts."

In order to promote the progress of science, not only must authors be induced to write new works, but also publishers must be induced to disseminate those works to the public. This philosophy has guided our country, with limited exceptions, since its beginning, and I am of the opinion that if there is to be a fundamental policy change in this system, such as a blanket exception for library photocopying, it is for the Congress to determine, not for the courts. The courts simply cannot draw the distinctions so obviously necessary in this area.

The court recognizes that the solution which it has undertaken to provide in this case is preeminently a problem for Congress which should decide how much photocopying should be allowed, what payments should be made to the copyright owners, and related questions. Nowhere else in its opinion is the court on more solid ground than when it

---

45

---

declares that the "choices involve economic, social, and policy factors which are far better sifted by a legislature. The possible intermediate solutions are also of the pragmatic kind legislatures, not courts, can and should fashion." In spite of this obviously correct statement, the court has bridged the gap which the inaction of Congress has left in the Copyright Act of 1909.

I agree with the court that we have no jurisdiction to order a copyright owner to institute a licensing system if he does not wish to do so, but I think we are equally powerless to assume the congressional role by granting what amounts to a blanket exemption to defendant's libraries. Without too much difficulty, however, we can determine the amount of just compensation that is due plaintiff for the infringement of its copyrights. If that should be done, it may very well lead to a satisfactory agreement between the parties for a continuation of the photocopying by defendant upon the payment of a reasonable royalty to plaintiff.

The following portions of the trial judge's opinion are made a part of this dissent:

I

Plaintiff, though a relatively small company, is a major publisher of medical journals and books. Plaintiff publishes 37 journals, dealing with various medical specialties. The four journals in suit are *Medicine, Journal of Immunology, Gastroenterology,* and *Pharmacological Reviews. Medicine* is published by plaintiff for profit and for its own benefit. The other three journals are published in conjunction with specialty medical societies which, by contract, share the journals' profits with plaintiff. The articles published in the journals stem from manuscripts submitted to plaintiff (or one of the medical societies) by physicians or other scientists engaged in medical research. The journals are widely disseminated throughout the United States (and the world) in libraries, schools, physicians' offices, and the like. Annual subscription prices range from about $12 to $44; and, due to the esoteric nature of the journals' subject matter, the number of annual subscriptions is relatively small, ranging from about 3,100 (*Pharmacological Reviews*) to about 7,000 (*Gastroenterology*). Most of the revenue derived from the

46

journals comes from subscription sales, though a small part comes from advertising.[4] The journals are published with notice of copyright in plaintiff's name. The notice appears at the front of the journal and sometimes at the beginning of each article. After publication of each journal issue (usually monthly or bimonthly) and after compliance with the requisite statutory requirements, the Register of Copyrights issues to plaintiff certificates of copyright registration.

NIH, the Government's principal medical research organization, is a conglomerate of institutes located on a multi-acre campus at Bethesda, Maryland. Each institute is concerned with a particular medical specialty, and the institutes conduct their activities by way of both intramural research and grants-in-aid to private individuals and organizations. NIH employs over 12,000 persons—4,000 are science professionals and 2,000 have doctoral degrees. To assist its intramural programs, NIH maintains a technical library. The library houses about 150,000 volumes, of which about 30,000 are books and the balance scientific (principally medical) journals. The library is open to the public, but is used mostly by NIH in-house research personnel. The library's budget for 1970 was $1.1 million.

The NIH library subscribes to about 3,000 different journal titles, four of which are the journals in suit. The library subscribes to two copies of each of the journals in suit. As a general rule, one copy stays in the library reading room and the other copy circulates among interested NIH personnel. Demand by NIH research workers for access to plaintiff's journals (as well as other journals to which the library subscribes) is usually not met by in-house subscription copies. Consequently, as an integral part of its operation, the library runs a photocopy service for the benefit of its research staff. On request, a researcher can obtain a photocopy of an article from any of the journals in the library's collection. Usually, researchers request photocopies of articles to assist them in their on-going projects; sometimes photocopies are requested simply for background reading. In any event, the library does not monitor the reason for requests or the use to which

[4] E.g., the November 1956 issue of Medicine has 86 pages, four of which carry commercial product advertising. The August 1965 issue of Journal of Immunology has 206 pages, nine of which carry commercial product advertising.

47

the photocopies are put. The photocopies are not returned to the library; and the record shows that, in most instances, researchers keep them in their private files for future reference.

Four regularly assigned employees operate the NIH photocopy equipment. The equipment consists of microfilm cameras and Xerox copying machines. In 1970, the library photocopy budget was $86,000 and the library filled 85,744 requests for photocopies of journal articles (including plaintiff's journals), constituting about 930,000 pages. On the average, a journal article is 10 pages long, so that in 1970, the library made about 93,000 photocopies of articles.

NLM is located on the Bethesda campus of NIH. NLM was formerly the Armed Forces Medical Library. In 1956, Congress transferred the library from the Department of Defense to the Public Health Service (renaming it the National Library of Medicine), and declared its purpose to be "* * * to aid the dissemination and exchange of scientific and other information important to the progress of medicine and to the public health * * *." 42 U.S.C. § 275 (1970). NLM is a repository of much of the world's medical literature. NLM is in essence a "librarians' library." As part of its operation, NLM cooperates with other libraries and like research-and-education-oriented institutions (both public and private) in a so-called "interlibrary loan" program. Upon request, NLM will loan to such institutions, for a limited time, books and other materials in its collection. In the case of journals, the "loans" usually take the form of photocopies of journal articles which are supplied by NLM free of charge and on a no-return basis. The term "loan" therefore is a euphemism when journal

articles are involved. NLM's loan policies are fashioned after the General Interlibrary Loan Code, which is a statement of self-imposed regulations to be followed by all libraries which cooperate in interlibrary loaning. The Code provides that each library, upon request for a loan of materials, shall decide whether to loan the original or provide a photoduplicate. The Code notes that photoduplication of copyrighted materials may raise copyright infringement problems, particularly with regard to "photographing *whole issues* of periodicals or books with *current copyrights*, or in making *multiple copies* of a publication." [Emphasis in original text.] NLM, there-

48

fore, will provide only one photocopy of a particular article, per request, and will not photocopy on any given request an entire journal issue. NLM, as well as other libraries, justifies this practice on the basis of a so-called "gentlemen's agreement," written in 1935 by the National Association of Book Publishers and the Joint Committee on Materials for Research (representing the libraries), which states in part, "A library * * * owning books or periodical volumes in which copyright still subsists may make and deliver a single photographic reproduction * * * *of a part thereof* to a scholar representing in writing that he desires such reproduction in lieu of loan of such publication or in place of manual transcription and solely for the purposes of research * * *." [Emphasis supplied.] Each photocopy reproduced by NLM contains a statement in the margin, "This is a single photostatic copy made by the National Library of Medicine for purposes of study or research in lieu of lending the original."

In 1968, a representative year, NLM received about 127,000 requests for interlibrary loans. Requests were received, for the most part, from other libraries or Government agencies. However, about 12 percent of the requests came from private or commercial organizations, particularly drug companies. Some requests were for books, in which event the book itself was loaned. Most requests were for journals or journal articles; and about 120,000 of the requests were filled by photocopying single articles from journals, including plaintiff's journals. Usually, the library seeking an interlibrary loan from NLM did so at the request of one of its patrons. If the "loan" was made by photocopy, the photocopy was given to the patron who was free to dispose of it as he wished. NLM made no effort to find out the ultimate use to which the photocopies were put; and there is no evidence that borrowing libraries kept the "loan" photocopies in their permanent collections for use by other patrons.

Defendant concedes that within the pertinent accounting period, NLM and the NIH library made at least one photocopy of each of eight articles (designated by plaintiff as the Count I-to-Count VIII articles) from one or more of the four journals in suit. Defendant also concedes that plaintiff is the record owner of copyright registrations on the journals. That would appear to end the matter in plaintiff's favor, for

49

§ 1 of the copyright statute (17 U.S.C.) says that the copyright owner "* * * shall have the exclusive right: (a) to print, reprint, publish, copy and vend the copyrighted work * * *"; and § 3 of the statute says that, "* * * [t]he copyright upon composite works or periodicals shall give to the proprietor thereof all the rights in respect thereto which he would have if each part were individually copyrighted under this title." Simply stated, this means that each article in plaintiff's journals is protected from infringement to the same extent as the entire journal issue. *Advertisers Exch., Inc.* v. *Laufe*, 29 F. Supp. 1 (W.D. Pa. 1939) ; *King Features Syndicate* v. *Fleischer*, 299 F. 533 (2d Cir. 1924).[5]

The noninfringement defense

Defendant contends that its acts of copying do not violate the copyright owner's exclusive right "to copy" the copyrighted work as provided by 17 U.S.C. § 1. The argument is that with respect to books and periodicals, the act of making single copies (*i.e.*, one copy at a time) is not, in itself, sufficient to incur liability; that the "copying," to be actionable, must include "printing" (or "reprinting") and "publishing" of *multiple* copies of the copyrighted work. The argument is bottomed on analysis of the copyright laws as they have evolved from 1790 to the present.[3] The early laws distinguished "copying" from "printing," "reprinting," and "publishing," and provided that the copyright in books is infringed by "printing," "reprinting" and "publishing" while the copyright in other works (*e.g.*, photographs, paintings, drawings, etc.) is infringed by "copying." The 1909 Copyright Act obliterated any such distinction. It provides in § 5 a list of all classes of copyrightable subject matter (in-

[footnotes]

[4] One argument made by defendant to justify the copying of single articles from plaintiff's journals is that each article is but "part" of a journal issue, which in turn is but "part" of a journal volume; and, accordingly, defendant says, its libraries have not copied an "entire" copyrighted work. Section 3 of 17 U.S.C. fully meets that argument, for it is undisputed that plaintiff could publish and seek copyright registration on each article separately. As stated in H.R. Rep. No. 2222, 60th Cong., 2d Sess. 10 (1909) :

    Section 3 [of the Copyright Act] does away with the necessity of taking a copyright on the contributions of different persons included in a single publication * * *.

[5] Congress enacted the first copyright statute in 1790 (Act of May 31, 1790, ch. 15, 1 Stat. 124). Thereafter, the statute was revised from time to time, notably in 1802, 1831, 1870, and 1891. In 1909, the present statute was passed (Act of March 4, 1909, ch. 320, 35 Stat. 1075) and later was codified as 17 U.S.C. (Act of July 30, 1947, 61 Stat. 652).

50

cluding books and periodicals), and says in § 1 that the owner of copyright shall have the exclusive right "to print, reprint, publish, copy and vend *the copyrighted work*" [emphasis supplied]. Thus, the 1909 Act, unlike the earlier statutes, does not expressly say which of the proscribed acts of § 1 apply to which classes of copyrightable subject matter of § 5. Defendant says that to be consistent with the intent and purpose of earlier statutes, the "copying" proscription of § 1 should not apply to books or periodicals; rather, only the proscribed acts of "printing," "reprinting" and "publishing" should apply to books and periodicals.

Defendant's argument is not persuasive and, in any event, is irrelevant. It is clear from a study of all the copyright statutes from 1790 to date that what Congress has sought to do in every statute is to proscribe unauthorized *duplication* of copyrighted works. The words used in the various statutes to define infringing acts (*i.e.*, printing, reprinting, copying, etc.) were simply attempts to define the then-current means by which duplication could be effected. It is reasonable to infer that in 1909, when Congress included "copying" in the list of proscribed acts applicable to books and periodicals (as well as copyrightable subject matter in general), it did so in light of the fact that new technologies (*e.g.*, photography) made it possible to duplicate books and periodicals by means other than "printing" and "reprinting." The legislative history of the 1909 Act says little, one way or the other, about the matter.[6] Nevertheless, §§ 1 and 5 are plain and unambiguous on their face; and the Supreme Court held as recently as 1968, in *Fortnightly Corp.*, *supra* at 394 :

    * * * § 1 of the [Copyright] Act enumerates several "rights" that are made "exclusive" to the holder of the copyright. If a person, without authorization from the copyright holder, puts a copyrighted work to a use *within the scope of one of these "exclusive rights*," *he infringes the copyright.* [Emphasis supplied.]

[footnote]

[6] H.R. Rep. No. 2222, 60th Cong., 2d Sess. 4 (1909) states:

    Subsection (a) of section 1 adopts without change the phraseology of section 4952 of the Revised Statutes, and this, with the insertion of the word "copy," practically adopts the phraseology of the first copyright act Congress ever passed—that of 1790. Many amendments of this were suggested, but the committee felt that it was safer to retain without change the old phraseology which has been so often construed by the courts.

51

See also the 1961 Register's Report, wherein it is noted at 21-22:

    * * * as several courts have observed, the right embraced in the repetitive terms of section 1(a) is the two-

---

fold right to make and publish copies.

    This right is the historic basis of copyright and pertains to *all* categories of copyrighted works. * * * [Emphasis supplied.]

The burden, therefore, is on defendant to show that Congress intended the statute to mean something other than what it plainly says. Defendant has not carried that burden.

It is also pertinent that the courts have liberally construed the 1909 Act to take into account new technologies by which copyrighted works can be duplicated, and thus infringed. In *Fortnightly Corp.*, *supra* at 395-96, the Court, in dealing with copyright infringement relating to television, said :

    In 1909, radio itself was in its infancy, and television had not been invented. *We read the statutory language of 60 years ago in the light of drastic technological change.* [Emphasis supplied.]

To the same effect is *Jerome H. Remick & Co.* v. *American Automobile Accessories Co.*, 5 F. 2d 411 (6th Cir. 1925), *cert. denied*, 269 U.S. 556, which stated at 411 :

    * * * the statute may be applied to new situations not anticipated by Congress, if, fairly construed, such situations come within its intent and meaning. Thus it has been held both in this country and England that a photograph was a copy or infringement of a copyrighted engraving under statutes passed before the photographic process had been developed. [citations omitted] While statutes should not be stretched to apply to new situations not fairly within their scope, they should not be so narrowly construed as to permit their evasion because of changing habits due to new inventions and discoveries.

Furthermore, defendant's argument that it may "copy," short of "printing," "reprinting" and "publishing," is irrelevant under the facts of this case. NLM and the NIH library did not merely "copy" the articles in suit; they, in effect, "reprinted" and "published" them. "Printing" and "reprinting" connote making a duplicate original, whether by printing press or a more modern method of duplication. *Macmillan Co.* v. *King*, 223 F. 862 (D. Mass. 1914) ; M.·Nimmer,

52

Copyright § 102 (1971 ed.). "Publishing" means disseminating to others, which defendant's libraries clearly did when they distributed photocopies to requesters and users. *Macmillan Co.*, *supra;* M. Nimmer, Copyright § 104 (1971 ed.).

Defendant's contention that its libraries make only "single copies" of journal articles, rather than multiple copies, is illusory and unrealistic. Admittedly, the libraries, as a general rule, make only one copy per request, usually for different users. But the record shows that the libraries duplicate particular articles over and over again, sometimes even for the same user within a short timespan. *E.g.*, the NIH library photocopied the Count I article three times within a 3-month period, two of the times for the same requester; and it copied the Count IV and Count V articles twice within a 2-month period, albeit for different users. The record also shows that NLM will supply to requesters photocopies of the same article, one after the other, on consecutive days, even with knowledge of such facts. In short, the libraries operate comprehensive duplication systems which provide every year thousands of photocopies of articles, many of which are copies of the same article; and, in essence, the systems are a reprint service which supplants the need for journal subscriptions. The effects of this so-called "single copying" practice on plaintiff's legitimate interests as copyright owner are obvious. The Sophar and Heilprin report, at 16, puts it in terms of a colorful analogy: "Babies are still born one at a time, but the world is rapidly being overpopulated."

The "fair use" defense

Defendant contends that its copying comes under the doctrine of "fair use" of copyrighted works. "Fair use," a judicially-created doctrine, is a sort of "rule of reason" applied by the courts as a defense to copyright infringement when the accused infringing acts are deemed to be outside the legiti-

mate scope of protection afforded copyright owners under
17 U.S.C. § 1. What constitutes "fair use" cannot be defined
with precision. Much has been written about the doctrine,
particularly its rationale and scope. *See, e.g.,* A. LATMAN,
FAIR USE OF COPYRIGHTED WORKS, STUDY No. 14, COPYRIGHT
LAW REVISION, STUDIES PREPARED FOR SENATE COMM. ON THE
JUDICIARY, 86th Cong., 2d Sess. (1960) ; Comment, *Copyright*

53

Fair Use—Case Law and Legislation, 1969 DUKE L.J. 73;
S. COHEN, FAIR USE AND THE LAW OF COPYRIGHT, ASCAP
COPYRIGHT LAW SYMPOSIUM (No. 6) 43 (1955) ; W. Jensen,
Fair Use: As Viewed by the "User," 39 DICTA 25 (1962) ;
L. Yankwich, *What Is Fair Use?,* 22 U. CHI. L. REV. 203
(1954) ; Note, *Fair Use: A Controversial Topic in the Latest
Revision of Our Copyright Law,* 34 U. CIN. L. REV. 73
(1965) ; M. NIMMER, COPYRIGHT § 145 (1971 ed.) ; SOPHAR &
HEILPRIN REPORT at 15; R. HEEDHAM, TAPE RECORDING, PHO-
TOCOPYING AND FAIR USE, ASCAP COPYRIGHT LAW SYMPO-
SIUM (No. 10) 75 (1959) ; Crossland, *The Rise and Fall of
Fair Use: The Protection of Literary Materials Against
Copyright Infringement by New and Developing Media,* 20
S. CAR. L. REV. 153 (1968). Some courts have held that the
doctrine is but an application of the principle *de minimis non
curat lex* and, as plaintiff puts it, "comes into play only when
a relatively small amount of copying takes place." Principal
factors considered by the courts in deciding whether a particular use of a copyrighted work is a "fair use" are (a) the
purpose of the use, (b) the nature of the copyrighted work,
(c) the amount and substantiality of the material used in
relation to the copyrighted work as a whole, and (d) the
effect of the use on a copyright owner's potential market for
his work.[10] While these criteria are interrelated and may
vary in relative significance, the last one, *i.e.,* the competitive
character of the use, is often the most important. *E.g.,* it has
been held "fair use" to copy excerpts from literary works for
purposes of criticism or review (*Loew's, Inc. v. CBS, Inc.,*
131 F. Supp. 165, 105 USPQ 302 (S.D. Cal. 1955), *aff'd sub
nom. Benny v. Loew's, Inc.,* 239 F. 2d 532, 112 USPQ 11 (9th
Cir. 1956), *aff'd by an equally divided Court,* 356 U.S. 43
(1958)) ; or to copy portions of scholarly works (*Greenbie
v. Noble, supra; Holdredge v. Knight Publishing Corp.,* 214
F. Supp. 921, 136 USPQ 615 (S.D. Cal. 1963)). However,
it is not "fair use" to copy substantial portions of a copyrighted work when the new work is a substitute for, and
diminishes the potential market for, the original. *Hill v.*

[10] H.R. Rep. No. 83, 90th Cong., 1st Sess. (1967), which relates to revision of the copyright laws, notes that these factors are the ones used by the courts. At 29–37, there is a detailed discussion of "fair use" as applicable to photocopying for educational purposes.

54

Whalen & Martell, Inc., 220 F. 359 (S.D.N.Y. 1914) ; *Folsom
v. Marsh,* 9 F. Cas. 343 (D. Mass. 1841). And it has been
held that wholesale copying of a copyrighted work is never
"fair use" (*Leon v. Pacific Tel. & Tel. Co.,* 91 F. 2d 484, 34
USPQ 237 (9th Cir. 1937) ; *Public Affairs Associates, Inc.
v. Rickover,* 284 F. 2d 262, 127 USPQ 231 (D.C. Cir. 1960),
vacated and remanded, 369 U.S. 111 (1962)), even if done
to further educational or artistic goals and without intent
to make profit. *Wihtol v. Crow,* 309 F. 2d 777, 135 USPQ
385 (8th Cir. 1962).

Whatever may be the bounds of "fair use" as defined and
applied by the courts, defendant is clearly outside those
bounds. Defendant's photocopying is wholesale copying and
meets none of the criteria for "fair use." The photocopies are
exact duplicates of the original articles; are intended to be
substitutes for, and serve the same purpose as, the original
articles; and serve to diminish plaintiff's potential market
for the original articles since the photocopies are made at
the request of, and for the benefit of, the very persons who
constitute plaintiff's market. Defendant says, nevertheless,
that plaintiff has failed to show that it has been harmed by
unauthorized photocopying; and that, in fact, plaintiff's

journal subscriptions have increased steadily over the last
decade. Plaintiff need not prove actual damages to make out
its case for infringement. *Macmillan Co., supra.* Section 1498
of title 28 U.S.C. provides for payment of "reasonable and
entire compensation * * * including minimum statutory
damages as set forth in section 101(b) of title 17, United
States Code." *See Brady v. Daly,* 175 U.S. 148 (1899) ; *F. W.
Woolworth & Co. v. Contemporary Arts, Inc.,* 344 U.S. 228
(1952). M. NIMMER, COPYRIGHT § 154 (1971 ed.). Moreover,
damage may be inferred in this case from the fact that the
photocopies are intended to supplant the original articles.
While it may be difficult (if not impossible) to determine
the number of subscription sales lost to photocopying, the
fact remains that each photocopy user is a potential subscriber, or at least is a potential source of royalty income for
licensed copying. Plaintiff has set up a licensing program to
collect royalties for photocopying articles from its journals;
and among the licensees have been libraries, including a

55

Government library.[11] Also, there is evidence that one subscriber canceled a subscription to one of plaintiff's journals
because the subscriber believed the cost of photocopying the
journal had become less than the journal's annual subscription price; and another subscriber canceled a subscription,
at least in part because library photocopies were available.
Loss of subscription (or photocopying royalty) income is
particularly acute in the medical journal field. The record
shows that printing preparation costs are 50–65 percent of
total cost of publication and that the number of subscriptions is relatively small. This simply means that any loss of
subscription sales (or royalty income) has the effect of
spreading publication costs over fewer copies, thus driving
up steeply the unit cost per copy and, in turn, subscription
prices. Higher subscription prices, coupled with cheap photocopying, means probable loss of subscribers, thus perpetuat-
ing a vicious cycle which can only bode ill for medical
publishing.

Defendant's amici fear that a decision for plaintiff will be
precedent for plaintiff's seeking injunctions against non-
Government libraries, pursuant to 17 U.S.C. § 101(a), thereby interfering with the free flow of technical and scientific
information through library photocopying. On the basis of
this record and representations made by plaintiff's personnel
and counsel, that fear does not appear to be justified. Plaintiff does not seek to *enjoin* any photocopying of its journals.
Rather, it merely seeks a reasonable royalty therefor.[12] Its
licensing program would so indicate for, as far as the record
shows, plaintiff will grant licenses to anyone at a reasonable
royalty. No doubt, plaintiff would prefer that all of its journal users be subscribers. However, plaintiff recognizes that
this is unrealistic. Some articles in its journals are in greater
demand than others, and many journal users will not consider

[11] There is no agreement, even among libraries and Government agencies, of what constitutes "fair use" in institutionalized photocopying. The Library of Congress will not photocopy copyrighted materials without permission of the copyright owners. Many other libraries follow the General Interlibrary Loan Code and engage in "single copy" photocopying. The U.S. Office of Education, through its Education Resources Information Center (ERIC) makes available current educational and research-related materials. ERIC will not copy copyrighted materials without permission of the copyright owner. See Sophar and Heilprin report at 39–46.

56

it economically justifiable to subscribe to a journal simply to
get access to a few articles. Implicit in plaintiff's licensing
program, therefore, is the idea that it is in the best interest
of all concerned that photocopying proceed without injunction, but with payment of a reasonable fee. That would appear to be a logical and commonsense solution to the problem,
not unlike the solution provided by the American Society of
Composers, Authors and Publishers (ASCAP) and Broadcast Music, Inc. (BMI) in the field of music and the performing arts. For a description of how ASCAP and BMI operate
in a context similar to this one, see *Hearings on H.R. 4347
and other bills before Subcomm. No. 3, House Comm. on the*

Judiciary, 89th Cong., 1st Sess. 194, 203 (1965) ; Finkelstein, *ASCAP as an Example of the Clearing House System in Operation*, 14 COPYRIGHT SOC'Y BULL. 2 (1966).

Defendant says that photocopying by NLM and the NIH library is "reasonable and customary" because it complies with a longstanding practice of libraries to supply photocopies of parts of scientific works to persons engaged in scholarly research, and is consistent with the terms of the "gentlemen's agreement," earlier noted. The "gentlemen's agreement," drafted in 1935, was the product of meetings and discussions between representatives of the book publishing industry and libraries. The representatives were interested in working out a practical accommodation of the conflict between (a) the legitimate interests of copyright owners not to have their works copied without compensation and (b) the needs of scholars and research workers for copies of parts of copyrighted works for private use in pursuit of literary or scientific investigation. The "agreement" was, in effect, a promise by the book publishers not to interfere

¹⁸ In his opening statement at trial, plaintiff's counsel said (emphasis supplied) :

The case has nothing to do with the stopping of photocopying. The Commissioner knows that an injunction is not available in this court, nor is plaintiff, in any case, seeking to curtail this use of its articles. Similarly, William M. Passano, plaintiff's Chairman of the Board, stated in a hearing before a Senate committee:

We feel that it is unrealistic and not in the public interest to consider restricting in any way the use of photocopying devices. They serve a useful purpose in the dissemination of knowledge. Since we, as publishers, are in that business, we certainly don't want to see the spread of knowledge curtailed.

To us the only solution to the problem is a simple system of royalty payments with a minimum of red tape. * * * [Hearings on Copyright Law Revision before the Patents, Trademarks and Copyrights Subcomm. of the Senate Comm. on the Judiciary, 90th Cong. 1st Sess. 976 (1967).]

57

with library photocopying under three conditions: (i) the library must warn the person for whom the photocopy is made that he is liable for any copyright infringement by misuse (presumably by making further photocopies), (ii) the photocopying must be done without profit to the library, and (iii) the amount copied must not be so substantial as to constitute an infringement. The third condition is implicit in the "agreement" which says:

While the right of quotation without permission is not provided in law, the courts have recognized the right to a "fair use" of book quotations, the length of a "fair" quotation being dependent upon the type of work quoted from and the "fairness" to the author's interest. *Extensive quotation is obviously inimical to the author's interest. * * * It would not be fair to the author or publisher to make possible the substitution of the photostat for the purchase of a copy of the book itself either for an individual library or for any permanent collection in a public or research library. Orders for photocopying which, by reason of their extensiveness or for any other reasons, violate this principle should not be accepted.* [Emphasis supplied.]

The "gentlemen's agreement" does not have, nor has it ever had, the force of law with respect to what constitutes copyright infringement or "fair use." So far as this record shows, the "agreement" has never been involved in any judicial proceedings. Nevertheless, the "agreement" is entitled to consideration as a guide to what book publishers and libraries considered to be "reasonable and customary" photocopying practices in the year 1935. It has limited significance, however, to this case. The agreement was drafted on behalf of a book publishers' organization which is now defunct and to which plaintiff never belonged. In fact, it appears that no periodical publishers were represented in the organization at the time the agreement was drafted; and, consequently, the "agreement" cannot speak for their interests or problems. See the Varmer study at 51, n. 9. Furthermore, the "agreement" was drafted at a time when photocopying was relatively expensive and cumbersome; was used relatively little as a means of duplication and dissemination; and posed no substantial threat to the potential market for copyrighted works. Beginning about 1960, photocopying changed character. The introduction to the marketplace of the office copying machine made photocopying rapid, cheap and readily available. The legitimate interests of copyright owners must,

58

accordingly, be measured against the changed realities of technology. Professor Nimmer in his treatise COPYRIGHT capsules the point at 653 :

Both classroom and library reproduction of copyrighted materials command a certain sympathy since they involve no commercial exploitation and more particularly in view of their socially useful objectives. *What this overlooks is the tremendous reduction in the value of copyrighted works which must result from a consistent and pervasive application of this practice.* One who creates a work for educational purposes may not suffer greatly by an occasional unauthorized reproduction. But if every school room or library may by purchasing a single copy supply a demand for numerous copies through photocopying, mimeographing or similar devices, the market for copyrighted educational materials would be almost completely obliterated. This could well discourage authors from creating works of a scientific or educational nature. If the 'progress of science and useful arts' is promoted by granting copyright protection to authors, such progress may well be impeded if copyright protection is largely undercut in the name of fair use. [Emphasis supplied.]

In any event, the "gentlemen's agreement" by its own terms condemned as "not * * * fair" the making of photocopies which could serve in "substitution" for the original work, and further noted that "[o]rders for photo-copying which, by reason of their extensiveness or for any other reasons" could serve as duplicates of the original copyrighted work "should not be accepted." Thus, the most that can be said for the "gentlemen's agreement" is that it supported (and probably still supports) the proposition that it is "reasonable and customary" (and thus "fair use") for a library to photocopy for a patron a part of a book, or even part of a periodical article, such as a chart, graph, table, or the like, so long as the portion copied is not practically a substitute for the entire original work. Other instances of library photocopying may also be "fair use." *E.g.*, a library no doubt can replace damaged pages of copyrighted works in its collection with photocopies; can make a small number of photocopies for in-house administrative purposes, such as cutting up for cataloging or

59

the like; or can supply attorneys or courts with single photocopies for use in litigation. In all those instances, and probably many more which might come to mind on reflection, the rights of the copyright owner are not materially harmed. The doctrine of "fair use" and the "gentlemen's agreement," however, cannot support wholesale copying of the kind here in suit.¹⁸

Defendant also contends that traditionally, scholars have made handwritten copies of copyrighted works for use in research or other scholarly pursuits; that it is in the public interest that they do so because any harm to copyright owners is minimal compared to the public benefits derived therefrom; and that the photocopying here in suit is essentially a substitute for handcopying by the scholars themselves. That argument is not persuasive. In the first place, defendant concedes that its libraries photocopy substantially more material than scholars can or do copy by hand. Implicit in such concession is a recognition that laborious handcopying and rapid machine photocopying are totally different in their impact on the interests of copyright owners. Furthermore, there is no case law to support defendant's proposition that the making of a handcopy by scholars or researchers of an *entire* copyrighted work is permitted by the copyright laws. Certainly the statute does not expressly permit it; and no doubt the issue has never been litigated because, as a practical matter, such copying is *de minimis* and causes no real threat to the copyright owner's legitimate right to control duplication and dissemination of copyrighted works. The photocopying done by NLM and the NIH library, on the other hand, poses a real and substantial threat to copyright owners' legitimate interests. Professor Nimmer discusses the point succinctly, at 653–54 of his treatise, and his language can hardly be improved upon:

> It may be argued that library reproduction is merely a more modern and efficient version of the time-honored practice of scholars in making handwritten copies of copyrighted works, for their own private use. In evaluating this argument several factors must be considered.[15]

[15] The potential pernicious effects of modern, institutionalized photocopying of copyrighted works (particularly journal articles) in the name of "fair use" is discussed at length in the Sophar and Heilprin report. The authors, at 24, characterize wholesale copying by libraries as "a non-violent form of civil disobedience."

60

In the first place, the drudgery of making handwritten copies probably means that such copies in most instances are not of the complete work, and the quantitative insignificance of the selected passages are such as generally not to amount to a *substantial* similarity. Secondly, there would appear to be a qualitative difference between each individual scholar performing the task of reproduction for himself, and a library or other institution performing the task on a wholesale basis for all scholars. If the latter is fair use, then must not the same be said for a non-profit publishing house that distributes to scholars unauthorized copies of scientific and educational works on a national or international basis? Finally, it is by no means clear that the underlying premise of the above argument is valid.

There is no reported case on the question of whether a single handwritten copy of all or substantially all of a protected work made for the copier's own private use is an infringement or fair use. If such a case were to arise the force of custom might impel a court to rule for the defendant on the ground of fair use. Such a result, however, could not be reconciled with the rationale for fair use suggested above since the handwritten copy would serve the same function as the protected work, and would tend to reduce the exploitation value of such work. Moreover, if such conduct is defensible then is it not equally a fair use for the copier to use his own photocopying or other duplicating device to achieve the same result? Once this is acknowledged to be fair use, the day may not be far off when no one need purchase books since by merely borrowing a copy from a library any individual will be able to make his own copy through photocopying or other reproduction devices which technological advances may soon make easily and economically available.

To the same effect is a statement in the Varmer study at 62–63:

> It has long been a matter of common practice for individual scholars to make manual transcriptions of published material, though copyrighted, for their own private use, and this practice has not been challenged. Such transcription imposed its own quantitative limitations; and in the nature of the event, it would not be feasible for copyright owners to control private copying and use. But reproduction for private use takes on different dimensions when made by modern photocopying devices capable of reproducing quickly any volume of material in any number of copies, and when copies are so made to be supplied to other persons.

61

Publisher's copies are bought for the private use of the buyer, and in some circumstances a person supplying copies to others will be competing with the publisher and diminishing his market.

Not only is such competition unfair to the publisher and copyright owner, but it may be injurious to scholarship and research. Thus, it has been pointed out that widespread photocopying of technical journals might so diminish the volume of subscriptions for the journals as to force the suspension of their publication.

Also, the 1961 Register's Report notes at 25–26:

> Researchers need to have available, for reference and study, the growing mass of published material in their particular fields. This is true especially, though not solely, of material published in scientific, technical, and scholarly journals. Researchers must rely on libraries for much of this material. When a published copy in a library's collections is not available for loan, which is

very often the case, the researcher's need can be met by a photocopy.

On the other hand, the supplying of photocopies of any work to a substantial number of researchers may diminish the copyright owner's market for the work. Publishers of scientific, technical, and scholarly works have pointed out that their market is small; and they have expressed the fear that if many of their potential subscribers or purchasers were furnished with photocopies, they might be forced to discontinue publication.

Finally, defendant says that it is unconstitutional to construe the copyright law so as to proscribe library photocopying of scientific or technical writings because such photocopying is consonant with the constitutional purpose of copyright "to promote the progress of science." That argument misses the mark. Article I, section 8, clause 8, of the U.S. Constitution grants to Congress the "Power * * * To Promote the Progress of Science * * * by securing for limited Times to Authors * * * the exclusive Right to their * * * Writings * * *." The word "Science" is used in the sense of general knowledge rather than the modern sense of physical or biological science. *See* Rich, *Principles of Patentability*, 28 GEO. WASH. L. REV. 393, 394–97 (1960) ; H.R. REP. No. 1923, 82d Cong., 2d Sess. 4 (1952) ; S. REP. No. 1979, 82d Cong., 2d Sess. 3 (1952). Congress has exercised its constitutional power by enacting, and revising from time to time, copyright statutes which are the method of, and provide a *system* for, achieving the constitu-

62

tional purpose. The system "promotes progress" by encouraging authors to write and publicly disclose their writings; by inducing publishers and entrepreneurs to invest risk capital in the dissemination of authors' writings; and by requiring other authors to create new writings, rather than plagiarize the old, all of which is in the public interest. *Mazer v. Stein*, 347 U.S. 201, 219 (1954), *rehearing denied*, 347 U.S. 949. Congress has broad discretion under the Constitution to prescribe the conditions under which copyright will be granted, the only express restriction being that any "exclusive right" must be for a "limited time." Nothing in the present statute, its legislative history or the case law suggests that Congress intended to exempt libraries or others from liability for wholesale copying of copyrighted works, whatever be the purpose or motivation for the copying. What defendant really appears to be arguing is that the copyright law *should* excuse libraries from liability for the kind of photocopying here in suit. That, of course, is a matter for Congress, not the courts, to consider for it involves questions of public policy aptly suited to the legislative process. In an analogous context in *Fortnightly Corp., supra*, Justice Fortas noted at 408 :

> The task of caring for CATV is one for the Congress. Our ax, being a rule of law, must cut straight, sharp, and deep; and perhaps this is a situation that calls for the compromise of theory and for the architectural improvisation which only legislation can accomplish.

See also White-Smith Music Co., supra, where the Court noted at 18, that "considerations [of what the copyright laws should provide] properly address themselves to the legislative and not the judicial branch of the Government."[16]

III

Several other points raised by the parties merit comment. Defendant notes that the National Library of Medicine Act

[16] There has been no dearth of activity to revise the 1909 Copyright Act. Some of that activity relates to library photocopying problems. See, e.g., Hearings on H.R. 4347 and other bills before Subcomm. No. 3, House Comm. on the Judiciary, 89th Cong., 1st Sess. 448, 450, 1133 (1965) ; S. 597, H.R. 2512, 90th Cong., 1st Sess. (1967) ; S. 543, 91st Cong., 1st Sess. (1969) ; S. Rep. No. 91–1219, 91st Cong., 2d Sess. 5 (1970) ; S. 644, 92d Cong., 1st Sess. (1971). For a brief history of legislative activity directed toward revision of the 1909 Copyright Act, *see Fortnightly Corp., supra* at 396 n. 17 ; UCLA Project at 931–38.

63

by which NLM was created (42 U.S.C. § 275, *et seq.*) provides at § 276(4) that the Secretary of Health, Education, and Welfare, through NLM, shall "make available, through loans, photographic or other copying procedures or otherwise, such materials in the Library as he deems appropriate * * *"; and that the Medical Library Assistance Act of 1965 (42 U.S.C. § 280b-1, *et seq.*) provides that grants be made to medical libraries for, among other things, "acquisition of duplicating devices, facsimile equipment * * * and other equipment to facilitate the use of the resources of the library." 42 U.S.C. 280b-7. Defendant suggests that by those statutory provisions Congress intended to exempt NLM and other grantee libraries from the copyright laws. As defendant puts it, " * * * the only reasonable interpretation [of the statutes] is that Congress knew that fair use would exempt such libraries from copyright infringement in the established use by libraries of such [photocopy] equipment." There is no merit to this. Nothing in the statutes or their legislative histories says anything about the copyright laws, and it cannot be inferred that Congress intended the statutes to be in derogation of the copyright laws, absent an express indication to the contrary.[16] *See generally* E. CRAWFORD, STATUTORY CONSTRUCTION § 227 (1940). No court has ever held that "fair use" applies to library wholesale photocopying; nor has there been a uniform and unchallenged policy among libraries and other institutionalized photocopiers on the bounds of "fair use." See note 11. Thus, it makes no sense to impute to Congress an intent for which there is no sound basis in judicial decision, or otherwise. The fact that the statutes authorize the libraries to make use, generally, of photocopying equipment and procedures, is not controlling or even very significant. Much material in library collections is either not copyrighted or is material on which the copyright has expired; and in either event, the material is in the public domain and can be freely copied.

Furthermore, the record shows that NLM, from the beginning, has been concerned about complying with the copyright laws and has never considered itself exempt therefrom. In 1957, NLM's Board of Regents discussed the library's pho-

[16] H.R. Rep. No. 941, 84th Cong., 2d Sess. (1956) ; S. Rep. No. 2071, 84th Cong., 2d Sess. (1956) ; H.R. Rep. No. 1026, 89th Cong., 1st Sess. (1965) ; S. Rep. No. 756, 89th Cong., 1st Sess. (1965).

64

tocopying practices and deemed them to create vexing copyright infringement problems. The Director of NLM was of the opinion that "sooner or later" the problems would bring "a test of the issue in the courts."

Defendant suggested at trial that payment of compensation to plaintiff for photocopying its journals would create a continuing undue and oppressive administrative and financial burden on NLM and the NIH library. Defendant has not pressed the point in its brief, perhaps because it is clear that plaintiff's right to compensation under 28 U.S.C. § 1498(b) cannot depend on the burdens of compliance. Nevertheless, defendant's point merits comment since courts should be mindful of the practical consequences of their decisions. Based on this record, defendant's fears are not justified. Both NLM and the NIH library already have administrative procedures by which they keep detailed records of photocopying. Both libraries require that written request slips be submitted by requesters of photocopies. The slips are a permanent record of the journals and pages photocopied. It would seem a routine, albeit tedious, matter to cull from those records the information necessary to calculate a reasonable royalty on the basis of the number of articles copied, or perhaps to come up with an acceptable formula for establishing a blanket annual royalty payment. Indeed, the evidence suggests that this is so. In 1967, NLM temporarily stopped photocopying articles from plaintiff's journals, as a result of plaintiff's charge of copyright infringement and requests for a reasonable royalty. NLM was able, as a practical matter, to flag all requests for photocopies from plaintiff's journals from April 27, 1967 to May 29, 1967, in order to refrain from copying them. On about May 29, 1967, photocopying was resumed and was monitored for about 90 days. Satisfied that the 90-day period was a representative sample, NLM found that it would have paid plaintiff about $250-

$300 if it had acceded to plaintiff's request for royalty payment. The Director of NLM testified that, in his opinion, this was "a very small sum—surprisingly small sum." Similarly, the NIH librarian testified that payment of royalties for photocopying "has nothing to do with the operation of the library in the fulfillment of * * * [its] function. It is an economic and budgetary consideration and not a service-oriented kind of thing."

65

Nor does it appear that payment of royalties to other publishers will create an undue or oppressive administrative burden. The Sophar and Heilprin report notes, at 58-60, that based on a study of the photocopying practices of U.S. libraries, less than 1,000 publishers provide the material photocopied by libraries, and that about 5 percent of that number provide about 40 percent of the material copied. This simply means that nearly half of the materials photocopied emanate from about 50 publishers. No doubt, the materials photocopied by NLM and the NIH library come from an even smaller number of publishers since those libraries are highly specialized. In any event, by using modern management practices including computers and the like, it would appear that NLM and the NIH library can, with minimum disruption, cope with the necessary recordkeeping.[17]

Postscript: The issues raised by this case are but part of a larger problem which continues to plague our institutions with ever-increasing complexity—how best to reconcile, on the one hand, the rights of authors and publishers under the copyright laws with, on the other hand, the technological improvements in copying techniques and the legitimate public need for rapid dissemination of scientific and technical literature. The conflict is real; the solution not simple. Legislative guidelines seem appropriate.[18] The Sophar and Heil-

[17] It has been suggested that there be established a clearinghouse for access, permissions and payments for photocopying of copyrighted materials. The clearinghouse would relieve institutional copiers of the burdens of royalty distribution and might also be instrumental in setting up blanket royalty arrangements, thus relieving the institutions from most recordkeeping requirements. See, e.g., the Sophar and Heilprin report at 82. The clearinghouse concept has also been alluded to in a congressional report:

* * * Despite past efforts, reasonable arrangements involving a mutual understanding of what generally constitutes acceptable library practices, and providing workable clearance and licensing conditions, have not been achieved and are overdue. The committee urges all concerned to resume their efforts to reach an accommodation under which the needs of scholarship and the rights of authors would both be respected. [Emphasis supplied.] [H.R. Rep. No. 83, 90th Cong., 1st Sess. 36 (1967).]
And it is interesting that Sophar and Heilprin found that librarians favored, two to one, the clearinghouse approach to the problem, even though many of those in favor "indicated a desire to settle an increasingly complex matter, rather than an enthusiastic approval of the idea." Sophar and Heilprin report, at p. v of the Summary.

[18] In 1969, several bills were introduced in both the Senate and House to establish a National Commission on Libraries and Information Science. Also in 1969, H.R. 8809 was introduced to provide for a "National Science Research Data Processing and Information Retrieval System." See 1969 Register of Copyrights Annual Rep. 6. Earlier, in 1967, the Senate enacted S. 2216, 90th Cong., 1st Sess., by which there would be created a commission to study and compile data on the reproduction and use of copyrighted works. The House took no action on the bill.

66

prin report, at pp. VIII-IX of the Summary, capsules the problem in a statement worth quoting:

From the viewpoint of the information scientist, copyright may appear as an impediment to the most efficient flow of information. It is apparently a blockage in an information system. Our early tendency was to oppose and try to limit the protection and control granted in copyright for the sake of efficiency. After careful analysis we no longer do.

There is a philosophical reason for not wanting to see copyright destroyed and there are a number of practical reasons. The philosophical reason is simply a belief that copyright is one of a number of ways in which our society expresses its belief and hope that an individual can continue his identity in a world of mass efforts by assuring the individual, his publisher or his association sufficient income from his ideas to maintain a degree of independence. The erosion of the economic value of copyright must lead to federal support of all kinds of writing and, of course, control.

The practical reasons flow from the philosophical reasons. Publishers, non-profit as well as commercial, will simply not be able to continue publishing under an eroded system. The scientific and other professional societies which, through their memberships, have done the most to develop information-handling tools and media are the ones most hurt by them. A means must be developed to assure payment to the copyright owner in return for unlimited and uncontrolled access to and duplication of the copyrighted work.

Our only concern and "vested interest" in copyright since we became interested in the problem "is to find a way to protect the 'exclusive Right' of an author to his 'Writings,' while permitting the advantages of modern information dissemination systems to become as useful as they may without weakening or threatening the economic urge and the need to create." We believe the two must become reconciled, not in the interests of compromise, but simply because both concepts are too valuable for either one to be permitted to severely harm or destroy the other.

KUNZIG, *Judge,* joins in the foregoing dissenting opinion.

NICHOLS, *Judge,* dissenting:

I join in the Chief Judge's able dissent, and add a few words of my own. I agree with him that the photocopying of copyrighted material, as described in the findings, is not within the judge-made doctrine of fair use, and it should

67

not be. The majority has posed a question, whose answer it triumphantly demonstrates, but it is the wrong question. The issue is not whether we should "stop" defendant's photocopying. Such a stoppage, at the behest of a publisher who refused to license on fair terms could well be unconscionable, in my opinion, but we have no such publisher before us. Plaintiff here is willing to license. If he did want to halt the photocopying, he would be in the wrong court here.

As the majority admits, we lack the power to enjoin. *United States* v. *King,* 395 U.S. 1 (1969). Under 28 U.S.C. § 1498, as amended, all we can do, if we find infringement, is to award reasonable and entire compensation. The idea we are asked to "stop" the photocopying I suppose can be elaborated as follows: our decision would be *stare decisis* in other suits against non-government libraries in which injunctive relief is expressly authorized. 17 U.S.C. §§ 101(a), 112. However, the latter section authorizes injunctions on terms. There is high authority under earlier legislation that courts can refuse to enjoin copyright infringements if they deem an injunction would be unconscionable. *Dun* v. *Lumbermen's Credit Ass'n,* 209 U.S. 20 (1908). Under the 1909 Act, the Second Circuit held in *National Comic Publications, Inc.* v. *Fawcett Publications, Inc.,* 198 F. 2d 927 (1952), refusing to direct an injunction on remand:

* * * We think it best to leave open to the district court the question whether an injunction shall issue, since that is always a discretionary matter.

The Ninth Circuit also recognizes that same principle. *Shapiro, Bernstein & Co.* v. *4636 S. Vermont Ave., Inc.,* 367 F. 2d 236 (1966).

The Senate Study on Copyright Law Revision, Committee On The Judiciary Pursuant to S. Res. 240, Studies 22-25, 86th Cong. 2d Sess., says at p. 127:

•   •   •

The present law leaves it to the discretion of the court whether an injunction will be granted or denied. It has always been the rule of the courts that an injunction is an extraordinary remedy to be used only where further injury to the plaintiff is likely and the equities of the situation are on the side of injunctive relief, and the courts have denied an injunction in cases where it was

68

thought that this remedy would be unduly harsh on the defendant.

•   •   •

In *Hecht Co.* v. *Bowles,* 321 U.S. 321 (1944), the Supreme Court construed the wartime Emergency Price Control Act as not mandating injunctive relief, although the language of the statute was more favorable to such a construction, than that of the Copyright Act. Mr. Justice Douglas said for the

Court at p. 329:

* * * We are dealing here with the requirements of equity practice with a background of several hundred years of history. Only the other day we stated that "An appeal to the equity jurisdiction conferred on federal district courts is an appeal to the sound discretion which guides the determinations of courts of equity." *Meredith* v. *Winter Haven,* 320 U.S. 228, 235. The historic injunctive process was designed to deter, not to punish. The essence of equity jurisdiction has been the power of the Chancellor to do equity and to mould each decree to the necessities of the particular case. Flexibility rather than rigidity has distinguished it. The qualities of mercy and practicality have made equity the instrument for nice adjustment and reconciliation between the public interest and private needs as well as between competing private claims. * * *

In view of the many persuasive reasons our majority adduces why photocopying by non-profit libraries should not be "stopped", I deem it an over-large assumption that an award by us of reasonable and entire compensation to our plaintiff would by *stare decisis* bind other tribunals, at the behest of other plaintiffs, to enjoin such library photocopying.

The amended § 1498 prescribes an award of "reasonable and entire compensation" which shall include the statutory minima under 17 U.S.C. § 101(b). Whether any statutory minimum is there prescribed in the case of a library photocopy of a periodical article, is a far tangent from our present inquiry, but I am satisfied, if it is, it need not be so prohibitive or punitive as to "stop" the photocopying.

Moreover, as to the question of fair use, I have difficulty regarding a use as fair, when a user benefits as extensively from the copyrighted material as this one does, yet adamantly refuses to make any contribution to defray the

69

publisher's cost, or compensate for the author's effort and expertise, except the nominal subscription price of two copies of each periodical. Defendant's libraries, and others, have attempted to exercise a measure of self-restraint hitherto, but there is nothing in the majority decision to induce them to continue, that is not more than counterbalanced by other material that will encourage unrestricted piracy. However hedged, the decision will be read, that a copyright holder has no rights a library is bound to respect. We are making the Dred Scott decision of copyright law.

I think the court also errs in inputing to Herbert Putnam, Librarian of Congress, an interpretation of the 1909 statute consistent with the court's. The brief for a group of amici put before us a 1908 regulation of that library which, the brief says, included this provision:

Photographing. Photographing is freely permitted. The permission extends to the building itself and any of its parts, including the mural decorations. *It extends to articles bearing claim of copyright,* but the Library gives no assurance that the photograph may be reproduced or republished or placed on sale. These are matters to be settled with the owner of the copyright. (Emphasis supplied.)

Assuming this is properly a matter for judicial notice, the omission to include it in the trial judge's findings (or to request inclusion) may perhaps be overlooked. Yet, as part of self-serving statements of historical fact in a brief, it avoids explanations such as an adverse party at the trial level might have furnished. The regulation possibly alluded to *articles* (*i.e.,* in common speech, short non-fiction writings) if it alluded to copyrighted printed matter. Why was not, *e.g.,* copyrighted fiction of equal concern? The explanation that suggests itself to me as possible is that the *articles* mentioned are, or at least include, three-dimensional objects, or artifacts. The provision is too ambiguous in its coverage to afford any indication of how Putnam interpreted the copyright law.

The 1913 regulation, in a new section entitled *Photostat,* deals for the first time with reproduction of two-dimensional material. The court quotes it. It includes no caution as to copyright. The former provision as to photographing is continued unchanged. It seems a fair inference that no copyright caution was considered necessary as to two-dimensional

70

material because the then method of photograph duplication of such material, known as photostating, was too costly, cumbersome and slow, to appear as a menace to holders of copyrights. Those of us whose memories go back to law practice in the thirties can take judicial notice that use of the method to generate copyright infringements on a major scale would have been unthinkable. A single copy of an infringing book or magazine article, produced by photostating, would have cost two dollars or so per page. If this recollection is carrying judicial notice too far, let us drop the Putnam argument altogether.

Finally, I must note the repeated alterations made in the trial judge's fact findings. Specifically:

New sentence in finding 6, that the requesters needed the articles in connection with their professional work, and used their copies solely for such purposes.

Deletions from finding 10 of part (b) explaining how copyright passes from authors to publishers.

Insertion in finding 17(b) that libraries' self-restraint policies are not abused or circumvented.

Insertion in finding 22(c), same effect.

Insertion in finding 39(b) that plaintiff's business is growing faster than the gross national product. This is irrelevant if true. Why not a comparison with the growth of the national debt? Or the total gate receipts of the National Football League?

Deletion from finding 39(d) of inference that plaintiff must have suffered some loss from photocopying and substitute statement he has failed to show substantial hurt. Trial Judge Davis also found, with record support, that at least one subscriber cancelled a subscription to one of plaintiff's journals because the cost of photocopying the journal had become less than the journal's annual subscription price. There was evidence that in another instance, a subscriber cancelled a subscription at least in part because library photocopies were available.

The relevance and effect of these changes is doubtful in light of the fact that the statutory minima under § 101(b) are apparently intended to take care of instances where a plain-tiff cannot prove actual damages. *Cf.*, *Shapiro, Bernstein & Co. v. 4636 S. Vermont Ave., Inc., Supra.*

71

I do not think these alterations were proper in light of the presumption that the trial judge's findings are correct. Rule 147(b). They also suggest that the court would have had difficulty reaching the conclusion it did if it had respected the findings as it should have done. If plaintiff's business is really growing faster than the gross national product or other indicia, without the court's protection, the place to take this into account is in the determination of reasonable and entire compensation.

FINDINGS OF FACT

The court, having considered the evidence, the decision and findings of former Trial Judge James F. Davis, and the briefs and arguments of counsel, makes findings of fact as follows:

1. This is a copyright suit under 28 U.S.C. § 1498(b). Plaintiff seeks reasonable and entire compensation for alleged infringement by the United States of certain copyrights in medical journals.

2. Plaintiff, The Williams & Wilkins Company, is a publisher located in Baltimore, Maryland. Though a relatively small company, plaintiff is one of the major publishers of medical journals in the United States. Plaintiff also publishes medical books. Plaintiff is a family-owned corporation, and its principal officers are William M. Passano and Charles O. Reville.

3. The Government agency accused of infringement is the Department of Health, Education, and Welfare, in particular the National Institutes of Health (NIH) and the National Library of Medicine (NLM). NIH and NLM are located in Bethesda, Maryland.

4. The petition was filed in this court on February 27, 1968, and was amended on July 23, 1970. The petition alleged infringement by reason of the Government's unauthorized photocopying of seven journal articles, identified below as Counts I to VII. The amended petition alleged infringement by reason of the Government's unauthorized photocopying of one journal article, identified below as Count VIII. The articles, and the journals in which they were published, are as follows:

72

Count	Article	Authors	Journal	Vol.	Issue	Pages	Month	Year
I.	The Genetic Mucopolysaccharidoses	Victor A. McKusick, David Kaplan, David Wise, W. Brian Hanley, S. B. Suddarth, M. E. Sevick, A. Edward Maumanee.	*Medicine*	44	6	445-483	Nov.	1965
II.	Supersensitivity and Subsensitivity to Sympatho-mimetic Amines.	Ullrich Trendelenburg	*Pharmacological Reviews*	15	2	225-276	June	1963
III.	Detection of Two Antibodies in Single Plasma Cells by the Paired Fluorescence Technique.	R. N. Hiramoto, M. Hamlin	*Journal of Immunology*	95	2	214-224	Aug.	1965
IV.	Fluorescent Antibody Staining	B. T. Wood, S. H. Thompson, O. Goldstein.	*Journal of Immunology*	95	2	225-229	Aug.	1965
V.	Chromatographic Purification of Tetramethyl-rhodamine-Immune Globulin Conjugates and Their Use in the Cellular Localization of Rabbit Gamma-Globulin Polypeptide Chains.	John J. Cebra, Gerald Goldstein	*Journal of Immunology*	95	2	230-245	Aug.	1965
VI.	The Stability of Messenger Ribonucleic Acid in Antibody Synthesis.	Velta Laxda, Jason L. Starr	*Journal of Immunology*	95	2	254-261	Aug.	1965
VII.	The Course of Non Specific Ulcerative Colitis: Review of Twenty Years Experience and Late Results.	Benjamin M. Banks, Burton I. Korelitz, Louis Zetzel.	*Gastroenterology*	32	6	983-1012	June	1957
VIII.	Occlusion of the Hepatic Veins in Man	R. G. F. Parker	*Medicine*	38	4	369-402	Dec.	1959

73

5. (a) Plaintiff publishes 37 medical journals, all of which are copyrighted. Of these, 26 are published in conjunction with professional societies, with the copyright being owned by plaintiff in 13 of such journals and the societies owning the copyright in the remaining 13. The journal *Medicine* is published by plaintiff for its own benefit, *i.e.*, not in conjunction with a professional society. The journal *Pharmacological Reviews* is and has been published by plaintiff since 1909 in conjunction with the American Society for Pharma-cology and Experimental Therapeutics. The *Journal of Immunology* is and has been published by plaintiff for about 50 years in conjunction with the American Association of Immunologists. The journal *Gastroenterology* is and has been published by plaintiff since 1946 in conjunction with the American Gastroenterological Association. The four journals above named are published with notice of copyright in plaintiff's name. Plaintiff has contracts with the above-noted professional societies, which contracts deal in part with copyright. Although there are differences in

phraseology among the contracts, such differences have led to no problems in dealings between plaintiff and the societies with respect to copyright matters. So far as the record shows, the parties to the contracts consider it the responsibility of plaintiff to enforce the copyright by granting licenses or instituting appropriate lawsuits.

(b) The agreement relating to copyright between plaintiff and the American Society for Pharmacology and Experimental Therapeutics (ASPET), under which agreement *Pharmacological Reviews* is published, provides as follows:

*   *   *   *   *

   5. COPYRIGHT. The Society is sole owner of the periodical but for the sake of convenience, copyright shall be taken out in the name of the Publisher. Procurement of copyright of each issue is the duty of the Publisher and the costs incident thereto shall be charged to the profit-and-loss account of the periodical. The Publisher may publish or permit others to publish excerpts from the periodical after publication but such excerpting shall not be so substantial as to interfere with the sale of the periodical.

*   *   *   *   *

74

   10. REVERSION OF RIGHTS. In case of bankruptcy, assignment for benefit of creditors, or liquidation for any cause of the Publisher, or upon termination of this Agreement for any cause stipulated herein, all rights conveyed under this Agreement by the Society to the Publisher shall revert to the Society forthwith.

The agreement was in effect at all times here material. There is no evidence that ASPET objected to, acquiesced in, or was any way involved with, the bringing of this suit by plaintiff.

(c) The agreement relating to copyright between the American Association of Immunologists (AAI) and plaintiff, under which agreement the *Journal of Immunology* is published, provides as follows:

*   *   *   *   *

   5. *PROCUREMENT OF COPYRIGHT*. The Association is the owner of the periodical but for the convenience of both parties copyright shall be procured by and in the name of the Publisher, and the costs incident thereto shall be charged to the profit-and-loss account of the periodical. *The Association reserves the right to have the copyright assigned to the Association if at any time in the future this seems desirable.* [Emphasis supplied.]

The agreement was in effect at all times here material. There is no evidence that AAI ever exercised its right to have assigned to it by plaintiff the ownership of any copyright registration in the *Journal of Immunology*. Nor is there evidence to show that AAI objected to, acquiesced in, or was any way involved with, the bringing of this suit by plaintiff.

(d) The agreement relating to copyright between the American Gastroenterological Association (AGA) and plaintiff, under which agreement *Gastroenterology* is published, provides as follows:

*   *   *   *   *

   (2) COPYRIGHT. The Association grants to the Publisher the exclusive right to copyright, in the name of the Publisher, and to renew such copyrights, all material published in the said Journal, and to publish the said work in all languages during the term of the copyright.

*   *   *   *   *

75

The agreement has been in effect since 1942. There is no evidence that AGA objected to, acquiesced in, or was in any way involved with, the bringing of this suit by plaintiff.

   6. (a) The Count I-to-Count VIII articles were published in their respective journals on or about the dates indicated in finding 4. The journals were published with a notice of copyright consisting of the word "Copyright," the symbol "©", the name "The Williams & Wilkins Company," and the year

of publication affixed to the title page of, and elsewhere on, each journal. In due course, the Register of Copyrights issued to plaintiff, with respect to each of the journals, the following certificates of registration:

Journal	Certificate of Registration Number
Medicine, Vol. 44, No. 6	B 231973
Pharmacological Reviews, Vol. 15, No. 2	B 49574
The Journal of Immunology, Vol. 95, No. 2	B 216406
Gastroenterology, Vol. 52, No. 6	B 653158
Medicine, Vol. 38, No. 4	B 809936

   (b) Only the issue of liability is now before the court; accounting, if any, is reserved for later proceedings. Defendant admits that at least one photocopy each of the Count I-to-Count VIII articles was made by defendant's NIH or NLM without authorization of plaintiff within the pertinent accounting period, as follows:

Article	Date Photocopied	Name of Requester
Count I	9/29/67	Backman
" "	10/5/67	Gabor
" "	10/19/67	Backman
Count II	9/29/67	McCallum
Count III	9/27/67	McEnany
Count IV	9/27/67	McEnany
" "	11/13/67	Reynolds
Count V	9/27/67	McEnany
" "	11/13/67	Reynolds
Count VI	9/27/67	McEnany
Count VII	10/12/67	Bird
Count VIII	1/11/68	Pitcher
" "	12/68	Young

76

The persons named above as "Requester" are all physicians or other professional medical personnel who requested from NIH or NLM copies of the articles in connection with medical research work or patient care at NIH or elsewhere. The copies were retained by the requesters who, for the most part, kept them in personal files as permanent documents for later reference and use, or put them in files available for use by coworkers or colleagues. The requesters needed the articles in connection with their professional work, and the copies were used solely for those purposes. The request by Dr. Pitcher of the Count VIII article was to NLM through an Army hospital library in Japan. All other requests listed above were to the NIH library and were made directly by the requester.

   7. The number of subscriptions in the year 1969 and the annual subscription prices for the journals involved in this suit are as follows:

Journal	Approximate Number of Subscriptions	Price
Medicine	5,400	$12.00
Pharmacological Reviews	3,100	15.00
Journal of Immunology	4,700	¹ 22.00
		² 44.00
Gastroenterology	7,000	¹ 12.50
		² 25.00

¹ Members.
² Nonmembers.

   8. Plaintiff's journals, noted in finding 7, are widely distributed in medical libraries throughout the country, are in the collection at the NIH library and are included on a list of journals of widespread availability compiled by NLM.

   9. (a) Plaintiff's function, as a publisher of medical and scientific journals and books, is to determine what is needed to advance knowledge in the field of medicine; determine who is qualified to write on that subject; and edit, produce and market their manuscripts. Plaintiff accepts manuscripts from physicians and related medical professionals for publication in an appropriate journal. The considerations which influence a contributor of a manuscript as to the journal to which to submit the manuscript include (i) the subject mat-

77

ter and length of the manuscript, (ii) the quality of articles published in the journal, (iii) the standing of the journal's editorial board, (iv) the nature of the journal's readership, and (v) the circulation of the journal. Contributors rarely publish their own articles because of the high cost involved and because acceptance by a leading journal marks the article as one of high quality. *E.g.*, *Gastroenterology* is considered the outstanding journal in its speciality field in the United States and probably in the world. Contributors submit manuscripts to *Medicine* because that journal publishes lengthy, definitive articles and is well-disseminated.

(b) A board of editors of each of plaintiff's journals screens the submitted manuscripts, and manuscripts suitable for publication are edited and revised, as necessary and within the discretion of the editors. Often, substantial editing is done by the editorial board; sometimes contributors are required to revise manuscripts prior to acceptance. If a journal is the official organ of a professional society, the society appoints the board of editors. The editors are responsible to the society and are compensated by the society which, in turn, shares with plaintiff the profits from journal sales, in accordance with the particular contractual relationship between plaintiff and the society. Revenues from plaintiff's journals are derived largely through subscription sales and also through advertising. The American Gastroenterological Association and the American Association of Immunologists get 50 percent of the profits from *Gastroenterology* and the *Journal of Immunology*, respectively. The American Society for Pharmacology and Experimental Therapeutics gets 90 percent of the profits from *Pharmacological Reviews*. Printing preparation costs are about 50–65 percent of the total cost of publication of plaintiff's journals.

10. Authors whose manuscripts are accepted and published by plaintiff, including the authors of the articles here in suit, are not paid monetary compensation by plaintiff; moreover, some journals require that authors pay a fee for published pages in excess of a preselected number of pages. Authors are, however, gratified when plaintiff publishes their works because of enhancement of their professional status, in that their works are screened by highly critical editors and are published in journals having wide dissemination and

78

high reputation. Authors, therefore, submit manuscripts to plaintiff for dual purposes: to disseminate medical information for the public welfare; and to seek recognition from the scientific community from which flows increased professional and economic opportunity. Most articles published in plaintiff's journals, and like journals, are the result of research work done under private or public grant; and sometimes a requirement of the grant is that the research worker will seek to have the results of the work published. Sometimes, the grants include funds to pay for excess-page charges to a journal publisher.

11. Authors whose articles are published by plaintiff usually purchase from plaintiff reprints of their articles (on the average, about 300) for distribution to interested colleagues. In general, the number of reprints purchased by authors, per article, has not changed over the past 10 years. Most authors distribute reprints free of charge to those requesting them. Depending upon the importance of, and professional interest in, a particular article, all reprints are distributed by authors within several months up to several years after publication. If someone requests directly from plaintiff a copy of an article appearing in one of plaintiff's journals, plaintiff first refers the requester to the author for a reprint; then offers to sell (either directly or through a licensed reprint house) a back copy of the issue in which the article appeared; and, finally, refers the requester to the Institute of Scientific Information, plaintiff's licensee for making photocopies. (Finding 36.) Authors who want to reprint one of their articles from one of plaintiff's journals request plaintiff's permission to do so. Others wanting to

reprint articles from one of plaintiff's journals usually ask permission of the author and also ask permission of plaintiff.

12. (a) NIH constitutes 10 institutes, each of which is concerned with a specialty of health and medical care. The mission of NIH is to advance health and well-being through the support of research in diseases, the support of educational and medical institutions, and improved biomedical communications. Generally, three types of activities are carried on by NIH: education and manpower training; communication of medical information; and research conducted by the various institutes. Research, as well as educa-

79

tion and manpower training, is performed by Government employees of the institutes and also by private persons and organizations supported by NIH grants. Biomedical communication is the function of NLM. (Finding 20.) NIH employs over 12,000 persons, 4,000 of whom are professionals and 2,000 of whom have doctoral degrees. In fiscal 1970, NIH spent over $1.5 billion for medical research, about $100 million of which was for intramural medical research. The balance was spent either for other intramural programs or for grants to outside organizations.

(b) Total national support of medical research, both Federal and non-Federal, has increased enormously in the period 1950–1970. In 1950, only about $160 million were spent. By 1970, the total spent was $2.7 billion. In 1950, the Federal Government contributed less than half the funds available for medical research. In 1970, the Federal Government contributed nearly two-thirds.

13. A library is essential to the conduct of medical research. A principal product of research scientists is their publications and publication of results is a vital part of research. NIH maintains and operates a technical library which is open to the public. The library houses about 125,000 to 150,000 volumes, of which 30,000 are books. The balance is periodicals or journals. The NIH library subscribes to over 3,000 different journal titles, of which 600 are purchased in multiple copies. The functions of the NIH library include acquisition, selection and cataloging of journal and book materials, preparation of reference services, response to queries for specific information, bibliographic services, formulation of computerized searches, a translation unit, housekeeping service, and a library copy service. The library's budget for 1970 was about $1.1 million, of which about $85,000 was for purchase of journal materials.

14. The NIH library subscribes to all 37 journals which plaintiff publishes. For about one-third of such journals, the library gets more than one copy. The library gets two copies of each of the four journals involved in this suit.

15. As an integral part of its operation, the NIH library operates a comprehensive system of providing photocopies of articles in scientific journals. Photocopying at the NIH library (as well as at NLM) includes making a photographic

80

copy of an article on microfilm, and then using the microfilm for further photocopying. The NIH photocopying service uses two Xerox copying machines and two Recordac microfilm cameras. The microfilm cameras are used in conjunction with a Xerox Copy-Flo printer to provide NIH personnel with permanent copies of journal articles. The microfilm is destroyed after a hard Xerox copy is made. NIH leases its Xerox machines from Xerox Corporation which it pays according to the number of pages photocopied. Microfilm used to photocopy articles at the NIH library is sent to NLM for processing. Such processing could be done by any commercial developer having the necessary equipment. Four regularly assigned employees operate the NIH photocopy equipment. In fiscal 1970, the library's photocopying budget was $86,000 and the library filled 85,744 requests for photocopies of journal articles, constituting about 930,000 pages. The average request was about 10–12 pages and the average cost per request was about $1.

16. Photocopying services of the NIH library are available only to NIII personnel. Members of the general public, while they may use the library, are not permitted to have materials photocopied. Two kinds of service are provided: over-the-counter and by mail. To get a photocopy, the requester must submit a request slip and an authorization slip. Authorization slips permit copying of either 20 pages or less, or 6 pages or less. The requirement for authorization slips is a budgetary limitation to hold down photocopying costs. Costs of library operation, including photocopying, are shared by the various institutes of NIII on a pro-rata basis.

17. (a) The photocopying policies of the NIH library have been essentially the same from 1965 to the present. If the library subscribes to but one copy of a journal, that copy is maintained in the library for the use of readers. If the library subscribes to a second copy of a journal, such copy will circulate among interested persons at NIII. Upon the request of interested personnel, articles in journals are photocopied at no charge to the requester. The library's policy on photocopying is that, as a general rule, only a single copy of a journal article will be made per request and each request is limited to about 40 to 50 pages though exceptions may be, and in fact have been, made in the case of long articles, upon

81

approval of the Assistant Chief of the library branch. Also, as a general rule, requests for photocopying are limited to only a single article from a journal issue. However, exceptions to this general rule are routinely made, so long as substantially less than an entire journal is photocopied, i.e., less than about half of the journal. Coworkers can, and frequently do, request single copies of the same article and such requests are honored. Also, there is nothing in the library's photocopying policy to prevent a user from returning month after month to get photocopies of one or more articles from one issue of a journal.

(b) NIH library personnel will not knowingly photocopy an entire issue of a journal. However, it is possible for a single user to make a series of separate requests which will result in the photocopying of an entire issue. The photocopy equipment operators are instructed to bring to the attention of their supervisor what they believe to be attempts to copy a substantial part, or all, of a journal issue. Nevertheless, because of the large volume of photocopying done by the library, it is difficult and impractical to police and curb such attempts. Substantially more people receive photocopies of journal articles from the NIH library than would copy by hand substantial portions of articles. Photocopies made by the library are not returned by the users. Sometimes the users make further photocopies from photocopies obtained from the NIII library to distribute to colleagues or otherwise. However, there is no showing that the library's policies have been abused or circumvented. Where the same person orders more than one copy the second has been for a colleague or to replace an illegible or undelivered copy. Nor is there a showing that the amount of the duplication of the same article has been excessive or unwarranted.

18. As a general rule, books (or monographs) which carry a copyright notice are not photocopied by the NIH library, even to the extent of a short chapter, without permission of the copyright owner. However, under special circumstances (the details of which are not clear from the record) and upon authorization of library supervisory personnel, exceptions are sometimes made to this rule to the extent of copying small portions, e.g., charts or graphs, from books (or monographs).

82

19. Materials (i.e., books and journals) not owned by the NIH library, and which are requested by users, are obtained by means of interlibrary loan. When an interlibrary loan is requested, the standard interlibrary loan form is used. Basically, the NIH library applies to interlibrary loan requests

the same restrictions on photocopying as are applied to requests filled internally.

20. (a) The mission of NLM is the exchange and dissemination of medical information. NLM began as the library of the Surgeon General of the Army, which was founded in 1836. Later such library became the Armed Forces Medical Library; and in 1956, the library was transferred from the Department of Defense to the Public Health Service and renamed the National Library of Medicine. The statute creating NLM is codified as 42 U.S.C. §§ 275–280a (1970 ed.) which, in relevant part, reads as follows:

§ 275. Congressional declaration of purpose; establishment.

In order to assist the advancement of medical and related sciences, and to aid the dissemination and exchange of scientific and other information important to the progress of medicine and to the public health, there is established in the Public Health Service a National Library of Medicine (hereinafter referred to in this part as the "Library").

§ 276. Functions.

(a) The Secretary, through the Library and subject to the provisions of subsection (c) of this section, shall—
    (1) acquire and preserve books, periodicals, prints, films, recordings, and other library materials pertinent to medicine;
    (2) organize the materials specified in clause (1) of this subsection by appropriate cataloging, indexing, and bibliographical listing;
    (3) publish and make available the catalogs, indexes, and bibliographies referred to in clause (2) of this subsection;
    (4) make available, through loans, photographic or other copying procedures or otherwise, such materials in the Library as he deems appropriate;
    (5) provide reference and research assistance; and

83

    (6) engage in such other activities in furtherance of the purposes of this part as he deems appropriate and the Library's resources permit.

    *   *   *   *

(c) The Secretary is authorized, after obtaining the advice and recommendations of the Board (established under section 277 of this title), to prescribe rules under which the Library will provide copies of its publications or materials, or will make available its facilities for research or its bibliographic, reference or other services, to public and private agencies and organizations, institutions, and individuals. Such rules may provide for making available such publications, materials, facilities, or services (1) without charge as a public service, or (2) upon a loan, exchange, or charge basis, or (3) in appropriate circumstances, under contract arrangements made with a public or other nonprofit agency, organization, or institution.

§ 277. Board of Regents.

(a) Establishment; composition; * * *
There is established in the Public Health Service a Board of Regents of the National Library of Medicine * * *.

(b) **Duties of Board;** * * *
It shall be the duty of the Board to advise, consult with, and make recommendations to the Secretary on important matters of policy in regard to the Library, including such matters as the acquisition of materials for the Library, the scope, content and organization of the Library's services, and the rules under which its materials, publications, facilities, and services shall be made available to various kinds of users, * * *

(b) There is no evidence that the Surgeon General or any other agent of defendant has issued regulations implementing 42 U.S.C. § 276(c).

(c) The basic function of NLM is to acquire books, journals and the like relating to health and medicine to assure that all medical literature is available at one place. In addition to acquisition, NLM indexes and catalogs medical literature by means of *Index Medicus*, which is a compilation of citations to about 2,400 leading biomedical journals. *Index*

84

Medicus is sold to the medical profession and enables medical practitioners to keep abreast of the current medical literature. NLM's catalog announces new publications and acquisitions by the library, thus providing a ready reference for other libraries.

21. (a) NLM has five operating components, one of which is called Library Operations. The Reference Services Division of Library Operations is responsible for administering the interlibrary loan system, which is a system whereby one library may request materials from other libraries. NLM also receives requests for loans of materials from Government institutions, medical schools, hospitals, research foundations, private physicians, and private companies including drug companies. NLM provides the same service to commercial companies as it does to governmental and academic libraries. Requests by commercial companies, particularly drug companies, account for about 12 percent of NLM's service. Upon a request for materials, NLM determines whether to loan out the original material or to make photocopies of the material. As a general rule, articles from journals, when requested, are photocopied and the photocopies given free of charge to the requester, so that, in the case of journals, the term "loan" is a euphemism. If NLM receives a request for a paid photographic service which otherwise meets the conditions of an interlibrary loan, payment is rejected and a loan or photocopy is furnished free of charge.

(b) To make photocopies, NLM uses mobile 35-mm. microfilm cameras which have an electrical power line overhead and can move up and down an aisle of the library. Full-size photocopies are then made from the microfilm. Most photocopies are made by such microfilm technique. In fiscal 1968, NLM received about 127,000 requests for interlibrary loans, of which about 120,000 were filled by photocopying. Applying the average of 10 pages per request, about 1.2 million pages were thus photocopied.

22. (a) Interlibrary loan requests must be accompanied by a proper form, the format of which is standardized and used by libraries and other institutions throughout the United States. The loan form, as a general rule, must be signed by a librarian. However, NLM will at times honor requests from individuals (*e.g.*, physicians) or nonlibrary institutions.

85

Upon receipt of requests for interlibrary loans, NLM stamps the requests by date and time, counts them for statistical purposes, and begins the sorting procedure. Generally, NLM does not know, nor does it make any attempt to find out, the purpose of the requests. NLM will supply copies of the same journal article to an unlimited number of libraries requesting copies of an article, one after the other, on consecutive days, even with knowledge of such facts.

(b) NLM is a regional medical library and serves the mid-Atlantic region. Requests for materials coming from regions other than the mid-Atlantic region are generally referred to the appropriate regional library, and the requester is advised to submit future requests to the appropriate regional library. NLM's stated policy in recent years is not to fill requests for copies of articles from any of 104 journals which are included on a so-called "widely-available list." Rather, the requester is furnished a copy of the "widely-available list" and the names of the regional libraries which are presumed to have the journals listed. Exceptions are sometimes made to the policy, particularly if the requester has been unsuccessful in obtaining the journal elsewhere. The four journals involved in this suit are listed on the "widely-available list." A rejection on the basis of the "widely-available list" is made only if the article requested was published during the preceding 5 years. Requests from Government libraries are not rejected on the basis of the "widely-available list."

(c) NLM's policy is not to honor an excessive number of requests from an individual or an institution. As a general

rule, not more than 20 requests from an individual, or not more than 30 requests from an institution, within a month, will be honored. In 1968, NLM adopted the policy that no more than one article from a single journal issue, or three from a journal volume, would be copied. Prior to 1968, NLM had no express policy on copying limitations, but endeavored to prevent "excessive copying." As a general rule, requests for more than 50 pages of material will not be honored, though exceptions are sometimes made, particularly for Government institutions. Requests for more than one copy of a journal article are rejected, without exception. If NLM receives a request for more than one copy, a single copy will be furnished and the requester advised that it is NLM's policy to

86

furnish only one copy. There is no showing that the amount of duplication of copies of the same article is excessive or unwarranted. Generally, requests for photocopies from books (or monographs) are rejected. NLM lends books (or monographs) for limited periods of time. In special cases (the details of which are not clear in the record), small portions of a book (or monograph), *e.g.*, charts or tables, will be photocopied.

23. (a) NLM, from time to time, issues statements to other libraries of its interlibrary loan policy. Its policy has remained essentially unchanged over the years. The statement of policy, as of January 1968, reads in pertinent part as follows:

*   *   *   *   *

Readers who cannot obtain medical literature in their regions and who cannot come to the National Library of Medicine in person may use the interlibrary loan service of the Library by applying through a local library *subject to compliance with the following regulations and instructions and the provisions of the General Interlibrary Loan Code.* A large number of titles should not be requested at one time for one applicant or one institution.

FORMS OF LOANS

1. The National Library of Medicine reserves the right to determine whether material will be lent in the original form or as a photoduplicate.
2. Photoduplicates sent instead of original material will be supplied without charge to requesting libraries. Photoduplicates may be retained permanently by the borrowing library, unless return is specifically requested by NLM.
3. Since this is an interlibrary loan service, multiple copies will not be furnished.
4. With sufficient justification NLM may lend complete issues or volumes of serials when such loan does not impair other service, but in no case will complete issues or volumes or substantial portions of issues or volumes be copied as a loan. Copying of complete issues or volumes may be considered under special photographic services.
5. Original material will not be lent outside the United States.

METHOD OF BORROWING

1. Borrowing libraries will submit *typed* requests on the Interlibrary Loan Request form approved by the

87

American Library Association. Requests made by letter or on other types of forms cannot be processed and will be returned to sender. Each item or item segment must be requested on a separate form.
2. Order of citation must follow directions on the Interlibrary Loan Request form.
3. Each request must be authenticated, in handwriting, by authorized personnel in the borrowing library. Unsigned requests will be returned.
4. It is expected that under all but the most unusual circumstances librarians will avail themselves of the resources of their region before directing requests to NLM.

*   *   *   *   *

SPECIAL PHOTOGRAPHIC SERVICES

1. Special photographic procedures are required to reproduce some items in the collection, and a charge will be made for this service. Cost estimates are available

on request. NLM will consider requests for copying items such as: portraits, photographs, etchings, and other pictorial work; text and line drawings; facsimile reproductions; long runs of periodicals to complete holdings.

2. Advance payment is required for all such photocopying when the requests emanate from outside the Federal Government. Orders for materials in which there is a question of copyright restriction will not be accepted for special photographic service without an accompanying permission statement from the copyright owner.

(b) NLM operates its interlibrary loan system in accordance with the General Interlibrary Loan Code, as revised in 1956. The Code states in pertinent part:

IX. *Photographic Substitution*

1. Time may be saved in filling the reader's request if, in the application for a loan, willingness is indicated to purchase a photographic reproduction as a satisfactory substitute should the original material be unavailable for interlibrary loan. This is especially applicable to periodical and newspaper articles and to typescript theses.

2. The type of photographic duplication (as a substitute) that is acceptable (*e.g.*, photostat; microfilm—negative or positive; record print; etc.) and the maximum price the borrowing library is willing to pay can appropriately be indicated on the original request. If preferred, the lending library may be asked to quote the

88

estimated cost of such a substitution before filling the order.

3. Photographic duplication in lieu of interlibrary loan *may be complicated* by interpretations of copyright restrictions, particularly in regard to photographing *whole issues* of periodicals or books with *current copyrights*, or in making *multiple copies* of a publication.*

4. Any request, therefore, that indicates acceptability of a photographic substitution, under the conditions described above, should be accompanied by a statement with the signature of the applicant attesting to his responsibility for observing copyright provisions in his use of the photographic copy.*

5. Requests indicating acceptability of photographic substitute in lieu of interlibrary loan that comply with the above provisions are to be considered *bona fide* orders for copying services. The lending library, if equipped to do so, may fill such orders with no further correspondence or delay.

24. Photocopies at NLM, for interlibrary loan purposes, are prepared using a microfilm camera and a Xerox Copy-Flo machine. Copying for in-house administrative purposes, oversized material, and material in oriental languages is done on Direct Copy Xerox 720 machines. Microfilm is destroyed after use. Each photocopy produced by the microfilm camera includes a statement as follows:

This is a single photostatic copy made by the National Library of Medicine for purposes of study or research in lieu of lending the original.

25. Since 1966 through 1970, there has been a steady decline in the amount of material or number of requests filled for photocopies through the interlibrary loan program of NLM. In 1969, the number of interlibrary loan requests filled was 110,573 and in 1970, 93,746. A principal reason for the decline is that regional libraries have taken on much of the burden of the program. The regional libraries operate in essentially the same manner as NLM except that some, if

---

*These statements on photographic substitutions are based on the "Gentlemen's Agreement" written in 1935 by the National Association of Book Publishers (reaffirmed in 1938 by its successor the Book Publishers Bureau) and the Joint Committee on Materials for Research (representing the libraries). For the text of this agreement see the *Journal of Documentary Reproduction*, 2:29–30, March 1939. [Finding 41.]

89

not all of them, charge a fee for photocopies furnished to requesters. The budget for the interlibrary loan operation at NLM in fiscal 1969 was $166,152.

26. The Count I, IV, V, and VI articles acknowledge on their faces that the research work reported therein was sup-

ported in part by grants awarded to the authors by the Public Health Service of NIH.

27. The Division of Research Grants of the Public Health Service is a service organization to NIH. Applications for grant support from NIH come to the Division of Research Grants, which determines the institute of NIH to which they shall be referred and the review group to which the application shall be assigned. Such group then reviews the application and determines its scientific merit, and also reviews the application's proposed budget with respect to, *e.g.*, salaries for personnel, equipment, supplies and services, travel funds, funds for the purchase of publications or journals, and funds for the payment of page charges and other costs of publications. The group's recommendation is transmitted to the appropriate institute. If a grant is subsequently awarded, the appropriate institute provides the funds and monitors the performance of the work under the grant. Grants are awarded on an annual basis and are characterized by the Public Health Service as "conditional gifts." NIH sometimes indicates at the beginning that it will support renewal applications. Renewal applications are administered by the Division of Research Grants. The scientific investigator under a grant award can pursue his research in any manner he feels appropriate, subject to limited budgetary control. Such investigators are not Government employees nor are they in the service of the United States; and the Public Health Service does not exercise supervision over the scientific techniques used in the research.

28. The Division of Research Grants, from time to time, issues policy statements with respect to copyright which set out guidelines delimiting the rights and responsibilities of grantees under NIH grants. The policy statements in effect for the years 1956 to the present are set out below in subparagraphs (a) to (d).

90

(a) With respect to grants awarded from November 1956 to 1959, the Public Health Service policy governing copyright was as follows:

When a grant or award is made without condition and a book or related material is privately published, the author is free to copyright the work and to make arrangements with his publisher as if the Government had not contributed support.

(b) With respect to grants awarded from 1959 to January 1, 1963, the Public Health Service policy governing copyright was as follows:

Copyright.—The author is free to arrange for copyright without reference to the Public Health Service.

(c) With respect to grants awarded from January 1, 1963 to July 1, 1965, the Public Health Service policy governing copyright was as follows:

COPYRIGHT The author is free to arrange for copyright without approval by the Public Health Service.

(d) With respect to grants awarded on or after July 1, 1965, the Public Health Service policy governing copyright was as follows:

Copyright Except as otherwise provided in the conditions of the award, when publications result from work supported by the Public Health Service, the author is free to arrange for copyright without approval. Any such copyrighted publications shall be subject to a royalty-free, non-exclusive, and irrevocable license to the Government to reproduce them, translate them, publish them, use and dispose of them, and to authorize others to do so.

29. None of the Count I-to-Count VIII articles resulted from a Public Health Service grant which imposed conditions expressly modifying the copyright policies noted in finding 28, subparagraphs (a) to (c).

30. The policy statement dated July 1, 1965 (finding 28(d)), was the first public statement by the Public Health Service that it reserved the right to duplicate copyrighted works which resulted from Public Health Service grants.

Prior to 1965, the Public Health Service had not addressed itself to the question of whether the Government should have

91

a nonexclusive license in works resulting from grant funds, though it had for some years been the policy that such works could be photocopied (up to 15 copies) for in-house administrative purposes.

31. The copyright policy of the Public Health Service, noted in finding 28(d), which by its terms was to become effective in connection with work supported by grants awarded on or after July 1, 1965, appeared in the *Federal Register*, in modified form, for the first time on April 2, 1970, at 35 Fed. Reg. 5470 (42 C.F.R. § 52.23 (revised as of Jan. 1, 1971)).

32. Dr. Victor A. McKusick, a coauthor of the Count I article, started research, along with several coworkers, in 1954 on the subject matter of the article. Work has continued up to the date of trial. The research was supported in part by funds from a Public Health Service grant; in part by funds from grants from the Health Research Council, a private trust; and in part by other funds which cannot be traced to any specific grant or agency. The manuscript for the Count I article was submitted to the editor of *Medicine* on August 19, 1964, and the article was published on December 9, 1965. Changes to reflect ongoing research were made in the manuscript by the authors from time to time, up to about 6 months before publication (*i.e.*, about mid-1965). After about mid-1965, any changes in the manuscript were editorial in nature, *e.g.*, citations to new articles added as footnotes, stylistic changes, and the like. There is no evidence that the article reports any substantive research work done under funds from a Public Health Service grant awarded on or after July 1, 1965.

33. Dr. Gerald Goldstein, a coauthor of the Count IV article, conducted research leading to its publication, which research was funded in part by Public Health Service grants. Such grants covered the years 1958 to 1966. The Count IV article was published in the *Journal of Immunology* in August 1965. There is no evidence to show when the manuscript for such article was completed, though the article states on its face that it was "received for publication" on December 18, 1964. There is no evidence to show that the article reported any substantive research work done under funds from a Public Health Service grant awarded on or after July 1, 1965.

92

34. Dr. John J. Cebra, a coauthor of the Count V article, conducted research leading to its publication, which research was funded in part by Public Health Service grants. The Count V article was published in the *Journal of Immunology* in August 1965. There is no evidence to show when the manuscript for such article was completed, though the article states on its face that it was "received for publication" on December 17, 1964. There is no evidence to show that the article reported any substantive research work done under funds from a Public Health Service grant awarded on or after July 1, 1965.

35. Dr. Jason L. Starr, a coauthor of the Count VI article, conducted research leading to its publication, which research was funded in part by Public Health Service grants. The Count VI article was published in the *Journal of Immunology* in August 1965. There is no evidence to show when the manuscript for such article was completed, though the article on its face states that it was "received for publication" on December 21, 1964. There is no evidence to show that the article reported any substantive research work done under funds from a Public Health Service grant awarded on or after July 1, 1965.

36. (a) Plaintiff has established a licensing program to cover various forms of exploitation of its medical journals. The program includes the following:

(i) Upon request, plaintiff grants permission, in the form of licenses, for reproducing a journal article as part

of a newly published book or for reproducing articles in other forms, particularly for use by educational institutions.

(ii) Plaintiff has received requests from Government agencies and others for licenses to make multiple copies of journal articles, and plaintiff has granted such requests and has been paid therefor.

(iii) Plaintiff has granted licenses for the distribution and sale of microfilm editions of its journals, including the four journals in suit, to University Microfilm Company, Ann Arbor, Michigan, and Arcadia Microfilms, Spring Valley, New York, in consideration for a royalty paid to plaintiff.

93

(iv) Plaintiff has granted licenses, for a consideration, to two reprint houses in New York to furnish a requester with a reprint of a journal article or an entire journal.

(v) Plaintiff has granted a royalty-bearing license to the Institute for Scientific Information, Philadelphia, Pennsylvania, to provide requesters with copies of articles from plaintiff's journals.

(vi) Plaintiff has granted to several libraries (Veterans Administration Hospital library in San Francisco, California, the Dugway Technical Library and the Wilkin Research Foundation of New York) a license to make, on a continuing basis, single copies of articles from journals in return for the payment of royalties. Such licenses, however, have not produced royalties to date and two of the licenses are no longer in effect. The license to Wilkin Research Foundation was entered into in February 1970 and provides for a royalty of 5 cents per copied page, with accumulated royalties payable yearly.

(b) It is not clear whether plaintiff's licensing program for libraries extends to the making of copies for persons not applying at the library building.

37. Plaintiff receives about 45 to 60 requests per week to make copies from its various publications, about five of such requests being for copies of single articles from plaintiff's journals. Requests for copies of journal articles are handled by plaintiff as set out in finding 11.

38. Plaintiff receives about $6,000 to $7,000 per year for permissions granted to individuals to copy journal articles (single copies and otherwise). Such receipts are in addition to royalties received from the Institute for Scientific Information, reprint houses and microfilm licensing.

39. (a) Between 1959 and 1969, annual subscriptions to *Medicine* increased from about 2,800 to about 5,400, though subscriptions decreased slightly from 1968 to 1969. Annual subscription sales increased from about $20,000 to about $60,000; and total annual income increased from about $23,000 to about $65,000. Between 1964 and 1969, annual subscriptions to *Pharmacological Reviews* increased from about

94

2,600 to about 3,100, though subscriptions decreased slightly from 1968 to 1969. Annual subscription sales increased from about $19,000 to about $21,000; and total annual income increased from about $22,000 to about $25,000. Between 1959 and 1969, annual subscriptions to the *Journal of Immunology* increased from about 2,600 to about 4,700. Annual subscription sales increased from about $36,000 to about $131,000; and total annual income increased from about $38,000 to about $185,000. Between 1959 and 1969, annual subscriptions to *Gastroenterology* increased from about 4,100 to about 7,000. Annual subscription sales increased from about $49,000 to about $155,000; and total annual income increased from about $108,000 to about $244,000.

(b) Between 1959 and 1966, plaintiff's annual taxable income increased from $272,000 to $726,000. In 1967, it fell to $589,000; and in 1968, to $451,000. Plaintiff's four journals in suit account for a relatively small percentage of plaintiff's total business; and over the years, such journals have been profitable, except that the *Journal of Immunology* showed losses in the period prior to 1961; *Gastroenterology* showed losses in 1967–68; and *Pharmacological Reviews* showed a loss in 1969. Profits from the journals have varied from less than $1,000 to about $15,000 annually. Plaintiff's share of the profits from the journals published under contract with medical societies has ranged from less than $1,000 to about $7,000. *E.g.,* in 1968, profit from *Pharmacological Reviews* was $1,154.44 (on sales of about $40,000). The profit was divided, $1,039 to ASPET and $115.44 to plaintiff. In 1969, net income from *Gastroenterology* was $21,312.08 (on sales of about $245,000) and $11,532.35 of that amount was offset by losses the previous year, leaving a balance of $9,779.73. The balance was split between plaintiff and AGA, plaintiff getting $4,889.86.

(c) Plaintiff's business appears to have been growing faster than the gross national product or of the rate of growth of manpower working in the field of science.

(d) There is no evidence to show whether any particular instance or instances of unauthorized photocopying of plaintiff's journals resulted in the loss of a particular form of revenue to plaintiff. It is also concluded that plaintiff has

95

failed to show that it has been hurt, in any substantial degree, by the photocopying practices of NLM and NIH.

40. (a) NIH (and so far as the record shows, NLM) has made no studies to determine the estimated costs over and above royalties which would be involved in paying publishers for photocopying part or all of their copyrighted journals. The costs involved in such an estimate would be essentially the salaries of the people who would make the necessary determinations. The Librarian of NIH testified that he is unable to make any estimate of such costs.

(b) In 1967, NLM temporarily ceased photocopying articles from plaintiff's journals. NLM was able, as a practical matter, to flag plaintiff's journals from April 27, 1967 to May 29, 1967, in order to refrain temporarily from copying from them. The flagging of plaintiff's journals was an administrative statistical operation performed by a library technician in the loan and stack section of NLM. On about May 29, 1967, NLM resumed photocopying articles from plaintiff's journals, and for about 90 days thereafter, NLM monitored such photocopying. Satisfied that such 90-day period was a representative sample, NLM found that it would have paid plaintiff about $250 to $300 if it had acceded to plaintiff's request for 2 cents royalty per page. The Director of NLM testified that, in his opinion, this was "a very small sum—surprisingly small sum." However, administrative costs involved in the payment of a royalty might be substantially greater than the royalty itself.

41. (a) In 1935, there was issued a joint statement by the National Association of Book Publishers and the Joint Committee on Materials for Research regarding the photocopying by libraries and like institutions of copyrighted materials. The statement, later to become known as the "gentlemen's agreement," was the product of meetings and discussions between representatives of the book publishing industry and research-and-education-oriented organizations, such as libraries. The representatives were interested in working out a practical accommodation of the conflict between (i) the legitimate interest of copyright owners not to have their works copied without compensation and (ii) the needs of scholars and research workers for copies of parts

96

of copyrighted works to use in pursuit of scientific or literary investigation. The "gentlemen's agreement," along with the introductory statement accompanying it, reads as follows:

> The Joint Committee on Materials for Research and the Board of Directors of the National Association of Book Publishers, after conferring on the problem of conscientious observance of copyright that faces research libraries in connection with the growing use of photographic methods of reproduction, have agreed upon the

following statement:

> A library, archives office, museum, or similar institution owning books or periodical volumes in which copyright still subsists may make and deliver a single photographic reproduction or reduction of a part thereof to a scholar representing in writing that he desires such reproduction in lieu of loan of such publication or in place of manual transcription and solely for the purposes of research; provided
>
> (1) That the person receiving it is given due notice in writing that he is not exempt from liability to the copyright proprietor for any infringement of copyright by misuse of the reproduction constituting an infringement under the copyright law;
>
> (2) That such reproduction is made and furnished without profit to itself by the institution making it.

> The exemption from liability of the library, archives office or museum herein provided for shall extend to every officer, agent or employee of such institution in the making and delivery of such reproduction when acting within the scope of his authority of employment. This exemption for the institution itself carries with it a responsibility to see that library employees caution patrons against the misuse of copyright material reproduced photographically.

> Under the law of copyright, authors or their agents are assured of "the exclusive right to print, reprint, publish, copy and vend the copyrighted work," all or any part. This means that legally no individual or institution can reproduce by photography or photo-mechanical means, mimeograph or other methods of reproduction a page or any part of a book without the written permission of the owner of the copyright. Society, by law, grants this exclusive right for a term of years in the belief that such exclusive control of creative work is necessary to encourage authorship and scholarship.

97

While the right of quotation without permission is not provided in law, the courts have recognized the right to a "fair use" of book quotations, the length of a "fair" quotation being dependent upon the type of work quoted from and the "fairness" to the author's interest. Extensive quotation is obviously inimical to the author's interest.

The statutes make no specific provision for a right of a research worker to make copies by hand or by typescript for his research notes, but a student has always been free to "copy" by hand; and mechanical reproductions from copyright material are presumably intended to take the place of hand transcriptions, and to be governed by the same principles governing hand transcription.

In order to guard against any possible infringement of copyright, however, libraries, archives offices and museums should require each applicant for photo-mechanical reproductions of material to assume full responsibility for such copying, and by his signature to a form printed for the purpose assure the institution that the duplicate being made for him is for his personal use only and is to relieve him of the task of transcription. The form should clearly indicate to the applicant that he is obligated under the law not to use the material thus copied from books for any further reproduction without the express permission of the copyright owner.

It would not be fair to the author or publisher to make possible the substitution of the photostats for the purchase of a copy of the book itself either for an individual library or for any permanent collection in a public or research library. Orders for photo-copying which, by reason of their extensiveness or for any other reasons, violate this principle should not be accepted. In case of doubt as to whether the excerpt requested complies with this condition, the safe thing to do is to defer action until the owner of the copyright has approved the reproduction.

Out-of-print books should likewise be reproduced only with permission, even if this reproduction is solely for the use of the institution making it and not for sale.

(*signed*) ROBERT C. BINKLEY, *Chairman*
Joint Committee on Materials for Research
W. W. NORTON, *President*
National Association of Book Publishers

(b) The practice by libraries of making photocopies has existed for at least 50 years. In the 1930's—and prior thereto—photocopying of books and like materials was done

98

principally by conventional photographic techniques. Starting about 1960, the new technology of electrostatic copying and other rapid, inexpensive copying techniques resulted in a dramatic increase in the instances and amounts of photocopying. During the past 10 years, the propriety of library photocopying has been the subject of many discussions at meetings and conferences of library and information groups. In 1957, the Director of NLM noted that "it is possible, if not indeed probable, that the years would bring, sooner or later, a test of the issue in the courts" posed by NLM's photocopying activities and the copyright law.

(c) Plaintiff's principal officers became aware of large-scale library photocopying in about 1962. Immediately thereafter, plaintiff's president made his views on the subject known to various library groups. In the course of exchanges with librarians, plaintiff's president learned of the statement called the "gentlemen's agreement" and expressed his views thereon essentially as follows: The statement is inconsequential to the issues of present-day photocopying because (i) it was written in the 1930's when copying processes consisted of blueprints, photostats or microfilm, processes significantly different from those principally used today, (ii) one party to the statement (National Association of Book Publishers) is a long-defunct organization to which plaintiff never belonged, and (iii) the National Association of Book Publishers apparently consisted not of periodical publishers, like plaintiff, but book publishers who were concerned with the publication (and unauthorized photocopying) of books (or monographs).

42. (a) In October 1966, defendant's General Services Administration issued a handbook, COPYING EQUIPMENT, identified by code number FPMR 101–6. The purpose of the handbook was to acquaint Government supervisory personnel with the various photocopying machines available on the market and to encourage Government agencies to make use of such machines in an economic and efficient manner. The introduction to the handbook notes as follows:

> With the dispersal of office copiers throughout Government agencies, the need for a good hard look at the economy and effectiveness of office copying services has become increasingly apparent. The uncontrolled acquisition and use of office copying equipment has often re-

99

sulted in uneconomical mismatches of user requirements with machine capabilities and wasteful practices in operating copying facilities.

The introduction goes on to say that large organizational units should make studies of needs for equipment before making substantial investments. It is further noted:

> Where such studies have not been made, an inquiry into the existing copying facilities will offer a high potential for savings. As a minimum, a goal of 10% reduction in overall copying and related paperwork costs would be feasible. This handbook has been prepared to guide managers and others responsible for office copying in providing economical and effective copying service which meets user requirements.

(b) The "Foreword" to the handbook notes in part:

> The impact of document copiers on Federal operations has been substantial just as it has been in commerce and industry. At this writing there are at least 202 models of copiers available from some 37 different manufacturers or distributors. The United States Government alone has installed approximately 55 thousand machines and the yearly cost of office copying is estimated at 80 million dollars. An increasing number of cost-conscious executives are concerned about the predictions that this cost could double within the next 5 years.

(c) Chapter III of the handbook is entitled "Legal Aspects" and reads as follows:

Copying Laws

Copying laws are almost in the same category as speed limit laws—people forget they are there. Although the former involves much less risk than the latter, the penalty can be much greater. Most documents which are prohibited by law from being copied have their source in State or Federal Government. A partial listing is shown in figure 1. In case of doubt, legal advice should be obtained.

Copyright Laws

The most frequently violated law is the Copyright Law: namely, that law which prohibits the copying of copyrighted material without permission.

The Copyright Law is intended to protect the publisher or author from plagiarism. It gives him the right to say who may reproduce his written or published work, and to demand payment for it. However, the current

100

widespread use of copying machines in reproducing literary works goes beyond the question of plagiarism. It is beginning seriously to affect the sale of published works, such as magazines, textbooks, and technical papers. Prior to this time, a user of such works desiring to have possession of a copy was obliged to purchase the publication if he could not borrow it for an indefinite period. Today, it is relatively simple to make copies of almost any printed matter by means of the office copier.

Because the copier has made it easy to reproduce published works, extra precaution is necessary. Where a notice of copyright is shown, either on the work itself, or by a general statement in the publication, the law is clear: it may not be copied unless permission of the publisher or author is obtained. Where doubt exists as to whether or not an item is copyrighted, the legal officer should be consulted.

Figure 1, accompanying Chapter III, is entitled "Material That May Not Be Copied" and notes in part:

> 1. Congress, by statute, has forbidden the copying of the following subjects under certain circumstances. There are penalties of fine or imprisonment imposed on those guilty of making such copies.
>
> * * * * *
>
> d. Copyrighted material of any manner or kind without permission of the copyright owner.
>
> * * * * *

43. (a) The Board of Regents of NLM (finding 20(a)), at several meetings in 1957, considered the problems of copyright with respect to the operations of NLM. The minutes of those meetings are not in evidence. However, such minutes are discussed in a letter dated December 29, 1965, from Abraham L. Kaminstein, Register of Copyrights, to The Honorable John L. McClellan, United States Senate, as follows:

> * * * * *
>
> The new law amended a 1944 Public Health Service Act, which in 1956 was further amended by the transfer of the Armed Forces Medical Library to the newly established National Library of Medicine. The Act provides, *inter alia*, (42 U.S.C. 276) that the Surgeon General shall "make available, through loans, *photographic or other copying procedures or otherwise,* such materials as he deems appropriate . . ." [Italics supplied] The 1956 amendment to the Public Health Service Act also pro-

101

vides for the establishment by the Surgeon General of a Board of Regents, which as a part of its duties is the [to?] prescribe "rules under which the Library will provide copies of its publications or materials." Since the provisions of section 398 are basically no different from the provisions of the 1956 amendment, it may be of interest to ascertain the administrative interpretation of that earlier copying provision.

A study of the minutes of the Board of Regents discloses that the agenda for the very first meeting of the Board, on March 20, 1957, included the distribution of a paper entitled Considerations for the Formulation of Loan Policy (of the National Library of Medicine). That paper contains a clear recognition of the copyright problem:

> "To start with, it must be pointed out that there are legal restrictions to the unlimited copying of published works; restrictions which are vague in some respects but which have been interpreted fairly definitely in most. The two most important inter-

pretations for this problem are that whole works may not be copied and that multiple copies may not be made."

This policy paper was the subject of discussion at the meeting of the Board on April 29, 1957, at which the recommendations were approved. It is significant that the minutes of that meeting disclose the following:

"Dr. Mumford [the Librarian of Congress] raised the question of copyright restrictions. It was stated that while the recommended new policy would not obviate the copyright problems, it would not raise more, and probably raise fewer difficulties in this area than does the current policy."

Further evidence that the Board was aware that copyright problems existed appeared in the minutes of the Board meeting for September 23, 1957, in the following notation:

"The Director [of the National Library of Medicine] expressed his concern 'with the continuing vexing problem of copyright restrictions.' He indicated that the Library is proceeding as circumspectly as possible, but that it is possible, if not indeed probable, that the years would bring, sooner or later, a test of the issue in the courts . . . The Director took pains to indicate that despite the difficulties of the situation it seemed clear to him that the Library could do no other than pursue its present course, since a very large part, if not the major part, of the Library's services is dependent upon it."

102

The foregoing would appear to indicate that, from the outset of the establishment of the National Library of Medicine, there has been an awareness of the existence of copyright restrictions with respect to the use of the copyrighted works in its collections. Nowhere does it appear that the policy-making body, the Board of Regents, considered that the above-quoted provision authorizing the Surgeon General to make the material in the Library available by "photographic or other copying procedures" was in any way in derogation of the rights granted under the copyright law to the proprietor of the copyright. On the contrary, the evidence indicates that the Library attempted to formulate a policy that would take due regard of the provisions of the copyright law.

* * * *

(b) In 1957, the then-Director of NLM, in discussing the problems created by NLM's policy of providing free photocopying services, stated as follows:

Let us now take a critical look at what has happened under these policies. Free photocopying has developed beyond reasonable bounds. For example, in a recent study conducted over a two month period, it was found that over 50% of all requests received could be filled by photocopying journal articles from 125 common journal titles of the last five years.

On the face of it, this is a need which the printing press, not the camera, is designed to fill. When a request from New York City is received for a photocopy of an article which appeared in last month's JAMA, it is apparent that the library is being treated as a cheap and convenient reprint service, and not as a library. It is felt NLM should not run a copying service *per se;* NLM must operate as a library, and all photocopying done should be an extension of normal library operations.

This statement was made in 1957 with reference to policies then in effect, before adoption of NLM's present policies.

44. The Library of Congress operates a photoduplication service by which it provides photocopies of documents for a per-page fee. In 1965, electrostatic positive prints (Xerox) were provided at from 16 cents to 85 cents per sheet, depending on the quantity ordered and other factors. A brochure issued by the Library of Congress, effective October 1, 1965, stated in part:

Photocopying is done by the Library under the following conditions:

103

1. The Library will generally make photoduplicates of materials in its collections available for research use. It performs such service for research, in lieu of loan of the material, or in place of manual transcription. Certain restricted material cannot be copied. The Library reserves the right to decline to make photoduplicates requested, to limit the number of copies made, or to furnish positive prints in lieu of negatives.

2. Copyright material will ordinarily not be copied without the signed authorization of the copyright owner. Exceptions to this rule may be made in particular cases. All responsibility for the use made of the photoduplicates is assumed by applicant.

There is no evidence to show the circumstances under which the Library of Congress makes "exceptions" to its rule against photocopying copyright materials.

45. The PRINTING MANAGEMENT MANUAL of defendant's Department of Health, Education, and Welfare (in effect in 1962 and 1967) stated as follows with respect to copyright:

* * * *

A. *General*

Material protected by copyright generally may not be reproduced in any fashion, including photocopying or similar techniques, without the express permission of the copyright proprietor. However, it has been the widespread practice of libraries to have single copies made of copyrighted articles to further scholarly research, without consent of the copyright proprietor. Therefore, Department libraries may make such single copies, but every precaution should be taken to assure that such single copying is done only at the written request of an employee to further scholarly research.

B. *Infringement*

1. Since the Government may be subject to claim or suit for damages, every precaution must be taken to avoid infringement of a copyright by an employee of the Department.

2. Employees should be advised that infringement of a copyright by an employee of the Department, not in the performance of his official duties may subject the employee to a suit for damages.

* * * *

46. The current and recent practices of NIH and NLM as described in the foregoing findings constitute a fair use.

104

CONCLUSION OF LAW

Upon the foregoing findings of fact, which are made a part of the judgment herein, the court concludes as a matter of law that plaintiff is not entitled to recover and its petition is dismissed.

Supreme Court of the United States

No.

THE WILLIAMS & WILKINS COMPANY,

Petitioner,

—against—

THE UNITED STATES,

Respondent.

PETITION FOR WRIT OF CERTIORARI

ALAN LATMAN
Attorney for Petitioner
200 East 42nd Street
New York, New York 10017
(212) 986–6272

ARTHUR J. GREENBAUM
COWAN, LIEBOWITZ & LATMAN, P. C.,
Of Counsel.

1

Petitioner prays that a writ of certiorari issue to review the judgment of the Court of Claims entered in this case on November 27, 1973.

OPINIONS BELOW

The opinion of the Court of Claims Trial Judge was unofficially reported in the United States Patent Quarterly at 172 USPQ 670. The majority and dissenting opinions of the

2

Court of Claims (App.[1] 1 through 104) were reported at 487 F.2d 1345 and 180 USPQ 49.

JURISDICTION

The judgment of the Court of Claims was entered on November 27, 1973. The jurisdiction of this Court to review that judgment is invoked under 28 U.S.C. §1255(1).

QUESTION PRESENTED

Does systematic library reproduction of copyrighted journal articles in their entirety constitute "fair use" or copyright infringement?

STATUTES INVOLVED

28 U.S.C. §1498(b) provides in pertinent part as follows:

"Hereafter, whenever the copyright in any work protected under the copyright laws of the United States shall be infringed by the United States***the exclusive remedy of the owner of such copyright shall be by action against the United States in the Court of Claims for the recovery of his reasonable and entire compensation***"

* * *

Section 1(a) of the Copyright Law, 17 U.S.C. §1(a), provides as follows:

"§1. EXCLUSIVE RIGHTS AS TO COPYRIGHTED WORKS. Any person entitled thereto, upon complying with the provisions of this title, shall have the exclusive right:

a) To print, reprint, publish, copy, and vend the copyrighted work;"

[1] Appendix hereto, which is being submitted to the Court separately pursuant to Rule 23(1)(i). References to numbers preceded by "Tr." are to the nscript of the trial.

3

Section 3 of the Copyright Law, 17 U.S.C. §3, provides in pertinent part as follows:

"§3. PROTECTION OF COMPONENT PARTS OF WORK COPYRIGHTED; COMPOSITE WORKS OR PERIODICALS. The copyright provided by this title shall protect all the copyrightable component parts of the work copyrighted,***. The copyright upon composite works or periodicals shall give to the proprietor thereof all the rights in respect thereto which he would have if each part were individually copyrighted under this title."

STATEMENT OF THE CASE

This is an action seeking reasonable compensation from the Government for copyright infringement under 28 U.S.C. §1498(b). The principal defense in what the court below called this "ground-breaking" suit (App. 2) is that the Government's system of reproduction and distribution of journal articles constitutes "fair use." The Trial Judge found for petitioner on the issue of liability, with damages reserved for later determination. The Court of Claims, in a 4–3 decision, rejected its Trial Judge's decision and dismissed the petition.

The action is based on the reproduction of entire articles from petitioner's copyrighted journals by respondent through its National Institutes of Health ("NIH") and National Library of Medicine ("NLM"). The reproduction is performed through a comprehensive system whereby libraries, relying generally on one or two subscriptions to a journal, regularly fill all the requests of library users for journals of petitioner and other publishers by photocopying the requested journal articles. Under this system several million pages per year are copied.[1] Thus, respondent's photocopying is not

[1] Respondent noted in 1966 its installation of 55,000 machines throughout the Government at a yearly cost of 80 million dollars (Finding 42(b)) and the serious effect of widespread copying on the sale of technical articles (Finding 42(c)) (App. 99).

4

casual or sporadic; its system is an integral part of NIH and NLM library operations.

Petitioner is a relatively small medical and scientific publisher whose journals are highly respected but have a limited number of subscriptions. Most of its journals are published in conjunction with nonprofit medical and scientific societies which receive from 50% to 90% of net profits, if any. Petitioner has established a licensing program to cover various uses of its journals, including licenses to libraries for photocopying.

Eight articles from four of petitioner's journals were among the many systematically copied by respondent. These articles were set forth in the petition in an effort to establish the rights of plaintiff and other copyright proprietors in this test case.

The NIH library photoduplication service employs Xerox copying machines and microfilm cameras from which copies are printed to provide journal articles, on a no-return basis, to any of the 12,000 employees at NIH. NLM is a library furnishing material generally to a network of other libraries and to other institutions, including commercial enterprises such as drug companies. In the case of journals, NLM (rather than the user) has decided to furnish reproductions of desired articles, also on a permanent basis, instead of lending the original. NLM's photocopying service is enhanced by its publication and sale of a current index of medical literature, which catalogs citations to journals of petitioner and other publishers and "thus advertises to the medical and scientific community which constitutes plaintiff's market, that certain articles are available free of charge in the form of a photocopy." (App. 41).

Respondent's system makes and distributes several hundred thousand reproductions of articles a year. Despite its purported self-limitations (established by reason, *inter alia*, of the danger of infringing copyrights) the system permits, and inevitably results in, repeated reproduction of the same articles.

5

In performing its photocopying, respondent leases its copying machines from Xerox Corporation, which it pays according to the number of pages reproduced.

This suit for reasonable compensation was not brought to halt or limit photocopying. It was undertaken to broaden the financial support available to privately published,[1] limited circulation, scientific journals whose survival is vital to the growth of scientific knowledge.

THE DECISION BELOW

All three opinions below recognized this case as requiring a landmark decision on the copyright doctrine of "fair use." The majority concluded that "on this record, the challenged use should be designated 'fair' and not 'unfair.'"[1] (App. 14). The "core" of the court's rationale was that: (1) petitioner (together with "medical publishers generally" (App. 23)) is not substantially harmed from the specific practices in question; (2) medicine and medical research would be injured by holding these particular practices to be an infringement; and (3) the problem of accommodating the competing interests calls for legislative action and until such action, the court should not place a risk of harm on science (App. 14). It is this last theme on which the court closes its opinion with the hope that "the result in the present case will be but a 'holding operation' in the interim period before Congress enacts its preferred solution."⁵ (App. 29)

³ The Trial Judge noted that alternatives to private publication would be either no publication or publication by the Government, with its attendant problems, including the danger of censorship. 172 USPQ at 676, n. 7.
⁴ In reaching this conclusion, the majority expressed "grave uncertainty" that the photocopying of journal articles (or any reproduction of periodicals or books) was covered by the word "copy" as one of the exclusive rights granted in Section 1(a) of the 1909 Copyright Act, 17 U.S.C. §1(a) (App. 9, 23). The Court took this "solid doubt . . . into account" (App. 9) in dismissing the petition.
⁵ The most recent effort to revise the governing 1909 statute commenced with a study program in 1955. This led to the introduction of a bill in 1964 and its passage by the House of Representatives, but not the Senate, in 1967.
(cont.)

6

Three of the seven judges dissented. Chief Judge Cowen's dissenting opinion pointed out the following:

(1) Upon analysis of the 1909 Act, its legislative history and subsequent judicial interpretation, photocopying of journal articles is indeed "copying," *i.e.*, "Congress obliterated the distinction, if there ever had been one, between the copying of books and the copying of other materials." (App. 32).

(2) Fair use is inapplicable because of the rule that wholesale copying of the kind here involved "without more defeats the defense of fair use."⁶ (App. 35).

(3) The latitude fair use affords science and scholarly works applies to a new author's need to comment on and discuss earlier works in the same field, and has no application to the bare verbatim reproduction here involved. (App. 35, 36).

(4) The so-called "single-copy-per-request" limitation of respondent is illusory and unrealistic because furnishing each of ten patrons with one copy of the same article is no different from giving ten copies to one patron. (App. 34).

(5) There is legally cognizable harm to petitioner resulting from respondent's operation of "a reprint service which supplants the need for journal subscriptions"

No further progress on general revision has been made in the House. The Senate Judiciary Subcommittee on Patents, Trademarks and Copyrights held hearings in July, 1973 but as of this writing no report has yet been issued. A dispassionate view of this 19-year effort precludes any assumptions as to whether, or when, a new law will be passed. Accordingly, the majority's attempt to decide the present case as a "holding operation" is, as pointed out at pages 13–15, *infra*, most inappropriate.
⁶ The opinion notes that the majority cites no decision in support of its rejection of the above rule (App. 35). The conflict created by the Court of Claims' decision on this point with those of the Ninth, District of Columbia and Eighth Circuits is discussed below at pages 16–17.

7

(App. 34) and operates "on a scale so vast that it dwarfs the output of many small companies." (App. 31, 37–42).⁷

(6) The award of reasonable compensation to petitioner in this case will not injure medical research. (App. 43–44).⁸

Judge Nichols, joining in Chief Judge Cowen's dissent, also wrote a separate opinion emphasizing that the question before the court is not whether photocopying should be stopped since curtailment of photocopying could in no event be the result of any decision by the Court of Claims. (App. 67). The opinion

points out that "however hedged, the [majority] decision will

⁷ The narrow subscription base and high preparation costs of scholarly journals make the loss of even a single subscription important (App. 55). Petitioner's income from permissions and licensing of microfilms, reprints and photocopying is also important. Though the sums may seem small, they are significant in financing journals, and will become more so in the future.
  Petitioner's blanket licensing system referred to by the majority (App. 24) would cost libraries supplying only their own patrons with photocopies, such as NIH, an average of $3.65 per year for each of petitioner's journals, payable along with the subscriptions. Regional libraries making reproductions for other libraries and NLM, at the apex of a massive national network, would pay proportionally more. These sums may properly be described as "a surprisingly small part" (App. 43) from the point of view of a particular library, but they are crucial in the aggregate to a publisher trying to keep scientific journals viable.
⁸ The record contains the admission on behalf of respondent that the payment of royalties to publishers for obtaining photocopies would not hinder the performance of the NIH library since this is merely "a side issue" involving economic and budgetary considerations. (Tr. 174-75).
  Medical research, rather than being harmed, would be benefited by reasonable compensation. This is because: (a) publication of research results is a "vital part of research" (Finding 13, App. 79); and (b) uncompensated photocopying leads to "a vicious cycle which can only bode ill for medical publishing." (Trial Judge's opinion incorporated in Chief Judge Cowen's dissent at App. 55. See Tr. 436; 986-87; 1301-02).
  The fallacy of the majority is demonstrated by simply considering the self-restraint of respondent and other libraries with respect to copying as much as a chapter from a book or "monograph" [a librarian's sometimes hazy distinction from a journal]. (Finding 18). Respondent's libraries have functioned and medical research has apparently proceeded apace despite the fact that libraries do not photocopy in this area without permission.

8

be read that a copyright holder has no rights a library is bound to respect. We are making the Dred Scott decision of copyright law." (App. 69).

REASONS FOR GRANTING THE WRIT

Despite the close division on the merits in the court below, all three opinions confirm that this case poses an important but undecided legal question concerning "fair use" of copyrighted works. In reaching and determining this issue, the Court of Claims departed from a fundamental rule of law in such manner as to create a sharp conflict with three Courts of Appeals. In so doing, the court has not only committed basic errors in copyright law but has also ignored its function under the jurisdictional statute, 28 U.S.C. 1498(b). Thus, the court below has misconstrued two important federal statutes.

The parties and their *amici curiae* below all agreed that these legal issues have immediate and substantial ramifications in the field of scientific research and communications far beyond the present litigants. The case thus involves application of established doctrines of copyright law to contemporary versions of information dissemination. Finally, this case presents these questions in a particularly appropriate context, with focus upon the relationship between Government and the individual, *i.e.*, the reasonable compensation, if any, to be awarded for Government use through modern technology of privately copyrighted material.

We urge that any one of these factors would justify the granting of certiorari; in combination, we respectfully submit that the granting of the writ is essential.

The sweep of the decision below has been carefully understated by the majority. The records of photoduplication necessarily maintained and disclosed by the Government have provided particularly complete documentation as to how library photocopying actually operates. This record reveals a comprehensive systematic operation, which includes a network of libraries throughout the country being

9

serviced by NLM. Under these facts, the reference in the majority opinion to its "being stingy rather than expansive in the reach of our holding" (App. 29) is, we submit, misdescriptive. The holding is necessarily expansive because it excuses a massive system of photoduplication—and of necessity all lesser photocopying activities—as "fair use." There are no limiting factors in this situation which would not be applicable in other situations. Accordingly, this case will simply be read, as noted by Judge Nichols, to "encourage unrestricted piracy." (App. 69).

1. The Current Applicability of The "Fair Use" Doctrine And The Duty of The Court of Claims Under Its Jurisdictional Statute Are Important Questions For This Court.

(a) *The Copyright "Fair Use" Question.* Resolution of the copyright issue here being tested has been long anticipated by scholars, administrative officials, legislators and the publishing and library communities. A definitive study of the subject observed that "unfortunately, there are no decisions dealing specifically with photocopying by libraries, or even with the narrower question of a person making photocopies for his own use." VARMER, "PHOTODUPLICATION OF COPYRIGHTED MATERIAL BY LIBRARIES" STUDY NO. 15, COPYRIGHT LAW REVISION STUDIES PREPARED FOR SENATE COMMITTEE ON THE JUDICIARY, 86TH CONG., 2D SESS. 50 (Comm. Print 1960). A director of NLM recognized that with respect to his library's photocopying activities "it is possible, if not probable, that the years would bring, sooner or later, a test of the issue in the courts." (Pltf. Ex. 38, p. 1375; Tr. 416). The Register of Copyrights similarly noted that this important question, which had not been decided by the courts, merits special consideration. See REGISTER OF COPYRIGHTS, 87TH CONG., 1ST SESS., REPORT ON THE GENERAL REVISION OF THE COPYRIGHT LAWS 25 (Comm. Print 1961).

It is thus not surprising that the majority opinion below called this case "a ground-breaking copyright infringement action" raising "troublesome problems" which "have never before been mooted or determined by a court." (App. 2). The

---

10

Trial Judge had stated that "this suit is one of first impression [and] raises long troublesome and much discussed issues. . . ." 172 USPQ at 672. The Trial Judge's opinion itself was the subject of at least seven law review comments[9] as well as innumerable reports in publishing, library and other industry media.[10] It received widespread international attention, including mention in a recent UNESCO document,[11] and was commented upon in some detail in TIME (May 1, 1973 at 62). In the short time since the Court of Claims' decision, its impact has been widely noted in the trade and popular press.[12]

The filing at the trial level of *amicus curiae* briefs was unusual and reflected the extraordinary consequences perceived by many affected groups.[13] The *amici* who have already appeared in this

---

[9] 41 U. CIN. L. REV. 511 (1972); 48 INDIANA L.J. 503 (1973); 3 RUTGERS JOURNAL OF COMPUTERS & THE LAW 328 (1974); 51 TEXAS L. REV. 137 (1972); 25 VAND. L. REV. 1093 (1972); 12 WASHBURN L.J. 235 (1973); 13 WM. & MARY L. REV. 940 (1972).

[10] E.g., PUBLISHER'S WEEKLY, Feb. 28, 1972 at 48 and 55; AMERICAN LIBRARIES, May, 1972 at 528; ADVERTISING AGE, August, 1972 at 53.

[11] UNITED NATIONS EDUCATIONAL SCIENTIFIC AND CULTURAL ORGANIZATION AND WORLD INTELLECTUAL PROPERTY ORGANIZATION, "REPORT OF WORKING GROUP ON REPROGRAPHIC REPRODUCTION OF WORKS PROTECTED BY COPYRIGHT" 5 (1973).

[12] PUBLISHERS WEEKLY, November 28, 1973, at 18; EDUCATION U.S.A. at 80 (December 3, 1973); WASHINGTON POST, November 28, 1973, at A24; MIAMI HERALD, November 29, 1973, at 20-A; LOS ANGELES TIMES, Jan. 27, 1974, Part VIII, at 1.

[13] At the Court of Claims level, five briefs *amicus curiae* were received in support of petitioner on behalf of: The Authors League of America, Inc., The American Chemical Society, The American Institute of Physics Incorporated, Association of American Publishers, Inc., The Association of American University Presses, Incorporated, American Society for Testing and Materials and National Council of Teachers of Mathematics.

Three briefs *amicus curiae* were received in support of respondent on behalf of: Association of Research Libraries, Medical Library Association, American Association of Law Libraries, American Medical Association, American Dental Association, Mayo Foundation, Robert H. Ebert, M.D. (in his capacity as Dean of the Faculty of Medicine, Harvard University), The University of Michigan Medical School, The University of Rochester, School

---

11

case themselves represent thousands and in one case millions of members. Each has in its brief below set forth in detail the respects in which the decision in this case will affect their members and the public at large. For example, the Authors League of America has indicated that it supports this action by a publisher because the principle involved not only affects authors through direct loss of income, but also "an even more drastic injury—the ultimate discontinuance of a periodical, journal or publishing house." (Brief *Amicus Curiae* of the Authors League of America, Inc., p. 3). Similarly, the Association of American Publishers and The Association of American University Presses have stated that their memberships, "non-profit and for profit alike, have a vital interest in the library photocopying issues presented in this case." (Brief *Amicus Curiae* of the Association of American Publishers, Inc. and The Association of American University Presses, Incorporated, p. 2).

This recognition of far-reaching implications is by no means restricted to the *amici* who have supported petitioner in the court below. For example, The American Library Association, in discussing the question presented by this case emphasized that "a decision would constitute precedent whose potential effect transcends the interests of the instant litigants." (Brief *Amicus Curiae* of the American Library Association, p. 2).

In view of these facts and the uncertainty engendered by the division in the court below, it is submitted that a prompt authoritative resolution by this Court of the copyright issue here involved is amply warranted.

(b) *The Jurisdictional "Reasonable Compensation" Question.* This action was commenced eight years after the enactment in 1960 of 28 U.S.C. §1498(b), the jurisdictional statute permitting suits against the Government for copyright infringement exclusively by action for damages in the Court of Claims. This is

---

of Medicine and Dentistry, American Sociological Association, Modern Language Association of America, History of Science Society, The National Education Association of the United States, and American Library Association.

12

the first such suit reaching decision and thus presents the first opportunity to define the duty of the Court of Claims under such statute. This is entirely appropriate because Congress, in passing this statute, was specifically asked by the Government to cover, among other things, the "ever-increasing danger" of infringement through photocopying machines. H.R. REP. No. 624, 86TH CONG., 2D SESS. 5 (1959).

In a striking departure from its established approach in patent and indeed other "taking" cases, the court ignored the task before it and denied reasonable compensation on the basis of its thoughts on what other courts might do in other cases. That the fears of the majority in this regard are groundless is demonstrated by Judge Nichols in his dissenting opinion and at page 18, *infra*. But aside from this, plaintiff sued in the Court of Claims because of activities by the Government, not by private persons. It does not seek an injunction which, of course, is specifically unavailable under 28 U.S.C. §1498(b). It does seek reasonable compensation from those who use its journals through large scale photocopying. This would supplement the income derived from those who use the journals by becoming subscribers, the objective being to gain broader based support for the ever increasing costs of publishing scholarly journals. The court's refusal to grant reasonable compensation here is unjustified and deprives plaintiff and parties similarly situated of their only possible forum the first time this remedy is sought. The only appellate procedure available in this situation is by way of certiorari, which is sought by this petition.

2. The Important Questions Involved In This Case Press For Immediate Judicial Resolution.

This lawsuit was commenced in February, 1968. During these

six years it has become evident that the technology of photo-duplication—a form of printing from which one or a thousand copies can be made with the turn of a dial—poses problems ripe for solution. The presence of problems of this type is confirmed by the cable antenna television issues raised in *Tele-*

13

prompter, Inc. v. CBS, Inc., Nos. 72–1628, 72–1633, which was argued before this Court in January, 1974. We are now at the point where, as conceded by the majority below, "the proliferation of inexpensive and improved copying machines, less than two decades ago, led to the surge in such duplication." (App. 18).

It is also submitted that courts, such as the Court of Claims, can and must face the task of applying the judge-made rules governing fair use cases such as this, without waiting for Congressional action.

We have noted the hope expressed by the majority below that "the result in the present case will be but a 'holding action' in the interim period before Congress enacts its preferred solution." (App. 29). But Congress has shown a distinct disinclination to act in this area in the absence of substantial agreement among the parties concerned. And the decision reached by the majority below, if adhered to, will merely reinforce adamance on the part of librarians[14] which will block any voluntary arrangement or satisfactory congressional compromise.

The "holding operation" philosophy also places this pressing problem in an "Alfonse & Gaston" posture. To emphasize the need for congressional treatment is one thing; to postulate a decision on this basis, even in part, is, it is submitted, virtually an abdication of the judicial function. Moreover, this approach conflicts directly with the legislative exhortation by the House Judiciary Committee that the "courts must be free to adapt the [fair use] doctrine to particular situations on a case-by-case basis;" for this reason the Committee (and presumably the House of Representatives in passing a bill in 1967) had "no

[14] An objective of the present lawsuit was to achieve legal recognition by librarians of the rights of copyright proprietors so that dialogue would be possible with the objective of reasonable accommodation. The clock has now been turned back in this respect to 1967 when the Director of NLM refused to consider any plan of payment to publishers until ordered to do so by a court (Tr. 75).

14

disposition to freeze the doctrine in the statute, especially during a period of technological change." H.R. REP. No. 83, 90TH CONG., 1ST SESS., 29 (1967). The majority quotes and then ignores this precise language in its opinion. (App. 26, n. 28). Plaintiff, and authors and publishers generally, are thus caught in a never-ending "holding operation" devised by the majority of the Court of Claims, unless and until this Court speaks.

The Solicitor General, as *amicus*, supported the grant of certiorari in the *Teleprompter* case, *supra*, because "it is uncertain when or whether copyright revision legislation will be forthcoming." (Memorandum, p. 2). The corollary is that courts must act, not as managers of an illusory "holding operation," but as adjudicators of existing rights. This is entirely appropriate in the context of the present case in which the compulsory license approach of 28 U.S.C. §1498 offers a unique opportunity to insure continuation of photocopying with a court setting compensation that is reasonable under the circumstances.[15] The result could serve as a model for other publishers and other libraries.

The fact that existing judicial procedures for copyright rate-making may be under the antitrust laws is of no moment; the systems have worked reasonably well.[16] Both the Court of Claims and other courts have the necessary powers under the copyright law to deny injunctions and award reasonable com-

[15] The case thus presents the very vehicle which was unavailable to this Court in *Fortnightly Corp. v. United Artists Television, Inc.*, 392 U.S. 390 (1968), the forerunner of *Teleprompter* on the question whether cable television

"performs" copyrighted works. The Solicitor General had there suggested that the Court render a compromise decision accommodating various competing considerations; the Court declined the suggestion, noting that such job was for Congress. 392 U.S. at 401. But in 1960 Congress, with full awareness of the risks of liability through photocopying, granted the Court of Claims the power to consider all factors in each case to arrive at reasonable compensation in concrete situations of copyright infringement by Government agencies.

[16] Judicial rate-making for copyright royalties is employed in the consent decree governing the American Society of Composers, Authors and Publishers. See, e. g., U.S.A. v. ASCAP, CCH 1940-43 Trade Cases ¶ 56,104; 1950 51 id. ¶¶ 62,594, 62,595.

15

pensation in this situation. If the decision below stands, however, this power will never be utilized.

3. The Court Below Misconstrued Two Important Federal Statutes.

(a) *The Copyright Statute.*

(i) *Misapplication of The Fair Use Doctrine.* The court below purported to decide this case on the judge-made doctrine of "fair use".[17] Since the key question in most copyright cases is whether the nature and amount of copying amounts to infringement, this doctrine has been aptly described as simply an attempt by the courts "to bring some order out of the confusion surrounding the question of how much can be copied." Note, 14 NOTRE DAME LAWYER 443, 449 (1939). The doctrine is not, as intimated throughout the majority's opinion, simply a subjective measure of a court's moralistic view as to whether a copying is "fair" or "unfair." The majority sets forth a set of distilled criteria in its opinion (App. 12) and then proceeds to ignore them in a complete departure from recognized principles of fair use. After expressing the doubt noted above that "copying" means "copying", the court proceeds to base its decision on eight factors. These begin with emphasis on the non-profit nature of NIH and NLM. But it is clear, as noted by Chief Judge Cowen (App. 36), that virtually every use by the Government is in fact nonprofit;[18] if this factor were to be determinative, or even significant, there would be no cases possible against the Government for copyright infringement. Yet, as

[17] The court assumed arguendo that petitioner was the proper party to sue, a point controverted by respondent below. Respondent did not press before the court below other defenses which had been raised at the trial including a license defense arising from certain Public Health Service grants because "these defenses have a limited impact." (Defendant's Brief, p. 9). These defenses are in fact completely inapplicable to certain counts in the petition herein and, accordingly, their determination either way would not avoid the necessity of resolving the fair use question which dominates this case.

[18] Of course, the medical societies for whom plaintiff publishes journals are nonprofit as well.

16

noted above, infringement by photocopying was one of the specific instances for which liability was provided in 1960. The majority's eight factors end with reliance on foreign statutes. Aside from substantial questions as to whether these statutes would actually excuse the activities here involved, the statutes merely illustrate that: (a) when a special exemption from the normal liability of the copyright law is desired, a statute is required and (b) the copyright laws of foreign countries are, as is well known, markedly different from United States law in a number of respects.[19]

(ii) *Conflict with Three Circuits and Need for Resolution by this Court.* It is not surprising that in ignoring established fair use criteria, the majority below was forced to depart from a significant and established rule of law. It has been explicitly recognized in the Ninth Circuit,[20] the District of Columbia Circuit[21] and the Eighth Circuit[22] that the doctrine of fair use is completely inapplicable to the copying of entire works. The Court of Claims rejected this proposition in the course of making its determination and could not have reached its result without doing so.[23]

[19] The majority goes far afield in time as well as place. In denying compensation in 1973, the Court below relies on alleged practices in 1935 or even

earlier. These are completely irrelevant by reason of respondent's concession in its brief below (page 46) that as late as 1958 "there was virtually no photocopying as presently practiced."

[19] *Benny* v. *Loew's, Inc.*, 239 F.2d. 532 (9th Cir. 1956), *aff'd by an equally divided Court*, 356 U.S. 43 (1958). (Parody not automatically fair use since "there is only a single decisive point in the case: one cannot copy the substance of another's work without infringing his copyright" 239 F.2d at 537). The *Benny* case is currently applied as law within the Ninth Circuit. See *Walt Disney Productions* v. *Air Pirates*, 345 F. Supp. 108 (N.D. Cal. 1972).

[21] *Public Affairs Associates, Inc.* v. *Rickover*, 284 F.2d 262 (D.C. Cir. 1960), *judgment vacated*, 369 U.S. 111 (1962). (Where verbatim copies of speeches are taken, the possibility of the defense of fair use can be ruled out at the threshold).

[22] *Wihtol* v. *Crow*, 309 F.2d 777 (8th Cir. 1962). (Educational nonprofit arrangement of musical song by high school choral instructor held infringement and not fair use because defendant had copied "all or substantially all of a copyrighted song").

[23] This is because the court agreed with petitioner that each article must be considered a separate work (App. 7, n. 6); therefore, copying an entire article is copying an entire work. This is explicitly required by Section 3 of the statute which provides that "the copyright upon ... periodicals shall give to the proprietor thereof all the rights in respect thereto which he would have if each part were individually copyrighted under this title." 17 U.S.C. §3. See *Markham* v. *A. E. Borden Co.*, 206 F.2d 199 (1st Cir. 1953); *King Features Syndicate* v. *Fleischer*, 299 Fed. 533 (2d Cir. 1924); *Hedeman Products Corp.* v. *Tap-Rite Products Corp.*, 228 F. Supp. 630, 633 (D.N.J. 1964).

18

tected work, subject only to the requirement that it pay the proprietor a reasonable compensation. Petitioner submits that the complete disregard of this approach by the majority of the Court of Claims in its first determination under the 1960 copyright reasonable compensation statute frustrates the legislative purpose.[24] For example, one of the three "core" propositions of the Court's opinion is that medical research would be injured by finding for petitioner. Reasonable compensation could not possibly have such a result, any more than reasonable compensation for the Defense Department's use of an invention would harm national defense.

The Court presumably fears that a decision in plaintiff's favor might be a precedent in cases between private parties where injunctions are potentially available. But as demonstrated by Judge Nichols in his dissenting opinion, courts may equitably withhold injunctions and determine compensation which is reasonable under the circumstances. This is a most likely result since neither the vast number of publishers represented by the *amici curiae* nor any other publisher has ever expressed any interest in an injunction against library photoduplication. Alternatively, fair use might well be found if a proprietor refused to license on reasonable terms. The court was in error here by completely ignoring petitioner's licensing program, which permits and indeed encourages photocopying simply upon payment of a modest annual sum constituting reasonable compensation.

CONCLUSION

It is respectfully submitted that this petition for a writ of certiorari should be granted.

ALAN LATMAN
Attorney for Petitioner

17

The error in both result and approach by the majority below results in part, we submit, from the absence of any controlling pronouncement on fair use thus far by this Court, the only reviewing authority of the Court of Claims. Both the *Benny* and *Rickover* cases (notes 20 and 21, *supra*) reached this Court but without producing any opinion of the Court on this issue.

(b) *The Jurisdictional Statute.* Congress provided for copyright compensation as a companion sub-section to the long-established provision covering Government liability for patent infringement. The operation of the two remedies is similar. The Department of Justice accurately described this patent provision recently as follows:

> "Under this provision, a patentee has no right to exclude or secure an injunction against such use; there is automatically a mandatory license to the government and its contractors. The patentee has a claim for just compensation, however, which may be brought before the Court of Claims.*** The original reason for this statute, and one that retains vitality today, is that *the government retains the right to undertake and carry out work involving the national defense and security, or other such public necessities, without being blocked from doing so by the patent system, although it should pay reasonable compensation for the use of the patented invention.*" [Emphasis supplied] THE BUREAU OF NAT'L AFFAIRS, 157 PATENT, TRADEMARK & COPYRIGHT JOURNAL, AT D-4 (Dec. 13, 1973).

As recognized by Congress, the Government in both patent and copyright situations must have the right to use the pro-

ARTHUR J. GREENBAUM
COWAN, LIEBOWITZ & LATMAN, P.C.
Of Counsel

[24] Cf. *Perma Life Mufflers* v. *International Parts Corp.*, 392 U.S. 134, 136 (1968) (Certiorari granted because lower court approach "seemed to threaten the effectiveness of the private action as a vital means for enforcing the antitrust policy of the United States.").

No. 73-1279

In the Supreme Court of the United States
October Term, 1973

Williams & Wilkins Co., Petitioner

v.

The United States

On Petition for Writ of Certiorari
to the United States Court of Claims

BRIEF FOR THE UNITED STATES IN OPPOSITION

Robert H. Bork,
   Solicitor General,

Carla A. Hills,
   Assistant Attorney General,

Harriet S. Shapiro,
   Assistant to the Solicitor General,

William Kanter,
Michael H. Stein,
Thomas J. Byrnes,
   Attorneys,
   Department of Justice,
   Washington, D.C. 20530.

1

OPINION BELOW

The opinion of the United States Court of Claims (Pet. App.) is reported at 487 F. 2d 1345.

JURISDICTION

The judgment of the Court of Claims was entered on November 27, 1973. The petition for a writ of certiorari was filed on February 20, 1974. The jurisdiction of this Court is invoked under 28 U.S.C. 1255(1).

2

QUESTION PRESENTED

Whether defendant's libraries, in furnishing single photocopies of journal articles to their patrons, made a fair use of petitioner's copyrighted journals, and thus did not infringe petitioner's copyrights.

STATEMENT

This suit was brought in the Court of Claims to recover compensation for the alleged infringement of petitioner's copyrights under 28 U.S.C. 1498(b). Petitioner claimed that respondent's libraries at the National Institutes of Health ("NIH") and the National Library of Medicine ("NLM") infringed certain copyrights allegedly owned by petitioner by furnishing to their patrons photocopies of articles appearing in journals published by petitioner. Respondent contended that in making such photocopies the libraries were merely making a permissible or fair use of petitioner's copyrighted journals and, thus, had not infringed petitioner's copyrights. The Court of Claims accepted respondent's contention and dismissed petitioner's complaint (Pet. App. 28, 29).

NIH is the principal federal medical research organization, employing over 12,000 persons of whom 4,000 have professional degrees. To support its medical research programs, NIH maintains a staff library containing approximately 150,000 volumes of which about 30,000 are books and the balance journals. The library furnishes to NIH employees photocopies of

3

journal articles pertinent to their research work (Pet. App. 3, 4).

NLM was constituted in its present form by an Act of Congress in 1956. In this statute, Congress declared the purpose of NLM was "* * * to aid the dissemination and exchange of scientific and other information important to the progress of medicine and to the public health * * *" and to make available such information "* * * through loans, photographic or other copying procedures * * *." 42 U.S.C. 275, 276(4). NLM is a "library's library," and furnishes to other libraries, under the interlibrary loan program, photocopies of medical journal articles (Pet. App. 5).

Both the NIH library and NLM have adopted and enforced guidelines to limit their photocopy services. Both require a written request. Both will furnish only a single copy of a journal article per request, and both limit each request to 40 or 50 pages. (Exceptions to the page limit are sometimes made in the case of long articles.) Both have rules designed to avoid excessive copying from a single journal issue. In addition, NLM will not fill requests for articles from the 104 journals included in their "widely available list"[1] (Pet. App. 5, 6, 15).

[1] A rejection on this basis is not made in the case of requests from government libraries, or in the case of a request for an article published more than 5 years before the request. The four journals identified in petitioner's complaint are named on the widely available list (Pet. App. 6).

4

The Court of Claims concluded that the library photocopying in this case was a fair use of the copyrighted material.[2] It rested this conclusion on the presence in this case of eight elements.[3] It noted that "probably the core of our evaluation" consisted of three propositions: 1) that plaintiff had not shown it was substantially harmed by the NIH and NLM practices;[4] 2) that the court was convinced medicine and medical research would be harmed by a finding that these practices constituted infringement; and 3) that, absent legislative guidance, the court should

[2] "The judicial doctrine of fair use [is] one of the most important and well-established limitations on the exclusive rights of copyright owners

.... Although the courts have considered and ruled upon the fair use doctrine over and over again, no real definition of the concept has ever emerged. Indeed, since the doctrine is an equitable rule of reason, no generally applicable definition is possible, and each case raising the question must be decided on its own facts." H. Rep. No. 83, 90th Cong., 1st Sess., 29.

[3] "We do not have to, and do not, say that any particular component would be enough, either by itself or together with some of the others. Conversely, we do not have to, and do not, say that all the elements we mention are essential to a finding of 'fair use.' They all happen to be present here, and it is enough for this case to rule, as we do, that at least when all co-exist in combination a 'fair use' is made out." (Pet. App. 28).

[4] The court refused to assume that this photocopying had an adverse impact on petitioner's market for its copyrighted works, since it was likely that the user of the photocopy would, if the copy were not available, simply do without the information, rather than purchase the journal (Pet. App. 20-22).

5

not impose such a risk of harm on these fields (Pet. App. 14, 19-25).[5]

ARGUMENT

The decision of the Court of Claims is correct. This case is the first one to deal specifically with the question of the copyright consequences of library photocopying; it is, therefore, of substantial interest to libraries, researchers, and publishers.[6] Nevertheless, since the decision is limited to the holding that

[5] The other elements identified by the court as indicating that the photocopying here challenged constituted a fair use of the materials were: 1) The total absence of any element of commercial gain to be derived from the reproduction, since these libraries are non-profit institutions, and the major users of the service are scientific researchers and practitioners who need the scientific materials involved for their work, and will not reduplicate them for sale or general distribution (Pet. App. 14-15); 2) Both libraries have reasonably strict limitations on the photocopying services provided, which effectively minimize potential harm to the copyright owner (Pet. App. 15-17); 3) The practice of library photocopying has long been accepted as appropriate (Pet. App. 17-19); 4) There is grave uncertainty about the prohibition on copying in the current copyright law, and the House Report on the proposed revision of that law indicates that library photocopying is a fair use in appropriate circumstances (Pet. App. 8-11, 23-27); and 5) The practice in foreign counties indicates that the library photocopying here is a fair use (Pet. App. 27-28).

[6] A holding that the photocopying involved here infringed petitioner's copyrights would substantially benefit petitioners and amici financially, since it would permit them to negotiate licensing agreements with NIH and NLM, and place them in a stronger position to negotiate such agreements with other libraries.

6

the photocopying by these libraries of these journals is a fair use of the copyrighted materials here involved, and disclaims any conclusions concerning the practice of photocopying in any other situations, the decision is in fact a narrow one, not meriting review by this Court.[7]

One of the reasons the court was careful to limit its holding to the precise facts of this case was its recognition of the inappropriateness of any attempt to establish judicially the broad principles which should govern the application of new technologies to copyright law, a matter "preeminently a problem for Congress * * * [since] [t]he choices involve economic, social, and policy factors which are far better sifted by a legislature" (Pet. App. 25). This Court has reached the same conclusion in *Teleprompter Corp.* v. *Columbia Broadcasting System*, No. 72-1628, decided March 4, 1974, slip op. p. 19: "shifts in current business and commercial relationships * * * simply cannot be controlled by means of litigation based on copyright legislation enacted more than half a century ago * * *. Detailed regulation of these relationships, and any ultimate resolution of the many

[7] Moreover, the very fact that this is the first case to consider the propriety of any library photocopying, despite the fact that photocopying of library materials in this manner has been a common practice at least since 1935 (Pet. App. 17), indicates that the issue is not as significant to those concerned as petitioners and amici assert.

7

sensitive and important problems in this field, must be left to Congress [footnote omitted]."[8]

The Court of Claims properly concluded, for the reasons summarized *supra* at p. 4-5, that the photocopying by NIH and NLM at issue here constitute a fair use of the copyrighted materials, rather than an infringement of the copyright. Petitioner's attack on this holding rests primarily on two grounds: 1) the allegation that copying an entire article can never be fair use, and 2) the claim that the court below improperly refused to consider petitioner's willingness to license photocopying by NIH and NLM in determining whether they were infringing petitioner's copyrights. Neither point is well taken.

As the court noted, the suggestion that the copying of an entire copyrighted work cannot be a fair use is "an overbroad generalization, unsupported by the decisions, and rejected by years of accepted practice" (Pet. App. 13). See New York Tribune, Inc. v. Otis & Co., 39 F. Supp. 67 (S.D.N.Y.); Meeropol v. Nizer, 361 F. Supp. 1063 (S.D.N.Y.).

The cases petitioner cites do not conflict with this conclusion, since they do not base their rejection of the defense of fair use on the fact that the entire work was copied. Indeed, in Benny v. Loew's Inc., 239 F. 2d 532 (C.A. 9), affirmed by an equally divided court, Sub rom. Columbia Broadcasting System, Inc. v. Loew's Inc. 356 U.S. 43, the court repeatedly noted

---

8 The court below noted that revision of the copyright laws is under consideration in Congress (Pet. App. 26). See also Teleprompter, supra, slip op. at 19 n. 16.

8

that "a substantial part" of the copyrighted play was appropriated. 9

Petitioner argues that the court below erred "by completely ignoring petitioner's licensing program" (Pet. 18), and that, because petitioner is willing to license photocopying by these libraries, no harm to medical research can be anticipated from a holding that they have infringed petitioner's copyrights. But

---

9 The issue in Benny was whether a parody of a work infringed the copyright. Petitioner interprets Public Affairs Associates Inc. v. Rickover, 284 F. 2d 262 (C.A. D.C.), judgment vacated, 369 U.S. 111, as indicating that there is no possibility of a defense of fair use when verbatim copies of speeches are taken (Pet. 16). But the court there stated only that the theory of fair use would not justify the publication of a work consisting in substantial part of quotations from a copyrighted work (*Id.* at 272). In vacating the judgment for an inadequate record, this Court noted that "as to [Rickover's] copyrighted speeches, [the court of appeals] remanded the case to the District Court for determination of the extent to which 'fair use' was open to the plaintiff," 369 U.S.

---

at 112.

Wihtol v. Crow, 309 F. 2d 777 (C.A. 8), the other case petitioner asserts conflicts with the holding below, held simply that "it is not conceivable to us that the copying of all, or substantially all, of a copyrighted song can be held to be a 'fair use' merely because the infringer had no intent to infringe [citations omitted]," *Id.* at 780. Instead, the court held, the proper test is whether the taking sensibly diminishes the value of the original or appropriates the author's labors. Judged by that test, the library photocopying here was a fair use. In any event, there was no proper basis for a defense of fair use in any of these cases. Benny and Rickover involved attempts to exploit substantial portions of another's copyrighted work commercially, while Wihtol dealt with an unauthorized arrangement of a copyrighted musical work.

9

the court did not ignore petitioner's program (Pet. App. 24-25). Instead, it correctly concluded that the determination whether a given use is fair, and thus not subject to royalty payments, cannot turn on whether the copyright holder is willing to license it at reasonable rates.

CONCLUSION

For the foregoing reasons the petition for a writ of certiorari should be denied.

Respectfully submitted.

Robert H. Bork,
    Solicitor General.

Carla A. Hills,
    Assistant Attorney General

Harriet S. Shapiro,
    Assistant to the Solicitor General

William Kanter,
Michael H. Stein,
Thomas J. Byrnes,
    Attorneys.

April 1974.

Index

Compiled by Susan Ruth Stein